W9-BXX-183

Moral Armor

Ronald E. Springer

authorHOUSE

1663 LIBERTY DRIVE, SUITE 200
BLOOMINGTON, INDIANA 47403
(800) 839-8640
www.authorhouse.com

First published by AuthorHouse 05/17/04

ISBN: 1-4184-1866-8 (sc)

Library of Congress Control Number: 2004093767

Printed in the United States of America
Bloomington, Indiana

This book is printed on acid-free paper.

Copy Editing by Jocelyn M. Strong
Cover Art by Jeremiah R. Springer

Dedications

The most profound impact on my development was made by Miss Ayn Rand—my spiritual father, my hero. You have no equal. For you.

For Sherry Murphy (L'Anse Creuse Class of '85). What can one small gesture do? This is what has grown from the seed you planted so long ago.

For Tina, without whom the need for such a work may never have occurred. "May God grant you the mercy that I cannot."

For Joss, who brought me back.

Thanks Mom, for working my corner and being my link to the Axis. Thanks to my riding companion and truest friend, Jeff Bartley.

To the teachers and executives in my past: Kenneth Poprave, who showed me strength and certainty while I was developing my own. David Kandt and Kurt Kurtenbach, who showed me the heroic trait of a focused, thoughtful interest towards those seeking self-advancement. Keith Pryzybylski who confirmed my faith in full, productive, jovial rationality. David Blair for his honorable and endless objectivity. And when the work is done, thanks to Terry Mullen and George Evans for helping me reach 200 MPH!

For all of the artists I have been exposed to and influenced by, inspiring all of mankind through the projection of specific, ideal human abilities, traits and exalted emotions—in their work and in themselves. Here follows only a partial list: Acura, Aristotle, Antonio Banderas, Michelle Branch, Warren Buffett, James Cameron, John Carpenter, Jim Carrey, Chevy Chase, Tom Cruise, James Dean, Dr. Barbara DeAngelis, Terrence Trent Darby, Laura Day, Leonardo DiCaprio, Clint Eastwood, Emilio Estevez, Ferrari, Benjamin Franklin, Andy Garcia, Jim Garrison, Bill Gates, Macy Gray, Hugh Hefner, Charlton Heston, Susanna Hoffs, James Horner, Andrew Jackson, Jesus of Nazareth, Helen Keller, John F. Kennedy, Stephen King, KISS, Lamborghini, Gary Larson, Bruce and Brandon Lee, Rush Limbaugh, Abraham Lincoln, George Lucas, Marvel Comics, McClaren Cars, Dennis Miller, Dr. Maria Montessori, Mandy Moore, Marion and Merit of M2M, Nightingale-Conant, James O'Barr, Gary Oldman, William J. O'Neal, Thomas Paine, Queensryche, Stephen Pearcy of RATT, Brad Pitt, Porsche, Robert Prechter Jr., Anthony Robbins, William Shakespeare, George Soros, Steven Spielberg, Oliver Stone, Michael Sweet of Stryper, Donald J. Trump, Tina Turner, Savage Garden, Sun Tzu, Sigourney Weaver, John Williams, Oprah Winfrey, Harry Wu and Edward Zwick.

Thank you all, for standing up and making your talents known.

For all of the artists yet to be acknowledged who work, day in and day out, shunning the world to pursue their passion. Keep going; do it for the glory of every breath you take. A star is born, long before the world takes notice.

My ultimate gratitude goes to Ludwig van Beethoven, who, during the years of this writing, reached through the centuries to give me the emotional support I needed from the "second self" I have yet to find.

Moral Armor - Contents

Moral Armor - Glossary

"Words are a lens to focus one's mind." —Helen Keller

Absolute—certainty that a thing *is* what it is.

Abstraction—the process of isolating certain elements of an existent's identity for the purpose of concept formation.

Anti-concept—a false and misleading proposal or idea, which keeps causal connections pertaining to the subject matter, immeasurable or indeterminate.

Axiom—a proposition that identifies the foundation of knowledge, upon which all further concepts are formed. An axiom's validation comes from that it must be used, in any attempt to refute it.

Concept—a mental integration of two or more things, possessing the same distinguishing characteristics, with their particular measurements omitted.

Consciousness— (an axiom) the faculty of perceiving that which exists.

Context—the background or field of awareness, within which, concepts are formed.

Dichotomy—a division between two sharply distinguished or opposing sides.

Entity—a thing of definite, individual existence and determinable shape.

Epistemology—the branch of philosophy devoted to the discovery of the proper methods of acquiring and validating knowledge.

Existence— (an axiom) the world of which, is the object of our perception.

Identity—the condition of being a specific existent, which possesses distinguishing attributes.

Identification—the second step of human consciousness, following perception. The act of isolating and describing the attributes of an entity.

Judgment—the act of measurement according to an applicable standard of value, gauging adherence to a principle.

Metaphysics—the branch of philosophy studying the natural, physical world.

Morality—an objective standard of action describing the rational, civil pattern of life-sustenance for Man, by adherence to which his stature is gauged.

Objectivity—recognition of the fact that reality exists independent of one's perceptions.

Radical—fundamental.

Sanction—to give approval to; to honor, support and encourage.

Subjectivity—implying that reality can be altered by the consciousness of the perceiver.

Unit-economy—as the direct perceptual range of a human being is limited, a vast amount of information must be reduced to fall within that range, in order to manage thought.

Volitional—you have a choice in the matter, which must be exercised.

Throughout life, you will
encounter many Spirit
Murderers who will hate
you for achieving what they
betrayed.
This is your armor.

Section One:

The Second Declaration of Independence

Chapter One

The Last Straw

"Sometimes, something so bad happens, the soul can't rest."
—The Crow

There is no need to be afraid. This image of dark vengeance is startling, I know. Pursuers tend to assume traits of the pursued. In a battle against open evil, this is the form which the good must take. You have seen me before, in the desperate need for a guardian—one who should have been there. I watched the betrayal you felt when no one came to rescue your innocence. I saw your tortured, valiant effort to understand what they had made of this world and why; so I left to discover the answer. I will not bring you harm. This hostile, vibrant force is protective; look closely: yes, that's right; strength, certainty and amusement; a portal to the world you expected this one to be. What did you think would be on the other side? I have returned, to pull you out and take you there. We are to be the victims of the soulless, no longer. Battered? Bruised? I know. But I'm back now, and it's going to be alright. Where was I?

It began as a wonderful dream. We met, exhilarated, living eyes full of hope, of love, of fantasies for our future. Intoxicated by the mystery of each other, so pure, so faithful, so devoted. All lies. The site of a plane crash; the decimation of my heart; shattered...blackened...transformed. Now I lay quietly, undetected, viewing the evil without a spiritual pulse of my own; detached, incorruptible, intransigent. No more values to seek or to lose; the perfect camouflage. The time for fear has passed. I look with steady, all-seeing eyes, upon that which has torn away my most precious possession. I vow to hold down my pain and last long enough to warn the others—my dying wish: to see those who still have a chance, lifted safely out of their reach.

Every day without her—my life's pinnacle, worked for, bled for, reached and discarded as an unspeakable fraud, is another day spent in front of a firing squad. The same feelings day after day; the stillness, the grim finality I chose, is better than the long, drawn out murder I was to suffer at her hands. Resurrection? One day; but I can't think of that now. With death, there is peace. Peace enough to do what I have to do. It was the last straw in a lifetime of unjustifiable inflictions; the last *sanctioned* violation. I'd had enough. The plague must be eradicated once and for all, no matter the cost. She drained me; not taking my life, but taking my will to live. Which is worse? Years of philosophical study could not shield me from what happened. Was it supposed to?...I don't know. But now, I have grown strong enough to shield what *I* sanction, and to blast the whole structure of evil, back into the dark ages. Then maybe, I can return to what I once was; maybe. Sometimes, when the fire of your will has gone out and your passion has been consumed, just knowing what killed you is enough.

Our Plague. Through every hurtful deception of others, every limitation, every act of cowardice, every evasive reaction, a voice inside you has said, "Don't turn away! *Look* at the treason; *remember it.*" You knew these evils were all connected somehow; that there was a principle outside of your range, left to future discovery. The time has come. We met for the first time, through the courage of that voice. Justice is what stepped through the shadows of the background, and now it has taken form. I have identified what no one has had the stomach for, and have returned with the defense from all the pain and hardships imposed on us that we never should've had to endure. Now there is a path cut to leave the anguish behind; a road to higher ground, but first we must return to the origin of the conflict and create a bridge to this new world.

For centuries, the world has suffered from a glaring yet elusive plague, which has kept men cowering in uncertainty, gun-shy in contemplation of every moral step. It has kept men from gaining their rightful pride and spiritual freedom, and from living their lives to the fullest. It has kept parents from handing down the most valuable traits they could give to their children, allowing their lives to flow smoothly and their relationships to be sound in turn. It has kept men from validating their own judgment, and left them open to any atrocity. It is responsible for erecting a wall of stress between their productivity and the enjoyment which that effort deserves. It is responsible for all of the heartache suffered by mankind, and has led to every disloyalty at the hands of its devotees. It has been a plague of *moral confusion*. There has been a very specific victim all along, within you and outside of you; and a very specific predator, within you and outside of you. The worst *premises* have been feeding their fear by riding and torturing the best through an inverted moral code, where the good is the evil and the evil is the good; a weapon most people have never conceived of or thought to question.

Morality, the crucial life or death, brother against brother, walk on eggshells issue—has always been the ultimate taboo subject. Since my earliest capacity to identify good and bad, I've watched in pathetic amusement the senseless, contradictory actions of my elders. It seemed so straight forward to make judgments and act accordingly, that I couldn't understand how moral issues could divide everyone into their hurt, indignant sides of foggy uncertainty and stubborn evasion. I believed that reality was real. From my earliest encounter with others to present day, I have watched most act as if it wasn't. Siblings sponged, connived and tortured as a means to deal with existence, and there was nothing they would not sacrifice to keep their illusions intact. We were taught that judging one's character and beliefs was to be avoided at all costs. The grown-ups around me were all so tangled in lies, reproaches and cowardice that their range of thought was barely able to project into the next day, and twenty-five years later, they have come no further.

Uncomfortable with my pursuit of knowledge and higher clarity on any subject, adults discouraged it with, "Who are *you* to know?" Curiosity about their self-destructive behavior was deflected with "Who are you to judge?" Their relationship advice was, "Don't ever talk about anything meaningful" (and discover whether you are compatible). As my understanding grew, their malice towards me grew. I was engaged in the forbidden; I was *looking.* Unable to comprehend their motives, I lived in moral confusion, suffering at the hands of subhuman beings for my willingness to see, to think, to judge and to act. It was almost as if my guardians believed that honesty was profane and lying was virtuous; that weakness and incompetence deserved affection while strength and ability deserved contempt; that awareness was destructive and blindness was kind. As a child, I looked up and saw that everything was backwards! Their teachings seemed to say that whatever gave me exhilaration for living was somehow wrong; and yet how could I renounce my sight, my hearing, my mind and body, and continue to enjoy life? By what means and through what senses would I then seek fulfillment? If comprehension, if seeing the truth, if deeply breathing the cool, fresh air into my proud, strong, able young body, boundlessly pursuing all the wonderful discoveries of existence, was evil, then why should men wish to live at all?

I never doubted myself; I thought they were idiots. They made all of life an unrewarding hell, until I discovered just what drove them. If moral judgment was to be interpreted and applied by men, then *they interpreted it wrong,* like every other primitive and dysfunctional aspect of their lives. The fault did not originate with their Bible per say; they simply tailored their moral view to cover their own fraud, while the productive were quiet on the subject. Before learning deception as children, all of us could see the source of hostility, of cowardice or of phoniness. If it began and ended in one individual, we knew it. Innocence is not stupidity. Lack of experience is not incompetence. We knew when we were hearing lies. We always did. It was their folly and its miserable result that I chose to renounce. I held my potency in reserve, longing for the day when the power to determine my course would match the power I felt while observing my world.

I've always had a special relationship with existence; a feeling that others didn't share. I was at home on Earth, glad to be alive, where the emotional response of others was to cope. The elements of nature were there to serve me; to be commanded by my direction, while others reacted as if some unknown beast was about to devour them. I would watch the same mistakes of my elders being made by the fear-ridden of my generation, and laugh; I'm not sure just when I began to consider it dangerous. With life experience and budding philosophical clarity, my contemptuous humor towards such self-abasing cowardice descended into a long, dark period of indignation, and then a fear of my own. The insanity was extrapolated deeply into business and world affairs; it marred everything in its path. I couldn't escape its influence and still couldn't believe that anyone took it seriously.

Operating so clean and efficient, I was eager to share my glorious road of achievement with others and longed for our worlds to merge. But in relationships as well as in business, I kept suffering that code's painful betrayals. Instead of the elegant atmosphere I expected, business was like an even more profane and immature high school. My most profitable ideas and efforts were scoffed at, and then stolen. Competence took a back seat to age, seniority or cliques. With friends and lovers, I was abandoned for being too successful, or I was used. They would not expand their concern outside of the inconsequential, and they ignored everything I needed acknowledgment for. Explaining to family a facet of industry unseen by my competitors, the response I would hear was, "But are you eating enough?" There was a whole level of my life I needed to share, and no one to listen. No one to understand. I felt like a freak because I was unable to erase this feeling: the feeling that life is a quest; a quest of the most crucial importance, allowing no primary time or consideration for the details. But my reward in any attempt to convey this was always a blank stare, and then something like, "Have you called your grandmother?" I could not bring my mind back to that level.

I could not reverse the priorities of my consciousness, and it took years to conceive of our fundamental incompatibility. I would meet a woman and have a similar emotional response to what I felt about my work; that our relationship was something epic, to be knelt before and carried out with reverence; a shrine of magnificence for us to build. I could see the beauty of our bodies and the beauty of the world together. I could feel the awesome power of life as almost audible, but it would be sunk with her complete reversal of claimed intentions. Fear drove everyone to wear masks; no one was what they portrayed. It began to ruin my enjoyment of life; time was being lost and it just wasn't funny anymore. I saw irrationality in every direction; my head wanted to explode, and I could sense that it was all tied together somehow.

I refused to give up. As my wealth and ability grew, so did my distance to others; not by my choice, but by theirs. I could not understand their discontent, and little by little, I lost everyone. Heartbroken, I couldn't see what I was doing wrong. I worked so hard; much harder than they did. Wasn't I good enough? It was incomprehensible to me that they could be responding with hatred toward the things I did *well*, but they were. Entranced with my style of living yet locked in social dysfunction, I stepped out. I stayed the intellectual course, trying to understand. I was sure that when I did, I would discover or create a world to match my ideals; my true homeland. I had glimpsed that world from time to time, as my means of its attainment grew more consistent. I could see it coming. Yet so ingrained was my tolerance of evil, that I had to be taken down in one final conflict before I accepted the truth. When I resurfaced, I found as in a rite of passage, that a shimmering, glistening, living morality awaited me. I finally stepped out of their reach. The rewards were clear and forever mine, but the evil was still there, and the war had just begun.

The Present Conflict in Morality. Just about every premise preached to Man under the guise of morality is wrong; often the exact opposite is true. Discovering this has not made my life any easier. When morality is inverted, it is the honest, the clean, the just and the rational that is considered controversial. When you have corrected this inversion of principles, you are speaking another language; even your physiological responses invert. As the language of good and evil has only two sides, those in the confused majority will classify you improperly and they will make you pay. There are so many fragile egos in the world, you'll feel like a bull in a china shop. A radiant spiritual health can appear frightening at times, and will become the rift between friends who are not brave enough to break from their conditioning. In my life, I watched them peel off in layers of honesty, and I could tell who would fall next, but it's just as well. They couldn't soar being chained to the ground.

I'm free of the Fear-driven psychologically, but societal interaction is unavoidable. And as *they* certainly haven't changed, the game goes on. I'm tired of being used; I'm tired of being considered the bad apple for being honest; I'm tired of being called ruthless and mean when standing for justice; I'm tired of being called arrogant for showing confidence; I'm sick of being called lucky for expending effort. We work and we work, hoping to see our lives develop into a logical whole, and every time we reach a sense of mature significance about it all, there is something or someone out there to undercut it. Notice the hostile silence of others when you do well, and the mocking compassion when you don't. Notice their veiled fraud of a smile in false approval of any accomplishment. Do anything too spectacular and you're treated like an outsider; but often, their companionship is worse. I'm tired of watching people avoid purpose and self-responsibility. Stagnation is always their noble sacrifice to their kids or their spouse, where any alternate path would (of course) have led to an achievement to match or exceed ours. Such excuses allow them to abandon the subject of purpose, squidding out in relief, to return to the safety of their shallow domain. I'm sick and tired of talking about little things. I'm tired of the inspirationally lethargic ignoring everything that matters. I'm sick of their attempts to delude us into giving up, slowing down and selling out.

What fun is there in playing it safe? The Fear-driven are moving towards an epitaph of "Should've, would've, could've." Ours will say "Did." I'm tired of seeing no one speak up to defend themselves or any of us against any injustice. Sometimes they vent about valid issues, but lose all backbone when facing their opposition; failing life and failing themselves. They damn the evils openly; *they do* understand. They can gage by rational standards when they're treated unfairly by a boss or a spouse, but nevertheless, they cave in and carry the burdens of moral default without protest. Then they actually reverse their moral response by condemning those who refuse to suffer the consequences of giving up along with them. Staring into the void of their basic cognitive unwillingness, you can explain until you are blue in the face, but they won't get it. They'll make sure they won't. Stand for anything and the first wave of fools will resent you; not on the issue, but for the capacity to stand. They turn against the fighters for truth, and in so doing, turn against themselves. They recognize the rat and nourish it anyway. At work, they cower under their bosses irrationality, and instead of wishing to correct the nonsense, they fantasize of taking over to impose their *own* irrationality on their subordinates. Powerless to fulfill this dream, they go home and impose it on their family. I'm tired of life in the muck. Why should it be muck? Why is it so exasperating and so difficult to get out of? What keeps us stuck at this moral level? If our enemies were all fire and brimstone they would be easy to see; but they're not so obvious. The battle hasn't been a swift, clean, violent clash, but a lethargic, smothering goo-offensive.

Their Predation of Innocence. A child stares with wide eyed wonder at the gigantic industries of Man: the huge vehicles, the rigs and trains that like a bloodstream, supply life to the nation. Watching his father in operation of this wonderfully complex machinery, he thinks, "Wow, my father is a giant." The man makes his living and is seen by innocent eyes as a hero. Then the child hears unsettling lessons that tell him that his father's role is predatory, that his making of money is vicious and that his creations are destruction. Nothing the boy can witness in his father's bearing suggests any malevolent intention. He sees only an active, able figure, intent on its task. Even if the work is dangerous, he feels an immense exhilaration, and strangely, safety. His actual response to evil—that sense of arresting fear—more appropriately describes the feelings he has for such teachers. Confused he remains silent, but inwardly he knows something is out of line.

Whether his father is a fisherman, a foreman or an executive, he isn't thinking of destroying the world, of cheating or harming anyone. He's thinking about the Visa bill that was due yesterday, or the overtime he needs in order to buy that bicycle for his son's birthday which he didn't budget for. He, like the rest of us, is keeping his family afloat and trying to make life comfortable in the process, and that's it. We are not evil. Often, life is too perplexing for us to consider having any motives at all, beyond earning a decent living and being able to enjoy it. We spend the majority of our days working, never having enough time to relax and reflect, and we get to find out every Sunday how black our hearts are; what evils lurk beneath our surface. Hearing this, a strange uneasiness washes over; we know we don't feel any *real* negativity, but we also know that we are supposed to just listen and accept. Too emotionally exhausted to consider making an issue of it and sensing no reward if victorious anyway, that is what we do. It is a big mistake: beyond that controversy lies the most critical values of living.

If we're brave enough to make a query, we'll hear something like, "A question reveals a doubt. You don't doubt your Savior, do you?" Stammering, we respond, "Well, no." Unarmed and uncertain, we feel safer to remain anonymous on the subject, fearing that a less than perfect understanding would reveal a moral flaw. But we would not fear condemnation for an honest question or error if its antithesis were not protected—appreciation and reward for maintaining a pretense, such as irrational perfection. Mankind would come out of hiding from moral judgment if an unquestionable, unaccountable force was not held to rule morality; if objective values were considered moral, such as the furtherance of his life; if he had the right to defend himself and to see morality as an issue of defense; if he were free to love the things he loves, and free to investigate their cause; if righteousness was not preached as an impossibility to hopelessly strive for; if he felt safe in seeking answers for his confusion.

It would be a different world for all of us if actual virtues were rewarded as we grew up. The dynamic motion of youth, fearlessly speeding along to their dreams could be all around us, as would be the marvels of their creation. But until recent history, the professionals in any field have not been acknowledged as the good, but damned as exploiters, highway robbers and fools. Nothing breeds hesitation in us quicker than watching our idols fall, physically and morally. Witnessing their hardships does not encourage youth or anyone else to follow. The bright future of a pioneer has historically been a daunting road of sneers, ridicule, intimidation, torture and sometimes even murder. How long have we been kept from emulating or even identifying the best, and for what reasons? The struggle would be palatable if we had a clear choice of good or evil, but I look around and I see that the *actual* good has no explicit representation in the world. As a result, only the bravest strike out on this path, while the rest dread stepping away from the skirt.

Good and evil are so intertwined in our culture that neither is independently recognizable, which of course was premeditated. This made it impossible to define guilt rationally or to refute its abusive misapplication. Everyone dreads the horrible feeling of a moral failure—the shame, the downcast eyes, the public knowledge that one has intentionally chosen the wrong—to rob, to deceive, to harm or to sponge. No one wants to be that kind of outsider. Guilt is a dreadful emotion to deserve, and very important to feel for the *right* reasons; but what if for the most part, we *don't* deserve to feel it? This inversion has us feeling guilty for making our living, for feeling good about ourselves and for upholding rational standards. Guilt is a correctional facility in itself for those who really *want* to live; but it is a brutal trauma to experience if undeserved, and is a sacrilege if imposed dishonestly. When you work hard and accomplish something great, then hear you are a greedy, selfish hater of those less endowed, you *should* be mad. When we reach our limit of tolerance and become offended, they'll tell us not to take it personally. I'm here to tell you, take it personally. Look at your accuser. Steady eyes will see the way.

The Road to Moral Clarity. Moral courage has freed me, and now I want to make it possible for others to step out of their reach as well, and lose the fear of being judged. I want to wipe out the reasons that drive men and women to practice an insincerity that just leads to their own unhappiness. I want to see to it that they are no longer victims, and bring them to a level of confidence where they need no longer make victims of others in turn. It is time to set the moral standard for human action: to make explicit, the nature of the motivations by which we *all* live. It is time to identify and validate the true sides of good and evil; to see what we really are, and decide what we truly want to sustain and to become. Don't be afraid. You're not about to find out how evil you are, but to step out of the darkness to discover just the opposite.

Actually, there is so much right about our personal and social actions in this world, that we have very little to fear in the way of negative self-discovery. The guilt in our lives is mostly unjustified and many problems we feel looming up behind us aren't even there. Still, it takes an unusual bravery to look. As we saw above, an inquiring mind is open to more than learning; *it is open to attack*. Intellectually, physically and spiritually we are bombarded with studies, opinions and statistics that classify us by our supposed flaws. Much publicity is given to medical doctors and psychologists who propose anti-theories which violate the very nature of their own disciplines; yet they are often heeded. Like the church, such professionals provide few solutions and provoke a sense of dread in the public, fearing that whatever traits we display will be labeled as the next malady. What they don't seem to understand is that by identifying and classifying what is healthy and right, often the bad just drops off. If you concentrate on advancing critical areas, you never have a chance to address problems or stress. They are simply forgotten. We could kill thousands of man-hours analyzing every known sub-classification of evil, nervously contemplating how *we* fit in, and still not understand what we should be doing.

I'm not going to waste your time. If you can read this, there is nothing essentially wrong with you! For most of the reading public (those who nurture and enjoy the process of abstraction), moral confusion is like walking out of the house with messed up hair. Nothing is essentially missing, it's just humorously unkempt and needs to be straightened out.

The actual purpose of morality has always been awry. When it is adjusted to its proper intent, everything else in life falls right into place. Morality doesn't start with a kind smile, a shared seat or anything between men. It is *not* primarily social. Morality starts when you open your eyes, look at the magnificence of the world and say, "It is." And then get to work.

Morality is not something you give homage to for a few hours on Sunday, then forget about while you're busy making a living. Morality is the *means* by which you pursue the goal of living, and to the extent that your activity has been constructive versus parasitical, what you've done for *your own* prosperity is directly in line with the moral progress of mankind. People know implicitly what is moral and immoral. Nature tells them. Other's reactions tell them. It is not difficult to evaluate what furthers the life of an entity and what hinders it, as it is not difficult to ascertain that *this* is the main issue of morality.

There *is* a crystal clear, non-contradictory structure for morality, and it is based on the nature of Man. This standard is not subjective, small and malicious, but objective, mature and honorable. The proper standard flows *with* life instead of defying it, requires no allegiance to the unprovable and vents no fundamental contempt whatsoever for Mankind. The true structure follows our pattern of cognition, and as the purpose of cognition is life, it reveals the structure of evil as well, in any break with the moral pattern. This natural process is the basis for sound mental health, sound relationships and provides the structure for mankind's proper organizations. It governs and can be seen in, all human action.

Morality's fundamental process is choice. Every choice you make serves one side or the other; either it is good, or it is evil. It either furthers your life or threatens it. Should the pride of choosing life be reserved only for when we help the needy, or should it be a constant medium of existence? The right choices and the right results, provide certainty. Do you ever wonder if you're good enough? Morally certain people don't have to wonder. Think you're a coward for being afraid of life sometimes? It is time to find out what cowardice *really* is. The correct standard returns morality to its proper function: that of a fascinating, constructive, life-shaping frame of reference; *not* a source of forbidding, dismal barriers. A morally clear mind is a stress free mind, and we are going to clean house. We are going to check every premise that drives us as individuals, for that is what we act on, what we judge ourselves and others by and ultimately, what we create as a society. More important is learning to identify and correct if necessary, the premises driving the other aspects of your existence, so that all of your motives flow together in one common life-furthering direction.

We are on a road now that is going to make your every step planted more certain. Imagine the feeling each time your foot lands, of "Yes, this is right." And the rhythm of another step lands thinking, "*This* is why I'm alive: I know where I'm going and why I'm taking these actions." You turn into the wind's warmth thinking, "No rational doctrine would damn the motion of my body or the thoughts that drive them, for they are so clearly and effectively taken to further my life." With such a standard, moral confidence would become apparent in your every thought and in your every action, as soothingly as you would gaze upon a sunset. When you look to nature, you will feel a special bond returning: a relationship you haven't felt since you were a child.

Life's Ancient Opposition

"She'll breed. You'll die." —Alien Resurrection

The True Sides. From the dawn of time, mankind has been in a class war; not between rich and poor, white and black or weak and strong, but between rational motive and irrational motive; between dependence and independence; between Fear-driven Man and Self-made Man. Civilization eliminated irresponsible savagery from social action, but not from thought. All men understand the ideal of living competence, but one kind desires to enjoy the benefits of competence while remaining incompetent; to enjoy the deliverance of a long chain of knowledge without expending the effort, bravery or discipline to obtain it. The productive men and women live by their own effort, but the parasites seek to live off ours. The producers obey their own nature, which the parasites attempt to defy. To remain alive, the parasites had to devise a means of extorting their sustenance from those who produce it, without being thrown off. What they had to secure was *our* acceptance of *their* supremacy; some non-debatable justification for enduring their ridicule and submitting to their guidance. Their arch-enemy became the perceptivity and self-esteem of their betters.

To gain control of a man, one must destroy his intellectual independence. To this end for millennia, the parasites have subverted every living premise, dividing cause from result, work from reward and pride from choice. Only the unproductive, the fear-ridden and the incompetent could psychologically benefit from keeping the productive, the self-confident and the competent in a state of moral uncertainty. So like any scheming dictator, they began stripping us of our defenses when we were just children. They took the radiant, shining standards of our love and made it unconditional. Original Sin and its modern descendent, environmentalism, damned the very nature of Man and robbed us of our innocence. They labeled us grafters if we worked hard, taking our honor and our pride. Money, a product of social stability and Man's civil means of exchange, was damned as the root of all evil. Any self-motivated action was considered destructively selfish, the pinnacle of which is one's life's purpose, while the pursuit of money was considered pure hedonistic greed. By denying us individual purpose, we became a society that could work for *nothing but money*. Their trap was complete and the circle closed.

Instead of encouraging the refinement of our competencies in preparation for life, they made their heaven a stagnant utopia of effortless treasures. Afraid of using their minds, they set up rules based on how they *wished* things to be versus factual reality, which only made life miserable for those who had to provide it all. Fed from birth ideas that were laced with cyanide, our pursuit of happiness was replaced with a battle against suffering. We were harnessed by an inverted morality brought to life through the eyes of panic. Like cancer, it grew into a system which destroys the rewards of life, limiting us and degenerating our living potency in mind and body. Life's ancient opposition is a battle against the nature of Man, against the pleasure of living and against existence itself.

Their Vile Substitution. Take a look at what is universally considered the domain of moral action: doling out soup to the poor, emptying bed-pans with a smile and being proudly victimized by the wretched: hand-outs, volunteer work and martyrdom. Proponents of this view respond to normal life in emergency fashion: wishing to seize what products they see, bandaging what wounds they see and cowering to whatever is an immediate danger; reacting to the now, as their consciousness does not extend much further. Morality to them is to answer disasters. Such non-intellectual beliefs uphold as our ideal—as our reason for living and as proof of our goodness—servitude to the most indigent, inattentive and unstable entities. In our quest for nobility, we inherently seek a shrine on which to stand; a hero's pedestal. They present to us instead, a hospital ward of living nightmares to attend to, which offend and retract every sense—without mind, without joy and without hope. Our typical exposure to their view is boxing up a few things for Good Will, canned food drives and at the extreme of dedication, a mission to some backward village to supply food and medicine. We have come to consider moral action to be the exception in life, *but not the exceptional.* No wonder a futile sense of drudgery accompanies all contemplation of morality!

It is particularly painful as we are wide open in that moment, expecting to experience a deserved elation. Do you think their timing is only a coincidence? Where does the pride we wish to express come from? What makes us wish to stand in the sight of the whole world to be admired? It comes from our life-sustaining productivity: a sum that grows every day; a source they refuse to name or honor. They hand to us as the climax of our triumphant productive effort, not a ceremony with the solemnity of Beethoven's Piano Concerto No. 5, but a stupid grin under a chef's hat, "giving something back" at the local soup kitchen, implying that our initial achievement was a form of robbery. Our most significant moral progress has been prompted and maintained by science and industry, and has gone completely unnoticed as such even by us, as we have been taught to believe that moral action means the *distribution* of goods and services required to sustain anonymous, immediate needs, without any consideration for their source. God we've been fools. The business of mankind—the production and exchange of products—is *not* evil, it keeps us alive! It is the *means* of civil human living. We fight to justify the existence of our business world, lacking the one weapon that would assure victory: the knowledge that it is *moral.*

In our time, where free trade has put so much distance between ourselves and our crudest needs, they wish to reduce the world's focus back to worrying where our next meal will come from. Their intention is to reduce us to the same terror of their own limited range. The truth is that charities, civil service and other such volunteer work are *very* minor league moral actions, if at all. And have you ever *tried* turning the other cheek to a criminal? So how was the hospital food? They tell us to permit and forgive any evil, therefore placing the whole burden of responsible action upon the innocent. Does it make sense that our moral worthiness is tied to whether or not we can catch a speeding bullet and reform the shooter in the process? Is there a rational moral code to follow for the time when we are not starving to death or dangling from cliffs? Why have they set moral standards to make sure that we can't be moral? Does the productive ninety-eight percent of the population need focus on the ailing two percent and fall victim to the criminal .01% in order to be virtuous? With a ratio of more than fifty-to-one, you can't possibly spend your life serving those in need. Does that mean that you spend the other ninety-eight percent of your life doing things that are immoral? In their code, that is exactly what they mean, and culturally it is accepted as a forgone conclusion. Why is the majority of life's activity not considered moral? Why is preserving the lives of the healthy and able, dismissed as hedonism? Does it make sense that morality is designed, not for our protection and fulfillment, but against it?

> *"It was on the tip of everyone's tongue. Tyler and I just gave it a name."*
> —Fight Club

Revealing Our Enemy. No one could guess by whom and in how many ways their passion is drained, but one term describes the enemy: Spirit Murderers. They come in many forms, all motivated by fear essentially and hate ultimately, with one common social goal: to design and skin the perfect victim. Spirit Murderers ride us, and hate us for our ability to carry them. So they try to rob us of our sense of living which holds adventure, endless possibility and personal significance, and replace it with the paranoia, insignificance and helplessness that *they* chronically feel. Now and then, we encounter ideals that do make sense and see creations that astonish us, revealing a human being's true dimensions to the world, only to discover the desolate tragedies these men suffered to bring such wonders into existence. Building a monument to Man is a delicate and heroic effort, be it a symphony, a skyscraper or the United States of America. The Spirit Murderer's have always had it easier because no matter what heights we reach, it's all downhill for them.

Victims can sacrifice an arm or a leg to survive, but not the nerve center; they cannot sacrifice their brains, which is why cognitive disintegration is the Spirit Murderer's primary attack. I know that most people cannot face that there is something missing in their thinking; to doubt their own conscious adequacy feels like a mortal blow. They have been taught to believe that a wrong move is proof of damnation; that to be imperfect in action is to admit their own worthlessness. But the truth is their teachers have violated the natural pattern of human thought—the logical accumulation of knowledge—often on purpose. They begin in ways you wouldn't suspect, gently undercutting with such questions as, "What came first? The chicken or the egg?" and because we falter in response to the unexpected, they claim the mind *by its nature* is unreliable. Wait a minute while I answer them: "Okay idiot, the chicken. Between the two it is the only one capable of sustaining itself in nature. The chicken came first, or more accurately, what evolved as a chicken. The existence of a living entity precedes its *attributes*—among them its reproductive process." Their intention becomes clear with what follows: other questions bearing no consequence in our lives such as, "So where do *we* come from?" "The scientific method has been disproved long ago" they say, because some obscure estimate about the universe was in experience found to be inaccurate (disregarding the incredible advances required to establish that fact). "That proves" they claim with glee, "that thinking is futile," and (forgetting that they are men too), "that mankind is a joke; everything he's ever done has been proved wrong. He can't get anything right; so why does he think he is so great?" Let me get this straight: We were wrong about gravity and it goes the other way now? Wow, this inconsequential detail has uncovered the folly of our existence. I get up in the morning and the sky isn't blue. Fossil fuels cannot be burned in cars, homes or power plants, which due to our inability to build, have all collapsed anyway. Our skyscrapers, tunnels and bridges have all been reduced to rubble by their simple revelation. All the planes fall out of the sky, there is no use for electricity or running water, Earth no longer spins in a day and we don't actually breathe air. Morons. They want us to believe that our "illusion of control" can be shaken by any senseless proposition they forward.

Reality has never been altered by their neurosis. Their claims are not a reflection of mankind's existential inconstancy, but of *theirs*. Look at their lives. What they actually want is to have us buy into what stopped *them*. What makes them think they can get away with such ludicrous nonsense? And worst of all, why do they? All that really happened in their scientific mishap is Man took another step forward. The human chain of knowledge got a little longer. Theories became fact, estimated measurements were made precise and our capacity for control expanded. Our means of acquiring and validating knowledge was implicitly furthered in parallel with our declared intentions, just as their declared intentions were to destroy that capacity. A man's rational faculty is not invalidated because fact follows theory, which follows hypothesis. Discoveries are limitless. At no time is it rational to stomp one's feet because knowledge is not automatic, because thinking requires an excruciating effort at times and because the world's secrets are not provided on a silver platter. Our database is in a constant state of accumulation and refinement. The efficacy of human consciousness is not "questionable" because new technologies supersede and new discoveries hone older ones; that is the natural progression of Man. But what was our response? We were silent: bearing their hostility until we could escape back to the clean rationality of our passions. What undercut our confidence? Why didn't we fight back?

We didn't fight back because we didn't have a defense for simply being human, and could never have conceived of the need for one. But at this point in history it is necessary. The beast has found no resistance in the flinching eyes of its victims. Defense begins with a fundamental sanction of existence: accepting that reality is real. You must understand what life on Earth requires of Man and accept the correct basis of morality: the preservation of human life. Cleaning your own epistemological structure will allow a pure internal harmony; a united front from which to defend against the evils outside. Then you must identify if those you encounter seek to further life or to stop it; to work with you or to ride you; to respect your rights or to negate them. It is a war of good and evil, and of all "shades of gray" in between. Anyone who doesn't want you to lead a rationally fulfilling life wants to kill you spiritually, as was done to them. Anyone who wants you to accept their shades of gray not only wants you to drink poison, but also wants to gain moral recognition for it.

Our productivity-generated spiritual wealth often leads us to assist and encourage those astray, back towards life, but you will learn that you can't. Progress is not what they are after. I for one am no longer willing to assume the exasperating burden of explaining the self-evident to those bent on misunderstanding. I'm done trying to provide a sunrise for a mankind that rejects the evidence of their eyes. To hell with them. The shimmering beauty of our glorious life-giving power may never awaken the living dead among us. Their fate was never our responsibility anyway; it was and is theirs. After years of futile effort, I accept now that I cannot save them. Instead with regretful diligence, I must draw my sword and protect us against them because they are many, and capable of great devastation.

We have all felt from time to time that morality was a steamroller, one with a malevolent driver, endangering everything in its path. Well morality *is* a steamroller, that is true; but with the proper moral armor, *we* are behind the wheel. In times of warfare, weapons can be overtaken and used by our opposition. That is what has been done to us for centuries. It's time to turn the tables. No matter what torture I for one have endured or will endure, the damage they can do now is limited. I know what moves them. To gain their acceptance and deflect their animosity requires that we be victims. I refuse to exist as a victim any longer. I refuse to let go of my dreams. I refuse to see the world through the vision of their panic. I refuse to cower to their supernatural threats. I refuse to *just live* with whatever irrational situation they present to us and to consider reform futile. I refuse to feed the rat. The world is ours as is our lives; ours to design. No longer shall we suffer the pain of knowing that that which should have been sanctioned was penalized instead. We are the adults now. It is time to take back control: of how we feed our minds, of how we live our lives, of what we choose as right and wrong, of what induces guilt and of what represents an obligation. Breaking free of their reign requires that you stand and declare what I declared to end my sacrifice: "*If you continue to make me pay for my virtues, they will no longer serve you.*"

Chapter Two

An Indestructible Spirit

"We are not sick men." —Bruce Lee

What if there were stresses that you were *so* used to, you didn't even notice the burden? In most communication with people, we hear insults to honor, to effort and to ability—to our own and to integrity as such—and in cutting to the chase, we let it go. What if this subtle repression of injustice is *precisely* what blocks you from enjoying *sacred* emotional rewards that you weren't even aware you deserved? What if it was *thee* barrier between you and the "reason for it all," and what if you found that it was placed there on purpose? Herein lies some of the great mysteries of life, and it's time to solve them.

What price would you put on being certain about the moral implications of your every action? Moral certainty is the most powerful human force, and there are astonishing planes of fulfillment that accompany its attainment. Unfortunately, dysfunctional premises drive illusory consequences in the minds of most, providing a sufficient barrier to these levels. The Spirit Murderer's don't wish the masses to reach them. These values rest in latent form, which if remain suppressed, allow the Spirit Murderer's to continue their game. What if solving this dilemma would allow you to reach the full maturity we all deserve an opportunity to feel? The Spirit Murderer's stand frozen, hovering over their fragile control of this powerful force, in dread of what will happen if full mass moral validation is actualized. Men will be freed and they will be thrown off. "Thrown off to die" in their minds, which rationally translates as, "responsible to face nature in the manner their victims do." As these rewards lay two levels

15

of abstraction from the typical range of human consciousness, they have gone undetected. As long as there was no one to make axiomatically valid ideals explicit, their secret was safe; but in recent history they have suffered a major setback.

We are in the midst of the self-help revolution. This is the time where the productive middle class has matured, spread its wings and is soaring. It is a fantastic time to be alive. Many people no longer feel helpless and are now in control of their own destinies, which is a much more significant cultural shift than just a generation coming into its own. The esteem they have generated is wholesome and real. It is the perfect opportunity for a philosopher to come in and reinforce the foundations of this movement, and therefore have a profound impact on all of the years ahead.

The human race is not deaf, blind or helpless, and we are now proving that en masse. With the promotional genius of men like Anthony Robbins, it is becoming generally accepted to model excellence in all fields and in all aspects of living. The traits which our heroes appear to so naturally assume are coming within reach of anyone who puts forth the effort to attain them. Philosophically speaking, the potency of human ability is being restored. This is such a wonderful step for a culture to take towards a moral existence, that I am sure men will have the strength to move into the next dimension and comprehend a moral code designed to convey a clear purpose for that excellence. We have learned how to spend our time wisely, to manage our money and to set goals. We have learned to build profitable corporations, to build healthy bodies and healthy relationships. Self-improvement has socially and psychologically moved into the realm of abstraction, where we are now beginning to effectively harness our emotions. Step by step, field by field, we are taking conscious control of our destinies. Sure, television news shows us nothing but crime and devastation, but I see a better-educated world around me and most importantly, a greater ability to link cause to effect and *act* on it, which includes an aggregate lengthening of intellectual range—both in capacity and time. On what many consider the brink of disaster, I feel an undercurrent of sound moral judgment in society today—a self-responsibility practiced by a growing number and identified as "en vogue." I see more leaders and fewer lemmings. At this point in history, it is time to make our moral countenance indestructible.

Along this road of progress, I'm sure you can recall experiences that have been turning points. Ideas you draw from constantly, which you couldn't imagine functioning day to day without; ideas that seem to lie at the base of every decision. What if there were still more powerful ideas that once known and practiced, became an absolutely priceless frame of reference? For all of the splendor you have achieved in your life, what if there was an awareness you could gain that would tie everything together and give great conscious meaning to your every glance, to your every action and to your every day? What if this awareness were to give you the grand, paternal feeling of looking upon all of existence as you foster those you have risen above, sharing your calm, your clarity, your love and your sanction for all that is possible to us? That is what I intend to fulfill.

Have you ever felt so pure a sanction of existence that you just wanted to tickle something? All throughout life I have maintained the boundless energy, the playful excitement and the unlimited possibility that we all started out with. Little did I know then, how much more I would encounter in the adult world. The clean reasons for friendship and romance, the stunning interests I've had in sharks, astronomy, philosophy, jets, racing cars and bikes has all followed me into adulthood. Life is a playground for adrenaline, with day-to-day development, refinement and increased emotional intensity. I left nothing to cultural dictates, and stayed open to the most fulfilling returns in all contexts. With experience and the power of vision, all elements of life now flow harmoniously. I see the parallels between our intimacy and our productivity, our morality and our physiology, our political affiliations and our art, and I'll bring that clarity to you.

The rewards just continue to gather more power and meaning, and among the pinnacles, I have found no greater interactive tribute to the incredible glory of Man than in visiting the Kennedy Space Center. Imagine being down in Cape Canaveral to witness an American space shuttle launch. Waiting for the countdown, your mind wanders, having time to appreciate the crisp, clean morning air and blue sky while you sit and enjoy the peaceful sounds of nature mixed with the motion of those gathered for the same purpose. With emotions fueled by spellbinding films and exhibits of their incredible struggle, you contemplate that sense of life that prompts men to endlessly explore; all driven to push the envelope, often at great risk to themselves. They carried mankind and technology along on their forward thrust into the unknown, to the crescendo of their final triumph—a man on the moon, which proved only the beginning. Here, you are a part of it, paying tribute to our present mastery in witnessing the launch of an orbiter, which is now building a space station. Suddenly the ground beneath you begins to vibrate, resonating with a deep, rich hum, which sweeps away your consciousness into a total focus on the craft. You look with wide unblinking eyes, barely allowing yourself to breathe, wishing to avoid the visual disruption of the rise and fall of your chest. The engines have been lit, and you can feel the pressure and heat of the air between you and the craft. As the countdown proceeds, your weight shifts, looking over the heads of others, astonished to realize you have been standing; not knowing when, or why. "Four...three...two...one," and the roar of the solid fuel rockets slams your senses way beyond anything you have ever experienced. A cloud pours around the bottom of the craft, engulfing it completely, spreading towards you and you think, "If the power and the heat were to engulf us all, oh,...just to feel what I am feeling now as the emotional height I've always wanted to reach, to feel this as my final salute to life, would be a precious blessing." The tip of the craft emerges above its cloud, and slowly lifts off with an incredible trail of fire, passion and thrust, as if it has joined forces with nature, harnessing and directing a storm to accomplish its will. Overwhelmed by the sensational rapture of your being, your eyes well with tears and you begin to pant in a pure, free, emotional release. With every sense filled so completely, you wonder if you'll even survive such unbearable pleasure. As it rises higher, the power of the sound diminishes; the shuttle lifts into the heavens peacefully—a red tailed comet—its firm touch releases, returning control of your body, but for the shallow breath of exhilaration still coursing all through you. Trembling in the aftermath, immersed so deeply within your soul, you find it difficult to walk, and you notice the same in others. You have been stunned and then laid back to peace, rocked by the incredible power, complexity and glory of Man; contemplating, "My god, *men* did this. Men erected a skyscraper and just shot it into space. If we can do this, we can do anything," and that is true. For the glory of that emotional release of all you can feel, which is a response to our highest potential, with the nature of the universe as our guide, we *can* do anything.

The most priceless reward of life is the ability to wake up every day with just such a wonderful sense of expectation; an awareness that you will have remarkable experiences of *your own* design that will make you feel so deeply, and so connected. The incredible power of Man is something we should all link to our own potentiality. Shivers move down my spine when I contemplate what each day might bring; the excitement, the risk, the adventure of life itself—of facing and conquering fears—is truly exhilarating.

Because of the implicit moral worth of our actions and its resulting confidence, it is going to be much easier for us individually to look inward at our own motives, to purify our body of knowledge and move to a new level, intellectually and spiritually. For example, picture yourself looking in the mirror. You think back and see achievement in your past. You see excitement in the present, and feeling a tingling sensation, your stomach drops, anticipating the plans you've laid for your future. This reflection is the life-force that makes it all possible, and which has made life worth living. Don't deny it, you *like* what you see! And you should. There stands a strong, progressive individual, on its way to its chosen and cherished goals. There is pride in that being, and there is beauty in that pride. For once in history you have to learn, not to take a hit, but the immense deliverance of taking a steady flow of self-compliments, because you know they are deserved. In today's world, the pursuit of our dreams seems limitless, and anything we want is just a 'plan of attack' away. Leading richer and fuller lives, we inherently *know* that our productivity is taking us in the right direction. As the industrious of Man, we now understand that our free expressions *are* the causes that reap mankind's glory; it's becoming obvious to all, but there are many crucial aspects of living which we still haven't learned.

When the space shuttle is prepped, every last detail is monitored to assure the health of the craft; its path, its platform, its fuel, its structure and its environment. Everything must flow perfectly or it doesn't take off. It is the same for a human spirit. This can be implied to mean that the craft is delicate, but that isn't true. Ballistic glass and a bullet-proof hull isn't delicate. The shuttle is designed to withstand the conditions it is expected to encounter in its traveled medium; so too properly, is the human mind. But how? Projecting what life should be and trying to live it, often feels like a soap bubble floating through the world. As light, as free and as easily punctured by experiencing the betrayal of values, by oneself or others. The difference is, as a bubble comes in contact with a thorn, its journey is over; not so for a damaged spirit. It goes on in a crippled state, kept in existence by the physical entity in which it is contained. One can wait for time to disassociate the pain, yet just when a benevolent medium returns, something else happens to smack it down in a self-defeating cycle. It isn't necessary for a spirit to be so fragile. The honest portion of this delicacy comes from a technology in its infancy; *not* in the nature of the medium. We can control our spiritual outcomes by assessing its nature, its environment and our direction, leaving nothing to chance. We can steer clear of thorns, making it safe for our innocence to return and flourish. We can plan for the world we live in, standing strong, tall and able, and move through it with a swift, preeminent elegance. *Moral Armor* will provide what is necessary to give your spirit a good solid feel. Instead of a soap bubble, it will be more like a run-flat, the high-performance tire that can still speed you along to your dreams with grace and style, even after a severe puncture.

Ingrained Spiritual Trauma. The self-help revolution's only clear flaw is that it doesn't define itself as *moral*. This absolutely crucial flaw can and always has acted as the wedge under the lid of hell. We have been humming along, blissfully unaware that a cliff lines one whole edge of our journey. Without explicit understanding of the moral justifications for our actions, we risk the loss of our most precious values or worse—the horror of seeing our efforts accomplish the will of evil. We *have* to face the issue of right and wrong and we have to face it head on. The next abstract step for us to take is to gain a fully integrated view of Man, of consciousness and of existence—giving sense, order and meaning to Man's life, to social actions and to all the tools we have been taught to use. With this knowledge, we can be sure that we are exercising our power responsibly and we can protect our right to exercise it. We can bring an end to what has been hurting us and secure human beings in their proper stature.

Intellectual freedom is a delicate and recent advance for Man, so the undercutting of our confidence has been easily perpetuated. The source of our spiritual fragility comes from a technology held back since Egyptian/Phoenician/Mesopotamian times, or about 3200 BC. The pharaoh's brute physical domination which worked so effectively for eons was given a spiritual equivalent as men moved into the realm of abstraction. When men invented language, the Spirit Murderers invented abstract distortion. The fear-ridden at all levels of society twisted every concept to mean its opposite in moral implication to keep men from comprehending their own value. Every attribute of Man was construed as a liability. Every desire of Man was considered a destructive impulse. Every sense of pride was turned into shame. Every advance was regarded as a moral affront by those who had to adjust their views or actions. Any means to rational fulfillment was trounced, and Man was cut off from achieving and enjoying his proper stature.

As all knowledge was claimed as coming from above, the creative faculty which brought mankind wonders it had never seen was considered a transgressor, and was often greeted with violence. In legend, Prometheus was torn by vultures for stealing the fire of the gods. Copernicus was forced to renounced his revolutionary scientific theories, while in the same dilemma, Socrates chose death. Even Einstein lamented that the true key to success was keeping your mouth shut. Most considered the realm of spirituality to be the unknowable and therefore the uncontrollable. The intellect was not given the same respect as the uncharted territories of the physical world, where the unknown was simply the undiscovered as yet. We were knocking down one barrier after another in the sciences, yet the structure of the mind itself was relegated to the *undiscoverable.* As mankind progressed, the scientists—the men who learned that nature to be commanded must be obeyed—began to encroach upon the domain of spirituality preached by the moral scholar's who sat beside kings. The scientific method was accountable and that clashed with the high priest's incantations, so free thinkers were forced to abandon the subject, leaving the field wide open to those who never intended to see mankind achieve a pure spiritual independence.

They proceeded to claim that Man was an unnatural being borne of conflict: partially of Earth, partially of spirit, irreconcilably at odds while alive, damned with a mind capable of nothing but misinterpretation and a body capable of nothing but pain. The irrational division of a man was coupled with an irrational division between men. Fraudulently viewing all of mankind as either totally untrustworthy if strong, and honorable but helpless if not, they demanded in haughty righteousness that the latter be taken care of, and service to the self-actualized mass indigence became the highest moral order. Somehow we were the only species on the planet not designed to fulfill our own requirements for living. Still, our weak limbs and useless minds were good enough to fulfill the needs of others, while another's limbs and mind were good enough to satisfy ours. The Spirit Murderers claimed to have solved nature's error, and like Frankenstein's monster, we were hacked apart and then reassembled with parts of each other.

A man was evil and unnatural to the extent of his self-sufficiency; he could not be permitted to act alone. The forfeit of one's own life to serve others became a moral code known as altruism, which in practice became a communal slave system often sanctioned by law, known as Socialism. Whether one's self was sacrificed unwillingly to domination or willingly to charity, the result was the same. No matter the benefactor, it was *the sacrifice of life* as a means of survival. What civil, rational men find necessary in only the most rare and tragic of circumstances was made a societal standard. Allowing no property, no personal ambitions and nothing precious to lay outside the right of seizure by our brethren, such a system pitted us all against each other. Our self-respect, our ability and our intelligence—putting our best foot forward—was no longer socially beneficial, but a mutual threat. Achievement became a toll road, enabling the deceivers to confiscate the products of our lives and/or determine their distribution *with our sanction,* carrying away our most sacred spiritual rewards in the process.

Imagine walking down the street with no right to the contents of your pockets, with even your smallest day to day preparations and simplest conveniences thwarted. *Hoarding* they called it. Imagine restraining yourself from showing any sign of ability or giving an opinion for fear of being enslaved or martyred. The cause of *Man divided, men divided* had the desired result: *Man neutralized, men neutralized.* No one could build. No one could grow. By destroying privacy and mutual respect among men, they avoided mass unity which could spur an uprising against centralized control. Just as Hitler planted distrust between members of his own party to avoid alliances that could oust him, the same was done *within* a man and between all men from the beginning. But such barbarism is ancient history, right? Our escape from religious persecution and totalitarianism was successful. In present day we can seek our dreams, own property and are allowed private lives. We have established civil order in society, launched ourselves into outer space and have harnessed the atom. We have come so far; so why are we still stopped dead in our tracks with the snide question, "Is that *moral?*"

It seems that anything is permitted, except what we really want. Walking into a review with your boss or into court, and though your mind might be saying that you have a right to ask for a fair shake, the reaction your body still has is that you are a slave. Our moral culture has ingrained us to go on submissive autopilot, feeling ashamed of our existence, feeling subservient and temporary—as if we exist on their grace—that this Earth is theirs and they have first right to it. We do not stand on common ground. For many, we react as if there *is* no common ground. That our *natural* relation is slave to master and that we must show respect for the irrational, because at any moment they can turn on us and take our lives, as they hold the whip-hand. The corrupters effectively stunted our cognition, and like farm animals have kept us within an intellectually tractable range. Our political system may be free, but our cultural ethics are still fear-driven. The irrational fundamentals that have allowed them to destroy individual lives and nations, are still in place.

The Lonely Road Inside Us All. The motive of spiritual undercutting is bad enough, but worse is what it is responsible for: senseless guilt, irrational fears, physical incapacitation, emotional deadening and dependencies on others or the heavens which go unfulfilled, as lives go unlived. The pretense of brother-love is abound, but we know full well that none of it is true and that we are very much alone. The rejection of reality denies us the process of *identification* and leaves us in an unrealistic limbo. Some take drugs to mimic the emotional states that rational premises would have generated naturally, while others take drugs to counter the pain and emotional conflict caused by our irrational code. I can sense the heartbreak in those trapped whom I pass daily—in hallways, in streets, in traffic—souls and bodies stiffened and aged by pain. Life promised so much once, a glory that never came. But underneath that is a cry for help, a weakness that screams, "I'm capable of so much more than you see, help me to find what I missed and I'll show you what I really am." There is so much untapped potential out there it is astonishing. The freedom in their souls has been stifled in so many ways and from so many directions that they have lost the capacity to recognize it. But one thing is clear: they're not enjoying life, and the problem is *inside* now. Missing the gratification of living is a tragedy played out by most of mankind. Drudgery becomes their medium which doesn't stimulate creative thought, but lethargy, leading to more drudgery. No matter what they try, all roads seem to lead there. They remain down on themselves and down on life.

If we're not having fun, what's the point? Life is only worth the effort if your spirit remains intact, meaning how you see the world, others and your possibilities. This is the most crucial human dilemma because *life itself* should never be the object of an unrequited love. I can see the dividing line which separates people from what they profess to seek in the statement, "Yeah, but." I see the tail-chasing mistakes, the pointless stress, the efforts that lead nowhere and the minds slammed shut to any path that would provide relief. They know there is a problem, yet can take no steps in the direction of their fulfillment. Stuck in a loop provided by popular guidance, they are left with so delicate an esteem they're easily shattered by a strong hand from either side. What happiness did they expect under the daunting sneers of those who tell Man his desires are selfish, his senses invalid, his body feeble, his actions harmful and his destiny Hell? With nowhere to turn, their feelings for life become conflicted. Any attempt to rise is blocked, stopped and thwarted, while they are encouraged by the plethora of mediocrity to coast downhill into degeneration. It is the nature of existence they end up damning as intended, while the code of the killers goes unquestioned. They learn not to expect justice, understanding or fulfillment; they learn to stand down, to *know their place* and to let go of their dreams. They come to believe that the only alternative in life is to feel torture, or to feel nothing. They expect pain as a result of any thought, so they shut off and disengage life, often never to be reached again.

Most of us haven't been paid for our virtues, and have lost the expectation of getting paid. You know what you should be recognized for; you inherently know what virtue is, and what is vice. You know what pride you have earned, and what contempt. But what you meet with in this introspective moment is more disturbing: nothing. You hear silence, see not a lasting glance of concern, approval or disapproval in your direction; not from Man, not from nature. The only response is the quiet, impersonal, unstoppable ticking of the secondhand on the clock facing you. You know how clearly the good you've done outweighs the bad, making it insignificant—and yet the world remains silent about both. You wouldn't mind paying the price for errors; you don't seek to hide. What you need is to pour out the beauty of your soul, but no one is there to see. They keep walking, paying no attention, and all that is left is loneliness, pain, heart break, rejection and hate. Often you conclude, "What's the point of being moral? Nobody notices either way." The truth is everyone notices, but they suffer the same barriers. In this environment, the last thing healthy people want to confront is the subject of morality; yet one of the most sacred forms of elation denied us is seeing our fellow men look upon our lives with the same pride *we* feel about it; to enjoy the common bond of our solemn dedication to progress, and to know in quiet serenity that their tribute is deserved. Instead when attention does come as in childhood, it is often in the form of torture. The pressure to conform to pretenses in society, schools and families is ridiculous. Ostracism for practicing virtue is a truly debilitating punishment, and few can survive it alone. The physical violations prohibited even in war are given no such protection on a spiritual level. We are slow tortured, and I can see why most don't make it emotionally.

The endurance of going on for years with nothing—no rewards outside of your own appreciation—with your reservoir of passion empty and only the stale residue of a memory—the awareness of how they loved you so much more when you were less—is tragically heartbreaking. *Moral Armor* grew out of that emotional delicacy, a precious respect for justice and a moral sanction I expected from the world and never received, to confirm my life-furthering attributes and actions. Even *without* respect for the judgment of others, it's very painful to feel the world doesn't want you, knowing that your virtues are what they reject. But in this moral environment, you have to be prepared to go it alone—to go without rewards from the outside. Until the beast is broken, we are all condemned to some level of desolation as we advance, and no, moral clarity doesn't make up for it. What is most important in the interim is that *you* know the true sum. Your spirit can live being shunned by the outside; it cannot live being shunned by the inside. You can bring into this world the highest image of Man now, or you can hold off for the social atmosphere that rewards strivers. But that could be decades. Why wait? Cry for an hour, but *live* for twenty-three. Do it for you.

The Worst Danger Might Be Right Next to You... I'm tired of watching a whole society struggling to bloom while their killing code holds them from it. I'm sick of seeing those who endure and rise to great heights only to have their accomplishments physically and spiritually confiscated by irrational laws or a plotting spouse, unable to fight back. I've watched my own kind get pushed around and led like poodles by family, clergy and the fools they've married, led to their own spiritual deaths—and to contempt for me, the absolute; the unremitting. There is a reason why people fight to preserve what harms them while sacrificing their highest values throughout life. Have you ever wondered what it is? Neurotic action is the offspring of missing, evaded or corrupt moral standards. Most of us experience their effects the hard way—listening to people twist morality in order to use us, to stop us or to penalize us, only to realize later that we were conned, while suffering the desperate loneliness we feel while striving for and reaching pinnacles of our own. It will continue to happen, but it would be worse to live a whole life never having known the true intentions of those around us; never having identified and accepted in full understanding, *their* psychological health as well as our own.

Who has scheduled your spirit for execution? Who demands your acceptance, but not your understanding or agreement? Permitting the negation of awareness will bring irrationality to power, while your aspirations are left to wander down uncharted roads. Either you pick up and use the tools given you, or you become a tool of others. Of whom in particular? Of those who told you it was moral to drop your tools. Whether they host black-tie benefits, pose alongside productive spouses or inhabit slums, the fear-based used their perversions to claw their way on top of us, using their victims as life-preservers. Sidestepping your consciousness allows them endless opportunities to hide their motivations. Clean motives have nothing to worry about; they *enjoy* an audience. Deadly motives loath awareness, and in self-defense, therefore demand it. My intention is to spawn a race of steady eyes; eyes that *see;* eyes that *know* what is being done.

...Or Even Closer. The first and most crucial battle is to be fought in an unexpected place: within us. As we have been inundated with corruption from the beginning of our lives, the first wave of enemies is now internal. They are anti-epistemological—anti-awareness processes—harmful patterns we have been cycling without question. We have *all* been victims of this system of cannibal ethics; there has been no way to escape it. It has infected every thought, inverted every image and mental projection and defined every self-hampering physical response. It has placed our living energy in the service of death, corrupted our rational long-term understandings, perverted our ultimate goals and destroyed our capacity to enjoy truly wholesome moments. Even when we have identified and solved our own conscious errors, it has often not been deep enough to counter the subconscious drivers which promote an unstudied reactionary defense. We stomp out what we see, yet like a weed its underground network of irrational connections regenerates it. The alternatives it offers all lead to the same brick walls: fear, malice, powerlessness and subservience. It saps our will, as cognitive hampering kills the capacity to look for answers. We come to fear the darkness they conjured within us, and to fear others.

What spiritual path are you on at present? Ask yourself how the inversion has drawn you in. What makes you murderously angry, people smarter than you? People with greater courage, independence and tenacity? People with greater integrity? People with more money? Or is it stupidity, pointless activities, lethargy, denial, the unwillingness of others to see, to learn and to grow, and all the resulting consequences? Does what you hate in others, reflect what you hate in yourself? If you hate another's ability, you have damned ability itself. On the other hand, if you hate another's incompetence and any incompetence you may have yet to overcome, *that* is a tribute to life. Can you achieve your own highest vision of yourself in the world of today? Do you believe it has a chance? Who has determined your view of Man? Those around you, an ideal potentiality, or the worst in your experience? What do you really wish for Man? Are they benevolent thoughts or angry thoughts? Are you afraid of human beings? Be honest. I was afraid for a long time. I had inherited the fears of those who came before me, and though perceptive enough to understand that my fears had no foundation, I had no ammunition to challenge them with; only strength of resolve, but no aim for that strength. The pain was mine to bear; the problem was mine to decipher, and upon solving it, the benefits were mine to enjoy.

We must come to recognize and eradicate the errors as they are encountered, or in other words, learn to get out of our own way in life. This is the journey now before you. Those seeking reform have to walk what appears at first to be a tightrope, but it gets wider and more stable once the elements are set into a psycho-epistemological routine (don't worry, I'll provide it). Enjoyment becomes more constant as causal factors become clearer. The right actions become automatic and the outcomes become easy to see, given either fork in the road.

It is important not to damn yourself along the way for identifying traits of character that are destructive. Being forthright is an opportunity for growth. This is the process of refinement, *not* a spotlight for shame. As they may bring detriment now, their resolution will bring a new strength, your experience of life will become more intensely passionate and true forgiveness—if necessary—will be deserved; from others and from yourself. The road of healing, of safety, of empowerment and ultimately of intransigence is a different length for everyone. You must start from where you are. You must be honest about where you are, in order to start. Hanging on to your illusions will only leave you further and further behind. Let go and you'll find firm ground just inches below. If you can understand that honesty is the greatest "leap of faith" in reason, that it will not toss you into an abyss, that it will not take your self-esteem but will bring you more than you could ever imagine, then you will be free. You will be well on your way to discover every answer you seek and every pleasure of living. And then your view of Man will change.

Ingraining New Patterns. Preserving a high spirited outlook is crucial to everyone, yet under society's mess of moral contradictions, there is nothing more difficult than spiritual maintenance. Cultural roots have us so off track, I'm surprised anyone wants to get out of bed in the morning. To most, a sense of invigorating pride and opportunity is inconsistent, uncontrollable and elusive, as if the stability of a human consciousness had a fragile nature. It doesn't, but under the ancient inversion, it *becomes* unstable. The whole structure of consciousness is meant to protect us, from the need of clarity, confidence and affection, to the safety we create in accomplishing what we know we must do, to the pride we feel by doing it right. Cause and effect can be identified from one end of it to the other, but we are vulnerable if we agree to pretend that the rules of the physical world do not apply to the soul. They do. There is no meaningful, lasting emotional intensity without acceptance of the concept of identity—accepting that existence exists. There is no long-term safety in relationships, business or law, without an organized and rational value-hierarchy, or in other words, without *standards*.

Our disconnection from rational standards is obvious in that we'd all like to live with great depth, passion and meaning, yet the trouble for everyone is...How? All men desire the same sense of ease in life; a sense of inner peace on a fundamental level. No one consciously desires dysfunction. Even when being irrational, we want our views to *work!* We all say we "just want to be happy," and then the fog rolls in and the epistemological chain ends. Happiness is so elusive and fleeting that most feel as if they are staring into a void, just saying the word. We all know what it feels like but few can describe it, and fewer can repeat the steps necessary to conjure it. But once the steps are known, it *can* be had as a constant medium of our existence. The path to an indestructible spirit is the *reintegration* of mind and body, of Man's proper relation to existence and of Man's proper relation to other men. The solution is had by looking to those untarnished by the problem.

There are people out there that are bulletproof spiritually, and they do certain things that make them that way. By conforming to the right code, they exist outside the Spirit Murderer's power. However, so few have reached an intransigent mindset—the soul of a hero—that it cannot be studied readily. If there were more such men in existence, its nature could more rightly be determined, but for now, we are left at the mercy of the sheer number who seek it. Such heroes embody a strength beyond strength; an impenetrable barrier for pain; a reservoir which holds a purity so potent that no foreign matter can survive past a certain point. By following their lead, it is possible to grow just as strong, to achieve all of our goals in a framework of our own design, to meet and surround ourselves with people we can respect and admire and to live a life largely absent of pain, contempt, boredom and senselessness.

The incredible meaning most come upon only once or twice throughout their span of years, you can come to feel a few times every day, and it will keep getting more and more frequent and more and more powerful. The full integration of mind and body is so potent a combination that no such individual can remain a follower; therein lies its danger to precedent. Your physical senses and their integrator—your consciousness—are the metaphysical inlets that open into a virtual ocean of knowledge and fulfillment. *Sensory perception* is the foundation of all exertion-generated human values including happiness, whose enjoyment is the bane and impossibility of those otherwise denied. *Honest* spirituality follows the clean rationality in the volitional nature of our being. *Pride* is a barometer, measuring the success of our choices.

As the human brain has a specific physical makeup, so too does the structure of its content. The function of a mind is identical for every man and cannot be altered, as the function of a heart or any other organ cannot. It has evolved into its most efficient design and can only be nourished by a proper diet, or starved and mangled by an improper diet. To flourish, we need certain nutrients in mind and body, and they go much deeper than you might imagine. So many things that you perceive as okay to leave approximate or optional, *are not.* The mechanics of the medium must be understood to fully exercise its power to achieve pure happiness, supreme confidence and a radiant self-worth. As in all of the other realms we have mastered, our control will remain precarious until with experience and introspection, we gain a firm grasp on its proper use.

The spirit must be worked and fed throughout life like any muscle, to maintain its strength. Like an athlete, it has a game to play—the game of life— and it must be kept in practice; otherwise, it will suffer in atrophy. All living things deteriorate from neglect. Still, its use must be *healthful*. An old martial arts instructor once said to me, "Any form is good, but some are better for you." I learned what he meant after training with Aikido students, most of whom wore joint supports for hyper-extension injuries, which often led to severe arthritis and the eventual quitting of the sport out of physical necessity. Such practice misuses the entity that acts—the human body. Likewise, evasion, repression, hysterics, emotional deadness and the desire for any causeless reward are all a reflection of the misuse and malnourishment of the human mind. A light, healthy spirit can never be conjured with a false smile and an affirmation. It is a state of mind that is earned—*achieved*—by a direct, focused, conscious effort. Such vitality is the natural result of enacting the correct life-furthering premises—a moral choice. The correct premises are identified by honestly experimenting with rational new ideas and by weeding out contradictions in the old ones. The pinnacle of emotional states has its own constant gauge, evidenced by a pure, vibrant emotional health. The closer we get to practicing the structures nature intended, the healthier we are.

There are ups and downs for us all, but someone with an indestructible spirit makes the right moves when things go wrong. They remain bright, awake and alive—ready and willing to defend themselves, actively seeking new clarity, willing to earn their own sense of significance and ready to enjoy their own existence. To come to this requires that we get good at being human. We have to learn how to *demand* human status; accepting and supporting that we *do* see, we *do* hear, we *do* feel, think, love and live. We have to learn not to buckle under centuries of ill conditioning by our opposition. It can be done. We must split, not our minds from our bodies, but from the irrational weight of that cross we all bear. The central civil issue in life is that we have the opportunity to experience our highest possibilities, in body *and* spirit.

Imagine a solid yellow line within your mind, which is the straightest path to your own ideals. It leads to that beautiful stranger, it conveys your truest style and your freest, most desirable way of being. If identified at all, most of us spend our time jockeying back and forth, fearfully and humbly criss-crossing the directness of this path. Learning to walk down the center of your life is a brave step forward. Bringing the heroic into your destiny will be a chaos of challenges as the defaults wither and the spirit blooms, with incredible new highs and frightening but clairvoyant lows; a roller coaster of emotional triumph that will make life worth living again.

What's really entertaining is watching those who emerge from the depths and struggle with their new happiness. They don't believe it's real. I get a kick out of it. They struggled against pain for so long with the tools of evasion, denial and false justifications that they're not prepared for an intense and consistent joy. They are so used to pushing feelings away that they are unpracticed in dealing with something they want to keep. They fear that it will elude them as in the past, and in panic, try to hoard it; but they have to break down and laugh, because it just keeps bubbling out of them. By practicing the correct causal factors, they've become a bunch of little happiness generators, and the rest of their lives are going to be like this. Instead of dealing with pain, they have the wealth of a new resource to contend with, and all the years ahead to discover the immense pleasures it will bring them. They gracefully learn to channel it, and every few months they step up to a new level. So used to being pushed around on moral issues, their new determination becomes a cherished facet of their lives.

Settling into this new code, those outside start to treat you with more deference, the exact deference you have come to associate with a trait you have worshipped and sought. Astonished, you'll think, "It's as if they believe I have that stature," and then you'll realize that your uncertainty with this level is rapidly diminishing or gone; that you're comfortable associating with peers on this plane, and suddenly realize that you are one of them. You've made it with one up; you're still moving. It is quietly exciting to watch yourself grow, and such deliverance always happens this way. You will see the day when you have the courage to do what was so recently impossible, and you'll do it as an afterthought. When you finish this book, you're going to feel a spectacular moral power. It will accent every thing you do, and your life will never be the same.

Chapter Three

Our Moral Vanguards

"We are all set to win, just as we are born, knowing only life."
—Enter the Dragon

Human beings have a natural affinity to do what is right as clearly as the need to breathe in, and I trust would always make that choice with the proper moral coherence. Being born and raised in a civil society, is it too much to expect that those who came before us would have provided such guidance? When a topic calls for it, we look with open eyes and questioning minds to those who hold positions of power and responsibility to reflect sound moral judgment. Yet whomever has been appointed or declared themselves the moral leaders of Man—priests, judges, politicians, professors; those we expected to see out in front—have mostly defaulted on this obligation. The university intelligentsia remain lost in unworkable utopias that they devise outside the laws of reality; our government accrues massive, unjustifiable debts that *we* have to repay; our courts have lost their objectivity and common sense and our spiritual leaders never had any. This is the greatest failure of our leadership on planet Earth, evidenced by the basic sense of unworthiness most feel: the steadfast, paternal accountability dropped throughout the ages; the careless logic, the lack of humanity and the lack of moral direction, all held back by cowardly, subhuman "get away with it" motivations. It is time to accept who the real vanguards are, *and who they are not.*

Living in a blessed era of peace has allowed us to realize implicitly that the most appreciable leaders are those who make the natural, practical flow of life more smooth and consistent. Our gratitude is owed not just to those who lead us to victory in battle, but to those who lead us to prosperity in daily life. As ninety-nine percent or more of our lives is not spent in fox-holes or running from tornadoes, it should be clear that *sound* moral guidance concentrates on long-range human progression, under the conditions that make settled life possible. That said, the essence of a Moral Vanguard's focus is to clarify and *make explicit*—to employ, protect and disseminate knowledge of the life-furthering attributes and actions of the best of men and their creations, in every context within the realm of their interest.

They exist in all fields required for Man's survival as do the sentry's of evil, so it is crucial that we learn to tell the difference. A true moral vanguard helps clear the way for men to live and to enjoy living. He teaches men to live independently by teaching them to think independently. He furthers ideas that foster and sanction the expansion of mankind's awareness of the world around us. Able to harvest the highest moral pride by his own actions, he seeks to exemplify and protect access to mankind's most sacred states of being. He knows that men have a nature that cannot be violated to their betterment; that a man owns his own creations by right and has sole authority to determine their means of distribution in trade. He acknowledges no authority over the actions of his person or over the product of his effort. Likewise, he doesn't try to do another man's living for him, never standing between another man and that man's own judgment. To do so would be to disrupt that man's life-generating power. He knows that the key to prosperity for a man and a nation is that men must be free; free to think, free to act and free to keep the results; *free* from being forced to pay for the lives of others and from bearing the penalties of their misfortunes. He doesn't attempt to secure values for himself or for others without earning them, as the champions of Welfare, unconditional love and government lobbies do. He never approaches others with force. He does not subject men to arbitrary rules that cannot be identified before breaking them (Antitrust). He does not seek his own sustenance or the sustenance of those he wishes to assist, by confusing, conning, barring, riding, robbing or murdering other men. A Moral Vanguard respects the sovereignty of men above anything he could gain if he didn't. Most importantly, the noblest can be identified in that they achieve their stature by life-serving means in a free market; by the voluntary consent of everyone who trades with them.

There are three main categories of vanguard as I define them: the *developmental,* the *abstract* and the *institutional.* The first deals with direct relations of Man to Man; the second, Man to Man's creations; and the third, Man to the organizations of Man. The actions of all three follow the same pattern for the same reason. For example, As Moral Vanguard, a president's realm is the good of his country, which implies the good of its citizens, *which implies a morality consonant with their nature,* which requires protection from physical force and the intellectual and physical freedom necessary to function. A producer's realm is the good of his business, *which implies a morality consonant with nature,* in order to harness the principles that make his product possible so that its production may exceed its consumption of resources, allowing sustenance and growth. The good of his business *implies a morality consonant with the nature* of those he employs, as no unnatural requirement can leave them free to function in the capacity they were hired for. An employee's realm is the fulfillment of his assignments, *which implies a morality consonant with nature,* by which to gauge the profitability of his actions in order to earn for himself and his family, their sustenance. A parent's realm is the good of his and her children, *which implies a morality consonant with their nature,* protecting their physical health and guiding the progress of their intellectual potency, leaving them free to expand both experientially in preparation for lifelong independent thought and action. A lover's realm is the good of his or her relationship, which implies a morality consonant with their shared spiritual and physical fulfillment, satisfying every sense, supporting their mate's expansion of potency as a human being and pursuing one's own. Notice a trend?

All living entities and their organizations must seek a course which allows an unhampered continuance in the flow of their lives. That flow is identified and preserved by a set of principles—*a moral code of action*—consonant with their nature. It is the philosopher's realm to define this code with respect to the nature of existence and the nature of Man. No instinct forces Man along a course of self-preservation. He must *choose life* by a process of thought, where the preservation and furtherance of life *is* the standard of value, and then take action accordingly. The body of knowledge that results from his correct decisions is a code of morality. A code of morality is Man's volitional equivalent for the concept of instinct. Moral Vanguards are the men who follow this code.

Developmental Vanguards. The first vanguards we encounter are those who brought us into being; our parents. They nourished our bodies in order to preserve our one cardinal value, our lives. If we were fortunate, they nourished our minds also, training us to carry on the life-process independently. The wave of guardians that followed were those whose intent was to shape us cognitively; our teachers. With the effort of comprehension, we found mentors wherever knowledge was to be had. It was their contribution that taught us how to carry out a rational progression from $2+2=4$ to understanding the wavelengths of light, and to convey that knowledge. They fostered our ability to identify what is and what isn't a correct answer, in order to make decisions wisely in any context of our future lives. In school, the right answers and actions led us to good grades. In life, the right answers and actions lead us to prosperity. If they taught well and we paid attention, we then join the world of production, the "real world" of the life sustainers where one's capacity for profitable actions is put to the test. We gain full competency by emulating the vanguards who do their jobs well. Upon mastering the realm of sustenance—which is to maintain profitability by outpacing what one consumes—we are free to rise to the limit of our ambition. Then *we* become the vanguards automatically by doing *all that is required of one;* by setting a sound example.

There are clearly a lot of should be's and if's in the above paragraph. Those who should be our protectors are often our corrupters. Some of us owe our very existence to a knee-jerk response in our parents, who sought children as a neurotic aversion in an attempt to fill the void of purpose. Lost on their own, such parents aren't aware of what kids need cognitively, and as a result can be abusive and neglectful. We all know of the dreadful records our public schools have, risking the quality of their lives and the future of America by putting a child's emotional state ahead of his cognitive structure (his very means to achieve self-affirming emotions). Executives and workers are often as inept as they are intelligent. It is quite common that we serve as a physical and spiritual punching bag for another's subhuman frustrations instead of receiving any healthy training; and upon *our* independence day, our ambition is all but dead on arrival. But it remains true that the role of parent, teacher and life generator are all *meant* to be the developmental guardians of the human race. Their contributions are essential and we must be forever cognizant of their impact, as they give structure to an individual's potency for the next levels of living.

Our most treasured response to existence, *our purpose in life,* parallels and motivates our highest intimate response to another human being; a romantic relationship. The charge we get from pursuing our dreams and winning, drives the need to express our deepest loving power. A romantic relationship is our greatest social experience and release; our most precious spiritual vanguard. We work conscientiously to develop and maintain our attractiveness to deserve the same in return—the best a spouse can offer. We practice wholesome values because we want the elation of true love, and with integrity, we *have* earned it. When we find someone who shares our style of living, our resulting fulfillment is priceless. But sometimes we have to spend years alone, and watch the passion we generate die on the vine. Popular psychologists tell us we shouldn't need anyone to be happy. So why are *they* all married? A relationship is not a dependency, it is a confirmation. Don't kid yourself; no one can keep his or her spirit fulfilled without personal intimacy when its potentiality is aroused by every passing smile. Love is a sacred reward.

Still, finding a suitable mate is rarely a cooperative pursuit, and can be a heartbreaking challenge. The torture of loneliness can drive us into the arms of those who harbor many unsettling characteristics. With foolish generosity we grant them faith, unable to believe their views on life could mean what they seem to mean. Slipping into an intellectual coma, we give our love completely (the only way we know how) and then tragically discover that the mate we've committed to isn't drawn to our hard won identity or any of the splendor we can create together, for any number of reasons. Here's one: They cling to you due to the shear, naked fear of facing life independently. You have been reduced from the sense of a gallant romantic partner to being a source of food. Confronted with the appalling reality that you aren't special to them at all—that the concept "special" is incommunicable to them—you fog out the knowledge that their favor could've been had by *anyone* willing to pay their deficit. With your last remnants of faith (they'll change), you continue to pretend that their mental range isn't one meal away from death. Equating your tolerance with weakness, they lose respect for you and attempt spiritual domination to secure their position. This leaves you to question: How does the one who professes to love me, consistently take actions of hate? Hmmm...A being spurred into action by negativity, yet passively indifferent to intimacy...

Or maybe they *did* choose you for your personal attributes, but furthering no life purposes of their own, seems to exert his or her greatest passionate response to you by relishing your physical or emotional pain; seeing your desires in life and in the relationship frustrated. They are so slow to provide comfort and so eager to help confirm your impotence in life. The worst default is your silent resignation to endure such hell out of romantic starvation; even though they have turned on you. Who turned on you first?

There will always be Spirit Murderers who seek to steal our potency. It is up to us to stay aware of who the *real* vanguards are; those who uphold justice and foster progress, privately and publicly, physically and spiritually, and who the impostors are in every context of our lives. Many claiming the title of vanguard are just the opposite. Both become easy to spot with the right tenets, to be fully spelled out in the following sections. But for now, understand that an imposter's energy is used to justify his own impotence, and his life's frustration exudes negativity. His focus brings about a sense of strain in those burdened by his presence; a sense of painful contradictions. In his life, everything is your fault; that is unless he runs into someone even more accomplished. Then it becomes theirs. When you cross paths with him, you breathe a sigh of relief when he is out of range.

A true vanguard carries around almost no negativity. He uses his energy to fulfill his dreams of which you may be a part, and his pride and peace exudes good feelings. When you pass *him* in the street, you can feel *life* walking by.

Abstract and Institutional Vanguards. The vanguards which our prosperity is most sensitive to as a nation are those who administer our legal and political structures. The fathers of our country foresaw encountering different forms of oppression. Just as Man designs durable products to withstand the natural elements, we devised a system to protect our life's constancy; to protect us physically from any kind of invader. It was a great idea which would take our minds off watching our backs and leave us free to achieve, individually and as a Union. We created an organized body to whom sole authority to use force against those who threaten the nation's people was delegated.

Our physical protection was its only valid function and concern. It was to leave all men free to pursue their survival by offering the results of their effort for a voluntary trade with others of the nation; our free system of commerce. Such a system was designed to protect the producers of life from the parasites of the living. The government was just an instrument of the people; it was not intended to serve as master; it was not to rule. It was to stand as guardian from any initiation of violence against men at any time; whether taking place in an alley, an office or a home. *We* as citizens take care of the rest. It was to respond to the *actual* use of force, where human lives are compromised by evildoers subjecting citizens to an *involuntary* circumstance. *All other human action is voluntary,* and therefore is supposed to be the object of their *guardianship.* Yet now, *perceived* threats are regulated; which simply means that laws are for sale. Any form of incarceration is a life-taking power, so such power must be exercised with the utmost care and the clearest reasoning. But what has transpired? The careful maintenance of individual freedom as technologies advance is clearly not the government's trend or priority. Our representatives have violated the Constitution, allowing the government to break loose of its essential function to permeate and decay everything in its path.

The evidence of degeneration is countless, whose aggregate result is our unjustifiable tax burden, our economic Fed-watching and the wild swinging in our scales of justice. There are now government agencies and government businesses competing in or constraining every major industry, most extensively in the credit markets; monopolies expropriating the benefits of freedom by those politically connected, to simply take it for themselves. In every instance outside its legitimate purpose, it has become a conspirator of the very evil we needed protection from, and now it is destined to enforce the irrational. On a common level, take for example the ludicrous injury judgments awarded by juries, the blaming of corporations for products used in self-inflicted injuries and the antitrust suits filed by our own government against private citizens who display the deepest vision, where a *less* successful effort on their part would have shielded them. Imagine working your whole life and rising to the top of your field, only to be attacked by those who reserve *the sole right to attack* in matters of business, who decide that *your* way is not the way to run *your* business any longer. Just when you should be getting the keys to cities and other honors, your brilliant ability to put together an organization that employs thousands and benefits millions is blasphemed and destroyed by the politician's "expert witnesses"—men who are unable to stay competitive with you for the same reasons and means by which they propose to restructure your business. You are someone who has been building a better world in your every thought and action. It has kept you up at night, gotten you up early, and given you a more genuine pride and satisfaction than any other endeavor. As a result, your company has been voted the best alternative by everyone who seeks a voluntary purchase in your industry. Does it make sense that you are considered an enemy of the country? There is no greater corruption, no greater self-abasement for a country than to take our highest and best—those who deserve our most reverent salute—and rob them of their control as we wipe our feet on them.

Throughout history, one empire after another has choked to death on its own red tape, and the first men to be sacrificed physically and legally—Abraham Lincoln, John Kennedy, Bill Gates—are always those of integrity in business and politics who are able to lead. Government is proper only as a consolidation of the right to use force against oppression. When wielded inappropriately, such as in initiation against private enterprise for a supposed "good cause," it acts as a catalyst to bring about such a policy's actual intention in defying nature; destruction. When this cycle begins, government becomes the most lethal enemy of the people, and only a return to sound fundamental principles can save them. Our government is no longer a pure vanguard of the people, no longer standing for American values alone, evidenced by our permeation of government enterprise, our trade status with slave nations and our debt-based currency system. It has become morally inconsistent and financially reckless, no longer guided but simply restrained by the original Constitution. Until and unless its motives are cleansed, we will continue to suffer a slow downward spiral back into another dark age.

The most prominent *opponent* of morality began its life as one of the first abstract vanguards, which is not at all unusual. I saw how religion could be abused as a child and have been at odds with it ever since, but in looking beyond my own experiences, I discovered a crucial and redeeming truth: Many people who seek religious guidance begin with an honest desire for an *explicit* morality. They want to find a clear format for living that allows them to feel good about their actions; they want to *know* that what they are doing is right. With all of the innocence of a child, that is just what I want, and have pursued since it was missed in my youth. Religion has dominated the subject for millennia; it is after all, *thee* publicly recognized domain of moral judgment, and was my first stop as well. As my studies continued to subdivide and move deeper, I understood that it was the intentional misuse of religion that I disagreed with, and *that* allowed me to relax. So if you follow the flow of thought which has full validation in the natural world, you'll understand that we quite possibly have the same benevolent motivation. If your religious premises are sound, they will not reject the nature of cause and effect either, *nor our means to discover it.* You will be able to identify which principles are life-furthering and which ones were "snuck in" to your faith over the centuries, to secure unearned benefits for the freeloaders.

Early on, religion claimed the title of Moral Vanguard. Yet at the Vatican for example, *actual* morality is lightly touched on and mostly avoided in fear of their follower's discovery that they have no clear idea of what morality *is*, and that what they have compiled is a very confused, obscure, semi-rational, semi-evasive definition. Their undefined and indefinable basis for explanations is not a means of validation. Identifications and conclusions suppose a rational chain of knowledge—an epistemological chain. You'll never witness their high priests in a public moral debate, vulnerable to having the world discover that they don't have a leg to stand on. They preserve some semblance of dignity by handing down their senseless edicts while hiding behind a locked door. They are apprehensive of any argument regarding morality, because they sanction and exercise no fundamentally valid frame of reference, and they never will. To do so would be to wipe out their remaining power. Clinging to their own self-limited interpretation of their chosen dogma, they remain hopelessly behind the rest of the world in the understanding and conveyance of moral action. Life does not flow with the patterns these men attempt to dictate, and the whole world knows it. They have lost their power to compete for the minds of rational men, and I wouldn't consider them a serious threat to western culture any longer.

It is to the productive public's intellectual credit that they have largely abandoned such sources for true moral guidance. Today, their statements are often treated on television news as entertainment. With the propensity of the press to exploit the obvious, discredit comes from claiming that they are "behind the times." But "times" do not determine the *content* of a moral code, only how it is practiced. It is their content and their means of its attainment which is unsound. Sound moral principles cannot go out of fashion; they are good for an eternity. For example, if you lived under censorship, openly sharing your ideas would get you killed; so until freedom is restored, in self-preservation the correct action is to withhold them. In a country of free speech and free men, your chosen career pays best when you openly share your ideas, so in self-preservation your correct action is to bestow them. When faced with the prospect of physical destruction, it would be immoral *not* to guard your life, by stopping or escaping those whose intention is to take it. In civil times, when one is able to address issues beyond sheer survival, it is morally right to expand the range of your knowledge and abilities, making life easier and more fun (as progress is a physio-intellectual necessity). "The times" change the form of our allegiance, but our objective remains the same; to preserve and further human life; vitally our own. The public's lack of explicit understanding on the issue is evidenced in that most do not recognize their daily, self-sustaining actions as moral. The Vatican's *actual* discredit is what is responsible for this: in their unwillingness to recognize that *Man's life* is the object of a rational moral code, and that *the preservation of life* is its purpose.

Understand that the populace may have lost touch with the Vatican; but they have not lost touch with religion as such. The world's most widely recognized set of moral principles became one of the first mass-scale abstract victim's of the Spirit Murderers. Religion was intended as a standard of action for men to live by, and yet it has been slammed into the wall and ridden into the ground just like any other unguarded value. Those seeking a buffer between life and the effort to deserve it have always been on the lookout for a means to obtain values without thinking or working. They saw how powerful a moral code is, how desperately it is sought by men, and they schemed to subvert it. It was their contradictions with the nature of existence that invented hypocrisy. Such a painful, heartbreaking and undeserved moral guilt—that one cannot be moral if one takes the actions necessary to exist; that one has failed one's Lord and one's self—is all they have to offer their followers now. It shocks me that someone can be stopped from pursuing knowledge, such as reading an important book or carrying on scientific or commercial work, due to the unsubstantiated condemnation of it by moral frauds. It is a frightening glimpse at just how primitive and influential their horror psychology, such as "You'll go to Hell if you even think it," can be. Through guilt or just the threat of potential guilt, Man can be controlled; and control of men is never a *true* vanguard's intention.

For the most part, religion, astrology and other popular forms of mysticism give me the creeps. It is not necessarily the mediums, but the interpretation and expectations of the audience that I find unsettling. As in religion, my contempt is reserved for followers who are willing to negate their consciousness (which true professionals in such fields will tell you is improper) in favor of external drivers. They float through their lives like pieces of driftwood, revering unaccountable forms of knowledge, while neglecting the provable and consistent ones. Abandoning reason, their fate rests in the stars or in the hands of others, but never in their own, where it belongs. Their future and esteem hinges on anyone's opinion, and the less it is substantiated the more it is heeded. Such people are looking for a way around thought for a very specific, self-abasing reason. Fools misuse mysticism, but it *can* be productively utilized by the rest of us upon reaching a certain intellectual level. The field is important as it often encompasses the cognitive unknown, mislabeled as the *unknowable*. Some attributes that are considered mystic, I am inclined to support. In time I expect to see them accepted as actual human capacities: as part of the knowable, natural world, releasing new keys to spirituality which the mind negating fools never could have achieved. Their contemplation is very interesting, but still I say to all of mankind, *master what is here*. Your mastery of and action taken on what *is* understood within a sound philosophy, is what provides you with the personal inertias that such mystic techniques measure and project. Their job as Moral Vanguard is to help you see where your momentum is leading. Master existence first, and then build to new discoveries. Whatever you find interesting, a clean philosophy will make your exploration of it efficient, decisive and more enjoyable. You will reach answers sooner and be able to move deeper; answering questions that right now, you could not possibly comprehend. Mysticism at best is a compass. A proper moral code is a global positioning system, 455 horsepower, and a full tank of racing fuel.

The true abstract vanguards are those who *project* ideals through specific mediums; the artists and the stars of field, stage and screen; those we voluntarily boost to their heights by *individual sanction;* by purchasing movie tickets, attending concerts, buying books, going to stadiums, etc. They are our public heroes. Not all celebrities are moral just as not all public sanctions are rational, but the mediums they reach us through are sound. The most significant medium of the abstract vanguards—when precision is required and nothing can be left to implications—is literature. It addresses the mind directly. Others such as sculpture, painting, music and film, can share what exalted states can be felt while living, but can't explain the means of achieving them. Next to literature, the most significant medium is what *does* show you; the productive coexistent activity of men: business. Actually, all of the tradable products of Man, be they automobiles, wedding dresses, medical skills or artistic creation, are subsets under the category of business. There is no greater moral education in action than American free trade; and the freer, the more refined the lesson. It is the best, as it addresses every possible subject of interest to human beings, tailoring lessons to every ambitious mind. Free commerce makes available every bit of marketable knowledge and makes careers possible in anything imaginable. Most importantly, it teaches men *the process* of utilizing a mind to its proper boundaries of productive creativity—a moral process. The ways to approach a career or business endeavor and therefore the sustenance of a life, are as wonderfully varied as the number of men on the planet, when they are free.

So what is *my* realm as Moral Vanguard? Simple. The protection, development and exaltation of all entities of volitional consciousness in their domain. To shield the world with my body if necessary, for I *know* by how *I* feel about living, the glory all of mankind could feel about their lives, and who deserve an unrestricted attempt. Now it is time to decide what *your* role is. Yes, there are things wrong with the world. Yes, sub-humans stand in our way. So what! We've all had experiences that end up limiting our emotional freedom through traumatic events and those who have hurt us, where we have to lock away a part of our heart—the part that grants faith—possibly forever. Such an experience was the genesis of *Moral Armor*. But there is still some part of us that needs to reach out and connect, and feel the warm safety we felt in an adult's lap. We *need* guardians. And then there's the side of us which is confident and sensual, that longs for the raw, primitive release of our deepest passions, that calms us and keeps us on track. But it's a jungle out there. The proper moral armor can lead us to those who are safe to turn to in these vulnerable instances; and any other time we care to be fully coherent of our choice. Such integrity is our foothold, for when it is time to stand alone.

Sometimes we must have it understood that we need to remain independent. That there are certain things we *don't* want help with. That we will find healing on our own, and in our own way. That we need solitude; to run away, to not call, to not consider, to just be alone and exist for ourselves, sometimes. I ran away to complete facets of my own chain of knowledge. I used to think, "I don't want help; I can do it myself." Now I know that what drove me away was the natural fact that one man's integration *cannot* be done by another. I cannot convey all of the peace this solitude has given me.

No matter what I have experienced, I have a priceless faith in mankind which grows from my own motives, actions and sense of life. I have always used myself as the gauge of moral action and for my view of Man, and so have you, whether you are conscious of it or not. Because of my introspection and all that has developed as a result, I know what we can be. What we are driven to do and what drives us, has a much greater self-impact than any action taken by others. You can never simply obey others who tell you what is right; you must judge for yourself. You must get away and take the time to understand. Understanding and choice is the essence of morality anyway. What we are and what we think is wholly our own; it is not to be determined or touched by the outside world. Whether or not others played a part in influencing what we have become, we still had to accept or reject the soundness of their authority. And whether we bothered to check their claims or not, what we have concluded is a reflection of our own intelligence and character. In our lives, we are and always have been the ultimate Moral Vanguard.

Our Heroes — The Living Generators

"I'd rather die a broken piece of jade, than live a life of clay."
—Bruce Lee

My blessing and my torture is that I've never been able to kid myself about anything. All of my life from one relationship to the next, romantic or otherwise, I've suffered the same ultimate rejection: rejection of my purity, of my depth and of my strength. The best of us love living so much that we cannot fake anything. Everything we are and everything we have must be earned, deserved and wholesome. We don't seek to protect social appearances for our self-worth, for our love interest, for our health or for our philosophy. We care only about getting it right, and we stop at nothing to discover it. Those who take the greatest chances and advanced their fields exponentially, names the whole world knows—men like Aristotle, Copernicus, Edison and Ford—men who clear the highest barriers in their time, have also suffered the worst denunciations and the cruelest punishments in return.

We watch cable specials about Napoleon, Gangues Khan and Pope John Paul, but centuries later, do we benefit from their existence? On the other hand, we move through rooms turning lights on and off, we drive our cars to work daily, we wear nice clothes and we take planes to vacation and business destinations. These are all products of another type of man; Thomas Edison, Henry Ford, Eli Whitney and the Wright Brothers. Isn't there an essential difference in the quality of their contribution?

They say but for a handful of men over the course of human existence, none of civilization would have been possible. Men to whom we owe so much— the mountain peaks—would give their lives and sometimes do, in their pursuit of truth. I'm exasperated at the world for resenting their quest to discover the next steps for mankind. Shouldn't the world hold sacred it's highest and best? Shouldn't it—if it values its own life, yet cannot equal their achievements— shouldn't it stand on the sidelines and cheer them on? Shouldn't the world just naturally want to follow them? Why try to suppress their importance? Why rob them of their glory? Likewise, *Moral Armor* is an answer and counterblow to all those who have called me cruel over the years, who have attempted to induce shame as reward for my virtues, to covet my achievements and to expropriate the value of my effort while attempting to conceal their evasions. The pattern is the same; it is to avenge those historically tortured and protect their spiritual descendents into the future that demanded such a statement and ultimatum.

Very early on, I felt the need to make a declaration of the terms on which I am willing to live and work in our world, but there was no guideline to be found. How was human effort to be expended on a mature, explicitly moral basis? I had to gather the fragments from history; from the wealth of human experience as well as my own, and integrate it all into a logical whole. Men may choose to disobey rationality and often do. But ultimately, they can't hide or deny who is wrong and who is right, who is depraved and who is honest, who has earned and who has loafed, who is brave and who is a coward. We cannot work with the physical reward of our effort stolen or confiscated; that would make us slaves. We cannot enjoy our work with the intellectual/emotional reward stolen; that is worse. That steals the value of life: spirit. History has shown that self-absorbed, self-guided Man brings life to others. Flowers bloom and life expands; hope, belief and happiness are made possible by his presence. Nothing justifies his martyrdom.

We as the self-motivated of mankind have developed an awesome personal power, and often take on burdens that are unjustified simply because we can handle so much. We watch the rest struggle to live, and floundering badly. We put up with a horrible level of insincerity, listen to intolerable shallowness for unbearable durations and pacify by letting them have their way, confident we can take the wheel if things get out of hand. Exuberant in our capacity to overcome any obstacle, we approach it believing that anything is possible to us. While in the moral mind of a producer this is a positively reinforcing affirmation, it is subject to an axiomatic caveat which, when unheeded will lead to the destruction of all that we hold sacred. The term "anything" includes all things evil; and often our own foolish generosity foils our plans and tarnishes our expectations.

We are all paying a price in stress, in frustration and in exasperating futility. Our chosen patterns of action *are* what bring about success, and if success is the result we desire, we cannot deviate from what we know to be true. We cannot let go of the wheel. They immorally consider our crucial actions to be optional, and *we know* that they're not. It is the source of all values that they reject on a private level, and at some point it gets political. All private evils have political manifestations. We have *earned* our prosperity, and the last thing I want to see happen is for us to lose control to the same demons as we have in our past. The heroes of mankind have always seen their ultimate goals frustrated by their inability to understand or express the moral foundation of their actions. The rug gets pulled primarily by the inversion of moral principles within *their own* minds. Secondarily by the moral subversion of others, and third by the simple absence of knowledge on critical social issues affecting every one of us. The unfortunate truth is that the tools of mass prosperity can be turned against mankind with the power of moral uncertainty and used for mass murder. They can and they have, repeatedly, throughout history.

Look at what had to be accepted in order for Germany to take the course it did in Nazi times. Conversely, look at what had to be accepted in order for America to be born. These great surges were driven by the philosophy accepted en masse. When the prominent in society build on Aristotle and Thomas Paine, the result is America. When they build on Kant and Nietzsche, the results are the horrors of The Third Reich. When they build on Hegel and Marx, the result is a very bloody Soviet Russia. Everything we do, everything we endorse and everything we allow to be done to us affects our quality of living, and the quality of living for the rest. We cannot make "anything" possible for others and we shouldn't try. They need to be held to life-furthering standards at whatever level their minds can handle. We should never be subject to the discovery that we unwittingly provided the means for neurotic aggression to succeed. Living Generators must be psychologically strong enough not to subordinate their premises to premises less developed.

Over the centuries, many evils experienced on a personal level have gained great social and political inertia. While our political system rests on sound moral footing, our explicit mass understanding of why, lags by over three hundred years. It is a great concern to the future of the world what is taught and passed down, but most importantly, just what is accepted on a grand scale. Moral philosophy is the fundamental driver of mankind, and has been throughout all of history. It determines just about every action we take and gets more sensitive as men make decisions together. We need to understand why men have chosen in aggregate the methods they practice, as there are always serious consequences. Once we know what drives any issue, we can be sure to side with life; which is to side with civility, sound purpose and competence. After all, whom do we want to see running the world: those who can, or those who claim it doesn't exist? Out of the two, who belongs here? Who loves it, and to whom have we always sacrificed explicit moral control?

The problem is so ancient and so vast that most philosophers will tell you that short of annihilation, no reform is possible. Should we nuke the human race and start over? No. For one, it isn't necessary, and two, the currently accepted view of morality, which drives the actions of "the moral majority," would result in a society suffering from the same errors. No such issue can be approached and solved as a group, primarily. As in ballet, the performers must be in shape and know the dance *before* any choreography can be attempted. Moral restructuring is the same; it must be addressed by every individual man in his own time and at his own pace. Your own moral clarity is the place to begin in any attempt to change society for the better. It all starts with one. If you were purely civil and morally empowered, then multiplied yourself by millions, you could predict how such a society would function. If you followed *Mein Kampf* then multiplied such an abomination by millions, you could easily predict destruction and bloody murder. If sacrifice is accepted as our standard, what Hitler did becomes excusable. Millions have been destroyed with the ethical perversion of our mass relations to one another. But jumping from the reform of oneself into reform of a society is not the next step either; a relationship with *one* other person is. When you've mastered a relationship with one other person, *then* you are ready to move on to moral contemplation for a society of men.

Our Social Challenge. It has been time for another Tea Party for decades, yet one hasn't come. While our society is advanced, twice now in history men have been freer and more morally wise on average: during The Golden Age of Athens and America during the 1800's, when our productive atmosphere was positively euphoric. But since then, our ancestors have allowed the moral degenerates of altruist slave States to infect us with guilt about our prosperity, through their inverted moral code. Such guilt is atonable only through the loss of our products and our money (the tools of civility), the loss of our peace of mind and respect for others, and the loss of control over that which we've created. Their code tells us that the highest moral action is to give up everything we hold sacred.

The Cold War may be over, but its beast is not dead. It lies dormant—preserved and nurtured by a fatal philosophic mixture. This veiled primitive psychology is *responsible* for our tolerance of living as fifty-percent slave without revolt as we do now in America. Successful men haughtily shrug off any forewarnings in the midst of their own prosperity, never considering it necessary to examine the true source of their wealth. They're ahead of the game, right? Well, the train is coming in many different ways, and our best have always stood on the tracks. Without moral grounding, they'll get creamed in a heartbeat when crisis does strike. The good doesn't always win, as Athens lost to Sparta. When a civil state faces a military state, a war's outcome favors those who like to fight and who *know the dance.* The Living Generators are fighters too; they don't pretend that an opposition does not exist, and they are not willing to live at anyone's mercy. We must come to understand how to protect the *source* of our values—human cognition—and to know in advance when it is threatened. The Living Generators know who their enemies are, as well as their peers.

The two types of men, the Self-made and the Fear-driven, tend to act consonant with their inner motivation in all things. We will come to understand them and see their actions extrapolated into all the realms of Man: relationships, art, institutions, and politics. We—with eyes that *can* see, minds that *can* judge and bodies that *can* act—will learn what is forgivable and what isn't, and to know the gravity of misgivings against a rational course of action at any level: personal, industrial or national. The direction of a society is determined by what its active individuals believe serve their benefit. In our lives, immorality should be reduced to its rightful identity; just a natural form of sediment. Like kelp on the ocean surface, we can predict encountering it and design appropriate intellectual protection. It *is* going to snag you from time to time, but it is no longer going to stop you.

Proper moral armor is like a boat: a well-engineered outer shell to deal with this natural environment while the softer, shock absorbing cushions carry the passengers in comfort. If you have ever fallen while water skiing, you know it feels like concrete. Imagine such continuous exposure, and then appreciate how purposeful and long-lasting the hull of a boat is. Man designed it to withstand the elements and achieve objectives that he could not withstand or accomplish with his own body. Our products are extensions of ourselves. Man answered this problem of existence brilliantly and continues to improve his answers as the sum of his knowledge grows in all things. His spiritual development deserves the same allegiance, aiming to blast through the sediment with the throttle pinned, on his way to his chosen goals. With seasoning, we'll be capable of using this technology to step again into forbidden realms, to prevent harm, to remove inefficiencies and to redirect outcomes in every little way that counts—in our lives and in its extrapolation to world events. Then, when we seek to change things it can be done simply, quickly and without violence.

If the intellectual range of the top one-percent on Earth is taken to a new plane, the rest will follow without question. These forty million people do not start from the Forbes 400 and descend from there. They are not measured by the virtue of sound financial accumulation alone, but by the combination of metaphysical honesty *and* productive efficacy. They use their bodies and their minds for the purpose nature intended. They are the most human of the humans—The Living Generators—the Self-made Men who intend to *remain* self-made. They understand that life is an act of constant replenishing in body and mind, and they don't use their advantages to secure a parasitical means of sustenance for themselves.

Nothing can exclude you from being counted among the prominent of mankind if this is the path you choose. Not wealth, degrees, positions, connections, citizenship or family name. It is a state of existence attainable by anyone who decides to pursue it. No one can stop you, and its rewards are beyond expropriation. The pursuit and its fulfillment are not primarily social, but are primarily between you and existence. As all great men do, we can develop ourselves to our own highest potency in every aspect of our existence that we care enough about living to remain conscious of.

If you are honest you can advance at an exhilarating pace, but socially, reforms struggle at the pace of an aggregate honesty. The American revolution took 156 years from our landing at Plymouth rock (1620) to our liberation (1776) and you can bet many of our lethargic inhabitants were opposed to thought, to freedom, to life and to civility, even under British oppression, and today's world is no different. Most of the populace lives in a state of panic—of emotional arrest— not knowing whether they are on track or whether they are wasting their lives, fearful to discover the truth either way. They live without certainty, without purpose and without joy. They think and make decisions as if every choice is life or death, where death always seems to have the advantage, and they bring into existence all of the impotence and misery that they themselves feel. Forget them and concentrate on expanding your own freedom and refinement. As moral leaders, we can build a better world with the most effective means: simply leading by example. This book was designed for the Self-made anyway; not for the slothful, the pretentious or the all-yielding. It is for the efforting, the honest and the successful—the way above average. It is for the morally invigorated, to help make their consciousness more integrated and their moral understanding more potent; to make their hides thick and their spirit high. Many of you have been in a cycle of consistent development throughout life or you never would have picked it up. For the rest of you, look in the bottom drawer, no, the shoe box in the back of the closet. Okay, open it. See that? That's your brain... hose it off, put it back in, and let's get going!

Chapters four and eight are comprised of new moral-philosophical technology. As the most abstract, they are the most difficult, so take your time; all moral action rests on them. If you're still foggy at the book's conclusion, read it again. I've read certain books over fifty times, as new experience clarifies their lessons. *Moral Armor* is a synthesis of 2500 years of philosophy; the bold headings address specific attributes of Man, making skimming and future reference a breeze. We use lights constantly; so should we reference their source. There will be a sense of familiarity to just about everything I'll name. Without knowing the content, you will still feel as if you *have* known, and here is why. It is the structure that is familiar, because all useful knowledge has come to you in this same format. You'll be able to sense my respect for human beings through advanced consonance with our proper means of comprehension. Now it will be deeper, more explicit and more precise than it ever has been. You'll find yourself settling in to the warm flow of logic, confirming for yourself that each step taken *is* in the right direction.

As you gain full cognitive responsibility for your own motivations, you'll begin to notice the difference between an emotional tantrum and a rational conviction, whenever you encounter an idea you are uncomfortable with. You will come to understand how your elders have been operating, and you will move past them. You will come to see that there is no value in maintaining their incomplete or irrational assumptions, knowing that the protection of the wrong ideas is a threat to your quality of life. You will begin to find safety and opportunity in the act of embracing the right ideas and in the pleasurable act of discovering them. The old consequences from defying reality which left you stranded with a shameful anger and a desire for emotional deadness will become senselessly immature—clearly the wrong path. There is no escape from existence, and any struggle to, will become too painful to bear. Evasion will become so suffocating that your immediate reaction to it will be to stand up straight, look openly at what is, and breathe in the pure fresh air of your proud moral choice: to face the world openly, as a heroic being must.

Eventually you will come to look at truths as the life-fostering blessings they are, and at your willingness to stand by them as the romantic transformation in your character that it is. You will become a scholar in your own rite as the great scientists were, calmly *observing* nature as it is, independent of what you might have hoped it to be. With the indestructible spirit of a Living Generator, you'll be one of us, and more so with every sunrise and every new connection. Openly dedicated to clarification, you'll employ new knowledge in order to live well, maintaining a pleasant state of fulfillment.

Moral Armor, like its spiritual predecessors, is a treasure map, and it leads to Atlantis. There are wonderful things to understand and wonderful emotional states to experience, once one *has* understood. We would all like to change the world and we can, but it must start with ourselves, and this is the road. To lift darkness off the Earth, one must first lift it from one's own brow.

As American law was designed to protect *the producers* of the nation by protecting *the productive capacity of a man*—to protect his life from violence and to guard the ownership of his creations—I want to see our society refined so that it protects a man's spirit as well as it protects his body. Our elders down through the centuries should have loved us more than to allow what has happened, to happen. The moral sanction of evil by the generators of life is up. Now it is our turn.

Still, the war will continue on many fronts, so be prepared for opposition. Due to morality's subversion, as a public officeholder, if you intend to uphold the tenets of the Constitution and pursue the endeavor with clear reasoning, you're considered a traitor. If you pursue scientific discoveries that clash with present views, you're considered crazy. If you disagree with degenerative cultural trends and seek to better human lives, you're considered behind the times. If you vent fresh ideas on the subject of morality, you're called insane. Mindless hordes will always try to batter us, but now the side of the good has a philosophical avenger. In such an atmosphere, it is honesty and justice that are considered controversial. So be it. The evil have always made the most honest, able and striving individuals pay for achieving in body and spirit, what *they* betrayed. Now they will witness *us* reaching critical mass: the radiant pride earned for accepting and practicing without apology, a moral code defined by *rational* standards. Unless we realize and accept that the premises we have suffered under for years do not come from God, but from men interpreting what the writers interpreted what the Disciples interpreted what Jesus interpreted was the message of God, as on any other grapevine, we are better off validating all moral premises for ourselves. As morality begins with the nature of cognition and cognition is an attribute of the individual, if you cling to the Bible and push its teachings after spending any serious time on this planet, you probably *are* crazy, which leads to the next point:

Warrior Note: *No valid morality begins with an external frame of reference.*

Every man is the owner of his mind, and if he must reference an outside source in order to find out what he thinks, he has sacrificed the moral power of his life. Morality is meant for our protection, and with the proper foundation as in all other civilized undertakings, our control grows with time—in scope and precision. The question of what fosters or destroys a human life is a mature concept linked to fact, and is not subject to wishy-washy interpretation. Pursuing endeavors which provide the greatest self-impact while respecting the rights of others is *by far* the most moral course any individual can follow. The greatest passion to be drawn from an individual is to be elicited *by* the individual. Such long days and late nights produced the light bulb, the phonograph and the personal computer. They've produced great works of art, beautiful buildings, and priceless literature. Such days and nights produced the defense and exaltation for this living pattern, which you now hold.

It is time for the premises of death to yield to the greater power: life and its immaculate patterns. The ominous evil you sense at times is just a midget behind a curtain, projecting a huge shadow. That's all. The good must regain control of this world. Take it back! Don't assume your elders know what they're doing. They don't. Don't make the emotional conclusion that evil has metaphysical power and that there is a natural bias towards it. There isn't. Evil gains its power only through the life force that is willing to serve it, and you have a choice in the matter. We are not tied; we are not forced into silent passivity or driven unalterably towards a future that takes from us our freedoms. If you're not treated professionally in a job, you can quit. If you're not treated fairly in a relationship, you can end it. If you're not treated appropriately in a store, you can walk out. If you're not treated civilly by a governing body, you can step away from society and create a voice for reform. We are as free as the risks and responsibilities we are willing to assume.

If you're going to be an outsider, be a good one, and know that you're not alone. Show the world that you are alive. Show them your motives and let theirs be seen. Let's see if the soulless can handle practicing their evils out in the open. Make no mistake, my mission is to restore moral potency in the minds of individual men—*the best*—to give them, not just a semblance of control over their lives, but *total authority*. As compensation, I want to see looking back at me, not a defiant tension, but a free sense of ease and recaptured innocence: the healthy, vibrant confidence of eyes that *know* what they're winning.

Section Two:

The Moral Warrior

Chapter Four

Self-Made Man

Part One: Validation of Origin: Concepts of Perception

"I followed all the rules—God's and Man's—and you, you followed none of them. And they all loved you more." —Legends of the Fall

There are forces in nature that cannot be stopped; they bring us to pinnacles, and sometimes they destroy us. We see and hear of great storms—hurricanes, tornadoes—striking one land or another, bringing relief or devastation, which parallel the emotional storms within all men. The heroes among men learn to channel and direct their storms, bringing to mankind the wonders it has never seen. They appear, displaying to the world their radiance, only to vanish without a trace. Some become legends. Held safe from their magnificent power, we are free to drop all fear and witness in awe, their astonishing beauty. The world will always reserve its most passionate response for those who look with their own eyes, decide with their own minds and take actions by their own standards–regardless of the opinions, laws, barriers or precedent of those who came before. They are the originators of thought and the fathers of honest effort who bring elegance to human stature, and a sense of glamour to precision. They are the Self-made Men, and their every generation faces nature alone. Accepting first and foremost that existence exists, they hold the most firm claim to this Earth, and to the extent that their premises are heeded, we as a people get to experience a touch of Atlantis.

Self-Made Man

Welcome, as the next four chapters are *our* world. We are those who are at peace with our maker, those whose dedication to civility and rational discipline did not rob us of our manhood. We remain in control, viewing our time here as *our turn* on this planet, and intend to match the glory of our forefathers, or surpass them.

Imagine for a moment a few candles burning, the crackle of a fire and peaceful music as light as thought in the background. The aura of this night is a setting for pleasant contemplation, accented by the faint howl of wind in the outer darkness. Drawn by an unknown urge, you move to the door and go outside. The sound stirred expectation of a chill, but surprisingly, the gusts are warm. Ascending the hill behind the country home, the long grass parts easily, as if welcoming motion. At the top looking back, a wonderful sense of safety washes over, in opposition to the ominous, darkening sky. The storm advances as if motivated by anger; sheets of wind challenge your stand and trees reel to remain steadfast, the grass hissing—the world is alive. As forces are set to embark on a violent battle, you are ready; for underscoring the howls moves a melody, untouched in the distant calm of the structure. With sympathy to any animal caught in the storm tonight, a brief chill runs its course, but turns to warmth in response to the glowing comforts that await. With an immense pride you cannot name, you feel a part of this great struggle, a contender, the master; and revel in the meaning of being a man.

We *are* the masters. No other beings can carry on regardless of storms, regardless of night, with no break in the flow of their activities. We don't live in defiance of nature, we live in harmony with all we've learned. We cherish the wind in our hair, the texture of the trees and the crunch of leaves under our feet. The smell of a world moving toward hibernation or of fresh new growth is intoxicating, and exists as a setting for every action we take. The glittering water and majestic sunsets bursting with color affect us with a fullness that feels nourishing to our eyes, and they are. Such stimulation expands and utilizes the full range of our tools, reminding us of their great capacity and preparing us to focus deeper, bringing us a warmth of confidence that we *can* understand, handle and appreciate our world. The senses through which we experience the glory of nature, provide us the gateway to fulfill our dreams and to reach all heights. This Earth is our home, and we are welcome on it wherever we can manage her forces. The wonderful relationship we share with our universe was made possible by the relationship we have with ourselves, through our sensate perceptions and our brave honesty to trust in them. But how did it all originate? What can we answer about our own origin and what is left to be discovered? Cozy in the glow of the fire, the distant howl a reminder of our pride, contemplation has us focused on the beginning of time. With the proper foundation, we can look into our possible future to confirm the course of our present. For years, we have looked to the stars and wondered what's out there. Let's go to them and look *this* way for once.

Cruising in a small craft from deep space, we gaze upon our spiral galaxy in the distance. Just over two million light years from M7, we are almost home. Stunned by its majestic beauty, we contemplate, "Wow, by sheer chance, a planet begins to orbit at just the right distance to the scale of a star to develop and sustain life, and here we are."

With every drawn breath, we all bear witness that this, the nature of existence, is the true foundation of it all—even if we aren't consciously aware of it. The evidence is all around us. There is only one way to consistently advance, and that is to recognize and respect the proper frame of reference. As our galaxy turns, fundamental calculations are effected. Earth's location relative to the stars—our early means of navigation—is not in the same place it was in Viking times. But the laws of nature, in the span of a human life and within the range of human use, do not fluctuate with enough significance to warrant account. They must be held constant and are for all human applications. From the darkness of space, we can see that we are the glorious sovereign beings of the planet—of the galaxy. We are the volitional entities, evolved without instincts and therefore without intellectual limitations, inextricably linked to the Earth's celestial environment, its rotational patterns, its composition and its climates. The rotational velocity of the Earth determines our periodic exposure to this radiant star. What we have named "day" and measure time by, sets the growth and retraction cycle of all living things—from amoebas, to flowers, to Man. We awaken and grow tired as a result, in tune with this duration, which determines the amount of expendable energy in our optimum workday. Our needs of nourishment, which then determine our sensate capacity for the coherence to meet those needs, have their origin in our planet's chemical composition. Our bodies are comprised of the planet's materials and require the same materials to sustain them. Everything we need is here.

We were designed by this Earth, and grasping that is responsible for our every step forward. The frame of reference which must have our cognizance and respect is the natural world as it is. The closer we come to identifying universal truths, the more useful the information becomes. It is the base axiomatic frame of reference to be held as absolute, and our adherence determines our intellectual depth, our range of concern, our capacity to project our own futures and our ability to take the actions to achieve it. Just as for animals, our senses have evolved to sufficiently detect the fundamental aspects of this world, and all validation of what is good for us or evil rests on them. Earth's gravitation defined Man's range of size and mobility. Our physical dimensions define the basic scale of the buildings we inhabit, the tools we use, the beds we stretch out on and the vehicles we travel in. We have designed our products around ourselves and for the conditions they will encounter in our service; thereby extending our range of power, travel and depth. The birth of an individual creates predictable requirements for the sustenance of that life which, in a civil aggregate, creates the base of an economy. Even our most solemn sense of self-worth—our happiness—is found in our capacity, exercise and deepest respect for our own creative life-sustaining potencies. Our romantic idolization of heroes—those of passionate energy who stand to uphold justice and remain true to truth—confirms this. In all that we are, there are no contradictions to find, and none in our true origin. It all makes sense, and can be traced by a balanced mind, step by step, through time.

We witness human activity from the beginning of life to its end, from morning until night—beautiful in its own harmony, all geared toward one goal: to fulfill the requirements of living. We think of *moral action* and its reward. We see the glittering lights of our cities—*our* stars—possibly unaware that they were originated by a moral process, to serve a moral purpose. Thought devoted to such advances has given us all that we have, and the human race depends on it. It is estimated that Earth has been here for thirteen billion years, and that Man has existed for over two million. After countless millennia, those who looked at the world with open, questioning eyes, willing to work for their values, road out the storms and won their peace at last, dispelling ancient myths with every new achievement. I have them to thank for this space ship and the technology around me, which has allowed such an incredible experience of life. To see the world from here and to know that there is no limit—that there is so much more to discover—is an honor. What happens when we reach a horizon? We find another. Just think, such excruciating efforts were taken to discover the principles necessary to build this craft which, with the Space Age, brought another consolidation of human intelligence. We now understand that space travel can exist on a large scale only if it serves industry—that is, human life. It can only be sustained by a free market system established and maintained on Earth—invulnerable to war—which generates a surplus large enough to allow us to explore. Just as freedom was necessary for economic expansion, peace is necessary for long-term projection, and within lies the confirmation for two hundred years of American capitalism and the bill of human rights upon which it rests—an example for the whole world to follow. As a man grows to be independent, the technology of this space ship also will one day be independent. As businesses and nations seek independence by means of prosperity, the sovereign entity at all levels is pursued as ideal. Peaceful productivity on Earth—a delicacy of thought and responsible action geared by self-interest on the part of everyone—is required to keep these ships flying. Another step is seen.

This technology has allowed us to observe other inhabited planets and watch their storms of men move through the same stages of barbarism into civility. We've seen their astonishment at every new discovery, frightened into believing fire and water were gods, possessing the choice to reward or harm them. The confident were tortured for effrontery as they faced these gods and experimented. As they began to develop concepts, Earth gods gave way to conceptual gods, emanating attributes such as wisdom, beauty and wrath. Eventually all authority consolidated under one god, coming full circle to take its proper form: the form of a man. Only one step precludes their meteoric rise as a galaxial species: final identification of the entity who has held the sole capacity of volition all along—themselves. The day they finally look in the mirror and see who has the definitive power to harm or reward them, to judge what is good or evil and to determine their fate is the day they reach full volitional maturity. Then, their chains will be off, and we will have many new friends.

In our experience, so rational a discipline was required to counter the ancient dissolution of consciousness and secure Man's moral footing, that it now seems insurmountable. Still, in contrast, the root of the misguidance was only the Neanderthal action of closing one's eyes, refusing fact and wishing that reality was something other than it is. To discover that the purveyor of so immense a malady was powerless all along is profound, but the pattern has been the same on every planet observed: consciousness aware versus consciousness dropped. It's so easy to see who is right and who is wrong from out in space. The mystics could never outpace Man's mind. It was our comprehension that originated every step; that conquered every barrier, placing new creations before the eyes of the world, which the Spirit Murderers could only sneer at, then attempt to subvert, steal or destroy. But reality turned out to be real. Proper evolution has continued, and here we are.

Our First Relationship. Ever since I can remember, as early as two, the Earth has been mine. It was given *my* sanction, through a pure, clean awareness, and its every glory has been mine as a result. I would open my eyes, look up from my crib and feel the exhilaration running all through my body at the start of a new day. This world held a new fascination at every turn. There was so much to learn, so much to do and so much to see. I couldn't wait for the adventure to begin, somehow aware that it already had. I would lie there and enjoy the simple pleasure of my own power of sight, the brilliant colors and the details I hadn't noticed before. As contrast improved, I could apprehend the flow of a curtain's motion and its relation to the gentle breeze that would follow. A visual phenomenon translated into touch, and the integration of my senses had begun. I could look at the world or focus inward, experimenting with the pleasant vibrations my vocal cords could produce. I was discovering all that was within my power, enjoying the capacity to improve my comfort by controlled muscular contraction—learning even then, that I need not settle for anything less than satisfaction, waiting for her to come and get me.

Life then was a constant exercise in sensory expansion—of learning the mechanics to control my tools of perception and mobility—and there were no barriers between the world and myself, beyond my effort and willingness to see. I wanted and needed the utmost clarity I could render and the purest concentration possible to be able to understand everything I came upon. As I grew into adolescence, adults attempted to introduce barriers—to claim that my senses were misleading, and I couldn't possibly be sure of myself. I rejected it contemptuously, but overpowered by those resorting to force, obeyed in silence and kept my private domain pure. Never once have I been tempted to doubt my own eyes, or the judgment of my mind. Confusion made me pause, but nothing spurred me into action except clarification. A wrong turn made me look deeper to make the correct course mine, which is Man's proper cognitive action. Why they would encourage us to violate our own nature was beyond me at the time.

Nature provides an advantage to every living species, making it possible for all to sustain and perpetuate life—advantages they were telling me to ignore. We watch the Discovery Channel in awe of the keen eyesight of the owl and the hawk, the agility of the cheetah, the shark's acute sense of smell—senses and abilities that give every animal an edge in its survival. We don't have to question their value. We know that the sharper the senses are for an animal, the more powerful its capacity to feed and protect itself, and this is true for Man as well. In addition, nature adorned us with the largest creative brain-mass, many times the size of our nearest biological relative, empowering us with full control over our consciousness. Instincts—if they exist at all—are a simple set of preprogrammed instructions that lead an animal along a course of self-preservation. Our reflexes can pull away from a hot stove without cognitive direction (the flexion reflex), but they cannot instruct us to build a house, plant a garden, or run a business. Humans are *volitional* beings—entirely self-guided. Our perceptions likewise, give us no automatic course of action. In order to survive we must make choices. In order to validate choices, we must identify a standard of value by which to weigh them, and the standard for Man and all living things is the alternative of life or death. That which protects and furthers life is the good; that which hinders or destroys it, is the evil. This is the implicit moral question in every human mind, spanning from morning to night, determining every step we take over the course of our existence. Rational judgment is life-furthering judgment. The conscious choice of life-serving action is a *moral* choice and is what keeps us all alive. Steering a car, crossing a street, selecting groceries, pursuing a career—these are all decisions originating through sensate perception, which begins a cognitive process of reflecting on our awareness of what will further our lives versus what will take it from us.

Self-made Man knows the moral confusion he was raised with was unnecessary. He moves from adolescence into adulthood thinking, "There should be sense made of all this." He knows what he would do if there were no one around to damn his actions; he would do just what he's doing anyway, but without pain, or fear, or guilt. Regardless of the animosity of others, he can see nothing wrong; nothing to condemn. We work to earn a flow of capital, which provides us with our base axiomatic needs: food and shelter—a moral action. We clear snow off our windshields, use our headlights and stay in our own lanes so as not to put ourselves or others at risk—all moral actions. We cross the street when it is safe, seek clean food and pay our bills to preserve the flow of our health and independence—all moral actions. We teach our children to respect the rights of others, to stand up for their own and to be aware of their surroundings—all moral lessons. Life actions are made to preserve its flow, and Self-made Man efforts to become cognizant of his every moral step. It is in the background of his mind as a constantly replenishing source of pride and life satisfaction. He is aware of our highest possibilities and greatest depths, and holds an endless love for those who strive to reach them. Even when in desolation, his example is the only one to look up to. The vast potency and grandeur of the individual astonishes him, through the choices *he himself* makes. He is enchanted with how honorable men can be; the bravery it requires and the power of the pride that follows. The spiritual rewards are so great, he could not imagine keeping any other course. He glances at most as they stagnate in groups, but pays them no mind as he can achieve so much alone. His ambition for moral action is unlimited and though refined in appearance and motivation, he is often bursting inside with childlike enthusiasm over new matters to explore and new roads he is eager to take. Looking from one path to another, he asks, "Where will this lead? And where will this lead?" And he can't wait to find out.

Self-made Man looks at the world alone. In his world, men can see, hear and comprehend. Walking into a wall with his eyes closed is all the proof he needs to validate the importance of his senses. He knows that the clarity of his perception determines the quality of his life. To depend on others at any fundamental level is intolerable, flying in the face of his struggle to become a self-sufficient adult. He is responsible for all facets of his life, and outside of a physical malady, accepts no ongoing assistance. All tools to be used for his survival must come from within. He thinks on his own, validating what he has learned from other men—validating everything—through his own experience and reflection. No fundamental delegation is done; all outside sources are the unaccountable, and to suspend his judgment in favor of another's higher certainty is to become a dependent once more. He makes all the knowledge important to him, his. Self-sufficiency is the base of his self-esteem, so he exercises and expands the range of every sense, while mastering the mobility and competence of his own physique to maximize his momentum.

Self-made Man doesn't question his capacity to think, to feel, to sense or to live. He knows he can, and his highest judge is himself. He makes up his own mind what makes sense and what doesn't, who is honest and who isn't and gets to the bottom of any issue with the clearest chain of knowledge necessary to act. He spends his time serving, creating and defending his own life and its peaceful progression. He inherently knows what is good for him or evil. Heroic Self-made Man didn't need to be told by clergy that an army overrunning his village was bad; he was already there, fighting for our freedom. He knows there are material and spiritual predators among men, and that he owes them no goodwill. He knows a thug is to be stopped, and a producer is to be rewarded. He knows that rational law is designed to protect the producers against the thugs, and shows his loyalty to values when law becomes corrupt, by maintaining his just course, regardless. He doesn't tolerate the idiocy that demands the subordination of his sensibilities; he is a fighter. He doesn't accept irrational premises that cannot be validated in the course of his own existence. He does not allow assertions to replace his perceptions. He moves unfettered at the comfortable pace of his own physio-intellectual efficiency, veering only when necessary, to avoid or stamp out whatever or whomever claims a dogmatic right to bar or stop him.

Part Two: Validation of Mind: Concepts of Reason

"...historically, dreamers have a pretty good track record."
—Sidekicks

With the incredible level of data collected in the medical and physical sciences, we have more than enough physical evidence to form a sound philosophy for Man. So many human attributes considered evil have been proven to be biologically natural, life-promoting structures, that the false-righteously stiff sit frozen, remaining backward as their control over morality is taken. Their stranglehold on innocence is succumbing to age, finally. Why did they fight rationality? The concepts of judgment, certainty and pleasure, which were considered impertinent, arrogant and selfish, have proven themselves to be derived by axiomatic needs—needs at the base of *conscious* health for Man—just as air and water are necessities of physical health. *Judgment* is the identification and acceptance of right and wrong; *certainty* is the established link of cause to effect, and *pleasure* is the reward for acting on the certainty of rational judgment. All were damned so that the imposed guilt could be used as justification to expropriate the values such concepts created. We were preyed upon by the Spirit Murderers all along, not for our vices, but for our virtues. Our sexual drives, our emotional propensity for constructive or destructive action, our degrees of intelligence; these are issues that as far as moral import is concerned, can be put to rest. There was and is, no mind/body dichotomy. There is no moral struggle of one against the other. There is no fixed, 'I can't help it' prenatal level of awareness. There is no struggle for control between the conscious and subconscious mind. The struggle is and always has been, between reality and the Spirit Murderer's unwillingness to accept it.

At one's first moment of conscious awareness, one sees the world, and is either afraid of it's complexity or is intrigued. One either immediately desires exploration or tries to back out. This initial reaction sets the stage for the manner in which one's mind will classify information or assimilate, from then on. The question truly is, "To be, or not to be." From the very beginning of cognitive responsibility, Self-made Man decided that he wants to live.

The most powerful emotion a man can feel is anticipation, and its antithesis, dread; the expectation of enjoyment, and the expectation of pain. Anticipation is a high *positive* energy response to existence driven by confidence—the projection of fulfillment—whereas dread is a high *negative* energy response to existence driven by inadequacy—the projection of doom. No other emotions can bring about so deep a personal impact: the trembling, the butterflies, the sudden perspiration—hot and then cold, a dry throat, and at the extreme, total incapacitation; all precursors of an outcome of crucial importance to the afflicted. Then there is the moment for some, when everything turns quiet: the purity of total focus, of absolute calm, the lock-on to a ruthless expansion of awareness, monitoring and maintaining only the key elements of achievement at peak levels. In this state of consciousness, the mind drops all inessentials and applies one hundred percent of its attention to regulating the expectations of one's conscious will. Access to this intellectual level is the province of the Self-made: the most purely earned state of personal accomplishment possible. From it, comes the wealth of the individual: the greatest advances, the greatest performances, the most passionate connections and the most powerful conveyances. Aware of it or not, Self-made Man utilizes this same process at differing degrees to satisfy all of his intentions, from the simplest to the most complex of endeavors.

Often these primary emotions can switch places without warning. Fear can easily turn into anticipatory exhilaration, because they are epistemological antipodes. Fear is easier to elicit, as it often precedes identification. It hits you just when you are faced with an input you were not prepared for; information outside of your focus. This is the critical juncture in every context, when a man chooses either to turn the lights on, or to keep them off. It is here, that the Self-made and the Fear-driven go their separate ways. Self-made Man goes on to achievement and self-satisfaction, while Fear-driven Man damns himself to stagnation and self-hatred. Perceptive bravery (courage) is Man's non-automatic, self-motivated, self-generated, conscious moral response to a new situation. As courage is not automatic, he must use discipline to exercise it; a moral choice. Choosing to identify the product of his senses (his perceptions) requires confidence in his ability to handle whatever is coming, in order to solve his life's concerns. Fifty percent of all heroic actions are done by untainted cognition—the "Yes, I see." The other half is being true to what is seen, by taking appropriate physical action.

Everyone feels uncertainty about the unknown, until its nature becomes clear. Self-worth is *not* a question of feeling fear or not; that does not define one's bravery or one's value as a person. What defines one's value, is how one responds. Some shrink according to their self-belief; Self-made Man expands according to his. But where does his self-confidence come from? It comes from his pattern of cognition. The pattern of life-serving human cognition is (1) sensate perception, (2) identification and integration into one's knowledge base, (3) creative response, and (4) result. Self-made Man can recall enough instances of his past to see the pattern implicitly; he knows the actions bettering his chances for success are contingent upon his remaining aware. His alpha-potency is made and perpetuated in this instance. Self-made Man develops to the point where he doesn't even realize fear *could* be felt; what he feels is exhilaration. The new is the unexplored; the startling is the adventurous and he anticipates his own triumph against any challenge.

Intellectual Efficiency. Every man lives alone in his mind. We are complete entities in ourselves, which means, 'every man *is* an island' in regard to his own life and consciousness. Every mind has a certain operating efficiency defined by its biological environment, then developed and maintained by the conscious will or degenerative random actions of its owner. It must operate at peak awareness in order to satisfy the basic moral requirement of a volitional being: to maximize its capacity to choose the path to life when faced with any alternative. Commanding it to act contrary to its nature or in excess of its capacity cannot work; it only results in dysfunction. We can see this in our driving speeds. An active mind can handle a more intellectually demanding environment than most. Just as one sets a stereo at a comfortable volume according to one's own physical requirements and mood, so one seeks to adjust the conditions open to one's choice, with respect to the integrator of one's perceptions (according to its refinement). If we are active, we *turn up* the environment by increasing our speed to a level that matches our intellectual efficiency. If we are forced to move slower, our mind wanders. It is our capacity to deal with the elements of existence (and freedom to do so) that determines our confidence in taking any action. Consonant with the flow of life, this level of efficiency and confidence ebbs and flows with our own physio-intellectual health and energy. If we act outside of our capacity, the result will be life-adverse; so in natural response to exhaustion for example, we drive slower. Every mind has its own speed and limitations, whose boundaries are to be pushed by and at the risk of the owner himself. The physical and intellectual efficiency of every man is determined by his own chosen focus and actions, and is a solid measure of moral stature. Acceptance, development and exercise of our full sensory and intellectual range is responsible for our level of comfort with ourselves, others and our environment.

There are different levels of efficiency to be sure. I define them on a scale related to the steps of cognition. The 1-2 level defines children mostly, as to remain Self-made, one must complete the metaphysical range of 1-4. But it can be completed in an isolated context prepared *for* him, where he operates at a very modest level in everything else, quietly and honorably. At the 3-4 level, he is career minded, morally questions ideas, and supports sincere intentions. Institutionally he may own businesses, be in politics, and provide moral leadership. At the 6-8 abstract level, he is a scientist in his field, and can have a global impact. He defines new knowledge, overseeing existence to harness principles for the furtherance of all. At each level, his range of effect increases, and his capacity to advance increases with experience. Maturity affects his level, as we all begin life at 1-2, and move on to contextually practice elements in the 3-4 level. How far one goes is a matter of personal ambition.

Neurobiology. In a truly stunning discovery, science has proven our self-chosen capacity in observing what physically happens as we think and automatize our processes. The mind is not an independent entity within the body, but an organ of the body—its regulator and driver. But it too has a driver: our conscious will. There is heightened brain activity in certain locations, relative to the type and level of exertion required for any action we take. With brain imaging techniques, this activity can be monitored and linked directly to its causal factors. That portion of the brain actually expands to allow greater sensitivity to a chosen stimulus, enhancing the accuracy of our perceptions and our means to deal with them. When we apply consistent effort to a particular endeavor, connections in the brain are reinforced so that more neurons can be devoted to the task. The body builds stronger connections for the processes given preference by one's consciousness. This doesn't mean that if a man is a plumber, it advances the 'plumbing' part of his brain. The biological augmentation supports natural functions of human cognition such as creativity, motor skills, memory and specific sensory acumen, which span an unlimited array of practical applications. Just as the blind experience a heightening in their remaining senses, hearing for instance, and touch for reading Braille, we experience a heightening of *our own design,* based on our individual practices. A painter will experience increased activity in the frontal lobes and will develop strong connections between the visual cortex and the supplementary motor area controlling the minute skills necessary for delicate brush strokes. This physically tailored awareness is a proven phenomenon in all living entities. Why? Because their lives depend on their link to the environment—the flow of sensory data, and in the blind man's case, the loss of one makes those remaining all the more crucial. For humans alone, our physio-intellectual structure adjusts to serve our own *chosen* premises. It designs itself to serve whatever we choose as most important to pursue. If the wrong methods were learned, they can be overridden by sheer will, and the body will physiologically adapt to further its new instructions. Change your premises, and it will change you physiologically; it's all up to you.

Confidence Displaces Instinct. All living entities run a cycle of accumulation, processing and the result, which is either a reward or penalty. Often considered an involuntary biological process, it is the pattern of cognition as well. The living patterns of Self-made Men all share this structure and can be seen at all levels of rational, civil human endeavor: free-market economics (Capitalism), sound business organizations, democratic elections, the evolution of the space program, Olympic training, choosing a career, the process of eating,...the list is endless. All human action has a purpose—an end in mind—and leads back to its origin; the elements which compose a single thought. The purpose of this cause and effect relationship is to produce *confidence*—an axiomatic need for a non-automatic consciousness—which acts as a constant barometer of physical and spiritual health. Animals supposedly have instincts to guide them—a set course to follow—so confirmation of sound cognition is unnecessary. All they need is a predictable environment to act in. Regardless of what is considered the primary causal factor, a disruption at any step affects the rest; it is a natural continuum. Studies have shown that when an animal's life-pattern of 'effort for sustenance' is interrupted with penalties when expecting rewards, it will quit eating—refusing to exist in a world it cannot comprehend—and this is true for us as well.

Confidence is the emotional aggregate resulting from the status of one's condition regarding the primary alternative—life or death. It involves data encompassing how well one's chosen premises are achieving one's desired ends—one's intellectual and physical health. Confidence attained is never a fixed state. It needs replenishing *even more frequently* than the body needs food. Confidence results from our every day-to-day action and it varies from brimming to anemic, just as our situations vary. I'm sure you can remember getting a job and suffering the embarrassment of a poor initial performance, which with critical apprehension was rectified quickly to your relief, as you settled into the work. Imagine reliving that experience every moment. Imagine if every right turn was supposed to be a left. If we didn't make most moves in life correctly, the stress alone would kill us off in no time. *Pride* or *self-esteem* is our awareness that our actions are correct. By adding to and building our confidence, they indicate that our ability to satisfy the requirements of existence has proven effective. A sense of prideful confidence is a part of the continuum for a rational being, a reward we have to earn and deserve, and which we *could not live without.*

Our Mental Structure. The elements of a single thought are the foundation upon which every wonder of Man has been built, and need to be understood explicitly if we are to comprehend and own any firm moral convictions. The most important phase in our ethical maturation is gaining explicit understanding of the structure by which Man accumulates and validates his knowledge. Most understand and accept that a healthy diet, exercise and posture for the body are ideal, yet do not grasp that a healthy posture also exists for a consciousness: the structure for an unlimited database, which only the discipline of reason can build and reference.

Being carbon-based, water and oxygen sustained entities, men require all the same nutrients to survive. The needs of water and oxygen are *axiomatic,* or in other words, are self-evident, foundational truths. Axiomatic needs are fundamentally irrefutable and reach substantially deeper than most imagine. They transcend these obvious physical associations to reveal links directly into conceptual processes. Every man's mind classifies information alike, building concepts in a standard pattern, and we either learn to hamper this natural design, or learn to act in accordance with it. The process is called *conceptualization,* and we run it at some level, all day long.

The proper means of cognition is in itself, an achievement. It is achieved, not granted—earned, not automatic—respected, not forced. And it can be learned any time one assumes the responsibility to do so. Nature to be commanded must be obeyed, and the proper utilization of the mind must be accepted by all those who intend to think, to live and to enjoy living—the aim of the Self-made. Accountable conceptualization *is* the abstract axiomatic necessity of life sustenance for Man. It isn't a separate issue to our need of air and water, but an extension of the same requirement, moving from direct sensate observation to conceptual observation—driven by the capacity of volition. Its first step, *perception,* is the open integration of clear, coherent sensory data. Perception must be used in any observation of existential matter, and in any communication with others. The second step, *identification,* is the mental effort extended to distinguish the objects of one's perceptions, their attributes and actions, for classification of all existential data along a rational hierarchy. To give them names—to name their attributes, to measure their motions and characteristics—is a hierarchy called an *epistemological chain* of knowledge.

Its links reveal the origin, components and ultimate purpose of any concept. Proper integration builds one's knowledge of the world into a non-contradictory whole, from which sound choices can be made. *Reason* is the process of making those sound choices, reflecting off this base to establish plans for the third step, *productive action*. The process of reason, or *rationality*, accumulates and unites every pertinent detail to arrive at a well-informed conclusion determining one's course of action. The fourth and final step is the product of all that has come before; the *result*. For Self-made Men, most often the result is a reward, a beneficial outcome achieved by intention, such as a positive emotional state, a thought provoking observation, a paycheck, or the United States of America.

Reward is often mistaken to be only a resultant factor, not a part of the process. Reward is not an element separate from cognition—not an isolated result that can be expropriated or divided in any way from that which it was borne—but contains vital, essential information to the soundness of one's cognitive process, and determines the steadfastness of course or of its correction. Another word for "result" in the cognitive process is *validation*. The moral import of this process is that it is *thee* life-serving means of existential control for Man, and every step is optional, though the consequences of their evasion are not. Nature cannot force you to compose thought; it can only force you to decompose. A man must accept life as his standard of value—as his basic referent—by choice, and conceptualization is the fundamental life-pattern—the definitive attribute of a human being. Self-made Man displays the cognitive willingness to exercise every aspect of the process until it is automatized, because he wants to live at the highest, most *human* level possible, to earn and enjoy the greatest pride.

From the Beginning. The first steps of a human consciousness as identified and trained in children by the world renowned Dr. Maria Montessori, were designed to explore and master the full range of Man's perceptual capacity. Her work focused on the subtle differentiation and integration of all facets of each sense, by comprehending the graduations of differing yet similar existents. Her blocks of graduating dimension in length, width, height, weight and shape allowed order to be established by sight and feel, by each sense independently or together. Her bells of graduating tone awakened the mind to the awareness of and differences in, tonal quality. Tactile sensitivity learned by assessing and organizing shapes and textures while voluntarily blindfolded, led into the simplified *causal connections* of round pegs into round holes. The tying of bows, fastening of buttons, snaps, and zippers transformed fumbling motor skills into practical, graceful motion. Her methods held the implicit truth that *differentiation* is the key to comprehension, which laid the foundation for sound independent judgment. Bringing sense and order to our perceptual tools is the springboard to an elegant, intellectually and emotionally mature future.

By training the *structure* of a child's consciousness, she prepared them for assimilating its future *content*. We use the four elements of a volitional consciousness—perception, identification, productive action, and reward—to validate and then store this data we then reference, in order to live. As a result, we have developed methods which measure and classify this data, according to the manner in which it was obtained. The first of our abstract creations was *language;* the second was *mathematics.* Their derivatives include the conceptual structure of *genus and differentia,* and the standards of measurement by which we identify and make use of the data received by each sense. Light and sound waves, the chemical compositions determining flavors and aromas, and the facets of touch: texture, pressure, temperature, sensual enjoyment and pain, can all be broken down into compositions and quantities along scales designed to be useful to Man. Such knowledge then leads to the means by which we can observe, measure and classify entities which exist well outside of our perceptual range. Every scientific and industrial instrument of Man is designed to extend the range of our senses, from the perceptual realm into the conceptual realm. We cannot see microorganisms, but with an electron microscope, we can. We can't grab radio waves from the air for our own enjoyment, but with a receiver, we can. We can't fight off menacing carnivores with our bare hands, but with the American Bill of Rights, we can.

Taking a few steps deeper can assure us of the proper foundation, as if digging into the Earth to view the roots of a tree. Moving from Dr. Montessori's mastery of our perceptual ranges into adult conceptualization, we should validate its origin. The answer lies in mathematics and the physiological workings of the human organism—in how we deal with individual existents and groups of existents. If a number of sticks were placed before you, how many could you perceive before having to count? Looking at ///, its no problem. Looking at /////, most could still reproduce the picture with little difficulty. Move to //////, and most minds hesitate, and have to count. But show six as /// ///, and one has no problem grasping it quickly. The reason is the separation, which is the foundation and purpose of conceptualization: to bring information about the world into our perceptual range, so that it may be dealt with efficiently. Five to six units is the limit for most people, myself included, where the mind begins to reduce the complexity of input to manageable levels, along one of two roads: the conceptual and the mathematical.

Remember the scene in Rain Man where Dustin Hoffman's autistic character counts toothpicks in quantities of 48, but cannot comprehend the concept "dollar"? That is an example of a mind whose full range is utilized perceptually, and cannot graduate to the next step of concept-formation. The perceptual faculty of a healthy mind permits only so many elements at once, and begins to condense information by the process of concept-formation, upon reaching that threshold. The creation of language and math is the means to that end.

Language and Concept-Formation. "I am." is the shortest sentence in the English language, and with a romantic imagination, maybe the first. The second was probably the first subversion: "I'm not." Having been developed at a primitive level some two million years ago, language was created for interspecies relations, and became the key abstract means for identifying, cataloging and passing on knowledge.

The origin of our language begins in the common vocal range of a man. A variety of individual sounds that can be made without strain were refined to comprise our alphabet, and form approximately 158,000 different sound combinations. They allow a concise, phonically-clear conveyance to be spoken and understood. Our system allows no meaning to the concept of "A," beyond its visual representation of the sound made. A fundamental advantage exists in this type of language, as its components maintain no fixed correlation to ideas. In contrast, the Chinese language has only 1,600 sound combinations, severely limiting the number of spoken words. Their alphabet is comprised of about three-thousand commonly used character-words (out of sixty-thousand) which define *preset ideas,* yet the combinations of our twenty-six are nearly limitless, as are our comparative advancements. Why? To hamper expression is to limit individual progress, which is to limit social progress; and this in part, is the reason the language spoken by the greatest number of people on Earth is rarely used outside Asian borders. Their symbols denote prior meaning, and therefore tax the creation of new meaning, skipping an essential cognitive step. Ours provides no ideas from which a consciousness must begin, allowing it an empty slate—full freedom to use the tool without the interference of non-self-derived, non-cognitive elements.

The definition of our every word denotes a specific, exact concept. Concept-formation is a sub-concept itself, of identification. The cognitive progression goes: existence, consciousness, perception, identification, concept-formation. It is obvious how the first step of perception precedes this second step of identification. To identify and integrate efficiently, one must see as clearly as possible to grasp and define the greatest number of attributes of any given entity. The simplest concepts are of perception—the words formed to represent physical objects, such as the concept *pencil.* All entities observed on the planet are given names, as are all attributes of entities. The observation of their attributes forms these sub-concepts, such as arms and legs—of a man, a dog and a frog, excluding the arm of a chair, as the subset *biological* becomes implicit in the trend. Such associations are created and can branch and be cross-referenced infinitely, given their relevance to human application. Entities spawn all abstract concepts as well, in attributes such as dimension, mass, energy, speed and trajectory—in the size of an atom, the energy of the sun and the speed of light. The definition of a concept indicates where it came from, pinpointing its location and differentiating itself from all other concepts on Man's tree of knowledge, and spawns derivative concepts of its own.

Practical use and clear conveyance of these concepts is a result of clear understanding, achieved by a focused mind. The discipline to understand them *exactly*, determines the quality of our actions and the ultimate quality of our lives. Words are like building blocks. They are what they are, they mean what they mean, and you can build what you want with them. When you discover or create something new, you combine words or signify a new word to describe it. Some understand the medium and built skyscrapers. Some corrupt good concepts to knock them down. There is a clear link to why the world's most popular language shares that stature alongside the world's standard of monetary value: the American dollar. One respects free will, while the other is stabilized by the exercise of free will. The existence of such concepts as passion, justice, rationality, precision, tenacity, effectiveness, intransigence and independence, presuppose great men of the past who *did* build and reached great heights.

The Tree of Knowledge. Remember those starlit nights of youth, lying on the hood of a car, contemplating the limitless galaxy and all of our possibilities? It implied future action, and was an experience of the exhilarating use of consciousness. The very term "question" is derived from the word *quest*. Those nights should have followed us into adulthood. We get so involved in our routines, that little energy is left to contemplate what we are all doing here. Topics concerning the universe, social movements and the boundless power of our minds can stem into anything, and most people haven't taken the time to understand the root of it all. The magnificent complexity of our civilization provokes thoughts that can branch off in countless directions. Most believe that every mind creates its own reality, that every branch of life has its own tree, and then it's too overwhelming a task to investigate them all. But how much simpler would it be if all branches led to the same trunk?

All sound concepts begin grounded in the axioms of existence itself, and consciousness as the faculty of perceiving existence. These concepts are not different for individual people; they are valid and useful for anyone who picks them up. We all use the same dictionaries as they all condense data about the same world. The axiom of existence spans and underlies the complete range of human awareness—of everything that will ever come within our grasp, encompassing the subjects of mankind's entire tree of knowledge. The parallel drawn between all branches of human intelligence, is the means and structure of their accumulation. As all limbs of a tree are of similar form, so grows our mental structure and the information it contains—all in this pattern of genus and differentia. If you zoom in, you'll notice that one branch is medicine, while another might be plumbing. Zoom in even closer and you'll see a detailed account of a limb or of the circulatory system—how it works, what helps or hinders it and how one repairs its internal and external maladies. While higher concepts of one branch save individual lives, concepts of the other make it easier to live those lives by feeding electricity, gas and water to all human establishments. Zoom in on the other, and its branches reveal the technical intricacies on the space shuttle, in complex machinery, in our homes, businesses, cars and hospitals. Other offshoots such as law on the branch of politics protect our freedoms and make life worth living. All branches of knowledge as all branches of a tree, live dependent on their trunk, and any separation means death for the limb. It is the trunk which is rooted in the ground—that gathers nutrition and provides the living energy to expand and reach new heights. In other words, any disconnection from existence invalidates a concept.

Healthy, valid concepts all serve the same ultimate purpose—providing data on which men can act. Each branch is held and furthered by the men who harbor that specific interest. There is no central location for the entirety of mankind's knowledge. The knowledge exists by grace of the specializations of every human being. We all build a knowledge tree, tailored to our own specific interests. The stability and worth of our tree depends on how deeply our roots delve into the soil of existence.

Building the Tree. Our epistemological structure is the father of all scientific classification. If you remember from biology, the animal kingdom is classified by the following tree: Kingdom, Phylum, Class, Order, Family, Genus, Species. The intention of this method of course, is to integrate data into a single whole. The act of gathering, validating and placing knowledge along this chain is *integration.* From any point on this tree to any other, a chain is formed. At any time, you should be able to see where you came from, where you are and where you are going. This should be true for any tree you amass on any subject. There can be no indetermination at any step. Indetermination is the end of every chain of knowledge—as knowledge is the defined and the determinable. A fuzzy element breaks the chain and cannot be considered knowledge until its full definition is discovered. There is no room for what 'might be' in fact; either it is or it isn't. Fuzz is where epistemological order ceases, waiting for and dependent on, the faculty of reason to deduce the subject's exact identity. Identifying the missing links in one's life and taking the steps to acquire them is the progress required of every volitional consciousness. A self-made rational man does not accept approximations into his epistemological chains, only at the non-useful (as of yet) ends. His judgment is based on sound reasoning, considering all of the elements necessary to draw conclusions. He is thorough in life, in order to thoroughly enjoy it. A step by step progression of logic is the convincing factor; the only means to *conviction.* The development of conviction is the road to *intransigence,* led by the practice and automatization of leaving no stone unturned in the validation of every premise.

Role of the Subconscious. There has always been this debate over the subconscious mind, and whether it is master over our lives and motivations, or servant. To Self-made Man, it is servant. What is the purpose of the conscious versus the subconscious mind? The conscious mind is the integrator, the organizer of percepts, from which concepts are derived, acted on, and whose bounty is then harvested. The subconscious is the *automatizer* of concepts frequently acted on by one's consciousness. It has no knowledge other than that which we give it, through repetition of our conscious effort. We pace ourselves with a certain practice until we understand it, then as it becomes automatic, it is released from conscious control and delegated to the subconscious, allowing the conscious mind to grasp new material. As our efficiency raises, our minor actions become automated, while our major goal remains conscious, and continues to expand in whatever direction our conscious mind chooses. If we make no determination of course, we float, and *still* get what we're after; it's only that "random mess" was replaced as the goal.

The concept of *will* is just the honest application of the process of cognition, of open perception—of honest identification—of disciplined, rational action and of gratifying reward. Human will is *not* a subconscious attribute, though prior automatization can serve to undercut our will or to fortify it. The subconscious makes no choices; *it has no faculty by which to make them*. The subconscious needs direction from the conscious mind. All it does is operate automated processes based on our accepted premises. If we automate unsound processes, it will operate them without question, and our resulting misery will continue as long as we evade the responsibility to correct them. Perceptiveness, evasion, introspection or its avoidance, are first set in motion by being the subject of the conscious mind. Whatever we dwell on, we train the subconscious to evoke and maintain. We control the subconscious whether we accept that responsibility or not, and controlling its automatization can produce fascinating results, to be explored in future works.

Role of Emotion. What part do emotions play in cognition? The hero of any story is always a just, strong, honorable mind, compelling an able body into action. Notice how his negative emotions are a reaction to the conflict and not an element of the solution. Notice how his elation is a *result* of his victory and the restoration of peace, earned and deserved *after* the battle was won; a desired result, but not the reason of success. Emotions are never sought for solutions to crucial problems—solutions of any problem. Notice how emotions are a reaction to a stimulus, positive or negative, which was a result of a happening or a thought. They are never the reason for action, but an indicator of an event's significance to our own conditions and possibilities. Emotions are strictly resultant factors. They ride the torrent of our environmental exposure, reading our health, pride, fear and pain with precision, revealing our own deepest estimate of a person's or a context's significance to us. All possible emotions are important—good and bad. They are estimates, giving an indication of the soundness of our course. As an intensity gauge, emotions measure virtue or vice, reward or penalty.

Emotions are not volitional phenomenon, but *the result* of volitional phenomenon; the result of choices. They are the finished product of actions taken earlier. Wherever they are encountered in the chain, they confirm the correct path, or warn of trouble ahead. They signal a fork in the road, indicating an alternate route, but they do not provide the map. Proper or improper cognitive effort is responsible for every human action.

Self-made Man considers his emotions to be just one of many gauges on his control panel, and patterns his intellectual effort to use his mind most effectively. He does not ignore them, but pay's strict attention, as to every other measure of health. He traces back through what led him to feel certain emotions, in order to continue their causes or to eliminate them. Once the source of an emotion is understood, it can be reproduced and harnessed as fuel; a concentration of power that can be used for some constructive end. He knows that if a negative emotion remains undefined, its power will rob energy from his sacred goals and possibly destroy them, along with his enjoyment of life. Morally, Self-made Man is motivated by the anticipation of all the pleasure that can be obtained by bettering his condition.

A mind at every turn chooses right or wrong, good or bad. It is simply a choice—a decision made—either based on reason, or based on non-reason. Fear and elation are not perceptual existents, they are psycho-physiological reactions based on the projection of dread and eagerness, which is itself a product of proper or improper conceptual effort. Emotions are a second-level resultant indicator; their implications are accounted for by reason, reason being the faculty of judgment which is rooted in your five-sense awareness, and is the only sound, predictable, repeatable base in which to entrust any decision.

Inertial Awareness. Forewarning information can be powerful, though quite unreliable, but I am beginning to pay closer attention to this facet of my being. I have had experiences in real life that happened first in dreams. One segment lasted for about five minutes. I was at a party. I knew who I was about to meet— what their names were, that we were standing by a circular stairway, that a pretty brunette would pass behind them—the detail was too remarkable to ignore. These people had no significance to my life and never would; I don't know why I was exposed to the information in advance. Déjà vu is a rare phenomenon we've all experienced to some extent, but I believe it can be made useful.

There are inertias that one can pick up on based on one's choices in life and one's likely future choices. Every choice we make immediately generates positive or negative energy; it immediately begins physiological preparation for the actions to come. This is a fascinating contemplation for me; an untapped cognitive ability I have termed Inertial Awareness. Its popular name is ESP, which is actually a way of saying what it is not. In time, I wish to find a valid philosophical link to what has been considered the proper domain of mysticism. I don't think it is mystical at all; it begins and ends in our minds. It is not a sixth sense, as it is not sensory; but simply an untapped facet of Man's integrating capacity. Thoughts, however complete in themselves, are not static. They have momentum; they are preceded and followed by other thoughts as are the motions of your body. Your intuitive responses are reflections of your own life's inertia, in a given context at the time of the intuition.

It is an amazing feeling to know in advance how things will come out at any range, long or short. I think of extreme sports, such as the sensation of a bicycle freestylist accelerating into the air on takeoff, reaching weightlessness, then falling back to the ramp. He knows by his approach if all will go well. He knows by his takeoff, how he will land; every fiber of his being can feel it before it happens. The smell of the air, his position on the ramp, the wind on his back, the feeling of the grips and pedals; his overall balance determines his overall confidence. This translates to any other activity. Making a business decision, walking down the stairs, driving a car on a winding road—you know what to expect; the pattern repeats. The inertia of now, indicates the inertia of the next moment. It is predictable.

All actions are energies whose 'abstraction to physical action' neurobiological link is yet to be discovered, but they can be used now for forward thinking. I take actions that further the inertias in my life—the paths I wish to see furthered. When I make a wrong turn, the inertias stop. I do what is necessary to get back on track. It can be any choice—the wrong person, a wrong business affiliation or the wrong approach. When it is correct or corrected, the inertias I wish to further are invigorated. As only the right equation will solve a problem of science, I believe that moral consistency is the key to make use of Inertial Awareness: the concept is integrity. Contrary to the claim of psychic hotlines, inertias do not determine your destiny; your premises do. As your premises evolve, your actions change; and so follow your inertias.

Turning the Tables. Why is the cognitive process so important to a Moral Warrior? Because when virtue is allowed to pass undefined, then so is vice. Sound conceptualization is responsible for all human furtherance. As nature determined our cognitive process, its proper utilization is at the root of every moral action. With the understanding of conceptualization comes the understanding of *every moral violation.* It is from the negation or perversion of proper conceptual construction that all twists come. The base of nonexistence—of that which isn't real—is derived from *that which is.* A negation of any one of the four elements—perception, identification, creative action or reward—allows a man to be taken advantage of, and a lack of its comprehension on our part dulls our sensitivity to the risk.

By virtue of the fact that we live, that which is harmonious with life is what we must respect. In our individual lives and in our history as Man, with an interest to see our code make sense it is rational principles we've supported, while ignoring, tolerating or opposing the senseless. We have been morally correct implicitly through our reverence for the joy-generating potency of our experiences, even in our memories. But without a clear standard to judge moral or immoral ideas, we were unable to get a fix on their identity, allowing them to recur in our own lives, in our relationships and in our law. Yet we still revere what is right: the ideals in Man that we cherish are his life-defending, life-furthering traits: the unflinching nerve, the candid honor, the powerful ability, the free, proud, radiant joy of a being who is calm, confident and in control—all elements of the four basic virtues.

A lifetime of evidence validating this process is behind the steady eyes and frightening potency of a Moral Warrior. The man who reaches the point beyond all doubt—the point of total conviction by rational means—who grew as Self-made, yet has spent serious time immersed in the world of the Spirit Murderers, who knows their evasions, their escapes and their denials, the man who learns to answer them in every context and watches them fold in their true impotence, time and time again, becomes *untouchable* psychologically. With pure honesty, there are no longer any psychological threats to fear. With full willingness to see ourselves, we will have eliminated them. The right shields are up; beautiful, clear, impenetrable shields, through which nothing can ever cut too deep. When you can breathe deeply and, with steady eyes, are able to see what's right and wrong and who stands where, no danger is ever too frightening; not even death.

Our pursuit of life is not evil and never was. Thought and knowledge are the tools of Man, and Man is their proper benefactor. The offenses borne against our pursuit were the actual evil, but self-defense is only the beginning. Once the way is clear, the freedom it affords—the clean pathways to new heights and sacred rewards—will open a whole new destiny before us. We amass within ourselves the wealth of a precision instrument, brimming with radiant activity; a controlled storm that took years to master, and we are free to create life in the most adventurous and exciting ways. That is our nature, our birth-right, our destiny and our glory.

Part Three: The Meaning of Life: Concepts of Purpose

"You won't be any good at all, unless you love it."
—The Perfect Storm

Peace: The First Necessity. Why is it that we no longer hear of men and women like Alexander the Great and Joan of Arc? They were fighters for freedom against any kind of oppression. They knew what they wanted—it was simple enough: to end the use of force against them, to gain the freedom to earn their living and to keep the results of their work. They longed for a society where they need not face constant perils; an environment where today's achievement could be furthered tomorrow without fear of it being demolished, confiscated or stolen. They wanted a world where their children would be spared the unnecessary hazards of predacious savages. They fought alongside those they inspired, fully willing to die for their dream, and became legends of human greatness. Do such people still exist? Where are they now? Hint: they are in industry. They had won their freedom to act, and now they are acting.

An industrial revolution is what happens when men are set free. It may have a name associated to a past event, but it is actually a human being's natural response to his surroundings when nothing stands in his way. Prosperity, *honestly* distributed, is what only freedom can regulate. Someone has to stand in every era—those who are part scientist and part adventurer—to speak and to lead. It doesn't matter whether the task is leading men to fight or leading them to produce; such men can do both equally well when called upon. All such men prefer prosperity to violence, but choose the latter when they witness corruption gaining a foothold on our civilization. Men like William Wallace of Scotland—the strong, reluctant warrior, the man of unimpeachable integrity and spirit seeing nothing but his right to be, guarding nothing but the integrity of men–will pick up their weapons again when the law tells them that the government monopoly on force allows the citizens no right to defend themselves against it. The warriors have not died off, and will never die.

Every successive generation asks, "What are we here for?" Moral Warriors are the men who have answered that question. We absorb the same fables, stories and legends—the great battles of good and evil—all sharing the same elements of innocence oppressed, to be quelled by innocence grown strong. We address the same universal problems as time moves on, passing to future generations the peace of ours. But for the most part, modern warriors use words now. We are free in America; we can speak. Words are swords without the "s," and they are powerful weapons. Every utterance of integrity is a blow to evil and a plus to the side of life. With our freedom of speech, the concentrations of evil have been disallowed a monopoly on Man's conveyances to men, and an unprecedented era of productivity has been the result.

Prosperity: The Next Step. The men who were driven by an overwhelming need to take responsibility and do something about evil—the leaders—are now answering the overwhelming need they fought for: their own fulfillment on Earth. The Moral Warrior lays down his arms and looks at the world. He sees ferrous elements glittering in the rock and thinks of the metal that can be extracted. He sees the violent flow of a river and thinks of the power to be generated. He sees the bounty of the forest, part of which is to be transformed as beams to become his home and the homes of others. His children can grow safely here.

Before long, thanks to those who have met the needs of civilization in these endeavors, individuals need not make the basic necessities their primary concern. Their purpose can exist far along Man's chain into abstract territory, furthering pleasurable concepts such as style, where an honest living can be made in as many creative ways as there are people. The vantage point of morality in action is often as witness to the pioneers of our past and present, following the structure of their course to define the motives, means and ends of the actual good. To the limits of their vision, they create and further our great industries and set the best examples for the whole world to follow. These are the men of purpose. They have a calling; a desire to see some specific end achieved, and the whole of their being is poured into its accomplishment. When they are finished, they find another. They spend their lives on growing, each concern more sophisticated than the one before, as a constant answer to why they live. With their every moment drenched in meaning as a result, they are the happiest, deepest, most devoted, and most genuine people on Earth. Their essential purpose acts as the highest abstraction in their epistemological chain, and all actions in life and all knowledge accumulated takes place within its framework. As a result, they acquire the longest intellectual range; knowing how every step they take will affect their lives, and are able to project their activities to the end of their days. With their purpose as motivator for every action, no energy is wasted. Their neurobiological development is streamlined and as a result, their chains of knowledge grow much faster and much longer than usual. These are the men who utilize the human mind as it was meant to be, and can show the rest how to actualize their greatest potential. Our appreciation for these men *is* our respect for life itself, as the axiomatic reason for purpose *is* life.

The Self-Made State of Mind. If men obeyed accountants, there would be no internal combustion engine, no airplane, and no light bulb; no steps taken on the untried and the new. A visionary is a man who holds his own view as paramount, motivationally equating the concept of investment with the concept of breakthrough, sensing the inherent risk in predictability. He is only at ease when he is safely out in front. He may weigh the ideas of others, but he never substitutes those ideas for his own cognitive process. If a visionary alters his course, it is by conviction; he learns the new facet as thoroughly as its creator, and accepts full responsibility for its use and result.

At any time, the effort necessary to reach spiritual fulfillment is dictated by the limit of our personal vision, which is also in a state of expansion over the course of our lives. As we mature, our undertakings must evolve to reflect our depth. The pinnacles of men embark on endeavors that encompass the whole of the world. They address the universal problems of existence and arrive at the next summit of questions to be answered. The most extreme of the pinnacles takes actions in life—runs errands, dines, works—oblivious to the world around him. People and the rest of the world are often just background. He has blinders on, seeing only the quickest route between two points; the issues of his mind and their solution. Self-made Man has instilled an automatic preoccupation that steals away the focus of his consciousness from others during all idle time. Confronted by people asking questions, he answers as he moves, not breaking stride when possible.

Like most people, I began my career in the pattern of a painful grind and cherished weekends, with torturous years and precious vacations. It was all backwards! Now, when I think of vacation, I think "To escape from what?" I love everything I do. There is no such thing as forever in human terms. Each second that goes by cannot be recalled, as it is ruthlessly subtracted from the span of our lives. No matter what happens—good or bad—we must enjoy our time here to our fullest capacity. No matter what we accumulate—money, fame, enlightenment—nothing compares to the satisfaction of squeezing every ounce of joy, passion and adventure out of our conscious hours. The goals of a Self-made Man are fully obtainable—even the long-range goals of his philosophers—and he expects to be rewarded without unnecessary delay. He accepts no undefinable gap between cause and effect; between required action and reward, as his time is too precious to be wasted. He expects both to be proven within a reasonable and *determinable* interval, and sets his hierarchy of pursuits accordingly. He shows as much concern for the expense of time as for the expense of money, and manages both in a businesslike manner.

All men have dreams, but their nature varies in regard to personal integrity. They all include riches and glamour, but his dreams differ from others in that Self-made Man exalts the *effort* necessary to achieve them. He knows that this is the source of his self-worth; not the *having* alone, but the earning. The capacity to *deserve* is the glory of any human being, in wealth, in love and in honor. He reveres the elements of the complete process—the chosen ideal, the training, the battle and the victory. His respect for time is a result of the crucial undertakings for which he wishes to spend every waking moment. When he does pause to look at the world, his glance is not that of a stranger, but of an appreciation beyond any depth the others could reach. When he looks upon men, he sees the same potential he feels about his own life, imagining their pursuits to be as profoundly important to them as his own, and his living eyes reflect the acceptance he feels in looking upon his own creations. His primary focus is his conscious purpose; his secondary is all other communication and action. Men are not a part of his inner world—they are not needed to achieve his goals—and consequently there is a total absence of fear. It is a world where no form of submission or violence need be accounted for, as there are no external authorities to undermine his course. There is only what he will do. And when he does take a break, he astonishes most with the untroubled lightness of his manner.

The Purpose of Purpose. As the Moral Warrior first fought for his freedom, then set out to satisfy the basic necessities of life before he could pursue other interests, we must do the same. Purpose can no more be separated from spiritual preservation than profit can be separated from physical preservation. Each is responsible for the other. The primary purpose of every human being is life itself. No further values are possible without life's needs first served. But beyond the sub-elements of food and shelter, there must be a reason for such effort's continuance: life's enjoyment.

There is natural resistance to life, and the most effective means of accumulating and spending the energy necessary to overcome it is found by selecting a reason to live—a purpose. Purpose itself has a purpose, serving a crucial role within a volitional being. First, overcoming this resistance sets a hierarchy of goals driven by personal interest for the individual to spend his lifetime accomplishing. Second, it steers the individual to embark on a path of self-development, inspiring commitment toward gathering the knowledge and ability needed to live and to satisfy his desires. Third, it lengthens his range and depth of thought, allowing him to see and consider the entire span of his life and set his goals according to the investment of time and energy necessary for the attainment of each. This assures the most productive and efficient use of his tools of cognition (cognitive steps 1 and 2), as a map for his creative action (cognitive step 3), and opens the door to the highest levels of spiritual accomplishment: the true maturation of his intellect. Purpose exists as foreman in the construction of our whole tree of knowledge.

At the top of the pyramid, our purpose guides and oversees all integration below, sorting what will help or hinder its attainment. All that lies beneath it is similar for every man—just existential data—yet without a central purpose, a human being is rudderless. Without a main intention there are no chains to run up or down, to set priorities, establishing order in hierarchies of importance. Without a central purpose, one floats disconnected to the whole of one's life and is unable to tell day by day, issue by issue, what is moral or immoral; what furthers or threatens one's goals and desires. We can be swept in any adverse direction by the ceaseless flow of data streaming into our senses every moment if we don't take conscious control. It must be gleaned of essentials by our ultimate volitional filter: our purpose, so the stream carries us closer to where we want to go. We have no choice in building a knowledge tree, but its value to us—what it will contain, its effectiveness and the purposes it will serve—is up to us. Having lifelong goals breeds cognizance of the long-range effects of any circumstance, to assure we don't end up in the wrong place.

The Rules of Purpose. A purpose, to be valid, must obey three rules: <u>Rule 1:</u> *All Purposes must be self-defined.* Our portal to creative action must be defined by our cognitive tools. It is not only an epistemological derivation, but a physiological one, determining not only what we will do, but where we must start and at what speed we can travel. <u>Rule 2:</u> *Purpose must be existentially based.* As it is an abstract concept derived from the biological need for cognitive integration, its subject must also be existential, exercising human thought and action applicable in our universe. <u>Rule 3:</u> *The central focus must be ourselves.* As the very architect of our capacities, purpose *must* revolve around us. A proper purpose does not require others or their agreement, or any specific outside cognitive power. As we move, we remain its constant center. Though we may employ others to see its facets to fruition, no one man is irreplaceable beyond ourselves. We are its essential contributor—the prime mover—without whom it cannot continue. Our purpose is a product of our consciousness and therefore dies with us, though our legacy may remain.

Self-Determination. As ninety-five percent of all blessings are self-made, our lives must be adventures of our own design. One individual can change the whole course of mankind, and with the right cognitive guidance, there is no telling what you could bring to the rest of us. But there is one caveat; your purpose must be chosen alone. Every part of you has a wonderful potency just waiting to be discovered, but you have to find your own way; your unique approach to experiencing your own highest view of yourself. There is no point in learning what you do not intend to use. If you are sitting in Geography class learning about European border laws, you'll have little incentive for retaining it. If you are crossing from Germany into Czechoslovakia on a near trip, you do. *Use determines retention* and therefore value, and the desire for use is the moral province of the individual. You don't have to know everything, and you don't have to consider everyone. The stimulus to elicit the energy necessary to establish order and coherently build our chain is found *only* through what draws our individual fascination, and men of purpose will tell you they can be aroused by nothing less.

True moral action is to work for our own self-interest and spend its bounty on our own sustenance and happiness. As we grow and expand by this means, we bring the greatest growth and expansion to the lives of others; but it must begin within, just as every flower must bloom before revealing its beauty. By learning your own endeavor, you form specialized knowledge, and bring its benefits to all you encounter. That you are the one to choose is truly a matter of spiritual life and death. The third cognitive element—creative action, demands that purpose be derived by the second, identification. There is no external controller in regard to this; full control resides in your consciousness. Purpose is a product of cognition, and can be nothing else. It is defined exclusively by the integrating capacity to be called upon for its completion—which alone knows its own sensitivities and loyalties. You alone know your physical and mental strengths and weaknesses; you alone know the true distance to your full capacity in all respects and your willingness to reach it. If you feel your own purpose is crucially important, you won't interrupt it for anything. The opinions of others may be weighed, but must never be allowed to override your own. A specialization is an independent derivation; unique and self-generated, as is its pride. Purpose is a road to travel where one should not look for a companion or a shepherd; nature allows no collusion. Like it or not, you are on your own. What we give our time freely too, or what we run to and immerse ourselves in during difficult times—given they are constructive—is the road to our passions. On this road, we will find what we wish to bring into existence: our purpose.

Range and Self-Impact. Our proper evolution as volitional entities drives a moral imperative: to ceaselessly investigate the efficiency and impact of our fulfillment in every aspect of our lives; to be self-sustaining at the highest level, physically and spiritually. The level of goals we choose—family, business, political or historic—is the longest-range *moral* contemplation and action open to us. What level of impact do you want to have?

In my case, I wanted to have a global effect. The range of my endeavors had to involve the environment I considered my realm, my home—the whole of the world. Primary metals were my first industrial interest, because they are in everything. After reviewing businesses to purchase, I realized something would still be missing. I felt that it was more important to discover and name this attribute, than any other benefit that I could bring to civilization, and to myself. I found it. It turned out to be the primary behind the discovery of primary metals, and of every other human concern. I look forward to helping people through this book, but first and foremost, *writing it* was what I wanted to do more than anything in the world. I gave up values which others could not fathom letting go of to see this through, but it was not a sacrifice. I valued *Moral Armor* higher than the money I could make in the interim, the women I could date, the trips I could take and even the Lamborghini I owned. My lifestyle was an aggregate of dreams itself, attained triumphantly, but they were the dreams of a younger man. After a while, my enthusiasm for past accomplishment waned, and I became hungry for more. I was no longer of the same dimension. I had grown in stature and vision and needed a more elaborate vent to channel my energy.

I gave so much to every past endeavor that prosperity in my new venture was a forgone conclusion. Having come so far in philosophy and in wealth, I knew my next attempt would be pointless if it didn't make the greatest *self*-impact. As our vision evolves, so do our goals. Our passion is an investment that must show the highest return possible, and I was finally free to concentrate on what I alone, found most exhilarating. Fed up with the weaklings considered by intellectuals to be the giants of thought, I want to show the world a philosopher who can *really* lean into it. That is my dream.

Self-Development. Self-made Man's life holds one main certainty—his direction. Subjects change often, particular interests and activities may appear random and are, only to the extent that they do not detract from his direction. That direction is his continued happiness and the furtherance of his life, physically and mentally. In essence, Self-made Man is after a ceaseless flow of new data to integrate. Learning to him is a warm, stimulating pleasure, because *he* chooses the subjects, and sees an immediate boost in the enjoyment of his pursuits as a result. That is what he lives for, not just the pridefully-earned byproducts of productivity, such as money and luxuries. He doesn't consider his education complete after four years; it's a lifelong commitment.

As an honest man, he looks openly, using his strengths to bolster his weaknesses. He rebuilds them, tearing down to the appropriate levels to ensure firm foundations, purifying his life by advancing his competence to live it. In facing and solving new problems, it is he that is built, day by day, step by step. Every day he becomes the master of a new skill, or master of one facet of a greater skill. He branches off at random to complete ideas and answer questions that form during other studies, all which serve one central purpose. He often forms a private library to *mine* the best minds. Our confidence exudes from knowing what we know, as we are able to walk our chains and revalidate any part of them, and often do. We maintain a willingness for reintegration long after our concepts are accepted as fixed and eternal, always interested to discover how new elements fit in. We stay open to new directions in the midst of valuable evidence and take the time to restructure if necessary. The purpose of an efficient flow of life never being far from our own specialties, we stay on the cutting edge. Why do we do all this? To see clearer. To live better. *To save time*—time to be spent on the unlimited discovery of our own joys.

Ultimately, Self-made Man's inner world revolves around just a handful of sacred subjects; his alone and his primary energy—his very life-force—goes to satisfy these endeavors. Limited to a lifetime, Self-made Man identifies all the key possibilities of life he wishes to experience, and then seeks to discover the means by which he can most effectively achieve and enjoy each one. His career, sports interests, hobbies, romantic involvement and parenting all require different traits and skills, and he makes a habit of accumulating and improving them. As his own view of himself is paramount, he looks deeply into the character of heroes, and works to acquire the attributes he wishes to represent. He is aware of the moral worth of his every action, so his esteem affords him to be fully conscious of his true ability in every context in which he lives. It is then easy to see where he is for any goal at any time, where he wants to be, and to move forward in their order of importance to him.

Training becomes as vital a part of his life as production. He knows that consonant with the flow of life, his abilities are in constant flux, and to stay sharp he must practice his skills. At times, he must accept back-pedaling in areas that need to wait while others take priority. The pleasure of a context that has advanced beyond the others need not be spoiled by one that languishes behind. He can grow by leaps and bounds in his work, be quietly tortured by a lack of intimacy and friends, yet still preserve the feeling that life is worth living. Joy from one activity cannot stretch to cover another; such radiance can only be reflective. But as his hierarchy is in place to control all of his actions, all values will be addressed at the right time. To stay up, he rewards himself regularly for practicing so sound a pattern of moral action. Scaled to particular actions, the reward may be just a candy bar, but one cannot wait until the final triumph to enjoy the elation of any consciously wholesome pursuit.

He may see inefficiencies in other areas of human life, but he cannot do everything. With respect for his time, he stays focused on his own interests, yet monitors advancements in the other fields that affect him to stay on the cutting edge there, too.

Nullifying Apprehension. There is no need to fear choosing the wrong purpose. Rational endeavors all share the correct fundamental premises: the preservation of life by civil means as its primary, the exaltation of its master as reward. There are so many endeavors to expand one's fulfillment that they can never be exhausted. Self-made Men search until they find the perfect fit. Even if you never find it, you'll have a hell of a lot better time looking than if you weren't. My first career was automotive design, the second was real estate, the third was the stock market and now I am a writer. In between, I gorged myself on philosophy, law, economics, business acquisitions and even considered founding a bank. I try whatever sparks my interest on this planet because I love being alive, but the pursuit of purpose certainly grows more refined as we gather experience. As we see farther, we can look back and understand why a previous goal suited our level at the time, and what made us move on. For example in my teens I could have trained to become a professional bicycle freestylist as some of my riding acquaintances went on to be. What stopped me was that I could not dedicate my life to it. My life's pursuit was still to be discovered and I knew if I tried to make my mark in freestyle, I would die inside. Likewise, if they tried to do what I do, it would be the same for them. They would feel trapped where I feel freed. Freestyle gives them a feeling about their lives which I could only experience through writing, and vice-versa. They could appreciate what I've done, but could not make it their purpose. So freestyle remained a sideline, while I kept searching. You must be able to say, "This is what I want to do with my life, or at least what I want to do right now." Take the first steps into purpose and further steps will be revealed. Reflecting back, I tried this and that, responding with, "No, that's not it," time and time again, but investigated each correctly. I had a serious interest to learn all I could about a subject, enjoyed it thoroughly, and worked hard to make it pay.

Outside of one's living purpose, other goals appear to be ends in themselves, but often prove to have significant value. Some such goals are not lifelong and just have to run their course. Starting out poor in youth, all I wanted was my dream car, a Lamborghini Countach. That dream led me to become a business owner, to study law, economics and finance—all knowledge I constantly draw from, long after the car has gone. With that experience, I realized my working hours should give me as much pleasure as the car did. Self-made Men watch their well-rounded educations take form, through their passions. We do things because they excite us, and when the thrill subsides, we move on to a different challenge. It's that simple. Discarding old endeavors is not failure; we simply close chapters in our lives, and with greater vision, open new ones. If we enjoyed the way we spent our time, we need regret nothing. This is life; the knowledge and experience from every venture is carried forward into bigger plans and deeper exaltation until the time comes for us to let go.

Sound Guidance. In any field you choose, you must care enough to want to operate at the top. You can go straight there in the privacy of your own mind with projection and try to think at their level, beginning with the end in mind. There is only one type of person safe to gain advice from: those who have taken your field the farthest. Whomever has obtained what you desire by private effort, is the one to ask or study. Those who have tried, erred and tried again are the primary source for sound, practical, experiential understanding, where one can learn the specialty as well as its proper method of development. The problem is finding them.

Heroes do not travel in herds. The training of sound practice can be all consuming, and most are so focused on their task that they have little time to spare for social interaction. That is why they leave most behind as they venture forth into their light. But by virtue of our respect for progress, fame for such a man is inevitable, and our exposure to them is made possible through what they have documented. Honing the skills of interaction with their science is their methodical process of advancement—the result of the steady pressure of application. *Tenacity* is this steady pressure. He sees the goal and learning what it requires of him, storms every angle until it is achieved. The consciousness most capable of satisfying its own ends is not mass-produced, but *tailor-made*, asking the self-made questions throughout life of "What am I living for? What do I want to be? What do I want to experience? What is most important for me to accomplish?", and letting nothing stand in the way of oneself and its achievement.

The most extreme feel they were chosen—that there is something they need to do, something the world must see, which only they understand and only they can bring. They have been ridiculed, thought to be crazy and tortured for their truth, but they all say the same thing—that it was worth whatever men made them pay. It was worth it. Horrendous obstacles are here for a reason: a test to see us grow past such challenges, to make insurmountable barriers look irrelevant, to challenge precedent and ultimately to cut our own path. They must be overcome to see our best prevail and determine higher standards. We prove our worth by facing a torrent of opposition—braving the storm to see our vision through to the end—an accomplishment that lived and triumphed due to the power of our will alone. We all need someone to believe in, and we are that someone. Legends don't die like a man dies. We have to accept the final stress of the decision to go forward—the contemplation before eternity—to embrace the point of no return. And we must go. Whatever is going to happen, will happen. The message must be heard in our words, and these words will live for us when we are no longer. They will live for all time.

Part Four: Life's Reward: Concepts of Self-Esteem

"If you done it, it ain't bragging." —John Wayne

Earned Greatness. The fourth cognitive element, the concept of validation, has many faces. The effect of so many causes, it first stands for justice. In this regard, the words *reward* and *consequence* are synonymous. For the slothful, validation is the hell on Earth they bring about by their own default. For Self-made Man, it is the glory of his existence. We are the men who see and hear, and trust those perceptions. We are the men who think and feel, and are totally honest about the conclusions we draw and the actions we take. We never, never, *never* drop our minds. We produce and therefore earn the stunning luxuries our freedom makes possible. Beautiful homes, exotic cars, sun-soaked vacations, a life with the mate of our dreams—it's all possible in this land of opportunity. The disciplined focus of our efforts, the intelligent choices and dedicated hours provides a steady climb to heights of our own. We know what we've earned and our work *should be* rewarded, and in America, it is; yet the most important reward is internal. The reward is self-esteem. It is our own ruthless sense of justice, knowing our own value and looking outward; ready to accept and give value for value in love and respect for existence and for others; with our greatest human bond reserved for those who live up to our standards. This is the spiritual stature of a Self-made Man.

Our Exclusive Medium. How nice it would be, as a ship has water as a medium for travel, if our minds had genuine enjoyment, expectation and light-heartedness as a medium through which to navigate the world. If only there were a clear path to follow, then the tear-filled divinity in most souls could come pouring out in total safety, with full honor and sanction. But there isn't. Self-made Man holds the secret to this pathway, often even from himself, as it is a product of traits condemned by widespread erroneous beliefs. By sacrificing our highest and enshrining our lowest, by worshipping the unknowable and ignoring self-destiny, such others have been *justly* denied this fulfillment.

Happiness—real, repeatable, consistent happiness—is had only by those who accept and practice its true foundation. It is not a random, causeless, selfless, undefinable phenomenon relying on mystical or intuitive elements which lie outside our power. It is a product of the proper tools of cognition practiced by the Self-made: perception, identification and purposeful action—of all that has come before—and one need only embrace the reality of its pattern. Nature, to be commanded, must be obeyed. Happiness cannot be had by seeking diversions that clash with our values, or by means which negate our consciousness, leading nowhere. It cannot be had by serving others. Self-made means *self*-made; not neighbor-made. No dead-ends, dependencies or freebies lead to happiness. It is instead, the radiance of a *fully valued* consciousness. It is a product of achievement. The code of the Self-made brings a man to the point where he is no longer *coping* with existence, but reveling in it. Following his lead, so serene a calm will develop in your control of life that you'll wonder how you ever got along without it. The radiant result of a moral existence as well as its most powerful motivation and product, is a profoundly private, self-serving personal joy.

Happiness is Self-Appreciation. Happiness is achievable midway up the axiomatic ladder, being the next link in the conceptual chain above confidence and pride. It is the *medium* of pride, as pride is the medium of confidence. Each can become a form of wealth; w*ealth* being an accumulation of *any* value above and beyond one's need to spend. Happiness is an accumulation of positive emotional energy to be enjoyed consciously, as it was borne constructively. It is not a man's job that is important, but his work; and science tells us that 'work' is any expense of energy which accomplishes an objective.

To develop as happiness, one's effort must serve sound, rational goals, but those goals can vary greatly. The desire to bring a new invention into the world, to go where no man has gone before, to close a deal, to be appealing to a certain quality of partner, to turn a faster lap on a racetrack, to express exaltation through art, these are all actions of joy; of pushing oneself to the next level in endeavors self-important to pursue. The joy varies only in degrees according to the personal significance and depth of the endeavor. It is a man's own passionate interests brought to life in a sound value hierarchy that leads to a consistently earned pride and a deserved happiness. Its depth determines whether the satisfaction is sustainable or fleeting. A surface goal gives off little esteem compared to a long-term goal of greater complexity, but both add to the plus side. The emotional reward for a small accomplishment can last only a few minutes, while the pride of something immense will be much more profound and lasting. Seemingly unrelated, both add to the plus column and both serve the same end; a tailor-made existence.

We select a favorite shampoo for the same reason we design and build skyscrapers. It is the act of creative, useful self-expression that displays to *ourselves,* our ability to meet our physical and spiritual needs, and therefore allows us to experience a sense of self-esteem. Happiness *is* self-appreciation and can naturally spring from nothing else.

The Rules of Happiness. The source of happiness has always been a big mystery, but not any longer. Think of a time in your life when you were most happy. Happiness is a bright, sharp, clear, light, radiant state of being, isn't it? We see blue skies, satisfied bosses and customers, a warm, stable home and meaningful relations. Happiness is associated to when things are going well—in nature, at work and in our personal lives—a reward for an unrestricted flow. It is a state of awareness where one needn't fear looking at the premises that caused it. In contrast, cynicism and malice—any kind of irrational negativity— is like mud: sticky, gooey, heavy, indeterminate, shapeless and dull—just like the premises that caused it, premises undesirable to reveal, premises we are going to wash away.

Self-help books declare thousands of ways to bring joy into life, but fortunately there is only one fundamental way. Generated by the sound pattern of cognition like all concepts, it has its own set of rules. First, happiness is a *state of consciousness;* the sole province of the individual. Since one can choose to actively think or to float randomly instead, then consciousness is a matter of choice. <u>Rule 1:</u> *Only those who choose to be conscious, can be happy.* Next, happiness requires a means to which this desirable state is the end. Once you consistently practice the means, you will have happiness as a constant. The means are efforts of thought and action, which result in self-appreciation. Forget those who lean on their parent's or their spouse's money and social position, because only one's *own* practice of virtue—the capacity to survive *independently* at the level one lives—determines one's true stature and self-respect. Therefore, <u>Rule 2:</u> *Happiness is self-generated.* The extent of our own thinking and the vital results based on it is the extent of our worth, *period.* Finally, <u>Rule 3:</u> *Happiness only results from the practice of life-patterns,* and is therefore inextricably linked to personal honesty. Happiness is a confirmation that one is on the right course in life, and that the course is worth sustaining (that life is worth living). Happiness is the natural result of the correct process of virtuous action—not the joy of escape, but the shining, glimmering pride of brave vision—of a universe worth seeing, of experiences worth living, of a countenance so appealing, of intimacy so moving, of adventure so exhilarating, of study and contemplation so engaging.

Virtue is *not* its own reward; it is a means to an end. Our goal in the pursuit of happiness is to expand our fulfillment by virtuous means in our every avenue of interest, to the end of our days. There are no short-cuts to self-esteem; the natural links of cause and effect run all through the pattern. From the axioms of existence and consciousness, to the honest effort of life, to the confidence of the means chosen, to their success, to the pride that follows, to the bravery to form new questions to answer, to the medium of happiness made possible only by the continuation of the process, the flow is discernible and fully accountable.

Happiness is a necessary, spirit-sustaining validation that life is worth living. Confidence alone won't do it. Security won't do it. These are sub-elements. A person can be brilliant, rich and active and still be miserable if his means have not addressed his most private heart-felt longings. There can be no compromise at any level of cognition, especially in regard to one's purpose. The most penetrating happiness is found in the knowledge that one's deepest, most personal desires are being reached. It is achieved by the steady, lifelong accumulation of one's *own* dreams, one after another. It is the trend of actualization that draws the deepest fulfillment; the deepest appreciation of self. Success begins with giving our true goals our best shot; then, win or lose, we know we haven't wasted our time here. This is where happiness becomes profound and the true meaning of life becomes clear—and priceless.

The Choice of Virtue: Ourselves to Admire. No matter what context happiness is experienced through, self-appreciation always lies at its base. Search the meaning in any happy feelings you've ever had and you will find a sanction of the value of *your own* being. This is natural and right. Happiness often seems to come from the outside, but it never does. The smile of a spouse, a solution to a problem, a raise in salary—is all existential data which must first pass through our senses, so our interpretations of meaning are alone responsible. Happiness is gained through our interrelation with ourselves, with nature and with others, generated by the soundness of what we view as important in life.

For example, experiencing pleasure from watching children or animals play can give you a sense of happiness, but the source of that happiness is the identification of what you regard as virtue. In this case, it is the recognition of your capacity to appreciate that special sense of existence children have; in their fearless awareness of the world and of people, in their innocent gaiety and the boundless certainty they display in the confident motion of their bodies, as beings who have not learned the imprisoning patterns of self-doubt (and maybe you can silently reflect on what has been wrongly lost in adulthood). Who hasn't been victim of the blatant staring of a two-year old in a restaurant and lived to tell about it? One level beyond attributes of character, the reasons we enjoy children, as in our own pursuits, affirm the efficacy of Man's senses (and their integrator, the mind) which *lead* to the fostering and preservation of life and its enjoyment. The anticipatory awareness of their wide eyes, eager to see, looking for the source of every unique sound they hear, their questioning expressions, open or retracted to the scents of the world—good and bad! Their able little bodies reaching to the sun, exploring, learning, endlessly invigorated by every new discovery awaiting them around all of life's corners—these are the pleasures of sensate perception and integration.

With animals playing, you get to see your appreciation and respect for social joviality, beings enjoying their coexistence, where the crucial problems of life have been solved, and one has earned the right to feel truly light, playful and open. If you look closely, happiness revolves around only two facets: your own confirmation, appreciation and respect for the pathways that lead to life; (1) its sustenance, and (2) its enjoyment. It is your awareness that what *you* personally value, generates a positive physical and spiritual bounty—a life pattern—and it follows that by witnessing its proof, you have validated and sanctioned your own reasoning power; a moral validation—and therefore have gracefully earned self-esteem.

The Levels Beyond Happiness. We've all heard people say, "If I could just be happy…" But Self-made Man doesn't stop there. He sees the road still stretching ahead, so in tow, we will go much farther. For every mile traveled he accumulates a new virtue and coins a new concept. From the conscious acceptance of existence, to earned confidence, pride and happiness, his next steps, like the others, build on what has come before. From how he deals with stress, to metaphysical honesty, integrity and existential consonance, these attributes lead to the next level of pride: intransigence and the exalted medium of full volitional maturity.

His strengths serve much more than what is historically considered as only a heroic defense against evil. Most can discern such traits in war, but often don't recognize their use in peacetime. Of what values are heroes truly capable, if their heights are only to be reached in times of horror? Attaining peace is only the first level. The power of their positive application towers over their use as a protective shield. Their actual purpose—what they were *really* designed for—is the pursuit of discovery, an epic stature and an unlimited joy. The true awakening is to see these same traits at work in productive endeavors, where the threat of destruction *does not* loom near; in the creation of theme parks, the making of movies, the building of spaceships, skyscrapers, multi-billion dollar assembly lines and their spiritual equivalent, captured in the quote "In His image and likeness."

If your goals don't make your stomach drop, you're missing all the fun. This makes America in particular, the hero's playground, where bare necessities come within easy reach of all, as a result of the sheer unleashed vitality of the most able. From here, Self-made Man rides the crest of his virtue, managing and advancing interests already brimming with positive results, radiantly youthful, drenched in unfathomable strength, justly on top of the world. And of course, with the relaxed bearing of a true master, he makes it look easy.

Dissolving Tension with Metaphysical Honesty. The indestructible spirit of the Anticipation-driven operates with little taxation. Seeking to be free of pain as a natural course, he watches stress carefully, to quickly and accurately diffuse its causal factors. His own survival demands a sound environment in which to flourish, so as the body wicks away toxins from the primary system, Self-made Man wicks spiritual toxins away consciously. Such an ability involves much more than being truthful with others; it begins with how we see the world. We cannot lie to the universe and defy its attributes. We can't ignore gravity and float away, or disregard sickness and be held immune. *Honesty* is the willingness to acknowledge that things *are what they are*.

MORAL ARMOR

Metaphysical honesty is sincerity with existence, as well as with oneself and others, which necessitates an unexpected level of intelligence and emotional discipline. It requires recognition of the separation between the products of men and the elements of nature, to understand what is in our power to develop and revise, and what must be accepted as unchangeable. Sun, wind and rain are products of nature. Continents, oceans and mountains will continue to exist, whether or not we do. The human design is also a product of nature, as is our sound cognitive process. As all things natural, that process is left for us not to create or alter, but to discover and obey. The whole of civilization, with its systems of mass-coexistence—its great buildings, industries and governments, its philosophies, sciences and arts—is the product of Man, and is entirely changeable. Both are to be mastered, but as one is discerned, the other is determined. The universe is known by observation, while our heights are borne of creative action.

Self-made Man's first creation is himself. His first obligation is comprehending the role of a human being, beginning with the most efficient use of his cognitive faculty. Developing as intellectually sovereign, he dispensed with the dogmatic interpretations demanding he feel guilty for his very existence. Operating as neither predator nor prey, he can see no need for men to feel guilty *in advance* of taking any action that would deserve it. Accepting only the *knowable* as knowledge, he saw through such guff and stopped fighting that he was human long ago. Only authentic, self-determinable evidence provides satisfactory validation in any field (not to mention the question of practical use), and he cannot conceive of any benefit that would justify overriding the source of his values, his mind. Accepting only what builds a reliable and traceable chain of logic, he is able to drop all unnecessary cultural stress in a heap.

Self-made Man doesn't suffer the mental mix of contradictions where reality is foremost on some issues, but where wishes and nonsense take precedence in others. By understanding what is changeable, he takes mature responsibility for it and drops the rest. He doesn't spend time locked in tension because he is too old, too young, too tall or too short. To chase his tail over what he can never change is a dead-end stress-inducing waste of imagination and instead, he uses his energy to determine what he *can* do with what he *does* have. He accepts what he is *in fact* and accepts what level of reward or penalty his current state of being deserves. He is concerned only with what lies within his power to improve, and works to widen the ranges open to him for his most crucial interests to get as close to his ideals as possible.

The aim of a Self-made Man is to become sovereign in all things, expanding his percentage of self-responsibility while reducing the uncontested outside conditions. Negativity comes only from the inconstancy of an entropic outer atmosphere, where he is subject to a myriad of unsound motivations. But as so small a percentage of his life and enjoyment is at the mercy of others, it matters little. He doesn't blame himself for circumstances outside of his choice. He doesn't agonize over being out of place, being liked or disliked. He no longer hides his virtue or frets over his inability to scale the emotional barriers of those unswayed by rationality. Beyond a fundamental respect for civil rights, the idea of conforming *socially* is foreign to him. So focused on his pursuits, he isn't concerned with what others think, say or do. He has dropped all cultural pretenses of duty to his neighbors, grants them rightful privacy, and is responsible only for himself and his own. Living by the action of his mind, he doesn't need people in any fundamental manner, so his relations with others are free to be wholesome and sincere.

When living patterns are acquired, it is amazing what just drops off naturally. He learns much faster by studying the functional versus studying the dysfunctional. There is no need to dissect every variation of evil known to Man, as evil will always mutate. Likewise, the variations of good are unlimited. Focused on solutions, the problems disappear. By seeing the division between what is possible to change and what isn't, between what is rational and what isn't, all unnecessary conflict within him is eliminated. Constant training to combat personal difficulties assures that he will overcome any obstacle he chooses to clear. The leftover stress he deals with is little more than what is typical of all living beings; hunger, physical pain, exhaustion, and the human exclusive; the excruciating effort of thought and the sometimes painful growth phases that follow. His key difference to all others is his absolute sincerity in accepting what *is*. Knowing that guilt results from the *chosen* practice of life-threatening evil just as pride results from the *choice* of life-furthering good, he is free to seek the only perfection possible to Man: consistently chosen existential consonance. That acted on, he can see himself openly and accept himself completely. As *understanding* is the pathway to life in facing the unknown, he is free to drop all inner tension and look, with all seeing eyes, allowing fear to turn properly into exhilaration. His sound moral standard of good and evil—of life itself—has set him free; and as it respects his need for coherence, he will guard it with his life, forever after.

Moral Perfection is Existential Consonance. So what is perfection? The only realm where perfection could have any significance is the realm of self-esteem, or more to the root, the realm of choice. Perfection in human terms is a reachable, ideal state of moral purity. To guard our view of ourselves is to be consciously aware of the moral root and value of our every motive and action. The perfection proper for a man to seek is to maintain existential consonance: to leave no contradiction unsolved, to always act in accordance with what is understood as moral and right. *Integrity* is moral perfection—one's overall flow with what reality requires.

Integrity is not applicable in individual contexts, which one can exercise in one context and defy in the next; that is the realm of honesty. Integrity exists in the context of life in general; either we have it or we don't. It is a living consonance, which transcends all issues. Having integrity is to have understood and integrated conscious life-serving premises in *all* of one's experiences. It is an integration of our overall actions by one common theme, that being the furtherance and preservation of human life, primarily our own. To have integrity is to consistently choose by *metaphysically honest* means, *existentially consonant* ends. In other words, it is to be aware of the moral implications of every action, and to act in their favor. It is the next step; a prelude to full volitional maturity and intransigence.

Just like happiness, integrity has its own set of necessary elements to be sound. It requires the identification of every facet of our existence which is under conscious control, as well as the continuous search for new ones, and the mastery of a life-serving pattern for each. We automatize these so they become routine, and then we are free to enhance them for the rest of our lives.

Full Volitional Maturity. The playfulness that some adults enjoy is always termed child-like, but it isn't immature at all. It is seen when innocence reaches the other side, *intact*. It is the natural cognitive reward of Self-made Man shining through unimpeded, with its proper results: a sense of joyous lightness, that no problem is too great, that the main point is to enjoy the process of living, that the essential requirements of existence have been met and we have earned the right to vent and revel in the sheer pleasure of being. To rediscover and reintegrate the openness of youth is a blessing to the true definition of maturity.

The Self-made typically wait to have little ones, because what they needed to learn from them, they *have* learned. All the traits we love children for, can be preserved or brought back to our own character. Of the four elements of cognition, only adults practice three and four (creative action and result) in regard to their ultimate purpose, yet we all retain a fundamental respect for one and two—perception and identification. It was our own derivation, which we blissfully share with the newcomers. Cognitive discipline is a key to maturity and an essential element of integrity. It is infinitely more fulfilling to exercise the entire process than to be sheltered halfway. We the adults, have moved on to a confident, creative response to our natural world—our productive effort—and have secured its sound result: life, and the boundless satisfaction we can achieve. We know what's in store for kids and we know it's built on the adventure they are experiencing now. We must display the balance of cognition in order for them to acquire it. The feeling that life *can* flow, that human beings *can* remain pure, that dreams *can* be reached—is the view of life Self-made Man passes on by example—through sound, educated decisions, by adhering to a sensible, proven standard of morality and in the countless endeavors he enjoys across the span of his existence. A mature animal has mastered the living functions of the entity which it is.

We are the dominant species due to our vast capacity of volition; the freedom of moral choice. Our pinnacle of maturity, the point of full blossom and the moral destination for Man, is found here. *Full Volitional Maturity* is defined as exercising the full range of responsibility offered by our capacity of choice. The result is that we automatize intellectual and behavioral patterns that foster a continuous progression. Organized to efficiently pursue Man's natural affinities—to live in accordance with, not in contradiction to, one's nature—reveals the dynamic lifestyle we were meant to achieve: a lifelong seamless integration of pleasant, productive physical motion, driven by a calm, guilt-free, active mind. It is his glory that Self-made Man *chose* to face existence in this way as an ideal state. His reward as master over himself is the zenith of spiritual nourishment.

See how it flows? From the beginning, the elements of cognition—wide open senses, emotionally disciplined identification and integration, creative action and validation—were all necessary to get this far. First, Self-made Man develops conviction in the correct process of cognition, through its proven ability to result in physical and spiritual bounty—*the achievement of self-sustenance and happiness.* Second, with the power to think and define life-furthering values firmly in place, he is able to question all the premises Man ever created, to revalidate what works and throw out what doesn't—the virtue of *metaphysical honesty.* The control of others over him is wiped out; the majority of his stress dissipates, and third, sovereign as a result, he is free to pursue true integrity. He weeds out any self-hampering ideas or behaviors in order to get his life flowing in the trouble-free direction nature intended—the perfection of *existential consonance.* His sophistication soars as his virtues blend into a pattern of lifelong advancement, where all of his human attributes are properly utilized—*full volitional maturity.* Intransigence adds the weight of experience—watching sound principles in action and winning—rooting out personal flaws to assure his practice matches the actual concepts, and tenaciously closing this gap. He reaches full conviction; not just agreeing with concepts, but *knowing*, through personal validation over time. A word on convictions: 1) A *conviction* is what one knows beyond all doubt. 2) What one knows is made possible *only* by a rational process of validation. 3) A rational process of validation requires the cognitive integration of sensory data which is formed into concepts that are provable through rigorous trials generating consistent results (obtained by isolating the elements of a context to measure a specific variable (which science calls control groups)), finally to be brought without contradiction, into the total sum of one's knowledge.

Intransigence. There is no greater power for a man or a group of men, than moral certainty. *Intransigence* is the point of full permeation of one's premises with one's person; the arrival and greeting of the full and final identity of *oneself.* You can feel its warmth pour over, coating, glimmering and protecting you; refining your own immaculate beauty, restoring serene pleasure and calm. Having lived the bounty linked to seamless concepts, our conviction stands behind their undeniable logic, and they become a part of us. This is the completion of the biological armor we've been building, upon the inner structure given us by nature.

In this phase, you'll reach the calm of a man who has made a final judgment about the origin of all validation—his own mind. He sees the world through his own eyes, makes up his own mind, doesn't cower and doesn't pretend. He stands openly and faces his world with a self-chosen view, unswayed by primitive influences, not requiring others to join or to confirm the validation.

This is invulnerable sovereignty. He knows what he feels; he looks right at it. He looks at the players and their motives, including his own, and he chooses the pathways to life, to growth, to the highest inner peace possible. He is independent, in love with all that is within his power, with the world and the greatness he can reach.

Indeed, our self-image determines our tolerance for evil. The clearer you see the truth, the less you'll budge from it. You'll come to the point where no stimulus, positive or negative, can cause you to suspend or drop any element of your process of cognition, or to live in defiance of your sound understandings. When no oppressive power—inside or outside—is allowed to interrupt your flow, your abstract structure takes solid shape, and begins to support you in turn. You start to recover the capacity for action without hesitation. To combine a peaceful inner calm with motive-driven energy is a stunning phenomenon; a feeling of so potent a power for living that you know *this* is the true emotional goal of morality and one of the greatest rewards of life. Having lost the capacity for doubt, standing tall becomes effortless, and no evil can slow your pace without getting itself run over.

At some point we get comfortable with the clashes necessary to achieve this. We know the only straight road to our goals is the one in our minds. Traversing this world requires a moral 4x4, where one comes to expect much experience off-road. You have to fight through the brush, absorb the shocks and *keep* moving. The most powerful men in history were fighters. They felt alive in their peace and equally alive while stirring it up. I fight for what is right, but that doesn't hide that I feel at home in the heat of battle; a competency acquired like any other. *Just* domination is in my blood. You don't have to go the way I have—figuratively speaking, the point of the arrow simply must be the hardest. You can find a calmer, more serene medium along the same path, but if the opposition knows that you are going to fight, they will likely seek an easier victim. It is better to be prepared for all one is likely to encounter. A Moral Warrior is someone who reaches intransigence. Through experience, he has developed such a comfort with the most difficult, most mature truths, that he lives, holding them before his mind in a place of the highest honor. He sees to the wall with so tried and true a conviction that he will die for them, but never surrender them. He is a rock.

A spirit need not be delicate; it can ultimately be invulnerable, but there is no hardening of what, by nature, must remain fluid. No level of intimacy is lost, nor ever need be; quite the contrary. With the worship of truth, all levels are enhanced. Concepts normally associated to fantasy, do have mortal equivalents. The concept of *invulnerability* applies to intransigence. The concept of *invincibility* applies to spirit and the concept of *immortality* applies to integrity. It is the state of being where we've gained the tools one would wish to gain, if we were to contemplate living forever.

Nothing will ever again hamper your independent judgment, or skew your ability to see clearly what is right and wrong. Your moral strength will convey to others that challenging precedent is okay, and the impetus for the reversal of corruption will have begun. Those around you will adapt to the proper ranges of action, and this virtue will begin spreading in ever widening circles. Regaining control over your own destiny and taking the moral power back is the ultimate joy of intransigence.

The Fountain of Youth. A stunning effect of *Moral Armor* and any other sound philosophical practice is the beautiful physiological transformations that occur over time. The human physical image is a reflection of our premises. People who are lost, often *look* lost; just as those who are confident, look confident. When I was eighteen, I saw no one older worth emulating, so I stayed eighteen. That joyous, youthful vibrancy, the immensely desirable resonating confidence, that unharnessed, unrestrained energy, the pure power of unquestioned action— these are traits not to be given up. I have the same *all or nothing* attitude I had then, and preserving that spirit is my life's pursuit; but one cannot stop the clock.

I don't mind getting older; because for each element nature takes, I add one. Intelligent awareness allows us to counter its effects, making the process of aging a graceful one, where we need not regret its march. Our living sum increases; we rise in stature, regardless of what is lost; making time our friend.

At any size, age or capacity, we must stand upright and live like human beings. Stripped of all inessentials, an entity should be only what it needs to be. Elegance is found in purpose, in a well-maintained physique and way of standing, whether it is a man, a building or a system of philosophy. Does it slouch, or is it clear-cut and proud? We all have unique physiology and it is our responsibility to achieve and maintain its most beautiful, ideal form. The fountain of youth does exist, and can be found in the philosophical statement, *"Form follows premise."*

The primary motor cortex of the brain, which handles the willed action of our muscles, reserves fifty percent of its mass *for the face alone*. Deep conceptual information can be read within the delicacy of our expressions. In a Self-made Man, one sees supreme joy, a confidence so complete it seems relaxed, and oddly enough, innocence—with no expectation of hurting or of being hurt—an openness that seems as if no danger exists. There is wisdom, energy, and an honest bearing so mature that it brings proper meaning to the concept of elegance. The repetition of graceful emotions felt by the Self-made, builds specific muscles of the face normally associated with beauty. Facial muscles used for smiling typically are considered high cheekbones. His confidence lends its grace to relaxed eyes, as to his arrogantly scornful smile; his certainty translates into a relaxed forehead; his playfulness results in animation, his exhilaration shows in the fire of his eyes. Appearing and vanishing instantaneously to the happenings of life, these traits give his face a real workout.

Much can be learned from the uninhibited Self-made; they can bring out our best, when we fully realize that we are just as free as they are, to do what we want. They awaken into a fresh supply of energy that washes over them every day, as a constant renewal. They spend it efficiently—controlling and heightening its production through nutrition, pleasure and rest—so that enough is available for rejuvenation. They are amazing—the way they walk, they way they look at you, that playful sense of arrogant pride, their energy—they strut! And that is how one should feel about living at any age. I love it.

Flooring It Morally. The intensities of all degrees of happiness (and any other emotion for that matter) are determined by their causal factors; therefore, *happiness is contextual.* For example, in the future, if someone asks if you are happy, you'll be able to say something like "In personal growth, yes. In my career, yes. In sports, yes. In relationships, not quite. In financial stability and prosperity, almost there."

Often, an element in our tree of knowledge may be acquired in one context, but is unknown to be an element in another. If you work out your arms you can lift more, but what else? You can throw a ball farther, swing a bat harder, and ride a bicycle more confidently. Your range of action has improved in every way those muscles are used. As the mind is no different, this leads to a fascinating benefit. This pattern provides the greatest opportunity in self-esteem, as we can never know in how many ways our capacity has expanded, with every step forward. Virtuous growth spreads exponentially, coating all areas of potential application, to be joyously discovered in time. As happiness is contextual, all other endeavors where an advance is applicable, holds a pleasant future surprise.

At this level, experience has proven repeatedly, the validity of our cognitive process. Life for us has become quite streamlined, fascinating and casual. At some point in his work, Self-made Man exceeds in virtue what no one can match, not an associate, nor a mate. He knows what to rationally expect from others. So, though a point of loneliness, he accepts it. This is his world, and the achievement needs to be for him, but there is an often un-admitted benefit: he no longer needs to check his speed. He drops consideration for their inability to follow, and surges ahead full speed, pushing himself for his own pleasure, without regard to limits. He rises above all with maximum grace and style, exalting his central theme which the outer world cannot touch: His exhilaration for living, for seeing justice prevail, for the magic colors of a sunrise, for strength, health and beauty, for the lovely smile of a stranger, for her scent as she passes by, for his dream marriage, for the unlimited opportunities to succeed, for the freedom to try, for his tear-filled love of being alive. And then he finds her.

Atlantis. Come into my world where so many universal problems are solved, and where youthfulness is a way of life. Welcome to a place of rest, of safety, of calm, where you are free to exchange the pain for elation and the anguish for fulfillment. Here, you are free to relax your face, your jaw and your eyes; to relax your shoulders and breathe deeply; to look at the world around you, and enjoy this wonderful setting for Man. Here, it is okay to feel exactly what you feel; to let it out if you need to cry, to explode with laughter when you feel like it, breathing deeply to savor this incredible sense of freedom. Here, you can do anything, be anything, and there is no need to be afraid. There are no masks, no barriers, and you are free to practice and to *not* get it right the first time. No one here expects you to be all things, but they do expect you to be working towards the goals and traits you desire. You are free to look at your own motives to see what drives you in all areas of life—to experiment, refine and idealize. You can make your life the sculptured work of art it deserves to be. Here you can develop true self-worth, to attain that radiant state of wholesome, valid happiness, which now will forever be yours to move towards—directly, openly, guiltlessly and with great passion.

Come to bask in the joyous, boundless power you felt as a child on a mission of discovery, in the crisp autumn air, running across a field and down to a stream, devising a means to cross it, not to be stopped. A being, radiantly capable in its own eyes, without doubt, without pain, or fear, or guilt. The glory began with *one,* just between ourselves and existence, and there is no reason for that feeling ever to die. Imagine the penetrating warmth of the sun on your back, the wind in your hair, the smell of a limitless living world all around, returning to a loving home to be appreciated for your sparkling eyes and innocent smile; held tight for all that you are and all that you aspire to be. And in time to see this radiance projected into adulthood, coming of age to the climax of your own epic sovereignty. You'll see it in the admiring eyes of the mate you've chosen to share your journey, who has the response to your person you've longed for and deserve. You'll walk among people who value your strength, courage and effort—your tribute to life. You'll enjoy a culture that cherishes your magnificent adherence to truth, to honor and to justice. You'll live in a country that respects what you've bled for; it wasn't in vain; we thank you. You'll see a society that rewards pioneering endeavors, touched by the influence of your dedication, while the worst of mankind looked away. Here before us, you can hold your head level and enjoy the sanction the whole world owes you. We see where you are going and we believe in you.

Imagine how completely you can love and trust, when this is the nature of existence. With the real possibility of Atlantis before you, suddenly your whole outlook is altered; you never want to grow old; you never want to die; you never want anything to change. Every day that passes becomes so sacred, that you treasure every minute; anticipating every dawn, thrilled with every sensual evening, with or without anyone else. You've matured as one center of this enchantment, a Living Generator. It becomes heartbreaking to see time slip, never to be regained. But for once, you didn't waste it. You lived. You lived. And the strangest truth comes to you, now that you love life as it should be loved. You can let it go without a struggle. When it comes to be your time, you are at peace; because you know what it truly means to be alive; and you are, at last. There will be no more wasted time. And no matter what curves life throws, from now on, you know how to preserve this romantic feeling, because it is not just between you and another, but has developed between you and this Earth, your home.

Chapter Five

Sound Relationships

"Not everyone believes what you believe." "My beliefs do not require them to."
—The Matrix Reloaded

A rational man socially interacts for the purposes of pleasure and productivity, the sustenance of his body and the fulfillment of his spirit. He does not use others as a buffer between himself and reality. His style of dealing begins with respect for the natural requirements of the species Man, with the same expectation in return: freedom from coercion in any form. His means of trade and communication rely solely on individual consent and persuasion, necessitating no subservience. Men form civilizations to make life easier by offering their specialization in trade for the specialization of others, which creates the internal and external production hierarchy of superior, subordinate and peer, customer, supplier and competitor. The prohibitive social classes of men dissolve, and the worth of a man is defined by his productive capacity: his ability, effort and civility. This encompasses all the forms a human being can take, as its inverse describes our enemies as well. Production's true opponent is not competition, but dictation (irrational regulation).

Moral men produce the relationships of master/apprentice, producer/ patron, associate, friend and lover—all of which are guardians. The Self-made seek relationships for the creation and production necessary to sustain human beings, for moral confirmation of their style of living and for its celebration. The social reward of living is a precious compensation for his own virtue and provides cues for directional improvements in the pursuit of his own life.

Our Fundamental Relation. *Individual* happiness is having all of our essential cognitive elements working together seamlessly for the fulfillment of our lives. *Social* happiness is having these elements understood, appreciated and practiced by those one inhabits the planet with to its noble end: our peaceful yet energetic rush of adrenaline for all that is possible everyday, to everyone. It is a man's essential dream—a projection of his dying wish—to spend the most time on the most precious subjects and with the most important people, a concept of utopia, as is actually possible.

All social virtues stem from individual virtues, as all groups are made up of individual men. His implicit sense of self-responsibility carries through; sound thought and action becomes responsible interaction. His productive self-discipline extends to satisfy social transactions by keeping his obligations to others. Respectful of the effort to bring his values into the world, he is cognizant of the efforts of others and respects their property and possessions. He never attempts to circumvent their cognitive action even in praise, but appeals to their reasoning mind.

The medium of exchange in material goods is money—our energy's equivalent. In spirit, it is *how that energy is spent*—love and hate. The biological parallel to objective standards aims love and appreciation towards life and the actions which preserve it, while hate and contempt is reserved for actions and premises which bring about its destruction. Self-made Man doesn't practice unconditional love; his condition is *life,* and all of the intellectual discipline necessary to see its implications: eyes that see beautiful actions, ears that hear beautiful premises and a mind that can tell the difference. Relationships form on the nature of *trust*, also a self-derived concept. To trust oneself is to know one uses the cognitive process properly for the fulfillment of life. Socially, it is to know others use the cognitive process for the same reason and make no intentional errors or evasions at any step. Honesty with oneself, is the prerequisite to honesty with others, as is love. It is through honesty that we communicate, and only through honesty that true connections to others can be established. All traits left undefined must be assumed as consonant with what has been shown. This bridge of faith is maintained until given a rational foundation, or until it is violated.

Our love shares the integrity of our work. Every time we switch on a light, some part of our minds should be saying "Thank you." Every day should be a form of Thanksgiving—our day to honor the creations of Man—bridges and ships, buildings and cars—to know why they stand, to trace the steps of their structure, and to contemplate all they bring into our lives. Self-made Man honors the creative actions of others, by practicing his own.

Self-made Man wants to see everyone reach their own form of greatness. Complete on his own, he needs nothing from them, and with the opportunity of freedom, hopes they will seek it. He wants to enjoy witnessing that "Anything is possible to me" look of youth in passers by, and seeks to establish it as the proper medium between human beings—strangers and friends alike. He wants to see them free, confident and active—unafraid to see and feel deeply, in *true* brotherhood and peace. Our goodwill starts when we look at the sky; it's a natural response to our environment.

The Line Never to be Crossed. When one encounters any consciousness, a special pattern of cognition is called into play—that of determining motive. Whether it is a dog or a person, their disposition tells of danger or safety, just as ours indicates to them. The pattern of interaction is a pattern of cognition for each involved, as entities of consciousness control all interactions. The specific steps of interaction are 1) Perception of entity, 2) Identification of motive 3) Interaction with entity, and 4) Result. All social action exists *beyond* the fundamental process of cognition, which is operating prior to the encounter as an individual faculty of life. One process presupposes the other; the two cannot be mixed. If we encounter a dog, do we involve the dog's thoughts with our own? Of course not, so we don't do it with people either. Social interaction is a secondary pattern, never to be brought into the first.

Self-made Man is historically notorious for refusing to mix his cognitive process with the process of others. He doesn't set out to be humble. He could stay home for that. He doesn't meld or compromise or sacrifice. In conference, he sifts through ideas, running suggestions through his own mind to verify logic before acceptance, then moves to the next juncture. His own rational discipline chooses the best course. He has kept the line clear, and by so doing, has alienated all those who cannot complete the first chain alone.

Communication between two bodies and all acquired knowledge must pass through his senses. His first relationship is with existence; and its truth must be his first loyalty. The guiltless man is true to himself, and runs at his own pace. He does not slow down for anyone. Those worthy can keep up, which is the filter to his ultimate social satisfaction. Anything less will cause pain, as energy expended at a lesser efficiency resonates at a lower intensity than his known ability. He moves towards his truth without consideration for anything it may do to his life and relationships; and with reflection, he sees it only makes them better. It brings about better situations and better people. Of course the old situations and relationships have rotted, but being saturated with the nutrition of fresh life every day, he can let them go with barely a backward glance.

It is due to the Spirit Murderers, that he built a level within him that is beyond all human reach. Not a closed door, but a crystal vault, open to view, but not to harm. What's in the vault? A collection of gems: 1) His sovereign essence, his purest perception and his life-giving power. 2) No fear and no concern for the views of others, and no hesitation in seeing what he knows to be true. 3) No room for the pain of regretting illusions that don't pan out; just a pure perception where all implications are clear and are accepted. 4) His sovereign love for existence, no matter what others make of it or try to do to him. 5) What he knows to be possible, what exists within him, and what he wishes could find its freedom in every man on Earth. 6) The peace of calm reflection necessary to tailor his fulfillment to his ever integrating, ever expanding sum.

Such a pinnacle of Man enters a room giving off an intellectual/ emotional vibrancy that affects all those around him. In awe, it can be felt, studied and enjoyed, but to be acquired, the energy source must come from within, in the same manner he acquired it. He knows that there are others who have been around the block, who know of the negatives out there and remain untouched by them. He knows there are others who have not made terms with evil and have not been tarnished by its existence. They know what greatness is possible and choose to practice *that,* while discarding the rest. They don't try to compromise, allowing it to wipe out their passion for living. They simply reject it as he does, and live their lives focused on their own enjoyment. This is where he finds intimacy. Self-made Man knows his colleagues across the spectrum will treat him with objective sincerity. With moral clarity between them and full awareness of their conformance, they have no qualms about judging or being judged. He maintains relationships with those who have a thirst for life, which means a thirst for discovery, a thirst for honesty, accuracy and for what works, because they intend to use it—not a thirst for blood. This is his realm—those who don't need assistance, and their honest, voluntary followers, all seeking a greater sum in themselves. They share their endeavors, their mutual interests, their personal triumph and the limitless future they see ahead. Their parallel is passion, allowing others to feel the same exhilaration as their own.

There are only so many people he can be close to in a physical sense, a small number really. Mother Teresa may advise to give our best to strangers, but this is totally incompatible with the moral standard of the Self-made. His scale of intimacy is deepest first, to whom he grants the most time. This begins *individually* with his purpose in life, and is followed by his most intimate social relationship, his spouse. The more people he wants to affect, the more *abstract* his medium must become. Some are so passionately dedicated to their pursuits, that they acquire fame, moving a great number with their work. As the number of people in one's sphere of influence moves to infinity, time decreases the potential for personal intimacy to zero. We then touch lives through abstract mediums, such as literature. As our cherished selectivity of individuals moves to one, our intimacy moves to infinity.

Compatibility Index. With our great power to deduce methods for success in every other aspect of life, how often is our solution for finding a mate better than sitting on a barstool and expecting our dreams to walk right up to us? Often an ideal mate is defined by physical appearance alone, along with an inessential, arbitrary grouping of psychological and experiential characteristics, such as family oriented, has specific musical tastes, or likes to dine out. Internet dating sites have made the search for a mate more intellectual, more sensible and more likely to result in fulfillment; but such abstract adventure could be aided significantly with a standard by which to weigh that probability. I for one have been dissatisfied with my choices even when my desires were met. Within my own philosophical experience, I still couldn't predict or fathom what killed one relationship after another. Dating younger girls, I often felt like a bowling ball fraternizing with a pea. It was always, "wasn't smart enough", "wasn't ambitious enough," or "wasn't mature and forthright", but the data was too wishy-washy to serve as filter for when the next one came along. Sensing a parallel existed, I needed to understand better who was suitable for me; not only for the woman in my life, but to understand my friends, family and associates as well; for all human relationships.

By identifying the moral process of cognition, an interesting facet took shape and I got what I was looking for: a standard for measuring human compatibility. This scale *reflects* the steps of the cognitive process, and one's adherence. Beyond the four key steps of cognition (1, 2, 3, 4), lies a like pattern (5, 6, 7, 8), in pure abstraction. People are grouped as 1-2's, 3-4's and 6-8's; the nature of the scale being cognitive efficiency—one's clarity in real-time and the *willingness* for clarity—one's integrity. Once the basic side of Fear-driven versus Anticipation-driven is defined for an individual, one then runs up the scale to assess their cognitive operating efficiency. The *rate* of cognition is the moral-biological equivalent of calculus in mathematics.

At the lower end of the scale, there is a simple cause and effect relationship with existence. The Self-made at this level are typically children, as we all begin in this world, and with sound health and full range of motion, he makes steady forays into the next levels. For him to remain at the 1-2 level into adulthood is rare. Such a man would be a day laborer, practicing a life pattern not encouraging or requiring abstract thought; so he won't often be found reading material that projects beyond the day to day range of a newspaper. This range permits subsistence, but leaves little opportunity for growth. The limit of his ambition and pride, are the fundamental tenets of human life: independence and good will. He exists at the rudiments of morality, in a fully hands on relationship with material existence. He is steady, trustworthy and good at what he does. With life implicitly being his highest pursuit, his spoken allegiance often revolves around the subject of competence. For him to respect the levels beyond him, others have to be as good at their job as he is at his. He keeps to himself and lives an honorable life, meeting his own needs and never being a burden on others.

The Self-made 3-4 runs the chain a decent portion of the time, and at his best, sees all four steps. The majority of mankind exists at this level, involved in the furtherance of some specific enterprise, which in essence is the maintenance of their own lives. Historically, they've operated on half-explicit, half-implicit philosophical essentials, striving for clarity all the while. He is much more open and social, interested in the world's political direction and enamored with our noblest. 3-4's produce the abundance of a civilization's wealth, and therefore are the primary target for predation. Within the 3-4 level lies the American middle-class, though it is not a financial division. Actors, doctors, politicians, executives—all those furthering the products and processes of the minds of others, exist here. Achievement-based fame is well within the reach of the 3-4.

A 6-8 runs the full chain without error and can advance it. He originates industries and the companies within them; inventing and creating without difficulty. His actions can change the course of mankind. He goes as far as human knowledge allows, often acting as the determiner of that limit. He advances science, industry and civilization, making contributions that result in cultural immortality; surpassing fame by making history. A 6-8 will operate at that level in his primary endeavors, and typically at a 3-4 level in all others. We all step down a number of levels when we look to other fields, but when we focus on truly knowing another individual, we bring our 6-8 capacity with us. His most excruciating effort is his most intimate pursuit, and with good fortune, his most intimate relationship reflects that intensity. Within him is the deepest tribute to Man; the deepest emotional capacity and the most intimate, heartfelt commitments. There is the greatest sense of justice and respect for civility, the purest integrity, the longest cognitive range and the most complex individual purpose. At this level, he has the opportunity to witness his own magnificence, and the magnificence of Man. His relationships are rich in understanding, rich in drama and bathed in romantic fulfillment.

Self-made Man is not limited in his relations by rich or poor, white or black, male or female. He sees bright eyes, dreams and the willing ability to reach them. The arbitrary classes of Man have dissolved in his mind, along with the guilt of adhering or not adhering to them. *The essential classifications of Man are fully cognitive.* This compatibility index is not an actual caste system, as no matter how high we go, we still begin with *perception,* while we exercise and respect the full range. Metaphysically, the 3-4 range is where we all *live.* Indeed, all 6-8 intentions return to find their realization at the 3-4 level, where there is a direct link to material reality. The more familiar you are with the steps of cognition, the easier it is to see where other people deviate, stop, or are having difficulty. Do they perceive and identify their perceptions, but become confused in its execution (1-2)? Do they see the true purpose of it all and get the result they want (3-4)? The point of tedious complication is their level.

Progress for all human beings is to move up in this chain. Improving intellectual efficacy is key to becoming a good partner as well. As a Self-made Man advances in the process of cognition, addressing and conquering his fears, he becomes compatible with new levels. With a lifelong pattern of development, there is no guarantee that his ultimate direction won't eventually deem him incompatible with the mate he's chosen; especially if he made the choice *before* his choice of career, but a more complex mind must satisfy a more complex need to be fulfilled. As he sees farther, he must strive to reach that vision. Deep dwellers cannot live, being dragged back to the surface every five minutes. Shallow dwellers cannot handle the pressure down below. Mixing the two becomes a struggle for life, to the benefit of no one. A 1-2 won't be compatible with a 3-4, just as a 3-4 won't be compatible with a 6-8. Each range thinks at a different speed, converses at that speed, and sees implications at that speed. Separations are painful, but spread out before him is the wild expansion of intimate possibilities to feel more than he has ever felt. The key to compatibility above and beyond initial attraction is understanding and acting at similar levels of clarity, at a similar rate. We can sense fundamental disparity. It is a spiritual necessity to find someone near your own level who is moving in the same direction in life, not more than two clicks apart.

Reading Emotions. Often, the Self-made overlook emotional vibrations—the whole truth—being so focused on deeper elements. The Fear-driven commit their entire intellectual range to the shallowest resultant factors, so often they are more adept in this realm; but we should learn to pay attention to emotional content also. Valuable rewards exist within such awareness when used for positive reasons, as well as the invaluable protection it offers. As half the primary motor cortex of the brain is reserved for delicate facial expressions, immense knowledge about us is vented through our emotions. *If this were not meant to be read and heeded, it would not be so significant a part of our biological makeup.* Its social purpose is *communication.* Our senses are so delicate, that we can read the intentions and mood of another, from across a room. We can tell if they are open to conversation, relaxed or nervous. You can hear epistemology in a person's voice—just as you can hear the hollowness of evil in a Spirit Murderer's. It is important to know what kind of emotions your *sound* effort is producing in those around you. If it is negative, you are dealing with Spirit Murderers—a waste of your time or worse. You are putting yourself in danger, spiritually as well as physically. If it is positive, you are likely on safe ground in both realms. How well you are received can let you know if you've found the bridge between yourself and any opposition between the two sides—a *one way* bridge, disallowing their premises to infect ours. Emotions are an excellent indicator to define whether you have been understood, while eyes serve as a window to the motives of others. The eyes are the barometer of conscience. Far above conflict, emotions are evidence of the most profound and devoted love between those of like premises, a reward we cannot afford to ignore.

What you are actually reading, are *premises.* You know when someone is performing the act of thinking; you can distinguish it. You know when he is in contemplation; trying to remember, trying to forget, or when a new idea pops into his head. Still, expression is cataloged as an emotional characteristic, as emotions are often the strongest expressions. It is not just emotions you are reading, but the full psycho-epistemological function or dysfunction of the entity; another's very moral foundation. There is an expression for every action of mind and every combination, as well as their emotional results. Most amazing are the expressions of guiltless purity, intelligence and active exhilaration reached by the Self-made, responding to life as if he just stepped off a roller coaster. Steady your glance and look at those before you; there is nothing—for the Self-made anyway—to fear.

Friends and Family

Friends come before extended family, as they are one's *chosen* associates. To have any meaning, the concept of "family" must exclude any preference due to incidental relation. To acquaint you with your true family, you have to see the essential division of Man: Self-made Man versus Spirit Murderer; *these* are the true families, even thicker than blood. Blood relation is the first caste system of the Spirit Murderer—the demand of respect and equal standing for something other than respectable action, precariously guarded by those who do not intend to trade on the level. Family must pass the same test as friends—that compatibility is based on values, not alms, and that the medium is good will, not obligation. Relatives or not, they are just human beings, and must be judged by the same impartial standard: the standard of life. What Self-made Man feels for family is the step *before* love—the faith-based promise to grant love to the traits within their grasp, which they appear willing and en route to achieve. Every man accepts his life as his standard of value—as his basic referent—by choice, and this choice determines his rationality. Self-made Man is supported in his sound, civil, life-furthering endeavors by his loved ones—family and friends—or he abandons them. Human beings associate for a constructive and joyful result, period. He doesn't associate with those he wouldn't, were they not blood relatives. There is no excuse for tolerating abuse, injustice or the burden of those who won't pull their own weight.

His own survival demands a sound environment in which to flourish. If he expects a sound business and political environment in society where the interaction is complex, then the corruption is not going to begin within his own family, where the interaction is simple. The pattern of family precedes and *predicts* the pattern of the others. He doesn't preserve relationships with those who subject him to any form of insincere or unjust action, or those who expect him to practice it. He demands the natural freedom that all humans require in order to function, just as he grants and fosters it in others. He demands the civility and fostering of virtue, or removes himself from their path of destruction at once. It's very simple; if they want to practice destruction, if they want to con and pretend, he lets them practice it...alone.

An indestructible spirit must operate free of unnecessary taxation; that being any deviation from the rational process of cognition. A Self-made Man gladly accepts the natural challenges of life along his sound, constructive path, but with contempt, he dumps immediately any request for the senseless—the blatantly false attempts to mask the vices of cowardice. Carefully controlling his energy to fulfill his quest is difficult enough; to carry the burden of his energy's destruction is ludicrous. He won't waste his time even to acknowledge death premises as an opinion to be considered equally valid to his premises which lead to life; *he will not relocate the battleground to be within him.* Negativity must come only from the inconstancy of an entropic outer atmosphere, and that is where he leaves it. Self-made Man practices that which is based on values, not pity, sacrifice or any self-destructive tenets. He cares about *life* and remains firm, cognizant and life-furthering at all times.

Contextual Limitations. A Self-made man can look at his family, and see in what issues they can be trusted and in which ones they can't. He knows their basic moral side, and he knows their intellectual level. His associations with them are contextual, and he maintains civil relations by limiting their effect on his life to those categories. This is done by identifying, accepting and appreciating an individual's *contextual* efficacy—isolating properly—without stretching virtues to cover vices on other subjects. The only trustworthy people overall, are those committed to wiping out their own evasiveness in every context in which they live and act. If one makes a study of love, one will be good at loving. If one makes a study of the natural world, one will be good at living. If one remains aware of cause and effect, one will be honest. These are all epistemological factors.

Self-made Man rids himself of destructive people and replaces them with the living, with little guilt expended. It is wonderful, the pressure that disappears when we surround ourselves with those whom are bright, passionate and industrious. Without the slovenly, our bitterness wanes. Left with students, teachers and peers, we feel alive, and all of our living energy is put to productive use.

The Approval of Those Who Count. Self-made Man has lost the need to confide in anyone, or to justify his actions to others. He no longer considers it; yet it isn't irrational to desire the approval of others. He has no desire to be an outcast, and little desire to fit in, but he knows that when he finds a Self-made individual or a room-full; he's right at home. He loves true camaraderie. To enjoy approval is confirmation that one is living among human beings, born able to achieve and appreciate greatness.

We spend the social part of our lives desiring to see traits we can look up to, and to deserve being accompanied by greatness is to reflect it. Unfortunately when misguided, we overlook loosely veiled sneers and grant a blind faith that others can identify values and view them honorably. Rational, productive men do not need any granting of faith. Within his true family, he no longer needs to set a false context in his mind, blanking out what people really are, in order to convey his pride to them. Respect for life and ability is already set; it is accepted, cherished and knelt to, by the Self-made.

There is a vibration that defines our aura, and it is this vibration in others that you pick up on when you interact with them. If your values and sense of life—your emotional response to your dreams and possibilities—is in sync, you will resonate with that person. Self-made Man chooses to develop this resonation alone, in his first relationship with existence itself. By this ability, he is capable of resonating with the greatest number of others, and to unveil his own soul mates much more efficiently.

Imagine standing at a party with a few of your heroes; the pillars of mankind, pausing for once, to enjoy the idleness which is so unlikely for all of you. Imagine yourself to be one of them, just feeling the radiant power of their overwhelming certainty, and their fully functional, jaded capacities for action. It is the parallel realm: the best in Hollywood, the best in business, the best in science and art, gathered by grace of their virtue. Each can appreciate and revere the other's ability, just the way each needs to be revered. As others kneel before what you hold as sacred—your passions—you display the same reverence for theirs. It is a personal interest in the subject of passion itself, its actualization, its practice and its importance to our own spiritual preservation. The parallel between you is the feeling that life is worth living, experienced through different mediums of expression, but with and through the same *physical* mediums—our moral cognitive approach, and through the same background—existence itself.

Absent this deliverance and along the road to its fulfillment, he settles for projections; the historic best are his ancestral friends through time. His physical lineage may determine significant attributes, but his *spiritual* lineage is key to the value of his being. We are never alone.

Human Development

A life of success, wealth and happiness is very complicated, and within the capacity to handle that complexity, lies the paternal pride of the able. It is not for everyone, yet it is the only road to true, sound, unquestionable satisfaction on this earth. The ability to succeed in the face of life's adversities and foster the next generations to do the same, are among the highest gifts one human being can offer another.

The Right Timing. Long before he attempts to raise another, Self-made Man knows he must master the entity he is. If he intends to be of any use to others, he must see to it that his standards reflect life's requirements to a "T." He spends his life answering questions, confident that he can deal with whatever he will encounter, and such life mastery is what he intends to hand down.

His wish to have children in ancient times, was after the war was won. When unsettling circumstances were evident, they did not intend to bring children into chaos. Its modern responsible equivalent is to have children after stability is achieved. His passionate career has taken off and no longer requires eighteen-hour days, and his romantic relationship is exactly what he wants. Kids fit into a grand scheme, along a couple's value hierarchy and life timeline. The endeavor is financially viable without interrupting his spiritual and material necessities, or those of his spouse. With respect for others, he plans it never to be a burden on those outside his primary relationship—so that seeing grandchildren, nieces and nephews will be a pleasure, not a duty.

He has mastered himself and his relationships and can convey healthy versions of both properly. His method for development reflects his own, instilling independence at the highest, proudest level possible—the cleanest rationality; the most straight-forward moral action, teaching them to run the cognitive process without fear and to interact socially without cognitive interruption. He teaches them to use their tools to meet their basic needs, to *master* these tools, so they can handle anything life throws at them along their tailored course. Learning to provide the proper frames for their greatest possibilities *takes time*, and he waits until the time is right.

Handing Down the Map to Utopia. The young can't see to the depth we can. They start by mastering step one, their perceptive tools, and move on to identification, grasping the rudimentary cause and effect relationship of existence. They have very modest epistemological chains, while ours are long and brimming with experience. We emit a confidence that often, we aren't aware of having, though they are. They look up to us, even when we have no conscious reason to expect them to. They figure there is a reason for our every action and trait, and they emulate them as a platform. The nature of our use of perceptive tools, our *pace* of thought, our depth of reasoning, our interactions with others, are all an example for what is appropriate in life. The majority of what they learn from us is wordless. It is the very pattern of comprehension we pass on to them—our brave, open, controlled response to every step, which in the inertia of its challenges, passes on our psychology as well.

POSITIVE, NEGATIVE, AND RATIONAL REINFORCEMENT

In the first years before a child understands the implications of danger that are found in the word "No," pleasure and pain are the only means of communication. There is no reasoning with a two-year old. Once bad behavior can be stemmed with cognitive penalties such as no dessert, belting them is no longer appropriate. Unless they initiate rude, violent behavior, no physical reprimand is sensible. The second *social* lesson we have the responsibility to convey to our children, is not to try solving problems by force. The first social lesson of course, is never to drop their mind.

You can't sell a kid on life-furthering issues with threats of death as the alternative, no more than you can sell him caution with the joy of safety. All living things grow towards values and are repelled by evils, whose clear division is seen only with the correct standard of value. Look both ways before crossing the street because you could get hit—not because of the life you would then miss. The first loss or the first gain is the primary focal point, where the balance of the argument are just the details. Harmful action gets a penalty, positive action gets a reward. Spanking and being grounded is the child's parallel to a few weeks in jail for an adult, to be used as sparingly as he is bad. He is to learn that any injustice on his part will be met with swift recompense—given that the standard of justice is rational. Life *is* fair when sound action gets rewarded, while no action or failed action does not.

We hear the promise of their futures in the line, "I can do it myself." True pride is the joy of witnessing one's own ability to satisfy a requirement of life. We can learn from others, sometimes intense, fabulous things, but as we were perceptive enough to pick up what was important, the glory is ours as well. The Self-made say "When the student is ready, the teacher will appear," and the teacher can be a person, a documentary, a book, or just the act of observing the natural flow of life. Schooling can come from anywhere, but it must be integrated within an individual's own mind, an action outside a parent's power.

Under balanced circumstances, a child gone right or wrong is not the parent's full responsibility; the road to choose is theirs.

As the child's capacity becomes abstract, we have to sell them on ideas. Enticement is management of an entity by what it loves. It is welcoming what the teacher intends, submitting to a trusted power—a safe acceptance of domination by an apt, charismatic guide. Coercion is management of an entity by what it fears; shields go up, and the entity stays on the defensive, acting only at times of maximum safety, volunteering nothing, offering the least risk possible. Coercion intends not to engage the rational faculty of another for consent, and therefore can make only temporary gains. Outside of emergencies, it is not a tool of the Self-made. Rational enticement is his ultimate form of civil influence, and is the foundation of most American advertising in concept. Explaining and giving reasons shows respect for the process of cognition. It tells them that they are people too, worthy of consideration, and provides the depth necessary to make responsible decisions. The sooner we begin treating them like adults, the sooner they will act like them. Still, we can only do so much; the one in true control is the life being trained. Kids have to buy in at every step.

Our contribution is to bring them our most valuable traits, and to see them fully armed for the world to come. There is natural resistance to life, which we struggle against to stay even and surpass, to gain the results we seek—that of life and fulfillment. *Perseverance* describes the steady actions we take toward the goals of our lives. We must prepare them to endure whatever is necessary to bring about the fulfillment they desire. We synthesize the elements of each attribute for training: our capacity to judge endeavors and overcome great odds, to outlast powerful storms and great spans of time to reach our deepest goals, to exercise the height of independent awareness, to defend sound living principles, to move physically and intellectually with healthy, fluid grace, to stand on the shoulders of our achievements and shoot even higher.

Fostering Pure Cognitive Freedom. Self-made Man teaches those up and coming to be independent. Among his desires is to see them fulfill their own highest possibilities, running the chain as they should, with no interest in owning or controlling them. He teaches them to think on their own, to validate what they've learned from other men—validate everything—through their own experience and reflection. Students must make all knowledge they intend to exercise, their own.

He advances another mind by simply answering the questions it asks of itself, or by showing the cognitive means of obtaining the answer. The latter helps to clear the way when pathways are hampered, showing the young how to use their tools to answer life's questions independently. He identifies the implications that surround a complex query, displaying the breadth that is possible to attain over time, and the knowledge is absorbed when they are ready for it. This is easy to determine, as *they* initiate at certain depths. They ask the questions.

The honest want their children to remain free from the parasites of any generation, who will try to hang from them. If children are shielded from anything, it should be religion, and any other sacrificial dogma inverting or perverting proper cognition; a moral crime. No knowledge exists outside the capacity of Man, and the farther those at the real limit go, the closer it is for everyone else.

Self made Man doesn't ask permission to become and to learn. He honors no caste system and no conqueror. He knows the hierarchy of Man adjusts with his every step forward, a viewpoint he passes on. He helps hone their tools, but doesn't choose their endeavors—leaving the greatest range of possibilities for their moral use open to them. He never dictates; they have room to move and confirm elements for themselves. They are free to run the chain, free to make mistakes and free to take their lives in any direction they wish.

Throwing Open the Gates to Their Future. Careers are so embedded in men, that as most knowledge is passed down within the framework of their field, that field is often chosen by his children. But essential, *axiomatic* knowledge is used in any field, and this is what must be passed down. Imagine if a lawyer chose his profession from deep personal interest, then saw his son choose law because he knew of nothing else. To his son, it's just a job. The father may encounter a junior counselor with the same passion he feels—the desire to make a difference—and feel a kinship he desires to feel with his own son. He *could* feel that kinship, if he steered his son towards the discovery of his *own* passions, instead of following in his footsteps. Passion—living fulfillment—should be the parallel in their lives to share, where career is only a medium.

Self-made Man knows what his children will go through; he's lived it himself. He knows of peer pressure, ridicule, bullies, cliques and from kindergarten, how early we can become endeared to others. As a parent, he doesn't deny that sex is a part of life, especially in teenage years. He doesn't ignore or try to limit their sexual interest, from playmates to crushes to dating. He never makes attraction out to be evil, sinful or wrong. By conveying sound values, he desires only to see their choices be wholesome and happy. With the complexity of a responsible, fulfilling life already instilled, he will see them making sound family planning decisions instead of the nightmare of mindless, unprepared teen childbirth. He faces life with them again, as open as his children are ready to be. He can see the phases of life before they come, and meets the challenge with a wise, tolerant bearing.

Most parents long for an open relationship with their kids; they claim to desire friendship, but they don't foster it. It seems they forgot what friends are. How do we deal with friends? Do we tell them what to do? Do we pretend puberty, relationships and peer issues aren't happening? Do we limit our friends, dictating who they can see, what they can do and what they can wear? Do we rifle through their belongings, invade their privacy and accost them, assuming the worst? If we take these actions, then we won't be close and they won't tell us anything. We won't be friends, and they won't even be friendly. At best, they'll tolerate us until they can escape. How we treat our kids is most likely how they'll treat their kids. Most battled this same oppression, only to nod off and have it destroy the peace a generation later. If you want to skip the belligerent and disagreeable phase, then wake up and stay *real*, Mom and Dad!

This is a good conversation to have at the age of about fourteen or fifteen: "Soon it will be time for you to take full control of your life. You must be prepared to do that, and that takes practice. I want you to begin to take as much responsibility over yourself as you can handle, right now. I'm here to help and answer any questions you wish to ask. I encourage you to ask others you respect, who live the kind of life you want to lead. I know that I cannot be your protector, softening the consequences of your lessons in life. So I'll do the only moral thing I can do, and get out of the way. I expect a payoff for the investment I've made in you. I expect you to be happy. I expect you to work with the passion and determination to make your life worthwhile, and to make your dreams come true. I believe in you, and I trust you will make sound decisions, not for my sake, but for yours.

Your coming of age preparation begins this weekend (maybe after a birthday). You are getting your own cell phone. You are getting your own credit card. We will work out a savings plan, so when the time comes, you'll have a down payment for the kind of car you want." Then you can go on to help them with job and career selection, help decide whether college is necessary, and help them map it all out. Self-made Man knows there is never only one chance to succeed. Kids can be wrong—the art is in recombining, experimenting and never giving up in the pursuit of whatever they wish life to be.

Setting a Sound Example. Throughout childhood, I looked forward to find heroes to pattern my life after. After eighteen, I saw no one around me worth emulating. I was what I wanted to be, and to follow the course of someone older would have required me to surrender one or more of my cherished values. I could not understand why it was necessary, and I could not imagine life improving because of it. So I quit looking for heroes, until one found me.

Often, teenagers think they have the whole world figured out, and the quality of their television gives them a good reason to think it. They've learned that sex and boldness conquers all, and at the sub-levels of cognition, it works. But after a few years of bar-hopping, manipulating others and being manipulated, they realize how empty it all is without the depth of intimacy and intelligence. It's as pointless as using foul language to be cool; so they look past the beer and cigarette ads to complete the picture of what life and love is supposed to be, and of what human beings really are. The true complexity of life is staggering, and most often, they reach that conclusion totally unprepared. Often, Mom and Dad were tacky, boring, controlling and unhelpful, and they don't want to end up like that. What is their alternative?

They don't need the luck of being born into wealth or rationality, and the Self-made need not consider reproduction a duty; Spirit Murderers will always produce more than enough mouths to feed in order to justify their passivity. The

Self-made need only to live the most fulfilling life possible in the sight of the world. Enough young people will use them as a role model—a being that just exudes health from every angle—not the bent work-horse that raised them.

The teens of any generation are at a divine turning point, when their wings grow strong, yet they have not mastered flight; and if we love them, all we have to do is let them know we trust them. Set them free to train their own cognitive functions, and set a sound example. Load them with personal responsibility to train their disciplines. We can treat them like people, because they are. We can give them the respect of a young mind—a new chance at greatness, not a source of irritation to be restrained. We don't have to force, cajole or threaten to get our point across. We govern by the Self-made quote which deals directly with life and is unafraid to expose truths: "See for yourself."

We experiment in our lives, just as we teach them to. We show our progress and its pattern. We show its reward. We face what must be faced. We admit wrongs. We reveal uncertainties. We deal with difficult situations and show the path to solutions. We show how important individual happiness is, through our own self-dedication. *We walk our talk.* Most of all, we stay real. Self-made Man gives them something to appreciate, even when they reach his age and look back, remaining wholesome, open and aware, with the honesty that only true strength can practice.

Deep Encouragement. Our value to them is that we can see farther than they can. We can give them hints about what lies around the next corner, or explore the result of any road they consider choosing. Future knowledge is all theoretical for them, so we won't spoil it. We should do all we can to sell them on their most fulfilling destiny. We need not involve specifics, but only the tools they use—their honesty and the projection of their dream lifestyle. We can't force advice, but we can tell them what we see. We can tell them they are lost if we have good reasons, and provide clear paths to answers they haven't discovered the questions to. Accomplished men in my past, through greater experience, have offered knowledge that has saved me significant time and stress. Pointers from the perspective of wealth are invaluable, and often the advice they give is tailored in response to one's particular challenge. It's alright to offer hard, frank advice; powerful people don't like to waste time either, especially their own.

Rational mentors don't reinforce false esteem, but reinstill the patterns that lead to true esteem. We trace and never let go of true cause and effect. We take them to the mountain tops as a lure for their effort; we offer implications and options, not groundless second guessing. We offer memorable quotes of support from wise men to keep them searching, to keep them thinking and to keep them striving. Paraphrasing Warren Buffet, we offer the projection that they can do anything, but never a sanction where they feel they can do nothing.

There is something even more powerful than a transitional generation such as ours; the generation reared under it. They will be a group more absent of fear, more clear and excited about their futures, than any witnessed by the world since the Industrial Revolution, and I can't wait to see what they'll do.

It's an astounding feat to overcome the moral confusion and fears that we've had, and go on to achieve wealth and happiness in our lives. It is another thing entirely to be raised as they will, never having these fears to begin with. The example we have set for them as self-responsible producers is our pride, and we do deserve to feel it. But there is much more we can do. This again, comes with perfect timing, as we are in the most active phase of our lives, and must begin planning the transition of our enjoyment more and more, into the intellectual. It involves blossoming in a worldly, moral-intellectual manner, reaching the full maturity mankind was meant to achieve by his design, and I think you, the top one percent, are ready for the challenge.

The challenge is to correct the structure of human institutional action, which lies within the young adult's realm of presumption through college years, but remains outside their grasp. We must see all human beings have a clean, safe, rational environment to thrive in, to see the young encounter beauty in the blossoming of their senses, and not to experience a constant recoil. It is in our power to see them grow into glamorous adults, exemplifying tact, class, elegance, pride, strength, productivity, bounty, fulfillment, honor, respect for themselves and respect for us. We must have them fully prepared for this world *as it is*, with a clear plan to continuously improve it. We must prepare them to demand fair treatment for all, never permitting themselves or anyone else to be ridden. It's time to shrug off the Christian weight of manufacturing slaves and martyrs. It's time to rid the world of the remnants of monarchy from mankind's savage and unfair past. Let the restructuring of unsound institutions be our greatest gift to the generations to come. We must rally around the best of the human race and the best within ourselves, to preserve the chance for all to live the dream.

Intimate Relationships

"If this is foreplay, I'm a dead man."—Cacoon

What we all long for, is to share our lives with someone we will miss all day long. Look at your past loves—what you loved was their life-furthering power, in all its forms, and this is no surprise. There is a clear link between intimacy and sound cognition. You breathe in and take in the scent of her hair. You look down her gorgeous profile, and think in pleasure, "Mine, all mine." You contemplate all that she is; not just this toned, beautiful body, but the wonder behind the smile, the active mind, full of deep personal interests, breathtaking to watch in their pursuit, capturing the special connection when she looks up at you in sheer enjoyment, as you look at her when hard at work. And when the day is done, we rest, speaking softly in candlelit serenity, holding hands and brushing close in passing embraces, winding down as our sensual energy stirs. We begin to lose coherency of the days events, seeing the one before us—so strong, so capable. We are drawn more and more to look, to smell, to touch— to fill our senses with the presence of this other. So often called "Being taken away," is to be so overwhelmed in our sensate capacity, "To be taken in *every* way" is more like it, to the greatest release of our true feelings and hopes about existence, our possibilities and our lives. Do you see a structure forming? This whole process follows 1) Perception, 2) Identification, 3) Creative Action and 4) Reward.

Love is a reward, whose provocation we learn in our relationship to existence. When a relationship follows the healthy lifestyle of a Self-made Man, love will emanate to others effortlessly. Many individual attributes flow straight into relationships, becoming key compatibility factors. Our own pace, our own courage, defines the range of mates who will be acceptable. When we like what we see, we know its value, we work well together and the result is fulfilling, we are ready to move closer. With interaction so positive at every step, both can commit to its continuance, forming a relationship.

The most difficult question in relationships is commitment: *when* to commit, *who* to commit to, and *what* to commit to. The more complex the consciousness, the more areas of compatibility it considers; so the more difficult the decision. Self-made Man can't have a lot of relationships, because he can't be indifferent to them. People take time, and if he doesn't invest in them, the effort won't be fulfilling. He can sample many, just touching the surface of each other, or he can delve deeply into a few and learn more intimately who he is. His long-term intention is to build an edifice; not a lot of sand hills, so he doesn't choose a social life of perpetual strangers. But there are valuable traits at all depths across the spectrum of individuals, and he can never be certain when or where he will encounter those who pique his interest. His outlook on relationships evolves as a result of their investigation, so he shouldn't commit too soon.

Our intimate interaction follows a pattern we will repeat continuously throughout life. It has many elements, each having their own art, which evolves with experience and reflection. First, we go through an internal process of *selection*, based on our own ambition for values. Second, we must approach and *initiate* conversation with those we find attractive, by making ourselves attractive to them. This is a numbers game; only so many will be receptive. Once we begin dating, we set precedents that determine how the rest of the relationship will go; so we stay real about who we are, where we're going, and what we want. Our essential compatibility is revealed here, stirring our anticipation for what is to come. Third, the relationship becomes *sexual*, sharing a facet of life withheld from the rest—the magnificent exploration of each other, and the deepest pleasure that can be had between us. Fourth, we span the day-to-day *conduct* of the relationship for however long it lasts; the medium of feeling generated between us as a result of how we treat each other and how we handle issues. Finally, the relationship is consummated by either moving on or committing. The process has its own expertise, and the reduction in initial and long-term stress alone makes it well worth learning.

Selection. Self-made Man can only *over*value the right partner by putting her *before* his living purpose. The proper hierarchy for a human value system is 1) Purpose, 2) Intimacy, and 3) Everything and everyone else. This is the moral course for a sound volitional consciousness, and there are no exceptions. Dedication to his own life is his first romantic connection, with existence itself. Once he has chosen his life's work, he is ready to choose someone who reflects its dimension. When he is in full agreement with his own direction, he has achieved a harmonic resonance with destiny, and there is no negative stress related to his purpose. When he encounters a match, the same is true. Romantic love is never a compromise. It is a flowing energy added to his own, accenting his happiness. Besides his purpose, nothing is more important than making the right choice. His relationship choice is a core accomplishment when done right in every way. It is there to lean on and to learn from, to reflect on the correct process of *winning* in life.

Just as in deciding one's own destiny, there is a big learning curve moving from temporary mates to permanent mates, which parallels moving from experimental action, to permanent patterns of action. Both are much longer roads without proper moral direction. Self-made Man doesn't even attempt a serious relationship before he has the basics of his life under clear control. He is financially stable and can handle the rudiments of life—he knows how to feed himself, how to dress himself and how to bathe. His appearance is neat and clean, as is his mind. His living space reflects how carefully he operates within his environment, evolving as respect and cognizance of other people and their possessions as well. As he addresses the challenge of growth and handles his own daily obligations, he interacts rationally and keeps his obligations to others.

Choosing a mate in any phase of life is incredibly dynamic. It is tailored to every individual as a sum covering a dozen general categories, and a few dozen minor ones. It becomes more difficult when family or friends try to play matchmaker based on some shallow cultural attribute which satisfies their perspective, but detracts from or fails to complement your central interests. Motive is everything. One potential partner may be further along in a specific context, such as makes more money, is more experienced or intelligent, yet an aggregate emotional sum will tell you your preference for one individual over another—their worth to you. One doesn't choose a mate on a scale of value between dueling suitors; but relative to *oneself.* This is highly personal, as only *you* know where you are, where you're going and how fast, establishing your hierarchy and preferences—intellectually, professionally, spiritually, emotionally, sexually, socially and recreationally. No one else knows what you have yet to learn or what you desire to experience and therefore, who you will mesh with best. No one else knows better psychologically, whether you are seeking growth and exhilaration, or just someone to hide behind; and usually what others propose is some form of this latter.

The truth about the significance of women to men and men to women, is that they worship each other; for proof, look at any effective advertising. Even if they can't, they want to. It isn't just sex; we worship all elegant human attributes when displayed most vividly, which hold a parallel virtue for both sexes. From self-projected ideal to actualization, people reveal their depth and self-worth by what kind of partner they submit to. It is here where one's true standards are uncovered. The Self-made looks for a match, no matter how long or hard the search. He works to complete the ideal social picture of his life, so that he'll have no need left unfulfilled. As his own comprehension and depth of all the facets of a relationship grows, his fulfillment grows. He continues to seek relationship knowledge throughout his life just as he seeks to advance his central purpose and intensifies their quality with what he learns. He develops many critical relationship areas to a point where his value is obvious to all. He recognizes that value and looks forward to a lifetime of rewarding someone deserving, who has spent their time developing themselves in the same anticipation.

Beyond cognitive honesty, all facets of being human hold potential for compatibility. The more elements that match, the more harmonious the union. Whether one is in possession of a particular trait or simply reveres and intends to acquire a tailored form, there is compatibility by implication. It's particularly valuable that we have a serious interest in each other's passions—work included. This gives the clearest understanding of the priorities of a mate's consciousness. Essential compatibility is to say, "I respect how you go about living." We must be honest in our evaluation of them for good or bad, and this process is lifelong. Sound relationships don't begin as projects, blind faith, or rescue missions; they begin with fundamental compatibility. We begin with a certain view of an entity. Upon witnessing a new trait, desirable or otherwise, we continually build and adjust our description of it. We don't grab hold of a human and try coercing them into compliance with the image we had originally, or what we project is possible for them, any more than we would do so studying an animal. We observe, catalog and draw conclusions from the true sum, not from isolated factors and not from hopes.

Among the many facets of an individual to be discovered, developed, and carried forward into relationships, it is our sense of life that we *must* have in common for it to last. We must know there is benevolence in the core of our hearts, which stems from how we feel about living itself. What we are looking for and what everyone needs psychologically, is a confirmation of our view of existence. We need a reflection of that tailored life we've created, in the person to whom we are devoted. It is the fuel of our spirits. Our passions will change over the years; but what never changes, is our devotion to making it all worthwhile.

Until reached, the ideal of his future mate's potentiality is always in his foreground. No day to day events are more important than maintaining a romantic sense of life. His projection is that of worship—of her and the wholesome traits she has worked for. His wish is to exist with this brilliant being; to become a dream team, completing each other. When he looks in her eyes—it isn't primarily her faith in him or his confidence in her loyalty that he values, but simply what she is. He fantasizes, not to have kids, but to have *her kids*, not to be married, but to be married *to her*, not to Jones, but to enjoy the risk of passion. To attain the adrenaline rush of saying "My wife," and feeling the deepest pride.

Our final choice should be saved for someone special—ourselves. Getting married, we can imagine an overwhelming elation vibrating all through us about what we have decided to do, reflecting on how devoted we are to each other. Projecting into our later years, we hold each other to say, "Didn't we do well?" We look in each other's eyes, feeling this incredible bond we spent a lifetime developing, and these children, who are a product of our love, respect and dedication to each other and our relationship—our creation. Our children in turn would know there is something adult that we share beyond them—something they aren't a part of, an intimacy they must grow to understand. It is the way we speak to each other, the way we look at each other and the way we touch. It is a pleasure to see them watch our peaceful, loving interaction in awe and romantic desire for what awaits them in their own futures.

Attraction and Initiation. Love at first sight has often been the target of refutation; mainly by those who cannot attract it. Is it possible? You bet it is! Love at first sight is linked to the concept of "form follows premise," and stems most clearly from the puppy-love of our first crushes in youth. First loves are our first rudimentary social connections to personal value. It grows well beyond that with time, but one can see crucial values in another—traits worthy of love—just by looking at them.

Beyond love at first sight, preparation is necessary for romantic encounters. First in the hierarchy of attraction is to please another's perceptions. Everyone appreciates someone who is clean, fresh, together and vibrant; the elements of beauty, most of which can be acquired. The first essential element of romantic beauty is sparkling, fiery eyes, conveying all that is possible in the anticipation of living. Second is excellent posture, being alert and aware with a backbone and no rolled shoulders. This conveys that one is joyously ready for exciting action. Third is respecting one's health and cleanliness, having low to no fat, being toned if not sculpted, and well groomed. Fourth, that one's overall facial structure and expression is driven by premise, with strong, hard, clear features. We smile with our eyes too, which should be steady, revealing joy, self-esteem and intelligence. Fifth is one's style and sensuality—our *way,* the mildly suggestive enjoyment of relaxed physical motion and frank interest. The sixth and final element is natural beauty—which can be maintained, but otherwise lies outside the virtue of the entity. All, even the sixth, can be changed, improved, and honed into art. As one develops towards a working model of excellence, inessentials which don't appear to reflect an ideal, get dismissed in the overwhelming positivism of other traits.

There is a very small percentage of people hopeless in the quest to spark romantic fantasy in the eyes of another. The majority have a virtual well of untapped sensual ability lying dormant underneath a layer of fearful evasion, unwillingness, or simple unawareness, through a lack of exposure to the possibilities.

Warrior Note: *If you ask the elderly what they regret most in their lives, it's never what they did, it's what they didn't do, what they held themselves back from doing. What if approaching her could alter both your destinies? Don't miss out.*

Traits desired must reflect traits acquired, so he must gain a conscious understanding of the level of suitor his aura will attract. With the Self-made traits of character, commitment to growth, emotional openness, mature responsibility, honesty, dependability, high self-esteem, positive sense of life and the resulting capacity for love, his options are good. If he expects more, then he has to *become* more. As one-half of the encounter, he must be comfortable approaching people he doesn't know. Engaging with confidence and without pretense is the key. Decent people are never rude to a sincere approach, but if he is nervous and uncomfortable, he can expect others to be uncomfortable with him. A key to removing the fear is to be complete *without* her. If his core purpose is established and his life is deeply satisfying, approaching will be much easier. Regardless, he doesn't expect to win until he has it mastered, and he keeps trying until he has. He works on what he wants to convey until women respond well. Just as he brings his mind into focus to perform in life, he practices pure perceptivity in initial attraction, consciously controlling his fear until his patterning has devoured it, where he can remain bright and alert, open and friendly. He engages as an adventure, using the adrenaline as stimulation to *heighten* his perception, not to limit it. Eventually he *enjoys* the thrill and risk of fully open senses. He is still dominant and sovereign, but not intimidating and not intimidated, ready to acknowledge her value alongside his own. He is a sexual being without regret or apology, and in the presence of a desirable woman, that interest always exists somewhere in his glance. He is the foundation, in control of himself and in control of them both, at her will. Once he has it mastered, he can relax and observe her half; what she brings to the table.

He does not limit himself as to *where* to find her. Often it's claimed that work is *not* the place to find a mate, but nothing could be further from the truth. Here is a place where both have a core mutual interest, much less superficial than the content of most dates and social gathering places. No activity could prove more affirming and consonant than how we carry out the business of life. If we can be professional about it, then management can too. At best, pursuing one's purpose is the most powerful realm to meet one's soul mate—there is no deeper, more dynamic a parallel to be made between individuals.

During courtship, he doesn't put extravagant effort or cost into activities he never intends to do as an established couple. He does normal things, at reasonable expense. He doesn't change his lifestyle to gain the relationship; it must fit within his scale and desired direction. He takes her to enjoy experiences along his own lines of interest to learn whether she can handle and appreciate them, as they share hers. Both contribute in turn, neither being shielded from the financial realities we all must acknowledge and respect.

> *"Erogenous zones are either everywhere or nowhere."*
> —Joseph Heller

It is said that men reach their sexual peak at eighteen. In my view, this is only true if their premises are wrong! Otherwise, it just keeps getting better. With deeper understanding, experiences are richer, fuller and far more satisfying. Sexual interest *grows* with the growth of one's cognitive capacity, and such expansion is lifelong.

Sex. Have you ever noticed that with certain people, you just can't seem to keep your mind on light topics; it always moves to more pressing things? You look at them, and you begin to dwell on more urgent needs. Your mind tends to wander toward other things you could be doing, and the thoughts may become overwhelming, but if you could just put that aside for awhile, and let it stir, the desire becomes absolutely explosive, and when you finally get what you've dreamt of, it is more satisfying than anything you could have imagined. Somehow, it's an experience that makes all life worthwhile.

Out of every five hundred people you see, one is a millionaire, and even more rare is that once in a lifetime love interest, who could bring into your life, all of the passion, fun and adventure you've ever wanted, affecting you so strongly, you can't help but respond. When you feel your heart beating in your chest and notice you're breathing heavily, it's a wonderful sign that it's right. Your body always seems to know first. A lustful reaction to someone can be much more than physical, depending on one's depth and their distance from one's dream. Lust can be based on seeing someone's wholesome *use* of sensuality. Tapping into the value behind the lust is the key. Our chemistry is strongest with those on similar wavelengths, and with the risk of honesty, such resonance can be deafening. There is a wealth of information in body language; the behavior of a girl with a crush, the glances reserved for lovers, the exhilaration of encountering someone worthy of fantasy, the motions and expressions she would make if you were touching her in the most intimate places. As a woman arches and curves her back, a man flares and is dominant, in a rocking, blinding, intolerable ecstasy nothing else on Earth can match. These are natural, gender-specific responses to sexual exaltation, properly guiltless, pure and beautiful in their grace.

A touch is a sanction of one's being, so Self-made Man isn't casual about it. He doesn't go around hugging everyone; it is too personal and too important to be misused. He reserves it for when he feels a sense of incredible connection. Thinking of emotion as a liquid, we have deep emotional pools within us. With those we truly care about, we can relax enough to let down our barriers, and allow our emotional pools to blend, surrounding each other in a glowing warmth, expressing our capacity for truly devoted love and friendship. When he sees his mate, it's as if there's an aura between them, and the warmth of that connection glows, as the rest of the world fades into oblivion. It sends a pleasant vibration all through them, which is a physical sensation, driven by their comfort with one another. It is so much, just to sit close to her and feel that wonderful sense of acceptance, which turns into a great warmth, and the desire to be even closer, which becomes a pulling, pressing need to have every part of him as close to every part of her as possible. He thinks of her naked body in his arms, her lips on his, his heart beating so hard he can almost hear it, the smell of her hair, the anticipation felt by every inch of his skin, longing to be caressed, and she responds. The desire to give themselves to each other is the act of saying "Yes" in their souls—"Yes, this is what I give myself to, totally. Take control of us, of me, this is worthy of my total release; this is exaltation."

Why is sex so powerful? It is the most potent experience of when joy is *inflicted*, just as a symphony isolates and inflicts the sense of hearing. Whether fast and aggressive or slow and torturous, it's all good. Sex is the desire to impart to someone the glory of your passion for living—of how euphoric and speechless you feel about this gift of life. No matter what happens in life, nothing matters as much as the desire to positively affect by touch, that which you sanction, and every reciprocation is a gift for your skin to react to. The most intimate causes your stomach to drop as your body moves to face it openly, willingly, in full submission and acceptance of the highest emotions life has to offer.

These zones are nature's way of leading Man and animal along the correct path. Our skin responds to a loving touch, just as a plant or a flower responds to the sun. Our spirits need fuel as frequently as our bodies need it. Sex is an essential means to acquire that fuel, being a celebration of life, our reward. Sex is the greatest opportunity to reaffirm our highest view of ourselves and of our mate, to sanction and bolster all we respect and wish to see furthered; to let them know we believe in them, that we need them, and that we stand behind their deepest fulfillment in all things. There is a vibration about all living entities, and lovers share a wavelength at the most important level. The resonating power of our mate's body is one of our greatest healing tools.

The effect a Self-made Man has on a woman is wild. It's as if being with him is a subconscious command to her body to bloom fully, and she does. Her reaction to him affects her metabolism, and her body begins to change. Her body knows, "this is it," and begins to prepare; filling out just the way she always wanted, accentuating the hourglass that nature had in store for her. She gets flushed, and carries a radiant glow wherever she goes. With him, she captures the essence of the woman she has always wanted to be. It is how he looks at the world, and how he interacts with her, that makes her feel mature, independent, in control of life, sensually in love with herself and the world—confident in a way that is permanent. It is no different for him when she is Self-made in her own right. He learns what a woman truly needs, and she encourages his growth towards her image of Man and her own ecstasy; bringing them both to a pinnacle of self-esteem and mutual satisfaction; a pinnacle that can and should become a glorious plateau.

In my own life I want to give that special girl the same thrill I get, when I run my hands all over her beautiful shape; so I maintain a beautiful shape for her. I have seen that look in a woman's eyes; the wonder, and the pleasure of the opportunity she feels she is being exposed to. And then I go on to be satisfying to every other sense she has. I want her heart racing when she thinks of me; I want her short of breath, of how full my lips feel on hers, of how safe and overwhelmed she feels, with my arms around her, particularly where the muscles touch her, the liquid tension, and the magic sensation of the pressure, of my fingertips, exploring every intimate part of her body, each one, independent, alive, with an unpredictable, thrilling plan of its own, outside of her control. A touch is a sanction of one's being, and I wish to share that, every time. Our openness brings us both to think and feel that a touch anywhere—a shoulder, a hand, is an intimate connection, and that conjures a feeling of inner warmth, that leads into a much deeper need, to be satisfied. Enjoying such intimate sensitivity makes it very difficult to get through the day sometimes, if anyone happens to touch one of us at work.

For the Anticipation-driven, touching his lips to any part of her is a treasured span of time, lived only for that action. It is an act of worship. It is a sanction of what she is, through his desire, and a sanction of what he is, through hers. That is the kind of feeling to preserve for a lifetime. They want each other's happiness, to just be, and love, and live with passion, and come together, for that emotional release that only they can give each other. True lovers are very comfortable with each other—they pal around, joke, touch, easily inspire romantic moments and are borderless. It is a perfectly comfortable, mutual form of prideful ownership. Knowing they have the future; they don't have to rush. Dedicated to values, each is committed to always be what they are, to maintain what attracted them in the first place. They want to thrill and be thrilled, so there isn't a gut to overlook or any irrationality to tolerate; nothing to kill the passion, and there never will be.

Relationship Conduct. You know when you're packing for a vacation, and you feel that almost unbearable sense of anticipation, where the adrenaline just *streams* through every muscle? Feeling that exhilarating response, to me, I think is wonderful, and should be our emotional medium. What would it be like, if every day with someone became a stimulating pleasure, where fascinating things were always being uncovered, and exciting new discoveries come up, allowing you to maintain a sense of awe—for me, there is no better way to live.

As a woman, wouldn't it be nice, to be with a man who treated you like a person for once, who didn't act like a dog on a leash, tiptoeing around to please you, but someone strong enough to trust you, someone who can joke and play, and pin you down, when you deserve it? You know how the most significant relationships have always had the highest highs, and the lowest lows? It was this conflict, rooted in passion, that drove you to feel more than you ever thought possible, and pulled more out of you, than you knew you could give. The best are always a roller coaster, that volleys between a sense of total helplessness, and glowing, radiant safety; but always, a healthy flow of violent, clashing, compelling emotions, and if you look back to those times, you never felt more alive. With the knowledge and means of its creation, you can look straight into the future, and know what you are in for!

One point of clarity when he comes home is that someone is there who understands him. When she crosses his mind, any negative pressure from life is gone. Just thinking of her potentiality, an enormous weight lifts, and his faculty of sight, hearing and thought no longer bring pain. His senses can tolerate what they see, as the core and majority of his intimate emotional exposure is so overwhelmingly positive. He is not trapped in a thankless life, and she is his proof. Their sacred relationship is built and maintained on pure honesty—consonance with their feelings, open about their fears, supporting, stabilizing, and fostering each other for mutual fulfillment. Private time is priceless between them. Little is on his chest; he doesn't need to talk about work. Work is like preparing a meal, a focused application of his tools. Self-appreciation is enjoying the meal and being nourished by it. Romantic relationships are the reward of life, the dessert. Seeing his mate should be the climax of his day. Along the food theme, he even appreciates seeing her eat; confident the energy it provides will be used morally.

Self-made individuals know they will never be "one" with another, and would never want to be. They know this poetic ideal is metaphysically impossible and are aware of its true intent, the exchange of independence for dependence. The entirety of their life is spent with only one person—themselves. They are thankful to have found someone who glides alongside so pleasantly. The pattern of life has them in constant appreciation of all forms of beauty; of anything and anyone who "has it right" in life. It is their ability to identify such values, which brought them together in the first place; a realm where they will readily connect with others as well. While a sound relationship is monogamous, they do not forsake interest in the value others may represent, or in discovering their own value to others. Flirting is legal; it can be an exhilarating learning experience. This does not mean that such an encounter leads to sex, nor does it sanction dishonesty. A Self-made couple is so focused on their endeavors, that no question of infidelity ever arises, or really matters. They've chosen each other to exist at the center of their world, and the deeper that world goes, the harder it is to uproot. We all like a sense of permanence uninterrupted, until we are ready to leave; but in a relationship, that choice and risk is in equal balance. The same values that he used to choose his mate, determines what he will find attractive in others, and there can be many. He in turn realizes there are other men out there that she will find attractive, and that he better remain competitive. Marriage is not a license for stagnation at any time.

Both take care not to get tangled up in the lives of those outside the relationship. In a sound relationship, man and woman are each other's first social consideration. He doesn't come to her looking for a relationship with her family and friends, and she doesn't come after his buddies. Playfully encircling her waist, he says "To hell with everyone outside of us. We come first." And hugging him she smiles, knowing how wonderful it is to be so mutually dedicated. With life being a puzzle, she fits just right in his arms; they chose each other for this reason. Together, they are a temporary reprieve from the rest of the world. It is their time to talk about their own goals and about shared experiences, independent of others. As their lives develop and unfold, this time helps them to stay on track, keeping their focus on what counts. He comes to her for reasons and standards of his own that she satisfies, and she recognizes that he is of equal importance to her happiness. He needs to know that he can touch her, hold her, stop her and just look deep into her eyes, anytime he needs to. No power struggle to gain an upper hand is necessary, and no one outside the relationship can come between them.

Who should be together long-term? Those who in unison, generate the most positive energy. In a proper relationship, the two work together, plan together and grow together. They are compatible if their goals match, and if neither requires sacrifice from the other. All decisions affecting both are made together, but long range decisions yield to the mind with the longest range. Both maintain their own financial responsibility, which is simply *cognitive* responsibility. Each makes their own money, and each controls that same amount. They remain independent together. He might say, "I have only one chance at this life. If I'm not free to live the way I wish, my spirit would die. It's the same for you. You have dreams and desires, as I do. We both have a full right to pursue them. Mine are on the table: my dedication to my work, private luxury, travel, kids at a specific phase of life or none at all, and a priceless intimacy. I hope yours are on the table as well. If you're sincere, I'll use my resources to benefit us both. If not, I'll have to use them to protect myself."

They have seen the trauma of unhappy coexistence, perhaps in their parent's lives, and are committed not to repeat it. No more domestic disputes or renounced dreams. No more shattered homes and battered wives. Just honesty, fairness and sound life-direction based on their mutual integrity. Together, they run through their mutual lifestyle interests subject by subject, to assure both are satisfied in life. Now is *not* the time for compromise. Each states "I'd prefer to allocate X time and X money to this endeavor, (be it kids, travel, housing, or business), in order to preserve my core passions and their growth. This is the hierarchy by which I intend to live." With core passions covered, the balance is negotiable. Neither tries to appropriate a share of their spouse's capital for their own stubborn interest; they want in life only what they can independently sustain. Neither should burden the other with gifts they could never afford alone. They must be disciplined to wait until they have accumulated the virtues necessary to maintain a desired lifestyle by their own merit. No partner is to be shielded from cause and effect to consider money inexhaustible; it isn't. Money is human energy, as is love. To waste either, or to spend it without the object's appraisal relative to the expense of effort (and whose), is a pattern of poverty. No endeavor is pursued until the timing is right for both and the money is sufficient, which sets their mutual value hierarchy. As they move forward in life, each addresses new plans and acquisitions questioning what is most urgent or personally valuable to have first, and seeks fulfillment in the proper order. If ever they part, each is entitled to the share their investment provided.

Pursuing their own independent purposes, the relationship can remain what it is in the beginning; filled with exhilarating emotions, the anticipation of joy and the freshness of continually happening upon something special. On separate tracks yet running parallel, there is always an aura of mystery about one another. The nature of this distance holds pleasant surprises and newness around every corner. They think independently, retaining the unique perspective each brings to life, neither being limited by the interests or abilities of the other. Self-governed, they remain free to stay or to go, in a checks and balances system that keeps both rational and fair, reversing the snowball cycle of repression, to the exact opposite result. They are both a source of additional positive energy for each other, never an energy drain; the basic intention and benefit of living in a civil society. With constant awareness of each other's value, their continual progression vents endless romantic appeal; and as a result, they court each other, *throughout* the relationship.

> *"Marriage is a great institution, but I'm not ready for an institution."*
> —Mae West

Moving On. We owe it to ourselves to find the best person we can to spend our lives with, but what if there was someone even more perfect for us out there? Loyalty to a relationship should never be treason to our own highest happiness. It's like driving an average car. It's ok for a while, but then you find yourself saying, oohh, look at that one... and you realize it's time to move on. Sometimes we outpace others as we grow in knowledge and experience, and our self-image follows; so should its reflection. Moving to higher values should never be the exception, but the rule itself. Still, with his kind of independence, a new relationship isn't required to prompt him to leave.

Often, relationships end in dysfunction for behavioral reasons, which are the result of epistemological reasons—the thinking and patterning of those involved. Therefore, they can end for *sound* reasons and in a rational way. A Self-made Man doesn't want to destroy his spouse or get even, if it is time for her to leave. She doesn't want his energy. They are both looking ahead. As their central power is within them, they can afford to show each other the highest civil respect, *by leaving each other intact.* It would be nice to hear someone at the end of a relationship say, "I know your life is yours. I'm thankful for the time we've had, but if you feel there is something more for you out there, you owe it to yourself to discover it. We only live once; we have to make the most of it." Whether they are making a mistake or not, whether their choice is prompted by intelligent expansion or by a blind, dissatisfied inertia is irrelevant. They own their lives, and remain free to see the world from where they are, and must learn all they can from that vantage point.

Often when we take on a relationship, we put ourselves on hold and get nothing done; a stress we bring with us. We are *taught* that we have to "give everything" in order to prove our love, which is the process of erosion. We pour all of our emotional and financial resources into the union, just to watch them walk off with it, or snub it without looking back. We suffer one ruined investment after another, until we shun cultural expectations and learn to keep something for ourselves. With reflection, we notice a steady return from our own interests, but from people, it's hit or miss. We do so well on our own with development so peaceful and straight forward, that we have to wonder if the single life isn't the better choice; but it's hard to be alone, and the last thing we need is another dysfunctional relationship. Why isn't the rational efficiency of our actions translating? At some point we have to question the contradiction, and find a solution.

Time alone is time for reflection on what went wrong, and how to assure success the next time. Self-made Man wants to be in love for real. He wants to *know* his mate is devoted to him and why. He must be wanted for the right reasons, reasons he respects. He has to know that he has traits that are valuable and worthy of love regardless; so that even when it doesn't work out, he can move on to love again. He wants to be respected for what he can do; to see his honor acknowledged and rewarded, not to see it cause him loss or unjust penalties. Above all this, he wants to remain *whole*. By isolating and mastering every nuance of difficulty he encounters, eventually his power to have a good relationship grows to astonishing levels; emitting a maturity that becomes very valuable to others. For an active mind, time alone is just as priceless as time with a spouse. Why? Epistemologically speaking, alone, it's the *trunk* that grows. Like saving for a car, the longer you save, the nicer the car you can buy.

Alone, he will miss having someone to dance with. It will hurt to leave valuable talents and abilities idle. He survives by drawing love from the trees, from the wind and from all of existence—his first love. He loves the motion of his body, the sun on his neck, the wind in his hair and how free he is to do anything. Imagine the facial expression of someone who has met the love of their life, and is contemplating all of the wonder of their years ahead. Self-made Man feels that way about his first relationship (Man's relation to existence). He knows it will be an extension, to feel it with his second (Man's relation to another). But half the equation is sound, and he can live his life romantically at this stage. He loves the life he has designed, and all the activities that bring him pleasure. There are many forms of love, so he keeps love in his life by practicing the others. When he is alone, it is his *purpose* that saves him. As a human being, his self must be the center of his concern. His primary focus is to construct an efficiently running entity in himself, whose maintenance continues throughout any relationship. He has reversed dogmatic sacrifice in moral self-defense—the key to the solution. When he is properly in tune to his own projects, it is difficult to give time to others, forcing them to match the quality of his endeavor. It allows him to interface and court with no appeals, and no demands. At his busiest, he doesn't even mind not having a mate; it's irrelevant. One could last forever alone, with this style of living. There is no sense of compromise in his existence. He loves being alive, and it's that much clearer that his next mate must be someone who values and operates at his level, someone who understands and pursues this pleasure as well, and won't try to take it from him. When he meets her, life just gets better.

Warrior Note: *One's own living sum must advance uninterrupted, regardless of relationship status.*

To lose invigoration for life is to lose the game, so he stays on course and achieves without her. He never again parts himself out by the incompetent code of sacrifice. It would be nice to turn his head and be able to look into another's eyes, acknowledging the pleasure they are experiencing together, but no one is there. He feels a stab of regret; yet if he accepted just anyone, that would mean he could not *conceive* of values, and there would be no accomplishments to admire and enjoy anyway. If he chose to compromise again as in the past, it would have the same result—the loss of self-respect, youthful vitality, and future promise.

The lone contemplation of ideals is much more satisfying than their violation and betrayal. Rather than endure a spouse who aggravates them, such phenomenal possibilities can exist untarnished, within him. There is a part of the brain that knows no difference between fantasy and reality—a proven biochemical stimulant—and his projection of ideals, however unreached, is a proper substitute. He doesn't knock himself for not finding the right partner to enjoy every step of his progression with. He knows how rare his own soul is, and is willing to wait. When it gets to be too much, he accepts the pain. He never fakes reality. He doesn't run, but looks right at it. He knows what he's feeling and why. He knows his emotional medium is looking for a payment which he has *earned*, but cannot satisfy alone. His torture is a tribute to what it should be, and one day will be.

Relationship Perspective. Given the current definition of a relationship's successful end—meaning marriage—it's true that most relationships don't ultimately workout; but maybe we're all looking at it wrong. Maybe they did workout. The concept of *relationship* is a branch of step two—identification—which in this context can be defined as *the interaction of individuals for a specific intent*. The Self-made intent is spiritual fulfillment, as the Spirit Murdering intent is predation. As with other concepts, we have to work with the concept, collecting knowledge for its application through experience, and then move on for better relationships down the road. Relationships are the *medium* through which we seek such fulfillment, not the goal in itself. Fulfillment is the goal, and like self-esteem, is tied to every interaction; another *variable* in life. Fulfillment indeed, is the *social* equivalent of self-esteem. We should not seek to fix or solidify our associations with others. We evolve and others evolve in so many ways and directions over the course of a lifetime, how can we *not* expect variation? How can we assume that our mutual development will flow together, and why should it? As in science and technology, we cannot and should not, commit to an outcome beyond our own vision. Like it or not, relationships will remain in flux, but with moral clarity, it will add—not to our fear, but to our exhilaration within them.

A perfect lifelong relationship with a soul mate may be ideal, yet most of us are in and out of relationships, hoping to find the right match. Out of those who do marry, how many actually found a soul mate? How many just settled for whoever was available and willing? There is so much to learn in life, I can't fathom giving away the right to pursue knowledge, even if that possibility is presented through the person of another. Most live within a state of repression, and I don't want to be one of them, which brings us to my ultimate relationship rule:

Warrior Note: *Don't plan for eternity until you can see that far.*

Time is precious; there is no forever in the context of human life. The one you will be with longest is *yourself*, and your happiness is the proper focus of your thinking. Relationships are pockets of time, isolated from the world as a private celebration of life. They *all* end eventually, through breakup or death. The essential is to bring to them and extract, an equal amount of joy. A relationship isn't successful because it lasts a long time, it's successful because of the feelings it generates and sustains, and the growth and fulfillment it imparts to those involved.

In the simplest language, we establish relationships to be good to each other, and must commit to this for its duration. I've learned as much from bad relationships as I have from good ones, though they are never to be tolerated for long. As long as I wasn't killed, there was something positive to carry forward—new facets or new armor. There are plenty of wonderful people out there who aren't complete, ourselves included. Compatibility doesn't have to be mathematically perfect every time; you learn as you go, trying not to repeat a lesson already lived. Even if you're ready to settle down but your mate isn't, there's no need to push it, and certainly no reason to end it. For example, imagine as thanks for some activity in which you were involved, a business offers you one of their Lamborghinis for a day. Would you decline because you couldn't keep it for thirty years, or would you experience its magnificence to the fullest, and then cherish the memory? Cedar Pointe is great, but you can't take it home with you. Just think if the wonderful opportunities you've had to love and to *be* loved, were taken away. I have cherished and will cherish, every encounter. They have shown me how wonderful people can be.

Fantasies. Imagine if you were to encounter some luminous being whose presence engulfs you in the warmth of his power—someone brilliant and mysterious, who answers an emotional need you had no way of expecting someone else to understand, awakening that special place where you hide your most secret passionate fantasies. What if he suddenly walked in and said exactly what you needed to hear, stirring you to feel so overwhelming a desire, that the only way to satisfy it is to just drop everything and leave with him, right now? We've all dreamt of such a romantic encounter. Who wouldn't enjoy being swept away like that? But for the most part, fantasies exist hidden within us, tailored to our desire. As we grow, they advance in depth and complexity, becoming richer and more fulfilling in a positive exercise of our full imaginative capacity. Like being on a beach, we get used to the shallow water before venturing deeper, and the deeper we go, the more exciting it is—the more pride we have in showing our willingness to face and overcome our fears. We struggle in the torrent and dive deep into the peace beneath it—a feat only possible by challenging all that has come before. In our return, we ride the surf as its master, then rise to enjoy the warmth of the sun and the ocean swirling at our feet, recovering the serene calm of certainty. From the beginning to the end, our adventure of life is positive. We carry forward the knowledge that we've been to the brink and back, in many ways. *We've lived the fantasy.*

The advice of most the world is that "If we love each other enough, we won't stray," yet few achieve it without painful longing, especially in youth. Such is the longing for a greater knowledge and exploration of people—even of oneself. I can hear the rest of this mantra; "*Worship one god and never invest in another. Serve one State and never honor another. Love one person and never experience another. Seek a dictator in every realm. Limit, deny and renounce yourself. Follow our rules. Suffer our fate.*" I can't settle yet. I'd rather take my chances and be honest. This is a struggle that through irrational guilt, pressures many people into premature commitments. It impedes collecting the knowledge and experience necessary in their pursuit to identify and find a true soul mate, someone who will reflect their deepest expression of vitality for a lifetime. Repression is a tax and by implication, without mutual freedom the relationship would become a tax. Ultimately, I hold a monogamous relationship as an ideal. I dream to have so pure and passionate a love for someone, that they *consume* all thoughts of intimacy. But I know we may not cross paths at the same level of interest or development. As painful as it is, I would weigh her value to me, and if she needs to learn more or I do, I would accept it. With the few times in life that a romantic fantasy is realized, personally I would grant it to her as I would my own rather than lose her over it, see her miss out, or have her hide it and carry the burden of an unnecessary guilt. Given the nature of her value to me, I know her fantasies would be wholesome, as are mine—to experience an exalted facet or discover an answer—about existence, about herself, or about her capacity for an intoxicating interrelation. She can live these rare fantasies and enjoy me as the heart of her medium as I enjoy her, and leave this Earth fulfilled; not limited by me or anyone else. If we stay together, the net result is that she becomes more important to me as she becomes more complete, as I do for her. We've confirmed our relationship. We've missed nothing intellectually or experientially—we are certain about each other—and can grow old together, in peace and harmony. From valuable experiences, our individual sum grows. If we seek values constructively, the fullness of our satisfaction shows in our future response to life and to others.

People don't have to be everything you've dreamt of in order to have a relationship, and you don't have to settle down, even when they are. The possibility of spending one evening with an extraordinary person is better than never living one's dream. When you come across critical opportunities in life, you must seize them and live your passion with no regrets. The fire of our passion does not just go out. It fuels us, or it destroys us. It must be managed; it must be fed. The pain of longing for a past experience is infinitely better than having to regret the suppression of desire. *Live the fantasy*. Die happy.

There is no point in questioning whether or not the slipper will fit, one day. Those lost feelings are meant as a rededication to what you are waiting for; given that you've identified exactly what you want. If you have, then the chances are very good. Such traits cannot be left to implications. If you are working to be the best you can be, then the right one and better experiences are still ahead of you; your love will not remain unrequited. Once found, if you continue to focus on the key elements which bring a relationship into existence, it can live forever—meaning indefinitely.

There is only so much time and so many people you can run across in your life, and so many more you will miss. The one you find may be right for you, but be certain that there are others. With 85 million singles in the United States alone—half the adult population—about *thirty thousand* possibilities exist in every age group and major city. It is always possible that your heart can be taken by another, more passionately and more completely. What counts most is that the one you're with brings positive feelings and experiences into your life, not pain, shame, distrust or anger. With a solid moral frame of reference, people can confirm for themselves what acceptable behavior is and what it isn't. They can see what is sanctioned by life and what is damned. Just as we all draw in air to further our lives, most will gravitate to the wholesome, meaningful, civil path. In a morally aware, rational society, satisfying encounters will become that much easier to find.

Enemies

Self-made Man in essence, doesn't often understand enemies, or how to have them. He doesn't understand disrespect; he doesn't understand the justification for negativity between rational beings—or what he supposes them to be. The nature of his own consciousness does not prepare him for the irrational. With his life's focus on generating and directing his own energy, their plotting hatred, jealousy and parasitism is inconceivable; a complete waste of resources. He knows there is something very wrong with those who spend energy in this way. He sees their open or veiled abusiveness—a glaring sneer or a malicious cowardice, poorly hidden under undisciplined expressions—and still can't quite believe it. The source seems abominable—so total a lack of self-esteem, that others become the roving temporary center of their attention, not to experience elation or hero worship, but for the exact opposite; to vent *their* greatest passion—the desire to hurt. Self-made Man doesn't often understand the attack, or the motivation. The Fear-driven seem offended by his very existence; a malady outside his power to solve. Its only solution seems for him to stop *being;* a demand he would never approach others with.

His enemy in any context is his antithesis—the Spirit Murder. I recall being disliked and feared, because I could always see much more than such people wanted me to. Implicitly I knew we were enemies, through something I was willing to see and something they refused to see. It was our pattern of consciousness that was incompatible; it made us mortal enemies. The Fear-driven cannot handle life's problems, so they cause others tension and loss, excommunication and violence. Conversation is refused: a point by point discussion would reveal their immoralities, so they avoid it or any other reasonable discipline, at all costs. Self-made Man can do nothing with the irrational; he can make no progress and find no happiness, so contextual isolation is the only solution. By habit, he isolates all forms of irritation and expands all forms of fulfillment; his cognitive pattern brought to social issues. His proper action in response to evil is to grant it no energy. He counters deception by stalling its pattern, denying the rewards expected by its use. He steps aside and lets their own poison consume them.

Typically, he dispenses with the issue of like and dislike, as he doesn't care what such others think, if they think at all. His self-esteem is not subject to their opinion. He pays attention to his own desired inertias, especially when stifled by association with another. Ultimately, he does not preserve relationships with those who subject him to any form of insincerity. He conforms to no subversion and remains on the level instead; naming what must not be named. Watching them scurry is his payment for the burden of its endurance. He *demands* the natural freedom that all human beings require in order to function, just as he grants and fosters it in others. He *demands* civility and the fostering of virtue, or removes himself from their path of destruction at once. When he is cornered with no chance of escape, he fights for his life—in premise as well as body—whether it takes place in a courtroom, or on the street. Death premises never get away with an uncontested acceptance.

As he approaches none with violence, he permits no such violation. Cognitive independence puts Self-made Man beyond the living need of parasitism, or any premise that leads to it. The disagreement of another is accepted, and respect for positions of authority over their realms of control goes without question. As long as his rights are not violated, no override is ever attempted. His response to those violating proper boundaries is self-defense, period—of himself and others—physically and spiritually. He views violence as a life-threatening insult, its initiation of which is never to be tolerated. When in danger, he counters force with the force necessary to stop it. Only those choosing force and its variants as a means of their physical and spiritual sustenance are the damned, *never* those who defend their right to life when it is threatened.

Chapter Six

Passionate Expressions

"He was an artist, and what he was, he was only through music." —Immortal Beloved

Everyone's life should feel like a sculpted work of art, and self-destiny is the name of the game. Those who seek exaltation by living means, will wish to experience and express it through every physical sense and their guiding power: the deepest, clearest, most tenaciously earned understandings and resultant emotions. Man needs to bring the deepest meaning of his life as well as his most profound and passionate expression towards it, into his immediate perceptual awareness. Since his struggle in the pursuit of values is lifelong, he needs regular spans of time where he can experience a sense of completion—the reward of his values having been achieved. Romantic art satisfies this desire. It shares the feeling of his goal's actualization, and the experience serves as fuel to carry him further. The intention of romantic art is to uphold Man's highest, to show him the reward for his climb—for his sparkling rationality, bravery and determination in the quest of life—meaning natural, organic life. Romanticism is a field of pure rewards for a life of challenge—the challenges of Self-made Man.

Imagine flipping through a magazine in a waiting room, and coming across a picture that you can't take your eyes off. You may not know why, but you are drawn back to it again and again, until you have to cut it out and take it with you. That is the response provoked by the best of art; it extracts a deep personal meaning; a fascination with the emotions and attraction it conjures.

125

Romanticism is a sanctuary for the best within us—where the results of our excruciating effort are loved, encouraged and fostered. It reflects the *gratification* in living effort. The realm of romanticism is the projection of rational, reachable human ideals, stylizing every facet of Man and existence, every kind of thought, every shade of emotion, every shape of detail and the grace in action of all living things—whose subject matter is inexhaustible.

Every art form isolates a limited number of physical senses, eliciting cognitive stimulation and appreciation for the depth and range of each. Painting enhances vision, music enhances hearing, yet all streamline and stylize cognition. They are a treat for every sense they affect—a wonderful reward and guide for their correct use, making sensate perception a pleasure, honing in on the very joy of living. The most significant works of art convey the purest, cleanest motivations and share with us their deference for Man.

The Artist and the Observer. A romantic artist shares the reward of his own mental state, revealing his deepest images of our stature and our environment. What he has chosen to present in colors, in landscape, in words, in musical harmony or in form is what he has trained his senses to focus on—what he finds most significant. To the extent that an artist is rational, his work will reflect living values. His choice of subjects is guided by his acceptance of existential reality. His style will reflect his own cognitive power; his skill reveals the effort and devotion he brings to his values. The highest art properly integrates subject matter, technical skill and meaning, idealizing the *use* of Man's perceptual and cognitive tools in the work's every detail. As an artist and a man, he has the capacity to *generate*, to create new depth and new ways of positively affecting the senses and of impacting the intellectual and emotional pool of his audience. At its best, romantic art helps Man to recognize what matters most, leading him to find deeper meaning in the range of his vision. By integrating the most prized attributes of a work's subject, the artist displays the order, structure and meaning behind moral awareness. The deepest and most moving pieces require the most pleasant concentration to enjoy, and it is proper that they be the most gratifying. Art is the most potent medium for exposing the essence of an artist's character, as well as that of the observer.

A man's sense of life determines his response to art—his view of himself in relation to what he accepts as possible to Man. All human beings take romanticism seriously. Their reaction to it, positive, negative or neutral, simply reveals the consonance or contrast of their accepted premises. From a consonant standpoint, listening to a symphony he might think, "This is how happiness or sadness (some particular emotion or cognitive action) feels to me." Observing a sculpture, he might think, "This is my image of what a man should be and can be." Watching a romantic movie he might think "This is how I want to feel about someone, and how I want them to feel about me." Reading literature he might think, "This describes me," or, "This represents my views." When art is disconnected from the real world or our current possibilities, he might respond with, "If I had superhuman traits, this is how I would use them," or, "If such a diabolical evil existed, this is how valiant men would fight it." In acceptance, his ultimate response is, "This is a reflection of life as I see it. In worship of life, this expresses my tribute."

Imagine observing the milky smoothness of a shapely woman's statue, then to feel the startling contrast of touch to discover it's marble. Imagine the tautness in the statue of a Herculean figure and *its* texture, which comes as no surprise. The highest art always projects the strongest man, the most stunning independence, the most beautiful physical form and poise, the purest confidence, and the most concentrated purpose—attributes that serve the challenge of life, which we admire and wish to acquire. The next time you walk through a gallery, by holding the moral standards of life and comprehension as your frame of reference, the art—good or bad—will make much more sense. Devoted to human life, I care for only one style, which is the subject of this chapter. The Self-made pattern of cognition *is* the means to create romantic art, as well as the means to achieve its projections in real life.

Art and Development. A romantic sense of life is first felt as a response to existence. It can then be felt with others, but as it is built on the achievement of independence, it can never be felt before. As our premises change, our tastes adapt to match the emotional content thrown off at any given time. As romantic art is a showcase for human virtue, its themes are universal. All men can identify the basic emotion conjured by a musical piece or a scene, but they vary widely in their estimation of its value. We respond most strongly to art that reflects the current depth of integration within us. As our depth of consciousness includes more than art, we pick the elements that suit us, and leave behind those that don't. When a work of art reflects our premises without contradiction, we will wish to add it to our medium of life. As we grow, we come to value elements previously not understood, and move past an equal number of others. Art is an evolving confirmation, continuously rewarding a man for expanding the power of his consciousness.

The structure of music can be defined mathematically, as can sight. Both operate via electric impulses, but this is only a physiological parallel. One needn't become a math wiz to enjoy music. What is considered pleasurable by a rational consciousness must exist within a certain auditory range. Music has the power to effect the emotions directly, as it rearranges the process of cognition to begin with the reward. It moves from sensate perception to emotional response, to appraisal, to understanding. *Emotions* are mathematical as well—the moving sum of the process of cognition—a living, resonant answer to one's experiences. Sound is a natural result of the motion of entities, emanating a state of harmony or tragedy to be picked up by those having the proper organ. In the nature of sound itself—of amplitude and frequency in the propagation of a sine wave— artists recreate the flow of life. Danger vibrates within a certain range of frequency, while its amplitude determines the scale of the danger. Tranquility has its own range as well.

Passionate Expressions

Life experience implicitly indicates the harmonic resonance of every human emotion to Man. For example, a child can listen to a symphony and get nothing from it, as he has yet to develop the depth necessary to experience the emotions and concepts it intends to express. As he encounters them in life, he will come to recognize and appreciate them in music.

Romantic Extensions of Art. I've heard criticism against the use of animals as the subjects of art, with the argument that art uplifts Man and should exemplify Man alone—and I don't agree. Why are wild animals so often used as symbols? The strong, proud stature of an eagle, the power and agility of a tiger, the alertness of an owl, and their total confidence show us beings who act on purpose and without the concept of doubt—a moral dilemma provoked by religion and altruism's undercutting of Man. What emerges for our contemplation is an entity acting consonant with its own nature. We extract the virtues we can practice in human terms, just as we do from superheroes. Art was created by Man *for* Man of course, but its subjects can cover all of existence and beyond, to the limit of what a man can dream and project.

Along this line, sometimes we run across products that dramatize the deep thought and care that was put into them—products that have the grace of art and preform exquisitely—so well designed, they bring a sense of glamour to their use, accenting our view of Man in the process. I consider them extensions of art, falling into a few main categories from least to most significant: 1) Products of all kinds, from disc players to hammers to furniture and appliances. 2) Automobiles and other forms of transit. 3) The architecture of dwellings, factories, parks and all other human environments. 4) The structure of a human being and human action—its physical style and style of thought, its health, beauty, elegance, tact, class and poise. 5) The structure of human institutions—their profitability, their timely pursuit of endeavors and their accomplishment, the interwoven psyche of top-down conveyance, motivation and coordinated action, and their stability and long range effects.

Man himself and his utilitarian creations cannot be classified under the strictest definition of art, as they do not serve the primary of contemplation. But they approach art, being as beautiful in form as they are in function, and personally, I get the most satisfaction from active participation involving the objects and entities I prize. I've always sought the most artistic surroundings as the medium for myself to become worthy of; be they cars, places, companions, or ideas. While photography is not classified as a primary art either, I find most of my visual inspiration through it; in periodicals covering exotic cars and locations, glamorous people and events. Though I grant romantic significance to sculpture and indulge the rare opportunity to enjoy it, I'd take People or Playboy Magazine over a museum pass any day (looking at mummies doesn't make my heart race). Perhaps this is just youth talking, but in my view, the most beautiful and successful people standing still or in motion are the attributes exemplified in sculpture anyway. In theater, I prefer the wholesomeness and intellectual depth of old movies. Notice the poise of actors and actresses in the sixties; the flowing poses lost in modern productions. Look at the musicals where half an actor's value was in motion and song, not just in memorizing lines or hostility. I miss the days when every perceivable facet of an actor's being was honed into art; when it was truly a profession. We looked up to our heroes in a much deeper sense then, as there was so much more to grasp and value in their conduct. It was a projection of the human ideal. Imagine what a man's bearing tells you of his character when he stands straight, looks alert, speaks clearly and moves decisively. The use of Man's body expresses his sense of life. The use of his mind reveals his worth. As an actor or an observer, his response to romanticism is a window to his soul.

We need a romantic release to renew and refocus, as we travel our own roads of self-actualization. Such excruciating effort is draining, and to have a chance to feel the state of arrival at one's ideal is all the motivation we need to stay the course. Literature is the most important, as nothing beats an explicit explanation of romantic premises, though I find music the most accessible: exaltation in four minutes or less! Literature requires a much greater investment in time. Notice we can't sit around in a state of euphoria for long however; nature requires that we top off our tanks and get back on the road. Those fully conscious of the virtue in their own progressive intent remain aware of this artistic link at all times, allowing romanticism to accent their every endeavor. It can be experienced any time one stays cognizant of one's actions; being aware of choices and of making *the right* choices, seeing their cause and effect together, at the greatest range one cares to define. Though art by definition is put in the box of "selective re-creation of reality," *all actualized* human ideals have artistic value and emit the emotions of glamour, which those who work towards them, deserve to feel.

Many people exist in a constant state of intellectual and romantic starvation. I have found very few vents—very few works of art that could give me the release I needed. Deeply moving, meaningful pieces are rare, but they do exist in every medium, such as film, music, painting, sculpture and literature. There are enough to hold onto, and once you identify that ideals are contextual, you begin to see them and feel them, everywhere. At the most significant level, listening to Beethoven or James Horner's *Legends of the Fall*, reading Ayn Rand's works or studying Greek sculpture or paintings by Monet or Vermeer, are among the only times I feel compensated for my effort. Other means stair step down in importance, though are still very positive, such as watching a deeply romantic movie, driving and studying an exotic car, enjoying a desirable companion, helping those bright and eager to learn, looking at the city, the mountains, the ocean or just moving through the world, breathing fresh, clean air. All feed a romantic sense of life.

The Life of a Purist

"The thorns of life wounded him deeply, so he held fast to his art...He lived

Passionate Expressions

alone, because he had found no second self. Thus he was; thus he died; thus he will live for all time." —Immortal Beloved

I'm not sure what level of consciousness allowed Beethoven's music to have so profound an effect on me. I would not have appreciated it at eighteen. It was my mid-twenties at the earliest when philosophy began to give me an intellectual clarity beyond my companions that I realized this pursuit of knowledge was separating me from the rest of the world. I could not turn back and be happy; I could not move forward with those unable to keep pace. I had to go alone to reach not just my own pinnacle, but a loneliness so complete in its torture, that it was beautiful to feel. It was and is a tear-filled honor. I've reached my goal so completely, that I barely have the emotional language to express it. Everything I imagined should be possible through it from a cognitive standpoint, has come true. In the process, I've become a mind free of all barriers, able to convey straight into language, the organic spiritual implications of good or evil at all levels.

I write for personal development as much as I do for others. It is a form of therapy, as all art is for its creator. It is my expression, my passion, and it addresses some of the most important questions of my life. It is not just about spiritual preservation and growth; for me it is the growth itself. The journey was made easier with the knowledge that others had lived as well, whose devotion to truth could be traded only for death; and Beethoven is my favorite to ponder.

An artist has trouble at times, for his unwillingness or inability to face opposition and share the forward vision that would explain his truth. That may come from the futility of past attempts, but regardless, his science is for himself. His passion is the art itself, not its conveyance; its meaning to him, not any meaning it may have for others. He doesn't approach others with malice, so being attacked is unfamiliar. He has no emotional dependencies, so he secures few social connections. Viewed as unsociable, the crowd is against him. Arguing his case is unfamiliar, so he presents his work, and must let it speak for itself. He is unbelievably stubborn; the execution of his work is not open to question. He doesn't care if anyone likes him; personal like or dislike is irrelevant; *objective evaluation of his art* is all that concerns him. With the crowd mentality each looking to the other to decide what they themselves think, he never reaches it. Often he carries the look of facing a firing squad, pinning his own murderers to the wall before he goes down. This is his selfishness of soul—a man who thinks alone without fear—as rational selfishness is most profoundly, an artistic attribute.

Rarely do we see an individual take his music where no one has ever been before; to master his instrument and make it do things no one has ever seen, opening their eyes to new possibilities. That is the true artist, and they exist in all fields—not just the popular ones. The excitement is found in the cognitive adventure that all pioneers take. A rock star writing a song he knows will be a hit, has much in common with a scientist who invents a new material that he knows will revolutionize industry.

It is interesting how we automatically expect everything in their lives to be perfect, but they are just people. Still, the true artists do have something that the rest do not: a pure devotion that opens all doors eventually, a devotion that gives them a satisfaction in life that is and should be the envy of the rest.

Beethoven, though light at times, is profoundly moving, touching a depth that Mozart and most other composers could never come close to. If I hadn't been scarred by others, if I didn't work as hard as I have to build my knowledge and get disregarded, trampled and used for it, I would not respond to his music so strongly. "Moonlight," conveys to me, "This is what I've brought to the world, and this is what the world has given me in return. This is how I feel about their response to my gifts, thus far." After what he suffered through, that Beethoven could still feel what he had to feel in order to write what he did, is astonishing. After enduring open public derision towards him, "Ode to joy" was his final answer to them.

As in Beethoven's case, it is not necessary for a genius to be so distant, but socially, very few people can satisfy a genius's emotional needs. A genius rarely begins life being considered a genius. He begins with a passionate intrigue with this world, and that drives a desire so strong to know everything he can about everything he encounters, that he comes to know more about his subjects of interest than anyone else, and can take the next steps. Socially, he looks for confirmation of how strongly he feels about living—about discovery and about the majestic limitlessness of all we can do. That is what he needs the people around him to reflect, and what he rarely finds. *They don't have to match his ability,* just his unguarded, passionate innocence; and he can tolerate nothing less.

If I had the opportunity to go back in time and talk philosophy with Beethoven, I'm pretty sure he would have kicked me out of his office. He would not consider relinquishing authority in any realm he practiced as a human being; even if it were not his specialty. The raw artist is beautiful in function, yet often neglects elements of life that could smooth his path. Lacking this refinement, he often suffers neurotic behavior, relationship dysfunction, money problems and incommunicability—acting as a barrier to his joy. He is notoriously messy and barely notices it. All passionate valuers work that way; he concentrates on essentials only—on the kernel of his values—and 'orderly' means nothing to him beyond the content of his consciousness. Comfort is not his primary concern and neither is harmony, all that can wait. Only production matters. The pain of dealing with life's administration is trumped only by the pain of time taken from his endeavors, so outside concerns languish. But mastering these facets and having them flow together would *serve* his work. The investment would pay great dividends in fresh, bountiful energy over a lifetime. Philosophical and moral clarity would profoundly affect his art, as well as ease his relations with others. The philosophy one accepts determines what one considers worthy of artistic expression, and surprise, surprise, all the most notable artists in essence, have held the same philosophy; the philosophy of the Self-made.

Passionate Expressions

I have encountered only four pure spirits in history thus far: Ayn Rand, Ludwig von Beethoven, Benjamin Franklin, and Bruce Lee; artists to whom no compromise ever clouded their truth. The history of art is a spectrum I'm rather new to, and I'm sure there are purists in all other fields as well. We should all seek those of honest motive as companions, with pure living motivations as primary traits to develop in ourselves. When you can introspect, "I sense something wrong in my motive; how can I make my intentions perfectly honest and perfectly clear to myself and to others?" When you have the bravery to do this consistently, you will have taken the greatest, most crucial step to correcting and streamlining your psycho-epistemological process, and your romantic experience and vision will begin to grow exponentially. As an artist or not, your living direction will be brought in parallel with the purist.

I know that no matter how much I do in life, it will only be so much. No matter where I stop, from that point others will one day carry the work further. I'll enjoy my life and my work much more if I get enough sleep, when I feel properly relaxed and properly rewarded. I take my time now, and cherish the action I've devoted my life to. As a result, *Moral Armor* will be as pure a romantic effort as my present capacity permits.

Fame

"The nice thing about being a celebrity is that, if you bore people, they think it's their fault." —Henry Kissinger

There are flagship cars and flagship people. With men of stature and ability in any field, so acute an effort advancing their specialty generated such positive results, that it brought them to prominence. Their position indicates they've justified our belief in them through the virtues they practice, and our respect for proper ideals is a down payment on the worth of our future being as well. In a free country, there is a fairer distribution of *stature*, as it is a direct result of talents empowered to climb to heights determined solely by their own will.

The Nature of Fame. All products that live in popularity contain natural elements of mass experiential validation. They face, solve or express, problems and concerns of existence. Every notable concentrates an audience—*who* they draw is a reflection of what they are and vice versa; the value of the audience itself is reflected in what they're drawn to. Fame is a relationship. As Self-made or as Spirit Murderer, one fosters and the other corrupts, but both further the road *chosen* or condoned by their audience.

Often, an artist or performer gains popularity by reflecting the mass mood of the moment. His work can be moral or immoral, reverent or irreverent, but either way, he provides his audience with an appropriate emotional release or response for a mood their mutual premises lead them to feel. The depth and nature of the emotion determines the range and term of his popularity. The Self-made are drawn to art that projects the joy of triumph, reflects the refinement of hard-won values, and either provokes states of rationally-based euphoria or confirms the intellectual loneliness of the pain and injustices they suffer. They are drawn to products that solve these problems. For those orphaned by their family and friends, concentrating an audience is a means of attaining one's *true* family, in the way we choose a spouse—by voluntary mutual interest.

The Dream and Its Reward. The healthiest motive for desiring fame is in order to gain the respect of peers for one's own valuable contributions; to reach them through *accomplishment* for the purpose of reward and further accomplishment. Recognition from the balance of mankind is just a consequence—hopefully positive. The intention is to become and associate with the best, the brightest and the most adventurous people on Earth, regardless of whether they are famous or not—the top one percent. That amounts to four million people in this country alone, and they exist in all other countries as well. With mass moral clarity, this percentage of the population will continue to increase.

The best artists do their work for their own pleasure, and if others like it enough, it can become their career. That should be the goal of every man; to do exactly what he loves in a way others appreciate enough to allow him to be immersed in its expression. Artists are in touch with the deepest part of themselves, so odds are, they are happier; and we should seek that same kind of happiness—to live just what fulfills us.

Fame of course, transcends art and talent transcends fame. Entertainment, politics, science, production—we have stars in all fields, known or up and coming, and they are our leaders. *Independent devotion to a craft* is the parallel, not just luck, timing or connections. There are tons of people out there who don't need schooling or grants to develop what *might* be there. It's there, crafted and honed by their will, having devoted their lives and all of their time to their passion. What they need is a world who is going to look, a world that can recognize greatness and have the self-esteem to say so. They don't need help with their work, they need only the honest, objective judgment of their observers. And a credit card number with expiration date. Just a joke, but the financial viability of a project is essential—it must be calculated. When the idea is properly designed to account for commercial value, the dream is then ready to come true.

Those who haven't made it yet think we're sitting on top of the world— and it's true. Who wouldn't want to attend events where we get to say, "There's so and so," and enjoy the awe of each others achievements? Everyone has problems, but *we* solve them. Who is really at the top? All those who practice the goal-seeking, rational process of cognition, followed by the sincere process of interaction. We are the truly proud—those of honest, healthy esteem—and we enjoy the rest as well, famous or not, by mutual appreciation for our respective goals, granting equal standing in each others presence. I love listening to a scientist speaking of new ideas, or an astronaut looking forward to a shuttle mission, or a fire fighter recounting a blaze, regardless of whether two other people have ever heard of him. I get to project myself into their journey and experience a parallel adventure outside my own chosen path. I love excitement and future pride coming from anyone, no matter how long a struggle lies ahead for them. I love the reflective glow in those who have accomplished wonders, looking backward and forward, surrounded in time by the grace of their own moral action, emersed in the pleasure available to all who face uncharted territory.

Some say fame doesn't change them. Should it? I'd say "Of course I've changed! The work is done and I've made it. This is my celebration." Fame is properly, a celebration of life. With the nature of one's fame being what one expected, it is a fourth step validation; an indication that all that has come before—logically linked—was correct. Fame *should* show a difference—a greater certainty—a view you can't get unless you climb the mountain. At its highest, fame is a *moral* acknowledgement; it is the world saying "Well done." Its value is profoundly personal, the social reward for achieving one's deepest moral ambition.

Here is *my* moral ambition: to achieve a world view like none before me, to bring order and moral clarity to all human action, to solve the greatest mystery of life, and free mankind through the purest form of epistemological processing. I'm Ronald E. Springer, a.k.a. *Moral Armor*. My unique ratio? One in *six billion*. This is my time to shine, so I'm going to have fun and be at my best, just as I get to watch the work of others and be enlightened or entertained by their creations. Presumptuous? Extremely. Pretentious? Never. I want the world to see me and say, *that* is an American. That is what is possible on Earth; a product of freedom—pure, strong and proud—possible to anyone who has the chance to live as a *human being*.

The Pattern of Fame. On a magazine cover for the new millennium, journalists were speculating on who would shape the next century. Flipping through it, I thought, "They seem to have missed me." Why's that? Why do we gain reverence only after we get the fame? Causes are rarely rewarded even within our own process—just creative action. When I bought my first Lamborghini, some were awed, but most still couldn't recognize the virtue which made the achievement possible, and hence, see no value in the five years I've dedicated to this work.

Where are the famous people of tomorrow? Are you one of them? There is a certain bearing of those with future promise—that of being unstoppable, but without tension; lacking any concern for being liked or approved of by others. They've made a final verdict on their own destiny and their ideas or plans, requiring no sanction from the outside. They can suffer deficits in any other aspect of their lives; in public relations, personal relations, or finances, but they are ferociously possessive of their work—their love, their creation—and will refuse to compromise it for anyone. They would appreciate a sanction of and for their effort, but ultimately they can survive without it and they must—until their talents become so potent, it is obvious to all.

For example, Benjamin Franklin worked diligently through years and years of effort of open willingness to reconstruct understanding. The result of fame and fortune was inevitable, and he knew it. Anyone who devotes himself to years of tenacious effort on one beloved subject, will become one of its best, a potentially famous, prominent spokesman in that field. Whether it is rock and roll, industry or philosophy, they are all businessmen, transacting the business of living, and in reaching new heights of their own, they will be well-known and treated with regard.

Trouble comes after we struggle to reach the top, then try to put a strangle hold on our success and popularity. Everything grows old; eventually, we must pass the torch. Go ahead and pass it gladly to the next generation of achievers. All too soon, they will need the maturity to pass it along as well. If you can, mentor what lies ahead for them. Be a part of their success, not its opposition. It's going to happen anyway, so we're better off to welcome the inevitable passage of time. The typical pattern of fame is like a roller coaster— the biggest hill is climbed first, you peak and then move fast and furious from there, often not realizing you're going downhill. Fame is no more static a value than is life. The question to ask isn't "How long will it last?" but "How many times do I want to climb the mountain?"

There is one tip to longevity; if your popularity is based on sound fundamentals of existence, your ambers will burn long after your fire dies down. Examples: Aristotle, the founders of the American Constitution, Beethoven and Bruce Lee. Next to personal exaltation, social acknowledgement and an ethically-based exaltation is a sacred reward. Just imagine being able to say, "At one time, I reached so high in life, the whole world stopped to look."

Axiomatic Longevity. As men mature, their spiritual needs advance geometrically. The works they choose to buy must reflect their own inner depth, and their choices stay with them for as long as the emotions it ratifies remain a part of their experience. The life pattern of nourishment, flourish, expel, and re-nourish, is physio-epistemological of course, but shows up in the realms of art as well, as art is an extension. An author or a musician must develop subsequent advancements, or the following withers and dies. A product based on wholesome ideas will live. A product built on a morally bankrupt foundation will not.

For example in music, if you try to adjust to what the music scene is now, you'll be mediocre. If you play to your emotions about your conflict with this age, you'll be good. If you pander, you'll fail; if you speak from the heart, you win no matter what. Be honest! Go with your strongest emotion, as it indicates your greatest problem, or its solution. It is so easy to be in when you're in touch with your own passions. When you are, you can *convey* another's passion for them—the magic of an artist—through music or any other medium. You can stay in touch with any age.

No one likes getting older. As we do, we notice rifts and incompatibilities with the younger generations. No matter our efforts to remain hip, the expanse of our vision puts us in another class, thank god. The media ceaselessly focuses on the latest and greatest glitter, stirring an emotional storm, which equates the loss of our youth as if it is the loss of our lives. Trying to keep up and stay young in the way popular advertising suggests is a futile pursuit, stultifying our own maturation. The Self-made lets go of this stress, and of what is no more. He embraces his future, and discovers that youthful vitality need never be lost. There is a whole life to live beyond our first twenty-five years; rich with togetherness, significance, discovery, and adventure if we seek it. There is a place for us, and a role to satisfy. We can watch the young move up the scale we've already experienced, enjoying their advance while we push the limits of ours.

What You Owe Your Fans. Beautiful, wealthy and intelligent people are like the famous in regard to society's treatment of them. A moral key to their character, an indication of their epistemological bias—anticipation vs. fear—is how they use their influence. Socially, do they use it to shut people out, to stir trouble, to take advantage or to bring others up? Fans want their heroes to be glamorous and beautiful. They want not just symbols to imagine, but to strive for; symbols that are real. A sparkling entity is wonderful to emulate. The moral role of a famous person requires no duty; it is simply as a proper role model. Mastering the conveyance of our patterns of fulfillment is a sacred obligation— almost paternal. One needn't use prominence to evangelize outside one's field, but only continue to earn their fan's favor by honing the expertise responsible for their success, expanding it and sharing its method candidly, to boost others and confirm their reverence for greatness.

As a role model, much more than a stylish outfit and the right pose is necessary. Possessing any clearly distinguishing attribute sets one apart and requires special skills to deal with the public interest or any disturbances it causes. If left uncontrolled, the attribute becomes a disenchanting impediment— for all involved. When the interaction would happen anyway, its *flow* should be by design. There is a wonderful dynamic involved with a star who really has it together. They move into a crowd with a plan and exit with a plan. Everyone is treated respectfully, and the entourage as a microcosm places the least hindrance on the flow of society around them; regulating but not stopping it. By managing these forces, we can spend more time in public and do it pleasantly, providing a safer, more positive experience for all, as well as a more glamorous impact.

What You Don't. As a fan, try not to be disheartened if you don't get the attention you desired. Celebrities are likely on their way from one engagement to another. They have to stay on track, which is often a key issue operating in the background of their minds.

Regardless of the honor in your motive, remember that this is a person who is harassed, followed, stared at and picked apart, who while holding their head high, must fight the media barrage constantly kicking at their shins. You can make any interaction much easier for them by adhering to the following: 1) Try never to approach during a meal. Engage them before the food is served or on the way out only. This is peace and quiet time, clean hands to eat food with time, and no talking or spitting complements over the food time. 2) Don't bar their way on a sidewalk. If they've stopped, it's alright to approach, but approach non-confrontationally and without surprise. Advancing strangers are intimidating for anyone—please be aware of it. The relaxation of lunch and shopping is their chance to be normal, and the experience is precious. Let the connection be visual alone. Autographs are no problem, but many celebrities don't wish to shake hands on the street. One clammy, sticky hand is enough for anyone to cringe at the prospect of encountering another, so let them be the one to offer. In my case, due to a biking injury, too firm a handshake is actually painful now. A wave, a smile and nod, or informal bows are the most appreciated forms of connection. 3) Don't trip over the world to meet them. If it seems that important, ask yourself if that's true for them as well. The prominent look *past* those uncollected, and it is those who maintain composure and tactfully observe from a distance who have their thanks—and their respect. The key is to *reflect* them; then you'll have their attention.

Fame is a value, but it can be equally wonderful to be anonymous, as negative attention is much worse than anonymity. At any level, we like to be appreciated for what we've done, but there are those who hate us for it. When they make a point to let us know that in person, it can be quite unsettling. Most prefer only to be known by and interact with those of good will, but it needn't taint our view of the world or of mankind. What is 'the world' anyway, but those we admire and those we don't? Helping to keep their private time peaceful and mature will shorten the distance between fans and celebrities, spiritually and socially.

Chapter Seven

Institutions of Good

"So far as possible, the people everywhere shall have that sense of perfect security, which is most favorable to calm thought and reflection."
—Abraham Lincoln

This quote of Abraham Lincoln's is in essence, the worldwide 6-8 level goal of a Self-made Man; *true* peace on Earth. It has never been clear however, just what this goal rests upon.

Sound institutions are built upon sound relationships, which are built upon sound cognition. All Self-made organizations share the same structure and hierarchy, as they are all designed by the same kind of mind. Productive groups who practice and preach ideals which bring freedom, peace and bounty to men, are the foundation of civilization. Self-made business and political leaders see the greatest power in truth, being open, honest and fully accountable for their activities. They make no pointed attempt to effect the lives or business interests of others, as others are not the means and therefore not the subject of their thoughts. They seek voluntary exchanges and enter negotiations with their own backbones, prepared to satisfy the terms agreed on. They put their best foot forward as good will requires in all endeavors with others, intending to leave a healthy impression as their only means to secure future associations. They enjoy the opportunity of a free market environment, as fixed rewards draw only yawns from enterprising men.

Throughout history, the Self-made have made our existence simpler, safer and more convenient. We don't face the elements with our bodies; we find ways to be protected while traversing the terrain. Moving through society, a business or getting an education is no different. We must maintain moral protection at every step—the awareness of a clear moral standard—so that we may put into perspective anything and anyone we encounter. To achieve certainty, one must be aware of sound moral principles—to understand their application and have the capacity to judge their use by others. Such honor is reflected in all romantic movies; it is the foundation of all heroic figures and actions, and is backed by all rational law.

Stand face to face with one other human being, and realize that trust— the integrity that you both respect and intend to live by a civil order—is all you have between you. In order to socially function on an abstract level—levels of cognitive construction such as learning, production and genuine enjoyment— one must be completely free of concern for any threat to one's life, and free of concern from any forcible loss. Add another person, and trust is all you have. Add five hundred, and honesty, rationality and integrity continues to be your guide. Add fifty million, and all that guarantees the character of men and keeps everyone from backing into corners, is trust. To trust is to feel comfortable about the actions and potential actions of the entities before you, which requires civil predictability, and that only comes with a clear pattern of cognition acknowledged by all, to which *every aspect* of human existence and interrelation is gauged— be it law, business, education or any other institutional entity that Man might form.

Motive is the most important premonition in the human world. Motive is what drives men to act. *What for* always precedes the *what*. If you know what drives a man fundamentally, you can forecast his every action. You can know him psychologically without knowing him through time consuming experience, and therefore expediently decide whether he is a proper candidate for whatever you are considering. You can see whether he would be good to work for, or if he would be a suitable employee. You can see whether he would be a good political candidate, jurist or spouse. You can extrapolate his rationale to see the kinds of institutions he would build. As every man is subject to the same standards, you can come to learn of yourself as well—your own motivations—and thus root out that which impedes your own progress in life. Without any interest in politics or international issues whatsoever, you may begin to see their connection to your spiritual destiny and that of your descendants, and be drawn in. With knowledge of the rational pattern of cognition, what appeared so vast and complex in world issues is now within your grasp—not only to understand, but to act on.

As human beings, the Self-made deserve to control all the essential institutions of Man. We should be in a position to assure that the rewards men have earned for their virtuous patterns of physical and spiritual sustenance, are received. It is the moral stability of *our* institutions that makes their interrelations and mankind's ultimate abstract goals, possible. Right now, we hold claim to about *half* our physical reward due to an unnecessary tax burden, and through the inversion of morality, are denied *almost all* of the other. As a result of historical moral barriers, the Self-made have yet to complete the 1-

2, 3-4, and 6-8 cognitive range and actualize our goals on a global scale. Our peaceful grace and generosity has always rendered us vulnerable in this regard, permitting simple acts of brutal violence to disrupt our long-term objectives of worldwide legal equality, fairness and civil order across the whole spectrum of human action. The essential institutional structures currently controlled by Spirit Murderers, must be recovered in time.

The heights we rise to are determined by a civilization's respect for axiomatic principles. When they are protected by law, the positive manifestations are unlimited. Self-made men have no 1-2 level organizations because none of us remain at that level. Being developmental, *education* is the only one that delves into it, so we'll start there, though education rises to guide the rest, across the span of time. Business and the civil flow of society—police, rescue, road and city planning—rest at the 3-4 level, while the longest-term objectives are shaped by the 6-8 level global vanguards, and we all contribute to each. Everything is driven by the stability of the foundation, which is why America has done so well relative to the rest of the world—why it has brought more wealth into the hands of more people than any other system of government. With moral clarity in the hands of the masses, our stretch into the future will contain more positive manifestations than I could possibly predict, and I look forward to witnessing them.

Education

As a huge fan and owner of exotic cars, I'm often asked by strangers how it is I'm able to afford them. I answer that *"I am able to afford them by the same process that is making you ask. I asked those who did the things I wanted to do and emulated them, gaining their abilities for myself. I then looked at my goals and interests, and chose that which had the greatest potential for financial reward."* As an adult, now wearing the shoes of my idols, I'm glad to answer their questions, or to put them in touch with someone who can. This is how the Self-made develop and pass on knowledge—by asking questions of others and of themselves. They are *drawn* to what they want—cars, relationships, careers— and it is no different with their education.

Doctors, businessmen and scientists have all of their knowledge organized by the epistemological structure of Man—all knowledge is. All the activities of Man are traceable and fully understandable by any other—time and willingness to acquire the knowledge are the only prerequisites. Even the running of a business empire or a country has base essentials, which anyone can understand. There is no need to fear computers or new technology. No need to ever consider oneself obsolete. Such are only tools to continually be made simpler, not more complex. Their purpose is to automate our tasks and simplify our lives, *freeing* our mental registers so that we can reach higher. One thousand years from now, their operation will remain designed to serve the physical and cognitive range of Man.

Philosophy. In our history, most philosophers have spent their time building useless theories and refuting others, often generating nothing new. The field was created by the passionate (Aristotle), heightened by the learned (St. Thomas Aquinas, The Founding Fathers, Ayn Rand), and ran into the ground by the malicious (Kant, Sartre, Marx). But all quietly performed revolutions in an era's thought, not necessarily for the better. It is time to bring philosophy back to its proper stature and place; to study and define the most rational, civil and invigorating approach to living.

How did Aristotle treat it? Implicit in his every action was the tenet that philosophy was for practical use, not the province for senseless utopias, or for pointless argumentation of the unprovable. A plumber in the role of philosopher could have done a more honest and better job than Kant, Nietzsche, Freud, Hegel or Marx. During the course of my writing, I inadvertently became a philosopher. Marx claimed that the essential division between men was economic; I say the essential classes of men are defined by the basic premise that drives their consciousness, and that all motives stem from within a man himself. Most used their minds to question whether or not the mind was of any use, and that became the limit of their contribution. The stinger for my work is, "Could I vent my philosophy in a job interview, and still get the job?"

Bad philosophers believed they could actually alter reason with words— to turn lead into gold—but only their fellow Spirit Murderers fell for it. The wise, to their credit, dismissed them, and the whole field of philosophy was tainted through cultural expulsion, prompted by those actually seeking sound, useful and intelligent moral guidance. The phonies removed science from philosophy, which made religion almost appealing by comparison, but they couldn't hide its truth and value forever. Philosophy *is* rocket science. It is a parallel field requiring the same depth and the real key factor—pure honesty. To the extent they are useful, such fields exist entirely without deceit. A rational philosopher has no interest in defying medical or scientific proof—new discoveries serve him. Only an irrationalist is at risk, pushing claims that are untrue.

With this work, I hope to return philosophy to its proper stature in education—that of coherently guiding Man to fulfillment in every aspect of his existence. Our education in essence, determines how we see ourselves, and its standard must be sound. A rational philosophy for living integrates *every single thing you know,* giving clear classification and clear links to where every bit of knowledge is coming from and going to. There is no limit to its usefulness, and that is a key reason for its debasement. How would you like to *know* beyond all doubt in moral issues, that you are right? What if such a capacity fortified your mind and brought you a peace and a resolve that you could never have known otherwise? If the people are spiritually self-sufficient, the con-man's game is up.

No matter what you do, philosophy will make you better at it. For example, I noticed that moral clarification resulted in such a state of inner calm that when I played golf, I lost my slice. When tension, or more to the point, chosen dysfunction, crept back into my life, my slice returned. When I faced the problem and solved it, my slice disappeared again. The stress of contemplating a difficult moral issue or an actual moral failure bleeds into your physiology, which manifests in your activities and is sensed by others. It is unavoidable. The only way to freedom and inner peace is moral clarity. Since realizing this truth, my vision has been restored to 20/20, which indicates a link between being *willing* to see and being *able* to see.

The Life Motive: Experiential Learning. If I'm away from practical business for too long, my ideas become impractical; disconnected from human experience and difficult to apply. Likewise, endless hours in a classroom can't hold a candle to experience. *Experiential learning* is head and shoulders above typical instruction, for many reasons. We use our whole body in application; not just our eyes and ears; there is no drifting off to sleep. We learn because we *want* to know; because the subject matter addresses some facet of the life we desire in our dreams. Self-generation is everything. Without the fundamental internal frame of personal preference driving assimilation, inefficiencies will be abound.

A certain level of individuals are beyond schools. They choose this very young; school is an exoskeleton they don't need. Their intellectual range includes all of existence, and inherently, wordlessly, these children know that the class subject matter is limited to the eyes of men who came before them, and that conclusions must be held off until their eyes see for themselves. They intend to (and will), integrate all matters important to them on their own, un-led and unhampered by any outside influence as all mental growth must be done. Knowledge itself is the product of individual men, expending passionate devotion towards their subjects of interest for the purpose of their complete understanding and use; not to pass tests. The knowledge existed *before* the schools did. Someone had to gather the information originally in order for it to be taught, and the life-furthering premise defining what to teach is based on why we learn—an awareness to be developed in all students.

Education is a business like any other. Only those who need it should pay for it, while competition should determine the success and quality of all schools. I agree with Benjamin Franklin that all citizens should be educated to the degree necessary to function in society, and that it serves them beyond all doubt. I agree with tax exemptions for parents who are dissatisfied with the record of public schools and pay instead for private educations. While home schooling is possible, I would never do it. If you're proven to be a good teacher for your own kids, you should be in front of a private classroom; otherwise, it is a senseless duplication of effort. Besides, kids need experience dealing with a wide variety of personality types and a wide range of ages and certainly their own. We learn a lot from other kids in watching and experiencing their attributes both good and bad; something Mom and Dad can't help us with. Besides, I couldn't imagine spending twenty-four hours a day with my parents hovering nearby. I couldn't imagine teenagers sitting there, taking *my* advice seriously if I'm not in a career that they intend to pursue for themselves. Past ten, it looks like a preposterous form of torture. The guff about outside forces causing them to go wrong is nonsense. There are certainly bad influences in the world, but there are many splendid forces as well, and ultimately, the prime mover is inside of them. Relax, and cut the cord. There are many facets of a purpose-driven lifestyle to be delegated—carefully, of course—and your child's education is one of them.

The True Worth of a Man. College could not contain me. The pace, the application—I had little tolerance for theoretical instructors who lacked real world experience. I left school because I wanted an education. Now, school is getting more tailored. It is beginning to reflect the true needs of commercial enterprises as well as fitting into varied lifestyles for students of all ages. But back then, self-help was in full swing, and I found the most valuable skills in the latest business and philosophy books, anything special interest written by a master, mixed with my own experiments. The self-help genre has answers for everyone; such programs make it a lot easier for the teacher to be in the right place at the right time. Formal education can be very valuable, but Self-made Man doesn't stop there. He seeks knowledge wherever he can find it.

I remember having questions about so many things—answers I was supposed to pretend to have already. I was made fun of for admitting my uncertainty, and those who taunted, would get hostile with any serious query. The best in each field were my teachers, through authorship—American presidents and statesmen, psychologists, philosophers and businessmen. They brought me up, but they neglected to mention the poor treatment the self-taught would suffer for our efforts. I reached a point of indignation, where convincing or seeking acknowledgment just wasn't worth it anymore, yet I was entranced with my style of living. I loved the advancement and the discovery, but those appreciative souls were few, and those who penalized were many. I was held up at another turning point. I couldn't give up my values, and I couldn't give up the world. If I continued forward, I was bound for more pain, yet I couldn't turn back and be happy. I couldn't shut down and conform. But pain from the outside never matched pain from the inside, so I kept going, to arrive at my own golden rule:

Warrior note: *One must be shameless about learning.*

I found many instructors who teach *and* work in their fields, and I took their classes. I found a mix of theory and practicality worked best for me—an apprenticeship education similar to that found in Europe, tailored to my interests alone, along paths acknowledged as commercially valuable. Such an education has cost no less—probably more as it has become a lifelong pursuit. But my conscience is clear—none of my time has been wasted and no false patterns have been ingrained.

There are great books written on every topic, great seminars, audio-programs and workshops designed to ingrain very specific skills, which you can walk out of the classroom with and use today. Anthony Robbins, Dr. Barbara De Angelis and many others to be found at any bookstore have passed on more expertise than you might imagine. Originally, self-help educators were classified with the religious TV charlatans selling eternal salvation charged to your Visa or Mastercard, but fakes are mixed in with every profession. The people who last, do so for a reason; often they are right. More right than anyone else. So right, it has made them rich, because they deliver on their promises. Tony delivers. Barbara delivers. Their work is responsible for some of the most well adjusted individuals and personal relationships on the planet. Donald J. Trump's business books hold some of the best advice I've ever seen, and he clearly leads by example. Often the best realize the value of their ability, and thank pride, they write it down. Warren Buffet, Ricardo Semler, Ayn Rand, Bill Gates—all deserve the highest praise for leaving us evidence of so many remarkable minds. How wonderful it is once again, to be so entranced by one's teacher.

Having taken control of my own education, it is hard to convey the immense pleasure I get from learning now. Learning is an adventure. Discovery is fascinating—out in the world and within my own mind. A mistake is just a mistake, to be corrected upon understanding. It only becomes a moral issue when it is masked and maintained, which is true individually, socially and organizationally. Having cognitive sincerity carry from one into the other is a terrific intellectual challenge. There are many business examples, but never have I seen a more honest, forward-thinking institution than NASA. Here is a group of people unafraid to admit the need to try something else. Perhaps the nature of their endeavor makes them more prone to adherence to the rational process of cognition—looking up to the stars and then solving the problem of reaching them. Mistakes can be made at any level—personal, societal, corporate, governmental—and rest assured with rational integrity, they can be corrected. I'm seeing calm, paced sincerity more and more everywhere I go—in traffic, in businesses, even at the post office—the result of our culture letting its hair down about how life must be. It's a healthy trend.

Everyone has their specialty. The Self-made yields to the mind with the most able capacity in any context, and takes charge when that person is him. If you are ready and able to lead, you must do it with the most active, alert and resolute countenance. It is my aim to concentrate the power of the ultimate virtuists; those who incessantly labor to advance their cognitive chains, formally or informally, degreed or not. The group of men currently focused on self-serving rational goals, based on nothing but rational actions are the most moral men among us. I've noticed at the other side of my journey, that we haven't given up the world as we thought. We blazed new paths for others to follow, and soon they will be traveled by the kind of quality companionship we desired. I've been willing to face any torrent necessary, but along this road, I've watched the sneers become quiet respect, and I'm very pleased with that; it means they understand now. Thank you.

Business: The Abstract Life of an Organization

A moral lesson can be learned (especially by the socialist-democrats), by witnessing America's finest corporations. They are the perfect example of men uniting in order to produce bounty—a fair, deserved, profitable result. Profit means that after a day's effort, you have something to show for it. Profitability is a sign of intelligence, not of greed. Profit in business is the balance left over from the process of production. A business has an abstract life, like a person, and profit is its lifeblood. Profit is the business equivalent of a man generating the physical energy necessary to allow the continuance of *his* life. Even in the process of learning, to end up with a greater sum is to profit intellectually. We see that plants and animals store food. Wealth and profit are fundamental patterns of life for *all* organisms—one, a form of potential energy stored to be made kinetic at our will, the other to monitor and safeguard our efficacy at the task of living. The notion that money and profit are the root of all evil has damned our ability to live. Money is simply a contract between individuals agreeing to trade their own best effort for the best effort of others. The paper money of a country stands for the total quantity of goods it can buy in that country. On an island with only a few people, money isn't necessary; we would simply trade the products of our effort directly, which would indeed be reduced to essentials. But in a civilization, it is easier to trade with a standard medium than having to hope a vacuum cleaner salesman has use for your stair-master. No, there is nothing wrong with the conceptual medium of money, nothing wrong with the honest, peaceful accumulation of capital, and nothing wrong with producing more than you consume, as *profit allows survival*. These are *essential* life-serving, forward-thinking, sound, civil and moral principles.

Like the biological structure of a person, a business is driven by its head. One's quality of life is determined by one's quality of thinking, as the health of a business is determined by the foresight of its leader. Business is a 3-4 endeavor, where the most successful are run by those who complete the cognitive structure without error. At the founding of every corporation is a man who knows *why* he is alive, and knows *how* to live. He is called greedy, but often the founder works for free; sometimes for *years* before his dreams take off. His lifelong surge is the desire to see how far he can go intellectually—brimming with productive activity to find the limit and never finding it. It's a game for the most profoundly moral. American business is magnificently complex, a most stimulating endeavor. An office to us is a second home—secretly more precious and more fulfilling than the first. Most Self-made become rich in their fluid human action, as wealth concentrates by civil means, into the hands of those most able to produce it. Knowing where and how to invest human energy, they are the masters of the medium. The basis of money is trust in the pursuit of human sustenance. The products of men will have the integrity of those who built them. Those who earn a fortune by moral means in a free system of exchange have accumulated a wealth of trust, and it *is* a rational measure of pride.

Sound Hierarchy. Abstraction is used correctly in the physical sciences and high-tech business, less efficiently in older businesses where the source has been lost, and often entirely inverted in government and religion. The man of greatest capacity at every level within the organization should lead. He should be chosen by his people, and replaced when he is no longer effective, as the life of the organization comes first. A business has a dynamic just like a human body, which gets sick if its focus strays—if it suffers dysfunction or comes to require a specialty which is different from that of its head. Each employee is a part of the company, and they contribute to or detract from its health with every action they take in its name.

At every level, men take specific aspects of existence and hone their specialties so that others will pay them to preform. The proper hierarchy of any organization displays expertise towards whatever it is they are doing; from the greatest life-giving power to the next greatest, and so on, but management is not the only direction determining the growth or value of an employee. One may specialize in the mechanics of business, or on the product itself, with no subordination in stature. Workers are valued according to the maturity, skill and efficiency brought to whatever it is they are employed to perform. A career path is defined first and foremost by the individual, and an artist for example will wish to practice his art, *not* manage other artists. Some prefer to practice a skilled trade rather than pursue a management role, or perhaps their life has been designed in such a way as to serve another primary interest. Regardless, management positions are not more important than those of the actual work being done; and often earn less. Only with the capacity to competently supervise the work being done, do they surpass others in the hierarchy. Managers should have some core medium of specialty which they practice as well—call them *working* managers. Without the exercise of a core medium, they are just secretaries. All positions should be vital to the welfare of the company, or they shouldn't exist.

The essential departments are already defined and understood in business: marketing, product development, accounting, production, and distribution. What must be defined is how people move *through* the organization and how they move *for* the organization. The corporate structure should eliminate as much overlap as possible. Departments must communicate of course, but a manager at any level should not be doing his subordinate's work or telling them what actions to take, no matter how competent he is. If he tries, he stands in the way of his employee's advancement and his own. Violating the process of cognition, he jumps in and provides *his* view of step two. He meddles with the employee's step three, and then denies them credit for step four at review time. Two analogies come to mind: in traffic, every driver must be responsible for his own vehicle; he has a planned intention and he carries it out, moving from point A to point B as instructed. The other is that of the human body: an indivisible entity, driven by millions of tiny blood cells. As blood cells each serve a specific function—to further the life of a body—each man fills a need, which the corporation's life could not do without. Such a cell doesn't have other cells nagging it along the way; it operates independently. It consistently faces opposition, which it handles on its own. If it fails in that action, it is removed by the body. Employees must be free to run the cognitive pattern for themselves. Responsible managers give employees clear actions to perform; handing out, not titles with undeclared expectations, but assignments with specific responsibilities. Provide assistance if you see them stuck or when asked, but otherwise, *get out of the way.*

An employer/employee relationship is governed by and must contain all of the essential attributes of any human relationship: rationality, civility, honesty, mutual interest and mutual benefit. Good managers don't require supplication in a world where force is banned; that is a psychological remnant of the past. If you deserve your position as a leader, you should be beyond tantrums, beyond neurotic dominance and be able to speak to anyone within your organization with objectivity and deference. Likewise, responsible employees are objective, sincere and perform tasks as or better than expected. They are emotionally mature and apply themselves as their interview promised they would. Satisfied employees and employers grow to be comfortable discussing the essentials of task and product that must be addressed, the intentions in business that must be addressed, and perhaps the life essentials of every man that can be shared. We all have dreams.

I've often witnessed a company executive looking for a way to persuade his people to stand behind the company's proud, long range goals as if they were their own; to display pure loyalty to *his* dream as if it was their own. If your campaign doesn't come with stock options, forget it. Such a mindset only comes with ownership. Mass support for another individual or his corporation above and beyond their own lives isn't sound—it isn't moral and it isn't ideal. All individuals work for *their own* health and objectives within the corporation— job satisfaction, advancement and financial reward—and they should. The company's health is a result of managing these forces wisely—having all of the independent entities flying in formation, while they are on your time.

The Pride of Competition. All sensible human activity, human organizations and human products are based on the preservation of human life, the cycles of human life and the range of comprehension of the human beings on this planet. They all operate by a 24-hour day; they respect the rejuvenation period of a human being, his daily range of travel, his cyclic dietary needs, and his necessary protection from the elements. These are primary needs. As a society grows more civil, it grows wealthy; secondary considerations—products expanding the joy of his existence—can be supported by the resulting economy, and in all endeavors of man, competition is born. When businesses try to steal customers from each other, it isn't actually stealing; there is no moral violation. No one has a right to patronage; all market activity is voluntary. If men dislike a product or if it is too complex, they won't buy it, and will find another way to satisfy their interests. This puts the investment of some companies at risk, which cannot be maintained for long. Our most complex products such as computers and software, will never extend beyond the range of an individual's comprehension for effective use; the free market will never allow such a breach. It's in every man's best interest that his products stay within the conceptual range and efficiency of the user and that he continually seeks to improve the attractiveness of his products to that end. In product development and experimentation, the best do a lot of arm-drags; we have to. When things don't work, we wipe the slate clean and try something else. The smarter we are, all other aspects of our lives experience this too; just as it's about time for a world-wide arm-drag of moral premises.

The battles between Self-made Men are civil, honest and fair—found in American business competition, the Olympics and corporate-sponsored events such as auto racing. The spoils go to whoever does it best, and whoever doesn't, often ends up working for whoever does. To lose a corporate battle is not a life or death issue, it's a spiritual issue, and a challenge to come back better, stronger and prouder than before, often catching the leader off-guard. It's fun! With a free economy, there is room for many levels of talent and of product quality— take cars for instance. We buy economy until we can afford luxury, with many different brands and styles to choose from. By competing, many entrepreneurs get to see how well they perform in the role of leader, and their ability determines their position among the great firms of the world.

Competition spurs discovery, and results in the aggregate efficiency of human energy. An advance of technology is an advance in wealth for all— regardless of how jobs are restructured for the change. The freer a field is, the better it is for everyone. Fierce competition, as in the computer industry, just results in more stars, greater talent, more numerous fortunes and a purer distribution of wealth than has ever existed. It is said that Microsoft has more millionaire *secretaries* than any other firm.

Spiritual Compensation. Morale is the most underrated, avoided and seemingly incomprehensible issue in business today. Bad morale has a silently devastating undercurrent; it is cancer to a business. Why is the subject avoided? Because it involves the mystical, uncertain realm of morality. Like it or not, managers are responsible for a happy staff. As a body is only as healthy as its cells, its cells must be healthy, and people are the cells of a business. People are obviously much more than protoplasm as they harness the capacity of volition, but as an analogy, people, like cells, have a specific nature which must be accounted for.

The focus of morale is often defined as the general mood of employees determined by the working conditions provided by management. While this is mostly accurate, one cannot discount the meaning of morale to those running the company. They want to know their people are happy, and would voluntarily honor their name. That irreplaceable sense of togetherness affects *their* morale, and lets them know they've done something truly special in their time on Earth.

Respect for one's superiors does not come from enforcing inessential issues such as strict start and stop times, if no loss to the company can be determined.

It cannot be had by steering people at every step instead of letting their natural processes function unimpeded. Decent morale comes from communicating to troops what is crucial to accomplish, providing the tools when necessary and leaving them free to achieve. All minds approach their work in patterns tailored to their own psychological makeup, and they must be free to reach the same end by their unique means. Any disruption causes spiritual dis-ease, the precursor to physical disease. The flow is delicate, but it can be fortified, and the freedom of individual action is the way. We are all professionals—employees and employers alike—no matter what we choose as a profession; the elements of cognition we bring are the same, as is our respect for those elements. It is the object of managers and leaders to understand the full epistemological chain of their business and its sub-elements, while providing information about the major nodes when necessary to those above and below, inside and outside the company. The resonance of a business is reached through a seamless employee, customer and supplier relation. There should be a clear, agreed upon purpose for the interrelation of the people. Everyone needs to know exactly what they are there to accomplish and who their contacts are, and everyone deserves to be acknowledged for its accomplishment. To be valued is much more than spiritual gratification; it is an assurance of one's living security. As most people live check to check, that comfort has very real psychological consequences.

When you buy a product, you study what it can do to be sure it meets your needs. When in management, you study what people have done, can do and desire to do, to determine where they fit best. Studying their résumé allows you to utilize their experience. Being aware of their thought process, you can see how it limits or serves them, what their level of skill is and what training to provide. Think of it not only as a means of advancing efficiency, but as compensation. If someone doesn't have to *cope* with their job but loves it, you will get a radical sense of loyalty from them. Compensation involves more than the sheer physical sustenance tied to money; it includes a sincere, mature work environment, advancement, self-destiny and personal significance.

All businesses and groups should have some type of acknowledgement ceremony. This ceremony should be directly connected to employee actions and those who benefit. Employees should be commended by the superiors they deal with every day. Not someone in the company they've seen pictures of but never associate with, though he may preside over the event. If the effect is to last, the complements must come from you, when and as you witness merit. We hear, "Don't get emotionally involved in business," yet to withhold our feelings is to be aloof of what level of fulfillment it carries. *Everyone* is emotionally involved. Thank them openly for making your life easier. Thank them for helping things to run smoothly. We are best off to control the cognitive actions that result in the emotions we most want to feel.

Government

"It is the duty of the patriot to protect his country from its government."
—Thomas Paine

The Separation of Church and State. It is difficult to characterize traits of human goodness and sound business policy regarding the interaction between associates, customers and suppliers, political representatives and citizens, without bringing morality into the picture, or more clearly, the discomfort of religious beliefs. Every business ethic is based on a deeper understanding of long term cause and effect of individual and corporate actions and an inherent respect for right and wrong, driven by a *logical* standard, which often conflicts with and requires defiance of religious instruction.

Short of conviction, most can only acknowledge some incoherent divine purpose as their motivation for achievement. Most attempts of spiritual integration in business or in the affairs of State are attributed to the teachings of God, but in fact, such integration is not the province of religion. I remember a quote from a local newspaper that said, "We want to make God's morality Michigan's morality." The problem is, God's morality isn't moral.

From birth we've associated our own goodness to our religious ties, never thinking to comprehend the possibility of another source—our own life-generating power. Throughout history, we've always been told that the purpose of morality was "to serve God." War-torn European citizens needed relief from this view, which from one dominion to another, kept men at odds. Our ancestors came to the New World to establish a civilization that dispensed with ideological struggle, based solely on a common standard: to respect that which is physically necessary for *all* men to survive in peace. The actual focus of morality in practice, is and always has been to preserve and further human life. This is the key to morality, practiced by our species and by every other living organism—to preserve and further its own existence, not from 1 AD, but from the dawn of time. Defining morality correctly allowed no interpretations that could subvert, seize or destroy our creations or our lives. It allowed no unjust guilt to accumulate, and no irrational criticism which would interest or be tolerated by a mature, introspective audience. A proper definition of morality leaves no foothold on the human body, and *that* is why it has been kept from us for so long.

Since the industrial revolution, all business activity has been damned by clergy as hedonistic greed. The profit we've made and the resulting pride of success earned, has been considered mankind's greatest evil. Animosity may have been justified when wealth was accumulated by slavery and conquest—hence the unearned, but nothing justifies guilt for accumulating wealth in an era of creative freedom, peace and voluntary trade. Facing aggression, who taught us to turn the other cheek? Who taught us in effect, that we can't fight back? Keep in mind that the Bible was not assembled and written until over *four hundred years* after the death of Jesus Christ and that the majority of its contributors were anonymous. That was more than enough time to exploit its powerful following, twisting its teachings to support the leaders of the day and in effect, distort the true purpose of morality. We've been told from birth that our senses are not valid, that "the only true knowledge is to know that we know nothing," that the only alternative to living for others is to run others over, that the only moral action is community service, that money, profit and wealth is evil and that concern for indigence takes center stage in a noble mind. While some quotes are attributable to bad philosophers and some are biblical, *both* are products of men.

Without instincts to drive us, a code of morality—our body of knowledge defining what is good for us or bad—is our primary means of survival. By spotlighting indigence instead of fostering ability, by giving preference to faith versus rationality, by supporting social adjustment rather than independence, by advising mercy towards guilt instead of justice for innocence, they inverted morality and turned it against Man. We were left with our purposes derailed, our ideals ignored and instead of a pat on the back for our effort, we were infused with an answerless guilt. Religion was just one of many tools perverted to serve a group of parasites and their minions—the Spirit Murderers—in order to raise the rest of civilization as their servants. This style of moral repression is why we have been allowed no connection between our healthy spirituality and the work we've done. We have never received the spiritual reward we've earned and deserved, by proper moral acknowledgement of the value of mankind's greatest productive endeavor—American free enterprise, and that fact reinforces the case for our separation of church and State.

"The more things are made, the more people will be employed to make them."
—George W. Bush

Capitalism. Some animals die in captivity. The Great White shark is one of them; Man is another. When his freedom is taken, his life is taken. The birth of our country was the birth of an idea of how men were to engage each other—for once having the courage not to cannibalize. Self-made Man sees that the vast majority of his experiences with other men are peaceful, and that dysfunction is rare. He sees both conditions as chosen and sees clearly which is to be sanctioned and which is to be quelled. No two philosophies are more desperately needed or are more intentionally subverted than morality and economics. And still, the subversion of one makes the subversion of the other possible. The proper morality focuses on the entity it protects—the individual. Economics focuses on the proper interrelation of those individual entities (not sociology, democracy, Communism or any governmental body, as is often taught). It would be clearer if we as a people discussed our social system by virtue of the actual principle which describes it, not Capitalism or Socialism, but economics. Government is an instrument of economics, not the other way around. These others are systems of economics, some which work and some which do not. In economic theory, the first suggestion of the use of force is *wrong,* and is the source of all further misapplication. Capitalism simply stands for the right of an individual citizen to make his own economic decisions—to use his own judgment in deciding what to buy and who to trade with. Any other system denies him that right—the use of cognition—and tells him what he needs and forces him to accept it. Capitalism is a product of metaphysically honest men who have reached full volitional maturity, who trust in and intend to foster the self-responsibility of their brethren. In contrast, any form of collectivism is a product of immaturity, power lust and neurotic denial.

We benefit from living in a civil society in countless ways, compared to what we would have on a desert island alone. But we are so focused on the living pattern of creation, there is no room in our consciousness for thoughts of those plotting against us. Our innocence is in that we don't even consider politics, and are mostly free not to. The battle of western culture and Communism is a relic of past generations for most of us—a political issue of our parents and grandparents—not particularly interesting. We saw Russia fall, Germany reunite and much of the world embrace open markets. Why would anyone think this trend is bad? That you can find a job that matches your own interests, that both you and your employer have a choice in the matter of hire and that you work steadily and receive a paycheck each week, the world has a political label for you: Capitalist, and a corresponding hate group. Capitalism is a system of voluntary exchange among men, which rewards the best foot anyone puts forward. After two hundred years of unprecedented productivity, the rest of the world caved in and acknowledged what at the outset, should have been obvious to all. It has stood the test of time, bringing more wealth into the lives of more people than any system in history, which won it global respect as the pattern to follow. But many nations still refuse to embrace it.

Out of all the systems proposed, the one Socialists won't experiment with is freedom. The most productive, civil groups of men, found in American corporations, are never considered as a template for other productive, life-serving civil groups. There is no "patience" necessary with freedom, as is called for in socialist States. The results of freedom are immediate—in growth, expansion and bounty. Walk into any grocery store and you'll see the combined effort of thousands of corporations and millions of people, all uncoerced and all voluntary. There are levels of economy—products for consumers and products for corporations—layers and layers of small to large corporations, which make the products for consumers possible. This is what is illegal under Socialism.

My job has been made considerably easier in that Western-style Capitalism has been proven to bring the greatest prosperity to the greatest number. Why this was ever doubted, why a system such as Socialism could gain any sort of acceptance by totally violating the natural requirements of the entity it governed isn't unfathomable anymore, but is certainly unforgivable. The good of others, or the "public good," can never morally violate the good of an individual. The individual *is* the measure. Look at their dogma and you won't see any complex and carefully deliberated laws, but only threats and reproaches—the result of an uneducated and undisciplined consciousness looking to defy itself. Some countries even voted themselves into Socialism, such as Great Britain, and the townspeople found out very quickly that they were to be used as kindling. Capitalism need not seek the destruction of Socialism—it need only wait for it to rot from the inside, just as it did. Capitalism on the other hand, completes the chain. It completes cognition, respecting Man's nature and securing the land for his *potential* stature. It leaves him free to choose his own loyalties, free to test his full adult capacities and leaves him free to do it all alone, without the fear of being devoured. To answer the age-old question fought over since the Cold War, "Who is going to build a better world?" That's right, the builders.

Responsible Politicians. Among a man's central purpose-driven interests, there is the civics of a nation and the globe to consider. Some are interested in individual businesses, and some are interested in this flow. Dealing with government policy today is properly what it was for the men of revolutionary times, who were private businessmen that came together to do what needed doing. Their honest efficiency was a side skill, a direct result of successful business practice and a strong work ethic. They didn't have degrees in political science. They didn't specialize in financially isolated socialist ideologies. Things had to be done, they know how to do them and they knew how much it would cost. The affairs of a country are not unlike the affairs of a major corporation, and of course the most important issue of peacetime prosperity is solvency and sound financial management. There is a proper need for politicians who can comprehend that the essentials of one life apply to one thousand, and to one billion. Those we select, win our confidence by showing they understand and can work with an integrated view of existence—how social interaction can only follow free individual action, and that our institutions must respect the sound fundamentals of both. A friend of the people does not provide men with freebies at any level. He frees them from the slavery of providing those freebies to other men, and protects us from any hostile actions—foreign or domestic. That said, I can't tell you how pleased I am to see an adult in the White House.

Many Presidents have become historic names, while others are all but forgotten. The memory of some are sustained by an incredible event, and others for their actions regarding incredible events. George Washington was historic even while he lived; there has never been another President like him. Lincoln's calm, honor and intelligence shined through the catastrophic realities of the Civil War, while Franklin D. Roosevelt's personal character is lost in the memory surrounding his period—the Great Depression and World War II. (The truth? He was a flake and an international banking puppet, as was Herbert Hoover before him, capping sixteen years of a fascist-dominated executive office). John F. Kennedy stood for all that a sound, loyal American *should* stand for—he was another Lincoln, while Johnson fed our people into the furnace, starting with his own predecessor. Ronald Reagan brought fresh new strength to the Presidency; he was wise and unique, like Washington. George W. Bush is another Andrew Jackson—my favorite President—the man who killed the private banking monopoly and paid off the national debt, both which *must* be done again. He flaunted the power of the Presidency as a true grass-roots American. As a result, he supported tariffs and dodged bullets; my kind of guy. He knew exactly what he was doing as chief executive, exactly who the greatest threat to our freedom was, and he wasn't afraid to face it.

A man fit for office has seen enough of the world to encompass an experienced view, so he is at least in his thirties. He has a solid legal, business and military background so that he is wise, realistic, profit and freedom oriented, and is conservatively attuned not to risk it. He is fully accountable, honestly using State funds for State obligations. He is passionate about America, respects the Republic, respects American sovereignty, our moral standing and our superiority among nations. He understands the truth of banking history and sound economics and watches the country's checkbook *closely*. He's seen it all, and he is no patsy. He knows when he's being lied to. He knows who's pulling who's strings, and he's not about to spend his life as a puppet for evil. He knows who he can trust, and when a picture is painted before him, he can still see right to the wall. He is not a master liar, but a master of reason. His job is to uphold the Constitution—an obligation by moral choice—and regardless of his party affiliation, his protection of the strong, independent, stable and healthy flow of the people is his highest awareness and responsibility.

The more facets a politician gains mastery of, the closer he comes to being worthy of the Presidency. Regardless of whether he ever attains it, he shows his respect for the Republic by never undermining due process. He knows his role as Congressman or Senator is critical to the Republic, that there is a balance of power to guarantee public representation, and his fully coherent dedication is necessary to assure that the conscious deliberation of issues and others are checked. He knows how cowards use power, and he isn't one of them. He is the fly-swatter.

The key issues to a man's and a country's survival which took me years to identify, validate and accept by purely abstract means, are contained in the first one hundred years of America's presidential speeches. Presidential priorities in brief are first and foremost, *order*—to secure the internal and external safety of the citizens. Second is the financial health and credit of the government, which assures the longevity and independent grasp of its power structure. Third is political sovereignty, or purity from foreign or corrupt influences detrimental to national security, prosperity and political integrity. Since the Federal Reserve Act was passed in 1913, we've had only one stable leg on the floor, and it's only a matter of time before danger besets us again.

No private interest should be granted a power which threatens the prevailing order. The conviction of our Forefathers should never be lost, and should remain at the base of any legislation proposed in this freest of countries. Man's motive power is his moral code. It was this dedication to moral values that made our society possible—a system designed to protect the human spirit, which has manifested itself as skyscrapers, spacecraft and long, peaceful, happy lives. It is crucial that it be preserved in its axiomatically sound, original form.

BENJAMIN FRANKLIN

The reason why Benjamin Franklin was so popular as a statesman and a general was because he treated human beings, *like* human beings. He didn't try to do their thinking for them. He expected them to be mature, and to make sound decisions. When this was expected of them, they did. Subordinates and peers felt *real* to him, in a way they had never felt real to anyone before. He looked upon you as if what you were going to say was important, and if you wanted any of his time, you made sure that it was. You could tell that he was listening. He was a man doing a job at a certain level, requiring specific information. He treated you like *you* were a man doing a job at a certain level, requiring specific information. There was no comparison of levels in his eyes. There was no pretense. When a man practices no pretense, you do not waste his time practicing one either.

Franklin was a man who respected existence and consciousness, verbatim. He knew that existence itself required him to practice specific attributes in order to advance, and he held it in his best interest to support a country that respected this requirement. In many other countries at the time and even today, rational cognition was considered treason, but his thoughtful innocence as a holder of public trust stuns me even now. He made every piece of reasoning complete in itself, bringing deliberation to an art form, and showed how *any* man, no matter how modest of intellect, can grasp and follow the moral path, when those of strength have the honor to present it. With so straight-forward, calm and thoughtful an approach, he stands as a monument to what is meant when we think of an American. With no fear of physical threat, what kind of a person would ever declare such a man as his enemy, and who does this damn?

Many politicians were shocked that Benjamin Franklin did not tuck public money away from the war effort into his own private accounts as so many other generals did. It wasn't that Franklin put the country's interest ahead of his own; Franklin knew that an act of cowardice was not in *his own* best interest. He knew that the fate of the Republic, to secure his freedom, was his highest self-interest, and that becoming a petty thief was not. Having brought so many ideas in politics, science and societal flow that are still in use, his use of moral energy was phenomenal—and timeless. In salute to him, his soldiers *drew* their swords; a display that enraged other generals who were jealous. That so purely moral a man has ever walked the Earth surely means a trail exists for the rest to pick up on.

The Constitution. Just as science looks at subatomic particles where existence cannot be subdivided further, Self-made Man respects the requirements of each individual life. All human energy must be generated. Every decision is a commitment to expend energy in a certain way. As energy is finite each day, it is finite in life. Man's hierarchy of values must be integrated in order that his energy may be spent efficiently. The Self-made work to become masters of their own energy, and in America, they are free to. It is this action that is the spiritual basis of his most sacred right—that this go on undisturbed—that no injustice impedes the processing of a civil mind—that each mind is the master over 100% of the energy it produces, and must remain so. Even what is considered the American dream is only a result of the *actual* dream—this base physical security. Human beings need very little, only a stable land and we'll do the rest.

Our Constitution bans force in all its forms, grants no pity for criminal action and provides no protection of zealots. It decentralizes power and spreads it around—granting sovereignty to all men, seeing his mind and path as endlessly unique and clearing the way for that potential. It steps beyond the Submission/Domination Axis into what interaction *should be* among men, and holds them to it. It dissolves all class wars, as anyone can reach any level they are willing to strive for. It provides a clear definition of *order* among men and in their relations to the government. Everyone is empowered to manage their own affairs—showing belief in the people, not just in a leader—and puts in place rules to restrain the government, so that the people are never at the mercy of one man's promise. Our Constitution fixes what can rationally be fixed, and leaves fluid what must remain so. Due to this, men have a stable environment in which to thrive.

FUNDAMENTAL HUMAN RIGHTS

Human energy is only safe where predation is disallowed by law. Only in America and other environments similar in design can there be great enterprises, allowing a man's energy to be open to the world and spread across a continent. It is only in the realm of legislation where predation is disconnected from sensate awareness, and losses are sustained with no awareness of a danger—where specific victims are chosen without their knowledge or consent. Self-made Man has gathered all the key variants of evil in social action, compiled throughout history to provide basic legal protection for every man's benefit, called the Bill of Rights. The most solid countries are those with a sound bill of rights, while those without are hollowed out shells waiting to crack. It is such a document that states *explicitly* that the purpose of a government is to protect its people, an end to which all other intentions must yield.

The great rights of mankind must *expressly* be declared, whose honor must supersede all other governmental action or statutes, if they are deemed by this standard unconstitutional. Its purpose in practice is to *qualify* power, to guard against legislative and executive abuses and protect would be prey against its predator. In all social realms, every man must be free to think, speak and disseminate his ideas to those interested, by his own means. To do so, no peaceable gathering may be disallowed—a lesson seen again in Hitler's Munich days, used as a way to avoid mass movements against a current regime. No governmental stand may be taken for a particular religion, religious persecution being the reason our settlers left England to begin with. As individuals can encounter others with violent intentions and officers cannot accompany every citizen, we retain the right to bear arms. This doesn't keep a people safe from tyranny as any third world country is evidence of; it is a street self-defense issue.

We are protected from unreasonable search and seizure as probable cause must exist, with a warrant stating the specific illegalities sought. The confiscation of our property for public use without just compensation is disallowed. The Constitution forbids depravation of life, liberty or property without due process of law. If we are accused of a crime, it guarantees us a speedy public trial by jury, for us to be informed of the accusation and to be confronted by our accusers. It provides protection for the witnesses and provides us with legal counsel. We are granted jury trials in civil cases as well. Excessive bail, fines and cruel and unusual punishments so well developed in the Middle Ages are all forbidden. These are all elements throughout history that men have suffered at the hands of Spirit Murderers, and with America as proof, men flourish without.

The Self-made fathers of America defined a set of rules that were straight-forward and enforceable by the courts. It is further stated that the rights listed in the Constitution do not deny others retained by the people; in other words, *the people come first.* All men, regardless of social standing, race, origin, religion, sex or age are guaranteed equal protection under the law. They may be punished *only* for legally defined offenses and taxed only by popular consent. The government is not our master. It is our tool, to be used and defined as we see fit, evidenced by the nature of our Constitution. All laws are based on the moral premises of those who propose them and those who pass them; as such, Congress should be the guardians of our fundamental premises. Our gage of their good or evil can be seen by comparing their legislative leanings to the Constitution's initial intent.

The overall sum of how Americans feel about their country can be seen in the elements of pride that citizens of any country would like to feel: 1) That our freedom of action is protected. 2) That respect is shown for our ability to think and remain sovereign. 3) The fairness with which our government treats all people, foreign and domestic. 4) The responsible use of force inside and outside of our country, guided by logical laws and forthright international agreements. 5) The protection our system provides, instead of the peril it could cause. 6) As a nation is just a large group of families, that our system fosters our best—in individuals and children—and doesn't look to rip us off. 7) That sound, mature, accountable men are in control, and are rewarded by the people for their integrity. To a great extent, this is what we have in America, which is a constant barometer of our civil virtues.

The rights of Individual Man must come before the rights of any groups of men. A mind must always be free to determine its own course. It must be free to disengage the intentions of others and dissent. Morality is itself implied by enforcement only against its antithesis, whereas otherwise no force is ever necessary. There is never a point to reach that requires retaining a loophole for seizure of anything. The rational interests of the mind are one, no matter how many individuals are involved. Civil, responsible men don't ask for sacrifices and they don't make them. Manipulation is not the game of heroes, nor their means of dealing with men.

Essential Services. The truth about society is that it is one big nothing. There is no such entity; it is an abstract concept, defining that state of interaction we face while moving from our homes to our work and back. All civics are properly designed to secure this capacity for all men. We have electricity and plumbing for human convenience, and government is for the same purpose. We don't live for *its* sake. Our stability comes from our social mediums being held constant— sound roads, sound laws and a stable money supply, securing unrestricted commerce between those in a policeable province. Our police force protects us from harm and protects the property we've made or acquired. Our armed forces do the same by protecting us from outside threats, be they invasions (planned disasters), or natural disasters. Our city planning and road commissions ensure an efficient flow between work and home. Our pleasure travel became possible only by establishing what we needed to live: trade routes. Civilization's priority is ensuring the flow itself, so roads come before houses (not meaning their existence, but their location). Our executive branch of government determines the use of our armed forces and all foreign relations, hostile or peaceful. Our legislative branch determines our policies towards other nations, as well as outlining proper legal relations between citizens.

Our societal organization provides for every likely mishap, so that we needn't feel guilty in not stopping beside every broken down car. With a clearly defined hierarchy of life—its interruption being the foremost issue to avoid— outside of a life or death situation, the stranded motorist gets a call to those paid for this purpose: rescue vehicles, tow trucks or whatever is appropriate.

What is most important to the citizens is *order*, that no form of anarchy be allowed to reign. To have a sound police department guarding the observance of rational laws, and by their very presence, quelling criminal action. It is not their position to dispense justice; it is only theirs to stop the use of force. Not to relieve their anxiety, but to use the minimum force necessary to restore the civil flow of society.

For one, what a relief it was to the country to see the 55 mph speed limit abolished. People can move again. High-speed limits keep cities small. They allow civilization to spread out, by bringing greater distances so much closer, which relieves congestion and improves business everywhere. The 55 mph speed limit was brought into existence based on a plan to conserve energy, which physics can prove was a mathematical fraud anyway. Limits, if any, are to be determined in the road design by its ultimate rational gauge—at what speed the populace chooses to travel it, so our officers can stop interrupting the flow and get back to real police work.

I remember hearing that motorists typically commit a civil infraction once every three blocks. If policemen were to follow every motorist, they would have lost their licenses by the time they got to work. With no one harmed or injured in any such instance, it's obvious that this doesn't damn the pubic, but shows the absurdity of such laws. Driving a car is no longer a "privilege" as the law tells you. Unless you want nothing more than the bare minimum out of life, (which is approximately how much thought is used by the supporters of such claims), it is a necessity. Unless you can support a family by walking to the corner store and working as a cashier, then long distance mobility is essential. It is our right and obligation to ensure that laws governing the roads are rational. To limit one's mobility is to limit his effectiveness at self-sustenance, which only breeds dependency.

These are my rules for driving: 1) Don't get killed. Know your machine in adverse conditions, and situations of aggressive recovery. 2) Be predictable. No swapping around mindlessly; those who do so are typically in a hurry to get nowhere. 3) No contact, no foul. Hey, driving can be hell. No laws can harness the public to insure safety to the most lethargic. From the highest Self-made to the lowest Spirit Murderer, everyone is out there. Nothing is so socially competitive as traffic. Quick adjustments, smooth efficiency, honor, swift logical calm, furtive moral failure, hedonism, senseless aggression, you see it all. Traffic is a deliberate reflection of subconscious morality—people drive like they live.

Traffic and local ordinances aren't the only set of laws to be reexamined. Every regulation requires money subtracted from our pockets for its enforcement, so we should be as frugal as rationality permits. The concept of *fairness* recognizes and respects the choices and the results of those choices, for every individual. Justice is done by maintaining proper credit or blame to those responsible for specific improvements or losses and holding harmless those not, in any realm. There are no victimless crimes that we should be wasting our money trying to collect fines against. For instance, the law needs to stay out of bedrooms and outside of any such *consensual* exchange, homo or heterosexual, right or wrong. Legislators cannot peak in to inspect for moral consonance. Of course, children have to be protected from physical and sexual abuse as they gain that right at birth. We don't have to sanction the epi-stems leading to such abuses, which we can see as clearly immoral, but it isn't our soul at risk either. Irrationality is its own damnation. Trying to legislate in areas that would require a KGB presence on every block and in every home, just clogs up the works. We have to trust the citizens until given a specific reason not to, and invest our attention and public money elsewhere.

Foreign Policy. America treats nations like we treat friends, neighbors or bullies, in response to how they act. The lending ratios used in an individual life are the same for a country. We don't lend what we can't afford to lend, and what they can't afford to pay back. We must guarantee our health, if ever we need to step outside our boundaries to help those in need or to counter an irrational force. Nothing we do for another country should ever be bad for ours. We should lend to friends and never to enemies. We help others in natural disasters, but never when we do not trust the motives or lifestyles of those in power. In that case, we invest our aid in a different way; by charging high tariffs to deal with us, and eventually, by toppling their regime and installing a civil republic.

When we see an unusual number of immigrants or defectors from a particular country, we know the people are not being treated fairly. We do not burden our people with the cost of feeding, housing and providing medical care for them. We instead weigh the military investment to free their country, so they can enjoy prosperity and freedom without leaving their homes. We impose trade tariffs on police states—*not* free trade agreements—with the express intention of taxing the corruptors. We call their loans, deny them war materials, gas, and oil and weaken their grasp on the noose they have around the necks of the people. Then, coordinated with those who wish to see their leadership made a moral, sound administration, we go in. Using the United States as the template, we set up a new government and show the people what is now possible to them. Our investment will come back one hundred fold or more, as we say goodbye to a liability and welcome a new productive nation into the realm of those free.

The United States is *the* moral authority; not the United Nations. The U.N. is proper only as a forum to vent and expose international concerns. It of itself has no country, and should have no army, no currency and no authority over us. Its power is limited to a combination of countries participating in any particular event which affects them. We make free trade agreements *only* with nations who match our productive capacity by morally parallel means. *We* are America; *we* decide; not the U.N. and their international banker's agenda. We're no longer tolerant of Spirit Murdering premises which promise to, but never lead to life. We take the immoral cripples out, and restore a canopy of peaceful, disciplined sanity for all to live under.

Offending America is synonymous with offending the Self-made. Cross us and we will squash you. There isn't a power on Earth to match ours. After any war, we would be back first, as our premises are life, while we would blast our enemies back into the Stone Age. Life and Earth are for those who want to live, and who practice living premises. Those who don't, we can make arrangements for.

American Armed Forces. The purpose of an army is not to fire its weapons, but to protect its borders and its countrymen. The military's function is to protect its country from all domestic, foreign and natural opposition such as civil outbreaks, invasions, storms or epidemics by whatever means is appropriate in order to return a secure, peaceful state of existence for its citizens. We as civilians, delegate our use of physical force to the armed services to represent us in foreign and domestic issues. The question to ask is who decides when the use of force is proper?

The military is going to want to do what they were trained for, but they must submit to the coolest heads who steer the nation politically. Military men will have their own political ideas—everyone believes they can do the job better than those elected—but the tail cannot wag the dog. A body lives by the direction instructed by its head; not from an arm or a leg. Our political leadership is just as essential as our armies. Armies are the body, policy is the brain. In leaving office, President Eisenhower said, "We must never let the military-industrial complex endanger our liberties or democratic processes." He said it for a good reason, as it killed his successor. Unfortunately, history has shown how evil those in power can be, but it isn't always so. Rationality can return, as morality is what drives policy. Despite occasional abuses, we have by far the most moral internal and external civilian and military force on the planet. How many other countries use tear gas and rubber bullets when possible?

Voluntary Service. There is a difference in public reaction to a civilian death versus a military death. We emotionally factor in that possibility for military personnel, given the risk involved in their occupation, versus what one would expect to encounter in private life. Military personnel and police officers should be well compensated for that potential—materially and spiritually. First and foremost, they should always have a choice of whether or not to serve in such a manner, including for whom and for how long. Volunteer armies are always the strongest, and there are just as many responsibilities to be addressed at home if some choose not to fight. If the man next to me is not committed, I don't want my life in his hands. If he can't handle it, he shouldn't be here and probably won't be for long. Let him support the war effort as a citizen, being useful in his own way; there is no shame in that. Let him object until he understands the issue at stake. No man should die for a principle he has not acquired. No man has the right to push another out onto a battlefield; it is a direct Constitutional violation of our right to life.

Sacrifice is leaned on mostly in troubled times, but it can become an abusive political instrument. No one wants to sacrifice—ever; and they are right not to want to. Great care must be exercised before political leaders decide to risk one single human life. If we were threatened with invasion, I would fight without question, even knowing my chances of survival were not good. Resistance to aggression parallels the resistance to death that nature requires of us every day; such a tribute to life is not a sacrifice. But to be forced to go and die for some dubious cause is a national disgrace, and suspicious intentions always surround those who advocate a draft.

Vietnam was a foreign policy disaster for America, showing the link between involuntary armies and unnecessary wars. A draft is not about patriotism, but about creating an expense account in blood for munitions makers and those who finance them. Its draft dodgers were totally justified. We must see to it that nations never degrade to the point where they must move outside their borders to expropriate wealth and spread violence, which is only an extension of those in charge suffering the same intellectual degradation. That war was a direct result of such fascist tyrannical powers seizing control of our executive office through the murder of President Kennedy, and they did here just what they do under Socialism; practicing their pattern to murder, pillage and destroy, at home and abroad. It should never be permitted to happen here again.

War is a minus-sum game to the mass citizenry—a pure expense in money and blood. Every building built, every creation brought into existence adds to our wealth and should be preserved. War just destroys it all, generating nothing but cost. No one benefits from war. No one wants to spend more than necessary, unless some intend to profit by it. Our foreign efforts are to assure protection and justice to our citizenry abroad, never to assist them in gaining property for themselves by military means. We must protect only what has been acquired by voluntary trade.

When we go to the Persian Gulf to protect American interests abroad, it isn't only the rich we are protecting. Thousands work for our oil companies, and all Americans benefit from their existence. Next to money, fuel is the lifeblood of our economy. Everyone who drives a car, lives or buys anything requires it. We as Americans are free to come up with another energy source, but if we don't, we drive what is available, and should respect that its fuel is a vital interest to our economy, and to our very lives.

The leaders who stem conflict at the cost of the fewest human lives are the greatest of heroes. The best solve issues on moral grounds, without ever firing a shot. As we must defend ourselves, this is not always possible, so we do counter aggression vigorously. The greatest men in government gear foreign policy to ensure a safe world for all of us to venture into, and they work to spread the *axiomatic means* to that freedom to all governments, who should want the same for their people. When they could care less about their people, we make them pay to trade with us, or refuse them altogether. That is the moral reason for tariffs—to deny slave labor an equal standing with our moral enterprises.

Look at any totalitarian or socialist government and you'll see few loyal soldiers, but many eventual defectors. No one defects from America. Here, every man's life is valuable. Every man has the right to live without subordinating his desires to anyone; and that is a land worth protecting—worth fighting for—worth dying for if necessary. If it came down to it, most Americans are willing to die for what America *is*—not for what it promises to be. The men of communist countries are considered expendable and are always left to die for "the noble ideal," ideals which their fundamental premises make impossible. Americans don't have to create illusions about their country's potential greatness to be proud of; it *is* great. It is the nearest to Atlantis the world has ever been.

Philanthropy

Whenever we come together, we stand for something, whether in business, associations or political groups. The Self-made stand for life, but outside of business, they've had few pure vents for sharing their glory in constructive, healthy, spiritual ways. They complete the moral structure of cognition and interaction, and further it into great enterprises, all along maintaining genuine pride and a clear conscience. It only gets strained when considering their deepest, most heartfelt hopes for humanity, and the substitute they've been given: giving money away. They know there is something wrong—something immoral about it. Of course that should be clear by now; the receiver didn't practice the pattern of life necessary to attain the reward.

We counter this by having all grants and scholarships awarded based on achievement, based on a future promise of life-furthering potential, which honors the student as well as the grantor. Honor must be maintained, as *meaning* is what we must satisfy.

The Self-made stay clean by never giving money to a dead end—by never seeing it poured down a drain into those who refuse to learn and won't try to better themselves by honest means. Our excess per *our* direction, should go to bring others to the moral balance of self-sustained independence—to make life flow more efficiently and safely for all those in pursuit of it. We shouldn't bother with those who have given up. In regard to them, we should follow their lead until they commit to changing their pattern.

We should be able to see the benefit of our philanthropy and enjoy the self-esteem it generates, every time we leave the house. No gift should ever feel futile. Opportunities for improvements are all around us. Look around; beautify your world, bring to life the beauty of your own soul in clear, obvious, visual ways. Fund the repair of roads and bridges. Add sidewalks and nature paths. Fund adding a policeman to an area you see as in need of attention. If you experience bureaucratic resistance, go to the people with advertising to circumvent any mindless authorities, or those who create problems because they "want in on it," for publicity's sake. Make philanthropic choices easier by having local jurisdictions announce work plans, in anticipation of contributions to fund public projects.

As we move up the scale into abstract territory, the effect of our grant has much deeper consequences. Never donate to universities without identification and moral understanding of what they propagate. Fund only those who defend sound, rational, coherent convictions—those who embrace the evolution of Man in educational techniques, tailored curriculums and the practical individual and social use of morally-integrated thought. If they are studying Marx instead of Franklin, drop them immediately.

Lend money to producers; don't just give it to consumers. Feed *dreams*, not vices. I was stunned to discover that Nikola Tesla spent a good twenty years as a pauper *after* he had been awarded countless patents for creations such as radio and the AC motor. Someone should've had the brains to back so incredible a mind when he was down and out. It's wonderful to discover new talent, but what about funding the research of proven talent?

Challenge irrational laws such as unnecessary taxes and antitrust. Check irrational lobbies, lobbying just to nullify their corruption. Buy our freedom back, and reform the system to no longer permit its sale. Challenge the existence of the IRS; challenge the 16th amendment. Wipe out our debt money system. Wipe out victimless crime legislation.

Consider joining forces with other philanthropists to create *full* reserve banks to compete with the teetering Federal Reserve banks. Provide simple interest loans for home mortgages, to compete with the compound interest-amortized scavengers. Finance your children and their children, your friends and their friends. Set up an equivalent of the Australian mortgage system which provides an interest shield to the borrower, so that he pays off his home loan in just a few years, permitting him independence much sooner, which can fund a business, children's educations, luxury, retirement or a nicer home in turn. Fund American independence from the secret banking government.

One of the best international attempts I'm aware of is the "Open Society" organization of financier George Soros, fostering nations to embrace free enterprise—an excellent attempt to bring backward nations to the 3-4 level of cognitive sanity and human respect. Another is "Sovereignty," a nationwide organization working towards a debt-free currency in America. These are the kind of plans that make a difference.

A more dangerous endeavor is that of Harry Wu, who has risked his life to document human cruelty, organ trafficking and slave operations backed by American corporations all over China. You can't turn over a product today without seeing "Made in China" stamped on the back of it—and what is the quality of life of those who've made it? He or she eats filthy food if any, sleeps in a dirt hole and is lashed instead of paid. This is an international extension of the Spirit Murderer's plan, which must be dealt with. Every individual is a source of wealth, which is theirs to direct by right, and securing their freedom will generate more natural bounty and dry up parasitical sustenance faster than any other method.

The Moral Warrior. We have seen what is generated by the rational, direct, civil process of thought across the full spectrum of human action. We can identify point by point, what we must defend, and now we know what we must become.

Moral clarity, fundamental confidence and spiritual autonomy is intended to bring our sole concerns within range, but they rest on another set of dreams. Our dream lifestyle of an endearing relationship, a flamboyant career, travel, a dream home and dream cars is all made possible and brought within reach by the abstract concepts *above* individual cognition, which are built *on* individual cognition, in sound relationships and sound institutions. We often miss the wealth we do have, which rests on the dreams of those in the 18th century on back: to be free, to have a right to one's life and property and to be self-governed. That fight is not over. Peace and civility are not sustained when the public stands down to oppressive forces, but only when rational human rights are respected and fought for, where sole consideration for the individual entity of Man is held as the key element defining any social order.

Before a Moral Warrior can come to be, he or she must have a reason to live, and a reason to fight for life's preservation. That reason is the lifestyle of a Self-made Man. *He* is the reason. The Moral Warrior's armor is acquired to protect innocence. It is an identity that anticipation-based minds assume, upon acquiring a resolute grasp of axiomatic principles. His commitment reflects his struggle: After years of torment, he stayed open to abstract growth, trying to understand why he was treated so poorly for living well. He discovered that it was not just a conspiracy against him, but was a hate tract against the best in all men. As an outcast, he spent his time alone—the only means of true inner peace—free of the random, pointless connections of those others, free of their range and of the stress in establishing any contact with it. He doesn't want to hate, but as he advanced further, he watched concern for his person and his struggle, vanish. The more valuable he became, the less those on the fringe of his consciousness honored him. He stayed his course of prosperity while remaining perceptive of the motives of others, no longer willing to pay penance for his virtues or to thanklessly carry the burdens of the evaders. He now stands alone with his brave, solemn grace and steady eyes, as the only human being that has fully earned that title, until he gathers the other lost children of Atlantis.

When you understand what great strides have already been taken, you'll see that our goals *are* possible. Every sound concept you have dreamt of is here for the taking; it's all up to you. At each new level, you will encounter much more grandeur than you could have imagined; here, real. An indestructible spirit sees romanticism in all realms—not that there aren't issues and wars to fight, but such a spirit *identifies* with the pride in our ability to fight them. To see beauty in our strength and beauty in our armor, in our conviction to decide what to shield against, what we stand for and *who we are* as a result. *We are,* the honorable at all levels and in all realms.

A Moral Warrior is needed to win a moral war, and this is one. This stance is transitional; there will be a time to put down our weapons and pick up our tools again, but for now and for a long time to come, we have to 'stay frosty.' Locked and loaded with the power of life, we must now learn our enemy. We must come to understand the structure of evil, and of all that threatens living harmony. The Spirit Murderers must be broken or turned. Most likely, they will *have* to be broken *before* they will turn. It is our prerogative *to develop* to where we can face our adversaries head on and see *them* cower for once, realizing their age-old fraud is no longer working. *To dominate,* when they see they've lost control of us morally. *To win,* as they roll over in shame and give up their game. Then to come back and teach that they need not fear us—that we will *never* relinquish moral control again, but mean them no harm, and will be glad to help them face life responsibly and grow, as now, they know they must. It will be difficult and painful, but it won't kill them—it will save those who can be saved. We must seek a true end to the *moral* Cold War; not the international bankers end of monopolizing all life and trade, but freeing the people of all lands, by freeing their minds.

Once axiomatic principles are accepted, it is astonishing how simple it becomes to identify the true motivations behind both sides of any issue. It is fascinating to recognize just where an idea is sound, and where it departs from rationality. The world can be changed simply, by holding those we encounter to a clear, sound, shining moral standard. True peace begins *within* every man. Quiet the individual and you quiet the nation. You now have a complete, morally-sanctioned format for seeing the world; a tool for honorable productivity that will spread joy and fascination in its exercise. With moral sovereignty lead by philosophy and discovered by science, you can now witness and participate in Man's graduation to an alien level of intelligence.

Section Three:

The Spirit Murderers

Don't jump off a cliff if you find some attributes of spirit murder in yourself. With life's ups and downs, we all display traits from time to time which are less than ideal, and are likewise repaid with less than ideal results. No one is bulletproof emotionally, and no one can be shielded from the influences of the world and its often disturbing, mass-supported moral viewpoints.

The hatred we should feel for immorality is often misdirected at the moral, in the same fashion and for the same reasons as why we as a nation immediately hated Lee Harvey Oswald; but he didn't kill Kennedy. We were conned on both counts and many others. Over time, the evil has branched out in countless directions of misery, but like all things, its key elements never change. It remains classifiable into distinct categories, to be identified in the following chapters.

We grow up facing a barrage of input from both sides, and have to weed through the mess to define ourselves. Fear itself is not evil. It's alright to be afraid. The key is to overcome; to not let it rule your destiny, and to grow strong enough to battle those who have allowed it to rule theirs.

A person is not damned for life because he chooses the wrong moral road in one issue or another, but if he stays the course after understanding he is wrong, he has damned himself to the pattern of self-destruction, along with anyone who gets caught in his snarl. Otherwise, damnation lasts *only as long as irrationality lasts.*

Chapter Eight

Fear-Driven Man

Part One: Denial of Existence: Concepts of Blindness

"Evildoers are easier; and they taste better."
—Interview with the Vampire

Hell. Having seen the world of Atlantis, where rationality shines and the best in all men is rewarded, we have acquired the weapons to remain untouchable. We have grown strong by the knowledge, and now we are ready for our journey into the underworld. This can be a descent into madness for the unprepared; conditions exist here that decent people should never have to see. Certain levels of contamination can scar by mere sight, but with our armor, we will traverse it in relative safety. Stay close.

Often we imagine Hell to be a great cavernous dwelling of jagged rock, fire and brimstone—dangerous, but exciting to a higher power just the same. Gung-ho, we can defend ourselves in that world, but that is not the true nature of Hell. Imagine forging this great blade; honing this hard, smooth body, then being sat down in a dirty, cold waiting room with sixties decor—staring at a green wall for hours. True Hell doesn't require armor plate to endure, but rubber gloves and clothespins. Hell is the immobility of being held back by oneself or others—by personal choice, culture or legislation. Hell is contemplating wonders forever denied to us, dreams that will never be reached, happenings that will never happen. Hell is contamination, the infiltration of filth and pestilence allowed to spread uncontested. It is disease left untreated; disease, not health, *welcomed* if you will. It is our better minds watching disease being given the right of way, while we are barred from providing solutions. Hell is not where *you* decide how best you are to live, but where others tell you. Hell is patiently trying to reason with the unreasonable. Hell is taking orders from our inferiors, stuck behind those who can barely handle 35 MPH when we could be doing eighty. It is where emotional "What ifs" rule, and thoughtful experimentation is forbidden. It is the energy of life drained and gone, the lethargic eyes too drawn to stay open and the ill-smelling bum who lacks the common decency to wash.

Socially, Hell is seeing our lives consumed, not to serve our highest ability, but to serve that bum. Hell is where high spirit is *not* fostered and *cannot* be sustained. Hell is where the cards are stacked in the favor of evil; where emphasis is placed on alleviating the burdens of stagnation versus protecting the foundations of growth. Hell is helplessness, where our comprehension is blurred, and our bodies are crippled. Hell is giving up—the decay of mind and body, the death of dreams, the offensive contraction of every sense and the defeat of every rational premise. It is where we must never set up camp. Hell is watching our living power wasted, forced to sit there and wait—who knows why. True hell is boredom, twenty-four hours a day. Not what you expected? No kidding. Hell is where *we* lose.

That of course is Hell from the viewpoint of a Self-made Man, a man of great capacity forced to sit on his energy. But while it limits *us,* it allows another type of man full reign in the use of his capacity. It allows him to posture as a leader in place of those who deserve to be there. It allows him to invert the *only* sound class structure of Man—sound motive versus unsound motive—and to invert human guidance, taking control away from the most complex thinkers and giving it to the least. Like rats roving over a corpse, it restrains his prey— allowing him to negate cause and effect and to check ability—undermining the best moral minds in favor of those with the lowest immoral aspirations. Our infection makes their survival possible. This Hell exists all around us today, and is *desired* by that type of man. Where does such a man come from? Why does he want to reverse everything? What advantages does he gain?

The Tragedy of Submission. A wealth of men cherish their time on Earth so much that they want to experience the best of everything—while at the same time, hordes of undifferentiated are pleased to settle for no more than any possible hand out can secure. Underneath the weight of such lethargy is the frantic clawing they are prone to, in response to their own sense of dysfunction. Hell from the view of Fear-driven Man, is existence itself.

Early on, some men suffer a panic attack against the very responsibility of vision and coherence. Perhaps upon opening his eyes and realizing an effort on his part is required to focus and to distinguish sounds, certain of his own inadequacy, he freezes. Utterly helpless in this warped, blurry world, the vibration he feels as the very undercurrent of existence, is a life-threatening intimidation. Unable to back out of the basic obligations imposed by life, with fear growing at an almost audible pace, it's too much; his terror of self-chosen action becomes so total that he claws towards any means of its avoidance. He runs *cognitively,* ingraining a behavioral pattern of constant disengagement and ends up only able and willing to see the world through the eyes and minds of others. In so choosing, he has wiped out his own identity, his first victim.

A dependency is an outside condition without which an entity cannot live, and a man's first dependency is upon those who sustain him. Beginning as a natural condition to be shed upon self-establishment, Fear-driven Man bucks nature and intends no separation. As he feels no individual graces—no positive use for sovereignty—it becomes implicit to his consciousness that we are all inexplicably tied to each other. He relinquishes control of his judgment and even his senses, to be superseded and overridden by any claim of other men. Wrapped up in how he sees others and how he is seen by others, the nature of existence is a bypassed or forgotten consideration.

Submission wins him nothing, because in renouncing control of his consciousness, there is no other power capable of assuming proper responsibility. His mind and life just stagnate. Fear shuts him down, breaching his connections between integration and sense. But as denial is the base premise of pretense, his white flag is never seen. He can identify rational standards, but evades them as soon as they are uttered, sensing danger. Ability, conviction and reality are not real to him; only the sentiment of others is. Sentiment is his life-blood and must be monitored carefully. To be pleasing to others is a life or death subject to him, and he negates his own choice to the point where if put into words, you would hear him say, "Tell me, does this feel good or bad to me? Do I like this, or are we against it?"

As one's identity is a result of personal choice and taste, his is replaced with whatever whoever is around him vents as a preference, until a more dominant entity comes into range. When alone, he faces an abyss—a void of identity—so he cannot be alone. Consonant with his own practice, he considers all human traits to be pretenses, designed to impress or frighten others. He must exist within others, as with nature denied and consciousness negated, no other form of identity exists. Sentiment begins as *his view of himself* held by others, and becomes *his view of existence,* held by others. With life seen only second hand, *men* become the first axiom of his existence, and all of his primary standards become social.

For other Fear-driven, it was cemented years later, forced into submission by those holding a greater physical power. They were bullied, most often when looking up to adults for guidance and truth, and instead found themselves subjected to violence for a host of reasons: the awareness of what they weren't supposed to acknowledge, innocent questioning in the presence of denial—an early attempt to reason—all squashed by crude adults threatened by the honesty of a child.

On one side he sees a malevolent universe which holds some dark, unknown peril at every sensation. On the other, he sees a menacing force much greater than his own, with no rationale to guide it. Reason clearly is not on the winning side. Stuck between the incapacity to face existence and men who disallow the process anyway—unable to deal with either—he gives in and uses his tools only enough to evade what he perceives as a danger.

As his *first* enemy is existence, his *second* becomes consciousness. Consciousness being the inescapable link to his first enemy and his only means to direct his elusion, he uses it to pull a barrier between himself and existence. The barrier can only be his *third* enemy—other men. He chooses to side with the least of these evils—the penalty he knows—subhuman brutality. He must face existence or Man to pursue his sustenance, and while existence is an unknown road, the road of deceitful appeasement is provided by those demanding his submission. Instead of considering violent actions to be evil, he comes to consider them necessary. As he is motivated by fear and others attempt to motivate him *by* fear, his conclusion is inherently confirmed. The tactics coincide, yet his own capacity is humbled in this regard. Instead of looking to how things should and could be, he accepts that submission to a dominant force is the proper human condition; that peace and honesty are only shields of mercy held up by the weak, doomed by design. *The Submission/Domination Axis* has in his mind, become inescapable and therefore *axiomatic*. The fundamental axioms of existence and consciousness have been replaced by the substitutes of men and their coercive relation to one another. Instead of independence, he looks forward to the day when *he* will be the dominant force and will no longer need to be afraid. Of course, he doesn't realize that his highest aspiration has been chosen by fear itself, whose tenets will henceforth rule his destiny.

A Fool's Paradise: The Birth of Altruism. Men are not born Spirit Murderers. It is an identity that fear-dominated minds assume, upon acquiring some sense of metaphysical potency in the successful disregard of existence. Grasping blindly for a substitute driver of his intellect, Fear-driven Man turns his focus to the task of securing a stranglehold on those who did not appear to default. He finds his home in a sub-structure that was prepared by other cowards over time; a societal structure requiring no mental effort—only obedience. In exchange for his servility, he gets protection from reality, which keeps him safely anonymous among the pack, hidden from the necessity of independence.

As all standards have been declared social by those he submits to, existence becomes whatever people want it to be. Threatening emotional intensity typically in tantrum form, *defines* existence, and reality therefore varies from person to person. Assuming the pattern of his masters, he decides this should work for him as well. Disconnected from self-support and its required discipline of focus, the sole purpose and activity of his mind becomes his limitless imagination. As the better men abandon such quests for unreason early, those who remain encourage it. He clings to them, and through malice, stupidity or in payment for submission, they pretend whatever he needs pretended, granting a pretense of whatever spiritual values he is too stunted to earn, fostering his distance from reality.

To his relief, he is satisfied that the natural world *need not* be obeyed or even considered, as he can attain his desires through these others—handed to him without causation. This unjust comforting allows him to disavow the world he fears, and disassociated, he looks at the world without dread for the first time. He need not examine it or anything else too closely; he can have whatever he remains cognizant enough of to wish for. "This is easy," he says—as easy as *his fear* needs it to be. There is no addressing any value's source or creation, no need to consider existence and consciousness, as men—not thought and effort—are his means of sustenance and esteem. Lost in illusion, he is free to dream up a world that need not obey even the natural elements of ours. As all causal factors have been breached in his experience, paradise begins with the *end* products of cognition, ready to be consumed.

In his world everything is free; treats fall into his hands from the sky; the atmosphere is set for his pleasure, his subjects bow to him and endless luxuries exist for his delight. He can claim that *by nature,* nothing is to be expected of him; that thought and its benefits should be automatic; that life should be provided to all as a minimum and require no effort. His guardians applaud his description of their heaven, and all effort toward these values in real life, stops. He receives love and acceptance without relation to his actions, and the traits he sees in others that cannot be had without effort—strength, ability, bravery—his guardian's assure him are unimportant and without consequence—the products of luck. With all values being automatic, all of his guilt can be shed or reversed. He can now conclude that those engaging in effort are the ones lost in folly, and he can safely look down on them.

There is only one problem with this world—it isn't real. Ultimately, none of it works. It seems to at home, but in the real world, the active, courageous boy wins the race, saves the day and gets the girl. The real world doesn't acknowledge his illusions. Here, there is no pride without achievement, there is no love without personal value and there is no life without effort. The girl he has a crush on doesn't know he exists; she has a crush on the boy whom his guardian's every statement has been designed to condemn. "Why would she want *him?*" he asks. Lied to and weakened by those closest, including himself, he isn't prepared to compete on wholesome grounds, and the breach between him and life has grown wider as a result. He ends up thankful that the girl doesn't like him, intimidated by what her expectations would reveal.

From the beginning, his successful escape from responsibility achieved no esteem at all, but left a void where esteem should have been. Regardless of his graceless guardian's pretensions, he couldn't escape after all. As he grows past adolescence, he continues to refuse acknowledgment of how the world works. No matter what his inner world redefines truth as, authentic standards prevail in every endeavor: the smartest go the farthest, the best looking turn the most heads and the most confident and capable draw the most respect. Dulled by evasion, grimaced in anger and stifled by fear, his spiral has begun, where no happiness, no pride and no feeling that life is worth living can be conjured—only random bits of momentary safety. He knows he isn't *really* living—that he's putting it off to avoid an unknown danger. He can even acknowledge that those who help maintain his front are fakes, but he returns to them for the consolation the outer world withholds—solace for an irrational contempt.

How to Make a Monster. Back safe in his world, he wonders why the values so freely available at home are refused him by outsiders. Regaining a sense of comfort, he is able to look out at those who did not fall to the same fear; those capable of experiencing the spiritual rewards of living—pride, satisfaction, love and happiness. He sees the way his dream-girl looks at her knight; he recognizes the virtues the knight represents, which makes such awe possible. In reluctant appreciation, he looks with the lost eyes of his greatest heartache—an injury never to be mended. He sees that not having the traits of strength, bravery and ability, *do* hold consequences; consequences too terrible to contemplate. Some undeniable knowledge within him admits, *"That* is what I could have been, had I not been so afraid." He could be enjoying the lifestyle of a Self-made Man: the adventure, the achievement and the passion. "All it would take is..." and fear overcomes him once again, to meet the arrival of the forbidden word—*independence.* He must look away, or he'll realize what the good is *for.*

His choice is either to acknowledge the highest and pursue its image, or to destroy the vision and any evidence of it. It is the destruction of life he chooses. He shrinks from the challenge; he cannot accept that the responsibility for its creation is *his.* He can't do it. He cannot risk failure and lost pride pursuing new values, when he must stand fast just to preserve the image of the faked values. But he sees life being lived by dynamic people, and cringes when he sees them win their dreams. "No!" he screams, in the face of truth. He can't make unreality real and he can't have what he wants, so he can't let it be possible for others. Instead of reverence for the good, he responds to his incapacity with so miserable a hatred, that he turns his cognitive power to the task of corrupting every living concept. He chops up what is left of his rationality, separating cause from effect, virtue from choice, value from love, productivity from pride and life from profit.

His make-believe world turns serious, not intent anymore on making the unworkable work, but on destroying what *does* work. He discovers that he is not the only one dissatisfied with what reality has given him—the contempt is widespread. He finds the way has already been paved—that his burdens can be transferred to the shoulders of the knights by way of a collusive thought process, developed against the productive by his fear-ridden predecessors. The battle has raged on for centuries, between independent men desiring civility and those impotent to pursue values, blindly requiring a blood sacrifice in every premise. His fear has chosen his side by default, and he is taken under their wing. His youthful choices are rationalized by formal anti-concepts. He learns that his fear to venture into the world was only his binding love for his family; that his submission to others was the ideal of selflessness and that his treason against life was his noble sacrifice for the nurturing of their own future killers. Masking that they live *through* others, they claim instead to live *for* others. They claim that "every man is his brother's keeper," disregarding the vast majority who need no keeping.

They held their wounds up before the world to be healed, and through sympathy, brought *dependency* into moral focus. Declaring this as the highest moral premise, they demand that all be chained to all, in an attempt to crush their prey by the very nature of their independence. In retaliation against existence and those able to deal with it, he is schooled to invert, corrupt, seize and destroy all human values. The innocent and strong are not to get away with it. Whether their blood is drawn slow or fast, there must be penalties for them too; the highest must be caned for being able. He learns to turn Man's tools against them, by infusing them with the same detrimental patterns that led to his own spiritual suicide. Afraid to live and afraid to die, he takes every possible action within his self-limited range to justify his stagnation and damn the responsible, relegating to his descendants the same lifelong torture.

He is not irredeemable, but as reform opposes his every conscious premise, we must interact from a point of safety. Developing that safety requires that we learn and accept what he has known all along. In other words, *know thine enemy*.

Part Two: Denial of Mind: Concepts of Irrationality

"It's what people know about themselves inside, that makes them afraid."
—High Plains Drifter

There was a reason our Founding Fathers said "We hold these truths to be *self-evident*." The ancient spiritual conflict has been a battle for control of Man's consciousness, and negation of mind is their primary tactic. The Spirit Murderers have undercut the Self-made every step of the way, to keep the genie of intellectual sovereignty in a bottle. Like every evolutionary step we have taken, it is a transitional phenomenon in human progress; life always breaks free to cover new ground, overcoming all forms of oppression and limitation. This time, our enemy is abstract—the hardest to detect—and therefore the hardest to kill. It lies within the minds of men—in the nature of the motives that drive every individual.

Parallels of Horror in Moral Thought. The best horror movies grip us, not only by fear of bloodshed, but by suffocating the very essence of our capacity to live. They put us in a situation where our senses are futile, and often deceive us. In the darkness, our vision is lost, every sound gives us away, and we dare not even breathe. There is no rationale in our killer and no stopping him. There is no shred of humanity we can appeal to, and no one to save us. Our minds cannot reason; the simplest choices result in drastic penalties; we fear every sight and sound, but wouldn't dare miss them. If we move, there is a penalty. If we stop, there is a penalty. To think is to face a terror too overwhelming to comprehend—so we run. We run without end, tired but don't dare sleep, hungry

175

but can't hold anything down, cold, bleeding—reduced to a panting, quivering mass, to be destroyed at any moment. Helpless, no action we take can get us out of harms way. At some point our perceptions blur, and we cannot fight any longer. Reaching the exhausted agony that begs to be rid of the burden of life, we give up, and wish to just have it end as painlessly as possible. This dread is at the heart of a Fear-driven Man, and as Spirit Murderer, is the state to which he intends to bring you. Regardless of motive, by following him, there would be no other choice.

There are many key parallels between what elicits the deepest feelings of horror in human beings, and the moral doctrines we have all been taught. Reading the Bible, you see the lure of unearned rewards, everlasting bliss, unlimited power over men and nature (the ability to throw mountains around) and you get it all, just for believing. You can see its shysters coming a mile away, shouting "Free this, free that: free, free, free," as the lemmings gather at their knees. In an uncertain realm, they promise the certainty of no judgment, no effort and nothing to worry about—but life doesn't work that way. Easing into it, aren't the traits they expound, *exactly wrong* for human beings?

No man of esteem would want something for nothing. Freebies don't conjure that lecherous grasping reflex in us as it does in the Fear-driven. These are benefits only a parasite would long for—someone afraid of living—and those who follow, give up their minds and deepen their own helplessness as a result.

If a man decides that working is just too much trouble and needs a living safety net as a result, that is his for the taking as well. Its immoral political equivalent is altruism (Forget about your needs—I'll take care of them while you live for me, and in united poverty, we'll starve to death). It takes the form of social systems set up in countries that claim will provide much more wealth to the people than is possible in America, and ends up doing just that—for the politically connected one percent—and slaughters the rest.

Between the presently declared standards of morality, the choice is to die on the vine or to be consumed. Whether such premises are generated by a church or a dictatorship, standards that take everything a man loves while he lives and leaves him for dead, have a common enemy—the mind—and the same result: stagnation and destruction. Furthermore, they all stem from a single source—an individual's *choice* of default. Most iterations of evil have followed the same pattern, which is the inversion of the non-sacrificial code Self-made Man has defined. The pattern of a fear-driven consciousness is 1) *Panic* in response to existence, 2) Intellectual retraction or *evasion*, 3) Destructive action and 4) Penalty.

He considers fear as the deciding factor of his welfare or injury and makes it the center of his focus—a target not to hit, but to avoid hitting—maneuvering to skim by unscathed. As he is always focused on fear, it is always near. Aware or not that his very actions are what cause him to be defenseless, this is what he propagates and brings into the lives of others. The irrational wishes of a Fear-driven Man are at the root of every human evil at every level; slavery, Welfare, Nazism, white lies—all are ways around facing what one fears.

Independent men need not make victims of others. The bloodiest regimes, the most savage crimes and the painful lives of lost dreams all began with a helpless slug at their core.

Death Premises. For the Fear-driven, most actions serve to avoid what it is they fear, and its hold on them determines the extent of their actions against life. As they become caught in their own spiral, the need of self-confirmation causes them to drag others down as well. A death premise or pattern is defined in that it produces no values; it only consumes them. It has no replenishing factors, ending in the detriment or death of the consumer to follow, once the value is consumed. The furtherance of an entity by death pattern is parasitical by design, as it must seek conquest to sustain itself. This pattern of action is as predictable as the patterns of life.

Beginning as a self-esteem issue, the first purpose of a Spirit Murderer is to 1) *Evade that any initiative in life is possible to them.* They *deny* the self-responsibilities of perception, identification, action and validation in order to avoid the shame that would overrun their defenses if they didn't. They have to negate the origin of human power and declare human futility to justify their own relinquishing of control. The second issue confronting them is the bounty they see us creating. They cannot allow our work to result in the pride they have cut themselves off from, so their next intention is, 2) *To remove sanction from our productivity as being moral and right.* The satisfaction of defacing Man's highest possibilities ends at their door, as the outside world is filled with outstanding individual achievements. Hatred for our potency drives the need to strip us of our rewards and destroy their cause—that potency. They have to prove to themselves and to the world, that our actions—actions they fear to perform—are devoid of moral value. That accomplished, they take the next step and declare them evil, which automatically declares the opposite of life-furthering action to be good. But as all human beings need material products in order to live, their third concern is, 3) *To secure a portion of our bounty for themselves.* The practical necessity of sustenance cannot be eluded, and it must come from somewhere. They grudgingly adapt to our system of trade, cheating whenever possible. Though damned by their code, our bounty is nevertheless taken and consumed for their survival—the expropriation of which is often disguised as a penalty to us for the sin of producing it. And last, with their stomachs full and momentary safety established, they intend, 4) *To make it impossible for us to produce any bounty at all.* They know we will go out of our way to produce—to continue being human. So they will make it as hard as possible—the vacuum of their esteem replaced with power, their pride replaced with malice. Disregarding what would happen if no production were possible, they clamp down wherever they can and dictate how things will be done, *or else*. But the nature of human progress doesn't recognize "or else," and their aims are sometimes exposed for what they actually foster—a slave/master relationship.

Freud said only one smart thing: *"There are no accidents."* First, they turn on themselves. Then they turn on us. Without being too blunt, killing is their passion and death is their goal.

Deception. Evasion is tragic—lies are insidious. To lie is to confess one's own living impotence—the personal conviction that life *can* be faked—that there *is* an alternate world that harbors bountiful treasures, much greater and much easier than the one that exists. Lies show one's *preference* for that world, a willing commitment to evade known facts in order to dance down the road of illusion, in pursuit of carrots which rationality forbids. The "get away with it" mentality sees *riches* as a result of dropping his mind.

As his mind has been a source of nothing but penalties, upon any difficulty, it's the first thing to go. Lies are a form of wealth to him, a way to be a coward and have the hero's bounty as well. His capacity for deception is the measure of his volitional dysfunction, and his resulting moral inversion. Given that a mind practices the pattern of what to do in any situation—meaning that it interprets the sides of threat and safety, and gravitates accordingly—it is clear that its metaphysical nature is unhampered—the individual is *not* retarded. His mind functions properly like a well-running car, yet as its choice of virtue is set to an irrational standard—faking that the road goes left instead of right—it steers off a cliff anyway.

The need to lie begins as a self-esteem issue. Valid self-esteem begins in a man simply by seeking the characteristics of existence that his mind is designed to identify—and that process cannot be faked. Such *sensory* evasion is a lie to life—a claim that these instruments bring not furtherance, but harm. It isn't true, and Fear-driven Man knows it. He knows that *inadequacy in its use* is what he fears; not the tool itself. *The falsification of esteem* is at the root of all lies—at the very root of Spirit Murder—and is the most disastrous practice as it makes all other human horrors possible. The essence of a Spirit Murderer and every element to be described in this section is about the cowardice of lying.

Lying is proof of a cognitive dependency—one cannot lie to a rock or a tree, convince it that it is a loaf of bread or a house and then benefit from the lie. One can only deceive a consciousness in an attempt to secure some undeserved value—even from one's own. White lies are the blackest, as they are delivered under the guise of friendship. They act as a wedge, separating the victim from his expressed ideal. Lies open a breach between the victim and truth—what *is*—hampering his ability to act, since reality is no longer the focus of his attention and is no longer protected, heeded, revered or respected. When unreality is tip-toed around and the true condition is overlooked, vices get away with a reward. But worse, all effort towards the proper value stops, as the victim is regarded as having reached it already. If he believes it, he is doomed to failure in attempting to display an attribute he doesn't have, competing with those who truly represent it. Believing he is in a different location on the road to his goal, with no chain of reason to tell him how he got there and no idea how to move forward, *he no longer moves,* and that is the end of values for him in that realm.

It wouldn't happen if merciful lies that defend stagnation were not held as virtues, but instead, the healing course of a mature, tactful honesty. There is no beauty in a premise that disregards justice, and no honor. One's fundamental worth and *only* value to others is one's *existential consonance*—one's bravery to see the truth, speak the truth and live by it. Being truthful, there is nothing to remember, only the logical derivation of existents and their attributes. Lying just makes perception the enemy. When one attempts to live in defiance of truth, then truth becomes one's toxin. Lies mark one's cognitive end in any realm, and where cognition stops, penalties start. A commitment to the unreal is the surest sign that someone should be *committed*. Reality is the last thing you want to have working against you.

Self-made Man cannot lie or fake; reality is hard enough to keep straight. To intentionally sabotage the process of identification would be an amazing waste of resources for anyone. He considers lying to be an incomprehensible violation of proper cognitive effort—that there is just no point to deception at all, or of dealing with anyone who deceives. He asks, "What point is there in seeing a tree, and pretending it isn't a tree?" Lies are dead information and can have no value. He cannot build with the results of a lie, and progress is his only concern. We cannot defraud existence to gain values and get away with it, any more than we can write bad checks. We end up getting paid back in shame and evasion, which have inestimable consequences on our self-esteem. The hard-nosed image often criticized of the Self-made, is that he cannot be swayed with unreality. His intellectual power is not evil. It simply allows those who compromise, no moral escape. With lifelong objectives in mind, he sees the long-term implications of choosing the wrong paths. Such compromise is a prison, locking his spirit and dreams away from the world when they should be free to expand. When we renounce what we really want, we open the gates to hell—our own personally tailored hell. We know exactly what we're missing and feel the twist of every knife in our unborn desire. We can lie to life, but life knows better, and makes us pay.

A soul is not sold in one dishonorable transaction, or in one particular default of reason. It is doled out piecemeal, in ounces of repression throughout life. *Repression* is the illusion that there is a value to be had in permitting an unacceptable element into an ideal, which just makes the vision impossible to reach. Whether involved in thought, a romantic relationship or a business deal, success in all has a specific definition made up of essential elements, where no deviation is permissible. To use different elements is to arrive at a different concept and a different destination. The willingness to repress is to be convinced that one will lose a greater value in being truthful. But if the situation provokes repression, is that value truly greater? Self-made Man knows better—often through painful experience—and will not build on any falsehood.

Evasion of Self-Responsibility. Fear-driven Man is not the creator of concepts or the identifier of attributes, so he starts by denying what has been identified by others. Having spent his entire life, from early development into adulthood avoiding the whole concept of self, his first fundamental evasion is the realm of self-responsibility. Reflecting on his own actions, he considers the attributes of self to *originate outside of self,* alluding to every other conception as the source. With personal misgivings he wishes the external world would account for, the responsible parties are hand-picked according to expediency—God, destiny, other people, society, luck, genetics, inalterable circumstances of the past—all take their turn in the place of his guilt.

He feels hate without any object of hate. He feels the emotion, then assigns a victim. Always wrapped up in some vain attempt to evade the shame of his own default, his mental effort is spent to hide the possibility of having any choice in the matter. We see it in the action that precedes an emotional tantrum—the stubbornly evasive desire to believe that something stands in his way, as an excuse not to try. He actually wishes that barriers *did* exist, to remove the mature obligation to act. The Self-made cannot fully conceive of or appreciate the power of his terror, and we're often left stunned when he plows through us to run the other way. It is no laughing matter; self-reliance is his greatest fear; he will kill or die to avoid the responsibility of independence. As our elation is incommunicable to him, his panic is incommunicable to us.

Panic *replaces* his freedom to choose. To him, there is no alternative, and as a result in life, no benefits. He'll tell you that it's not his fault—that nature made him this way and that he has no choice. He can only use what he is given, and it is unfair if someone else was given more. He'd have you believe that at the precise moment Einstein's cerebral cortex was being developed, his mother ate a Power Bar. Because his own mother apparently didn't, he gets to ignore free will, personal effort and rational discipline, and claim that the surplus of a productive man rightly belongs to him as well. He cannot permit himself to except that ability is a *volitional* development.

He believes that if he can convince others (and himself) that motivations and results can be nothing but indeterminate and that competence is an inalterable, unchosen physical or God-given trait, then his inaction poses no moral default. But if it were not for choice, there would be no individual character. There would be no thought and no science; there would be no progress, there would be no fun and there would be no love. Choice gives us all a unique identity and allows us to build the value system by which we live. Ultimately, choice shows you *exactly* what people are.

In the pursuit of values, the process of cognition is not optional. The freedom to think or not, doesn't dismiss one from its responsibility, or from the fact that to discard it is to cut oneself off from all the spiritual values of living. As our consciousness cannot be forced to provide values by anyone, that includes ourselves. It cannot work properly by any random means, but only by controlled discipline. Without accepting the proper means of cognition, there are no values, no esteem and no passions. There is only pain and hopeless longing, brought about by evading one's first obligation—to accept reality and to live accordingly.

Consciousness is Imagination. There is much criticism about the role of comprehension in human destinies, by those who wish to set it aside as a non-causal factor. To the Fear-driven, the content of the mind is soup—a mixture of chemicals not defined by conscious will, but *defining* conscious will—unreasoning drivers that prove he is not to blame, while simultaneously proving that achievers are not to be praised. The chemicals decide *for* him and determine his behavior, chemicals that are *just there* for some reason, whose existence or nonexistence is to be juggled with diet or sleep, but never by self-discipline or any volitional consideration. His focus then, is to prepare an environment to conjure chemicals that will make the right decisions, leading to prosperity in all things.

Striving to evade the responsibility of thought, he wishes to believe that the abstract world is simply imagination where nothing commits him to anything; but it isn't true. Imagination is only one facet of cognition. In a Self-made Man, there are many wonderful and varied actions of mind, whose biological/chemical trail is so eagerly sought by the effortless. There is the action of solving a problem—looking to the fundamentals of existence and rebuilding scenarios until solutions are found. There is the act of discovery in the physical world, of wide open senses eager to absorb it all, to be enjoyed and stored within his experience. There is the cognitive discovery of a mind following all the implications of new data, combing through his intellect to improve prior understandings and make new connections. There is the action of verifying that an idea or a conclusion is true. There is the exhilarating romantic projection of one's own future. These are the living actions of mind: evaluation, judgment, reflection, creation, discovery and there are countless others. The Spirit Murderers have an anti-path for every one of them, which all funnel back to their causeless, effortless ideal. There is an immoral, life-taking path for every virtue—be aware of it. But for the most part, a Spirit Murderer prefers to remain primitive, and attempts to replace all actions of consciousness with the one requiring no discipline—his limitless and therefore useless imagination.

Sanction of the Irrational. To a Self-made Man, even his imagination has a productive intent, but the subject of purpose is foreign to the Fear-driven. Spirit Murderers aren't creators. They have never reached the conceptual level of consciousness which gives one full appreciation for creative activity. They prefer to remain in the nearsighted untaxing range immediately before them, unable to differentiate what is man-made from what is earthborn, unwilling to separate imagination from thought and unable to think independently. The mental isolation of attributes for classification or any other phase of thought, is just too complex. They never had to work for values in their cognitively sheltered childhood, and unconditioned for that tenacity, they stay focused on the pavement just before them.

Exhausted by the simplest cognitive effort and in tantrum against being lost, they dance around saying "See? La, la, la, I can get away with being irrational! It isn't killing me!" and in that twenty seconds, they conclude that discipline, because it is not forced on them, is unnecessary for the rest of their lives as well. Thought is a realm outside the power of domination, and perhaps in rebellion against the oppression they've submitted to, they drop their minds, saying "See? I have the power *not* to use it. *That* is my stamp of individuality." We all have that power, and it defines or *defies* our pride. To use it is to acquire pride for the choice of life. To abandon it is to conjure the pestilence of shame for the choice of death, first of spirit, next of body, but this is one realm where they feel they can get away with it. They can say "No" in the face of truth, and nothing immediately bad happens; they suffer no visible harm. With no one to stop them, they come to agree that their minds can be as fluid and as wishy-washy as their teachers profess, where anything goes.

They come to believe there are no facts—only opinions, and their opinion of what is good and evil, of what *works for them*—sheltering their esteem by allowing no investigation into their motives—is no less valid than any other. They say, "It *has* to be right; my own guardians encouraged it. They said there were no answers, so that means my *non*-answer can't be wrong." In defiance, they evict from their lives, all those for whom there *is* an answer, and left to grope for self-esteem, they wonder why their free reign against cognition is not resulting in any fulfillment. The truth is, what "works for them," *doesn't work*. They couldn't act like a fool in a job interview and expect to get the job. They couldn't drive a car so carelessly and keep their license. Exclaiming what, in any practical avenue of life will bring not rewards but harm, they try to run a life by such means, and as in all other realms, it results in nothing but penalties.

Lacking the courage to admit the source of their shame, in moments of quiet desperation, they sense regret for their life's course. Misery bleeds through as their nature cannot be repressed and comes to haunt them in their hatred for the independent man—the one who did not drop the responsible structure of his consciousness, who now enjoys all the benefits they long for. In place of the passion they could feel by using their minds to satisfy the natural human need of self-confirmation in choosing life-furthering values, they feel passionate hatred toward those who *have* achieved it. You can witness Fear-driven impotence firsthand, when a discussion about their course of action gets heated. You need not be a genius and explain or expect refutation of a rational pattern of cognition. The next time you hear "That might work for you, but it won't work for me" Ask, "How does your method work?" (Blank stare). "What are the steps?" (Looks at shoes). Their actual steps are 1) Feel problems looming, 2) Evade them and 3) Suffer—and they've earned it.

Impotence of Mind. Needing to hide their fear at the basest level, they attempt to negate the power of the mind by negating its very existence. When that doesn't work, they rely on claims that the mind acts as a tool of distortion, not of precision. They frame our intellectual development throughout history as exploded fallacies instead of a positive view for what actually happens: greater precision, for lives lived better and longer. At any point in time, we have solutions to problems, which are established from our grasp of the issues. As our knowledge and techniques advance, we reintegrate our data to provide more efficient and often revolutionary solutions. *Reintegration,* an essential element of cognition, is most often used as an example of the futility of all knowledge.

They say, "With more experience, we know our conclusions will change again, so why waste time thinking we are correct right now?" or, "Everything we thought we knew, has been disproved." Who in the world thought it wise to give these people press time? Doesn't everyone hear the blatant whining? They stomp their feet because knowledge is not automatic; because life for human beings is a constant process of ever expanding integration. These are people who wish to be relieved of the burden of being *human.* They look down on those trying to understand, saying "Reality *cannot* be understood; it is just a subjective illusion, different for every mind." Treating their cynicism as if it were forward thinking, they'd rather sit back and wait for everything to be finished and perfect.

Those who spout such nonsense are never responsible for great achievements; and likewise, those of achievement would never spout such nonsense. Initially, I couldn't even conceive of this type of dishonesty. Thinking is our basic act of choice—our fundamental virtue and our *only* means of self-worth. Why would anyone try to discredit it? Spirit Murderers have none, and vent their self-dissatisfaction by condemning the capacities of the human race in general. Misery loves company.

They dance with glee when hearing of what is touted as a failure of science—a failure of Man—and proof of his cognitive inadequacy. As the Self-made seek confirmation of their life-furthering power, the Fear-driven seek confirmation that it is hopeless. They joyfully discredit our efforts, perhaps comparing our tenacious progress to their perfect God, and attempt that same automatic stature that they don't have to work for. They claim to be perfect, and then do nothing to rattle that possibility. Asserting that perfection means never to slip on a banana peel, never to make a wrong move, to always look perfect without a word or a hair out of place—to face so immense an impossibility and maintain its image, they cannot move. They fall prey to their own irrational standards—a mistake Self-made Man didn't make.

We did not fix the results of our intellect, basing our worth on any single successful instance. We made no unnecessary presumptions about the world or about ourselves to live up to; we just kept working to solve the problems. If we expected every experiment to work, there would be no need to experiment. The majority of failure is not fatal; it is not a pride issue for a rational man. A pride issue for a rational man would be to quit, or not to try in the first place. But the Fear-driven don't accept that. They rejoice in temporary relief when we fall short, needing to believe that to try is as futile as doing nothing. They expect to see us give up. They long to see their own worst view of themselves confirmed as a condition of *all men,* eager to paint the Self-made as clowns to be laughed at. Could you imagine if Thomas Edison had to face a room full of Spirit Murderers snickering, hooting and hollering at every one of his ten thousand attempts? You'd be sitting in the dark right now. But we shut the door to their influence, and as usual, eventually we succeed, and the floor drops out from under them once more.

Self as a Standard of Evil. Fear-driven Man avoids all possible actions of self, as the self is the medium through which all his pain is received and perceived. The self implicitly becomes his standard of evil. The risks of life and death are most felt through his reliance on others, and *the self versus others* becomes his gauge of well-being. If others are pleased with him, he feels safe. At odds with life when alone, he sides with the others and gauges the quality of his life by the success of his placation.

Never trusting himself to begin with, all attributes of self—in his projection of morality—are to be mistrusted, while all actions of any outside force is to be acknowledged as wholesome and superior. Just look at the general negativity publicly encountered by mentioning any *self-serving* intention. Showing enough concern to keep oneself alive is considered hedonistic selfishness, while the pursuit of happiness is practically equated with slaughter. Isn't it clear? The Spirit Murderers consider life *without* sacrifice to be a warpath, while blood sacrifice is considered *honorable*. Their intention is to remove true morality from life, and morality in practice becomes the pursuit of evil—something a human being cannot bear. Their morality is inverted.

They do not see that a proper, thriving society is built on the sound function of each individual in that society, and that necessitates adherence to the proper standard that life requires: existence itself and our awareness of it. Sound civilization stair-steps from sound coherence, to sound individual, to productive groups of mature individuals. Still, self-hatred drives the Spirit Murderer to wipe out the individual. To cover their cowardice, they must destroy the possibility and moral value of individualism. They pretend that any action of *the self* is vulgar, improper, destructive and at the extreme of their own capacity to deceive, to be insane.

This brings us to a philosophical rule: *If men preach selflessness, selves will be destroyed.* If they preach unconditional love, the conditions will be deplorable. There is no sacrifice in the world of the Self-made, no blood drawn for others and no selflessness. In ours, the self as consciousness, is all: to be nourished, fulfilled and exalted. It is the entity which makes all further societal values possible but *not* by its sacrifice; only through its fortification.

Self-esteem becomes a much more sensitive issue for those intent on faking it. We shouldn't be too surprised that a Fear-driven Man would consider his own actions of consciousness to be unnatural when not involuntary. His esteem is anemic; he can never afford to be wrong. He cannot admit to his patterns being anything but perfect and outside of question. Esteem being an inescapable necessity of life, its lack tortures him throughout his every day, and he grabs onto every twist of truth possible to cover it up. Concurrently, Self-made Man pays attention when esteem is ailing, and works to remedy the causes to get himself back on track. Locked in angst against any attempt at its honest means, Fear-driven Man puts himself in a constant struggle to suppress what his emotions are telling him: that one layer under his unwillingness to see is a feeling of naked terror. This terror comes from the self; the feeling isn't good, so he blames the self and in impotence, looks no further.

It's the self that nags him day in and day out for values. It is the self that constantly wants and needs these things—food, water, warmth, love, stimulation, luxury—with no automatic means offered to achieve them. He hates the self because it doesn't relieve the axiomatic need of esteem for free, and never gives him a moment's rest. A source of nothing but agony, his only answer to the constant nagging of the self, is to kill it. He intends to convince himself and others that his inaction is a virtue. His God snaps his fingers for values, so, created in His image, *effort* is out of the question. He chooses to have faith because it's so much easier than thinking. Wishing becomes the good; working becomes the evil, where to deny life to self is considered moral. *Self-denial* he calls it? It is so simple: he damns what he never intended to pursue in the first place.

Emotions as Instinct. Fear-driven Man prefers to believe that his emotional drivers are instinctual, as no investigation of ensuing responsibilities need follow. He patterns his intellectual effort to surrender to his emotions, and thereby hampers his perception. He conditions himself to disengage proper cognition at any touch of fear, and negative emotions become his primary cognitive guide.

Free will allows Man the misuse of reason. That choice is a part of his nature, and serves him in a way of crucial importance. That he can take the wrong road isn't a contradiction, but an essential attribute of volition—the basic determiner of his pride. Still looking to abandon the controls, he whines that the process to be natural must be automatic; that the direct consequence of any motion his body makes in response to any random emotional sum must turn him in a life-furthering direction, leaving out the proper action of mind—evaluation. But human emotion is not the equivalent of an animal's instinct (and I am beginning to believe that instinct as well is an invalid concept). Animals use sharp eyes, calculated movements and peaked awareness to stay alive; not the evasive eyes and lethargic stumbling of the Fear-driven trying to skirt responsibility. Animals don't negate their minds; they exploit every tool possible to them.

Emotions do not encompass the whole of the data available to Man or to animals. We have sensory organs that gather information, a body that can carry us to pioneering discoveries and an unlimited database to build and reference, to reach objective conclusions. The choice to isolate and be steered by emotional content does not exploit our human advantage and proper potentiality—the capacity of judgment—but instead misdirects our cognitive process, exercising a negative potentiality. Emotion is only a gauge on the dashboard; it cannot assume the wheel. By negating the mind's many other gauges, our lack of instinct leaves us nothing to fall back on and only leads to physical and spiritual annihilation.

The power and exercise of choice based on *all* elements of our human capacity—sensory data, accumulated knowledge and experience and yes, emotion—*creates* morality, which defines our spiritual destiny and well being as well as our physical. We are given these tools and can build anything we choose with them, as we are self-made. Our volitional complexity makes possible a state of existence that animals cannot reach—the *pride* of choosing correctly—choosing life. With every new intellectual height reached, there is a resulting emotional parallel, a reward unattainable to lower levels. By negating choice, Fear-driven Man can't even revert to being an animal. He becomes sub-human. Animals kill for their survival, broken into a few main reasons: to eat, for defense and to eliminate the competition. Spirit Murderers kill first and foremost to evade their own natures—a primal sin.

Animals offer a valuable perspective in regard to morality. Naturally limited to a modest level of choice, they have little capacity for self-deception, and outside of predation, rarely take any false actions. As predators or herbivores, *they are what they are*—it's simple and it's clean. With people, you never know.

An early distinction applied to Man is that of "hunter-gatherer." Well, cats hunt and squirrels gather; does this mean we are a type of cat-squirrel? Or does Man have attributes unique to Man, which "hunter-gatherer" does not acknowledge? When an animal's genus and differentia is defined, its *type of consciousness* is a part of the classification, as a fully volitional consciousness is the key to Man's. Implicit in this scientific breakdown is a being's self-sustaining, self-preserving characteristics: *what* it is, is what keeps it alive. All the willed actions furthering the life of *any* being are moral actions for the entity. The automatic functions of its body further its life as well—that is their purpose, and is the template nature has given us to follow (yet without guiding consent, such functions lie outside an entity's character and moral appraisal). *All* automatic functions of *all* living organisms act for their preservation and likewise must be the purpose of our *chosen* actions.

All men are homo-sapiens, but the title "human" is reserved for those who exercise the proper life-serving cognitive functions of Man. The word "human" is a *moral* term, just as the word "subhuman" defines that state of existence which is *immoral* for Man. We have all taken human and subhuman actions along the road of life, so this must be isolated contextually. A man can operate morally in business, advancing a product—a human action, then go home and beat up his wife—a subhuman action. He can inspire a group—a human action, repress himself in a meeting with superiors—a subhuman action, and then take it out on a subordinate—a subhuman action. We as men must make constant choices, all of which are sources of life-furthering pride, or of self-withering detriment. It is *our responsibility* to see every conscious choice serve the human side—the side of our sustenance, pride and progress.

Self-made Man takes great pleasure in the process. To him, every choice of emotional control, judicious honor and intellectual mastery is another opportunity to feel good about himself. Fear-driven Man hates it, as such rational discipline is a complex action of self. He hates his own nature and makes choices only when no other alternative exists. He is tortured in the process whether his action is correct or not and whether he deserves reward or not. To the extent that he negates his volitional consciousness, he is a subhuman being.

Exoskeletal Frames of Reference. With a world of proof to the contrary, the Fear-driven exist as the only beings who see fit to consider the idea of their own universal impotence as a plausible and acceptable natural condition. Accepting his consciousness as imaginary and the whole of the world to be an indeterminate flux, he *causes and reinforces* his own sterility. By sidelining existence and consciousness, he feels no grounding and seeks to steady his feet with the rules, conditions and unquestionable authority of others. With his outer world as formless as his inner world, he needs *something* of substance—a hard outer shell to handle what he cannot deal with independently. Since by his own estimation, nothing inside his skull is of any use, external frames of reference replace his middle cognitive actions: identification and the creative actions of mind. His ideal, fervently pursued with a vigor to match ours, is to successfully remove choice from his life. If the choices are made for him by a source that can neither be doubted nor questioned, then the responsibility has been shifted, and in his mind, he has won his security. But the desire to negate choice is the inadvertent desire to wipe out morality. By attempting it, he is cut off from all the benefits which only moral action can provide—pride, confidence, enjoyment and love.

Crutches are *temporary* supports for a weakness, to be discarded upon attainment or recovery of independent action. In physical life, crutches are sound, but in the realm of intellectual weakness, they are often dishonest. They exist not to help, but to take over. Acquiring strength and skill and then moving on is a part of growth; relinquishing control is not. For the Fear-driven, crutches are not temporary, but a permanent scaffolding for a building that never gets completed, though it is certainly finished.

The extent to which he clings to others is the extent of his own confusion and fear in each context of life. In the act of rejecting his own judgment at any level, he abandons his only *internal* frame of reference for the collective and unquestionable (unquestioned) code of conduct. He then filters his own actions by their expectations to assure compliance, as self-esteem now comes from the outside in the form of approval or conformity. Improper emphasis is now on the "good opinion" of others, which is the consideration of non-essential values as if they were essential. Fear-driven Man ignores existence and uses men as the *means of perception* to draw his metaphysical conclusions, which leads him to treat irrational filters also, as a means of perception. Others become his eyes and ears, and their false frames become his track to run on.

Fear-Driven Man

The most timid and basic social subordination is to fear the power of another's consciousness, and *others* are the first false frame he finds. We've all known people with so loose a grasp on their own rationality—so easily spooked—that they can be stopped by saying "If you read that or listen to that music, you'll go to Hell!" They give you the 'deer in the headlights' look, which transforms into the primitive terror of expecting some mystical force to descend upon them. To a human being with full control of consciousness, it is truly humiliating to witness. As one must accept or reject a premise to determine one's moral stand, dropping their rationality negates their very moral responsibility. By turning into a nobody to avoid the incomprehensible retribution of displeasing an unknowable power, they become a pawn of evil to be steered, and they asked for it. Those who side with evil are only those who submit their minds.

Other people are the foundation from which all other false frames spring. Others sell him the second false frame in all its forms—faith. As rational validation is inherently processed by him as a threat anyway, he is offered faith as a replacement for reason as driver. Religious, social or otherwise, he simply tells himself that the thinking has been done for him and can be safely relied on. There is no need to confirm it and no need to delve into its motivations; it only need be accepted without question for it to work (not to *actually* work, but to replace discipline with submission as the means, and to replace confidence with approval as the end). People will accept him and he gets rewards for taking one step closer to his automatic ideal, subjugating the painful process of thought. As he grows, more frames follow, some valid, some not, but none are rationally meant to replace his own judgment. Fear-driven Man doesn't see it that way. To him they are a chauffeur, an excuse, a defense, an identity, a fall guy and an alibi. Whether it is a popular culture, peers, school, elders, authorities, political parties or unions, he just desires anyone who will tell him what to do, and grant him the positive view of himself which his own sense of justice denies him.

Exoskeletal frames of reference attempt to replace the internal frame that guides a being throughout its life: a process that can only remain fixed in the fundamental tools of its accomplishment—tools to be used alone. Late teens to early twenties are particularly crucial, as youth are seeking a foundation from which to launch into their futures. The lure of unearned rewards is strong at this stage, especially to those with a great deal of uncertainty in the quest for independence, vulnerable to the organized immorality which is in place against them. The Fear-driven, longing in angst to avoid the necessity to operate their cognitive functions, are given an out by such social framework. They welcome it.

Formal education can be valuable, but not as a pattern for living. They teach conformity and obedience, not the structure of thought. Their hallmark is memorization, and merit is defined not by individual ability, but often by the quality of individual pretense. False frames *don't require* judgment and actually discourage it. If you realize all the students must see through before they can view the world itself—religious doctrines, family obligations, collective requirements, educational, peer and authoritarian pretenses, social pressures—to be moral becomes *to be without mind,* without independence and without sovereign identity. They end up with layer after layer of rules and regulations for living that so obscure and inhibit reality, they can barely function. Stacked one after another directly in front of their vision, the weight of the burden is too great, and the decisions of their lives can no longer be managed. False frames are like Coke bottle glasses over 20/20 vision.

Around false framers, you will find yourself stopped, trapped—your dreams and desires halted by senseless limitations and required obedience to irrational demands. Their frames withhold the dissemination of knowledge to *cause* timidity. They then attempt to rule the minds of others; *the mind* they fear and *know not* how to use. To interpose one's judgment with that of others is to violate the nature of the entity—to suspend and restrict his tools of survival and to leave him defenseless. Self-made Man saw this coming and knocked them all aside. He wouldn't let anything stand in the way of the world and his view of it. We don't jump through hoops; we find our own way, practicing no formality beyond a strict intellectual discipline. Our minds must remain free to function and our bodies must remain free to act on our reasoning power. Self-made Man designs his own filters to sift his affairs. He decides whether or not he agrees with prevailing principles and regardless, chooses the path to life. He builds structures which allow the greatest number of options to remain open, accepting nothing that replaces cognitive action or inhibits the process. He makes sure he has the correct frames for the proper applications. To the extent that outside principles are rational, he respects them. To the extent they are unsound, he seeks to correct them. He is a man. He does not consider himself to be helplessly subject to another's limitations, stupidity, ill-will or parasitism.

RULES FOR RATIONAL FRAMES

Frames of reference are not difficult to validate. Rule 1: *No frame of reference is valid whose verification of authority lies outside the range of your physical senses, outside of your capacity to define and outside of your right to question.* Since before the Inquisition, to question a moral authority's right to sacrifice your life has been considered heresy. This view has spread to include other hopeful benefactors of homicidal altruistic principles, veiled by the claimed good of a family, the public, a State or a nation. With their system of morality, they claim physical and spiritual values are only enjoyed if they are destroyed, and then proceed to confiscate your valuables—goals, dreams, money and privacy, saying it's for your own good. *No one* holds that right over you, and no one ever will.

Rule 2: *No frame of reference is valid which relies on maintaining the immeasurable and the indeterminate as its purpose, its technique, its damage or its reward, while naming a very specific cause, culprit or benefactor.* Cause and effect from purpose to fulfillment must be traceable. For example, faith has always claimed Man to be evil by nature, and granted God the esteem of all good, with proof of neither—concluding that Man must be stopped. Sacrifice of individuals is a claimed historical necessity of a nation's welfare—for the children's futures, for protection against emerging enemies, for the purity of the Aryan race. No link of *supposed* cause to *desired* effect can ever be established. In our first steps of comprehending the enormous cycles of the Earth, man-hating environmental protesters extrapolate straight-line calamity from every measurement taken. If the Earth is cooler, we are headed straight for an Ice Age, and it's Man's fault. If it's warmer, we are headed straight for an inferno, and again it's Man's fault. Supposedly intervening to save this fragile planet, it isn't the problems they wish to solve, but the living actions of Man they wish to stop. The course of every such crisis shows solutions provided by the men of thought and living action, never by the men of tantrum and demand.

Rule 3: *A frame of reference must have a valid context based on a human need for the standard, and all must rest on the fundamental axioms of existence and consciousness.* Frames such as mathematics, science and language are elements that foster and reinforce the power of the individual in dealing with nature. They aid him in the use of his consciousness, allowing complex evaluations with no outside interference. Rational laws such as the American Bill of Rights and self-governed capitalism protect him from the grasping sub-humans who are unwilling to face nature alone. Proper frames of reference accent the individual's capabilities; they don't limit him or provoke dependencies. They lay a foundation that best allows men *by the nature of their metaphysical attributes,* to flourish. In essence, proper frames not only allow experimentation and discovery of better methods, they *sanctify* their pursuit.

Still, many valid frames have been infused with self-defeating, human-limiting guidelines over the course of history. Capitalism for one has been beaten to death by those claiming its attributes to be *exactly* those of its antithesis—Communism. Still, there is no duty required for each of us to approach these realms and sort them all out. It is up to you only to decipher the truths along strains that *interest* you—to follow what works and to discard the rest. In seeking your highest pride and enjoyment, you will have performed such a purification. Other avenues of life will be cleansed by those whose passion is likewise consumed in them.

Putting Spirit Murderers in their own trap, if we *are* driven by God, our conditioning or any other circumstances beyond our control, then our own private interests *are* the result of that affinity, and our proper course and highest efficiency is to pursue them.

Their Withered Tree. The growth of a tree can be planned; unneeded offshoots can be clipped to focus nutrients on a few select branches, and on the trunk. Self-made Man's accumulation of knowledge is identical. He furthers what is most important to him and trims the rest, until and if he decides to pursue the others as well. When he does, he has a much more stable base to work from, and the effort to accomplish the new task is small compared to the size, power and efficiency of his system. His knowledge tree becomes like a redwood—wide and towering—shooting up to the heavens like an organic skyscraper. On the other side, Fear-driven Man rarely addresses the subject of his knowledge base; he allows it to be dictated to him by his outside frames. The result is most often a short bushy thing, crowded with inessential offshoots that keep up appearances, but lead nowhere. So much energy is sapped in feeding the different snarls, little is left for expansion of the trunk. His has many trunks, much smaller and weaker than normal. Self-made Man has one—consciousness—firmly rooted in the soil of existence. The Fear-driven starts trunks according to every false source they believe is responsible for their lives—mysticism, wishes, family, peers—one for each outside frame of reference. Often what provides essential stability—the trunk of consciousness—is undernourished, becomes withered and never bears its proper fruit—the emotional reward of self-worth. The others bear nothing but poison. Poorly rooted, eventually it breaks free, dries up and tumbles with the wind, to be blown around as listlessly as it was created.

Neurobiological facts still apply to those who reject self-determination, though one who negates his senses will receive less data through them. Ignoring instead of analyzing, their biological structure simply fosters what they choose, reinforcing excuses and parasitism while Self-made Man's structure reinforces the skills required for living.

Ever notice how we associate larger pupils to honest, intelligent people, while evil is often portrayed and experienced with those having small pupils? Denial affects the senses as well, and they are less prone to 'let the light in.' Within the range of their proper function, the senses will contract to avoid or expand to accept, according to the will of the entity. The full system energy of a Fear-driven Man is lessened by will, and among his neural pathways, those leading to evasion and falsifications grow the strongest, while those determining his minimum required effort follow. The pathways and connections which could make his experience of living so much more powerful, remain thin, weak and undifferentiated.

He considers self-development impossible—the insuperable and forbidden sanctuary of luck—and so it remains. The anti-concept "Either you have it or you don't" imposes no responsibility. His subconscious, often claimed as the driver, still provides the only function possible to its nature—to automatize common elements of the conscious mind, leaving it free to integrate new information—or in his case, to *dis*integrate it. The actions of mind are what he wishes to avoid, so his subconscious keys off his fear and automates his defaults. Ingrained with the practice of disengaging, these patterns become second nature and denial becomes an automated subconscious attribute. Social standards become inseparable to his means of cognition, and nonessential frames become essential. His fear-driven base is so deep in the brush, he is often no longer aware of it as the source of his plight. As far as he is now concerned, this is how the mind works. Cut off from the higher reaches of his own intellect and from the most sacred emotional states, his mind is dimmed to twist and contort new data to suit his illusions, streamlining his own destruction.

Preserving the Indeterminate: Anti-Concept Formation. Words do not command reality, but only describe it. They cannot be tailored to an individual's wishes or weaknesses, and they do not alter existence. They are as rigid as scientific measurements, and the more precise we are in their use, the brighter are the benefits they make possible. But to a Spirit Murderer, words are a way of stealing: an attempt to loot the value of a concept's true meaning by stretching it to cover what it doesn't actually describe. In most circles, anti-concepts exist unchallenged, spreading and perpetuating without resistance, and to the trained ear, their death rattle can be heard in every sentence.

A concept is a mental integration of specific attributes. A word's clarity determines its usefulness, which is the whole point of defining it. An *anti-concept* is a mental integration of *variable* attributes, subject to the interests of the wisher. It allows the user to hijack valuable concepts such as love, courage and honor and install his own defining characteristics. A definition that lets any attribute comprise a thing, evicts it from the realm of identity, of measurement and of focus. When *anything* defines a thing or a concept, *it no longer exists.* Anti-concept formation is the ultimate cognitive sin. It is not just the corruption of language, but of comprehension itself. In tribute to Aristotle, I call this "A is Anything."

Spirit Murderers intend to reverse or negate all attributes of Man and existence by any means possible. As we stair-step up, they head back down with whatever we've created, beginning as early as the first human accomplishment. Their effort has shadowed our progress along the whole means of abstract evolution: language. We use language to build; they use it to destroy. Did you ever notice when conversing with the Fear-driven, that you never seem to be talking about the same thing? They bob and weave to avoid any clarification which would leave their true motives exposed to open daylight, and avoid any subject they are afraid to discuss, even while discussing it. Consonant with the mislaid formation of their consciousness, so such a being uses language—not to clarify, but to form his Fear-driven view of it: obscure, uncertain and out of control, without purpose or structure, to justify how he lives. His fuzzy, half-understood definitions can mean anything, or more to the point, nothing, and their insubstantiality leads him and anyone who listens as usual—nowhere. But his lethargy is not without cause. There is a clear motive behind their inexactness: language and concept-formation are inverted to serve their opposite intention; to subvert and break cause and effect. Not to build, but to make building impossible.

There is always a dual motive: to cover their own default and to destroy those who did not. If you're wondering *what* beget *what* in chicken or egg fashion, application to the self *always* comes first. They want to sever the relationship of cause to effect primarily to mask their own default. To accumulate every bounty and damn its *actual* producers, is a secondary consideration.

If they can mix and match cause and effect, they neurotically believe they can realize their imaginary world. The concrete-bound mentalities claim implicitly, "If I can touch it or taste it, then perhaps it *is.* If it is of the mind, then I get to make it up." Because a concept is not a material element like a rock or a tree, they think they can get away with subverting its identity. But such folly has never resulted in the values they try to cheat. This is the only time when they exclaim the great power of the human mind—the supposed power to turn their intellectual sludge into grandeur. Their method is simple. They see desirable products or traits in others and detach the benefits from the work expended to achieve them. Then, they reattach the benefits to whatever random actions they themselves have taken. They disconnect the guilt, shame and poverty *they* suffer, and plug *that* in as the result of the producer's effort, in place of his rewards. It's easy—the producer works and gets no thanks for it—no reward, while the Spirit Murderer is free to remain irresponsible and incapable, gets treated like a king and enjoys the looted bounty. It may sound like a foolish child's game and is, but it has grown into the foundation of many religious, philosophical and governmental systems around the world.

Still, it doesn't work; not on an individual level and not on a national level. A man can cannibalize, but cannot assume the stature of his victims. He can steal their property, but he cannot reproduce the bounty which he efforts only to take. The productive cannot be drained to serve the nonproductive without collapse of the system, on any scale that it's practiced. The only difference is the time necessary to hollow out a larger capital base, revealing the sickness with the final crumbling of the structure; but truth, facts, honor and justice are not enough to stop the Fear-driven. The something for nothing, 'get away with it' mentality respects neither reason nor boundaries, as they are psychologically tied to their end. Under the pretense of confirming the fluid structure of the mind, they approach the psychological safety of never having to face reality, and for the Fear-driven, that is too big a carrot to ignore. It is a quest they will never drop, even though its true confirmation would be a descent into madness, which some do reach. But most Spirit Murderers exist in a state of neurotic dysfunction—angry and helpless—and function just enough to make it to work each day, grudgingly adhering to the minimum level of civility society requires. The only discipline that keeps them together—that instance of proper conceptualization—is what they fight. *Integration* is the action of mind that fits new pieces into the puzzle of life. The purpose and inevitable result of anti-conceptualization is *dis*integration. He achieves no pride in this folly, he just makes the puzzle impossible to solve. Domination and temporarily successful deceit do not carry the sense of self-worth that pride does, as they require victims. He can stand alone no more than a beggar can. He achieves no spiritual bounty, but only wipes out the values he wished to seize, and further distances himself from ever reaching any.

There is no way to escape cause and effect—it is what it is. Life fulfillment and emotional health are achieved by *all* men in the *same* basic ways and for the *same* reasons, as why we all use the same dictionaries. Concepts are what they are and mean what they mean, regardless of who's using them. They describe conditions of existence that can be encountered by anyone. When encountered, they are given names to differentiate them from all other concepts. To use a concept's name when its conditions *do not* exist, does not bring its rewards about. Yet as we form concepts just as we build homes, plants and skyscrapers—*for use*—the immoral man sits back and expects that one day the book titled "My Way" will drop out of the sky, packed with the definitions that allow him wealth and grand spirituality for nothing—for his guarded lifestyle of total irresponsibility. It will never happen. Sloth by any other name is still sloth, as is fear. Confidence, pride, love and self-worth are made up of the elements they are made up of, regardless of the names chosen for them. The elements are determined by cause and effect. They cannot be cheated and are not negotiable. The clear definition of virtues places all men on a moral map, showing each his distance to their attainment. Spirit Murderers pretend the map shows them sitting upon the crest of virtue in all cases automatically, which leaves him stuck where he is.

There has never been proper philosophical separation for the *moral* sides of concepts in *any* human language, and that can result only in confusion for the human mind. Looking in a dictionary or thesaurus and you will see that nearly every word has a life-serving and a life-taking definition that is supposed to mean the same thing. Every word will have a synonym, which is actually a metaphysical antonym. The expropriation of the benefits provided by the life-serving concept is the motive behind equating these words. Being inconsistent, it is obvious that no rational standard defines their poles. Intentional? I consider it a missed step in the progression of reason—perhaps an over-emphasis on etymology—but the proper standard *is* life, and someday it should be straightened out. Otherwise, such inconsistency can mask a Spirit Murderer's philosophical intentions, fostering a host of insincere games. By equating moral words with immoral ones, it allows the actions of a moral man to be described with immoral words, while an immoral man can have his actions softened or justified with moral synonyms. They can bait and switch—saying things one way and implying another meaning in expression or tone—leaving victims with plausible statements, attached to improperly negative undercurrents. They can do the same to give a positive spin to evil propositions. Such subversion is their key means of distorting reality to rob the glory of our virtuous action and its product.

Motive is everything; if someone is hell bent on viewing virtues negatively, he can find the words for it. If he wants to put the best light on destruction and slaughter, he can do that as well. But the man who *is* a man, uses words objectively and doesn't waste his life. He looks for the words that give him the most complete description of what it is he is doing, and outside of propriety, he needs to hide nothing. His mind flows with the logic of truth and his body follows suit. He can breathe deeply, and watch the darting eyes, eager to evade his steady glance. He can note the inconsistent gestures, the manic energy of a flight from reality, which the creature is attempting to conceal. He can watch these things calmly and make the decision not to deal with it, isolating the potential impact it can have on his affairs, until the creature matures into a human being.

Non-thought. Most of the fear-driven use abstraction improperly, if ever. Even what they call "thinking" is not thinking at all, as you cannot trust their means of differentiation. What anything means, is simply *what it means to others,* and they often only parrot what they hear, as believing and repeating is easier than thinking. Ask him what he thinks and you'll hear "The Bible says" or "The newspaper says..." but never his own judgment. Asking him to drop his frame and answer alone, and he is lost. A viewpoint derived not from existence but from other's views of existence—*beginning in others*—does not qualify as thought, or as one's opinion. Thought is an independent process; an opinion on any subject must be self-derived, revealing links back to the foundations of existence. His mental content was accepted without knowledge of its derivation—without awareness of the roots leading back to its origin—and he therefore lacks the capacity to work with the knowledge itself.

He often shows impatience with the true process of cognition—a matured form of his childhood tantrums—considering it not so much a threat anymore, but as stubbornly unnecessary. Immediate results are always the expectations of those who seek the effortless, but in trying to cut corners, he only turns off the greatest depths of his mind. He can handle the immediate result of direct cause and effect, being simple to witness and ignore; but he has no patience for enduring a multi-step process. You can feel his predefined sneer—the emotional charge building as he grows eager for its release. He indulges every opportunity to express contempt, and won't consider any enlightenment that would substantiate its withdrawal.

As the natural enemies of thought, the vast concentration of Spirit Murderers are limited to the lower levels of cognition. By choice, they share characteristics with early Man and the tribal primitives that still exist today. Held back by will or by nature, little is possible to savages. At some subjective parallel, they believe all of reality is controlled by demons—subject to the unknown in its very form, where entities can vanish, appear or mold into a threat—and they leave as much of existence as possible in that category. The elements above simple cause and effect for a 1-2 level Spirit Murderer are not considered to be within the capacity of Man. Their two piece opinion however, is its own avenger—to damn with only a few facts has an alternate short-range equivalent—to *love* with only a few facts. They give their favor without firm identification and vent their dislike with the same willingness to approximate, and wonder why they can maintain no consistent respect or happiness in their lives. The error and malady is the same—a mind too lethargic to form rational standards and adhere to them. There is no escape from the penalties of a shoddy intellectual effort. Living by the shortest range, they remain vulnerable to obstacles that could easily be avoided. Concepts, dreams and ideas are always impossible to those who do not seek the validation of their premises. Instead of that effort, they prefer to plant into their epistemology the possibility of the impossible—of the morally exempt—a process which forms no chain. Such an attempt is not rational, but neurotic cowardice, and only leads to further stultification.

The Fear-driven suffer the spotty reasoning of a selective reality to avoid effort and blame, often acknowledging its simple elements and refusing the existence of complexities. With a fifty-piece puzzle in front of him, he tries to draw conclusions after he gets a few pieces. He justifies this with the same animosity which negates the valiant effort of a man and replaces it with luck—that such discipline is an unconscionable imposition. Instead, he wants everyone to pretend that the picture is complete, and that he is justified to move beyond it and he does—straight into a void.

Its symptoms show up in what Ayn Rand called *package dealing,* where approval of any part is necessarily approval of the whole. There is no breakdown, no cognitive separation, no clarification allowed—just blind approval or renunciation. This is the unwillingness to abstract, to evaluate the attributes of entities. A context is a setting, a background for an event. As one moves through one's knowledge tree, each new vantage point is a new context—the point from which one is looking at the world. Fear-driven Man cannot follow, or just doesn't want to. The anti-conceptual mentality has reached the limit of his abstract capacity, or the limit of his tolerance for it. He is left behind, and reacts to the new conditions as if they are false, seeing them as inconsistent with the old context. They *are* inconsistent as we are in a different place intellectually, but they cannot or in tantrum *will not,* keep up. For example, he sees one link in a chain of knowledge and considers it the whole. He hears a radio program on a subject, feels a bond with the commentator's negative bias—an opportunity to sneer—and considers it a complete description of the event in question. He mimics the commentary as if it was his own, without consideration for a better reasoned argument. He makes no attempt at a macro or micro understanding, no effort to scale back to see a wider view or to zoom in to identify its elements. The introduction of any aspects not discussed by the commentator blindside him. Without the radio program, he wouldn't know what to think, *or how.*

This is the birth of Ayn Rand's theory of *context dropping,* which begins as a lethargic byproduct of cowardice and grows into a deliberate means for the irrational invalidation of sound reasoning, as well as the irrational *validation* of unsound reasoning. An anti-conceptual mentality will raise wages without expecting the product to cost more. He'll cap consumer prices without regard for the price of energy. His actions senselessly destroy, putting companies out of business and starving individuals—physically and spiritually.

Separating cause from effect to ignore originating factors and consequences is the chief means of context dropping—ignoring the existence of the full chain in fear of one's capacity to handle the living process of managing it—but there are other forms. Calling us "insignificant specks of dust in the universe" takes us out of the context in which we *are* significant—our loved ones and our loved pursuits. Measuring us against impossible standards is another. Context isolation, dropping or any other kind of evasion is obviously not a refutation or a proper ground for action; it is immaturity or worse—the inability to think, or to "run the chain," as I call it. It's frightening to see how many of them end up Vice President, as lacking the functional capacity for thought disqualifies them from leadership. They may enact faulty reasoning to suit their fraud or malice, but I'm inclined to think that often, they just missed the bus.

The Fixed and the Fluid. The Fear-driven simplify standards by not having any. Actually, standards are unavoidable to any human, and theirs are defined as usual—by default. Early on, they identify *the good* as any value experienced which requires no effort. *The evil* is anything they fear, and whatever causes them to face it. Often, that's as far as they take it, and naturally, the mind falls into the latter category. Parasitical from day one—believing all are tied to all—standards become not primarily existential, but *social,* and backwards, they look to their social links to define what is *existential.* Too lethargic to form standards on their own, they live off of what *others* have created, involve themselves in *others* as a purpose and look to *others* to form their values. People tell them what the world is, and in fear of facing it alone, they accept what is told to them second-hand. Disconnected from fundamental judgment, they must pursue self-worth by gauging their own adherence to exoskeletal frames. The Fear-driven typically avoid the physical sciences, away from any association with an emphasis on true standards, where such observation could blend into their psychology to positively reinforce their emotional control. In the sciences, the rules are rigid—they do not account for fears, and remain unaltered by tantrums, pleas for mercy or patience—and that poses too many questions. $2+2=4$ has no give; it simply *is.* It can't be cheated, lied to or threatened, and this provokes the most extreme discomfort in a Spirit Murderer. It exists outside his power—outside his world. The world will pay no tribute to a man and grant no harvest, without his understanding of it. To understand it is to exercise an attribute of self, and the *concept of self* is their enemy. Science wipes out their whole basis of reality—an unconscionable threat. They intend to negate facts and stick with rootless opinions, so in effect, all standards remain in flux, as they vary from person to person, influence to influence. For the Fear-driven, standards of good and evil remain whatever they want them to be, and magically adjust in pace with their own degeneration.

An actual standard is a means to gauge adherence to a principle, placing the measurable attributes of an entity along an applicable scale of unit value. An *anti-standard* is a rejection of the capacity to measure—a stature granted automatically, not requiring effort or mind. Morally, it is the rejection to stand *alone,* along a scale of virtue. A false standard negates all liabilities of the individual while providing the individual with rewards. It glorifies his current state as the pinnacle point of departure, molding itself to fit, rather than permitting valuations where room for improvement could be seen. This simply means that if he is to determine a hierarchy, he is only to look down. Relative standards between what the men around him uphold (oddly enough defined by the true standards) are all he can see, and ignoring all above him, he compares himself to the lowest to say, "I'm not *that* bad." Being higher doesn't hide that he needs to compare himself to the deplorable. He feels no need to be as high on the proper scale as possible as is the quest of a Self-made Man, but only a smidgen above the stature of others, which too is often a lie. As his self-esteem is derived from others, his herd instinct of not outdistancing the pack is of greater value to him, and quells all desires to rise. Their justification can be found in the saying "everybody does it." Standards of relativity are the tools of the unselfworthy. They have no self, and gain no esteem from climbing the ladders of virtue, as there is no self to please.

An anti-standard must allow no adherence to itself—adjusting the target to suit their flawed aim, like moving the basket to catch any wild shot. Reality as far as their concerned must bend to account for their moods, emotions and tantrums. You can imagine them in their threatened misery, yelling, "This *is* happiness! I *am* happy, damn it!" They ignore that the problem exists and could be solved, because the only means to the solution is the enemy they dread—cognition, and the first hurdle to clear is accepting what their default has done to their pride. Chickening out instead, their false route to esteem drives them to claim that there *is* no default, that the mind is capable of anything, that concepts can be whatever one wants them to be, and that there are no fixed means in body or spirit by which a man must live. Close off one nostril and you'll know how simply and drastically it will affect your life. Existence *matters*. It all matters, but they need to believe our brains have no structure or form—as if they were liquid. The reason? A dual motive again: first, to fix the impossibility of addressing what they fear, allowing to remain fluid only what aids their game. Second, as a death premise breeds dependency and dependency requires victims, they fix the restraints to move freely over the soon to be corpse.

From a Spirit Murderer, you'll hear nothing but approximations about facts and final verdicts about unknowable dementia. The fixed is not the world he cannot change—the rotation of the Earth, gravity and the new truths of nature that science reveals every day. The fixed is his desired superiority *over* nature: the power to tell nature what it is and demand that it oblige. He fights to nullify the rational process of validation—the commitment to reality, the process he fears—and fixes his inability to perform. He fixes the impossibility of personal action—that goes without question—but his excuses remain dynamic, as do the accused sources of his own guilt. His emotions are free to run wild, and are to determine how reality must submit at his every random turn. For a group whose slogan is "There are no absolutes," they hold as utterly absolute, the impossibility to pin any responsibility on themselves. He holds fixed his own barriers to progress, a human's capacity for talent, his opinions, assumptions and what knowledge he has worked for. He has no tolerance for it to change—to always advance as science does. It is either fixed or it is wrong, because in fact, it has been memorized, *not* understood. He can't catch it unless it stands still. You can feel the lack of foundation to his assertions, always delivered offhand, tainted with belligerence or condescension as if self-evident, to avoid questioning. Part of its indication is the forbearance not to look past its utterance, somehow aware that a void would be faced. Whenever he rides the edge, he freezes, frightened at the extent of his knowledge, but this is the threshold of learning—the pioneering step, considered great adventure by the Self-made. Either an individual questions and explores all that has gone before to validate and build on it, or he shuts his mind to secure the illusions of its validity, and can take no steps alone. The sad truth is that in his knowledge, he might be right, but he'll never reach conviction, being unwilling to identify the elements of his view. Fear overcomes him, and memorization is his way around it. He submits to the teachings without question, feeling he has no right and no capacity to question, and upon reaching a position of authority, he then denies that right and capacity to others.

Spirit Murderers cannot afford admitting to an accurate definition of good and evil—they wish to allow no clean, rational view of innocence on one side or total contamination on the other. They see 'no need to go to extremes,' in other words, no need for purity and no need to disinfect. Whenever I hear this, I think of the research laboratories or the dust and dirt free environment of the space shuttle pre-loading bay. I think of micrometers and other precision instruments measuring phenomena well beyond our sensory grasp. I think of the complex readouts on digital displays, where some miniscule variation can make a roomful of scientists cheer, or rise in astonishment. I think of my constant pursuit of pure, moral clarity and all it has given me. No need? The Fear-driven imply that the pursuit of exacting standards is a manic, destructive interest such as those of Nazi skinheads, but it obviously is not. Still, a goal-driven man is treated as an outsider because his creations are accomplished alone. The pack had nothing to do with it—they unite to lie, cheat and hate—not to produce. The only extreme their pack ever partakes in, is slaughter.

The pursuit of pushing the rational envelope cannot be taken out of context. In this realm, it gauges adherence to a principle, therefore, another word for 'extreme' in this context is *true*. Extreme fitness is good. Extreme beauty, love, devotion to truth, accuracy, purity, physical awareness, knowledge, happiness, bounty, are all powerful forces that serve the living, if one is willing to gather and practice them. Then again, living is not always one's intention. To avoid extremism is to avoid white and black in the context of identification, which is to avoid exactness. They say, "We are all just shades of grey," except for the best, and of course, the worst. Acknowledging the best imposes a fundamental obligation and a brave honesty beyond most—the act of reverence. Not acknowledging the best is part reproach—in defiance of those who are truly alive and truly moral—part cowardice, in the attempt to dodge a valid guilt. Not acknowledging the worst is a psychological limitation, but driven by the irrational dread of discovering a mirror image, which is also valid. To permit no extremes means nothing is quite hard or soft, but remains shapeless and undefinable, reflecting the content of their consciousness. Such an object—a lifeless, spineless blob—cannot be projected like an arrow can. It cannot gather any inertia and never does; therefore, it poses no threat to the esteem of a Spirit Murderer.

The whole intention of *Moral Armor* is to glorify and preserve the spirit of the highest type of human being: the arrow, the Self-made Man, and his possibility exists only because there *is* a hard, clear, realistic extreme to aspire to: the moral purity of seeking the life-furthering path in all things. Not to measure each man by an elastic standard as life does not grade on a curve, but for each entity seeking to enjoy its existence at the height of its own capacity—whatever that may be. A by-product of this is to publicly shatter any false esteem such proponents of the grey lay claim to. The last grasp they have on the spirit of Man, the only power they ever had; their sacred moral inversion will fall to me. *The game is up;* we know what you are doing, and there will be nowhere left to hide. But there is a big difference in how we will deal with our enemy. They will not be put to death as is the ultimate social goal of the fog-summoners, but the greatest horror for the Spirit Murderer, to be put to work in the service of earning their own esteem by civil means. No longer will a cushion be allowed between cause and effect for the immoral. For once they will face the true consequences of their theories in practice. Those who are willing will learn that there is *nothing* to be afraid of. Those who aren't, will be their only victims.

Part Three: Evasive Action: Perversion of Purpose

"Madness unleashed respects neither reason nor boundaries."
—WWII Adage

We hear that the good always prevails, but the truth is often, the best *don't* win. They get taken out by weapons that are not in their arsenal. If the only human danger were crude gunman, burglars and other easily identified criminals, common law would be enough to safeguard civilization. The real danger is philosophical subversion, the false ideas behind human action in thought, relationships, art and the social institutions designed for the supposed benefit of all. The confusion suppresses motives one level lower, to hide the true premise and intention of either side: that of life or death. This isn't accidental, of course. When an army is in front of a large gun, it will mix with the opposing side to nullify the weapon. This is what the Spirit Murderer's have done with their default. If they can keep it from being seen, they can keep it from being annihilated. Their death patterns are interwoven throughout all living structures, intending to choke the virtue out of them eventually. Sickly enough, in our own moral confusion, by apologizing for our capacity to live, we have woven ours around theirs as well. It is time to choose sides openly.

A random thug harms us *once;* moral subversion harms us *all day long, every day of our lives.* These enemies cause the inadvertent worship of evil, and a profound hesitation to do what is truly right—especially in regard to independent judgment. Philosophical subversion has us supporting foolish and embarrassing moral premises, with many futile and destructive consequences. It has parents wishing for their children's success, while unwittingly working for their destruction. The extra effort of reinforcing them with unquestioned moral dogma only serves to hollow them out, making success *more* difficult to achieve and life's enjoyment nearly impossible. Growing up, I heard the same mindless explanations everywhere I went, the same rehearsed quotations, the same heated theatrics and the same spiritual threats. I found it shocking that the product of adult minds often became raving lunacy. Struggling with such hand-me-down moral nonsense led me to the discovery of what it was *actually* damning—life and cognition.

With the moral brainwashing I suffered, I remember the extent to which I was drawn in. I'd be driving along thinking, "If I adjust my seat back a little more, I'd be perfectly comfortable," but I wouldn't do it. To do anything totally for myself was regarded as wrong—as selfish—so I would delay doing it, or try to *ignore* that I was doing it, so I didn't have to feel guilty. I'd feel guilty about taking extra creams for my coffee. I'd feel guilty for getting a good parking spot, being first at a light or standing ahead of someone in line. Now tell me: is this a sound preoccupation for any productive mind? Why did I torture myself? Because I took this morality very seriously, not realizing that insane torture was its intent, and the more introspective its victims are, the more thorough is its harm. The consequences go much deeper than such shallow diversions; they go right to the wall. I see it all the time, people pandering to senseless expectations such as selflessness or sacrifice, trying not to be hit by the opposing accusation of selfishness, accepting its liabilities without question and submitting to its penalties rather than thinking their way to freedom by invalidating these false premises. I see irreparable damage done to lives spent masking the neurotic insufficiencies of spouse or family, while their own priceless desires are surrendered to the void. Even the presidents of vast companies, exercising the height of intellectual complexity have put no effort into an *independent* understanding of morality, and what it does to them. They never ask the crucial question—whether or not the premises they serve are rational; *whether or not they deserve any guilt in the first place.*

The malady reminds me of a comedy I once saw, where two catholic schoolboys were waiting in line for confession. Divulging their sins, one remarks something to the effect that he masturbated eighty-five times and told three lies. The other boy being more savvy, helps mask his disturbing problem by changing his confession to masturbating twice and telling *four* lies. Like a crack in the sidewalk, false premises always breed loopholes—a means to cheat the system in order for life to continue, but most are not so inventive. For those without integrity, morality becomes a hustle; for the straight forward, it becomes guilt. Most process the cheating as one more moral flaw, pushing them further away from the actual truth about themselves.

The tragedy of individuals trapped under unnecessary stress is rampant, while issues paramount to their self-esteem go hidden and unaddressed. It has put Man in the position not to maximize his moral actions, but to *lessen* the effect of false moral penalties on his life. They have us looping, using our ingenuity to evade a senseless guilt, instead of using it properly to follow our dreams. We're all stuck in the process of mitigation, when at any time, we could choose to just drop their code—the unchosen obligations and false burdens—altogether.

Otherwise, the resultant manifestations into false epistemological chaining are endless, always degenerating into the senseless sidetrack of deflection and justification on one side, and the gluttonous determination of punishment and value seizure on the other. The fiasco burns energy for no productive purpose, driving the victim to cave in on himself and fry, like an adding machine run amok, while he is stripped of values by his accusers. Doesn't it sound familiar? Like hoodlums keeping your mind occupied while others go through your pockets. It is a vast problem, and begins as an exclusive outgrowth of the fear-driven mindset.

Enterprise of Mind. When a man gives in to fear and reduces himself to a helpless quivering mass, it infects everything he does. It changes his approach to life from one of utility and enjoyment, to an awed struggle to covet and preserve pleasing illusions, with reluctance ever to exercise his mind's proper function. The strain of reality never gives the Fear-driven a moment's rest, so to him, peace is impossible. As his ideal is a mental state undisturbed by thought, his outward manifestations are simple extensions of this desire. To him, the projection of peace and prosperity has a very different meaning. A semblance of peace comes only after conquest, which lasts only as long as it takes to digest prior pillaging. Clinging in fear to life, his death premises must be fed with new victims, as he is, like it or not, a living being. Prosperity to him is a constant flow of unearned goods. His first motive was to get all he wants—not to earn it, just to get it. But such gluttony is quickly identified—even by him—as a distraction, and his mind presses on for the true means of satisfying a natural craving—a productive (or destructive) endeavor.

Life allows no negation of purpose. To maintain even the most rudimentary comprehension, all men must practice the mechanics of mind at some level. A man's enterprise of mind—his fundamental purpose—*is* his expression of self-esteem, or his evasion of its lack. If a pointed plan is not chosen in life, random integration and disintegration *is* the resulting plan. Life lived in an orderly, controlled, structured way is a *human* attribute. The structured is the intelligent; the noble. The Fear-driven have no regard for order in their lives, as order is defined by a hierarchical value system—a patient construct of the rational. He senses order not as a sound intellectual frame, but as a cognitive straight jacket, limiting him in a way that is intolerable. It's too clear, permitting no cover, no fog and no blanked out safe haven for his falsified esteem. It is this place he values above all: his oasis of thoughtless, blameless, obligation-less freedom. When a man is freed from the responsibility of life—from profit in body and mind—he is disconnected from all responsible courses of action. When he is left to float, he is able to distort life's purposes and to live without sound purpose. Negating his mind and riding others, he can propose and pursue any evil without regard for consequence. An independent man would never have time for that. With the maintenance of his physio-spiritual life as his chief concern, the efficiency of that quest would drive his every thought. When a Fear-driven Man is free not to consider life, *he doesn't*. He contemplates its opposite. When someone presents him with the irrational, he pursues it.

Fear-driven Man becomes absorbed in anything that allows the essential questions of his life *not* to be addressed. Even what seems a normal, logical involvement can be chosen by unhealthy fear-based motivations. Dating, friends and children can be a product not of personal desire, but of panic over the question of what to do and who to cling to, erected as a barrier to their own secret dreams. *Spirit Murderers start with themselves.* His enterprise is wholly in fraud, in a manic interest not to face his core default, and he spends a lifetime building a defense against it. Whatever cleverness he possesses serves to fake to himself and to others that his default is something other than it is. His underlying theme in constant self-reflection is "It isn't true." His only belief in the power of the mind is in the success of his evasions. He says, "If existence is whatever I want it to be, then what I did yesterday didn't happen. It is wiped off, even out of the minds of those who witnessed it. I can move ahead with a clean slate, ready for new filth." What he doesn't realize in the folly, is that most everything he enacts or supports, addresses his weaknesses directly.

Consumed with the protection and concealment of his flaws, he works hardest to validate his own futility. He reads the riot act on why goals aren't possible and why his destiny is not in his hands. Let him have the floor and you'll hear how not even tomorrow can be planned, that discipline can't be expected of men, how they'll squash any attempt at virtue, how morality is hopeless, how ability can't be learned, how no one can know anything, that men are evil cannibals by nature and the world is going to end any day now in chaos and calamity. What he is actually describing is *himself*, his hatred and fear for life and the fragile mental structure he's built. Stop him in his blind fury, and he might see that *he* is the one with human arms and legs dangling from his mouth.

If he can get you to ditch your mind and join him in his trench, then he feels justified to relax into his panic. "I *should* feel panic," he wishes to confirm. Without an illusory barrier, he faces a void, and on the other side, the truth of his own chosen impotence. He'll fight like a dog to declare the focused and determinate as evil, allowing his indeterminate heaven to reign—his only image of self-esteem—or more accurately, the only shutter hiding his self-hatred. All he has to do is harp on it long enough and menacingly enough for it to be true. Where does it leave him? Stuck with his aversions, safely as he sees it.

Let him go on and you'll hear of his illusory jackpot—the sales pitch that all values requiring effort to achieve in our world, require none in his. His virtue is not earned by work, but by lack of work. All of our earned pride and happiness is a preposterous illusion, and all of his illusions are a command. His heroics portray not the courage of action, but of inaction, not the beauty of strength, but of weakness, not the honor of rewarding intelligence, but of emanating pity. He need do nothing to meet these standards. Stepping farther, the practice of virtue—productivity—can be considered selfish treason in his world, and all treason, a virtuous sign of faith. As no mind is recognized, contradictions cannot be exposed. As there is no process of validation, no errors can be invalidated. His goal is to devise an environment where he can feel significant, without doing anything significant. He believes that his "get away with it" mentality has created an alternate universe where he can be powerful too, without representing the virtues required. But the truth is "his world" isn't a world at all. To describe any part of it, he must give it form by damning reality as a point of departure. *It is the inverse of the world that exists*—nothing more. It's our world minus effort and responsibility—our world minus honesty, where a man lives not by acts of will, but by wishes. The joke is on his followers: eluding to a world where one's mind is replaced, only spurs the dilemma where one's mind becomes powerless.

The Abyss: Irrational Invalidation. Why is it that the last to be accepted as true, is always what every indicator pointed to in the first place? Why does it take so long for anything truly moral or rational to catch on? History is filled with stories of men overcoming great odds—obstacles often put there by other men—and accomplishing the unthinkable. They were fought every step of the way in the name of *avoiding* unsubstantiated disasters, while the achievers created railroads, factories, power grids and the electric light. We hear how our acts of creation will bring destruction—a destruction that never comes. We are the Evil West: evil because our laws protect the rights of every man regardless of his "connections," the connections that determine whether you live or die in those other countries. The best of the West work uphill against howling protests stirred within those intimidated by our endeavors, while our advances are enjoyed in silence. Everyone forgets the fight, but we don't. Most of us can't conceive of how the populace can fall for the senseless, foundationless ravings of our opposition. Can't they see through the malice? As a consequence, we as the Self-made are left more desolate, and with a strained respect for our fellow men in general.

What if there was a pattern to it? As humans, our every premonition tells us to follow our gut—to discover and name the proper course for our every endeavor. Essentially in innocence, that is all we as the Self-made are doing, every step of our lives. The Spirit Murderer's fear tells them *not* to follow their gut, and to disallow it to others as well, knowing it leads to the truth—about themselves, about the true purpose of life and about those they damn. In avoiding proper coherency, here are some of their key means of invalidation.

VALUE INVERSION: HIS FALSE HIERARCHY. Morality to a volitional being is the basic mental tool of life. For a Spirit Murderer, it is used as a weapon of destruction. A carpenter's hammer is a tool designed for a moral intention—to produce the benefits enjoyed by a civil society. In the hands of a psychotic, it can be used to kill. The main premise of a moral man is *life,* and he is proud of the volume of his tool chest—of the many ways he can bring it about. The main premise of an immoral man is *death,* and he derives significance by means of his arsenal as well—of the many ways *he* can bring it about.

If you were to imagine the Fear-driven structure of mind, it is a constant, willed reversal of normal intellectual flow. Like an intestine turning on itself, everything is inside out and backwards, with every muscle tensed for the purpose of inversion. Never intending any correction, it is fully dedicated to the completion of its reversal, believing it will arrive at the world *as it wishes it were.* Have you ever righted a rubber band just to see it twist itself back again? Inversion is his steady state, where he feels most comfortable, not because it's natural, but because he is so uncomfortable with the world as it is. *To back out* is his first premonition. Any step towards clarity is a step in the wrong direction, summoned by what is considered evil to the success of his fundamental goal.

In day to day experience, we'll see a Spirit Murderer approach values in a specific pattern. 1) He mimics the simpler values, 2) Claims the more complex values are a gift or the result of luck and 3) Claims the highest values are impossible. If he can't succeed in ignoring them, he'll attempt to neutralize their positivism, or declare them a vice through judgment by improper standards. In the meantime, he'll attempt to steal, deface or destroy them, as they exist contrary to his view of human possibility. If *he* can't have it, neither can anyone else.

In dealing with non-values or vices, his pattern is the same. 1) He pretends not to have them, 2) Claims they are the result of bad luck, to blame others or 3) To claim that nothing better is possible to Man. If he doesn't succeed in concealing them, he'll attempt to neutralize their negativity, even declaring them a virtue to be worshipped, replacing true virtues. In secret, he prizes his evil as a reproach to life, works to preserve and foster it and ultimately works to confirm his stubbornly irrational view of existence, by *empowering* it.

In contrast, Self-made Man treats all human values—necessities and luxuries—in a very straightforward manner. He seeks to earn them, considers them wholly possible, worships their grandeur, studies their every attribute, decides what he wants and maps out their attainment. He treats non-values with the same pattern, just reversed. He seeks to eliminate them, aware of their ominous threat to his life and spirit if he doesn't. He studies their every attribute to know their danger and step by step, flaw by flaw, maps out their eradication.

> *"You know, it is easier to pull a trigger, than it is to play a guitar."*
> —Desperado.

Easier to denounce than to give a carefully reasoned argument, easier to stab than to suture, easier to demolish than to build, easier to submit than to think and easier to form a gang than to form a treaty. These values require what the Fear-driven lack: a calm, patient discipline with oneself and one's task, beginning with cognition. Such a perspective violates his pretense of automatic, effortless perfection and implies an obligation he is missing the path to practice. Its lack is the result of practicing its opposite—irrationality—and his whole means of premise construction is off as a consequence. It requires him to come face to face with an aptitude that by his unrealistic standard, *he is supposed to have already*—an impossible esteem predicament for him.

A key misdirection in the field of psychology is attempting to catalog every instance of such pathology. The Fear-driven combinations of default and senseless reasoning are *infinite*, multiplying as fast as it takes him to cower in response to any looming responsibility. All forms of psychopathology begin with the intentional or unintentional, self-assumed, dogmatic or cultural, misplacement of existence and consciousness in one's hierarchy of values—placing consciousness first, *before* what it is conscious *of*—to believe consciousness to be a power determining existence itself, versus its true role of observance. This is the choice and difference between *objectivity* and *subjectivity*. If the argument of the subjective were put into words, it might go something like this: "That idea is useless or wrong, because it is not yours. You have no right to use it, mention it or benefit from it. It is invalid because it was learned through the effort of another mind, and since it was *his* reality, not yours, it is inapplicable to any other human being." Psychology is *not* the study of human thought and action—*philosophy* is. That semiconscious behavioral elements make up the vast majority of human action and relegate themselves to psychoanalysis is due to the present moral limitations on cognitive advancement—*not* due to a fault in the nature of the species.

Whether he is attempting to validate a false premise or invalidate a true one, his regard for facts is the same, as is his pattern: escape. All *rational* validation or invalidation is arrived at by a like process: looking for consonance with or contradiction to, existential evidence. Self-made Man macro- and micro-studies every element to understand what it is, what it does and how it fits in. He identifies the essential characteristics of an idea or an entity, isolating and analyzing *with no fear to see*. The better defined his object, the closer he can come to enacting the causes which reap his desired effects. This is the anatomy of rational cognition, whose *antithetic* process is the acceptance or rejection of ideas *without* gathering and analyzing measurable data. Instead, Fear-driven Man *avoids* measurable data and reaches for the immeasurable elements, to reinforce his cognitive shield. He follows no fixed pattern of identification and has no respect for analytical methods—for anything defining a thing, which cannot be *something else* in the next moment. He abandons such discipline, being most comfortable with "maybe" this and "maybe" that, with no constructive point and no intended conclusions, beyond confirming that approximations are the closest one can come to understand anything. In reason he will agree—having to—but he still won't act on reason. His senses will be heightened to find the slightest justification not to, instead of his natural responsibility to look deeper. He'll maintain a pose of conformity while in your presence, bursting at the seams to defy it once you are out of range. He doesn't delve into anything. He doesn't want to know what anything is, what anything does or what it fits into. He is not integrating and in tantrum will not, until the standard is reversed in favor of his false premises.

CREEPING DEATH. Still, as *self-potencies* are the drivers of all human action, subjective outgrowths are all powered by self-acknowledged potencies of the Fear-driven (even their confirmation of impotence). They will only do consistently, what they believe they can—an action of true esteem; therefore all evil actions are accomplished through living means. To mask and protect his flaws, he inevitably places his power for living in the service of death.

Ever have someone breathe down your neck, implying violence as the consequence of opposing their view? Of course, we all have. During their physically potent years, force in place of reasonable persuasion is a popular alternative for the Fear-driven. Clinging to an automatic advantage such as size, he wants to believe that a victory won by violence is proof of his superiority, which in his delusion is to transcend over all other realms, but domination doesn't determine rank in thought. Compensating for non-thought, he tries to *force* his errors to be true by wiping out whoever or whatever says it isn't, but it does as much good as punching and kicking at a rainstorm. Facts are not altered by intimidation. No link is added and no advancement is brought about, except those of medical treatments and arrest records. From an abusive spouse to Soviet Russia, nothing but physical and spiritual harm is ever accomplished by the introduction of violence, on any scale.

It gets really frightening when Spirit Murderers combine this with religion. They say "My erroneous frame of reference says something is evil," —a lesson memorized with no chain to back it— "and that justifies anything I do in its name" —a license for slaughter. Religion becomes a template for destruction, sanctioned by an anonymous source that supposedly did the reasoning for them. They need not convince their opposition, but only wipe them out, as disagreement alone declares them evil. The Fear-driven hold their worship of God and faith, pitted against self and thought, instead of attempting any integration, because they intend one to replace the other. Faith then as they preach it, is a form of lying, and attack is a form of escape. It is not reliance on a higher power, but the simple abandonment of cognitive effort, and then of civility. It is much easier to submit to faith and brandish force, than to stick to the discipline of the chain.

SLANDER. As an alternative to violence and instead of facing an issue, he'll try to discredit you through a tactic known as *straw man*—properly damning an evil trait, which in truth, you *do not* possess. Setting up his straw man and then knocking it down is the photo-negative of a white lie, where the liar tries to gain esteem from a valuable trait which *he* does not possess. We see it often in politics where they prey on scandal, called mud-slinging or muck-raking. They'll exclaim, "Your idea is wrong or you're evil because you slept with someone, said something, did something, are a Christian, aren't a Christian…" in an attempt to stretch damnation for an irrelevant issue over a relevant one. We hear "*You're* not degreed," implying that we are not licensed to think and must accept without question the mental contents of those who are. But their quest for credentials—never facts—is a substitute for acquiring the capacity to properly gage competence. They can never face an issue head on, and instead lean on whatever takes the focus off, not just the issue, but off of a rational process of validation. In all awareness, it must be no fun at all to need discredit others in order to maintain one's own assertions. To mud-sling is to seek a scapegoat for an evasion of moral guilt—you are being framed *as* evil or incompetent, *by* evil or incompetence.

Often-times, he needs even less than a false rationale to damn. Does 2+2 *not* equal four because you hate your math teacher? Of course not, yet in less straight-forward situations, we hear "I don't like him, so I wouldn't believe anything he says." A nonessential attribute serves as barrier to any valuable conveyance—a big nose, a gruff voice—any disenchantment their unconditional love is supposed to overlook, is enough to sever their comprehension. I say, liking each other is beside the point. What is, *is*. Even lower and simpler along this strain is attempting to shame an action or a value. Once in my marina on the Fourth of July, I was passing by some drunks (I'm guessing), who were slurring god knows what, pointing and making these full-bodied gestures in my direction. I stopped and looked at them in curious amusement. Having my attention, they stepped it up, then noticed others watching them and stopped abruptly in embarrassment. I didn't get what they were after, but I knew their essence. Spirit Murderers sneer, because it is an action *they* find most frightening. To me it was meaningless.

When focus is misdirected *off* of validation, it heads towards a host of non-constructive alternatives, all with the same results—the impotence of mind and of Man. They'll say, "Someone else said something else, and I agree with them," still without any reasoning, or my personal favorite, "No matter what you say, it won't change my mind." This is a blatant affront to proper epistemological structure and personal growth. The less thoughtful they are, the more they rely on superstitious and mystical threats—"You will go to hell just for thinking it," claiming that the issue violates a predisposition or belief and therefore *cannot be* contemplated.

Unproven predispositions or muckraking, are only a fool's self-protection from *epistemological showcasing*—revealing to others how well their mind works. You'll face a plethora of chauvinistic bias before any sense is made or accepted. "Anything relying on the senses is necessarily invalid, as it was *your* senses, not mine." "What's true for you may not be true for me." "What works for you won't work for me." Such attempts pretend that existence tailors its identity to every individual, rather than the truth: that an individual must tailor his identity within the constraints of reality. Speak common sense or the uncommon levels above, and you won't get a word in edgewise. Knowledge? Success? Answers? These are not what he's after. He needs to think that a success overshadowing his own is possible only by sinking lower than he did. I get bored quickly, so my rebuttal to a parking lot debate is "I won't argue the validity of my premises on success versus yours: my premises earned this car. I'm the one with the Lamborghini." Still, he'll listen to everyone except the guy driving out of the dealership in it—the only one to tell him that it *is* possible, and by *moral* means—what he is afraid to hear.

FALSE ASSOCIATIONS. A lazy chainer grasps the most rudimentary connections and will not effort beyond them. Thought is so great an imposition that he grants as true, whatever connection is made most easily, and shirks any further investigation. Rather than invest the effort to correct them, he lives a life riddled with cognitive errors, compensating simply by refusing their acknowledgment. Faking that a greater depth could never override his base connections—his only self-grasped conclusions—no deeper argument can stick. No <u>doubt</u> you have experienced the hopeless trauma of demystifying an issue for someone step by step, only to find that you've gotten nowhere. He chases his tail, clinging to his own initial observance—loyal to the chosen limit of his cognitive power—even after his verdict has been clearly disproven. With someone eager to learn, you watch them grow and they surprise you with fresh variations—fun for teacher and student. With him, it's back to square one, again and again. Explanations are a wasted courtesy; such a mind cannot tell the difference between sound competent effort and incompetence, due to his own. Unlike Spiderman, he can't sling a web and swing to a new conclusion.

How exciting it is to discover new vindications, to no longer be bound by senseless condemnation, to be suddenly freed from inefficient patterns, punishment and a guilt so old we didn't even realize we carried it. The Fear-driven don't share our excitement in such a release. A step in a new direction is an unwelcome burden, another chance to fall flat. Barriers are safety to him, a reason to stop. He bounces along the path of least resistance, sightless and mindless, ricocheting off of any cognitive pressure, wishing the road would just end. Bio-chemically, this leads in only one direction—decay. He wanders through a maze of semi-acknowledged, semi-evaded data, placing degenerative elements in his chain, whose every offshoot is sick. The short, snarled branching guides his life to nothing but dead ends while bringing mobility to harm, with him at its constant center. His mounting incapacities result in a well-deserved low self-worth. The glass house of esteem he builds *requires* a retaining wall of insubstantiation to keep it from crashing down, and hence, he is locked in a downward spiral.

A Manic Waste of Time. Time is the enemy of the inspirationally lethargic. It is the constant reminder of a wasted life, which is why the fool always wants to kill it. Those separated from any passionate pursuit, kill much of their time by whatever means—food, drink, television—to avoid the suffering of unsatisfied hungers in life: for love, for achievement, for any wholesome, self-fulfilling value. This lethargy is a result of fear, which is the real cause of their unhappiness. They do not believe in themselves enough to accomplish anything significant. The issue is a lack of self-esteem, safely buried under the rush of the common maintenance of life. Some do what they call "partying" —inhabiting bars, fogging out their minds, gathering a mob of friends, anything to stay occupied on a shallow level so as not to face their void of self. Its ultimate mutation and twisted idol is known as the "Player." Nothing says "pointless existence," more loudly than a twenty-four hour social life. Others claiming to have grown up, shed the party life, and instead squander their time with family endeavors—gossip and errands—with the same depth and hollow reward. They take concrete, short-term actions, with no view or range stepping past today into the realm of deep personal desires, fantasies or ideals. The key element is still missing. Like wedging a size ten body into a size six dress, nothing strains a grown mind more than remaining at the level of a child's. They blank out the possibility that greater fulfillment exists, and as simple reason tells them they should be looking for answers, instead out of guilt, they turn against their cognitive faculty—and choose not to be fully aware of anything.

The activities that keep them so busy are of no significant, crucial importance to them. If they were, we would see a clear product emanating from their effort—great enjoyment or a personal advance of some kind—a growing elegance with every year, not the degeneration we witness instead. Most of them live in a state of chronic tension, a manic relationship with time, unable to remember what it was they did from hour to hour, or why. They string a row of days together with the same sum, then a row of years, until their life is gone. I can't even conceive of an infamy worse than to spend a life of passionless activity or dull inactivity, never having known what one wanted, what would've satisfied, what would've stitched it all together into a completed whole and made all of life worthwhile. Instead of looking for answers, they hold out for its end—the end of time which they experience as pain—a false association made early and built upon ever since.

In contrast, it is very painful for the Self-made to sit and listen to the irrelevant. Self-made Man doesn't gossip or habitually talk about other's lives, because he *has* a life. He couldn't imagine wasting mental effort considering what other's choices should be, and working through their issues. He is busy enough with his own. He has no interest in examining the motives or conditions of others—no need to process it whatsoever, as he is totally independent—unsteered and unalterable from the outside. The guilt, pressure, and animosity which the Fear-driven often succumb to—the result of holding irrational filters in front of their view of existence, acknowledging the expectations of others as if they were a metaphysical requirement of self-sustenance—Self-made Man doesn't even notice. Such interference can result only in time lost—an intolerable predicament. Likewise, dependencies cannot catch up to him. He won't drink, take drugs or overeat due to the intellectual down-time involved. He has no desire to escape reality in the first place, as he holds no premises which necessitate escape. Time is the medium through which his elation is experienced—his very power over life—and is a respected ally. He feels something like treason in wasting it—a violation of *why* he lives. If he allowed two hours of his life to pass without any sense of passion, he feels he has cheated himself, and *that* is when guilt and pain would follow. Wasted time is a wedge dividing you from your happiness, or as the Self-made declare:

Warrior Note: *Purposeful time leads to exaltation; idle time leads to spirit murder!*

Emergency Ethics. A favorite story of mine has a young man skipping clams that had washed ashore, back into the ocean. Another man approaches him and looking down the coast, exclaims, "Why bother? You can't save them all; it doesn't matter anyway." Reaching for another, he replies, "It matters to this one." Now, this can be interpreted in two ways by either mindset. That it is our duty to spend our lives helping every slug that falls short of life's requirements, or as a profound respect for *every* life—for life *as such*—to be prized first and foremost, by the one who is living it.

Succumbing to one's own fears leads to an irrational bias favoring the unearned in all things. In situations of emergency, the means to basic existence such as food and safe shelter are desired first hand *without regard to their source:* they simply must be had or life cannot continue. This may be true, but to the fear-ridden, *everything* is an emergency. They seek to make their fears *our* priority at every turn, saying, "What are *we* going to do? We need food and we need it now; there is no time to discover the means of its creation or to investigate the cause of our plight. It exists for whatever reason, and it must be quelled or we will die. Oh, and four hours from now, it will happen again." If their panic convinces us that a valid crisis exists, then individual rights and conventional approaches are beside the point, and they've justified their seizure of our bounty to address it.

We've all encountered this in their view of love: "If I were drowning, would you give your life to save me?" Their focus is not on values to be shared with one another, but on what values are to be destroyed. The injuries of those contemplating our commitment to prevent their demise, then extend past metaphoric disasters to infiltrate all aspects of life—rent, comparative luxury, love—the pursuit of any value for which they refuse to pay full price. With no forethought into the consequences of their actions, they may indeed face one disaster after another, but these are not life-threatening instances and do not provoke the obligation for others to come to the rescue.

A true emergency is defined as a sudden and unexpected crisis requiring immediate action to mitigate loss. It is a condition of existence where human life cannot be sustained. A ship sinking, a house burning down, an earthquake, a tornado or a car-accident are incalculable, non-repeating, tragic events which require immediate attention to restore the normal flow of life. The penalties of incompetence, general poverty, denial, cowardice, lethargy and dependencies—the basic challenges of life with which we *all* must deal, are *not* among them. Still, we hear 'disaster scenarios to prove our moral worth' everywhere, implying that emergencies are the standard by which to gauge all moral action. They have convinced mankind that to be moral, there is no alternative to our destruction. Their psychological motive is to convince themselves that negating their minds was the right thing to do: that their panic is justified. To that end, they need to convince us that calamities are a daily occurrence which demand our constant attention, that life is a series of unavoidable perils, and all we can do is huddle, disperse what goods remain and wait to be killed. What is true?

In 1999, approximately 44,182 people worldwide lost their lives to disasters of any significant magnitude—floods, hurricanes, earthquakes, plane crashes, shipwrecks and the like. With an estimated world population of six billion, that totals 0.00001% lost. With more accurate data on the United States alone, four percent of *deaths* for the same period were attributed to accidents, amounting to 0.0003% of the U.S. population lost—*less* than those lost to the flu. With figures such as these, there are no grounds to consider mankind as precariously clinging to life.

I've always been shocked by the moral commitments expressed by others in regard to this. On a plane a woman once told me that she would fight to get the oxygen mask on her child before securing her own. She disregarded the medical fact that the child can pass out and recover in the time it takes to assure she maintains consciousness, but would die if the mother passes out first. This is how thoughtlessly twisted false morality can be—to risk their own children for the shallow boast of what they'll give to save them—ahead of the circumstance which *kills* the child in the very next instant. But the Fear-driven place anything ahead of taking cause and effect even one more painful step. Her dramatic moral tribute was to give her life to save her child, even though she would never know if she put the mask on right and whether the child survived at all. She thinks, "My moral stature is in question" and her response is *to die to affirm it*—not to stay in control, not to think—not to live. I was horrified for the child, but I know the false premise—*sacrifice*.

I can hear popular morality's followers saying, "I've done all that was asked of me. I've sacrificed my time to the lowest, loved those who deserved none, forgiven private moral atrocities and kept nothing for myself, yet I'm not happy." No kidding, your morality has prevented it. You consider it noble to sacrifice your fulfillment as the first answer to anyone's needs—needs that never cease—and wonder why you're not fulfilled! You're not set up for fulfillment. The error is in accepting premises without investigating their validity, and instead just trying to live with them. The first sacrifice of the Fear-driven was their minds—*their self,* so likewise, the first sacrifice they demand in their hostile agitation, is *our* minds, minds that question why. They brought us to the point where we seek happiness by practicing the tenets of spiritual destruction, ingraining patterns in us whose harmful results should be obvious. Happiness requires not sacrifice, but *the renunciation of sacrifice.*

It takes plenty of effort to define and uphold high standards, to weigh situations rationally and make proper decisions and to judge what is lovable and unlovable. Most the Fear-driven are unwilling to put forth the effort required—for happiness, or any value. They lack the cognitive discipline to gather the data necessary for the proper validation of anything, and are dishonest, just enough to cover their lethargy. The rest have been stopped by moral subversion and the immense pressure to conform to it.

It is much easier to sacrifice one's life than to live it well, much easier to act from panic than to think things through, much easier to give up than to press on and much easier to accept poor conditions than to challenge them. When people feel they are forced into action with no idea of what to do and only a hampered means to identify it, they destroy—themselves, others and their own happiness. When the civility of a rational mind is negated as one's means of survival, conquest becomes the only alternative. Men at all levels become in their realms what their leaders are in theirs—cannibals. We hear them shout, "Women and children first!" though most women refuse to be classified with the helpless any longer. Rejecting the inversion of human value which leaves him to die, their hedonist equivalents shout "Every man for himself!" and in likewise avoidance of cognitive responsibility, *he* struggles to steal the life-jacket of daily sustenance from others. Neither considers the possibility of calm thought and peaceful action. By their own anti-logic, this brings about an important caveat: If morality is defined by emergency situations that rarely happen if ever, then is it irrational for the Fear-driven to conclude that they will never have any use for it? Emergencies don't happen often enough to practice moral principles, so for the rest of life, we are left without moral direction. They have us thinking that without their emergencies, we cannot achieve any esteem, implying that outside the act of sacrifice, we are being immoral. With their attempt to restore moral value to daily life, their code of sacrifice just brings death and harm into civil situations.

Sacrifice. So what is sacrifice really? Beyond an offering to a deity, Webster's dictionary defines *sacrifice* as "the act of giving up, destroying, permitting injury to or forgoing something valued for the sake of something having a more pressing claim." This definition has been subverted to mean giving up a *greater* value in favor of a *lesser* one. Making a sacrifice in current morality would be resigning cleanliness to filth, wealth to poverty and health to indigence. At an abstract level, it is to discard pursuing the life you want and settling for a life you don't and to give up the powerful romance you dream of, in preference to bland safety. After the expense of effort to better one's condition, why would anyone in their right mind throw it away and return to their previous level, or possibly end up below it? There is no flow—no continuation of gathering nourishment, processing and expelling in the concept of sacrifice. Once a sacrifice is made, the object consumed must be completely regenerated, but notice how sacrifice gives no pattern for creation and production—only for expropriation and consumption. It is a death pattern. If a process cannot sustain one man alone, but instead uses him up, considering his life not as the goal, but as expendable fuel for another purpose, then it is wrong by design—it is evil. Its continuation is found only in new victims. Life is a precious, irreplaceable value: the pinnacle focus for all personal and governmental protection, and it begins with the individual. When the sacrifice is life, no regeneration is possible.

If your house is burning down, you scramble to save what is most precious—the greatest value generating powers. We save the living first, on down the hierarchy—irreplaceable productive efforts, accumulated wealth and fond memories—the non-essentials can be replaced. Spirit Murderers reverse this, beginning within themselves, to let the most valuable elements die first.

Under sacrifice, who's lives take precedence, and why would women wish to shed this opportunistic privilege? In the matter of deciding the hierarchy of sacrifice, the most able—those with the greatest stockpile to loot—are always killed off first. In matter, the Fear-driven seek to destroy the most productive, in spirit, the most coherent. Spirit Murderers consume value from the most obvious to the least. Those *most able to sustain life* are sacrificed in favor of those who are *least able*. Women have implicitly realized that the highest value and pride a human being can feel, regardless of what they make us pay for it, is this status—the independent status of "I can."

It doesn't make much sense to kill the breadwinner and leave the rest safely ashore, only to die a few days later. By sacrificing the productive, the race is that much less likely to survive. It reminds me of a story I once heard of an Indian custom: When the elderly felt they were becoming a liability on the tribe, they would go off into the woods, sit under a tree with their arms tied above them and go to sleep, never to come back. They let go of life to keep their people focused on maintaining the strongest elements of the tribe. This has profoundly moral implications. For one, that their need of assistance was not to be a primary consideration of others. Second, that when self-sufficiency is no longer possible to an individual, his pursuit of values is over, and spiritually, without self-esteem, so is life. In this predicament, they chose to exit gracefully. If I were in an emergency situation in old age, I'd prefer the young to have a chance to reach my age as well, not see them give their lives to save mine, and still, it would not be a sacrifice.

The view and use of the term sacrifice has become so shopworn, its actual meaning and moral impact has been obliterated. If you accept temporary hardships in order to secure a long-term gain, these are *investments*—necessary elements of a goal's attainment, *not* sacrifices. If you stay home and study rather than go out and party, it is not a sacrifice if you value a degree more than a hangover. The concept of sacrifice applies only when the result is contrary to your own desire, and leaves you with less. Sacrifice chops away parts of your life until there is nothing left. It is another impossible moral concept, though the concept itself is quite real. Taxes are often a sacrifice. Past essential services such as police and fire protection, the drains down which we see our money being poured are much less a value to us than what we could have done with our capital. The sacrifice of *self* is possible through the negation of mind, and is the personal guilt of all Spirit Murderers.

Sacrifice is the destruction of values—death by slow or fast torture—nothing else. It is *not* a moral concept, but one of the most corruptly milked anti-life concepts of the Spirit Murderers. It is not about what is moral; it is about the destruction of those who are. If you agree to spill your blood for a cause, what will follow is not divine serenity, but requests for more. The anti-virtue of self-sacrifice was borne of the Fear-driven's core default—how they came to be. The moral discovery leading us all out of the woods is that the demand for sacrifice is the cannibal's answer to replacing their surrendered self with the self of others.

Sound morality is not defined by borderline cases, infinitesimal percentages or poetic delusions and neither is sound law. Sacrifice in civil times is clearly well outside its contextual borders. In ethics it is an instrument of those who simply intend to leave you with less. It may tragically occur in 0.0003% of situations, but 99.9997% of the time, we live by *another* standard, which is the exact opposite of sacrifice. Only consistent, repeatable results are suitable to form proper concepts, to build and regulate civilizations and to back scientific advancements, allowing mankind to progress. What defines true morality—just as in nature, just as in breathing—is the peaceful accumulation of physical and spiritual nutrients for the preservation and advancement of life—primarily our own, just what most of us do every day.

Infirmity Worship—The Destruction of Heroism. Lies are a cognitive dead end, and rarely go past their initial cover up. The deeper they go, the more tangled the liar becomes; so to avoid suffocation within their own homespun version of non-identity, they have to escape the mess and leave the snarl behind them. The longest-term actions of the Fear-driven therefore often reflect their *true* malady, in what they stand behind and support. If they feel for the weak, they *feel* weak. If they back a labor union, they feel slovenly and wish to guard the condition from reprisal. *They ask us to worship the sick, as a semiconscious acknowledgment of their own condition.*

Their psychological motive is the exact inverse of the Self-made. We worship the strong, the able and the competent, because we actively seek to expand our own strength, ability and competence. They break with our living format in seeking appreciation for flaws, but *appreciation* is still sought. Their contradiction is that all living entities must know that what they're doing is right—that what they're doing is good—and they exist as the only beings on the planet who attempt to deceive themselves into believing that the actions of demise can bring about life. We respect living values, and practice living patterns to attain them. *They* claim to respect living values, but practice *death* patterns to attain them. Health, wealth and prosperity is touted on both sides, but while one side initiates the precursors to make it happen, the other does not, and its proponents spend their lives trying to cover it up by having the world reverse its idols. Then of course, they are just as surprised when their ends match their means, and they achieve destruction instead.

Less than two percent of the population actually has a physical malady that impedes their ability to sustain independent life. It is an insignificant moral consideration, certainly not a standard by which to gauge the normal, flowing value system for 98% of day-to-day human action. Most disorders are *chosen*, whose consequences are to be paid for by the afflicted, not by those who chose better. The whiners play impaired to escape their fundamental human responsibility. As with emergencies, they need us to serve their lifelong indigence in the same way, not questioning its source. Beyond a free ride, infirmity worship is intended to accomplish a specific motive: holding crutches as a badge of honor, leaves Man no incentive for learning to walk. By subverting heroism *away from* a valiant struggle and *towards* dabbing a drooling mouth, they have destroyed it.

Selflessness. Selflessness is the anti-concept of stepping out of oneself as the only means of performing moral actions—an utter impossibility. It demands that you place others ahead of any routine consideration for your own survival, requiring that you make decisions, having no interest or stake in any cause you support or any action you take. It is a flagrant defiance of logic and moral judgment. Claiming the best self must be selfless is as senseless as claiming the best airplane must be *plane*less. It is another term to cause looping—hesitation and thoughtless self-destruction—but is masked to mean virtue, charity and love for others. Most know selflessness as a vague moral concept: the act of surrendering what they truly want, to settle for what they truly don't. It has been ingrained in them that to want anything for themselves is to admit the intention to sacrifice others. Spirit Murderers deny the possibility of creation or work, so they view any attainment of wealth as an act of robbery. For the Self-made, a self-sustaining or *selfish* action is simply the cognitive act of evaluation, coupled with the moral choice of life—*the act of valuing*. To be *selfless* is to have no self, to wipe oneself out of existence in regard to all one loves, to reflect no judgment and to display no pride for personal value. Without a self, who then is to love? Without a self, who then is to live?

For years people denounced my goals, focusing on the most visible results, especially the exotic cars. With a not so well concealed sneer, I'd hear against my Lamborghini, "Was it *all* you had *hoped* it would be?" I'd reply, "It turned out to be more significant than I ever thought possible," but missing the effect they sought, they were no longer listening.

Because of that childhood dream I learned the real estate business, law and economics. The study of law led me to history, philosophy and psychology. Even the deflection from my proper course which brings me before you now, was still only a product of that dream. On the other side of the goal, I was raised from the poverty level to upper middle class, all due to action taken on an innocent, childhood inspiration. I've been able to give gifts of world travel to those I've loved and have shown them wonders they'd never seen. I evolved as a center of knowledge, wealth and life, whereas in their fully altruistic interchangeability, my critics can still barely get themselves *or others* across the street. Still, my effort was damned for years as immoral. In some circles, it has come to the point where breathing is considered a selfish action to be apologized for, where the first hedonistic action is considered *thought*. The Self-made know better, and treat any mention of *selfless* expectations or *selfish* denunciations as an alarm for the acute awareness of motive.

Every human being is a sum of virtues. If you become a greater sum, the world is richer for it. Selflessness demands the opposite: that you skin yourself alive, gauging your moral worth to how thoroughly you can rake over the most sensitive, intimate areas of your body and mind, without reaction. By their code, if you are self-abasing enough to catapult your clean body into stagnant filth, you win, but not if you're still breathing. Selflessness requires sacrificing the products of *individual* action based on a sound value hierarchy, *without the means to derive one*—a self. It implies that the only alternative is to hedonistically destroy others—to be *selfish*—leaving no room for and never mentioning…civility—a rational coexistence between men. Our honorable system of payment for services rendered is *evil* to them, as they do not intend to pay. Likewise, they don't ask for payment, because they don't intend to produce anything of value.

There is no selfless giving, without a self that *does* the giving. *Nothing human is selfless.* Be warned: If the beneficial actions of self are to be consumed in selfless channels, the enterprise is a con. If they continue to demand selflessness, fine. Let them have exactly what they are asking for. Tell them "Selfless service? Selfless love? No problem, my *self* has nothing to do with it." There are all kinds of charities I have been generous to in selfless dedication, my self was never there. My self gave nothing, and it will stay that way until I see them acknowledging the value of *every* self; but by that time, graft-style charities—dependents on dependency—will have disappeared.

Sooner or later, we had to come to the truth of the matter: haters of the self-serving, hate *themselves*. Spirit Murderers have destroyed themselves—the *self* they hate—and claim it a virtue for you to follow suit, to subject you to the same constant torture it has brought into their lives. But a *self* must do the work of life, so like a vacuum, they suck the self out of you to replace the one with which they live at odds, substituting their body as its benefactor. Hang on to it instead. One's self is an endlessly exciting exploration, unless of course, one has no self—and that is the key to the riddle.

Turning the other cheek. What is the first thing that typically comes to mind about Jesus? That he died on the cross—the very symbol of Christian morality. We seek to do right, and look up to see him dead as sole explanation of how. The Spirit Murderers want you to make a similar sacrifice, every day of *their* lives: to die and suffer loss for their sake. They tell us to "bear predations," which can only mean to tolerate falling victim to predators, to live like animals and to be consumed. Of course they neglect to mention that *they* are the predators who will benefit. In response, some thoughtlessly surrender their lives with eloquent statements such as, "I'd rather go gracefully to my maker, than to take another human life." Talk about ringing the dinner bell for cannibals. It is not what Jesus intended—not for the masses to follow him on the cross, but its real statement: *to make no compromise with evil.*

In any confrontational situation, it is treason to the civil flow of life to respect an aggressor. It is ludicrous to permit his destructive intentions an unrestricted path, while wiping out our peaceful aims. It is a violation of justice to withhold the penalty of removal from circulation, those who violate the rights of others.

So what did Jesus really mean by permitting himself to be struck again? *That the initiation of violence accomplishes nothing but violence.* That the solution to end slavery was ideological—not to fight fire with fire, but to fight fire with *water*. He wasn't demonstrating the immorality of self-defense against aggression (self-defense *is* moral), but the futility of choosing bloodshed by mankind's leaders (Barabbas was a rebel leader). He did it to prove a point— *not* to lull men into tolerating abuse. A Self-made believer would say, "I'd rather *send* a predator to be reformed by his maker, than to leave the world subject to his danger." Strength is *not* practiced by showing tolerance for all spiritual and physical pestilence. The height of moral stature is not gained by enduring abuse, remaining peaceful and unshaken in the face of aggression. The Self-made *counter* force to stop its use, and look good doing it.

The day he died amounted to 0.0001% of his history, yet it backs 99.9999% of our supposed moral lessons. It wasn't Jesus who perverted martyrdom into a moral symbol—that was done by others. It wasn't his own murder that he wished to hold up to men as his greatest achievement—now the symbol of his life and philosophy—that as well, was done by others.

It is time to disassociate morality from acts of murder, and place him in our minds and in our symbols, in his proper setting—walking through the world, bringing the bright freedom of moral awareness to those he encountered. It's time to stop worshipping his death and start worshipping his life, and the lives of true heroes throughout history—the Self-made and self-sustained—what a man should be.

Unconditional, Selfless and Free Love. When you pick out a Christmas tree, do you just grab the one closest to the car, or do you apply a set of standards? If so temporary a value cannot be withheld from scrutiny, then how could our deepest values? Unconditional love is the mother of all anti-concepts, the spiritual pinnacle of the irresponsible and un-worked for, eliminating the Fear-driven's two chief enemies: thought and effort. On the part of the grantor, it is the escape of determining standards; on the part of the grantee, it is the escape of upholding them.

Before I understood the issue, I would fantasize about what kind of woman I could make a lifelong commitment to—the one I could love "unconditionally" —the smell of her hair, the beautiful smile, the lovely figure and a depth of purity, intelligence and passion to match my own. Eventually I realized that in order for me to love her unconditionally, she would have to meet such rigid standards, that her predefined virtue became Condition City! I was told my concept of it was all wrong (I had mistaken it for complete confidence in another person). The purpose of unconditional love I was told, was *not* to project ideals and dream of an enchanted future to grow to be worthy of, but the unfiltered adoration of whatever drifts along at any time.

With some rationale still prompting them to conceal their vices, the Fear-driven throw a white sheet over what they consider to be undeserving of love, and assert that "To be virtuous, you must love what's under it, never identifying the object of your love and never desiring to." Of course, this wipes out the value of coherent rationality. I knew that no one of esteem grants approval to what he is disallowed to understand or identify. Goodness need not hide; no one of self-confidence ever need fear *any* truth or discovery. What I was to discover in the long run, was that no honest man who respects life makes a stupid game of virtue. I noticed that those preaching it had little achievement to their names, while those who had, were always quiet on the subject. Then I saw the fundamental approach of unconditional love—to suspend consciousness: *the key element disallowed in the concept.* Love, a product of evaluation, was to be given without exercising *the tool* of evaluation—the mind.

When you think of devoting yourself to another without reservation, is the image it conjures like mine—that of someone ready-made, or is it of a flabby, foul smelling, ignorant, abusive grease ball? Remember, unconditional love is *without* condition; selfless love is *without* cognitive appraisal; free love is *without* spiritual compensation. All are something for nothing, which in the physical realm is called theft. These anti-concepts consider any preferential image abominably, to be a moral *affront.* No attribute selection or value filter is allowed, leaving only a dumping ground onto which any refuse can be thrown. What made it possible for them to treat the highest value Man can grant or receive, with less care than we exercise even to choose a can of vegetables?

I'm sure you've experienced a partner who became angry if you mentioned what you loved them *for,* as safety for their precarious esteem hinged on the reward remaining causeless. Naming specific traits imposed an obligation for their continuance, revealing a potentiality whereupon the love could be withdrawn. Unconditional love tries to kill that potentiality, by denying the cognitive steps of *perception and identification.* Identifying the knowledge necessary to derive an estimate of individual character—the traits worthy of love—is a frightening prospect, a responsibility they lack the courage to face, not to mention living up to that knowledge. Spirit Murderers cannot accept that love is a reward for merit. They are still cowardly babies, hoping to remain in safe harbor and get it as a grant *as in their youth,* so to initiate the fraud, they try to *give it* as a grant.

Unconditional love is the coward's formula for fixing the game in a way nature does not allow. Only a coward or an evader wishes to get the trophy whether he wins or loses, in contradiction to the known rules of the game. He wants to pretend to take the risks, but not be held to the rules if his performance proves inadequate. His elder spiritual equivalents (who have given up on all goal-directed action) know the game, and try to cheat the concept of love to cover anything he happens to do or to become. The surest way to stop achievement is to pull it out at the root. Answering youthful contemplation such as, "What should I do to be the best I can be?" their response is, "You need do nothing," *as they did,* and hence, no future threat to *their* esteem. Whatever the motive, the cheaters succeed not in spreading or receiving love, but only in mangling the pathways to the true concept within themselves and their victims, nullifying love's value to them, destroying the quality of their relationships and irreparably harming their futures.

But what has it done to us? Civilization can't shut its eyes to shoplifting, homicide and all the crimes in between. If no one were held accountable to rational standards, societal breakdown and anarchy would result—we know it; we've seen it. Still it is considered a beautiful gesture to forgive *any* atrocity on a private level, though it spawns the same disorder. The pursuit of spiritual values ceases when a controlled format for their identification is abandoned, resulting in moral chaos. A beautiful gesture? It isn't beautiful ever to be thoughtless. It isn't responsible to reward anyone for ill practices, to deflect the consequences of their actions so they can't and don't learn, or to settle for less than our own virtue has earned. Milking our pity, they secured our consent to overlook their misgivings *as a moral action* and in so doing, we unwittingly damned our own virtues as *immoral*. If that which hinders life is to be valued, then that which furthers life is not—it's one or the other. The result was inevitable. If that which hinders life is not condemned, then that which furthers life *will be*. They claimed we must love everything, but we found virtues quickly excluded— didn't we, as moral sides were again recognized once their inversion was in place. The innocent are treated like criminals and the criminals are treated with compassion. Spirit Murderers will suddenly conform to a value structure when it is bent to serve their evasions, and what remains distinctly unforgiven has always been success.

They made us feel guilty for our fulfillment in the presence of their pain—*guilty for practicing the moral patterns of life* and for gaining their proper result—pride. They successfully transmitted the bitterness which dwells in their own hearts—the second key to their *true* plan—*no reward for anyone*. Our only real guilt is that we fell for it. They've taught it as sinful to enjoy the natural flow of our passions, to distrust our invigoration and encouraged us instead, to suffer the abrupt stop and go of a practice which our senses are *constantly* telling us, is wrong.

They damned the true cause, purpose and meaning of attraction—the pursuit of a reciprocal living power as a reflection and a completion—pushing us instead into tolerating a disjointed, fumbling incompetence. They know our natural affinity for uncorrupted values would endure as sure as we breathe, and would become a well of guilt for them to feed on. Our passion and desire for life was turned into a weapon of torture, to the very extent that we permitted ourselves to feel.

And if we choose not to feel? Obedience to their code holds the damnation of its own logic. If you consent to loving the contemptible, *cringing* becomes your confused expression of love. If you agree to love what you are indifferent to, it is *detachment* you will project. If your fear of ability mutates as a brimming love for the helpless, the death of dreams becomes love's association—*the truth comes out anyway*. Can you see the disposition of most priests and nuns emerging? They have become just what their view of love propounds—sterile, distant and passionless. These variations hold one thing in common: what they call love is actually *the abhorrent toleration of spiritual toxicity*—agony, boredom, stillness—and their false concept of love propels them towards harm and decay, into a roving center of death. Disgust by any other name is felt as disgust, distrust is felt as paranoia and emptiness is hollow. The true concept being practiced is not to be concealed, and comes out in senses dulled by pain, toil and an unrewarded life.

The truth about unconditional love is that it shares the same source as race hate—a non-objectively-founded, non-cognitive appraisal. As an appraisal is an act of cognition, a non-cognitive appraisal is a contradiction in terms—an impossibility. To love without reason is as destructive as to hate without reason. Why sidestep appraisal? For the same reason they wish to dodge the cash register in a store—to get away with life without practicing the virtues required by life. In sidestepping appraisal, one also sidesteps justice. Instead of the good rightly rewarded and the evil penalized, it is the good that is penalized and the evil rewarded—though the reward is illusory. Uncovering its true intent, unconditional love is a reproach, in hatred for all human values; the values it was created to defy. It allows them on a spiritual level, just what they desire on the physical—to get away with murder. Disallowing comprehension leaves us no means to tell decay from furtherance or enemy from friend—their own state of mind. If a premise doesn't sanction life, it sanctions its opposite. It's time to let them have what's coming.

Those who claim to "love everything" aren't spreading love: their imbecilic pretense just brings the world another example of self-chosen retardation. All those who believe they can skip the performance and hand out the prizes are not capable of love at all, and bring, not value to those they claim to love, but harm. No one can succeed in practicing unconditional or selfless love, and to the extent that people are sane, they don't try. Conceptually its true meaning is *mindless approval*—a contradiction in terms. Approval presupposes a mind that approves. Love, presupposes a *self* that does the loving. As they deny Man his perceptions and perceptions are sensory-based, by their own definition, *it is senseless*. Mindless love benefits no one; not even the mindless. It isn't love, and it isn't moral at all; it's stupid. If your supposed love can be had for nothing, then that is simply a declaration of its value, which *is* nothing, and of the inverted moral premises which gave it that value.

True love is not the all accepting, all forgiving garbage can they claim it to be; it is just the opposite. No one who *deserves* love and knows it would expound such an anti-concept, whether he's received the honor he's earned, or not. Only those who are worthless by their own estimate would, and do. Love is a precious reward—*an appreciable response to admirable traits*—and every human being, from the most innocent child to the most wicked, seething Spirit Murderer, knows it. Sound appreciation is a response to that which benefits *the living*, in some way. Love stems from the same values which drive us to seek the cleanest drinking water we can find. The *standard of appreciation* for a rational man is *life*. Its purest form can be obtained only by the practice of life-furthering virtues, seen by a countenance healthy enough to acknowledge them.

Can love be selfless? Never. Cognition is an attribute of *self;* love is a *result* of evaluation—an action of cognition—an endearing appraisal of a person, place or thing to oneself (including self-respect) and can be nothing else. *Love does not exist* without the intellectual depth to judge what is virtuous or not, and to practice and convey the life-furthering value structure from which it comes. One's intellectual depth *determines* one's depth of feeling, as well as its value to others. Self-made Man tolerates no tolerance of evil, *most carefully* in his concept of love. He forgives no practice which knowingly results in disaster, and permits no betrayal to life by placating its contaminants. Coming full circle, the goal for a moral man is in fact, to seek complete confidence in others based on *objective evidence*, possible first, only by gaining complete confidence in the integrity of his own actions. His love is granted only to the premises leading to life, just as his hate is validated by the premises which take it. Keenly guarding the purity in his concept of love is his most honorable tribute to the joy of living.

The Illusion of Infallibility. Spirit Murderers view Self-made Men as those who can do no wrong. It is the denial of Man's natural pattern of function to expect men to live in a state of perfect action—to be infallible. Their own pretense of false perfection drives the belief that infallibility is *necessary* for achievement, which it isn't, and they revel in seeing us err, enjoying the shame they expect us to feel at slipping on a pretense which we never practiced to begin with. The truth is that *their* premises tied perfect action to egoism, and in attempting to mimic our earned stature, we see their false-egoism most blatantly in the insincere refusal to admit any wrong-doings on their part. False perfection and false egoism are based on the same default, to avoid identification of the sub-elements which make our success possible—rational thought and tenacious effort. These they fear most of all.

The Pretense of False Perfection. For centuries, perfection has been preached as a futile, hopeless ideal, an unobtainable height that men must be measured against, yet can never reach. The Spirit Murderer's definition of perfection requires that Man not be human. Animals trip, stumble and fall out of trees, but Man cannot gain approval if he remains subject to the laws of gravity, to the inconsistency of meteorological conditions or if he is not aware of all knowledge *in advance* of its discovery. *Man* cannot be considered perfect as long as he is subject to the natural flow of life.

Webster's dictionary defines perfection as: "complete in all respects; without defect or omission; sound; flawless." This is a proper definition, but the contexts most often used regarding Man are wrong and demand clarification. Flying in the face of reasonable expectation, they measure his worth by whether he manages not to stumble on an uneven sidewalk, never spills anything, never gets sick, never says the wrong thing, never gets angry, never pay's a bill late, never disobeys a law, never talks back, never disappoints, has the perfect house and the perfect family. One mistake—one sneeze and your damned.

So what do most people do? Some try to maintain this impossible pretense, making themselves and those around them miserable, while the rest accept that Man can be nothing but imperfect, and end up *more* prone to degeneration. All of them avoid looking inward with a humble sense of unworthiness and guilt, fearing to find out just how imperfect they actually are. When a man succeeds, he'll often accept congratulations in silence or *deflect* honors, reluctant to recount the difficulties of his quest. For one, he knows his secret passion—pushing himself to the limit—is not viewed fondly by most. It is feared, envied and hated and he feels the tension against its acknowledgment. He knows what tenacity was necessary to fulfill his dream, and in mild embarrassment—knowing he is to be judged by a standard which claims that winners achieve success automatically, overnight—he knows he cannot live up to it. This dance of self-doubt is unnecessary. Look closely and you'll discover that what false perfection actually damns, is human cognition.

Rational perfection for Man does not require everything he does to be on cue. The concept of perfection is inapplicable to whether or not he encounters circumstances that catch him off-guard, but to *what he does about them*. Perfection applies not to whether a man trips, but to whether he attempts to recover, versus the preference of falling on his face. Not whether he never gets sick, but whether he takes steps to cure his illness and to prevent future illness. Not whether he never gets angry, but whether it's properly a response to injustice. Human perfection is found in the dynamic realm of volition: identifying and choosing the right course—the moral course—in every important issue of one's life, simple or complex. *Moral consistency in choice* is the true gauge of perfection, but false perfection accomplishes a number of parasitical goals for a Spirit Murderer. 1) To impose guilt for later redemption, 2) To justify his own misgivings "Nobody's perfect," 3) To look down on Man, 4) To kick him when he's down and 5) To keep his focus on *what is expected* and not on *what matters*.

The proper human countenance weighs all metaphysical conditions in his capacity to consider—calculating their effects to streamline his intentions. He moves through the world according to his own plan, and must interact with, oppose if contrary and harness if possible, the forces he encounters along his journey. Part of that journey, is learning how. He spends a lifetime honing the skill of processing data related to his causes, always becoming a greater, more efficient sum, and the result of living well is his highest pride. He rejects all irrational elements held as impediments before him by lesser men, knocking their fear aside to grasp the essence of an issue and gain proper footing. This constant upward thrust is Man's living will—the survival of the fittest—his answer to the question "Live or die?" The quest he was reluctant to describe earlier, which the discovery of its application to themselves makes the Spirit Murderer's equally reluctant to hear, *was in fact* his pursuit of true epistemological perfection.

Our true worth is not to be measured by an irrational standard. From our willingness to breathe and focus our eyes to our life's work, our self-generated productive effort determines our worth, and we add to the plus side with every moral decision—every decision that serves our betterment, to no one's harm or loss. In a Self-made Man, his life-preserving provocation is instantaneous; he isn't defeated in advance. He leaps to his feet, willing to fight for life until the end—of the storm or of himself. This is true of him in peacetime as well, channeling his energy into realms of no lesser spiritual consequence—the tenacity to succeed no matter what it requires of him. Now *that* is heroic moral perfection.

Metaphor/reality swapping. We hear speakers and read articles that weep for the whip-driven slaves chained to their jobs, who then propose legislation that will put real chains on the country's employers, forcing involuntary conformance to cowardly demands. We know that workers exist in their jobs voluntarily, and can quit whenever they want. We know that employers can offer a position and a salary to those qualified, and we can accept it or say no—neither has the right to resort to force. American free enterprise is not a slave/master relationship, but metaphorically it has always been treated as one. Voluntary involvement in American business has never been cut-throat competition; that is a mob term. From the Industrial Revolution, the mud has been hurled at every man with the vision to rise above the others and climb the mountain on his own. Without the writer's poetic chains, there is no justification for his animosity. Either his readers cannot tell the difference between metaphor and reality, or the 'get away with it' mentality simply appreciates the lines being blurred in their favor, anticipating an undeserved windfall if they act as an injured party. Their intention is not to achieve equal opportunity for the less endowed—they already have that—but to return to the violence of the dark ages and emerge above our greatest men as their master.

While being a simple cognitive violation easily seen through, its success is staggering—the irrational yet accepted business-killing union demands on management, the crippling laws passed against voluntary commerce, the outrageous awards granted in parasitical lawsuits—all achieved by appealing to a melodramatic loss, impossible to validate or measure—a realm considered higher than reason because no one understands it. Do consumers really care about the nationwide $1.49 settlement on a pair of $100 shoes, when a pricing discrepancy was prosecuted as "intent to monopolize" by our government? Should McDonald's pay two million dollars to every idiot who burns themselves on coffee, for pain and embarrassment? To nurse their delicate psychological health after a stressful and emotional chase (believe it or not), should police officers be encouraged to beat every motorist to death who takes too long to pull over? Was the man crawling around on his belly really a life-threatening situation for the officers?

Metaphor and reality swapping is driven by the desire to be rewarded for irrationality. The Fear-driven think "Wouldn't it be nice if I could spill some coffee and retire," and as juror, they allow someone else to do just that. Their generic question in all contexts is, "Wouldn't it be nice if we could *wish* instead of think?" and every attempt to make it possible just dims humanity with infection. In one moment, such jurors cause patiently, carefully accumulated capital to be dislocated into channels that will further short-range irrational goals instead. The money becomes stolen integrity, promoting a market for lower class concerns, whose existence relies solely on the spread of the infection, robbing mankind of a brighter future.

False Equality. It is said in our Constitution that "all men are created equal." Spirit Murderers extrapolate this *past* a man's creation, to claim it is a lifelong chain on all men obligating them never to outpace each other, and if so, requiring an equal distribution of their wealth to compensate for all human attributes which are clearly *not* equal—honesty, effort, willingness, et cetera.

We are all born into different economic and moral situations, national origins and climates. We develop to different heights, weights, health, intelligence and chosen character. We are given a host of core metaphysical attributes by nature, and with umbilical separation we must assume responsibility to hone them to their greatest efficiency. The least important traits on average are hereditary, while the most significant are *volitional*—meaning chosen by us. We all have special hopes and dreams, which are private and personally important. We all vary in our ambition for their pursuit, and this produces the Self-made bounty which a Spirit Murderer sees as worth looting. Recalling Forrest Gump who becomes a millionaire even with numerous—including mental—handicaps, would the fighters for supposed equality *desire* to be retarded? No, it's his money and honor they're eager to divide amongst themselves. Take away subversive language, and it comes down to the simple abrogation of virtues created by those willing, in favor of those who aren't.

The perfect contrast is that the Self-made all strive to be *unique,* while the Fear-driven want to blend in and hide—mirrors reflecting mirrors in endless monotony. From the faceless masses, they demand that all men be provided with a prosperous life as a minimum on which to build, unwilling to start where nature starts us all. Who is to provide it? The pursuit of equality past legal protection from violence is just another slave/master form of cannibalism, as confiscation is their only means to achieve it. Equality is a legal concept only, meaning no man is born with special governmental privileges denied to the others, period. It doesn't pursue happiness *for* them, or grant them any products that must be produced by others, but only clears their path of the unnecessary obstacles witnessed throughout history by outlawing violence and fraud among men. For once, it sanctions a human being's freedom to rise as high as his will carries him. It does not apply to private situations such as inheritance, or to the *supposed* unfairness of being subjected to stupid parents versus the grace of intelligent ones. It is not *unfair,* as no one has the right to mitigate such circumstances, but only unfortunate. Poverty-stricken parents are going to have poverty-stricken children, at least initially. Rich parents have rich children initially. They have a better chance because they witness better traits. It is the parent's traits handed down, whose abrogation would be a violation of their rights. Spirit Murderers would say something like, "If the poor decide to have children, the rich parents should subsidize them so that the poor children can have as equal a chance as their own." Or, "It's not the child's fault that he was born poor." It's not *ours* either; it's his parents fault. The poor are poor for a reason. Spirit Murderers are Spirit Murderers for a reason. And that reason disqualifies them from ever giving advice, or of having their viewpoints considered in a rational world.

That those of greater ability, effort and tenacity should live under threat of confiscation by those less endowed or less willing, is an abomination. That the smooth functioning ideas of a thoughtful, civil discipline should be subordinated to the unworkable tantrums of those demanding equality *as measured in asset value alone,* but never in effort, is deplorable. Moral? Like hell it is.

FALSE SPIRITUAL EQUALITY

Those who negate the mind have no choice but to swing from one annoying pretense to another. The quest for *spiritual* equality amounts to a grant of unearned snubbing, damnation, hatred, contempt, divinity, sanction, love and forgiveness. They swap from overly nice to overly not, avoiding what would allow no predispositional bias: objectivity. Objectivity requires thought, and thought is what they wish to avoid. Their unquestioned inner trauma or pleasure determines how they'll view the world each moment, instead of judging men and situations as they are encountered. Its proponents often swing from the unreal euphoria of a wonderful world full of wonderful people, to the raving lunacy of a terrifying world, full of evil bloody killers. It reminds me of an incident that happened on a jetliner some years back. A religious zealot was walking up and down the aisles, tapping people on the head to give them his blessing, spreading his love until a stewardess asked him to sit down and stop bothering people. He blew up and attacked her, was restrained by passengers and arrested upon landing. The intellectually destabilizing factor from positive to negative is the same: *the desire for a fixed societal interplay for fear of exercising real-time rational judgment.*

I've been through the gauntlet of the "undifferentiated as virtue" —the attempt to hold all things and all people on par as an equal and unqualified value—too many times. To hold a pre-established view of the world is exhausting and unnecessary, always leaving one unprepared for encounters with whatever does not conform. The game gets old fast. To view people in the best possible light, burdening them with a level of virtue they cannot uphold is just as destructive as subjecting them to unjust accusations. I know where it leads because I've done it myself—straight to immature nonexistence—an epistemological dead end.

We are what we are, and *objectivity* is the only mature gauge of human worth in any context—physically or spiritually. The best should be reverently studied, with effort put forth to acquire their traits; never to blank them out of our minds; never to shackle them and seize their rewards. Kill the golden goose, no more eggs. Speaking on behalf of the able to the unwilling, "It is not our fault that you are stupid; it is not our fault that you are afraid; that is your burden. Drop your weapons and fall in *behind* our children, *observing us* to learn and grow, because we will not carry your deficit any longer."

Materialism and Profit. Desiring to get the most out of life, life's lovers intend to earn and therefore *deserve* the best the world has to offer. Materialism is an anti-concept which damns this desire as a spiritually bankrupt, destructive pursuit. In the most rudimentary separation, it considers the body and mind to be two halves of a man with no interconnection, and more often than not, declares them to be fiercely at odds—the modern equivalent of religion's "man fighting for his soul." They claim they can put him back on track, exclaiming that spirituality can only be achieved by renouncing all material interests and necessities. The anti-concept is further narrowed as no intellectual pursuit is considered spiritual, omitting whatever could offend the non-thinking, non-producing man. In true Fear-driven fashion, they look down on the physical world where they have no power, and look up to the spiritual where they have no responsibility.

In their world, spiritual pursuits must yield no hard-earned clarity or material advantages, just some empty, unquestionable, eternal bliss. Has anyone ever asked why? Why is *that* spiritual; because it's the Hindu's answer? Centuries of monks have passed through time, sitting Indian-style in silence with steepled hands and have brought to the world a value amounting to exactly...nothing. Their credo is *mindlessness* as the price of spirituality and *stagnation* as the price of peace—not a healthy pattern to follow. Why renounce the material world? "Man's greed" would be their response, and the only way around wanting something improperly—as the Fear-driven see no alternative— is to want nothing, the only way for them not to harm is not to move. But greed or any desire, great or small, is only wrong when one seeks the unearned. *Greed* as defined by Webster's dictionary, is "an excessive desire for getting or having; a desire for more than one needs or deserves." It has a very negative connotation, yet can simply mean as stated under *greedy,* "intensely eager." It is another word twisted to draw a moral conclusion in advance, to assert that a strong desire is *wrong in itself* to be damned, regardless of whether its means of fulfillment is honest or dishonest.

Are people that "never have enough" truly evil? Beginning with the obvious, a human being is an entity of matter *and* consciousness, requiring material *and* spiritual products to sustain itself. Should we damn our bodies because they are never done consuming food? Every day, on and on, nourish, expel, nourish, expel—the simple nature of the entity. Did it ever occur to you that Man's spirit runs the same cycle? Spirit Murderers often deny this nutritional cycle, reaching a point where they decide they are done learning— what I call the Finished Product. They stifle the expansion of their knowledge, yet expect to continue to gain spiritual values, never seeing its link to their unhappiness. Man can no more settle for a fixed amount of achievement, than he can exist with a single breath of oxygen. Happy people do not seek or settle for an intellectually or physically static state of being, at any age. There is no such thing as a mindless body or a bodiless mind, and a man cannot live lacking either. To survive, he must continue to feed both. You may hear about their wonderful out of body experiences, but what do you think their body was doing while they were off floating in no-man's land? Keeping them alive is all.

They dispense with our ambition, saying "There are *non-material* ideals to consider." That's true. The non-material ideals are the *abstract* ideals of a Self-made Man, which make grasping and seeking the material ideals possible, and they are outlined in the previous section. With our own neurobiological understanding, it is becoming clear that there is no real separation between mind and body at all. All living organisms have specific nutrients they must pursue in *both* realms. But how is this done? Proper spiritual nutrition is found exactly in the creative activity of bringing abstract ideas into material reality, which they damn, not first in buying the goods, but in *producing* them. It's exciting to come up with an idea and see if the world will go for it. Win or lose, I keep running this process over and over—I love it! I love the opportunity to buy the products of another's genius—simple inventions like my tool-grabber, things I've imagined but haven't the time to develop, and revolutionary new ideas from people who've spent passionate time out on an epistemological limb I'll never have to walk alone. The passionate endeavors of others have brought such wealth into my life, that in my thankfulness, I don't know where to begin. Maybe from the harnessing of fire, to the invention of the wheel, to Aristotle's laws of logic, to the founding fathers of America, to Benjamin Franklin's experiments with electricity, to Thomas Edison's light bulb, to Henry Ford's Model T, to IBM's personal computer and its unlimited applications, to the exotic cars I treasure— these are all products of Man which I benefit from greatly, and had no part in designing. All were considered foolish ostentation or evil upon their inception, in malicious fear of the creative faculty from which they came, by those whose productive significance history never seems to record.

Very few people are wrapped up in "over-consumerism" —shopping themselves silly as a manic attempt to replace spiritual fulfillment. Such an addiction is an aversive dependency just as alcoholism or gambling, but in these others, the remedial push is to get their act together. There is rarely a call to *separate oneself from oneself,* and reformers focus on those afflicted; they don't declare it to be a worldwide epidemic. Their solution for this supposed rash of greed is only to relegate our time to idle prayer or to a cruder material pursuit they can understand, such as farming. Only in socialist slave-pens such as China, does a society need to focus solely on the preservation of Man's body, a need their political system consistently fails to meet. Freedom translates into innovations for efficient farming requiring less labor, releasing individuals to create new products and new markets. Those who want to stop men from producing whatever comes to their mind as a salable product, then dictate to them how they will spend their time, their money and on what, are the ones to be criticized. America's wonderful bounty of products is the result of every man's right to exist being recognized, and that's all. Breathe easily when a man is after money and luxuries he is willing to *earn,* because when he isn't, he is after control. The Spirit Murderers are the ones responsible for wanting the unearned in *both* realms; the problem was created by them, in self-restraint supposedly solved by them, and the Finished Product was its result. This cold, mindless, dead relation to matter and spirit has nothing to do with us, so we should leave them to it.

Self-made Man *can and does* act without harming. He *can* want properly. Most forget that those accused of being materialist, often put many unpaid years into their fields before any profit is realized, if at all. And profit, damned for centuries, is the basic necessity of life, the requirement that one stays ahead of even—in body and spirit. It is the third step of cognition, the act of creation—the hope of prosperity in *any* realm in which one dares to dream—that brings the human spirit to life. It is the fourth step of cognition—validation, whose equivalent in work is profit, which determines whether one remains on course. Whether one's interest is commercial, romantic or both, it is *not* evil or wasteful as the Spirit Murderers claim, but *essential:* the very fiber of our self-esteem, and the key to the deepest spirituality a man can ever hope to reach—and they know it.

To know that one's divine inspiration has a productive purpose—that it brings joy to others and prosperity to ourselves, that our energy serves a sum, not to be lost in the past, but a value to be brought forward with every day of our lives—develops an inertia that will supercharge our exhilaration for living. As a result, all thought and action becomes tied to prosperity, as it should be. The structure of every mind assumes the correct hierarchical order, and gains the capacity to project across the span of its own existence, bringing to fruition a height of personal significance, almost too precious to contemplate.

False Proverbs. After a while, cultural trends form to reveal the Fear-driven's favorite approaches to impotence. Here are a number of common sayings that have their root in cowardice, and have been an endless source of moral irritation for Man:

"There are no absolutes in life" or "Nothing is certain" versus the vast knowledge of unchanging natural standards discovered by Man, every step up the ladder of science and 99% of all human action. You don't have to speak to a nuclear physicist to verify whether or not there *are* absolutes; ask anyone with a checking account. The next time you hear this, ask the speaker to go step on a rake a few times, to see if he notices a trend.

"Judge not, lest ye be judged" versus the coherent identification of a man's adherence to life-furthering principles, *as well as one's own.* Negating the value of judgment is a disastrously stupid anti-concept, implying that thought itself is an act of evil. It claims that if your mind runs the process to determine the location of entities and their actions along a hierarchy of value—the cognitive means of human life—that you have committed an abomination against morality. Jesus meant that men should not judge each other *falsely,* by irrational standards—nothing more.

The way this statement is most often used implies that it is *immoral to think.* If that is so, then the brain is useless. If they declare the brain to be useless, then why respect the content of theirs? If all they can say is Bible this and Bible that, they can't think for themselves. They are followers—not leaders, and can only lead you to your own spiritual demise.

When someone says they **"didn't have the heart"** to do or say something—it means they're being heartless, and it's true. Gutless too. We don't have to kick someone when they are down, but when they're *asking* for help, a tactful, objective emotional discipline is called into action. In practicing conveyance of the pure truth with regard to their state, you grant more than just consideration for their feelings; you communicate belief in their capacity to reach the human stature they seek, and then, it directly attributes to yours.

"In this day and age", "At this time," and "In this environment," are valid only when drawing a map from where we are, to where we want to be. But for the most part, these false claims imply the necessity of compromise with, acceptance and submission to, current levels of corruption, while justifying the speaker's passivity to think further, to be honest or to act.

"That's old-fashioned", "That's out of date," or "You have to change with the times." Likewise, lacking the foundation of sound judgment, the untried and new is also not to be trusted, ala "It's never been done before." The anti-pioneer has to see it done by others and gain their estimate before a side can be chosen. Riding the emotional current of others, what is out of favor with the favor-providers is automatically out of favor with him. This may be suitable to clothing fashions, but they want to apply it to physics as a universal axiom, allowing them to discard all sound frames and play it anything goes. In their culture it always becomes folly to be responsible, intellectual or enterprising, and fashionable to be an aimless, unhappy bum.

The truth is that time is irrelevant to the validity of any concept dealing with organic life. Just because a premise was identified 2500 years ago doesn't make it any more or less valid than a discovery of five minutes ago. Sir Isaac Newton's Laws of Motion still apply, as do what led to their discovery—Aristotle's Laws of Logic. Axioms are good for *all* time, regardless of when they are discovered; and the opportunity to be concerned with such a luxury as fashion, remains possible only as long as men respect them. Likewise, Fear-driven premises were wrong 2000 years ago, are still wrong, and always will be.

"If you want it *bad* enough." Negatively enough, or just intensely enough? A strong desire is *not* evil; that is precisely why it is labeled as bad.

"You have to give something back." Originally a mob custom, this false premise is stretched to stain essential human productivity, implying that working or owning a business is a form of robbery. As a normal civilian, you need give *nothing* back. With our unnecessary tax burden and subversive moral environment, it's the other way around.

"Not everyone can be wealthy." In addition to the blatant unwillingness to lift a finger, this statement implies that wealth only falls on the lucky from the outside. Individual human action is the driver of prosperity, as it should be. Everyone can be as wealthy as the effort they are willing to expend. Wealth essentially is a result of personal action, the equivalent of work accomplished. As everyone has their own person as an energy source, it is possible to all. We are all responsible for our immediate environment; whether we empty the garbage or let it rot, whether we live in a pigsty or not is up to us. Money is the mass-acknowledged measure of wealth, but the forms of wealth are infinite. In spirit, every chain of knowledge is a form of wealth, as is the effect of every virtuous cause. Among these are the tenacity for wealth's accumulation and our life-serving plans of action. The feeling of wealth in application is different for every one of us, by attaining satisfaction of what we truly want. A fisherman may desire the latest vessel or a fleet and the ability to yield the greatest bounty, while that would be a painful distraction for another. Another's enterprise may be the construction of great buildings. Another may imagine a fleet of exotic cars and the capacity to drive them expertly, right to their limits. Still another may desire a beautiful landscape, a clean canvas and the time and skill to fill it. Men have infinitely different dreams, yet all share the same format, revolving around money, time and skill. As long as *we* remain the source of our dynamic wealth—not a rich spouse or parent—the door to our deepest self-esteem remains open.

"There is good in the lowest." The fear-stagnated have to look below themselves to feel tall. We as the Self-made aspire to one day reach our hero's stature; we are always looking up and ahead. The Fear-driven always look for value in remote places, excluding wherever it is most obvious. Mining for that minute percentage is only a diversion for the guardianship of what they consider as the overwhelming sum of their being—incompetence and evil.

"He or she has potential." *Everyone* has potential. What you should be looking for, is kinetic. A body in motion can be turned onto the correct path, but a stationary object requires an enormous effort just to overcome initial friction. Have you ever moved a large piece of furniture alone? The first effort is the hardest, then it slides much more easily. Objects in motion tend to stay in motion, just as still objects tend to stay still. If one's predisposition is to do nothing, you have an uphill battle on your hands. Stagnation is chosen out of fear. Forced into action, the Fear-driven look to dig and dive right back into another foxhole. They seek safety—not rewards, which is why they stopped in the first place. Don't kid yourself; they have to get out of the hole alone.

"Happiness is fleeting." Happiness to them is an unpredictable, unreliable and inconsistent sense of euphoria whose source cannot be identified, practiced or maintained. There is a payoff in accepting no solid definition; it wipes out the personal responsibility to uphold the standards that would lure it into their lives *as a constant*—just like love.

"A person is a product of his environment." As far as they are concerned, all cures as well as all actions, originate outside of them. Yes, your life and character are molded by many causative factors, but you are responsible for managing *all* of them. Their effect on you is your *objective* pride or your *subjective* guilt. Either results from the effort you put forth into the construction of your own value filters.

"Grow up!" They invert their conscious effort to reinforce in themselves and others the futility of Man's aspirations—that to grow up is to give up. To stand by convictions is to be cold and cruel. To tell lies is merciful; to be honest is rude. That passion is comical, and comedy is cynical. The attempt to twist these definitions is to fake to themselves that what they gave up wasn't worth reaching anyway, and they veil their true fear by hijacking the virtue of maturity—but they aren't. They have let themselves down, and wish to mask their own secret heartbreak.

We all decide what is sufficient to stop us. It is rare to encounter someone who doesn't stoop to the dishonesty of declaring values no longer to *be* values, once they've given up their pursuit.

"Loosen Up!" They want us to loosen up, but notice that we have few, if any, manic tendencies. Why do you think that is? We can bring relaxation to others with our confidence like no one else can, yet *we* need to relax. What they actually mean, is that as one lets one's hair down, we should learn to let our premises down—to loosen our grasp on consciousness—yet *their* grasp is the reason for their mania. Self-made Men are masters of living, so reality is never the subject of their escape. We have it down so well that we can spin our wheels, work hard, be light, be serious, do anything, buy anything and go anywhere, all driven by our deepest passions in life—now that's freedom. The barrier they wish to break down is our unwillingness to accept data on faith, which means without passing it through our filter of cognition, and to consider such mindlessness to be virtue. Without a firm grasp on reality and purpose, one cannot and shouldn't be able to, relax.

Here are a number of other falsehoods as the Fear-driven use them today, versus the true moral attributes they covet:

"Patience is a virtue" versus pushing past barriers to accomplish one's objective regardless of the opposition's desire to stop you. "Money is the root of all evil" versus acknowledging the innocent, wholesome prosperity which results from the mature civility of voluntary exchange between men. "Speed kills" versus the speed *differential* between vehicles involved in a collision and the actual culprit, irresponsibility. "Man is a creature of circumstance" versus self-responsibility. "It takes money to make money" versus creativity. "It is easier for a camel to pass through the eye of a needle, than for a rich man to enter the kingdom of heaven" versus the proper honor and heroic reverence for the vast majority of the wealthy, who earn their money by the consistent practice of honest means. "God-given talents" versus acknowledging the tenacious effort of the moral. "Pride for wealth is the ultimate evil" versus the self-esteem possible only to those of independent judgment. "Luck" versus the earned and deserved. "Unlucky" versus lazy and afraid. "No man is an island" versus independence. "Better to play it safe" versus a fully conscious and responsible, pioneering attitude. "We're just insignificant specks of dust floating through time" versus proper contextual significance. "No one can prove anything" versus a rational progression of thought.

Such statements are driven by the secret desire to see their victims fail, as they did. Their eyes are on the inevitability of falling short and returning to safe harbor, *not* on making it. The extent to which a man knowingly clings to anti-concepts is the extent to which he fears to live, and is the extent to which he is *not* living as a man. Such falsehoods are countless; these are only what have most often irritated me. Let your own understanding of life-furthering standards, uncover and weed out the rest.

Part Four: Their Logical End: Penalties

"Irrationality is its own damnation." —Me! I said that!

We have seen the first three elements of cognition for the Fear-driven: evasion of reality, evasion of consciousness and deceptive action, and here is its reward: nothing but penalties.

There is a clear link to why cartoons portray angry people with storm clouds overhead. The sunlight which gives us life is itself a high frequency form of electricity. We all function by electrical energy, and an electrical storm strikes whatever is most vulnerable. It transfers a build-up of energy from one place to another—in their case, negative. Positive or negative, no one can hold a charge for long; it must be dispelled. Self-made Man lives his life gathering positive energy, a wealth to be spent lavishly in controlled directions from powerful purpose-driven action at his highest frequency, to relaxed ease at his calmest. No matter what anti-concepts Fear-driven Man invents to mask his actions, his defaults continue to result in vast negativity. He builds a great concentration of pain, which finds its release in fury and mental breakdown. It is a collapse of the restraint of sanity—his fundamental intention achieved—poured onto anyone who crosses his path.

Years go by and our Self-made capacities deepen. Our depth of feeling grows, as does our pride. In this time, the Fear-driven become more irritable, shorter range and still their advice never changes: "Give up, slow down, play it safe..." Focusing on excuses, twenty years can pass with little to no progress in his life-strands, and often times he suffers their regression. *He* expands in subsets of evasion and corruption, his expertise reflecting that of the Spanish Inquisition: the devious anti-reason creed which relies on an unquestionable, unprovable authority, to vindicate himself and condemn others. He grows more efficient at bringing to the surface everything he hates, while suppressing everything that matters. He gets to his emotional results quicker—anger, hatred and pain—and can be as instantly callous, phony and track-covering as any soap opera tramp. All actions of the Self-made accumulate as the sum of their stature, while all actions of the Fear-driven accumulate as festering toxic waste. Experience has cut his ruts deeper, and he has only gotten better at lying to himself.

For the Self-made, imaginary flags go up throughout the world as markers to lead him to his goals and to confirm the value of living. For the Fear-driven, flags go up to *justify* his negative associations. Stepping on one rake after another through his own default, his focus on the negative is unavoidable. To him, every stubbed toe is proof that happiness is a futile pursuit; every mishap in traffic is proof that it is a god-damned world. It becomes ingrained in his very physiology to *seek* the negative as a confirmation of his premises—as his summation of life—where his capacity for the prediction of disaster gives him a semblance of self-esteem to keep him running. Self-esteem is as essential to life as our heart and brain. Faking it is his means of wicking toxins away from his primary cognitive functions to sustain a living efficiency—just as the body moves fat away from the major organs—but both can tolerate only so much abuse before they falter.

When a Self-made Man battles negative pressure, he doesn't destroy himself. Directing all energy whether it be positive or negative, he says "To hell with it, if they don't like me now, I'll really give them something to whine about," and becomes even more. A Spirit Murderer doesn't attempt to harness the energy he generates for *any* living purpose. Through random disintegration and thoughtless waste, he is left with no reserves to combat the pain of his own subjectivity, no relaxed grace to foster elasticity, and he is left to spiritual starvation, a brittle composure and an impending physical doom.

Cacophony of Contradictions. The gap in his logic of course, is the missing step holding him accountable for his actions that has been passed down for centuries. It is tragic: all we've heard from our elders which they've heard from theirs—the stagnant, evasive demands not to be questioned, the unrealistic expectations they forced down our throats, the whole of their "or else" philosophy—none of it worked for them either. All of the unfounded, unsupported assertions we've ever encountered were the hasty product of Fear-driven Man, no matter his age or position—a man willing and eager to work with a cacophony of contradictions, distortions and outright fraud. Watching him in action, he damns the senses and all individual capacities as such, but will ask you to pay close attention, while learning to shut your mind, close your eyes and follow him as if to say, "Listen carefully... There *are* no senses!" His religion preaches a world we can't have now, virtues we can't apply now and leaves us with no direction for the one that exists, counseling us only to follow the same aimless surrender as his own. Arguing the unintelligible, his morality damns wealth, without consideration for whether it was earned or stolen (negating the productive source of life and denying justice to the honorable). *In fear* of moral action, he preaches a heaven of effortless treasures, and then wonders why casinos are coming up around him. Feeling worthless, he preaches unconditional love, and wonders why brothels follow. He shuns cause and effect, but it piles up his losses unrestrained; he cannot escape the illogical flow and practical result of his own senseless theories. Conviction being certainty over a proven body of knowledge and his morality supporting a negation of the senses which provide it, he *has* no convictions. His hatred for life spewing from every default, he *must* discredit reason to survive spiritually, and only succeeds in discrediting himself.

Still, he will do anything to make his unworkable wishes work, to avoid the discovery that he has no standards, save fear. Rebelling against the incoming stream of data, he fights his own consciousness, his tantrum claiming that knowledge should be preset for his automatic manipulation, and all requirements of life should be a birthright. He accepts no difference between life-essentials and inessentials, no difference between right and wrong, and works to shield himself from ever identifying its necessity. "The mind can do and be anything," he exclaims, refusing our living processes, and makes unreasoned decisions at whatever level he manages to operate—personal, national or global—fighting to force others—and existence itself—to accept his unreality as being on par with the reality he will not face. Cultural inertia has helped him do it, as without moral clarity in society, individual status has borne no relation to competence. In the sight of the whole world, he has been free to make decisions and cope with life from his fear-driven mindset, and has succeeded only in making irreversible and unrecoverable, life-destroying mistakes. From every edict of the papacy to FDR's "New Deal" welfare-state disaster to its sister, Soviet Russia, mankind has been plagued with the mass pursuit of one mindless expectation after another, the result of every Fear-driven longing of freedom from the responsibility of self-sustenance. Red, dead, malicious or just confused, his utopia requires no healthy guiding premise, no honest judgment, no proof and no effort—nothing to worry about. Whew! But life doesn't work that way. Trying to reason *without* reason, he accomplishes nothing but ludicrous insanity, and reality checks into him like an NHL superstar at every step.

The Spirit Murderer's fundamental contradiction is in choosing an enemy against whom he cannot possibly win and remain alive. He fights existence, but he exists none the less. He hates this world, but he has to live in it. He damns the tasks of living, but he must perform them. He does everything a living man must, but he does it for evil. His every action intends to interrupt the flow of the proper patterns of life—to slow, stop or destroy—yet he feels as much anguish in a traffic jam as the rest of us. He ends up getting dragged along the path of mankind's advancements—kicking, screaming and negating our value every step of the way. He clashes with existence in a fight that is unnecessary, as there is no one opposing him. In his punching, kicking fury, if he were to look up, he'd realize he is alone. Existence does not oppose him on conscious terms. Ultimately he learns that the only way to defeat existence, is *not* to exist.

Stress and Anguish as a Medium. Every decision a man makes is a fork in the road indicating his prime intention; one leads to life, the other to death. We all make mistakes from time to time—decisions based on fear that lead us in the wrong direction temporarily, until we see the penalties and correct our course—but a Spirit Murderer chooses this as his constant. A Self-made decision is the choice to venture forth into the unknown, to conquer it, making it the known, the mastered, and then venturing further. For the Fear-driven it is quite different—an immediate disengagement. He initiates a stream of justifications as his alternate path, amounting to nothing more than the cancer of cognition, and his many well-deserved forms of neurotic anxiety. These are subjective outgrowths, unbuildable structures which permit his sub-tenets—evasion of existence, consciousness and sound purpose—which he relies on and attempts to work with, but lead only to misery. There is no escape from reality: If he looks, he'll see that the sum of *his* stature as well, is and only ever has been his minute accumulation of Self-made attributes and actions.

Human beings are premise driven entities. Our automatic functions give us a head-start as we work to automate more and more processes over the course of our lives, to grow in stature and power. We are meant to follow their lead and move forward, but Fear-driven Man tries to operate in reverse, to break their patterns. Along any particular line, his desire to evade existence and thought, immediately suspends all further virtue. No, he doesn't reverse reality or even reverse his consciousness; he only causes a cacophony of contradictory motives and actions thrown among the rational human motives and actions needed to live, like sand between the gears of his mind. When he violates the proper flow of life with impossible desires, his body tries to obey his consciously chosen direction and succeeds only in clogging up the works. He promotes his own stress in forcing conscious control over non-conscious processes, resulting in nothing but dysfunction and confused physiological orders. Emotional stress is the body's warning to us that we are using *cognition* improperly.

What is that disease where the victim twitches so much, he could rattle himself out of his own chair? Feeling our heart pound, having shallow breath, a dry mouth and having our body firing off senseless gestures is just what we've all suffered to a lesser degree when confronted with an uncomfortable situation. Twitches and stress are the result of the desire to have reality be something other than it is—our body's response to unrealistic demands. Physical processes, because they must act in harmony with their natural purposes, cannot act in contradiction to them and only become hampered and dysfunctional when illogical control is attempted. Wishing to control elements outside our power, we only lose control over ourselves. Whenever a physical inconsistency is felt—a pain in the chest, brain or ill control in one's muscles—if it is stress-driven and often it is, then something must be faced. A Self-made Man has the courage to look, knowing in his deepest maturity that he won't be sorry. He trains himself to engage immediately: to learn its sub-components and conquer them. Learning time after time that there is nothing to fear, he no longer associates his instigation to bravery, but moves on to the patterns above. As a result, the state of the Self-made is an active, youthful relaxation; nothing in day to day life is outside his power to deal with. He is not without tension, as solving problems to his interest certainly tests the limits of his endurance. The key is that his energy is productively channeled, and he learns to cope with high levels of responsible activity, developing grace under pressure. Ultimately his devotion makes it look easy, and the pathways to his pride appear automatic, even to himself. This is where virtue becomes *second nature*.

On the other side, the ill tension suffered by the Fear-driven which shows so clearly in their faces—struggling with muscles not meant to be controlled—is his *denial* in action. Fighting himself, he accomplishes little, and what he does accomplish comes at a much greater emotional cost. Most often he side-steps his incapacities by evading the dangers altogether, never conquering his pounding heart or any other symptoms of trauma. Choosing dead-end interests over any crucial, self-serving purpose, he believes he can escape the potential of future disappointment. By never trying, he ends up with the angst and desperation of living a lifetime with a broken heart. He is devoted only to what is easiest for him—the path of least resistance—and never develops any skill for the dynamic courage which would bring peace and calm. Necessarily then, he can never develop the productive endurance or the intellectual range to project goals which would make the effort towards them worthwhile. His alternative to depth and clarity—things that must *not* be seen—by himself or others—leaves him stuck in the shallow, miserable loop of their concealment, and he never even learns who he is.

COMMON PSYCHOLOGICAL MALADIES. Stress has very real, very serious effects on our health and our term of life, its worst physical effects being chronic sickness and rapid aging. A body hampered by the senseless is derailed from its proper duties and must let them slide. As a warning, the first attribute it abandons is appearance. One's physical appearance is the most delicate indication of our welfare that the body can muster. The brain lends a large mass for control of our facial structure, in part to show early signs as a preemptive strike against illness—physical or spiritual in origin. Depression is a spiritual sickness, with denial as its root. No one stays depressed without it. *Anxiety* being one level less suppressed, has fear as its root. Fear-driven Man is rundown by premise, and as a result is more prone to all forms of sickness. A man who has chosen evasion as his means of dealing with existence shouldn't exist, and self-destruction—rapidly wearing out his organs and no longer replenishing his health—is nature's way of putting him out of his misery.

One's self is defined by our depth of commitment to bring our greatest truth into being. Fear-driven Man brings *no* truth into being, so he lives without an identity he is willing to admit, and spawns the plethora of psychological disorders ever recorded by Man. *Behavior* is determined by whatever one chooses to tie to one's esteem. The pattern of Fear-driven Man *is* the pattern of neurosis and fundamentally its outgrowths are all *phobias* of reason. Who is surprised? Not adhering to the concept of identity causes *identity crisis.* Evading sensory perception and identification causes *panic attacks,* leaving him lost, helpless and afraid. Living without goals results in there being no point to his existence. He is a speck of dust floating in the universe, and aww, he feels insignificant. What did he expect to feel when life is approached as if it has no meaning? Did he expect it to be meaningful? He got what he asked for—no confidence, no self-esteem and no means to achieve any—for in the base of every *voluntary* mental disorder lies his default—his first three elements of cognitive action—life's essence unseen, unprocessed and unsteered.

Disorders mutate with every cognitive violation, but fall into predictable routines. Here are some of them: Ingrained social dependencies result in over-elaborate cognitive structures built on the opinions of others—leading to *paranoia* and *exhibitionism.* The threat of not being approved of leads to *pandering, persecution mania, violence* or hermitic *withdrawal.* Chronic disbelief in one's capacity for independent survival causes *obsessive-compulsive disorders*—such as lying, gambling and stealing. Present dissatisfaction and hopelessness for the outcome of future action elicits *depression (their form of projection).* The absence of sound purpose forces a substitute, from the simple—*overemphasis on family* and *overeating*—to the complex—*drugs* and *alcoholism*—to cover the true vice, *cognitive procrastination.* Mismanaged energy and the guilt of untended dreams leads to chronic *insomnia.* Anxious hopelessness and loss leads to hypersomnia (over-sleeping). True *guilt* results from taking actions known as contrary to life. *Desperation* is being backed into a deep enough corner to know that for his premises, it's too late, and he now faces a real threat to his life. The psychotic joy of relishing the *true* outcome of his premises is called *masochism* or *sadism.* In all psychological maladies, you will find a negation of one or more of the proper elements of cognition.

There is no form of natural illness that results in one's statistical choice of harm being greater than one's choice of good: there is no honest bias. With an involuntary cognitive break, one could not tell good from evil and the result would be a coin toss. If the consistent choice is evil, then so are the premises driving it. We were not structurally designed to carry the dysfunctional mediums of crisis, self-inflicted injustice or unhappiness: these are man-made problems. Due to his own cowardice, Fear-driven Man doesn't know where to put his hands or feet, he doesn't know how to act, who to be, what is expected or when. Suffering these burdens without a moments rest, he swings between presumptuousness and humility in life—swaying from a dominance he cannot impose to a subservience he need not feel, in a fit of chronic psychological trauma—and considers it normal. But evidence that it's not, shows in that he seeks not to solve the mysteries of his life, but to find a way out. If you've come to the point in life where your only true satisfaction is to contemplate leaving it, you're doing something wrong.

All Doors Closed to Reform. Just about everything a Spirit Murderer does— even his redemptive efforts—is corrupt. The ultimate result of his evasions are needs that must be met by any means, and emotions that must be evaded at any cost. I am always shocked at the extent to which a Spirit Murderer will go to preserve their illusions. They will sacrifice themselves, their children—the whole world—to evade their responsibilities just as steadfastly as we work to fulfill our dreams. Any tragedy will be endured; they seek evasion with equal fervor. Evading is what he *wants* to do; he is a professional at subversion, testing and acquiring every iteration—every escape. If he senses that a brave realization must be faced, he responds by using his mind's fullest capacity to stamp it out. His precarious esteem must be preserved at all costs; not by discovering and collecting the missing pieces, but by evading any possible answer to the questions that must never be asked. His greatest fear is to find the worst about him to be true, and be left to witness his own naked worthlessness—exposed, undeniable and worst of all, unchangeable.

Self-made Man touches pinnacles throughout life, peaking and returning to his comfortable medium in open display of his strength and as his deepest tribute to greatness. Fear-driven Man lives behind a veil, dipping into his black hole of treachery as a window to *his* soul, and then returns to his negative neurotic medium. Only in times of severe personal crisis where the consequences of his actions are undeniable even to him, can one really know him. Being brought to justice reveals the vulnerability which comprises his only genuine moments with others, and that insecurity is *his* deepest truth.

Often his reformers—personal or professional—have no inkling of the kind of psychological leverage he applies to maintain an irrational course. This is his specialty, his most personal endeavor, and his reformers want to take it away from him. They offer this loathsome replacement of *acknowledging* cause and effect—what he's worked so hard to avoid—so he bites the hand trying to help. Uncivil people do not learn by civil means. Given the socio-psychiatric trend of looking outside him for the answer to his character, his attempts at reform are likewise insincere. Playing on this, his clinical effort is just another confidence game, and through his web of lies, rests his undertone of hope—that his doctors will slip and reveal the secret to finally make his unworkable wishes work. Practically his intention becomes to learn enough not to get caught again, leaving him free to continue his actions undetected. To him, "If you don't succeed, try, try again" is an inspiration for the tenacity of fraud.

When he fogs out his mind, the evil is born: it begins to churn, and creates a vortex which must be fed. As the inventor of this trap—its creator and sympathizer—his straightjacket spun for the world has been woven instead around himself. In seeking exemptions from truth, he loses the power of consciousness and the pattern of rational thought. His lack of experience in the responsible world disallows him to function in it alone. Every fork in the road is a temptation to defy his enemy—reality—and any sound decision is grudgingly considered a sucker's move, and a missed opportunity. Indulging his weakness at every turn leads right back to his constant flow of penalties. There is no escape without renunciation of the process, which is nearly impossible as it is a substitute structure for his very life force—self-esteem. His energy is immediately sapped by the thought of conforming to a rational structure. Reform is equated with *giving up*—to surrender his false premises and the world he wants, in abominable favor of the premises which make it impossible.

It is okay to help him *when* he seeks clarity, but the truth is most often, he doesn't want to learn. He doesn't want to be more than he is, he doesn't want to know that anything more is possible to him and he doesn't want to know that he is doing anything wrong. His equivalent of integrity is the refusal to acknowledge defaults and errors. He refuses to recognize his problems as his and would rather loop in patterns of self-hate deflection, coping with a world left undefined and accepted as indefinable. He wants to be declared healthy with *no* examination, preferring to live with the pestilence without acknowledging it or considering it good (unconditional love). He claims to have tried everything he could to make his plans work—except honesty—and damns a moral man for believing that *his* method—accountability—is always right. *Of course* a Self-made Man wants to be right as *the right* is the life-preserving, but he would never sacrifice honesty to get there. A Spirit Murderer *has* to be right because his premises allow no means of recovery from being wrong, so he looks to the entropy of nature or society to provide the inertia to get him to his specific destinations automatically. Still wonder why he gambles? In his fantasy, he floats to his goals on a cloud and is free to sneer at the grunts below, who earn their way. The unknown *must* be the answer, as it is the only answer acceptable to him.

Ask him what he thinks he's doing and you reach an impasse, differentiating it from a parallel feeling in a producer—confidence in his outcome. Producers know exactly what they are after, and that knowledge fuels them. Like a lemming on a cliff, the Fear-driven must have the unknown awaiting them on the other side, and spiritually they share the lemming's fate. Implicit in the definition of neurosis is disregard for any possible clarity or solutions. "*A neurotic will fight any identification that the danger can be averted.*"—Ayn Rand. For him, a cliff lines both sides of his life; one of truth, the other of his own destruction. Destruction holds a lesser terror.

I had to learn the hard way, just how much I wanted to live and just how much the Fear-driven didn't. Motivation to do good or evil is carried out by the same living source, and their passion to die can match or *exceed* our passions for living. It all depends on the energy generated, and such weeds have the predatory inertia to choke out any delicate flower. If you think you are smart enough to turn them by intellectual means, you will learn otherwise. They don't want to turn. Reform is simply adapting to the moral process of life. To see, to learn, to grow, to love and to feel good, is in direct contradiction with their means of self-preservation—*no greater emotional clash exists.* He doesn't see his capacity to fake reality as a crippling debilitation; *he prizes it.* As long as he feels empowered by lying and fogging out his mind, he doesn't stand a chance.

Physical and Emotional Stillness. As his fire of youth burns out, his zest for creative fraud fades as well. It has brought him nothing but clever excuses and empty triumph, a sustenance he has not earned, a guilt which he has, and instead of a blossoming, the spread of decay. His effort in life has been to *not* look, to *not* see, to *not* acknowledge, and collecting his reward, to *not* live. He realizes that after years of laughing at greatness, of extinguishing any spark of talent, of stomping out any passion for living, in preaching human impotence—he has reached it.

Lacking the energy for another step forward, he slows to a crawl. His hearing slows, his comprehension slows and like a warped record, his spirit whirs to an end. Life then becomes a different set of automatic functions. Ironically, he gains his dream world of fixed expectations, but it isn't the enchantment he envisioned. In place of the attractive, loving spouse, he has the safe indistinguishable one who couldn't find better, grows disturbingly larger and won't leave. Everything about him says, "I give up." His posture succumbs to his premises, his skeletal structure follows, as does his gut. In his own shameful state of flabby neglect, he deserves nothing more than he gives. He has lost all feeling for others—his shrinking arousal undermined by chronic exhaustion—but for those two minutes a month, he hopelessly recalls what it's like to be alive. He has lost all contact with the physical world and couldn't step down a hillside unless it was paved. Instead of his dream career, he often works just enough not to get fired and is paid just enough not to quit. He lives for the same boring actions in constant repetition, with no element of surprise and no projection of activity past his next meal. Cut off from his future he stares two steps ahead, unwilling to look up and face the limitless depth of its obligation and the life he could have, still before him. In any brief flicker of discontent, he sees so many elements lacking—so many undisciplined strains to relearn—the overwhelming responsibility to get from agony to elation is just too much. With his weak patterns, he is unable to project his gratification five years into the future, so there is no incentive to try. Five years goes by and once again he repeats his mantra: "I'm too old, it's too late, they wouldn't give me a chance." His life force never having seen its proper purpose, is worn out with an ugliness no strict discipline would ever inflict. Having relished the fraud in every false virtue of his code, he has fallen victim to them all and is now *dead* to every joy in life. He struggles to get out of bed day after day, year after year, with only one desire left: for it to end.

Aging without grace, he is no longer lost in the pretense of the moment, being lost to begin with. The moment left without him. To spend decades of life on the fence without recording any achievements or stature from one's experience is beyond tragic. With no courage to make positive decisions, he stays at the same level—living hand to mouth intellectually as he does financially—and may not appear to have advanced in premise towards life *or* death, although visible degeneration makes his intention clear. Believing he can make no decisions, take no action and safely escape responsibility only wastes his gift of life and condemns him to a self-chosen retardation. Remaining in intellectual limbo pushes all of his values into limbo as well. He is stuck: He cannot generate the positive emotions he wants and wishes to stop the emotions his premises do conjure, but won't alter his actions. Suffering *incompetence* in the physical and spiritual realms, his answer to both is stillness—to not move, to feel nothing—to walk on eggshells around his own shattered sense of life, and to suffer the insignificance of never having existed.

Every lasting incompetence involves facets of the endeavor which a person is unwilling to acquire. He is unwilling to break things down further, unwilling to accept his cognitive or physical action as any less than ideal and forces indifference to the advantages he could enjoy through its remedy. Indifference to values is the coward's emotional safety net. He counters inadequate action, not with correction, but with inaction—the scared rabbit response. He places himself at the top of every pyramid as the Finished Product, where there is never anything to learn and no further expectation for growth—nothing to threaten him—and unwittingly earns the resultant penalty—no healthy emotions to feel. He is truly helpless, and in escape from its identification, all that is left is to continue the march towards his true goal: "Biologically, stillness is death."—Ayn Rand. Indifference to values is the greatest crime of consciousness—to be dead to one's own experience—and is the greatest penalty for acting out of fear. True Hell *is* indifference, in any context necessary to life.

Does it matter then, what style of self-destructive dependency he chooses? Drugs, Drink, Affairs, Robbery, Family? They are all used to stem the same thing. *Social dependencies* make the cognitive process unnecessary, while *chemical dependencies* make the cognitive process impossible. They are all a replacement for pride—an essential physio-spiritual need. They bide their time with replacement purposes while developing replacement premises, until there is no turning back. Dependencies are the result of *low self-esteem,* and low self-esteem is by far the best indicator of ill spiritual and psychological health. To the extent that fear and tantrums construct their premises, they are not human, and the only choice left is whether to slow down to slug speed or high-tail it to Hell.

Insanity and Suicide. Neurosis is the confused mental state resulting from an attempt to work with illogical connections, by choice or error. Its honest side is driven by inexperience attempting to utilize a corrupt moral or societal structure, which exclaims that the unreal *is* possible and that the unjust is moral. Its dishonest side is the unwillingness to accept the cause and effect relationship of honestly linked ideas, attributes and actions, which serve the purpose of our cognitive function—life's furtherance. Neurotic anxiety is the *result*—being trapped with the unrewarded effort of nothing working, yet refusing to acknowledge and remedy the cause, with no end to the torture in sight. A Spirit Murderer is a neurotic from the word go, but just as Self-made Man advances throughout life with true commitment, the Spirit Murderer has levels to graduate to as well. This is what lies beyond.

The anguish of investing so much in his view and reaching nothing he had dreamt of, takes its toll. All of the creative fraud, all of the intimidating triumphs, all of the predatory scavenging—the whole of his effort in life—were hollow material victories and outright spiritual failures. There is no pride in fooling fools, in consuming what couldn't be earned honestly or in sneering at those above. Tearing them down did not make him great. There is no monument to him and there never will be; it was all for nothing. He has wasted his life and destroyed his relationships. He has brought no joy to others, only strain, distrust and one mess to clean up after another. No one really loves him—he can sense what his presence does to others—no good feelings are left, and they would prefer to avoid his ordeals. If it wasn't for altruistic injustice, he could never have gotten away with so much. At times he feels so desperately guilty for those he's hurt, the shame is unbearable, and he can no longer face anyone. His pain is limitless and flows in all directions, as do his regrets. He lives a life that is worse than worthless, as it brings others nothing but losses and torment. With self-hatred as his only objective evidence, he realizes they *should* hate him, but it is hard to continue apologizing for actions he cannot stop. He sees the poverty, devastation and unhappiness around him. He knows he caused it, and worse, he knows this is all his future will hold. No pot of gold, no rainbow— only emotional stillness, the shameful rot of decay and in his worst moments, a jail cell. Unable to control the urge to commit his atrocities, there seems only one solution: kill the source. With one less roving predator, humanity would certainly be better off. Given his lifelong stance against honest effort and the monumental commitment necessary to change, reform is an almost impossible alternative. He would have to start over and face all he has run from, from day one. Once again he is tempted to take the easy way out, but this time it *is* in the best interest of all, and outside of reform, the only redemptive action left to him.

Another alternative is a total commitment to non-identity: insanity. Upon reaching the breakdown of living futility caused by anti-concepts accepted so completely that he can no longer move, he sees himself in the open for the first time, and recognizes the true nature of his goal. His terror of the actual world is so total, that to completely abandon his rationale is his only relief—and last escape. Ferociously unwilling to surrender, he clings to his illusions and drops the rest, and implodes into his own inner darkness. For the first time in his life, he knows calm, a peace broken by any contact with reality. With this choice, he moves from neurosis to psychosis—incapable of life-furthering action, unsafe for others to encounter and unsafe alone. Of course by premise he wasn't safe to begin with, but his actions become simple, obvious and blatantly destructive. He can be friendly and semi-coherent in one moment, and whirl to kill you in the next. There is no dividing line any longer: no reason, no structure, nothing left uncorrupted. His eyes can relax out of focus, his face can relax, there is no concern for him to hide his choice now. Now his senses *are* invalid. He shifts in and out of coherency: some elements connect, most do not. Now his mind *is* useless. There is no conscience, no plan, no motive save evasion. He can no longer build: all constructive elements and all structure above are lost. He sees only what he wants to see. He has accepted non-identity as on par with identity, giving it equal footing, and takes action on either without regard for the intermediate filter of identification. Sensory perception no longer comes first. The senses are no longer counseled as to the factual existence of entities, their attributes or his setting. He has dropped the difference—the line between imagination and fact—allowing his mind to see and interact with illusions as if real. This is the abandonment of cognitive structure, the containment and restraint of sanity, which the neurotic drops into now and again, believing he can force his issues. Psychotic behavior is the depth of his inverted pinnacles, from which he returns to a less vile neurotic medium. It is what they call "temporary insanity," believing it not to be a normal pattern of action for him. It is, and one day he won't return.

Evaporation of the line between pride and guilt, between right and wrong, between thought and wish, is the goal of unconditional love, self-sacrificial slavery and the injustice of any mercy towards evil they've ever touted. It is the state to which they wish to bring you, and the sum of all they have to offer. This is where it leads—their holy, non-profit, non-material, "everyone is his brother's keeper", "no one is responsible for themselves", "life should be free" morality— straight to disaster. This is irrationality matured, in its full and final form.

"Yours was the code of life...What, then, is theirs?" —Atlas Shrugged

In the final analysis, there are the men who live, and the men who fight to stop it. You can see it in their faces—submitting to malice, to pain, to their own death—embracing instead of fighting what they know to be wrong, what they know to be contrary to life. Yet in defiance of all they know and can confirm, they wear the proper expression of the ultimate negation of mind—a pure, robust terror, complete in its final intention: murder, insanity or suicide. Most criminals and mental patients fit this profile, and at the extreme end up in jail, institutionalized or in the graveyard. The rest whose existence tarnishes our civilizations, are just different degrees away from these. The sacrificial offerings of altruism as an ideal society? These are the elements of cannibal insanity—not a higher mode of life.

To the Spirit Murderers I say, "You came into this world with dreams. You cowered into the role of an agent for evil. Instead of making an honest attempt to achieve, you gave in and became a killer of dreams. You run, and hide the truth of your murderous plans even from yourself, in a desperate quest for personal identity. We know the truth; no one is impressed with what you're doing; your intentions are not noble. No matter whom you stop, rob, maim or kill, by these means you will never be worshipped, wanted or loved. By your own choice and hand, *you destroy life.* Congratulations: you're nothing.

I know we are a serious threat to you. We are and will be, until you let go of the fear and free yourself of illusions. It is not us that you must kill. It is the dead controlling the living within you that must be eradicated. If you don't seek your dreams, you become a vacuum that sucks the dreams out of the rest to balance pressures. I'm going to take your victims away from you and let you collapse. Your vacuum of relaxed morals *loses* for you the moral men, and draws in the immoral. Your world will become all cannibals with the same bag of tricks, and no innocent food left to fall for them. That is the reward for the life you have chosen; that was its goal. Your altruist cannibalism is impotent—being stillborn in premise, it has no existence—no life. Seen in the open, it will lose world influence once and for all, and will make no further advance.

I've set out to take your power—the spirit destroying motives you've used to fill the void caused by your own spiritual emptiness. My Generators will take back every form of control you have over the living world. You're not even a danger anymore; just a momentary annoyance like a mosquito, bringing nothing but irritation, to be swatted or incarcerated, whatever is necessary to isolate ourselves from the misery you cause. Your premises are powerless; *reform or starve.* The game is up, brother."

Chapter Nine

Parasitical Relationships

"People who need people" just get in the way.

All Spirit Murderers see a world of achievement that exists contrary to what they have accepted in their inner circle as possible to man, and react with so seething a hatred that their greatest passionate release becomes the destruction of those capable of dealing with the world as it *is*. Their psycho-pathological dysfunction is derived by so overwhelming a sense of inadequacy in life that they panic, and counter their default by trying to claw their way onto the backs of their betters. They ride us and hate us for our ability to carry them. To cover their esteem-shattering actions, they renounce honor and truth in favor of the rosiest picture that can be painted of their own weakness. Watching us succeed, seemingly without strain, enjoying the impossible concepts they live in chronic terror of—calm creation, light-heartedness and harmony—their doctrines allow them to damn our means as evil, granting them a smoke screen to hide their true motive; but they cannot hide completely. Their negation of reality does not define them as a separate and superior species. The functional, human part of them is needed to sustain the dysfunctional, and such self-incapacitation and illusory folly conjures so low a self-worth that to survive, they must turn their focus outward.

Beyond justifying their stagnation, their balance of creativity is spent to find another way to satisfy unfulfilled needs, and the energy and product of others is their intended reward. In place of a self-involved pursuit, their purpose becomes domination over us. Once they've sold others on their whole internal game, they move to inflict its true penalty as well—torture, and they fight to puncture the life preserver they cling to. What begins as a private act of cowardice, becomes socially deliberate. What is first designed to cover their own defaults is then used to harm others. Not builders but expropriators, they look not to what they can do with the Earth, but what they can do to men, in defiance of Earth and Man. Suffering is their medium, which they are intent on bringing into the lives of others. Self-actualization is what the Self-made call it, but instead of limitless prosperity and good will, Spirit Murderers wish to hear others screaming, just as they scream inside. They seek to defile ability and all they fear to practice, and exalt its opposite as a reproach against *life itself*—believe it or not—something very shocking to unveil. This is a neurological pattern—not the monopoly of any particular faith, but chosen one by one, a private, humiliating, heart-wrenching intellectual default. Whether a man expounds a particular faith, is agnostic or atheist, it is a certain *mindset* that chooses destruction, of which dogma is only a justification.

Spirit Murderers act predictably when they feel their positions are threatened. They know that by rational standards, they are *not* men. They feel naked before the world and choose to kill that vision at any cost, rather than risk awareness of its validation. As a pocket definition, a Spirit Murderer is someone who opposes the natural flow of life. 1) He is unwilling to commit to existence as such, 2) He is unwilling to consciously accept the process of cognition and as a result, 3) He is unwilling to pursue life independently or allow others to do so. The only reason a man cannot mind his own business, is that he finds no pleasure in the sovereign exercise of his consciousness.

All independent prosperity is an affront to his claim of Man's fundamental helplessness. Violating cognition, they process all observation and depth as an attack. As evasion is the intellectual equivalent of being cornered, they are always one step away from open violence—from their own destruction, or yours. The world of neurological disorder is a frightening place—a world where sensory evidence is futile, where reason has no leg on which to stand, where no existential argument will be weighed or considered—ultimately spawns a primitive creature intent on taking your life, all claws and no mind.

Cognitive Index. Spirit Murderer's reach every level of intellect, as their default is one of cowardice, not of mental efficiency. At the 1-2 level, their crimes are crude—material damage, rape, fraud, robbery and murder—while their institutions are likewise crude, kept in motion with confused ideology such as the religious fanaticism of terrorists, the racial supremacy of the Neo-Nazi's and the Ku Klux Klan, the government paranoia of small town militias, and the cling factor of teens in street gangs. Fortunately, with an air of instability and no productive medium to display any value in their activities, they never gain any trust or public acceptance. They hate other races, other countries, other sports teams and other car manufacturers. They must choose sides regardless of whether a choice is necessary, and their answer to those who chose differently is violence.

At the 3-4 level, their crimes achieve the same ends, but are better thought out. Their organizations are functional though destructive, such as Social Security, organized crime and labor unions. Their justifications appear semi-viable as they complete the cognitive structure, though often with great error. Their ideas often endure, as they've reached the level of abstraction where they can shield the causes of their effects with propaganda, while their victims often haven't reached that level. Many institutions, labor unions for example, have Spirit Murderers at all levels, from the lowest who enforce their principles, to the middle who are typically silent cowards, to the party leaders who generate the twisted logic that permits their extortions.

Spirit Murderer's at the 1-4 level are a tangled mess, as steps are deleted or replaced with social substitutions. Their ingrained denial is invisible to them, so every unseen premise hits them like a car wreck—quite entertaining to witness actually. 6-8 level Spirit Murderers see what the tangles are *for*, and guide the process to ends of their choice. All waste precious energy. If the mind is busy defrauding, it's missing a lot. Every leak must be plugged with an excuse, spending much more energy than life consonance would, and dropping them a few notches on the scale.

6-8 level Spirit Murderers are very rare; most kill themselves upon full acceptance of their own futile discourse. The rest of the Fear-driven have shut down access to that depth and never get passed functional neurosis, but exceptions do exist. Their rarity indicates safety, but one is enough to alter the course of mankind—especially when the indeterminate is permitted in any part of the Self-made's cognitive process. Spirit Murderers at the 6-8 level can have a global impact, such as Hitler, Marx and Kant. The sophistication of their crimes can be so complex, that at times the results can never be traced back to their source. National and world institutions such as communism, fascism and altruism can determine civic and moral inertia, harming millions at a time. They are responsible for initiating wars, unsound currency control, irrational law and assassinations, all serving the same end as the lowest—satisfying the desire for the undeserved.

To him, his competence justifies submission on the part of others. His intellectual superiority once established, is to be obeyed, not questioned. He doesn't believe the fraud of his own dogma as the lower levels need to. He sees the true intention, the true victim and the focus of his hate is clear. At the 6-8 level, he knows exactly what he's doing and can efficiently calculate his butchery. A 6-8 Spirit Murderer's motive will be to see how low he can drive others, how much he can inflict and how thoroughly he can control them. He wants to look down on all of mankind from a point of superiority as the king or queen of pretense, all subject to his unsolicited kindness, all subject to his impotent wrath. Even his power is a substitute for our kind, the kind that draws followers. His requires motivation from the other side—a bayonet. The 1-4 level mistakes he makes are intentional. It's a good joke on the rest of the world to enshrine the lowest and allow it to run amok.

Fortunately, the Fear-driven don't usually rise to any significant level in society. By the anti-virtue of self-limitation, they stay on the bottom, fearing to be measured alone. While all Spirit Murderers dream of 6-8 level conquests, 1-2 level action is typically settled for. Yet their anti-thinking still infests better minds through the associations of unproductive spouses with the productive and the social circles they inhabit. It's not difficult to sort out who is who. In determining the character and worth of another, the question to ask yourself is, "Did this person earn his or her own sustenance, or are they riding someone?" And no, housewives and socialites don't count as workers, if divorce or disinheritance is the only way to be fired. A person's respect for values—true respect—is made most glaringly evident when losses can be real—when there is no safety net devised outside of one's own ingenuity. The preservation of an individual—his thought and application—is *never* to be a joint effort between men. The only proper way to develop sound moral judgment and secure the personal worth of an individual is for each to carry his own burdens of life.

Most individuals are a mix of both sides: a mix of attributes of value among attributes of harm. All have a central theme and intention, which overall, places them on the side of good or the side of evil. Those of the lowest cognitive structural adherence are the most consistently evil—the Spirit Murderers. As this section deals with harmful attributes, expect no positive feelings. Their scale of intimacy is a scale of enemies; their scale of emotion is a scale of negatives. The motive behind every action is the inverse of all that sanity indicates, and the closer you get, the more destructive they are.

Melding Cognition with Interaction. *Others* are a Spirit Murderer's means of perception, but they aren't zombies—they still struggle with internally driven desires, so they try to steer the cognitive process from the outside, through deception, flattery and violence. Of course, reason isn't chosen. Their response to an individual problem is a social answer. They crouch behind the rocks during our step 3, hurling insults and stoning us for its attempt. Then they spring out at our step 4 to seize our reward. The untried and the new is evil to them, because to them, the pattern of comprehension is evil. Evading consciousness, Spirit Murderers are free to eliminate steps, break the process up and replace steps with the effort of others. They *meld* the process of cognition with that of interaction—a fundamental relinquishment—something the Self-made would never do. The process of perception, identification, creative action and reward is replaced with, "Tell me what I see, tell me what to do, tell me what is true." If they don't like the answers, they find another host. They follow the frames they are given, knowing an element is missing—their own judgment, but that has a bonus: they are no longer responsible for the results.

Sociology should be the study of the most efficient means of human interaction. Instead, it is this melding—the pure interruption of independent judgment. For the Fear-driven, the process of interaction *cannot* lie beyond the process of cognition because for him, it is a key ingredient. "We're all in this together" is his motto, beginning with his own physiological motion and control. *United we stand, divided we fall* has its use's, but it certainly doesn't apply to cognition. *Divide and conquer* is more appropriate. Once born, we have no physical link to others, and all premises stating otherwise, cease being valid with that separation. Any collaboration is a secondary consideration. No action, voluntary or involuntary, that violates the proper process of cognition and self-sustenance for an individual, is a moral action. No mix of cognition with interaction, of "putting our heads together" to take the place of individual thought, is a moral action. But social "connections" are his substitute for *causal* connections, which leads to his next step: Predation.

Predation. Have you ever wanted to die at the height of an accomplishment? Why? It was because the rest of life was such a drag by comparison due to the moral status of the world, that you knew it wouldn't last. Overcoming the necessary barriers was undermined by a plethora of the unnecessary, and it became more of an ordeal than an adventure. None of our actions earned the open moral appreciation we expected and deserved, and in some ways, our accomplishments made our lives even harder.

Moral men produce. The rest *attack* producers, which substitutes for their production. The moral purveyors were more concerned with those who stayed home in the safety of competence untested—or incompetence unrevealed. The purveyor's ideals reflected no human productivity other than to shun and damn; they chose not to teach, but to cater instead to the state of their keepers—those of uncertain faith and dubious career. It was their only chance at an audience; they knew the producers couldn't employ their ideas and wouldn't listen to them anyway. Confident that no one could miss the value of our effort, *we left them the subject of morality.* We thought our devotion made us the model for excellence, but they revealed their true stature and feelings by turning on our every living premise. They've created their illusion. Now all they need is someone to pay for it. By defining spiritual ideals impossible for men to adhere to or reach while remaining alive, the Spirit Murderer's negated the entirety of our virtue, and infused us with an irrational sense of unworthiness: a guilt which must then be atoned.

All human action is an answer to existence. A Spirit Murderer negates existence, and then all of his problems stem from *existential inadequacy.* He learns that the only way to live without one's brain is to hijack the conscious power of others. Fear-driven Man seeks others primarily for direct physical sustenance, using them as a buffer between himself and reality. Any association with him requires a loss for the other party. The only alternatives in the desire to have it all without thinking or working, is to sit in misery without it, or to take it from someone else. His means of procurement and communication rely on deception and violence, necessitating subservience of mind and body. His only means to survive is to victimize. By all rational standards of interaction, he is a criminal. Such is how the relationships of predator/prey, host/parasite and slave/master are brought into the realm of Man—all unnatural dilemmas for volitional beings. Still, even a carrion man acts with purpose. If a victim isn't willing, he will lose interest and move on. Man has no parasitical nature; it is solely a matter of default. Abandoning reason explains their state and the state they need to bring us to as well, for safe feeding. His focus on the weak travels under cover of compassion, but is actually the means of creating an easily dominated adversary. When a being can no longer protect itself, it can only wait to be picked off by the nearest predator.

Blame of course, does not lie exclusively with those in control throughout history. It is not a paranoid conspiracy of a few key men, but of specific ideas developed by the Fear-driven—a system of layered fallacies generated to cover the trail as contradictions were met and left unanswered over time, advanced by those sharing the mindset of the tyrant. Once one coward gets away with something, the others come running to see how far it can be pushed. They want a guarantee from another that their own inconsistency defies, so they stick with what their inverted morality allows them: to turn on their betters and demand wealth through guilt. When production is not sought, *predation* is the only alternative. It begins with individual cognitive default, and expands among those like-minded. All of their false concepts are brought into social use to create a full system of cover, blame and parasitical sustenance. They move from simple individual robbery to complex social robbery, setting up institutions that promote the pilfering of material and spiritual wealth, which the able produce in such abundance. *Abstract predation* at the 6-8 level is no longer directly comprehensible—one never encounters the criminal—and is outside the victim's power to stop. From unnecessary taxation to unfair laws to unsound banking practice and foreign policy, predation lies along all the mediums of existence for Man, and from the beginning, it was and is intentional.

An entity that practices no civil life-sustaining patterns is a value vacuum—a cannibal nightmare—a one man physical and spiritual crime wave. Current morality *is* the morality of criminals—fused with plunder for their benefit. Their whole morality is designed to conceal and whitewash predation, used by men who don't feel they should be held by the same standards of reality. There is no point in seeking within their souls a higher feeling or intent. There *is* no higher feeling or intent in them. When you seek it, you're exposing a vulnerability and you'll see it used against you. A value revealed is a value attacked. We must protect our accomplishments—physical and spiritual—or they will be taken. If we are uncertain of our own worth and negotiable on the definition of what is proper to value, we will draw a predator.

We need to draw them a simple diagram, "This is food," with a schematic of fruits and vegetables. Then a frame that says "This is not," with a picture of a family. Don't respond to their cries in foolish sympathy; a carnivore cries too, when it is denied its meal. It starves when its methods fail, and starvation hurts. Their pattern results in a capacity insufficient to sustain life. Patterning for lack *necessitates* seizure, while damning the capacity for abundance exonerates it. Those who choose not to complete a sound process of cognition should have no access to its rewards—certainly not when they are consumed dishonorably. They deserve only what their effort produces, and to be taken out of circulation if they pursue another's—until they adhere to the proper pattern like responsible adults. Wishing for the unearned is a spiritual felony. Plotting for it is the essence and mark of damnation. If the closest to greatness you can come is to draw its blood, its time to rethink your life.

We have been undercut precisely to make us crumble when asserting our right to exist without being flea-bitten. Under this system there is no way to be happy, and it is designed from our first steps to our last, to keep us from building a way. If cause and effect are breached early, it makes the understanding of complex subjects with multiple causative factors, impossible to contemplate or interpret. They have allowed us no clear moral definitions or understandings, funneling us to reach an international weak point: at the moment of moral assertion, we lose all confidence in ourselves and in our moral worth. We accept our own demise, and we submit. They want to oil this killing machine with our blood, I know, redirecting the producer to comfort the life of the killer. The lice will ride us for all we're worth, until we come to understand their game and shrug them off.

We *will live* to see the moral hierarchy clarified—to have our devotion to advancement take the place of honor it deserves, far above the bland virtues and anti-virtues with which they've burdened mankind.

The Submission/Domination Axis

"One hundred thousand lemmings can't be wrong." –Graffito

For the dominant and the subservient, all life begins with submission; it's the gauntlet through which all Fear-driven are borne. His first experience is submission to physical existence—an enemy offering no alternative, to whom he ascribes the power of a malevolent consciousness bent against him. His aspiration is to assume the dominant role, and in defiance, trounce on existence in turn (Being an internal conflict, the Anticipation-driven can grow right along side and never realize this struggle exists). As cognition is the first to go, next is civility. Spirit Murderers derive their societal structure according to a wolf-pack hierarchy, whose attributes stem from physical violence. Violence and threats are only one side of the psychological coin however; the other side never got that far, and is still submissive.

Sharks and shark bait need each other. The dominant needs someone to dominate. Irrational dominance by its nature is parasitical. It doesn't work without victims. Knowing only the pattern of submission, fearing to face nature when no structured force exists for them to submit to, the submissive can't be alone either; it is a mutual dependency. Their views of existence and of their own individual potentials are alike—powerless. One side fakes reality, takes no constructive action and submits, feeling no potency. The other side fakes reality, takes no constructive action and lashes out, drawing on a single potency—the power to destroy. Both are limited to the same physical capacity, but one exercises it, while the other will react only when cornered. Differing only by degrees of passive/aggressive certainty derived from their own physical strength relative to others, were they to reverse roles, the result would be the same. Both have given in—submitted to the same error, and have assumed their sub-level places. They are simply two impotent sides of the same intellectual passivity—the patsy and the killer, the squasher and the squashed, the dominant and the submissive.

The submissive is impotent in body, so his path to freedom and esteem is imagination. The dominant permits the unreality of the submissive, as it is that unreality which honors and does not challenge his dominance. They team up, as in "Your premises, my power." Abandoning reason is their tie, being self-restrained to the level of perceptions without regard for their causative factors. They believe there is no alternative to force and docility—that it is an *axiomatic* relationship—an unavoidable means of interrelation. They cannot conceive of any other means, because they cannot conceive independently. The act of claiming faith as their substitute for thought, leaves the connections of logic outside their power. In true submission/domination form, *wishing* and *force* comprise the two extremes along the scale of intellectual impotence. One acts, one doesn't; neither thinks. Neither is willing to be held to rationality and a civil order. Both are permitted by the other, the freedom to destroy all logical discipline. When reason is dropped, its void is always filled by variations of the Submission/Domination Axis and the resulting inertias of mass default.

All Spirit Murderers can be subdivided along the submission and domination axis. In dropping reason, the majority of their cognitive makeup comes from others. They do something I call *Premise Hijacking*—where even their professed desires are not their own. They are hijacked from others, believed to be pre-thought-through and pre-valued; prepackaged for desire and acceptability by the moral appraisal of those hijacked. They struggle to keep up with the Jones's, hitch-hiking on the motion of their trends. From queen of the homeless to high society, they try to impress, focused on what they think others expect of them, posing throughout life to derive their own stature. They praise with the crowd and damn with the crowd; they don't think. As soon as someone stronger takes a position, they storm to that side. Having lacked an argument for choosing, no argument can sway them. *Relativism* determines their resistance to oppression; how others react determines their rebellion or acceptance, and gives shape to mass movements and other forms of hysteria—lynch mobs, riots and manias—all of mindless intentions and violent ends. In the Irrationally Dominant's mind, stealing is self-restitution. In the Submissive's mind, alms is self-restitution. The premise of mob-rule, the combination of stealing and alms in Altruist Communism—of all chained to all as an ideal—is its worst outgrowth.

The Irrationally Dominant. The Dominant can often deal with nature; it is the consciousness of others and his own in this regard, with which he cannot deal. His body is a form of potency and it substitutes as often as possible for any cognitive requirement. He is of potent body and impotent mind. He fosters a selective reality—industrious in required areas, but abandons the proper pattern in the rest. In fearing life, evasion, confusion, deception and violence become his tools of coping.

From childhood into adolescence, he is disobedient without reason, unruly for its own sake. He won't listen. He won't reason. He likes to pick fights, and likes to insult and be disrespectful as he tests for boundaries, pushing others to feel what he feels—the extreme tension of being one step away from explosion.

For the Fear-driven, existence, identity and esteem come from the outside, so he must be sure that you know he is there. Most obvious in his teen years, he becomes a danger as he tries to get your attention. He has to assert his physical dominance not only to gain power over you, but to validate control over himself. As his actions lie outside of reason, a constant struggle for power in any realm of interaction ensues. He often confuses his own sense of feeling threatened with an attack, and he counter-attacks, not relative to his adversary, but relative to his own level of fear.

He has no tenacity for peaceful, disciplined, coexistent activity. All of life must be on cue around him, where even telling you what to do is an imposition and justifies his abuse. In his most cowardly form, he waits for privacy to show you his darkest and truest attributes—providing a front to the rest. He won't share himself, as all he could reveal is panic. His life isn't what he wanted, having feared the responsibility of desire. Fundamentally unwilling to be productive, he equates earning a living with torture. To him, blood money funds his painful life, so he's notoriously cheap, fearing he could never make it again and wouldn't want to anyway. A man's worth comes from that which he brings into existence, but his power brings only misery. He abuses others—his wife, his children, his dog—to convince them that they represent the level of worthless evil that he himself feels. He makes his own family suffer a personal holocaust, twisting their souls and strangling them with misery. The truth behind his tantrums states, "I can't lead! I can't guide us to any values; I can't even lead myself. I don't know what it means to be a man; my only link to it is that I can hurt you."

When nature removes his dominance through age, he retains the faculty of denial—none of it ever happened. His final stop in life is the determination to evade acknowledging the devastation his manner of living caused. How can he evade it? Simple; he is a coward. That's a pattern he has practiced all his life.

FORCE. His social cognitive action revolves around pleas and threats; pleas to the holders of power and threats when the power is his. He must flare up in order to avoid being attacked, whether the threat is real or illusory, to protect his esteem or to gain it. He cannot tolerate anyone disrespecting his pseudo-self-image. He wants obedience, not agreement, subservience to dictation, not consent. The next time you hear his threats, stop, look and listen. You'll hear damnation of just that: looking, listening and questioning. Reveal any of his truths and he becomes a raving lunatic—that is his pattern. He's practicing spiritual domination—kill or be killed—and one leads to the other.

The base social immorality for which there is no forgiveness is the initiation of force by Man against Man, and this is his specialty. Knowing nothing else, he tries to stretch his mechanical advantage to cover areas where it does not belong—to control the elements of intimate relationships, politics, law and commerce—and only moral confusion permits it. He sees that for whatever reason, through confusion, pity or the desire for power, other men often accept his burdens and tolerate his lies without challenge. This allows him a settling, the comfort that a safe haven does exist for him in the world, and is an opportunity to repel borders. There are many variants to force as well, all of which have fraudulent intent—the attempt to secure values by deceptive means with no intended remuneration—whose target can be a material product, or an escape from cognitive responsibility. All imply violence.

Most common and effective is the simple *lie*, an immediate offshoot into non-identity. He commits *robbery*, the blatant action of stealing the living product of another. He *enslaves*, stealing the very life of another. He enacts what I call *psychological ambush*—the disruption of civil expectations not easily quelled by the meek, which itself has many derivative physical and theological threats. His harsh, heated delivery preys on another's ingrained willingness to submit in order to restore calm. Psychological ambush begins as fraud and ends as a prelude to violence, intending to extract submission by exploiting our natural response of alarm. There is *fraud* itself, the devious gaining of confidence in one realm to be stretched over others, as a means to bring about future loss for the victim and gain for the predator—the action of a con-man. Fraud is just a delayed, premeditated form of robbery. He *tortures:* reaching futility with thought, he strikes whatever bars or potentially bars the path to his answerless, unquestionable dominance. He rapes, tortures, maims and bullies, building to his climax of technique and ultimate end—murder. He will do anything to satisfy his inner hunger, a self-designed pathology based on fiercely dedicated contradictions. The Fear-driven are dishonest even in withdrawal. When his ploy fails, he does what I call *squidding*—the confusion smoke screen—a complex construct delivered too quickly to process, ending in a fast change of subject in order to elicit cognitive surrender through an expediently closed issue. He escapes to see wounds heal with silence, time and distance, unable to face them. The key element missing in all his phases of action is sincerity.

He wasn't ready to lead and still isn't. Someone else needs to be the man. Belligerent aggressiveness is a mask for cowardice, as is callousness and insincerity. Cowardice underlies the need for power over others, and his lies and violence give him that temporary control. He believes if he can give a beating and take a beating without flinching, then he is a man, but the only meat that doesn't react to punishment is dead meat. It is the same spiritually; there is no music in the irrationally dominant. All harmonic waves have been destroyed by his military march, and his trampling of flowers *doesn't* foster their growth.

If allowed to rise, his ultimate aim will be to rule by the standard of irrationally violent dominion alone—as a dictator. There is permission only for praise—there is no speaking against him. There is no knowledge permitted beyond his own. All cognitive action he doesn't practice will be disallowed, and the contrarian books burned. There is no questioning or exceeding what he does, no being of greater value to others, as that implies a greater worthiness and a threat to his rule. Defy him and he'll subject you to every evil imaginable. Placate and you can evade it for a while, but he'll need his fix—his actualization of all he efforts towards—to choke the life out of anything in range. As force creates nothing, his focus is the conquest of all existing assets from land to art to talent, but ultimately, the truth will come out once he accomplishes a key campaign. All he really wanted was destruction, beginning with the destruction of cognition and ending with barbarism—a dog-eat-dog, cannibal society. Even serial killers can't hold a candle to the misuse of political power and the subsequent mal-direction of human energy. More unnatural deaths are associated to the actions of Subhuman Man than to any other single source. Throughout history, these deaths have been in the name of so-called *noble experiments,* such as communal ownership of all, ethnic cleansing and the industrialization of a country for the sake of world prestige (Stalin) and their truth: Nazi-style purges, legally sanctioned confiscation (Socialism), forced-labor camps and wholesale slaughter. Slavery and warfare—internal and external seizure of values—all reaching extremes through government sanctioned action, have the Submission/Domination Axis to thank as their source.

Is it simply a question of the strong over the weak? No, Self-made Man exudes a sense of strength that is of no harm to anyone. The display of his living mastery *is* his dominance, and the brilliant pride associated to it is his reward. Strong people don't need obedience; they have nothing to gain from it. Chickens and quitters, no matter how well disguised, do. They must destroy us physically because they cannot face us intellectually. Why does he need power over others? *To get what he wants from them.* Why does he need anything? *Because he is not independent.* Why can't he approach them with his request directly? *Because his request is not honest.* Fear is his driver—the common bond he feels in all contexts and brings to others with "Tell me what I want to hear, *or else*." Murder sometimes, is just one less person to convince.

Slavery. The Irrationally Dominant's dream is the environment of our mortal enemies in Islamic Fundamentalist regimes, who hold their country's hostage and use children as private whores and first battle waves. They murder, rape, beat and rob as their normal daily flow of action, lifting a finger only to pick amongst the values around them, leaving horrific emotional scars on their victims, never to heal. He desires all the same actions, but in Islam, the law protects the offenders instead of the citizens. He wishes to practice the same— feeding off and using people, destroying their creations, interrupting their flow, seizing their bounty, shattering their emotional stability, their innocence and their lives—all in order not to face his own state of worthless panic. Only a coward needs to approach life through an intermediary.

He is not alone in this; most doctrines hold slavery as their ultimate moral commitment to Man. Christianity for instance, holds that the pinnacle of moral action is self-slaughter, that true peace and harmony can only be achieved by accepting that one's life is the property of others, not forced, but through voluntarily agreement. Riding the mind, their satisfaction is to force others to exercise the mental faculties which they refuse, coercing their victims to take action in contradiction to the proper intellectual function and well-being of a human entity. Their communal commitment to the less fortunate becomes a gun aimed at the able, saying "Do what we tell you or die." It is almost impossible to contemplate our own deaths, but Spirit Murderers have no problem contemplating how to sacrifice others. They generously spill our blood in benevolence toward their fellow neurotics. Considering sacrifice a moral concept serves to shield the abrogation of rights, permitting them to say "If you won't give us what we want, we will *force* you to be moral," and their contrived retribution sparks a scramble for what has been created—never how.

Physical slavery carries with it a much deeper cognitive torture: the placing of one's fundamental purpose into the hands of another. It limits the better men to the cognitive levels of the oppressors or considerably lower, trapped in the mindless repetition of their demands. They hit the nail on the head for the worst possible human violation—control of a biological entity by a source outside the entity. This is not their primary, however. Their primary is to hijack the mind and body of another and instill it with the defaulted task of keeping *them* alive—done mostly by percentages in today's world.

Slavery is strictly a concept of *human* relation, considering human beings to be a product like trees or cattle, to be chopped, slaughtered or like batteries, used up and disposed of. Throughout its forms, it is defined as any human system set to benefit specific men at the expense of others, be it energy taken or fields of action forbidden. Modern methods of slavery are less crude and much more subversive. The killers put us in compromising moral dilemmas to force unhappiness, to take control of our actions and to redistribute the product of our effort. They do whatever is necessary to transfer the living energy of the individual to whatever power is dominant—a state, a group, a creed or just another individual. Ignoring their well-voiced contempt against materialism, notice they attack those with the most assets to take—the American middle and upper classes. In essence they think, "If we just pass laws that give us the right to the property or persons of others, then we can live much easier, and the law will protect our position over them, instead of protecting them from us." With the organized power of the state behind them, no one can defy their neurosis. Through this structure which morphs as chartered monopolies, subsidies, welfare, predatory taxes and interest, they can feed off people they never have to see.

Sacrifice is the modern word for slavery, and it *requires* a submission/domination system. To give one's life away *is* to be a slave—no matter the benefactor. By this premise, a man must consider as his moral primary, not how his life will be lived, but how it will be destroyed. He is asked to consider the suffering of the world, not its health. There is no need to address or study the healthy as they don't need assistance, which eliminates drawing any roads to recovery, or the subsequent discharge of the "healer" or the slave. Self-made Man can answer disasters much better, as he is focused on the preservation of calm, but that is not what the welfare preachers want. Watch closely—they do not regard your actions as a virtue if there is no sacrifice involved. You gain no approval if you are not harmed. The reason? Sacrifice *requires* parasitism, tying us together—it justifies their position and forces us to miserably impose ourselves on others, as they do.

As fear drives *them* to act, it is fear they intend to elicit in others. As psychology (emotional/behavioral reactions) is where their cognitive limit is, it is primitive psychology they attempt to use against men. In facing their ethical questions, it is always the "sacrifice of life to prove your worth" scenario. At any time, he has a fistful of false assertions to offer, all resting on the hope that they won't be questioned, as their means of derivation likewise must go unquestioned. Present morality is riddled with false assertions and false opposites, whose purpose is to attach negativity to positive elements to mask their value—stealing their moral impact and disrupting their pursuit. If his assertion fails, his reciprocal is an equally damning submission/domination alternate—all he is willing to acknowledge—so that he can get what he wants either way. His only alternative to Christianity is immorality (a Christian must atone for the sin of his existence, and likewise, immorality demands atonement). His only alternative to self-sacrifice is hedonism. His only alternative to charity is personal misery. These false paths form epistemological structure that leads to stagnation, looping and the demanded renunciation of consciousness—the destruction of self in favor of *any other source*. All lead back to slavery.

Sacrifice rewards flaws, even though nature refuses to. Rewards are taken from those who did not err—the only ones who have what they're after, and who practice the true alternative of their every premise. Any forced contribution is slavery. The pursuit of a moral life which *is* the pursuit of happiness, has nothing to do with others. The pursuit of happiness is not an endeavor of slaves. Through productiveness and personal fulfillment, the action of pursuing your passion through work *is* your social contribution. Simply not being a burden on them, *fully discharges* your duty to others.

Sacrifice is easy for Spirit Murderers to propound; they have nothing to sacrifice. Self-sacrifice is an indication—not of Mother Teresa goodness, but of incompetence. To give a part of yourself away is to admit the inability to exercise the proper function of that part—the inability to make it pay for itself. You are a physiological whole. There is no way to part yourself out and survive too. The call for sacrifice is the surest sign that a leader needs to step down.

Torture. From Medieval times and before, Spirit Murderers have shown their inventiveness with countless ways to dole out punishment and few if any, ways to celebrate human greatness. I think of all the ways human beings have tortured each other throughout history—the dungeons and chambers of horror I've seen all over Europe—and it just turns my stomach. What some sub-humans are willing to do to others, reveals a level of moral atrocity decent people should never have to see.

To torture another is to give voice to a Spirit Murderer's own angst with sensory tools. Those who want to torture the senses are those tortured *by* them—nagged by the incessant flow of data, which they refuse to classify and use rationally. Their intention is to expand every source of pain—to bring negativity to every pour—to kill men in every way imaginable—and they are inexhaustible on the subject. There is a medieval torture for every imaginable sensation, but little if any cognitive advancement for that time. Such heinous violations were all claimed to be provoked and justified by their victim's inability to adhere to corrupt and often-impossible moral standards. The positive use of sensate tools was considered evil, so their passion delved into its opposite.

Efficient in agony, maximum infliction was and is their goal, and their senses are heightened *only* to this end. For once they acknowledge the senses, which they otherwise claim to be invalid or non-existent. The only way they are willing to explore them, is in agony. It is a reenactment of how they feel—their tempting of fate, the thrill of facing their own deepest fears—to see others helpless and under the power of a malevolent force bent on their destruction—the subject reversal of their borne affliction.

In daily life, he starts at home by making war against his family, driving them to reflect his own inner state of misery, futility, betrayal and lost hope. He keeps them fearful in order never to be challenged or questioned. Instead of fostering development of the young, he sees them as moral competitors, and preys on the smallest tree as a helpless victim to steer, mold and easily dominate. Instead of teaching and providing clarity, he manipulates with confusion and fear. He kicks the dog and abuses the children, where molestation is just the sexual release of the same torment. To reassert his view of his own maturity, he seeks an adult confrontation by beating or harping on his spouse—another frail adversary. The alternative to accepting his confused reasoning always comes as insults or violence. Cognitively, he is still a child bully on the playground. All he has to do to settle his conflicts is get mad, but conflicts are never settled in this manner, so he is *always* mad.

While Spirit Murderers try to hide their ugliness, it often comes out anyway; it's never just domestic. There are certain areas all humans partake in: home life, work and society, where society at a minimum is simply the action of getting from one to the other. His scale of abuse operates as high as his ambition permits—in his company, debasing his suppliers and associates, or in civics, enslaving provinces, states or nations, including his own. He doesn't let you merge in traffic, doing everything he can to defeat you. To merge is to beat him, so he has to get you back. In his mind you've taken advantage and he has to prove to his ebbing and flowing audience that he is no patsy. With his consciousness scattered amongst those others, the senseless becomes essential to his esteem. Not interrupting the living flow of others when possible causes him to feel subservient—to feel you've won. Make a mistake and he rides you with his horn blaring. His productive effort amounts to the same: backstabbing, playing games, befriending and then badmouthing. In the office, he makes a big deal out of your mistakes, amplifying the negative. He lives to dismiss civility and get even, regardless of whether anyone holds motivations against him. Think about it: this is someone whose self-esteem is at risk in traffic, or just being looked at. How stable or fulfilled could he be in the important areas of his life? It's agitation he feels, and it's destruction he wants—to annoy, to pester and to irritate you in the way his fears and failures irritate him. If he has to win in traffic, it's a sure sign that he's losing in life.

At his least harmful, he simply bad-mouths and pesters. At his worst, he robs, tortures and murders. He breaks into your home while you are sleeping. He stalks your wife and children. He mugs your parents. He keys your car. He can rob you in ways you've never dreamed of, but he has. He lives by such methods and is fulfilled to see others in pain. All the lowest atrocities you've heard of, he is responsible for. In the worst countries, he is protected; there is no one for you to call to stop him. Even in America, corrupt moral premises feel for him and forget about you.

The Fear-driven live in angst to please and love to torture. The pleasing is faked, the torture is real. Either way, any desire to impose is a violent intention, and both are a response to the same motive—irrational self-sustenance. His primary doesn't involve us, it involves faking to himself that a better view of existence is unreal and impossible, and he will lash out to the extent that we display anything beyond his panic-tinged grasp. He believes so totally in his servile framework that he lavishes the opportunity to display his secret malice against his masters, negating that the predicament is a creature of his own default. If there is no way for him to expropriate, he destroys. The intention in all cases is to wipe out value. The manic urge to stab, to rip and to burn flesh, the unimaginable agony of contemplating the pain and witnessing it from a point of personal safety, is a reflection of his struggle with cognition. To revel in torture is a confession of personal dysfunction—of the discontent of fundamental aimlessness—of the trauma of experiencing life as pain. The tantrum of never feeling good feelings is to amplify it, just as an explosion of violence is from a build up of negativity. It's a crescendo, which is a relief to be rid of. The Self-made crescendo in contrast, is an explosion of joy—singing, dancing, intimacy—all good feelings, in celebration of life.

Self-made Man hates any kind of misery. To hear babies crying or to see those sick or injured, just tears him up. He wishes for their pain to dissolve and to see them restored to health as quickly as possible. Intentional torture is an unspeakable violation of his view of a civil existence. It is a mind off its epistemological tracks, focused outward in frantic escape. To him, the senses are meant to feel good, as much and as often as possible. His premises are responsible for this positive view of sensate perception, and for providing so pure a medium of enjoyment. He knows that pain is mostly unnecessary, and is often stemmed by premises alone. Proper living and proper virtues require no pain. But by skewing every evil into virtue, by blocking out and barricading himself from the truth of his choices, Fear-driven Man can consider his virtue equivalent to be *carrying* the burden of pain—a concept they've successfully saddled us with as well. Pain is an indicator that something is wrong, not a virtuous experience. The virtue is in its extinguishing. Pain isn't a virtue, it's a *warning*. It is not the time to stop and feel exaltation as they intend for us, but the time to look for and stamp out its cause. They wish instead to get us to ignore the warning as they do, to the same end. Misery loves company.

Rape. To *rape* is to take forcibly what he believes he could never earn, and has no intention to attempt. He can accept sure things only, in end item fashion, never thinking of the sub-elements. There can be no rejection and no error. Often considered spite for women, it is spite for the deserved. He thinks nothing of the torment he inflicts—a hopeless slant begging for death, which he has already inflicted on himself. With no regard for human rights, he views others as property to be joy-ridden and then ditched before he gets caught. In its purest form, the stalking of a complete stranger, it is death penalty material. Subjected to true forcible rape, a woman definitely has the right to kill her aggressor if she can.

Murder. The motive behind ending a life that poses no real threat to one's own is purely the pursuit of a Spirit Murderer. To snap and kill over neurotic fears such as a spouse leaving, a public or private shaming, for robbery and political motives or to kill randomly is indefensible and of the lowest degeneration, from bad to worse in that order.

The pinnacles of feeling for healthy human beings, are exalted states. The Spirit Murderer's equivalent is an absolute dedication to non-identity— the forced loss of life—the cannibal ethic which reveals his true identity. In watching life go out of the eyes of another, he actualizes the morbid fantasy of his own demise—just where his premises are leading—the final goal. The peace he seeks—possible only to the glassy stare of the non-valuing, non-thinking and non-feeling, to whom self-sacrifice and destruction no longer matters—is that of the dead.

BETRAYAL. Spousal betrayal at least has the excuse of his emotional world crashing down unexpectedly—a spiritual death in itself. Due to cheating or just being dumped, violence is still inexcusable, as with him a like future situation will still put someone's life in jeopardy. In his mind, those he values are his property, and they lose freedom of choice by choosing him, a view fueled by religion's "Two spirits becoming one"—a metaphysical impossibility. His argument amounts to, "I won't snap as long as I need not face the world as it is"—meaning as long as all intellectual discipline comes from the outside.

GAIN. The most common reason to kill reflects the Spirit Murderer's most basic default: his own sustenance. The 1-2 robs instead of works or simply works to plan robberies, taking money and other valuables to meet those most basic needs, bludgeoning any resistance that may startle or oppose him. Past food, he steals for drugs to escape the guilt of what he's doing. He is the most primitive form of cannibal. To kill in order to live is to admit that he cannot handle the requirements of life. He pursues what he desperately wants by undeserved means, exasperated by its cause and unwilling to understand it as his victim has. He attempts to seize it, no matter the consequences—the ultimate failure of his mind. If he is to live, then someone must die. Murder is so heinous a violation, he must be constantly on the run from his own emotional sum. If his true esteem caught up to him, it would amount to implosion.

On up the scale to where intelligence matches treachery, his 3-4 and 6-8 brothers accept his basic premises, yet justify *their* butchering in the pursuit of spiritual values. Helpless to constructively seek mass acceptance for poorly thought-out or corrupt ideals, they address them with real murder. Their way of making a difference on a topic they claim to care so much about, is to do something about it, and what they do is hack, poison, crucify and slaughter those who disagree. In the name of life, they bomb abortion clinics, kill their doctors and torment their patients. To stem what they consider the initiation of force within a woman's own body, *they* murder, cajole and harass—the essence of their medieval psyche—and display the futility of their own ineffective reasoning. Regardless of the subject matter, be it abortion, race or class privileges, their answer is the same—fanatical lynch-mob violence—their inner state and the pinnacle of their own thought process brought to full sunlight.

Beyond that, his approach to decimation and murder becomes much more secretive. As in the Kennedy assassination, his political atrocities are designed to seize the machinery of state to pursue a war agenda for whatever plunder is possible inside or outside the country. His conquest seeks to eliminate the competition and achieve population control by disrupting cultural trends adverse to his own pathological bias. As a mask, he intends to enforce whatever he feels is best for the country (though a country is no better than the ideals it is collectively *willing* to fight for), so he tries to circumvent their agreement by purging any key opposition, looking down the Spirit Murdering scale for the gunmen to carry it out. His system and his type must be in control; he has no patience for civility or to accept the possibility of his ultimatum's failure when force can change the outcome. His reckless pursuit of power—alone or in a group—is the panicked desire for irrational domination, nothing more.

At all levels from 1-8, as their plans cannot move forward without murder, it is a form of terrorism. Terrorism is his answer to the pursuit of what he considers as moral. Terrorism is his means to achieve it. The truth be told, it's all a front anyway. He doesn't care about the long-range bliss he projects, and will offer no way to secure it—it remains as undefined as his justification for killing. To kill as means, is to seek destruction as end. In any collective effort, the first to be wrong is the first to use force against others.

COVER-UPS. Some actions are so dark, their existence cannot be admitted even to himself. He strangles the voice that could announce his guilt, to stem the loss of others discovering what he doesn't want them to know—usually an act of evil perpetrated on another—physical molestation, harm or some other drastic illegality. What he does to children, to women or to anyone unwary reveals so unspeakable and morbid an evil, that there can be no forgiveness and no justification. He knows that to be caught, his own death must follow. Out of all the purposeful human endeavors on Earth, *this* is what he chose: the pure destruction of innocence, of trust and of life. Killers at organized levels have their dirty-work done for them, but that just creates another trail to extinguish, pay off or suffer blackmail to, in fear of it ever being made public. Thank science that it is now practically impossible to kill without leaving a DNA trace. As technology and rational law has extended our life expectancy, it has also extended our power to see much deeper than a killer's fit of rage allows *him* to.

TERRORISM AND RANDOM MURDER. Dysfunctional in life, look at his style of efficiency—the desire to take as many people with him as possible—those who denied him his unreality. To mow down random and nameless victims is to wipe out those neurotically purported to be in coercive control of his consciousness. Relinquishing his own control yet fighting theirs, at wits end, all that is left to him is murder-suicide; not to give up and reform, but to annihilate the source of what defies his defiance. Their massacres always target those of the highest stature and greatest innocence. At home, it's those of the most civil, disciplined, independent thought. Abroad, it's Americans and children.

Extermination is a Spirit Murderer's ultimate argument. The denial of life and freedom lies at the end of his every road; it is the penalty for disagreeing with him. It is his means of incentive along all paths, be they business, legislation or private relationships, but don't be fooled. The ability to destroy us cannot mask the *necessity* to destroy us—the intellectual default and resulting cowardice that requires the chained death of their betters. For a parasite, murder is the ultimate form of power. These are beings who are proud of it, proud of throttling ambition and proud of fraud. He looks fiercely into their eyes as he chokes the life out of them, saying "I hate you and all the rest; I hate human beings; *this* is what I think of them," and with his release, he is refreshed until the hatred builds up again. The reversal of virtue in some is so complete, it is unspeakable to encounter, and the only solution is to turn and run. They may feel remorse at times, but they still kill. There is no sincerity, compassion or mature understanding that they won't spit at and try to destroy. There is no strength, wisdom or moral value in being stoned to death while trying to reason with the unreasonable. To stay and argue necessitates a bridge—a means of communication with evil. This is a bridge to burn. Attempt no communication and get out. Abandon *all* those against whom your civil life needs a defense.

The Submissive. To witness the nature of the submissive first hand is downright medieval. These fear-based, quivering, miserable hulks, without mind or reason, hope that through your pity for them you'll grant their pseudo-reality. We've all encountered the type. Eyes that say, "I'll let reality be whatever you want if you protect me, and promise to like me." Such a person's conviction is dependent on the verdict of another, hence fundamental submission in life. They plead on their knees *not* to know that the standard of good is life and justice. This is what true pity is reserved for—the scared human animal, self-castrated, cowering before life.

Permitted their feeble esteem extortions, it's amazing how they blank out the cause of true glory and insert their own causes when they are allowed to assume its place, through the foolish generosity of some moral man. To witness the birth of haughtiness, just give a complement or a gift that is worth more than they deserve, then watch the show. Submissives are all talk. The submissive will complain of injustices, but when you stand up for them and challenge those in control, they won't support you; they will shrink off until it's over. Whining *is* their protest in life, and it goes no further.

In conflict with a submissive, to them their view is more pardonable because it is weaker. They automatically grant the role of dominance to their adversary, whether they wish to assume it or not. They justify their own moral treason by playing the card of weakness, believing those stronger must withstand any emotional torture as recompense for imposing their strength. As they submit to force in the physical world, the realm they are permitted control over is the spiritual, and between the two sides, it is *their* ends which often guide that force. The real conflict begins when their adversary isn't interested in dominance. Their role is lost; a discussion based on mutual respect is not possible—and cannot be endured. Civility is out of the question; it leads to reason, and their stamina falls far short of that. They are prepared to submit, thinking, "Why is he trying to convince me? Why doesn't he just *take* what he wants?" The submissive considers reason to be weakness—a reflection of their own pleading, and will try to assume the dominant role. They shift from dodging a violence that isn't there, to imposing their own. As well, the dominant only sees reason as a greater power when it doesn't submit to his rants. He then attempts submission, destruction or escape. To him, *to agree is to be out of control,* is to be submissive. Neither believes control can be earned, so neither attempts reason. Both swap sides in times of crisis, but they won't think.

Submissives expect nature to respond to them the way the irrationally dominant expect: everything must be on cue around them, or they're hurt by the world. They implicitly say, "I've submitted! I've done my part! Now its existence's turn to give me what I want!" They expect a reward from nature for their submission, but there is no reward, only decomposition. Most submissives never achieve their professed intentions, yet try to counsel those of us who do, to follow *their* lead. Our advice is futile; what works for us cannot possibly work for them. Somehow, their existence defies science, and the natural laws that would commit them do not apply. Some way, some how, the world should change to allow them to accomplish their aim without any effort, ability or thought on their part. Notice their pure stamina for troubles, trifles and complications as that is their life. Notice their complete lack of stamina for exercise, steady progress, intellectual exactness or wholesome feelings, as to them, self-generated life-furthering actions are the impossible. Talk about something tragic, trivial or mindless, and they can go for hours—trauma perks them right up. Convey any productive depth and they just go to sleep on you. They are so hopelessly dependent on their unreasoning dysfunction that they will do anything to preserve it, perpetuating their own torture and exasperating others.

"You are a slave. You were born into bondage—a bondage you cannot see or taste or touch—a prison for your mind." —The Matrix.

Voluntary Enslavement. The Submissive focuses on cognitive infliction, while the Dominant focuses on physical. There is always a group of patsies for the killer and it is their job to deliver themselves, their children and anyone else possible to their destruction. Many of those selling peace are only seeking your peaceful surrender to evil premises, and they can win only through intellectual submission.

The dominant doesn't typically create or enact subversion; he just takes what he wants—me, you, any value. The submissive side tries to get the same irrational benefits voluntarily—to evade the violence they've too often been subjected to as well. Physical torture is the province of the dominant, but the submissive have a wicked parallel: the subversion of morality. One nuclear blast is nothing against the constant wear of unreason; its plague withers and kills just the same. Instead of a tool to *aid* human progress, morality has been used as a weapon against mankind for over 2000 years, and likely from the beginning of time. The Spirit Murderers cannot afford to have you discover morality's true value; the responsibility it would impose on them is unthinkable. So instead, it has been used for torture. There is no more devastating a spiritual infliction than to be accused of being morally unfit; there is no more debilitating a threat than to be considered cognitively inadequate. There is no more embarrassing a demise than to be subjected to physical destruction at the hands and limitations of an inferior mind.

Guilt is the spiritual fine for a known moral offense. When subverted, it is a submissive tool to make us feel bad about feeling good—a pure inversion. The submissive form doctrines, the dominant enforce them, causing the natural reward we expect for our virtue to be countered with a human penalty. They drive guilt as deeply as possible into our every endeavor. They have us believing that if anything is for ourselves, it is evil—it is against others. You are evil if you breathe, evil if you live and most importantly evil if you think (to think is to take advantage), which must be atoned for through service to those who don't. They control the pattern of service as well. Practicing damned virtues yet wanting to live, stemming desire yet wanting to love, if our leaders tell us its evil to sit down—something in life that we can't avoid doing—and we believe them, we'll accept whatever their punishment is, having willfully violated a moral premise. Now our energy is guided by atonement. Forcing us into subservience to their inessentials is at once their evasion of moral responsibility, their infliction of harm and their means of significance.

How did they get us to fall for it in the first place? Without a rational standard of good and evil, it was easy. Following our culture without question, we have come to believe that certain patterns *must* be respected, and it is *this* that limits us from clearer moral abstraction. Everyone has to enact sound principles if life is to continue, so all life actions are fair game to be labeled as evil but "necessary," such as sex, work or personal ambition. Subjects of damnation are kept in flux, as inconsistent, unpredictable moral requirements assure dependency. Our views are held accountable to their shiftless nonsense, while their own kind are permitted exemptions from it. If you wish to secure any further value, you have to join the gang. You'll be harassed or die until you do. Sound familiar? They think our emotional pain is less devastating than their fear, but our awareness makes it fuller—driving us to drink or to some form of evasion as well, as their mix of non-reality with our reality has often made life unbearable. It is a curse to see farther than you are allowed to rise. A plethora of contradictory feelings are borne of this: part guilt in their spotlight of supposed violation, part injustice, part embarrassment to be counted among such short-range Neanderthals, part torment for not having the words or the backing to fight it. It doesn't actually matter if you buy into it. If they stop you from advancing spirituality, if they stop you from making the correct moral connections, that is enough. If they can alter your course in any way, they have earned significance in their eyes, and control is their primary intention. We know it; at some point, the inertias to our values stop. Certain conditions destroy them—specifically, anything that takes our destiny out of our hands, determinable by the depth of our own vision. If that vision is hindered, our advancement is frozen, and their position assured.

We must be independently sure that our guilt is rationally earned, as it is a key tool of slavery. Add religion and it becomes a business. *True guilt* is only derived by personally enacting a known wrong, which includes allowing a known injustice to pass uncorrected, or failing to act within one's capacity to safely stem loss. The rest of their projected sociological harm is just a dead end of false epistemological chaining, performed by those too stupid and frightened to live. Those who think it is some diabolical plot, it is simply what they have done within themselves—their own default at every step of self-responsibility. The Spirit Murderers wish you to forever be a stranger to your own consciousness, as they are to theirs. A confused mind cannot form a solid opinion about what they are doing and pose no threat to stop it. They are slaves to non-identity, and through their premises, can only make us slaves to it as well. Their "Green" *this* and "Back to nature" *that* is simply the wish to reduce life for all, to what it is for them—a bare struggle for survival.

Ridicule. Walking down a train platform in Lausanne, Switzerland, I came upon two French-speaking girls. As I passed, our eyes met, I smiled and kept going. On the way back from viewing the schedules, I glance their way again with no particular interest other than a pretty face to see, but instead saw malicious eyes and a contemptuous voice trying in English, "You loser." I looked at her briefly in humored astonishment that I was important enough a site to openly degrade, and as she read my thoughts, she lowered her head, seeing what she was...then I marveled at how far I'd come. Two years earlier, such a thing would've been devastating; one year earlier, I would've been drawn into her hell long enough to give a hurtful or frightening reply, but now I never missed a beat; my owned rhythm took precedence. I saw her essence and answered the little murderer as she had earned: identification and *dismissal*. The simple, effortless dismissal of all that which intends to harm, degrade or steal, the playful, relaxed view of life from those deserving its bounty.

It is interesting and useful to identify the nature of what she did, as being single so far, I've run across a number of times. She struck what she viewed as the worst possible blow one can deliver to the esteem of another; but what one defines as good and bad, harmful or harmless, depends on one's standard of value. A person's concept of what *is* the bad, is exactly what the Fear-driven would expect a virtuous soul (an intransigent mind) to have contempt for. Of course, with an erroneous standard of value, right and wrong are equally subject to error for them. The structures they attempt to build upon are flawed by design, and crumble when encountered by someone of healthy premises. Such people will act with suspicion of the consciousness opposing them, consciously expecting the same betrayals they themselves commit, and subconsciously dreading the vast unknown which they refuse to define, even to themselves (One's most complete understanding of Man is of oneself). Their construct is part irrational, part assumptive and unable to trace the conscious flow of a moral man based on *his* values—as to do so would be an act of esteem suicide.

The standard they fear dismisses all irrational, foundationless disapproval and accepts only soundly motivated communications between individuals. It holds that one's self-worth does not rely on the opinions of others, but relies solely on one's *self*-estimate of one's own capacity to sustain and enjoy life, and one's willingness to utilize that capacity. No foundationless assertions can rattle an individual who holds this premise. In the case of the girl, she had no basis for condemning me, as she knew nothing more than what visual perception permitted. If this principle is valid, then the same is true when approaching someone you find attractive. They know only what you show them—the tip of the iceberg. If they decide to say no, it means very little. Social action lies beyond cognition. Self-esteem only dies by suicide. Only its pretense—its dishonest attempt—can be killed by others. Self-worth is earned prior to any contact with the outside world.

Embarrassment itself is overrated—just a meaningless and temporary sense of personal shame—humorous in my opinion. You could fall down the stairs with a full lunch tray in front of a thousand people, and still maintain your integrity. People amped in the triumph of ridicule are the prime victims of such petty disturbances, discomforts and disapproval—a symptom of a much more important issue: raw sensitivity to their own life's socially parasitic discontent, and the fact that its cause is *intended* to remain elusive. They live in a prison of their own design and they hold the key, which they lack the courage to use. Freedom is a greater threat to them than prison. For a Self-made Man, there is no payoff for criticizing others. He has no perversion of premises that require it, and no time or emotional energy to spend on dead ends. Insincerity is moral self-incrimination; it is a lie to oneself. No decent, brave, happy person ever employs it. I watch insincerity closely, because it is not a reflection of others, but of the futility of one's own stillborn aspirations. If I see it in myself, I know I have more work to do. In other words, if you are looking down, you are no longer climbing.

Still, we learn as children the power of ridicule. Beyond simple rottenness, it becomes excommunication or public stoning, a taste of power along the same line—feeding the sick curiosity of watching another living organism die, physically or spiritually. It is at its worst when the moral standard is inverted, and it is the good who must endure it. Any mud thrown at an ideal is ultimately thrown at oneself. One's animosity towards values is one's distance from them. Every great achievement has been accompanied by torture, from name-calling to excommunication to murder. It isn't easy to go on knowing the world is laughing at you, with the cultural nobility of people who lived two hundred years ago as sole sanction for your actions, while facing the rest as the one no one cheers for. The superior performance has no allies.

It grows more pathetic as one moves into high society. There are no spirit-murdering levels of affluence—they act alike at each—as if no causes need be referenced, and as if referencing them is of poor taste. Ascendancy requires that they run a mental calculation of your worth in their caste system relative to their own, which determines their poise. Many live their lives looking as if they are drenched in preservatives, haughty, cynical, on the perpetual lookout for something to look down on, to sneer at, to disapprove of and to look the other way when true value and passion is undeniable, and when someone's deepest dreams are being fulfilled. It becomes easier to bear, with the knowledge that under their malice lies shattered dreams, hopeless longing and an unreasoning fear that drives them to the diversion of changing their center of focus to you.

Victim to Murderer: The Compromiser (Their Frankenstein)

"You never got out, you simply added yourself to the things they ran—you were the first to give up, and give in." —The Fountainhead

Often we hear stories or see portrayals of a successful man who has reached a mid-life moral crisis. He realizes there is some spiritual value he has missed, and instead of coherently seeking a new facet of his being in addition to that which he has demonstrably mastered, we see him *turn* on all he has achieved. Broken down by animosity, he surrenders to the popular dogma which damns his previous actions, to say "Here, take this wealth earned by a rational, disciplined progression and use it to satisfy your thoughtless, aimless, self-chosen sickness and poverty." How could he give up? Perhaps because he faced a void alone, condemned to be an outcast precisely for his practice of virtue, which those around him did not share. He gains acceptance only when he lets his virtues slide, and the movie lasts only for as long as his assets hold out. Rarely do we see him use his great strength to bring that same living potential to others. It is always the sacrifice of his productive morality to their wastefulness—a hand out from what was accumulated by the process he *isn't* teaching, and which the maggots don't wish to learn. Yet the wealth unless otherwise gathered, would have made the unearned jubilee impossible.

The unfortunate evidence of the Spirit Murderer's cultural success is found in the support of their prey. The most tragic social error of a producer is that through his foolish generosity, he often creates the illusion that a value can be had for a much lower price than reality sets. Perhaps as reality won't bend, he feels he has to. Perhaps he is afraid of being measured by an irrational standard, knowing his closest lack the stamina even to tolerate his standard's conveyance. Regardless, he skips instruction and explanations and rushes to catch their falling self-image. The first to respond is the first to be attacked, so he silently carries the burden of their malice, expecting it to last only until they recover, but they never do. Blame mounts on blame, he accepts the tenets of his own illusion—that half-truths and half-lies can save a person, while other half-truths and half-lies can damn a person. He spends his life faking the esteem of the first, while trying to dodge the bullets of the second. Unable to reason with the unreasonable, he gives up and permits others lower standards while holding himself to the impossible, defying justice to balance esteem between them. He never questions their motive.

I've heard from time to time that the most successful are also the most unhappy, that intelligence is not effort-driven but only a physical attribute, and that any wealthy person effectively stole his loot from society. What is worse than these claims, is their acceptance. What leads such a producer to self-destruction? It isn't our ideas, it is toleration of their defacement. It is permitting ourselves to live among those who refuse to acknowledge or respect them. We are the honest and hard-working, and we are treated by the liars—those who claim moral superiority by the *peace* of non-thought and non-productivity—as if we are murderers, thugs and thieves, as if our goals and dreams are crude, crass and evil. They have pushed all of society's fabulously productive industrial innocence into the lower class, equating us with the mobsters who must posture to whitewash their reputations. They, the guardians of shame, have sold out sincerity to make room for the Hitler's of the world to thrive.

The worst trait of most victims is that they don't even know they're victims. Even his ancillary actions have been planned by a source outside of him, tested and honed by generations of studied psychological default and cowardice. The victim's toleration causes it; the Fear-driven knows victimization need only be tailored to their prey. Lost in the question of what others will think, tied up and harassed by dogma, unable to let them down in a drastic mix of cognition with interaction, the compromiser becomes responsible for the emotional stability of others. They harp on him, pretending their scornful disapproval of a premise—life or death in nature—is sufficient to damn it. Wearing him down with pressure and negativity, reason brings him no advantages—only frustration and pain. They hen-peck him to where he doubts his own judgment, bringing his very perception into question. Tortured *by them* for his clarity and weakened *by nature* for incoherence, he soon doubts his own sanity. — With so few to support his logic and so many against, he gives in and follows the peckers through the process of identification. They push as far into his cognition as he allows, mixing his living effort with a sense of displeasure and betrayal, masked as the moral failure of *his* interaction—a cognitive criticism impossible to ignore. It is then his responsibility to preform all creative actions, and he exchanges the rewards for a hostile peace, in atonement for his guilt. He exercises his great power through repression, submitting his mind to the will of those less capable, using his great skill and discipline to achieve their shallow aims—aims no productive person would be interested in pursuing and which the shallow can't reach alone. He holds *only himself* to the facts of reality. Shamefully having to consider it an attribute of strength, he endures the pain they inflict and holds back from hurting them with the truth about themselves. Perhaps he doesn't realize he has accepted suffering for his virtues, while permitting them to escape unharmed for their vices. His strain spares them the earned pain of not facing reality, while he is *not* spared *because* he faces reality, solves his problems and succeeds. He is left as miserable as if he had never used his mind in the first place. He fails to achieve their joy, and only succeeds in destroying his own.

The key fundamental compromise is the surrender of reason. By breaking up the elements of cognition, he is practicing the process of a Fear-driven consciousness, but what does *he* have to fear? Obligated to generate another's happiness or stem their negativity, he ends up controlled by the pattern. He is then led around like a poodle, ingrained to proactively stem any imagined displeasure—the moral horror where submission becomes the means of personal achievement—a scramble for pride by the standards of evil. There is another name Spirit Murderers give to those who valiantly subordinate themselves to others: pushover. One person is never the central cause of another's negativity or the center of another's life. If one claims so as a loving dedication *or* as a hateful reproach, either way it's a trap.

Gun-shy of contempt from his spouse, his family and to preserve outward appearances, he feels he must posture as the representative of any mob-approved state of being. From the outside, it looks as if a giant is trying to wedge himself into a shoe-box which the Fear-driven all find so roomy, believing they will accept him and no longer see his differences. He's not fooling anyone and will only fit when they break him, which they will sooner or later. The breaking point is where he can acknowledge their pattern as irrational, yet plans to beat them to the punch by doing what they want before they become hostile. His open awareness is serving evil. They have what they wanted—the perfect slave. His proper action would be to openly show the pattern to fulfillment and its reward for them to follow, but that of course is not what they want. Any such attempt provokes the look normally reserved for insects, "Don't try to impose your filthy evil on me," —where life and the use of one's mind is the evil. They want *his* generating power on *their* terms. Not using his intellect in the spiritual realm, he left morality to others and gave them the fuel to invert human ethics. He became their workhorse, their torture subject and their prize: The Compromiser.

A compromiser believes in rational ideals, but permits the notion that rational discipline is not the only way to achieve them. Harnessed by evil, he is damned to fight in favor of his own destruction and that of his fellow Generators. He fails to stand alone and ask whether his accepted premises serve life, and looks for an irrational middle ground—a balance between good and evil resulting only in an anorexic, guilt-ridden good and a plump, blood-sustained evil. A balance between good and evil implies that they *both* get what they want, but it never happens. As the good have nothing to gain from the evil, the premises of independence and life-production are bent to serve the premises of dependence and life-destruction. The living balance to seek is *not* between good and evil—not a mix of right and wrong, part truth, part lie, part health, part disease, part filth, part cleanliness, part freedom, part slave—but achieved in the efficient practice of *living premises alone.* The premises which serve the bio-spiritual entity of Man—every man—*held to like standards:* that of a rational system of values derived by a rational process of cognition.

Warrior Note: *Mixing cognition with interaction paves the way to spiritual suicide.*

The most difficult battles in life will be with the Compromisers, due to their intelligence and productive ability. An otherwise rational man who is willing to fake the character of others for any reason whatever, cannot be trusted. By closing his eyes to injustice, he damns perception itself. He accepts his position and that of all the Self-made as evil, and becomes an anti-vanguard of the race. Looking across their lives, they wrought devastation by spirit murdering moral standards, with little energy left to pursue their own. The evasive producers will use their living energy to maliciously protect what they have accepted by default as the moral, so we must contain the harm they can cause. It is their fault the Spirit Murderers reach as high as they do; their faith opened the door and permitted their poison to infiltrate every realm. Death premises are dangerous and to be feared, only when practiced by the compromising Self-made. The Fear-driven have no power alone, but with *their* premises guiding *his* creative action, they built the atom bomb. When dealing with evaders—Self-made or not—one cannot rely on respect for the tools of cognition—truth, justice, rationality or reason. They attempt to set all essential elements in reverse. This being impossible, only destruction can follow. If we value our lives, we must step aside. Until they understand that a life-respecting system *does not* require victims, we have to insulate ourselves—our businesses, our institutions and our private lives—from their Fear-driven psychological limitations.

By isolating ourselves, he'll no longer be around other humans—only these predators. He'll be forced to look at the nature of those he's submitted to, to see their success versus those he's turned against, and he will reform. If not, he'll reproach his peers, saying "I'm strong enough to carry them. I can still achieve. It didn't stop me. I can handle it; you're the one who can't." *Sure* he can; it only took his joy, and stripped the very meaning out of his life. Being despised has become bearable; it's now harder for him to be liked. He can no longer accept any positive appreciation for his person, as being honored is incompatible with his pattern of reaction. He finds himself guilty of the ultimate esteem obscenity—losing respect for people, *because* they like him. This undertone implies that his observer is expressing appreciation for his evil—evil by his own admission—a drastic link between friendship, appreciation and moral failure. The potential combinations are infinitely abominable. Wholesome interests stall him out just as negativity did in the beginning, and he moves down immoral paths he would've considered unfathomable in his youth. Congratulations, you're a pretzel. He loses the people he wants to keep, and is driven further from his personal goals. As soon as he chooses irrational burdens, he falls behind those who don't—those he admires and would prefer to be with. But the turkeys are there waiting, and he's one of them.

What is he afraid of anyway? He props up their esteem; if it wasn't for him, their reign would collapse. If it wasn't for him, they would be powerless. His effort to avert their demise has always been thrown back in his face. They never picked up his pattern and if he stepped aside, he would cringe to see what their true incompatibility has been all along. Left to their own devices, they would have no choice but to pick it up, to find other prey or to become plain criminals. It was *he* who stood in the way of justice. It was *he* who allowed the premises of evil to trump the premises of good. It was *he* who permitted the desecration of life and by his own living power, honored that which he despised, gave it precedence and brought it to bear. His effort didn't even help them; it made them worse. In his defense, it is time to end the treason; to see the truth and let the chips fall where they may. People who make you live under threats, pressure and constant disapproval don't love you. They don't love anything.

There is no armed neutrality to be tolerated between good and evil; the evil must be put down.

Between them, only he has the power to change. He must break free. There is a whole world of Self-made awaiting his redemption. If he doesn't come back to the side he was born on, evasion will destroy him with my complements, and his time is running out. Moral self-awareness will run through the world like wildfire and soon there will be nowhere left to hide. In loyalty to what he was, it will grind every wet bit of whatever is left of him, out of existence.

Warrior note: *Our resistance to them must reflect their resistance to virtue.*

As with Scrooge, his opponents claim it's his meanness that made his success possible, and often convince him of this as well. By disassociating productivity with virtue, they justify redistributing the products of the minds of others by a process incompatible with life. They have the best serving the lowest—those who generate nothing—not by conveying the Self-made pattern of productivity, but by bowing to the Spirit Murderer's pattern of cause separated from effect. Familial demands, charitable foundations, money grants—this is how the fledgling Self-made get tangled and earn shame for their effort instead of what they could have had—solemnity and a moral-intellectual scope and power beyond anything their charity could achieve. We have always been taught that self-sacrifice is the symbol of honor, but look at it: *sacrifice is a question of murder.* When the sacrificing begins, the Compromiser will do his duty and hand us over, according to the moral law he has no right to question. He crawls on his knees to the guilty and only stands against his betrayed own—the Self-made. He lives with a heart broken by his own hand, in constant torment of a cowardice he dare not acknowledge, and he won't knock off your parasites until he gathers the courage and self-worth to shake off his own. The producers get sentenced to public shame, while we watch the killers destroy all we have lived for and our every higher motive, in the name of progress. We're much guiltier than they tell us, not for their reasons of course, but for standing down. It is treason not to defend life and all that leads to it.

To maintain their game, the sanction of the victim is needed, so like a mouse kicking an elephant, they must get him to accept that he is powerless. They do their dance around us, knowing there is a great danger to them in our implicit premises. Realizing for ourselves what that danger is, is to discover that the power is ours.

Toxic Friends and Family

"Are these people your friends? Well no wonder you came looking for me."
—*Pretty Woman*

Family are the first people we encounter—our implicit protectors. We have no reason to expect them to be enemies. Giving us life, it is life we would expect them to want for us. However, our first wave of injustice was the double standards imposed by family members expecting exemptions from judgment. They attempt to get away with physical and intellectual abuses which would never be tolerated from strangers. Just when you would expect a change of attitude from indifference to intimacy, they show less interactional integrity at home, not more. There is no exclusion from Spirit Murder for family members, as family comprise all of their early experiments. It serves as their springboard into life to determine what people will let them get away with. The reason we've heard "Never do business with family" is the altruist morality. One party is always counting on unfairness, while the other is unable to demand restitution, obligated to forgive, forget and endure their financial and spiritual losses without a peep. If justice is sought instead, it would tear the family apart. The victim always faces a double affront—the con and the insult. The cheater gets his esteem propped up by those who place blame outside of him; the cheated gets the cold shoulder for bringing him above board. The victim isn't considered by the cowards as family-oriented or group-oriented. If he is not a human slayer or one who submits, he is not a team player.

To the fear-driven, family is a guarantee of sustenance and effortless esteem. It means protection, blind approval and an unlimited account to whom restitution is unnecessary—his first non-profit organization. Family is a source of unquestioning support, a scratching post that must tolerate any violation, and as such, is his model for all of society. He holds fast to that ambition within his realm of control, but no matter how convincing his illusions are, he sees those outside who do not conform. He watches in horror as the Anticipation-driven jet past. He doesn't really make friends or choose intimate family relations; he makes bonds against this common enemy.

Sub-humans come together—in families, friendships or any other association—to make life decisions with anonymity and to drain the blood of the living. As this first is a cognitive essential, they typically hunt in packs, like most carnivores. As conspirators, they defraud existence to survive, while providing moral exemptions for each other's passivity. As self-sufficient people needn't drain others to survive, the Fear-driven cannot acknowledge any value in independence—only danger. Anyone outside the group—anyone who doesn't cling—is the enemy. They preach unity as a moral premise in itself. *Unity without context* is essential and beyond question. They then attempt to confront existence by ganging up on values and those who earn them. Where they cannot extort, they destroy. They are resolved to be parasitical—to get their free lunch, no matter the cost. It validates their world, so they have a vigilance to match ours. Their arguments are so littered with self-deception, it is a waste of time to try and help them. Their tears are shed for missed or lost plunder—for the loss of any side-track which forces them onto a rational path. Con-games, insurance jobs, slip and fall lawsuits, baby traps, double-dipping welfare scams—their world revolves around ripping off governments, corporations and other individuals. Society has one concise word for those who make a mess of their space, invade that of others and uncontrollably destroy whatever is in their path—losers.

When forced to account, they feel *they* are the victims, and get migraines from honesty—a common response to an unfamiliar effort.

Their friendship and loyalty is based on the sidetracking of existential reality, in favor of an attempted adherence to another's limitations—where appreciation is the homage paid, not to exceed them. Notice the contradiction of his pride in having so many of these "friends," yet he is unwilling to get close to any of them; closeness is an attribute of individualism. He straddles between the fear of self-determination versus safe social expectations, where pleasing others is his claimed source of fulfillment. The cord of life is only so long; it cannot be plugged into both premises at the same time. Such is two sides of the same behavioral action—the unwillingness to pursue essential values drives him to seek cover in the form of a group, a leader or a given system, to take the place of thought. The actual value of the leadership, friendship or affiliation, is willingly and safely beyond his comprehension. Cohesion is the rule, and his malady grows into seeking people as a purpose itself, versus seeking companions to share in the glory of living.

Their value inversion is evidenced in that in speaking to someone of certainty and discipline, they become afraid—feeling the sense of a trap, and desiring to return to evasion and semi-consciousness—the actual trap. You'll notice that they will hold onto any moral failure of yours, eager to see you out of control, unhappy, angry or drunk. They have a heightened sensitivity to the misgivings of people they consider virtuous, and monitor them carefully. If we try to fit in, they hold them against us, considering them the moral errors they are, yet will let their fellow mediocrity off the hook for the same malady, including themselves. Notice their endless stamina for trivialities, yet they show none for the meaningful complexity of achievement. The cowards always leave us to take the hardest steps alone, but it *is* proper for them, as it marks their point of departure with our moral/cognitive compatibility. His motives cause us to look away in shameful disgust. He looks away from ours as well for the opposing reason; what it would reveal about himself.

When you pursue objectives the majority of people do not understand and aren't willing to grasp, the pressure to abandon your quest and conform can be horrible—how foreign an individual, unique purpose is. No one can afford to deal with that at home. Self-made Man tortures people with less significant ambitions, and draws tremendous contempt from those with none. He watches the degeneration of friends and family around him over the years, driven by our culture's inverted morality and their incapacity to defy it. It's as if one by one, through their own weakness, they are taken. Closer and closer the Neanderthals come, until he finds his closest looking at him with hollow eyes, eyes cut off from passion, reversed in their identification of value and actually pursuing destruction. Just as in *Invasion of the Body Snatchers,* they scream when they recognize a being who is still connected with that world of personal wants and desires—of passionate ambition and meaning—rousing the others to swarm and devour him.

How difficult it is to be doing what we love and were meant to do, and have no one to support it. With no social/spiritual reward—no social accomplishment of step four—our mind will act incongruous with our highest good. What family and friends don't understand or effort toward, they will impede. Being faced with their penalties instead of encouragement just burns us out, so often, we try to bridge the tension by taking those we care for along. We need to see ability in others. We need to see others striving for something, going somewhere, accomplishing goals of tremendous importance to them—our deepest bond of intimacy. We get drawn instead into spoon-feeding the helpless, all because we can't afford to let our image of what they could be, slip. Their nurtured promise is our only tie, a thread that once broken, will cast us outside. Eventually, in horror and bitter futility, we witness them wipe their feet on all we've taught them and criticize us in childish resentment behind our backs, revealing their true stature. We are just delaying the inevitable—their path *is not* up to us. Self-worth originates from one's *own* adequacy to live; nature forbids any other derivation. If you practice self-sacrifice, it turns unavoidably into self-hatred, then into hatred of others, as the natural process of toxicity deflection requires. If you are going to be an outsider anyway, be a good one. Respect your highest means for generating positive energy and *reach for the stars*. Gather your strength and leave them behind.

Beyond a spouse, children and business ties, most human relationships—family in particular—are redundant and costly. If you wish to grow, you will find it very difficult to do if you spend any significant time with them. Your family, purposely or not, will make you pay for what you are trying to become. They will expect a continuance of the traits you may wish to change, and the disrupted expectation will not be welcome—especially with the non-goal driven. We must not squander time with people we wouldn't otherwise, if they were strangers. All relationships should bring us up, provoking mutual respect, admiration and goodwill. We gravitate naturally to those who complement our interests and abilities. To that extent, the relationship is valuable. We are held to the rest in a state of anxiety; a pattern we know is harmful. They should be dropped, or given as little time and therefore behavioral influence, as possible. In contexts where others are irresponsible, they should be allowed no active role in our lives—putting them in a place of no consequence, where the only victims of their thoughtlessness will be outside of us.

It isn't constructive to attack family; family is too important for those within to try getting away with lies, violence or irrationality. All social action is an extension of individual action and is governed by the same standards. The true concept of "family-oriented" is found in the choice and practice of *correct* civil values, not the altruist fantasy of exalting criminal attributes. Do not maintain contact with those who would see you subjected to injustice. They can't sort it out—it is a cultural moral failure, and *they are in on it*. There is no way to promote a disciplined rational interrelation and progression among Spirit Murderers. They know it; it is more often the Self-made, who don't.

Irrational Parenting

If a kid asks where rain comes from, I think a cute thing to tell him is "God is crying." And if he asks why God is crying, another cute thing to tell him is, "Probably because of something you did."—Jack Handey

The Wrong Decision. Stupid men and stupid women are dysfunctional on their own. They are dysfunctional together. Their answer to fix everything? More people. Babies are the one gigantic liability people can assume in America without credit or common sense. At upwards of four-hundred thousand dollars to raise a child responsibly these days, if you didn't take specific actions to earn and plan for that expense, you cannot afford it independently. Affording a kid is like affording a Ferrari. The stature for extravagance takes time to earn, and requires a tenacious discipline to reach that economic class. Being a responsible parent is no different. If you can't afford to buy a median priced home with all the trimmings, you can't afford a baby, and probably haven't accumulated the knowledge necessary to raise one. This however, is a luxury the Fear-driven indulge in. Most have kids because they don't know what else to do with themselves. They don't know what's next, where to take their lives, or where to take their relationship. There is no order to their lives, only what they saw their parents do. Life for them amounts to adolescence, dating—uh ho!—a baby, marriage and game shows. Unable to stop their own biological maturation, they develop an adult mind with adult needs within a being already trapped by prior errors—so discontent follows, then fighting, divorce and poverty. Then they do it again.

To some, having children is a form of involuntary companionship, an unthreatening presence that demands little cognitive action. They claim this route because kids "keep life simple." Isn't it simple enough? They extol the simple joy of children and spend their lives looking at the floor. What's so interesting about it? Someone has to grow up, take adult action and advance the world. Instead they waste their early productive years stagnating at the level of baby talk when they should be building a solid future, and through productive action, learning the true nature of consciousness *before* they commit to another, or try to raise another.

The most laughable cowards are the moral missionaries. Everything in their lives, as if a flower blooms with their words, is "for the children." In youth I recall overhearing, "If I didn't have kids, there would be a void of time I wouldn't know how to fill." Exactly. Children, when not a planned occurrence along a romantic sketch of living desire, are a substitute for the frustrated need of achievement. Kids are just *other people.* Thought and spirit are the exclusive domain of the individual. There is no social endeavor that trumps the moral value of individual action. That action must generate more than enough to feed ourselves, whose surplus feeds them as well, not by social concern, but by purposeful productive ability. One's purpose in life must be self-defined, whose core is to be pursued and accomplished without assistance. Any living purpose requiring people is by its nature, neurotic. It is the confession that one does not know what to do with oneself alone; that one cannot live independently and be happy by the functioning of one's own brain, meaning that for this person, *life is not an end in itself.* Worse yet, if a central purpose is not defined, one cannot convey its importance to another. They can't teach happiness and can only pass along their own status—slave, master, predator, host or parasite. Their blissful concern for the children doesn't earn them jack for respect in anyone past the age of five.

Some generate liabilities for the free ride our legislators permit, using a combination of the above excuses. "We can't afford it" becomes "We need not consider the expense. The government will give us $X for the production of each baby. The government wants babies—babies can be our enterprise. If we control costs and push the remaining burden onto the shoulders of others, we won't have to work." There is nothing as heart-wrenching as a hungry child? Well, it's nothing compared to the collapse of a nation by internal corruption. En masse, they and their sympathizers including those responsible for such laws, are responsible for all segments of overpopulation, of rent-control slums, inner-city crime and societal breakdown. The shortest-term thinkers and those willing to submit to them, always have the longest-term disasters.

Handing Down Malignancy. Children may begin bright and eager to face the world, but are often inundated with the conditioning of their fear-ridden predecessors speaking of lost dreams—taken by no one in particular. Their guardians appear learned, but seem *not* to damn the worst traits in men. In facing life's greatest question, venturing into their future lives based solely on the hopes of an untested mind, they are offered an alternative. The fear-preying lure of their elders is to stay common and small. In place of goals, there will be duty. In place of love, there will be dependency. In place of identity, there will be pretense. In place of understanding, there will be orders. In place of agreements, there will be domination. In place of respect, there will be power. In place of standards, there will be social sentiment. In place of reason, there will be faith. In place of dignity, there will be sacrifice. In place of progress, there will be culture. For their submission, they are offered unconditional acceptance.

Schooled evil has a nightmare advantage over unskilled virtue. Against a more complete and experienced evil, adolescent innocence stands little chance. With a wider certainty in the field of corruption, such cowards always seek to dominate the unformed. They have many more methods than someone newer to life or to a given context who walks a fragile line for the first time—carefully forming his epistemological trunk prior to branching. Imagine four-year-old eyes, staring up at evil—guilty of the sin of perception, a trait crucial to the survival of any living thing—serving animals, but damned in Man. Not helping to arm him for life, this evil is intent on knocking the weapons out of his hands, forcing him to give in to the void, which will be filled by patterns of expropriation, designed in response to their own fears. Youth must hesitate, not because nature requires it, but because social flaws and immoral conditioning get in the way of truth. A desert island youth would skip this phase.

There are only two ways to corrupt a human being. *First,* by direct physical harm or its precursor, threats of consequence, as such action disrupts the function of the entity. *Second,* by providing a context that makes it okay for the entity to harm *itself,* to convey or frame thoughts in a way that *sanctions* the debilitation of the victim's own life-furthering potential.

A mind disconnected from living usefulness cannot convey the importance of ability. A mind relishing the spectacle of getting away with anything, disconnects its offspring from virtue. With each generation it *de*generates; the victims are driven further from the grounding patterns of cause and effect, further from rationality, further from morality and further into its inevitable results—self-hatred and stagnation. The hidden desires of the first generation become the open desires of the second. The third acts on them, not realizing the dreams of the first, but the true end, dysfunction. First, they go to unwanted jobs arguing that they shouldn't have to, then raise children who aren't employable. They in turn abide by laws which they claim limit their rights to the work of others, then raise children who steal. In each successive generation they wipe out a level of values, and the ability to identify them. They shorten their own intellectual range, and stunt their children's in turn. By stunting any means to a clean sense of self-worth, their children are that much more willing to participate in what disregards it.

The correct philosophical knowledge has been available for thousands of years—predating Christianity—held back by parents and leaders who prefer to see their children's hampered, helpless spirits die just to stave off the fear of discovering their own unnamed inadequacies. They *chose* our pain and limitations in order to hide from their own. Men are brought into the world fully armed, with no need for tampering of any kind. It is the Spirit Murderers who slowly take his weapons from him. Their method to bring about submission, helplessness and penance, breeds Self-made Man's antithesis: the dependent. This method of creating zombies to do the bidding of the Fear-driven is identical to their own pattern of degenerative development. When he doesn't have to acknowledge ability—human beings shrink back to a level he need not fear.

I know how social trends work; I know *Moral Armor* will have many opponents. There will be mothers screaming their hatred, safely aiming it away from themselves and towards me, delivering their children into the hell of their own stagnant processes, forever unwilling to face and except responsibility for the result of their own actions. Instead of mature growth, they'll commit the ultimate evil—the spirit murder of their own offspring—sacrificing them to feed the headless monster of their own denial.

It took a long time to realize what the older generations have been doing to the younger, and I can see why many turned to drugs. We're worse off because of what they've had us automatize. We were harped on if we did bad. We were ostracized and ignored when we did too well. With no path to harmony, escape is sometimes the only option. The moral default of our elders has made life intolerable for everyone. Enough is enough. Many of them don't exercise their power responsibly, so it is time to take it away from them. No more power over us and over the world's future. No more running it into the ground. Their true error, intentional or not, is that they use their consciousness improperly, and they don't want to redeem their errors. How many lies do they intend to take to the grave? By understanding the nature of consciousness and the sound moral base for all thought and action, we can reveal the true moral sanction for how we live and interact every day. Then we can break free from their domination and see the world honor the new management.

Not Letting Them Think. We all implicitly know that anything questioning the process of cognition itself will be met with massive irritation, making us want to respond with "Don't question my capacity to think." Their moronic reasoning to show how logic is derived, provokes the thought, "Don't try to tell me *how* to think." Forcing their opinions down your throat earns the response, "Don't tell me *what* to think." Some parents show no respect for personal boundaries long after childhood, straightening your clothes, your hair, invading your privacy—incessantly buzzing around you like a mosquito. This belittlement implies incompetent dependency—a fundamental insult to Man or animal—any way you slice it. These actions tick *everyone* off, at any stage in life.

Their children are a test bed for ill technology—the grand experiment— saying "In this child, the great dream will be made real," and they hold them to their own irrational standard of how they wish life to be. They experiment with violence, as if forcing kids to practice the senseless can make it succeed, and then take aggression out on them when it fails. They trounce on their children's right to life by their gift of life. They punish them for having preferences. They force them into unchosen activities, pushing them into unnecessary competition in areas they care or don't care for, straining kid's friendships and taking the joy out of everything. Eventually their children accept patterns of repression, whose unchosen and unhappy situations follows them into adulthood.

Breaking life down into philosophic essentials, the motives that drive ideas and actions either go on one side—the side of life, or on the other—the side of death. Maybe five percent of parents I have known had a conscious understanding of intellectual essentials and could convey them effectively to children. Thinking is exactly what they don't know how to explain or train. Most wouldn't want to harm children if they knew better, but often they don't and at some point they made the choice *not* to know. That is their guilt. The crucial point is that their actions affect the child positively or negatively according to existential cause and effect, regardless of their claimed intentions. So what do they do? They try to live their lives for them. They buzz in their face like an insect and never leave them alone, saying "Why do you have to do it my way? *Because,* that's why. Do you want to be grounded? Don't question me." They offer no chain, make no attempt to teach one and penalize children for reasoning through what doesn't make sense to them. Riddled with cognitive errors and brimming with inexperience, they'll refuse to spank their child as a moral stand when pleasure and pain are the first rudimentary connections a child can make, and their children never learn to respect social boundaries. Instead they'll attempt to *explain* the ramifications of being good or bad when it's still well outside their cognitive range. Some hit unjustly, choosing violence as the constant solution instead of responsibly engaging a child ready for more complex understandings. A smothering parent will choose their children's diet, their interests, their friends, their schedule, their career, their mate, you name it, claiming to care. They will be hated, and as the children grow, both will make each other miserable. When the kids leave, don't expect to see them for a long, long time.

There is no justification for our every action being checked by another. Alone, we can relax. We can try new things, test and entertain conclusions with no need for immediate validation. There are no disagreements to have and no justifications to clear with ourselves, only dysfunctions to identify and inefficiencies to overcome. Few things are more valuable than a safely executed mistake. There are questions in life that *need not* be answered on the spot. Experience with the cognitive process itself will provide the completed picture; kids must only remain free to exercise it. Parental interference is a confession that they don't understand the cognitive process themselves, and don't trust their children to use it either. It is *inappropriate* to attempt to raise another consciousness until you have mastered your own.

Imposing Their Future. In contradiction to parents who try to force children down a certain path, individual purpose *must* be a product of cognition, if it is to sustain the spiritual health of the entity to choose it. Even if the choice is wrong, the individual learns the process of selecting self-generated interests, which has countless daily and lifelong applications. It shows him *how* to value. When a rational man is wrong, his thought process *retains* the format for discovering the correct answer. Wired to never being wrong, it is the Fear-driven's skewed, incomplete perception which has buried the format for this discovery, and destruction *becomes* the product of their cognition.

No two human beings will agree on the course each other's lives should take in regard to private interests, *nor need they agree*. In tolerating another's opinion on this subject, we end up with the sense that they entered our inner sanctuary and never wiped their feet, or that our sanctuary is where they *chose* to wipe them. The feeling is inevitable in any field of specialization when we attempt to make consultation a cognitive element, or when it is forced on us. There is no sincerity in violating cognition to make this choice for another, be they friends, children or spouse.

Individual purpose is a key variable in the equation of life—different for everyone. It cannot be chosen by another. Only *we* know our location on an epistemological map. No matter what others think is good for us, they are in a different place, and no override of our consciousness can bring us to their location. Our central purpose and life structure must be our own unforced conclusion.

False Encouragement. Often people believe a child's esteem must be reinforced—one reason why kids prefer to watch dad do something productive versus suffering as the fishbowl between fawning Aunts. Children must learn that a joyful state is a natural reward, and that it does not stop with adolescence, but is theirs to earn and deserve for all time. What they often learn instead, is that enjoyment is causeless and that their elders are phonies. Children don't want to remain children; they want to be adults. It is the purposeful action of adults that piques their curiosity—a mystery outside their present range. The true intention of Spirit Murdering adults can be confirmed in that future success is considered a betrayal, as their shallow malice follows this mindless demeanor.

I've been badgered all my life by the second-guessing of the Fear-driven, which such losers consider "encouragement." What was their contribution? They blurt out, "What happens if you fail?" *I'll try again.* Or, "You know, not everything works out as you'd like." *Which is why I stay limber in my approach.* Or "If you fail, we will still love you." *But if I succeed? Don't worry, securing your charity is no concern of mine. This* is what they call wisdom. Their theme in life and their God, is failure. That last statement is most alarming. What spurs contemplation of withdrawing their love in the first place? The answer is the threat of accomplishment. No book on success talks like that. "Why don't you scale back?" *Why should I?* "Why don't you quit while you're ahead?" *Because I'm not a coward.* "Now is not the time to be taking chances." *When is?* Why don't you consider what a risk you're taking?" *My risk is calculated.* Why do you want it so bad?" *Because I'm still alive.* "How can you be thinking of this when the world is falling apart?" *Because it isn't.* "It's too soon!", "It's too late!", "You're too old!", "You're too young!" *Nonsense, but so what?* "No one has ever done it before!" *Why do you think I'm doing it?* "Pioneers are the ones with all the arrows in their backs." *So stop shooting them.* To interpose the idea of failure at such a critical point of dreams is so monstrously destructive, I almost can't fathom the motive, for the same reason I don't go around tipping garbage can lids. They are fools—all of them, prepared only to break you down and salt your wounds, which is all that popular morality has taught them to do. If you make it, you'll hear the snide remarks from the same people, "When is enough, enough?" *When I'm dead.* "Why can't you leave good enough alone?" *Because it can be better.* "Have you thought of what *others* need?" *No.* "You don't care about anyone but yourself, do you?" *I'm considerate to those who are considerate of me.* "You think you're *so* good, don't you?" *I have nothing but life-furthering attributes; why shouldn't I?* If you ask what they would change about you, it always amounts to removing the same key virtues: strength, clarity and discipline. Permit their counsel and they'd say, "That's not the way to run a human being!" Then they'd knock a few holes in you to release all the energy—to waste it, saying "Loosen up! Slouch! Get comfortable! Talk about meaningless nonsense! *Now* you're one of us! *Now* we approve! Sit around with us and we'll teach you all about The Welfare!"

283

A Self-made Man's ambition for knowledge, his pioneering spirit and his desire to live well is limitless and he will continue to expand it, never giving credence to the idea that enough is enough, as so many lethargic souls attempt to convince him of. They hem and haw about impossibilities and back projects only after they are a proven success, still looking with the stupefied awe of witnessing a miracle, *no step closer* and *no more willing* to adhere to a disciplined rationale. As the living product of their own advice, they chase their tails so much it's surprising they're not in better shape. Far be it for them to ask the successful how to *be* successful, but when their approach contradicts a means you *know* to be more efficient, you can expect to hear, "Can't you be supportive? I'm trying." *I've seen trying. Trying looks more like a salad.* At a certain level, you can relax and have fun with the banter. They have no chance of luring us into passivity any longer, so why not?

Setting a Bad Example. Their illogical banter is all driven by neurotic denial—one of the most horrific traits to hand down. When reality is faked, everyone is betrayed. When an issue of life cannot be faced, then one favors death. The veins of thought and offshoots such as relationships must wither, until the virtue of honesty is injected to bring them back. When there is some piece of reality one is not willing to see, all those who are even remotely affected, are harmed. Instead of being the loving spouse, the caring parent and the loyal friend, one becomes the enemy of the good, the stuntor of growth, the polluter of purity and the corrupter of innocence. The worst social consequence of such cowards is the infection of uncertainty they pass on to their children, destroying their pathways to self-esteem as well. Their children come to identify denial as an acceptable pattern, and the quality of their lives goes into a spiral. They deliver children to their own demons, leaving the attainment of their dreams in the same state of empty, wistful longing. If one cares so little about oneself *not* to clarify knowledge and live at the highest level, then one will not care what happens to others, or more pointedly, will harm them *intentionally*. They knock them down, slow them down and do everything to stop them with their wishy-washy, semi-coherent, panic-tantrum under the guise of concern for their welfare. Through the anti-concept of repression and sacrifice, this is what some adults have been telling uneasy children, is good. Teach them self-sacrifice and it is their *self* that will be destroyed.

With moral inversion, cruelty quite simply has become to uphold standards, as kindness has become bending them to suit whatever weakness is displayed by another in the presence of their sobs. The truth is it's cruel to show the world in your thoughts or actions, a practice which is harmful to the life of a human being. It is cruel to leave those who trust you, unprepared for life. It is cruel to show a child poor eating habits that resulted in obesity or any other form of dependence. It is cruel to impose illogical sanctions on them in the name of discipline; kids know what makes sense. It is cruel to waste time and share the burden of pointless activity with others. It is cruel to show unchecked tantrums—that one can reach adulthood *without* grace or self-control. It is cruel to show them lies and denial, planting in them the idea that it is acceptable to deceive. It is cruel to not attempt to be all you can be. Future generations may follow your lead, and if you are going nowhere, you will have helped to destroy them.

The example we set for society is defined by what we practice ourselves. "Do what I say, not what I do," simply translates into children who will say the same to their children. Each one of us contributes to the shape of those around us, and their view of mankind through our interactions with them. We can show them honor, graceful wisdom and other great possibilities that Spirit Murderers often suppress. We can uphold the true moral standards of life as mature adults should, or we can be cruel.

Seduce and Destroy

"If you marry, then marry a fool, because wise men know what monsters you make of them." —Hamlet

Do you remember the video of the old woman who was nice as pie to the parents, then beat the crap out of their infant when they left? That is how Spirit Murderers treat people who get too close to them. If they were forthright, they would say "Some people just don't know how to take abuse." Or "I'm looking for someone who thrives on boredom and an occasional beating; that special sense of bitterness we share." Spirit Murderers get into relationships, not to experience love, but to avoid it. They're not after serenity or any internal or external peace offered to them. When it is available, they twist it into misery. Why? *Confirmation that happiness is impossible is a key to their enterprise.* It is strange to imagine someone seeking an intimate relationship in order to avoid intimacy, but that is just what they do. The Self-made wish to have their deepest seen, but a Spirit Murderer's greatest fear is to have *his* deepest seen. Substitutes for sound fulfillment occupy him at less intimate levels—so even relationships are a form of escape.

As a result of their irrational cultural dogma, there are many things the rest of us now practice that are equally harmful. We are all so clever to expect betrayal and to be the first to damn. In five minutes of meeting someone, we have them nailed down and classified; we know exactly what they are. We're unprepared for the patience to watch love develop, but when the natural need for intimacy in our lives becomes overwhelming, we enter relationships we know are wrong and then spend months if not years, *not* being so quick to judge, giving every advantage and side stepping every doubt, when we *know* the truth. Our hopeless expectation becomes to meet someone new and then wait for the inevitable.

We fake to ourselves that the ill, incompatible traits we catch glimpses of do not exist, just so we can experience the incredible feelings of love. We do it to have the opportunity to express the profound feeling of being alive, showing how much we appreciate it and to express how great our capacity for love is, in return. It's worth the falsifications, isn't it? So are the lessons. Yet the evils settle in under the skin of our relationship, coming out as cancer, to destroy it eventually. And what hurts are not the traits we kid ourselves into believing didn't exist, but our surrender to deception as the only means through which we could gain this value. We reflect on how fruitless the search for wholesomeness has been, and we lose hope—not a healthy result. The answer isn't abstinence, but exploration, admitting that they have traits we want, others we're uncertain of, and remaining perceptive to define if these other traits are moral and the fault is ours, or immoral and the fault is theirs. Experience reveals each trait's significance, a mate's patterns and their distance to ours. We choose the path to life, expand in knowledge, see more clearly what we're after, and then narrow the search.

Finding one's soul mate is a result of knowing oneself in final form, and that takes time. To do so, our closest relationship and loyalty must be to truth, as it supersedes all other relationships. No rational individual would demand that we surrender it. By all means be close to people, but be closer to reality.

"When I meet a man I ask myself, "Is this the man I want my children to spend their weekends with?" —Rita Rudner

Poor Selection. Spirit Murderers may select mates at random—whoever is willing—but mostly they choose through fear, anger and low self-esteem. They give up on life, and settling into it, hope their sacrifice is everything they wanted but were afraid to pursue in the first place. Instead, they bring about the hell they dreaded. They openly seek the safety of a substitute mind that will work beyond their own capacity or willingness, but their honest desire is for the destructive traits which match their own. Relationships don't typically last for Spirit Murderers, so a trend clearly develops. Tired of the fraud they stage, they need to let their hair down, so they alternate in relationships between victims and destroyers, seeking the first for sustenance and the second for self-actualization. Running these simultaneously, if only in their mind, is their only way to cope. Mixed up in their desired reversal of reality, they begin to withdraw all values given the victim, while showering rewards on the destroyer. Their mask comes off, killing the golden goose. Once the goose is gone and her life-needs must be filled, the destroyer splits too. Then she looks to repeat the process with a new victim and a new destroyer. (What role did I play? I was the cash cow who took off his bell).

One need not be a pimp or a whore to operate on prostitution premises; such action is common, and spiritually its practitioners reach the same end. When looks wear out or they just seek to settle down, it's all dollar signs— mates are interchangeable. They treat relationships as if it's an escort service assignment. They pretend they like you. They pretend to be what you want. They lay down and let you use them not out of desire, but because it is expected as compensation for access to your sustenance. You wonder why she ignores you during the work and prefers to hang with her friends, spending her time socially getting high or drunk (unearned emotional states), but is willing to accompany you to enjoy the result of your effort (unearned wealth). Is it clearer now? Is there any contradiction? All the relationship will lack is serenity, intimacy, love, passion and respect. You can give them love and companionship, but what they really want, is an annuity. If they dropped the act, they might discover that they *do* like you, but they won't. They don't like anything, including themselves. If you hear "I can be bought," the going rate for ground chuck is $3.39 a pound. Such an admission is the acceptance of human beings as cattle—a link to slavery. They are willing to give their most sacred embrace—not to emotional fulfillment, but for naked survival—at any level open to them. What men realize implicitly is that sincerity will not win this girl. What they must show is not their purest and practiced best, but their most practiced deviousness—a craft mastered only by fundamental cowards. Cowardice breeds insincerity. Insincere people are manic pretenders—they are not happy. No matter how pretty she is, if she is insincere, be thankful she is making someone else's life miserable, and not yours.

The non-parasitical side of poor selection just doesn't think. There is no range or scope to their preference, only surface qualities. An honest creature is attracted by beauty and confidence, while ugly cowardice repels them. This association begins with sensory data—the reason we fall for beauty alone, early on. It grows with experience into an abstraction of beauty, which includes the intelligence, energy and integrity of the individual who is the object of our desire, but the lethargic never look past appearance. They stop, believing a beautiful person has all the bases covered. They couldn't be more wrong. Posture is only an indication; it is up to reason to validate their character, but any greater depth even within themselves remains a mystery.

Physical beauty is much more common than the intellectual effort required to live and act with sound judgment. Nevertheless, here are some reasons I've heard for marriage: nice butt, nice car, nice family, likes 80's music. That's fine for starters, but for them it never gets any deeper: that's why their emotions turn on a dime. Love to them is a fad, as significant and as deep as their initial preference. Defining compatibility based on looks alone indicates a host of additional errors, which never permit clear understanding of oneself or anyone else. How do they hope to qualify a mate for the next ten thousand steps, without the knowledge to see two steps ahead? That is the danger of having adult equipment and an immature brain, capable of making decisions that bear a crucial lifelong impact. If she thinks the excitement of all night parties or sex in the bathroom defines the kind of man she wants, then she deserves the level 2 rewards it will yield. If their union is the result of preferred musical tastes and nightclubs, then their joy will carry the same depth as a hangover. What does experience tell us? If inessentials define you, you're still a child.

Unthinking women consider a dominating man to be an alpha male, as he has a force she cannot match; but if he instigates trouble when he is not in danger, then he is actually acting out of cowardice. He is evading cognition and will exercise any outlandish violence and screaming necessary to avoid identification of whatever it is he is running from. Strap him down and ask him a few crucial questions and he's toast. Admiring him as her image of a man, she *defines* her probable fate and the unhappy, submissive position she will assume. Force is only proper for situations of danger—nothing we should be subjected to in a modern civilization. In relationships, this power is meant to protect her, not to threaten her, to guard her against the savagery of others, not to subject her to it. When such a man initiates violence against a woman to compensate for his own immature stupidity, she should leave him and pursue more responsible men. This is true for anyone in his path. Withdraw his victims and he is helpless. The dominant position represents a moral opportunity to use strength wisely, and is an opportunity for all in the hierarchy to appreciate the sound use of any strength existing above them, and anywhere else along the chain.

Often I'd see beautiful girls with Neanderthal guys and be horrified at my incapacity to land them. I'd ask myself, "Can't she judge the difference? Can't she see?" After talking with many, it struck me that she *is* that guy—in better packaging. Flakes date flakes. Deal with it. It is our own flakiness that comes out when we waste our time with them.

DENIAL IN SELECTION

Have you ever wondered why the do-gooders, the social workers and the Bible-brigade ignore a true producer, but stand valiantly behind someone they know *won't* make it? Do you think that is an accident? My first love left me because my "light shined too bright," and she couldn't see her own. It took years of torment to understand her motive. It wasn't that I wasn't good enough, but that I did things *too* well. I would show her some great achievement, trying to give her the hope I knew she couldn't generate alone. I heard criticism instead of appreciation; evasion instead of acceptance. She saw my results, saying "Yes that, but not with the effort you had to expend. I don't want to know why or how, because your way doesn't interest me." She was willing to sell herself experimentally for wealth or security, but would never experiment with the honest, the able and with their means of living. Fearing the dreams of her youth, I saw the hands of mediocrity reaching up to pull her back down, and ultimately, I knew they would win. I lost her to another, but not due to his merit. He won her for the distinguished character he failed to achieve—a fear to match her own, and a contentment never to question and never to rise. She did us both a favor; we weren't compatible.

Every relationship is at the mercy of the shakiest epistemological ground. She'd given no level 2 reasons to distrust her—those within her range—but she *had* given level 4 reasons. Those prone to the Democratic fantasy where their wishes cost someone, but they need not consider who, those who assert mysticism as fact yet ignore all rational derivations, pose a red flag. If you want to get the truth about another's ultimate premises, religion and politics are the places to do it. Watch for anyone who argues for premises you view as below them; *they're not.* Such are justifications for future intent, and their lives will come to reflect them sooner or later.

Compatibility amongst Spirit Murderers is only in their joint hatred of ability—otherwise, their evasions go off in different directions. The Irrationally Dominant looks for someone who could never equal him; he needs the assurance of superiority. The Submissive looks for humble safety; they bring little, so they settle for the same. One is never more than 50% of a relationship and never less. If you believe you are, you chose poorly, or you have more work to do. If you *need* to be, you have a confidence problem either way. Those of premises incompatible with life, to that extent, are compatible with *no one.*

I can see those driven by anticipation by the look in their eyes, being bright, excited and alive. When I see nothing in their eyes, it is still a reflection of their premises. What matters most is in the entity before you—in what their actions have made of them. If their level of achievement doesn't reflect yours or your achievable aspirations, you'll never have adequate respect for each other. One cannot love another to the same extent if a like dimension of values is not practiced; if life is not loved as much. Do you want a Ferrari or an AMC Pacer? Because, *we love in the manner we live,* and I wouldn't want any lethargic eyes choosing *me* for a mate.

Warrior Note: *One's relationship with another can never be more valuable than one's relationship to truth.*

Unconditional love is the savior of the Fear-driven, who wring every last drop of insanity out of it. They push aside supposed inconsequentials such as weight—meaning *health, beauty*—meaning a harmonious flow of features and *posture*—defining productive intent and awareness—key elements that *do in fact* lend significant evidence to understanding another's character. They give us instead the unfit alternative—to find something truly repulsive and try to love it, challenging that virtue can only be attained if we don't gag. They say love is blind. By this standard it's also fat, stupid and ugly.

Love is the product of dynamically moral judgment, which weighs every known action and assigns value accordingly. It is a barometer of virtue, a constant reminder and indicator of whether or not one is on track in life. To say *anything* is fine is to say "I don't judge, weigh or determine anything of value; I can't tell the difference. My brain is completely useless." Real love isn't possible to anyone who considers proper cognition to be too big a chore. The key to the value of love is an active mind, capable of identifying and appreciating rational life-furthering values. Let them decide what is more valuable, you or their denial.

My faith in the sanity of mankind is in that they *leave* relationships that give them nothing, the very nothing they were taught to expect through selfless, unconditional love. If there is nothing in it for them, they split, and they should. Those who fell for it were often seeking a way around effort and cannot love anyway. Those who think and value and therefore *can* love, can see the subversion for what it is. As a caveat, if your partner yearns for this kind of pointless love, be warned: regardless of your virtue, you are being "loved" in this exact way.

THE MASS AVERAGE

No one enjoys being considered a public utility, and no one enjoys the knowledge of using them. But I've heard the whore's equivalent out of normal women when they say "I can have any man I want." Why does a quiet shame always follow to undercut that pride? Because it is an admission of reliance on one's own beauty, a secondary consideration superceding all other human values—and also, that it isn't working. The thorn is that this power only works among the submission/domination crowd, with a mate who is not looking to love her, but to use her, or one who doesn't feel worthy. Such shallow pride can be felt as long as one doesn't look too closely at what type of people it reels in. Most mistake this sense of false-pride for confidence, but it isn't vanity, its vulnerability. She conveys, "This is all men are, and this is all I have to offer," and the creeps—male and female—come running, while the decent suitors no longer take her seriously. If she pursues the submissive, preying on his fear, her future is limited to petty psychological manipulation, disrespect and self-hatred. The truth is she's trapped in the axis, and until she can be sincere, she isn't worthy of a better man.

Believing she can have *any* man just equates her love with the standards of a garbage can. It is once again a desire not to judge, but to be passive, with a multi-prong penalty. Believing that men are interchangeable wipes out her capacity to see a true match. There is no adequate substitute for thought and tenacious effort. Beautiful people have to practice wholesomeness to validate and deserve love, just like everyone else.

Lacking the power of sexual choice, men often practice another version of the same error. He believes he has to provide a bottomless expense account for her enjoyment. He's afraid he can't be himself and have her like him. He can't struggle with bills, he can't be uncertain, he can't cry, he can't feel, he can't be human. He displays the expectations of the mainstream at the price of his own happiness, and hurts her as he misrepresents the truth about himself. He fosters her dilemma by *implying* through these actions, that she must be bought, and perpetuates his own stress by spending his life maintaining a cushion between her and existence—between life and how he actually feels about it. He ends up with what he was *looking* for: a woman who has to be supported and who he doesn't respect, and wonders why his life has arrived at an unsatisfying sum.

Then, there is the opposite, a man afraid to show a woman his strengths, believing he must placate her delicacy by reflecting an inordinate level of sensitivity, instead of just being what he is. He ends up with an unbecoming and unnatural softening of male features—a blurring which takes her job away. That isn't what a woman wants. She *is* the softening. She softens our hard edges, otherwise, what use would we have for her—or her for us?

We all struggle to be appealing to mass expectations, but *we don't want* the mass average; we want someone special. Be yourself. Whoever can't handle it isn't suitable anyway. When fishing for a mate, don't stick your pole in a cesspool. Your chances are better seeking the freshest water, not the biggest tank.

Conduct: Breaking One's Mate. Spirit Murderers can turn on you and leave. They can turn on you and stay. Misery is their medium, so it is not a factor for ending or maintaining a relationship. Their relationship conduct is consistent in one medium: damage. Out there in the world's mix of Spirit Murder and Self-made, there's no guarantee which side will be your next encounter. What is guaranteed, is new knowledge and experience, and for the alert, new armor. We stair-step up as they stair-step down, and we attempt a relationship as we pass. It fails. Then, we continue to move in our opposing directions.

Spirit murder knows no gender, but certain forms are statistically gender specific, such as male violence and female deception—the easy way out for both. She neurotically pursues submission from her man, constantly trying to take control. She puts him down and undercuts his every living desire. Instead of supporting the traits she desires in a man, she works for his destruction. She does everything in her power to make sure he knows he's not enough, but she doesn't leave. The male equivalent won't let her work—the veil of custom simply denies her the opportunity to pursue self-worth. Both put you in awkward positions due to their irresponsible behavior, and harm your reputation with those you respect. They talk behind your back—the person to whom you grant the most trust, bad-mouths and pins you to the wall, where everyone learns the true value of your intimate relationship, but you. They need someone to blame, "All of our problems are *your* fault. It's *your* fault I drink; it's *your* fault I'm abusive and it's *your* fault I cheat. If you weren't the way you are, we'd be happy." They want *you* to pay for what *they* are. They want to break you.

On the luckier than deserved end, they try to bring you down to their level, attempting to sell you on their style of degeneration. If they disturb your purity, they will feel they earned their place alongside you. If exploiting your weak points and needling you fails to elicit humble reform, they move to the next level and try to lure you into evil. Their goal is to see you aimless and unsure, to see you drunk, to see you waste time, even to see you cheat. They need a reflection of themselves, to affirm their sin's continuance.

They distrust without evidence, coping with their glass esteem by making you walk on pins and needles around their chronic fear and suspicion, doubting you, expecting the worst every step of the way. Being worthy of trust, it is unjust; no one deserves that kind of tax. If you get fed up and leave them, the "unknowable" reasons for your departure will hurt them forever with no intention to look or understand further.

They damage your relationships with friends and family. They damage your possessions, saying "Don't I mean more to you than everything else?" As if King or Queen, their position in your value hierarchy justifies the surrender and abuse of all those below, and they cover it with, "If you loved me, the things I do wouldn't matter." And pushing you into unthinking servitude, "If you loved me, you would do anything I asked; you wouldn't question me; you wouldn't doubt." Right, you'd voluntarily accept a dictator in your life—the Fear-driven's well-known style of default. In the worst nightmare, you become an accomplice to illegalities—drugs, violence, fraud—and their financial irresponsibility bankrupts you, wiping out your credit as well.

They profess to love us and claim their intention is to contribute to our joy, yet all they contribute to is our pain. When the opposite of their declared intentions is achieved, then that *is* their true intention. For them, the desire for destruction is like a sex urge. They have to do it. You can have long, painfully clear discussions with them, explaining your total commitment. You could say, "I know I'm not crazy, I conveyed something that was perfectly rational and they blew up at me anyway. So what am I missing?" You missed that they don't operate on reason. You didn't choose someone rational to convey it to. Don't expect to win them over with devotion, compassion, love or honesty. Don't expect clear reason to make any difference. They can see clearly that in their life with you alone, you are the only one to take advantage of, and they still can't stop themselves. They must as all must, seek confirmation of their own premises, which is to bring destruction to the premises of the living. Forget any outside source of reclamation; they will fight progress and only attempt to *re-actualize* their environment when removed from it. Accept the truth of their cannibal nature and move on.

They can't help but secretly respect rational values, and could never live with themselves if they gave in to that love. So they fight to die, as we fight to live. To accept us is to damn themselves, which is true for us as well. Each tries to undercut the other and the result is proper—disaster. For the times when we feel battered by the shallowness and distrust in the outside world, our home must be a resting ground—a sanctuary of sanity. We must hold out for someone who won't batter us at home.

NEGATIVE ASSOCIATIONS

Not all spirit murdering action has malicious intent. There are subversive forms of torture rooted in unsound patterning, which cause alienation and emptiness where connection should be felt. Many have honest intentions, yet have been sold premises of destruction outside their capacity to identify. They practice them unaware of the danger until it's too late, as the relationship comes across a spiritual vortex and gets pulled down. For example, popular morality never gives you credit for your virtues, so it follows that you will fail to recognize them in your mate. She works for reward, but the reward doesn't reflect the effort she expended. She deserves appreciation for it, perhaps withheld because your not getting it either. *We end up associating callous disregard to each other*. No such deficit can be maintained for long. Present morality teaches us to give up all personal goals and desires, to submit, to compromise and to sacrifice in order to become *one*—a metaphysical impossibility. As a result, we lose our identity, as to make a personal request is to be guilty of hedonism. *We end up associating identity crisis to our union.* With selfless love, it is considered a display of strength to have no needs. No longer an individual, we fear opening up, which would reveal that we are still individuals. It can also be fear of what others will do with the information you give them, possibly from reflecting on how you personally have misused the information of others. *We end up associating emotional sterility to each other.* This morality tells us to follow our heart, not our mind, so cognitive self-doubt surmises that reality is *determined* in their judgment of us—right or wrong. *We end up associating a void of helpless dependency to the relationship.* Decent people or not, such patterns bring nothing but harm and must be corrected to achieve any form of prosperity.

Another negative association is that many mistakenly approach a relationship as "get it off your chest" time or "let it all hang out" time—what become the elements of a relationship's destruction. Often work worries are the essence of one's focus, bleeding through and tingeing everything else with misery. We've heard, "You aren't here, you're still at work." The purpose of both places has been inverted; our most important relationship becomes a dumping ground in order to maintain psychological efficiency at work. It is the need to transmit toxicity—an individual problem that has gone unaddressed. Continued venting will cause mates to associate boredom and stress to each other, and it will destroy the relationship eventually.

"Am I a coward? ...That I...must like a whore, unpack my heart with words."
—*Hamlet.*

Venting is the after burn of cowardice: of those who have not learned to convey displeasure, disagreement or to just carry on productive conversation in a mature and tactful manner. Instead they shut down, and have to accept the self-loathing of private humiliation. If one can't deal with work issues at work, it is likely that one can't deal with relationship issues at home. If a relationship is to be sound, you have to have *yourself* sorted out first. Until you commit to yourself, you should not commit to another.

With our most intimate, we share our deepest view of the world and of Man. If that amounts to smut and toilet humor, the magic dies fast. There are certain things that need to remain private if a satisfying image of each other is to be maintained. It is with our mate whom we share or psychological medium. Is it a medium of discontent? A Fear-driven medium exemplifies, not the best of their body and mind, but the worst it can do. Spirit Murderers replace joy with malicious humor; they replace their life's future projection with cynical blindness, and properly banish all affection to darkness where they need not face its shameful disparity with the rest. If they prefer to share disgusting habits, ask yourself "Why do they find it important to show me this trait? What are the implications of its alternative?" Crass smallness destroys romance. Lack of awareness or disregard for bad habits or mannerisms is a toxic negative. There should be no abrupt or adverse actions to repress—nothing we see leading into negativity—just peace, relaxed stimulation and enchantment.

SEX

To him, sex is expected versus deserved, an automatic attribute of the relationship, unrelated to his conduct. He drifts away even then in a one-sided fantasy with a one-sided end, detached and unable to express himself emotionally. Sex remains a mission of blind and deaf discovery, if it provokes more than interest in release. For her, sex is used as a means of control, to influence or emaciate. It wins her the relationship, but once in, she begins to penalize him for his every desire and action. Sex is her greatest opportunity for negative infliction, belittlement and ridicule. She doesn't initiate. She responds coldly or refuses intimacy altogether. Orgasm to her, simply feeds a momentary rush of life into a dead body. Treating it like prostitution, she welcomes him only when she's after something. At the pinnacle of her own self-contempt, she submits to and embraces what is *not* her image of Man, acknowledging she has failed her image of what a woman should be as well.

Another danger is to hear "Men run this world and sex is a woman's weapon to get what she wants." Such a woman fundamentally destroys her capacity for valuing by betraying the purpose of her most personal, intimate need. It becomes just what she says, a weapon, which means someone is going to get hurt. When sex is anything other than one's own precious, private desire, it is a confession of inadequacy for living. In this particular context, more damage has been done to more people than any other means, by the actions of those who, due to their own weakness, could not afford honest motives. She creates the illusion of love and throws away the value of living for herself, as there are no higher values to seek. She goes on, pretending to herself that she enjoys living through the accumulation of material assets and ostentation, and in the meantime, subjects anyone she crosses to her callous poison. Her default revolves around the statement "That's how the world works," and unwilling to defend her spirit, refuses to accept that she has any alternative. Did her weapon work?

The worst is where sex becomes perversion. As growth is associated to all endeavors of Man, and with sex being a physio-spiritual activity, it must advance in some direction. With a disciplined life-consonance, it grows more personal and fulfilling with every passing year. With a killer's cognition it moves along another strain: degeneration. It becomes public; it involves all ages and relations; it becomes involuntary. Breaking through every barrier of decency, it welcomes all impurities in the most open salute to depravity next to Nazism. As the pinnacle of unconditional love, it brings all social immoralities together, reversing our deepest tribute to Man.

INFIDELITY

"If you don't inhale, it's not adultery." —*Presidential musing*

Who has heard, "Wait! I can explain!" Well, with moral clarity, *so can I*. They *should* say, "Just put the facts aside for a minute and consider my pathology." Infidelity is not just deception. It isn't the innocent desire for the affection one isn't getting at home. It is the psychological desire to provoke or witness, the triumph of evil over good. It is first and foremost self-deception as all spirit murder begins, and becomes damage to others as one leads one's own premises astray.

Different Spirit Murderers cheat for different specifics, but their motive is always the same: to show spite for life and human beings. Everyone decides individually how to spend his or her own time. The Player spends his time trying to pick up every girl that catches his eye. With an established relationship taking so much time and emotional energy, a multiple pursuit is a clear sign of misdirection. Time lost to trivialities is subtracted from one's own depth. Such men are cut off from their own rational fulfillment, and fill the void with conquests. They view women as things, not as people, and they desire them as they desire things—without the volitional consent, mutual desire or fulfillment of the women. He needs to prove that he can have what he wants, not whether there is any point in wanting it. He seeks a sense of self-esteem, something that cannot be had by any form of self-appreciation achieved outside of witnessing one's own cognitive efficacy. He wants to know that he is worthy of living, but he goes about it outside his mind, through the women who favor him, instead of the only valid means of happiness: self-motivated, productive personal development and the resulting individual creation. The playboy is viewed as an ideal for narrow-minded men to reach, but in actuality, he is an irrationally miserable, short range neurotic. He claims to be after sex alone, but notice he cannot stay with the same woman for more than a few rounds. He is caught in an existential conflict: using tools set to respond to an experiential value progression, yet morally stagnant, blindly pursues what his premises are designed not to satisfy.

There is nothing wrong with refusing to settle down until you know what type of person you can trust and desire for a lifetime, and that takes years of experience to define. To be of any value, relationships must be an honest pursuit; lying at any point of the journey is unnecessary. When a mate cheats, they cheat not only on their spouse, but they cheat themselves. It is their integrity that is betrayed. If one isn't honest with others, it is because one isn't honest with oneself, and won't end up with someone compatible. If you settle, the need for what you truly want will come back to haunt the relationship. You will make your mate pay for what they lack—what you did not have the strength to hold out for.

A mate who cheats on another with you, will cheat on you. A mate who breaks up with you for superficial reasons, went out with you for superficial reasons. If a mate has no self-absorbing purpose, watch out. The more valuable their partner, the more they will want to cheat. They are parasites on esteem, and with the risk of disease, parasites on bodily health as well. End the cheating and get a life; it isn't manly, womanly, powerful or mature, and has nothing to do with your partner.

Exiting without Grace. Spirit Murdering relationships usually end with some kind of trap. Whether they stay or whether they go, this is where the truth comes out. They did their part of the work—the lies, the fraud, the posturing—now it's payday. Their crescendo is to get a cut of *your* life forever, as granted them through neurosis, child support, settlement or alimony, and they intend to cash in. Parasitical destruction was their plan from the beginning, so they cannot leave you in one piece. They refuse your freedom, never having respected fundamental human rights to begin with (which divorce laws permit). If you don't accept that you're their property, they stalk you, making your every move a peril. They brim with anticipation in their desire to inflict as much damage as possible—to damage your belongings, to disrupt your plans, to wreck your dreams, in neurotic vengeance against your rational expectations—their only means to show you or anyone, how powerful they are. Never will you see them more energized, more fluent in action or more fulfilled as when they are threatening or harming you. They aren't looking into their own futures—independent projection is not their pattern. They are absorbed in a terrorist's wish—to plant a bomb that will blow up your life without lesson or forward value, with only malicious hatred as their parting signature.

MARRIAGE HUNTERS

Advancing through dependencies in the surrender of all dreams, this group of cowards plot to chain themselves to another who represents a living power they cannot match. A woman with no productive intent indicates a *non*productive intent, making her very dangerous to get involved with—a life-altering trap such as pregnancy or a marriage ultimatum is likely. Life becomes a challenge to fulfill their *replacement* dream: to stay home where it's safe and do nothing. Rather than pursue the splendor possible within and outside of them, they long instead to endure a daily anguish, where they can just wait around to die. It must be the most embarrassing thing to admit: "I'm a housewife." It's like saying "I'm a door knob." Dogs are kept, not people. With respect for the undervalued service stay-at-home Moms render, here is my contribution: they are all slugs.

I can hear them now, "No, *we agreed* on a host/parasite relationship; it's voluntary," or "It's *his families* money, not *his* either," implying that self-esteem suicide is a mature, adult choice if openly acknowledged. With skills as a housemaid worth minimum wage, upon divorce the man wonders why Miss Worthless goes to court and makes the "agreement" *involuntary*. "Why can't she support herself?" he asks. Could she in the beginning? Did you respect her judgment then? The nature and power of her prosperity is *everything*. If not, then it is going to be your prosperity. It defines her as a person, as yours defines you. Current law implores you to accept it now, or you'll pay for it later.

When a woman is willing to leave a man who won't marry her, she neurotically wants the state of marriage more than she wants the man, or the state of happiness. The man is interchangeable; the goal of marriage is not. To be married without consideration to whom is a desired reversal of cause and effect, as one who wants wealth and distinction and won't consider the steps necessary to acquire it. To her, a relationship is a lot of posturing to gain commitment. If she feels anything at all it's a bonus, yet it is likely considered a hindrance—a weakness. Upon completion of the goal, she perpetuates the fraud in impressions on others, attempting to capture the self-esteem and fulfillment she was irrationally pursuing through the state of marriage.

This relationship-killing ultimatum is imposed to gain her own confidence through the forced commitment of a man—a *self*-con game. The true source of relationship security comes from an introspective estimate of one's self-worth, and a like confidence in the value of another. Through such awareness, any time together is precious. Healthy partners know their values can never be fixed. The ebb and flow of life keeps them striving, and this steady pressure to succeed is constantly emitting romantic appeal. It is senseless to throw away a satisfying relationship because a partner isn't ready for legal ties. Paper won't change your feelings for each other.

If marriage is pursued and permitted as an end in itself, it will simply exemplify her irrationality in future pursuits. If her greatest achievements were gained by whining, agonizing fear, then her life was a fraud. Those who end relationships on this issue haven't matured enough to conduct them responsibly, to cherish deserving their values or to respect the meaning of life. She believes the state of marriage itself will bring about the process of emotional health she hasn't learned to practice. She hasn't accepted the actual elements emotional health is comprised of, and until she does, married or not, has no chance to reach it. In the interim, she needs to get a job. People must work, and there is a name for those who work in the home: Maid. Don't marry the maid.

PREDATIONAL PREGNANCY

We constantly hear of crackdowns on "dead-beat dads," but the topic of how they often originate remains hidden and deserves serious light: *Dead-beat Mothers*. Imagine if a toy company put out a realistic product for Christmas that had kids screaming, "I want Baby-Waste Your Life! It comes with a work book and legal kit on how to lie, how to sue, how to apply for welfare, the various addictions I'll employ when it blows up in my face and all the excuses I'll need for why my life is not my responsibility!"

Why are girls given dolls, when we all know what a disaster a baby actually is for a young girl? Why are we shocked, when unprepared for constructive dreams, *that* is what they choose?

Motherhood has always been played off as a moral symbol beyond reproach, so in panic, she moves straight for its cover. The truth is it has little moral worth. Anyone on I-75 at rush-hour knows there is little risk of the race dying out. Defaulting on life, her first goal is to have her future assured—to force a man into a position where he no longer has a choice but to support her. But the more critical goal is in effect, an inverted life projection: to ensure an alibi that will neatly dispose of her productive years. Whether the trap works or not, she fears life, and in withdrawal, seeks a justifiable diversion she can handle. Her enterprise of mind is *evasion*. Its subversive application is children—avoiding the subject of achievement by meeting the most rudimentary needs of others. *Others* become her achievement. Trapping a spouse is among the worst long-range acts of malice, as it permanently affects so many. If he recognizes the con and refuses, how unattractive it is to have children without a husband—not by virtue of an accident, but by her own stupidity. How indecent it is to expect family and friends to help shoulder the burden of that choice. Being questioned about her incomplete picture, we hear defensively that she *could have* taken a Self-made path, but just *chose* differently, then she scats. It's always a bluff. Probe deeper and you'll find no chain—no all-life-orchestrating principles—just the kid as purpose. When someone won't share their depth, nine times out of ten, it doesn't exist. Babies are *not* the final frontier—though they serve as that mask for the Fear-driven. As a faulty pursuit of esteem to the point of psychosis, she will sacrifice anyone to realize her goal: having babies with no thought to the future, without consent of mate, without means, without sense, without end.

There are certain levels of living that no one has the right to affect, including your spouse. First is your purpose in life. Second is the choice of rewards for your own effort, of which she too, is an extension. Pregnancy in this case is a grasping attempt to take your living energy and spend it on her own bumbling course of destruction. If she is willing to derail your life without your consent, she doesn't care what happens to you and it's just the beginning—the tip of the iceberg. At times, some men try to secure a relationship through pregnancy, but inequality under the law makes this issue gender specific. As the laws are biased to women, the knife is in their hands.

The Fear-driven lie their way into relationships, they lie about their dreams and then try to take you both in a direction opposite of their declared intentions. To foster this, a woman is given a clear legal pattern for transgression upon a man. A man must finance the endeavor, regardless of what a woman does to conceive. When deceptive action has no legal relevance, a serious bias exists for evil to thrive. Among these cases, here is the type of insanity it manifests: a woman slips into a bedroom at a party, has sex with an unconscious stranger, has a baby, sues him for support and wins. In another, a nurse fondles a hospital patient, inseminates herself in the bathroom, has a baby, sues him for support and wins. Theoretically, a woman could break into a sperm bank, inseminate herself with a sample from a dead millionaire, then sue his estate for support and our courts would give it to her. While serving a jail sentence for the break in, she can get rich collecting his royalties. There are countless cases of equally asinine yet more conventional deception, which is all *predation,* period. Such a woman believes the state of motherhood is beyond any moral question, and backed by our courts, is free to commit any atrocity to achieve it. What are our legal guardians thinking? I wouldn't trust such a Judge to preside over a toaster: *fraud is a felony.* Holding one person accountable for another's actions simply exonerates the guilty party. The legal and *moral r*esponse to securing values through fraud in any other realm is time and restitution, but in this case, the penalties are reserved for the victim. It's a good scam, knowing your victim is legally defenseless—given the certainty you won't be murdered for it. It is the most convenient way to steal the life-force of another.

Only one reason makes a woman violate the sanctity of her romantic relationship: it isn't sacred to her. The man is only a medium through which the goal will be attained, but he isn't the only victim—the child is also a medium. The violations she is prone to, indicate her likely dysfunction with the child as well. She can treat that relationship as haphazardly as she treated her relationship with him. *Social* dysfunction is predicated on *cognitive* dysfunction. A woman who wants a child with or without a sound relationship, does not respect the need for a father in the lives of her children. She is perfectly willing to let them feel that hollow, rejected, emptiness that is conjured when a parent leaves, along with its complex psychological implications, of which she herself was a likely victim. She *designs* heartbreak into their lives and hands down an ill pattern for human relations, which will likely be perpetuated. She doesn't know *how* to have a wholesome relationship, she hasn't developed the discipline to respect basic human rights, and will not be able to pass them on. If he tries to step in and make a difference, he is legally chained to a neurotic who has no obligation to act rationally, but has the full power to override his and continue running wild in the attempted moral validation of her own illness. He can't defend the child from the inconstancy, malice and evil in the world when it comes from its own mother. He is forced to work with her as equal partners—someone whose actions would get her fired or incarcerated under any other circumstances.

In debates over social ills, political leaders claim "The real problem is unwed mothers." Our own President has said it, yet the government honors their pattern. Current policy is to say "You're actions are foolish and wrong, but fraud is okay, we'll close our eyes and force someone else to cover it." We are the adults, but our judicial confusion with moral responsibility effectively means that this plight is guided by a bunch of scared teenage girls. Holding them to no standard of right and wrong simply allows their pattern to go on uninterrupted. With our years of experience, our senseless answer is to provide sacrificial charity wrung out of an involuntary contributor, and in response, the girls conduct themselves as any welfare recipient would. When sustenance comes from an outside source one need not understand, one is free to play it deuces wild. Nine times out of ten, if she knew she couldn't get away with it, it would never happen.

The inertial implications are equally troubling. Sapping Self-made ambition is the worst possible spiritual infliction against individual life, and for the country as a whole. His aggregate output drops dramatically when he realizes his country is willing to subject him to such injustice. If he cannot keep his property by the right of its creation, he will produce no more than he consumes. Ideologically, if he is violated in proportion to his ambition, *ambition* is the target—a Communist premise—and that is what gets killed. When Spirit Murderers get control of laws, the last thing you want to be accused of, is prosperity. His expropriation is a violation of justice and civility, and therefore weakens the cultural-moral structure its practitioners are commissioned to reinforce. All human action is nourishment of an idea or a desire, rational or irrational. In this case, the energy of innocence is granted to further the intentions of evil—and individuals have only so much energy to spend. The branches of innocence are denied nourishment, while the branches of evil are allowed to flourish. Tolerating this kind of abuse feeds our country's demise, as it brings this risk to every man. America is just a group of families. If a man is not protected until he finds the life he wants, he won't support the one he was forced into, or the country that forced him. Sound friendships and families are built on respect for individual rights. As sound family is the foundation of society, its violation is a foundational weakness for the country. Multiplied by millions of insincere cases, the country's cultural inertias slow, breeding spiritual and economic decay—a lowering of human dimension—for both men and women. If government leaders consider unwed motherhood a deplorable issue, then the law cannot support bringing mongrel families into existence—it must break the pattern.

If individuals are undecided about a future family, they must plan for the fact that no birth control method is 100% effective. There is a moral choice to begin with that cannot be overlooked: the agreement between partners to *have* children or *not to* and when. No trust is more crucial to the individuals involved, and shattering that trust is not outside the court's authority to acknowledge. A violation of trust is the basis for *any* legal suit, and is the court's obligation to determine innocence and reward it, as it is to determine guilt and punish it or in this case, to grant it nothing. Since the 1960's, we've had the capacity to agree on children and on what to do if anything should happen—an essential element of compatibility. Still, we hear "If you didn't want children, you shouldn't have had sex." If couples have sex twice a week over the course of a twenty year relationship resulting in two children, sex was had .001% of the time for procreation. The other 99.999% of the time, it was for the sake of the sex. Do we see bikini-clad models and think lustfully of diapers? Does a woman see a gorgeous guy and think of a minivan and a fat ass? SEX IS AN END IN ITSELF. If not, then it is a form of prostitution. Unplanned pregnancy is no longer an irreversible malady hopeless to challenge, and if one changes the rules, both lives need not be taken off track. Every step up the ladder of science has brought more of Man's life within his power to decide—the opportunity to control a facet of existence, versus leaving it to chance. Every new choice represents an obligation by those involved to adhere to the choice made, and it's about time the courts recognized it. One can be honest or dishonest, which determines our integrity and the justice of our stand. As science changes our lives, we no longer need honor falsely imposed, outmoded expectations. If the man opts out from the beginning, no further obligation is warranted.

No matter what altruists wish, human law cannot violate the laws of nature. If justice fails him, he will seek his own by retracting his living power, as he should. His life is treated so carelessly, yet the squawking begins only when he chooses to practice the pattern pushed on him as well. There is no compassion for him or his situation, no concern for his financial well being—like her and like most politicians, no fiscal responsibility whatsoever. If that's the pattern we are using, why should he be different? He thinks connivers don't plan, but they do— as completely under the table, as he does on it. Their same intellectual elements are crawling down strands of evil. In their altruistic generosity, legislators forget that if the producer can't live, neither can anyone else.

There are enough people on the planet; surely there is room for justice. The law must acknowledge the father's right to live, and guard him against this kind of fraud. By serving honesty, it serves the child. When you pull a weed, you have to pull it out by the root—never rewarding evil or anything branching from it. Her pattern will be broken by a simple withdrawal of legal sanction. A woman must understand that if she makes a decision against her vows as wife or partner, that just as such a decision was made, she will face the consequences alone. As in all welfare reform, she will then have to look to the discipline of self-responsibility, and will weigh her choices more carefully. If she refuses abortion on supposedly moral grounds, she'll have to come to grips with what her principles cost.

THE CHALLENGE OF REPUDIATION. In a serious relationship or not, this can happen long before he discovers her true motive. He senses something is awry, only too late to do anything about it. It happens, and too many faulty motivations are involved to let it slide. Suddenly she expects marriage and a whole life she planned without his consent. Projecting his acceptance of this fate, he knows how it would unfold: the man she trapped would change. He'd be kicking her ass every day for stealing his future, in part to evade the guilt of letting her do it. She'd try to leave, and for his sacrifice, he wouldn't let her, thinking *"You* got us into this. You took us off course and brought us to this bitter, futile state of misery. You've damned us both and you're going to *stay* damned."* Then he'd spend his years living for spite, patiently waiting for those vulnerable moments to show her how little he cares, and at times to look at the beauty of the world and regret how they came to waste this sacred gift.

If she goes ahead against his wishes, then he has an important decision to make—whether or not he can live without her. If she takes action as if his fundamental direction is in *her* hands and he stands down, he might as well bend over and have her strap one on, because he's no longer the man. Dropping contemplation of that disaster, he sees the truth: that *his* life isn't *her* property.

That his expense of energy must be granted by his own willingness, and that the solution is to spend as little of it as possible in any *unchosen* direction. Still, it's hard to take such a stand in life, especially if he hasn't fully comprehended life yet. He can't help but ask, "How can I fight this? What are people going to think? What woman will want me if I fight?" Actually, it's just the opposite. It's immoral to roll over and play dead when you're being attacked. *They know* what such women are about, and better women will only respect you if you fight injustice. Only the sub-human, wishing to reserve the possibility to act likewise, would despise you for it. Those are the women to avoid. He hasn't the energy nor the time to pursue his own blossoming and this unwanted burden as well; one destroys the other. This is the type of sadistic choice where someone must be sacrificed, a position the Self-made never require, yet which the Spirit Murderers are constantly forwarding. "Why did you trust her?" others ask, as if trust was the irresponsible action. They school us to put faith in people, and when we do, *we are destroyed.*

For others to side with the trapper, and see *her* ends achieved with *his* means in spite of his own chosen course is so monstrous an injustice, it could only be the reflection of her own conscious premises in them. Their fundamental incompatibility is that he is *working* to accumulate the talent and energy necessary to ensure success in life, while she is *praying* for a massive liability that justifies failure. Out of fear, she's after blood, *not* love—two very different things, and her supporters honor that pursuit. To a Spirit Murderer, *any* relationship necessitates compromise. They intend to sell you out, to justify the weakness responsible for the unfaced, unresolved, corrupt relationships in their own lives. Forget them. A man doesn't forfeit his life if he sleeps with a woman. If he is not treated as an equal in all decisions, he's being set up for slavery. When consideration is dropped for him, he must drop consideration as well, or be consumed. It's all right not to be ready, and with the wrong partner, you'll *never* be ready. It's all right to refuse being pushed down any path, until you are prepared to traverse it. Such violations must be fought (by civil means); one's spirit must be preserved, *no matter the cost.* Never help anyone who makes it impossible for you to live. You'll find that if you fight insincerity, life will reveal a better class of women to you, and a more elegant style of living. Cut your losses and find a mate who deals from complete sincerity, and nothing else will matter.

Relationships and parenting are too important to be indulged in casually. A man has a right to wait for the conditions he finds conducive to his being a good mate and father—conditions of his fulfillment, safety and honor—and he has a right to retain his resources until he finds it. It's fine to grow roots at the right time, but never *unhealthy* roots. We all must learn how healthy roots grow, and that takes experience. It is never learned by *permitting* victimization; there is no room for insincerity in ongoing human relationships. It is each person's responsibility to find a mutually agreeable partner, together to develop a stable environment, and take the next step when both so intend. It isn't sound to start a family before both are certain they want to spend their lives together. It isn't practical to force a partner into an unchosen situation. It isn't healthy for anyone to embark on a financial course well outside their means. Children must be a product of love, trust, mutual respect and sound life progression—not of fraud, contempt and aimlessness. Waiting for the right time, our future children will be given much more spiritually than what a drained, unhappy parent could share.

Beautiful families are the product of man and wife planning *together;* never are they born of malice. If the issue was treated properly as under contract law, the result would be vastly different. A woman would know she cannot prey on others to achieve her dreams and would make more responsible decisions. He could move through courtship and no longer fear the predators who lie in wait. It would return the moral and financial confidence all men deserve, and we could watch both genders go on to achieve wealth and happiness by rational means. How much cleaner the ethical atmosphere would be, not to mention the healthier relationships that would be initiated under the sound principles of sincerity, sanctioned by law. Until then, *deny control* to those whose vision and ambition is no greater than lies, diapers and soap operas. Deny control to those whose ambitions *exceed* that, possible only with the means of others.

The world is full of Spirit Murderers who will try to take control of your energy and use it to pacify their own madness. For all men, an unwelcome pregnancy is viewed as an immediate threat to our survival and our control over it—which is why the leading cause of death for pregnant women is homicide. Maybe when the worst of your gender stop trying to trap us, the worst of ours will stop killing you.

Pimps and Whores, Oh My! Spirit Murderers sacrifice whatever value is most expedient, beginning with those handed to them by nature or by others. Prostitution isn't just a 'no alternative' heartbreaking choice to sustain themselves—not in a free society. They get a charge out of evil—it is the defeat of rational reality—of goodness. Giving their own bodies for anything other than love is a triumph, proof that they don't have to adhere to life. If one trades affection for another medium of value such as money, the inevitable result is impotence and spiritual death—such mediums cannot be crossed. Yet this realm is the only possibility for them to gain a sense of power and control over their own existence—a ready product to be sold. Put them in a suit in an office or boardroom where achievement must be a product of consciousness, and they turn into worthless cowards. They have no self-esteem to engage in the process of thinking. Their living purpose is so inverted to the clean, the honest and the rational, that their achievement becomes an intended affront to all nature requires of them. Though Spirit Murderers at this level may be worms, all writhing and twisting amongst each other, there is no sound basis for its suppression. Prostitution is its own penalty; it is the same with alcohol and drugs. If no loss has been claimed by those involved, no restitution should be sought. As long as sex is consensual between them, there is no right of the law to limit the medium of consideration—be it respect, desire or dollars.

Gays. Never have I seen more social paranoia than in these people. Their percentage of unwholesome activity and voyeurism relative to heterosexuals is extreme, placing them at the far end of the Submission/Domination Axis, where all esteem is derived from social acceptance. The closest they've come to it was in the late nineties when we saw girl teens kissing other girl teens, but the damage was minimal. Shame as the young matured brought them to the correct path, and implicitly revealed to them the true structure of the movement: personal hatred and fear of the opposite gender. The difference between genders is not cognitive, only physical. Gays must view approaching the opposite for a sexual relationship as a tremendous threat, so cutting off all sexual intentions is a way to cope with them. They need a guarantee of safety from rejection, where the surrender to the lowest of their own gender is much easier. I can only deduce from limited exposure, the actions taken which reveals their foremost concern and therefore their cognitive level—their neurotic preoccupation with public acceptance. Sexual choice is not fit as a public issue. Fortunately their numbers are small as are statistics for retardation or for criminals, and that is the way it will stay.

Enemies

"Only a fool fails to learn from the enemy." —Adolph Hitler

Spirit Murderers need strict social classes of men to maintain a sense of safety and identity. They define the abstract worth of a man by a *non-achievement based stature,* such as inheritance, seniority, race, gender, social position or affiliations. The true dividing line among men is Fear-driven versus Self-made; all other differences can be transcended, but the Fear-driven will do anything to keep this from being seen. They *want* to hate—it is their cognitive fourth step release—and they don't want that release to be taken. Hate is their freedom from rationality, and in this form, is the substance of defeat. When one clings to an external frame of reference such as religion, political preference, racial bias or social customs, it is *cognition* that is feared, *and all that which substantiates it.*

Though locked in misery, for companions or enemies, they prefer other Spirit Murderers. Another Spirit Murderer is a *safe* enemy, one who wars on his terms, who he has a chance to win against. There is no peace or harmony, and none is sought. Just fear, claws, flesh and teeth—the world as they need it to be. They are compatible in incompatibility; no form of illusion will ever match another, but their aim is alike—to actualize their world of constant turmoil. They are content in constantly trying to out-maneuver each other and out-lie, fulfilling and perpetuating their submission/domination relationship. The version of reality for every split second depends on who is dominant, and is accepted until he is toppled and replaced, in the ebb and flow of insanity. In a Spirit Murdering microcosm, all take turns as victim and predator.

Sexism. The misery women have endured in their fight for equality and for recognition of their ability—powerless to change the minds of others, parallels our fight: moral recognition for self-sustaining action. The demeaning need to prove oneself where others pass solely by grace of their gender or race, is the same as those who challenge precedent with sound reason, having no one willing to listen. Through the Submission/Domination Axis, Spirit Murderers have brought all human interactions to where they must be defined as win or lose, and with their views of men and women, it's no different.

It is unfortunate that many women feel inadequate relative to men; it isn't necessary. Saying "I'm a woman. Society doesn't consider me as good or as important as a man" is as pointless as the "I'm too tall or too short" routine, spending one's life in tension against unchangeable facts, instead of expanding the range of what one *does* have and *can* build on. It is senseless to rebel against our own identities and the hierarchies we exist along in the context of life. A lesser physical power is *not* a sign of lower worth, but the simple mechanics of calculating the forces present. If you encountered a stampeding elephant or a speeding car, would you try to reason with it, or get out of the way? The essential difference between men and women is physical; their cognitive power is *identical* and this power encompasses the majority of an individual's worth. All of us practice submission and domination in its proper realm every day: the Neon yields to the SUV, the SUV yields to the Mack truck and everyone yields to a train. Metaphysically we all know each pattern and assume one or the other—not just among men, but among all entities of mass and inertia that we encounter—our children, a tennis ball, it's all physics. In immediate reaction to a temporary danger or as a lifelong awareness, anyone in a submissive role assumes more subtle traits as a pre-warning system for their own welfare.

Where women are submissive to the dominant power of men, they develop the capacity to sense emotional resonance—the origin of *women's intuition*. It is an indicator of tranquility or hostility—a confirmation of peace or a warning that danger is imminent. Men don't develop it as acutely, as they needn't feel physical danger in the presence of a woman. Still, this wolf-pack hierarchy exists between men as well, whether they acknowledge it or not. A thin man knows a fat man could sit on him; he knows the inertia of a larger man is much greater than his own. The key difference is that it's not a constant peril in his life; for the most part, he is in no mortal danger. Nothing justifies the wolf-pack hierarchy seeping into abstract realms. Force knows no reason, which is why it's not a proper pecking order for a moral civilization. Still, it exists between animals in nature and is embraced by the lowest of men, so we must remain cognizant of it.

Physical power is not obsolete. A man must use it in many ways, and must develop confidence in its use—to be confident that the morally right can put down any threat. The health of our bodies determines our life-span and we must exercise its full range of motion; we must experience all it has to offer and extend its mobility just as we extend the power of our consciousness. Whether man or woman, children or elderly, to protect and develop our mobility is to protect our independence. Still, when push comes to shove, *men* are the human masters of violence, so no, there should never be a woman President. The President is in control of our armed forces: no woman should be in a position of that kind over men; it is a perversion of natural law. As a man, I couldn't fathom accepting war strategy from someone I could kill with my bare hands. Women who butch out trying to beat men at their own game, have a psychological preoccupation that disqualifies them from leadership positions anyway. Such a woman fights her own neurotic submissive bent by trying to reverse roles, instead of stepping beyond the struggle into objectivity. Emulating metaphysically-male traits, she practices the subjective behavioral offshoots that the irrational imposition of force leads to, to arrive at a miserable pseudo-equality that is of no greater value to anyone. The bilateral gender roles of protector and procreator will always exist. Sometimes we all have to fight. I'm all for Girl-power, but if there are competent men around, let them handle it—as nature intended.

Back in the old west, you could look at someone wrong and wham! They'd kill you. Nowadays, it's the same with militant women. Look at them wrong and wham! They sue you. Women's Libbers are guilty of the same sin of cognitive collusion—that *others* define them, that others must deal with them in a tailored way, or their glass world is in jeopardy. They claim productive women should be a part of their cause, but what they sell them is an inferiority complex—believing they must convince every contrasting opinion and fight every transgression. Not to dodge every obstacle, but to be stopped up by every one of them, claiming they've been violated. The problem was born when our metaphysical differences pushed their way into abstraction, where they don't belong. I don't know how often the typical man thinks about sex, but for me, I'd say constantly. If you're appealing at all, men are going to think about it. If you can't handle it, try baggy clothes and a mask. We all estimate each others attractiveness; women are just more subtle about it. Our incapacity to judge our chances, a bad joke or a crass comment however senseless and distasteful, does not justify a transfer of our assets to you. Be a man! Just deal with it.

In the working world, integration is the answer, where by personal encounter every consciousness gets to witness the fact of our like cognitive power for itself. Equal pay for equal work is of course deserved, but should be *quit* over, not sued for. There will be many supervisors who need to preserve their ancient view of women. His intellectual effort may be acute in business, but is lethargic in everything else. He thinks at work because he has to, not because he enjoys it. He didn't try to gain a valuable spouse and ended up with a huge house hog. Stereotyping doesn't stop at the desire not to think, it is also a means to cover one's own shameful submission to it. Fostering her false-limitations helps him to avoid facing his own failure to choose better. For him to accept the true potential of a woman is to accept that he married "man's best friend." Happiness implies divorce and acquiring a level of attractiveness sufficient to secure someone he respects, whom he has no energy to pursue and has lost the capacity to deserve.

You will be held back as he tries to prove his illusion through you instead, so just find someone braver to work for.

Racism. There is perhaps no greater spiritual war or a more false endeavor, than that of racial superiority. Those *for* racial solidarity lose their best to the torrent of capitalist freedom, were anyone can be anything they are willing to work towards, breaking ethnic borders as a side effect. The most dynamic sweep aside such inessentials in their upward surge to fulfillment. For that, we must leave the nest and its cohesive safety and focus purely on human essentials—those of all humans, not just our own race or culture—and market our wares to the world. The backward people cannot dismiss their culture; they hang onto it like Linus hangs onto his blanket. Producing no unique identity of their own, they cling to it for identity. Supposedly a symbol of pride, it is actually quite the opposite. We've all seen foreign flags on bumper stickers and jackets, women dressed as if they dragged the sheets off the bed with them, hats that look like a tornado landed on their head and the goatee and bald-spot beanie—all unusual, all ungainly and all out of place. These are not productive displays, but the exclusionist statement they need to feel safe. Instead of engaging in personal growth, they try to reverse the process, looking into their background for attributes to bring forward and accentuate. Fear to venture out becomes identity crisis, which becomes false pride and a border *not* to be crossed. Preoccupied with reflecting an aggregate of meaningless ethnic inertia, "fitting in" to them would mean surrendering a crutch, *not* a surrender of convictions. While many minorities fail to dissolve inessential differences in the melting pot of integration, America's key racial issue has always been between white and black.

Most people imagine African life as television has portrayed it—as a primitive people with no technology, practicing religious rituals even more senseless and irresponsible than ours. They believe blacks were simply taken from places where they ran mindlessly through the jungle, but the truth is their homes were settlements not much different from the American colonies at the time. All civilizations have unique rituals, but most of their time was spent in essence, as ours is now: working for the common maintenance of life. Their villages were ransacked as by any conquering army, and their people were taken. Imagine that happening to us today by another nation, or to individuals who are abducted—their very lives stolen—as we hear about now and then, a nightmare for anyone.

Slavery was brought to the New World in the 1600's, spreading from the Caribbean colonies of European States and South America, but it was a part of human history from the beginning. America *inherited* slavery—it didn't create it. From the start, slavery was acknowledged as a blatant violation of her true principles. The Founding Fathers had a choice: accepting slavery in the southern States and facing Britain together, or dropping the idea of a unified country. The South refused to ratify the Constitution otherwise. The founders did it right; they allowed America to develop its own sovereign inertia before abolishing key impurities with time and pressure. Blacks weren't alone however; there were white Irish slaves as well in New England, and the policy of indentured servants continued; even Abraham Lincoln's ancestors were white slaves. No one rational is proud of slavery. The honorable men of that time did the best they could.

Ultimately, the unsound economic policies of The South put the whole country in jeopardy, allowing European financial interests to prey on their foolishness, intending to split the nation and give the halves back to England and France, which spurred the American Civil War and an end to slavery. Since then, integration has been difficult. When a violation is defined by race, there will be guilt by association. It's like expecting the criminal and victim to live together without malice. In Ancient Egypt, the slaves left. America chose the hardest way—learning to trust one another. It was the right thing to do.

After a war, there is a period of reconstruction and healing. What about spiritual reconstruction? How does a race recover from a mortally wounded pride? The pride and stature of a people is an ongoing phenomenon, a cultural and transitional inertia throughout history, with societies rising and falling at different times, unfortunately making the same mistakes over and over, such as Germany. As Ancient Egypt was winding down, Rome was evolving. As the Romans wound down, the Nordics were coming into their own, each developing in time from the equatorial origin of Man to his expansion northward. Each expanded their domains by conquest and bloodshed, stabilizing their reign with lessons learned from those earlier. Finally a Melting Pot formed on a new continent, with laws designed to assure the safety of individuals of *any* ethnic background. Barbarian conquest was ended at one level, and a true civilization was born. It's obvious that African natives never should have been left out. Feeling down and out as a race or a gender, it is difficult to accept having fallen, but it becomes irrelevant when you realize that historically for one, it's temporary, and two, the slate is clean for something new. Other than Hollywood's depiction, what past greatness do blacks have to reflect on and recover to?

The known origin of life for Man is Africa, and from Africa, came the first great civilization. Ancient Egypt excelled in mathematics, astronomy, language and civil structure, contributing to the vast potential of human cognition and laying the foundation for future societies. They proved that men are fully capable of controlling all they undertake with astonishing outcomes, and showed the world the power of the human mind. We still stand in awe of all they accomplished. Most aren't aware that the Ancient Egyptians, with their incredible wealth and glamour, were a black race, as so many historical referents verify—Aristotle for one. I think it would be extremely cool to descend from them. In defining ourselves, should we be limited by nation, race or family? Being of German-English descent, should I consider Churchill or Hitler as my ancestor? Can we choose the best of our past, or must we dwell on the worst? Must we choose from prior patterns and occupations, or can we drop them and cut our own path? Is our self-image and lifestyle determined by us, or by others?

Romantic history is what you make of it; in this regard, *imagination* reigns; not fact alone. Our link to historical pride is in the traits we honor and wish to practice. Every race has greatness in its past, which is now ours to match. Who from the past reflects your views? *Spiritual* lineage is infinitely more significant than physical; we can all project ourselves alongside our heroes and strive to deserve their stature. We are most intimately, descendants of those we admire.

RACIAL EPISTEMOLOGY

Race is a valid scientific sub-classification of species—recording point of origin, climactic influence, differing attributes, strengths and vulnerabilities. People can be divided any number of ways—nations, races, families, genders—but the division stops at individuals. The cognitive process of men and women of all races is obviously identical, and its disciplined adherence is the moral measure of all. As the process is alike, individual and social behavior is *equally prone to error* as well, often in the direction of peer or cultural sentiment. When physical or spiritual rewards are sought—personally or collectively—due to ancestry, the action is racist. When physical or spiritual penalties are inflicted—personally or collectively—due to ancestry, the action is racist. There are no minority rights versus majority rights to balance out, for the purpose of equality. There is no set of rules for one race different from another, but only rights addressing the metaphysical nature of Man *qua Man. Political* equality amounts to equal protection before the law for *individuals* as the smallest minority, and that is where equality for human beings *ends*. No Self-made Man wants to be just like everyone else. His stature is earned—the product of his own fire.

Racism is fundamentally a mask for self-hatred for the 1-2 level Fear-driven of any race. The state of the world and the state of their lives are always someone else's fault, and another race is a convenient target. To judge an individual or a group as evil *or good* by inessential traits is to run the epistemological tree improperly. They violate the structure of logic to negate the very basis of morality: choice. Who would use mismatched bits of truth to arrive at unwarranted assumptions? Spirit Murderers. They categorize people and moral action by inessential divisions and leave information out—they have to. A key result of cognition is classification itself, which is what they refuse to exercise honestly; it would lead to revelations they cannot afford to contemplate. The fear and condemnation of outsiders is just an extension of the fear and condemnation of thought. Interaction *follows* cognition. If thought is faulty, whatever is built upon it will be dysfunctional and unpleasant. Prejudice is important to be aware of, as the morons of any race are always a danger. Black or white, we are better off to know who is a bigot and who isn't; it indicates their likely neurotic limitations and general unreliability in other realms.

Who among any past society was responsible for a civilization's achievements, and who was responsible for their atrocities? Can a logical division be made? Enslavement is a secret dream for the Spirit Murderers of *any* race. They will always seek to expropriate every physical and spiritual value they can identify. It isn't a majority inclination, but an individually based, fear-driven power lust. It has many forms and many agents, but always the same result. It leads to the spirit and physical murder of both; the conquered are demeaned and destroyed, while the conqueror incites tyranny and in time, destroys his own society. In all contexts, it destroys not only the value sought, but the true means to achieve it as well. He destroys his own pattern to pride by reducing men to predator/prey, and in the dominant position, he is the more contemptible. More often, the entire population of a country is enslaved by its leaders through their altruistic generosity of "redistributing" the energy of the healthy. In time, the country succumbs to the axiomatic vulnerability that infirmity worship causes: internal corruption.

Blacks and Jews have borne the most recent historical persecution, but history could exonerate the white race if the next step were recognized: that the Jews who built the pyramids were in fact, enslaved by the black race. As usual, the Pharaohs—the Fear-driven political leaders of that time—took credit for the pinnacle Self-made accomplishments in all fields, while preying on the conquered Hebrew masses. Their worst enslaved a people, while their best created that civilization's marvels. In American history, our worst enslaved a people, while our Self-made created *this* civilization's marvels. With that clarified, we are *all* free to choose which side we will join.

There is no guarantee that we will agree with the actions of others in any division we belong to. There is no guarantee that we will not be swept into some insanity that has targeted one of our divisions. All we can control and all that really matters, is the one indivisible entity: ourselves. We must remain a point of unswerving objectivity, running the process of cognition properly if we intend to preserve a shred of sanity. Otherwise, those irrationally subdividing will separate effort from reward, action from responsibility and human beings from their lives, to reach their ideal society where anything goes—anarchy. The ultimate purpose of civilization is *privacy*—the protection of our own person and personal property—so that an individual can break away from any mob and jet along his own path, without risk of destruction. Until men understand that any action taken by anyone has everything to do with their essential cognitive responsibility and nothing to do with their nonessential attributes such as race or gender, this risk will remain.

FAMILY PATTERNS

Some families pass down great charisma, showing stability without concern for outside judgment, while others pass down dysfunction and addiction. Instead of instilling dreams and the possibilities offered by freedom, most pass down their hate. In today's world, this is where you will find racism—in housewives and grandparents—in those outside the productive loop.

In 1865, there were 4.5 million blacks in America. Given that 200,000 served in the Civil War, war effort versus population statistics indicate that 3 million lived free in the north. That leaves 1.5 million living under southern domination at the time. Currently, America has 36 million black residents.

Slavery was a malady of only *four percent* of the current black population, yet is a historic blight passed down by their majority today. The percentage of whites actually taking offensive action against them may be .01%, yet holding the past in front of them, the percentage they are conditioned to blame is 100%.

Physical handicaps are bad enough, but most are cultural—some forced on us by enemies, but most by those claiming to be on our side. Conditioned handicaps are most often *familial,* who in essence convey to us "You can't because *they* won't let you, *as they wouldn't let me.* It's not your fault or mine, we must stick together. You realize you can't win, right?" They conspicuously ignore the black entrepreneur magazines, evidence that others of the same race can and are doing well. There is a payoff in persecution; with no chance to rise, there is no *pressure* to rise, and *that* is the true guilt they wish to shed. Their form of denial intends to shield them from seeing that *they* are the failure, not their race. Fear-driven blacks treat their best like outsiders. They don't stand behind them, but alienate them as traitors. If they speak clearly, if they are industrious and organized, they are ridiculed as "trying to be white." Criticizing individual success itself as a white conformist compromise, they support instead those causing upheaval and violating the civil flow of human action; not to foster peace, but to prevent it. They call their enemy "The Man" meaning the white man, a simple classification by color—not even smart enough to identify him as the *subversive* white man. They convey that coherence, self-responsibility and success are *white* traits, or in essence, that *life* as a pursuit, is a *white* pursuit. They've equated color with America and made themselves the outsiders. This can only amount to one peril: a Spirit Murdering internal race war.

They fell for a *moral* division based on inessentials—a hierarchy of race, which doesn't exist—instead of ignoring it and working towards integration. That bred distance, and forced them into the supremacy mindset. It moves the fight to lie inside those who accept it—just as the Spirit Murderer's wanted. Buying into such sociological poison as "Folklore is at the heart of self-expression and therefore at the heart of self-acceptance" (Alice Walker), something an individual can do nothing about, the Spirit Murderers can say, "There, we have him looping. He'll burn *himself* out now." He is then damned to become a Spirit Murderer as well.

The solution is to drop ancestral anchors and live your own life. Take animals for instance, they don't hand down all the bad things that happened to them. Cows never see it coming. Historical knowledge is appropriate in a political context—not in paranoia. Don't burden the future generations with patterns of seasoned, impotent malice; don't limit them to the fate of the racially handicapped. *Design* the life-pattern you will pass down. By keeping hate in front of them, by revisiting the horrors and giving them an out, pretty soon they will accept it. The pattern is the same for success: by keeping dreams in front of them, by revisiting the elation and giving them hope, pretty soon they will reach them. Feed your dreams and they grow beyond your wildest imagination. Feed your pain and it grows too. Focus on the values or on the obstacles: the choice is yours.

INTEGRATION

Racial pressure for those ingrained with a bias is like having to go to the dentist every day. The ratio of black to white in America is approximately six to one. As blacks encounter whites more often, they are going to be more used to it. This can result in two behavioral directions depending on their psychological bias: feeling consistently harassed, or having a controlled, predictable expectation in the encounter.

Harassment is felt only when one is not in control of one's life. I never realized blacks felt afraid of whites; I thought we were afraid. Seems stupid to think that after slavery, but actually, there is nothing historic about it. It is an issue of interaction between individuals—nothing more. I recall imagining the notion that blacks all knew each other, preferred each other and would conspire against me. Maybe in their youth as well, blacks imagined whites all knew each other, preferred each other and would conspire against them. It is clear now that this is numerically and now organizationally impossible. All humans walk through the world essentially alone. They have the capacity to interact constructively with a few individuals per day—a very small number really. There might be fifteen people in his work environment whose names he can readily remember. Outside of that, the rest he encounters of his or any other color, often remain strangers.

We all read attraction and danger signals alike: there is much more we convey physically, than just our color. In initial encounters, I've witnessed such a malicious hatred toward whites, I thought it would become audible. Intelligent people can tell the difference between the surface discomfort of another and irrational resistance. If the barrier cannot be overcome with sincerity and warmth, they automatically move on to better people. Everyone should understand that as an axiom, *insincerity is based on fear,* whereas discomfort is simply due to inexperience. Projecting a prejudiced, predefined betrayal is a sure way to kill any positive connection with others. Probe into such a person's cognition and it amounts to "Everything should be automatic. Everyone should like me, no matter how I act. In a perfect world, I shouldn't have to earn anything. It should be given to me, as it is given to whites. Life should be easy for me, as it's easy for whites." (Whites aren't given anything. Life isn't any easier for us. We all work to survive, we all struggle for happiness. Put in the same numbers perspective, there are five others that look just like us, so favoritism by race is impossible). Looking further will reveal no mature, organized approach and no tenacious action—just skirt-tugging fear, laziness and hate. Paralyzed by fear, their energy ferments and becomes bitterness. No matter their excuses, they are simply the Fear-driven, running patterns of their own Spirit Murder.

In the melting pot, Self-made Man doesn't view racial limitations as a reflection of himself. He considers it a detail—a temporary irrational advantage or impediment—not the deciding factor of his life and future. The deciding factors of his life are within him, never relinquished—never outside. He knows that for every three that say no, one will say yes, and he plays the numbers. Only a handful of times in life will others take specific actions against him. He leaves the fight outside where it belongs, and continues to pursue his own wealth and happiness, and he achieves it. In philosophical essence and of any color, *he is* the Self-Made, confident and in control of himself, running the patterns of living fulfillment.

Given the complexity of social integration, it is never going to be perfect. People are always uncomfortable with different people. Those unused to the experience are on uncertain ground, and will be unsettled. Individual experiences must be managed by the discipline of those involved—otherwise, expecting automatic preference is an attempt at mind control—another Fear-driven dream. On a trip to Germany, I was out of place; they knew I was different, and treated me differently. They didn't owe me anything for my discomfort; *they* were uncomfortable too. I faced the same foreign sense returning home, in that the native Detroiters were different to those to whom I had grown accustomed. It is our own discipline that must answer this dilemma, with courage, grace and eventually, invigorating cordiality. The more integrated we are, the more comfortable we are, and the more we realize we are all essentially alike: just people, each a unique individual with a limited group of friends, each the center of our own universe.

AMERICA

Many minorities born here are raised to believe that America is a system set up against them, though foreign born minorities brought up under truly oppressive political systems know otherwise. America wasn't set up *for* white men, though it was set up *by* white men. There is no white power conspiracy in existence today beyond the insignificant and powerless fanaticism of 1-2 level Spirit Murderers to whom all outsiders are the enemy, and from which everyone has legal protection.

For Americans, our flag is a symbol of pride. Our country dominates in most realms because we are free to make things, free to air them, free to sell them and free to keep them. We have so great a productive inertia that our wealth permits a strong defense in our desire to preserve it. As a society, we have the lowest level of corruption in the history of Man; but to some, the American flag is considered a facade for corruption. For a communist nation, their flag represents the gang of the moment—confused ideas they don't agree with and protection for those holding them hostage. I was astonished to discover that many blacks of our own country are raised to believe that our flag represents the same evil.

During this research, I anticipated encountering the same purity of injured innocence seen in European literature before their voyage to the New World. Unfortunately I found a serious subjectivity in black leadership and their current view overall is no more objective. They consider the only things right about their current economic condition to be the freebies—freebies *involuntarily* paid for by someone—a direct contradiction with freedom. I expected to find calm, wise sensibility, but found their leaders instead to have a politically naïve, pre-Cold War Marxist something-for-nothing bias, with eyes shut to the consequences—drastically immature. History has taught them nothing. Like any politician, they claim responsibility for a founding share of America's virtues with no hand in her vices, as does the rest. Often, they just want to see whites "get ours," while they unwittingly support the dogmas responsible for their own enslavement. They feel their people struggle on the bottom, but with a Marxist doctrine, they will stay there. They seem to believe being free means life is supposed to cost nothing, so in effect, our brand of freedom is a lie. Communism claims to offer that free life, naturally bankrupting every country to embrace it as it devours itself in ruins and slaughter. Nevertheless, they align themselves with Communism, along with the poorest and most hostile countries (there's a clue), under America's equivalent, the Democratic Party. They encourage contempt for the country—not its fortification and the creative development that *is* possible to their people and all people. Their actions reveal no deeper a motivation than to get elected, and attempt popularity by preying on the hostilities of the greatest number, as Hitler did. Teaching the patterns of our country's demise and their own to follow, they are more interested in fueling their own hate than conquering the false premises that bar them—within the country and within themselves. They fail with good reason, as historical reflection undermines the hostile nature of their fame.

The political Spirit Murderers destroyed the economies of Ancient Egypt, of Rome and of The South, all based on the same premise: something for nothing; yet still, most democratic and black leaders ask us to repeat that tragedy. I've heard them claim that having to work for one's sustenance is a white economic trap, and then propose solutions already disproven time and time again throughout history. They seem to long for their perfect world where everything is free as they imagine it used to be, but that past world isn't Africa. In Africa or any less free nation, they would spend *more* of their time on basic sustenance, not less. Dissatisfied with politicians and searching deeper, I found rationality where it is usually found—glistening in the constructive, non-hysterical Self-made of their own race—private enterprise. The most responsible always have some personal achievement attached to their names—not just fanatical rambling.

Despite her flaws, America is the most sincere nation on the planet. Our Fathers acted in a way unprecedented in human history—not taking advantage of the populace just because it was possible, but through the Bill of Rights, showing respect for the use of human energy, with awareness of what it could mean for mankind—a more perfect union of individuals. Our country may violate its own premises in many ways, but we have the most solid foundation to work with on Earth; there is no reason to give it up. Past atrocities were never sanctioned by the majority anyway; it simply took time to reach the necessary level of mass intolerance to do something about it—the point to where it affected everyone—and they fought a war to change the system, not just for you, but for themselves. Don't step away, step inside; the Founding Fathers are yours too, and in the case of Thomas Jefferson, that could be a literal truth.

As long as blacks consider it America vs. blacks, as long as black familial sentiment fuels white vs. black, nothing is going to change. The essential division of Man is *cognitive:* Self-made vs. Spirit Murderer, period. An individual is either objective, or he goes *nowhere;* it's the same with a country. Every man can make his home better by creating a better life for himself, structuring a step by step, goal by goal life plan and making it happen. He must understand and acquire a political premise proven to be successful—that of hands off, voluntary commerce: Capitalism. Stand behind a winner; stand behind America. Blacks in the 1800's were an unfortunate victim of history, but moving forward, out of all the nations of the world, America has it right. Look at our Bill of Rights. Compare it to the rest of the world and look at the results. Of all men by law, Americans have the greatest opportunities in life.

From the black dominance of Ancient Egypt to the Chosen Bankers of Israel to the pursuit of Nordic supremacy, the fight for racial superiority has been spiritually crippling for anyone wasting their time in its attempt, as well as those within range of their malice. It's demeaning and untrue, but worse still, is seeing such irrationality actually have its way. The fact is, we all encounter and have to deal with different levels of intellect acting on life or death motives; that is the cross-section of society.

The answer is no longer forgiveness; the answer is objectivity. Forgiveness was earned with a break in the immoral pattern—the granting of just freedom. There is no one left alive from that period to forgive. All those born under freedom whose great-grandparents were not, deserve a one-time allotment of...nothing, just as the rest of us are entitled to. There are no victims in retrospect. Honest men don't ask for subsidies and sound policies don't grant them. Whatever you want, you are free to produce it. You'll have to grow strong enough to struggle through the plethora of unbelievable morons as the rest of us do. Don't expect anyone to cut you a path. All civil men need is a community where we can move and act without being harmed—that *is* America. America is not a place where your dreams will be reached *for* you, but where you are free to make the attempt, which is all a civil human being has the right to demand. The Chosen People who carry the world forward are not a specific race, but only the productive and rational—the Self-made.

There are plenty of cool black people and plenty of cool white people. There are many losers of both as well. None of the whiners on either side are cool. No incoherent, lazy, fear-ridden moral impostors ever are. The negative stereotypes on both sides will always disappoint those with more productive traits, so we all must grow beyond them. How you ever been in a job interview where the manager looks at you in wonder and leans over to ask a coworker, "What *is* that thing?" No? Seriously, if your mind is on a racial clash, odds are good that the adversary you've just created is aware that your primary interest is not personal productivity. If you believe it has the power to stop you, it will.

No one appreciates being burdened with another's senseless emotional power struggle. Often, the accusation of racism is a mask for cowardice, in words that would be "I'm afraid in this context of life and I don't know what to do." As most do when they're afraid, they follow the pattern of submission, but often, there is no one to submit to, and they're left lost. The proper pattern is to pursue the knowledge they are missing; to break with the Submission/Domination Axis and become independent. One company addresses just about every growth issue an adult faces—Nightingale-Conant Corporation (call 1-800-525-9000 for a catalog). Once you're firmly in the saddle in life, that fact will be conveyed just as clearly.

It is no fun to feel like a threatened outsider anywhere, but whether the danger is real or just an inherited Fear-driven cover, it must be overcome independently. That underdog feeling is the same rejection felt by unsuccessful courtship, peer ridicule, college cliques and other exclusionist situations. Rejection is painful, but freedom doesn't mean an automatic sustenance, automatic rewards or that others owe you anything. Every person you meet isn't going to prefer you over all other human beings. Every day isn't going to be the best day of your life. Every girl you ask out isn't going to say yes. Political freedom means that others can't take physical action against you, period. The rest of life is for *you* to finance and build. The truly successful of any race knows this and can relax. Look at how they view racism from the top: it's a non-issue. A 6-8 knows that human stature is determined by cognition alone—including a man's actions, as inaction is a cognitive malfunction. He also knows that fools won't recognize this. He knows that when he faces prejudice from another—of a different or of the same race—that he is dealing with a 1-2 level Spirit Murderer in this context. The better men *know* racism exists at the lower levels of all; they are too wise to waste their own time, energy and emotion—so they disengage them immediately and maintain relationships only with those above. The rest are *looking* for a reason to give up, so they seek out potential racist indications in others to justify their own stagnation. A Fear-driven Man looks to complete the sentence, "I *can't* because..." and lets nothing stand in his way of a semi-plausible, self-convincing excuse. A successful man says "No matter what it takes, in the long run, I'm going to win. *Nothing* is going to stop me."

Race is just one element of who we are, and is meaningless intellectually. Races, like kids, are just *other* people. True identity—our soul and fullest moral potential—is defined by our deepest parallel: our like cognitive power, and our own willingness to exercise it. What are *your* dreams? It's your life. What are you doing to make it better?

Self-Made Man versus The Spirit Murderer

Now let's get to the *real* issue. Why can't we as the Self-made avoid being hated by the Fear-driven? Because no one can hide what they are. What they see to hate is the initial processing of *existential information,* regardless of whether we attempt to appease them. They know that what they said or did was picked up by our perceptiveness—that we *know* and are willing to *see*. We conveyed to them in that moment that we are not fundamentally afraid of *life,* regardless of any other neurotic problems we may have yet to overcome. If a Self-made Man caters to the second-handers in their social void, in trying to fit in, they see him as the most offensive of all posers. He unknowingly mocks them by trying to hide the two values their view of existence makes impossible: power and certainty. Such tribalists recognize an independent man immediately, reserving an insidious hatred for anyone who doesn't practice their all-excusing virtue: the all-accepting, undemanding approximation of existence and consciousness. The process of someone with a fear foundation is immediate deceit—to fake understanding, to parrot principles, to memorize utterance and gesture with the expectation of drawing a favorable response. There is no actual processing of the occasion other than red light, green light— "approval or disapproval from the consciousness before me." They know that *reality is real* for us—that life is real for us—and *that* is what they cannot forgive. The Self-made will always have one or many in a group take a strong, malicious dislike for him without ever speaking a word. His very existence is an affront to them—the upright posture, the steady, scrutinizing gaze, the arrogant smile, the untroubled forehead and youthful vitality—it all adds up to the only passionate response you can expect to see from a Spirit Murderer—the evasion clouded desire to kill.

The Fear-driven enter a trap of their own design, forever unwilling to consider their own actions as the cause of their plight. A futile struggle against existence ensues. Their ideals damn human abilities: the natural requirements of life they have no choice but to practice as well to some degree. Cut off from any fundamental means of self-esteem, they have no choice but to wander in a fog, never identifying what is appropriate for an individual to seek in life, or how. Their own inverted moral culture stops them from the outside, while denial—or the preservation of the indeterminate—stops them from the inside. They seek to cover low self-esteem by accepting no fixed identification of their position, or of the pathways that could lead higher. Without rational standards, purpose can be anything (as planned), which necessitates that any potential happiness *must remain causeless.* The result? A bland, shapeless emotional medium, filled with the torment of personal insignificance. Spirit Murderers are intimidated by a confident means of cognition, that is why the more pure his adversary, the more monstrous we appear. Fearing independence above all, they are drawn into groups by the bond of a common enemy, and are easily steered to do the bidding of the like-minded at any scale left open to them. My proof of their inverted morality is in that their greatest fear is not a murderer, but any man who tells them their course is wrong—any man of clear conscience, rational discipline and youthful vitality—a creature glad to be living. He in their eyes becomes the evil, the man not to be encouraged, the man to be destroyed.

We will conflict with anyone who isn't Self-made to the extent they are not, in any realm of their lives. We've all observed what they're after first hand. Paying close attention is the only way to convince ourselves of the truth behind their motives. Experience has put us before many firing squads, where what men take aim at are all the virtues and values that make life worth living. We must throw lines way out in front of ourselves and be pulled through all kinds of trauma to reach our goals. This is the same line and test they use for their goal of evasion. This is how Fear-driven premises steer a life right into the tank—eyes on failure, doom as inevitable and heart-wrenching malice toward the victories of others. They are committed to rebellion against the concept of *identity* (existence) at all levels—through the destruction of those who represent *identification* (consciousness). By displaying its creative response and reward— relaxed self-confidence, enjoyment, awareness, elegance and poise—we become the targets of evil. We may try to excuse them by claiming "they know not what they do," but one must identify a thing's nature to except or reject it. To say "No!" is to *understand*. They see achievements they did not fight for, and they must take on the task of wiping that knowledge and those beings, out of existence.

Warrior Note: *We must be as ruthless about virtue as they are about evil.*

If the Fear-driven were honest and sought what was best for themselves and for others, there would be no problem, no tension, no tolerance issue between the morally healthy and the sick. Self-made Men are not intolerant with those having the wherewithal to make an honest effort. Spirit Murderers effort instead, to lie. Sane, moral men practice their discipline for physical and emotional rewards: for principles and ideals, all too aware of the trauma they would experience otherwise. The insane endure physical and emotional trauma to avoid this discipline. They are cowards on the most important level, the freedom and preservation of their own spirit. Their spirit is in spirit prison. They hide the key from themselves and claim they don't have it. They poison it, starve it, take jabs at it and do everything in their power to make it miserable, but keep it alive so that it can feel pain. They love to stab ours thru the bars when we let them get close enough, every time we foolishly grant them an undeserved moral pardon. They are Spirit Murderers, torturers of the living, whether they have the capacity to understand and the honesty to admit it to themselves, or not.

Don't look away! Look at them. You can pick up anything and if it is precious to you, they are going to want to take it away; not to enjoy it for themselves, but to take your enjoyment. *Us against them* has always been Fear-driven vs. Anticipation-driven. The greater the offering you show them, the greater they feel is their stature in destroying it. They want our money, our products, our admiration, our love and respect—a false sense of themselves, all unearned. They want to decimate our positive outlook, our confidence which they call arrogance, our productive capacity which they claim is greed, and our romanticism and dreams damned as selfishness and grandiosity. Most of all, they want our certainty. They prey on those whose concepts are unformed, and do all they can to keep their victims unaware and uncertain. They have done this by promoting the incompetence of Man's mind, by perverting the whole intention of morality, and by destroying our ability to fight back. To keep people from knowing, it is the capacity to know that must be destroyed—reason. Guilt is their primary weapon, as it demands atonement. It provides ready stock for the con-man's dream, primed and unpaid for, and works exactly like the "live off the interest" ideal of every hopeful lottery winner. Guilt is our highest interest debt; it can suck the life out of you, as downcast eyes don't scrutinize. They want revenge; not for a moral failure, but for a lack of moral failure—our lack of subservience. The motives accused, are actually the motives of the accusers. No longer will they get away with blaming the victim. There will be no more plea-bargaining our spirits through falsely admitted guilt.

Deep down, the subjectivist believes evil will win, so he joins it; but the evil man lost when he renounced his spirit by giving in to fear, and he can never win as long as he practices that which devours the living. The truth is, Spirit Murderers are powerless; *we* provide the fuel to make their premises work. Don't kid yourself into passivity though, because they'll keep coming. Your rational efficacy in life is matched by their *irrational* efficacy, which they use to take life from us. All Fear-driven intentions harbor this evil. They will always exist, trying to wedge their way into our grace. It takes great power to rise, and like throwing a stone in the air, it takes nothing to fall back—nature does it for them. Fear-driven Men choose to default on their human responsibilities, and then nature reduces them to the least complex entity—mold and decay. Don't allow the entropy within you to aid their game. Remember the Self-made tenet that *all* knowledge is a blessing, and be ready to use it when things are at their worst. Fake nothing for Spirit Murderers, or they will reform the very life out of you.

Spirit murderers attempt a strangle hold on every human value, and no greater hate could be reserved for the person who creates those values— who does his job and lives his life well. Consuming values is all they know and all they wish to know. They want a buffer between themselves and thought, between their actions and their consequences. You *are* that buffer. Respecting no boundaries between men is not an offshoot of brotherly love, but of burglary, whether the victims are willing, or not. Jails take people who cannot coexist civilly, out of circulation. Immoral beings likewise, if only in your personal awareness, must be confined to the contexts where they can do no harm to you and yours. We must fight their resistance to life and living patterns, and we must use our natural tools to do it. We can no longer permit the simple fact of being human, to be damned. To them I say, *"You can learn from us or you can try to kill us, but there is no other course to take. We now have the moral clarity we needed; we have the steady eyes to pin you right to the wall. We know what you're doing. Surrender or die."*

Chapter Ten

Expressions of Contempt

"Don't set out to raze all shrines—you'll frighten men. Enshrine mediocrity—and the shrines are razed." —The Fountainhead

Spirit Murderers can be just as passionate about destroying values as the living generators are about enjoying them. They need the imagery of impotence to confirm their stand, just as the generators need heroism, and they pursue it with equal fervor. Irrationalism in art is evidence of this. History is littered with the distortions of those at odds with existence in every artistic medium, such as film, music, painting, sculpture and literature. Their intent is the degradation and destruction of human potencies and values, by means of cognitive disintegration. They seek to corrupt beauty, purpose and discipline in preference to the repulsive, the aimless and the indefinable. Such artists are made popular by their spiritual equivalents and are tolerated by the rest through moral confusion. Those without progressive intent must conjure a state of semi-consciousness to disguise the nature of their motives. They prey on the fact that we don't know what to make of their work as it repels and undercuts conscious identification, challenging a moral standard that no one is prepared to defend.

It grows worse when they *are* clear in their objective. Over human history, more damage has been done with a pen than any bomb ever detonated (Karl Marx, Immanuel Kant). Being the deepest cognitive link, more is done to kill moral inspirations by the Spirit Murderers of literature than anywhere else. Notice that the title "literature" is given typically to fiction, while nonfiction is considered science, expelling it from the realm of art. The concept of art therefore, implies fantasy and inaccuracy—what is *not* real. Hence, they give us goals outside human reach. They enshrine everything below us. They teach us to sneer at everything, permitting nothing to be serious or sacred—disallowing reverence and any pattern leading to it. They shame all we desire so that wanting becomes an evil, and its sacrifice becomes the means of personal achievement. They prey on our confusion, bending the meaning of cultural inertias as a means to devour our strengths. Through their abstract equivalent of force— subversion—art becomes something other than the expression of the highest and best. It becomes a confused cacophony of mixed elements generally accepted as art, regardless of talent or motive. If they can degrade us in song, they will. If they can degrade us in paint or sculpture, they will. The lack of a clear-cut moral standard *welcomes* this opportunity.

> *"Art is a selective re-creation of reality according to an artist's metaphysical value judgments."* —Ayn Rand

Their Motives. Art is a re-creation of *reality*, meaning its subject must be *intelligible* to be considered art. To prove this, in observing art, the first question posed to our minds is "What is it?" Then we ask of ourselves, "What does it mean?" We notice what skill has gone into the creation, noting the complexity of colors and whether the brush strokes were carefully planned, or if paint was just thrown at the canvass. Can the work stand on its own, providing a complete meaning to contemplate, or does a story have to go along with it as a crutch and an apology (van Gogh)? The cognitive pattern we use in art criticism is reordered as perception, identification, reward and evaluation. Rational art *makes sense*. Irrational art requires that we discard the cognitive pattern as in all spirit murdering endeavors, and melt into the illusion of its value. They expound disorder and chaos in life and thought, confirming the impotence of their every perceptive sense—confirming the fog. The artist shares his own willing dissolution of consciousness by presenting objects as Man does not perceive them: with no moral theme, no lesson and no warning (Cubism and Surrealism). He shares his resulting mental state as well—that of being confused, malicious, bitter and lost. His work often has the same feel of mediocrity we see from the lethargic in all other realms, the shoddy grade school effort of someone who doesn't care about their work. Minimum competencies are fine for regulating the sound flow of society, but they are not to be exalted. If he makes any contribution at all, it is only a new bent on unintelligible distortion.

To the extent that an artist is irrational, his work will reflect the perversion and destruction of living values. With the false premises of Spirit Murder driving his effort, his psychological bias will reveal a great hostility, fear or the deadness of no feeling whatsoever. As he evades the possibility of exceptional men, he exemplifies the commoner (Impressionism). Unable or unwilling to prosper or succeed, he presents life as misery, poverty and submission. With malicious fear towards the beautiful, he mars their glamour and defaces it by subtracting other virtues such as intelligence and integrity, or makes his subjects as indistinguishable as his own comfort requires. Disturbed by integrity, he makes such characters impractical and destined to fail (Existentialism). No one gets away with integrity: as in soap operas, he throws doubt on the motives of every character (Dostoyevski). As any extension necessitates, their art is subject to the same inconstancies *they* are prone to. Paraphrasing Ayn Rand, with no capacity to integrate, they reduce language to grunts, literature to moods, painting to smears, sculpture to slabs and music to noise, giving us an example of what existence is like to someone with an empty skull. They need not understand the highest to trash it. All they need to do is indulge the worst of their premises.

His approach is the opposite of the purist—mastery over social action as central focus. His success pivots on his connections. The more monstrous his work and the more it is accepted, the more he can justify being what he is. He can rate himself on a scale of evil as opposed to a living scale, to exclaim, "See, I'm not *that* bad." Instead of fuel, for the irrational, his art is the permission to stand still and do nothing—an extension of his own evasion. What he accepts *as* art conveys to him that values are unattainable, resistance is futile, fear, guilt, pain and failure *are* mankind's pre-destined end and he is not to blame. His passively uncommitted sense of life communicates one key attribute to his audience: impotence. It is the mindset of the Spirit Murderer attempting to gel into life-like potency, but only able to achieve and reveal triumphant malice, hatred for existence, vengeance against life and its best, the defeat of human values and the reassuring illusion that evil has real power.

The cultural barometer of who is winning the fight for the soul is shown through the acceptance of art. The Self-made intention is to expose men to the possibility of reaching the heroism portrayed in Greek art. What the disintegrators intend you to become, is a useless, shapeless blob. For a Spirit Murderer, art is a tribute to parasitism, dysfunction and death—a socially driven desire to mar the stature and creations of others. As artists, they attempt to convey that men are ridiculous, and judging by their own lives, they have good reason to think it.

Art is not intended for pointless contemplation. It is not a product of indifference as the non-passionate, take it or leave it endeavors which the Spirit Murderers stir about in, called pass-times. The value of *all* art is found in one reflective question: "How does this make me feel about life?"

Man's Response. A rational observer finds challenge and reward in his preferred style of art; it is a meaningful form of rest and reward. He will be hostile to a poor or jumbled artistic effort. Dislike for art does not negate its esthetic merit, however (Rembrandt, Picasso). Partial integration is a common result of an inconsistent moral code. The irrational artist will choose some disastrous mix as his subject, sometimes applying a fantastic ability to a pointless or evil notion. Imagine the painting of a grand ball room, colorful flowers and a dynamic couple dancing romantically at its center. Make them both fat, and it just kills the beauty of the concept.

The lost, the limited and the impotent are drawn to entertainment that confirms that state. As projection is an act of abstraction and their capacity to deal with the unknown is what they fear, they will not respond well to compositions that convey anything too specific to them; it isn't safe. For instance, primitive music justifies the dissolution of self and of consciousness. It reassures fans that their stupor is appropriate. To the Self-made, music conveys our passion for life, and a powerful resonance brings order to our energy. To the Fear-driven, it conveys dysfunctional dominance—a power and a backbone they don't have. Ours is a setting, while theirs is the substance—the purpose itself.

Stunted Development. If you don't advance in your work, your musical tastes and artistic interests won't advance either. There is nothing deeper you will need to confirm, convey or require an outlet for. A testament to this is the dilemma rock groups suffer; if they want to advance, they often lose their following, as many of their fans are stuck. That or they cater to the high school crowd well into their thirties and beyond, instead of maturing along with their original fan base. Either way, a shallow premise was in style which served to spread their popularity, which is then lost with the change in trend. They are outlived by musicians who reach something much deeper in Man—compositions that require greater discipline and knowledge to create. Look at our female teen artists; they begin their careers with lyrics about flirting, friends and games. Then their lyrics reflect the approach and trials of womanhood, then of prostitution (just kidding). As their range of experience grows, their emotional range deepens and so follows their expression. Some evolve as the trends change; they master the surf and ride it expertly. The rest just get more dysfunctional.

The inertia of our own premises determines our response to all forms of music. For one, most jazz makes no sense to me; its joy seems pointless and I find it miserable to listen to. Discovering Beethoven, I responded with "*Oh*, this is my soul...in music." Listening to Jimmy Buffett, my mind said, "I haven't given up; I don't feel this," and I couldn't tolerate it. *Rap* is all right for teens with parental issues, but beyond that any serious interest is degenerative. As an extension of nursery rhymes, rap extols no exalted emotions; it is pure pretense. It must be difficult for rap stars over twenty to stick with the senseless vulgarity and all of its dead end subject matter, just to keep their audience. Some show tremendous musical talent, but as of yet, little maturity to develop it into a more stable form and following. *Heavy metal* brings a brutal, military approach to harmony, often with an angry, pointed flow. It can be driven by intelligence and therefore be useful, or by hate and be a complete waste of time. As one acquires the maturity of rational living action and a parallel respect for others, as with rap, its premises are all but dropped, but we can hang onto its energy.

The power of some *techno-music* is astounding. It is like the beat of a heart: the beat of life. House music is pre-conceptual—even pre-perceptual. It emulates the automatic functions of the body that do not require cognition, therefore falling outside the actual definition of music—but it is not without value. The petty strain that had gradually accumulated in my life-medium over the years was wiped out in a few hours at such a club, leaving an unusual calm as the only evidence of its existence. There was no stress or doubt left—it literally pounded it out of me. I can't sanction the lifestyle of those who live for such places (if you added up the self-esteem in the club, you almost could've made a whole person), but I cannot deny that with such a grounding, I was able to appreciate all that is beyond it much more thoroughly. Of course, die-hard clubbers can't recognize anything beyond it.

No music is essentially harmful, unless maybe you throw the CD at someone. It is not an educational tool, nor does art cover enough ground to be an accurate moral gage. But if it has a scale of evil, Jimmy Buffett's lyrical contribution is as destructive as any heavy metal group or rapper sanctioning aggression. Why? What is worse, committing a crime or providing an ideology that is indifferent to morality? He sings that it's okay to give up, to go nowhere in life, to be passionless, helpless and worthless, *in your own eyes*. Just have a good time (how?), blank out your mind and waste away. Yet other than setting a bad example, such is only a confirmation of impotence, and therefore poses no real threat to anyone. The Self-made have too clear a purpose to be derailed by life-defying pretenses. Intelligent people don't spend their weekends recovering from hangovers *or* gunshot wounds.

Ultimately, we like what we like and that isn't wrong, but it does indicate where we are cognitively, and the question to ask is *why* we like it and where our preference is leading us. Is it constructive or not?

The typical reaction to the presentation of shocking trash, glamorized indigence and flaky simplicity has been moral confusion—not knowing what to think as a consequence of not knowing *how*. If we enshrine men of vision, grace, beauty and their expressions, then mankind has a standard to live up to. If we enshrine so-called "art," such as feces on a statue of the Virgin Mary, then men won't. It isn't art just because it's in a frame. It isn't literature just because it was published. The sound of a jackhammer is not a definition of music. Professional art doesn't involve basketballs, ribbons, papier-mâché or glue. If it looks like something that will be thrown out after the show, you know what to think of it. If it's not art, it's garbage. When they blow their nose and put a frame around it, they just want to see how far they can push indignation—to see others cringe, as they do while looking in the mirror. If there was a backlash, such "artists" wouldn't fight. They'd collapse at the first sign of resistance, because their quest is a bluff. Public acceptance of personal misery is not worth fighting for.

People reaffirm their view of man and existence in their every conveyance: work, conversation, sex, politics, art, entertainment, you name it. In their every action, they show you what they respect, and therefore what to expect of them in that context. For life-haters, destruction *is* their expression of love. They use their creativity—their same life giving power as ours—to advance the destruction of any value they encounter, considering it a threat to their malevolent view of life and of Man. Granting them significance can only exacerbate human development. There is no need to fret over the crude nonsense that is popular with fools—it is not a stamp on the fate *or* the stature of mankind. With art being the voice of philosophy for any era, some critics point to its degradation in fear of what is to come. Let me just say, a society that propels a romantic masterpiece like James Cameron's *Titanic* into one of the biggest box office smashes of all time, is *not* doomed.

Infamy

"One doesn't love God and sacrilege impartially. Except when one doesn't know that sacrilege has been committed. Because one doesn't know God."
—The Fountainhead

How often have you idolized a particular star or businessman, only to find out that they suffer from a vice you thought was well below their stature, interest or capacity to resist? Perhaps they reveal that they were dope fiends or were addicted to pornography, cross-dressing or shoplifting. Maybe they suffer from alcoholism, indulge weird phobias or mindless religions—unable to find constructive use for their time off. Then as icing they make a beeline for non-identity, saying "I'm so insignificant" next to this or that. Their pride in shirking the virtue of their own achievement is so sickeningly predictable. It reveals submission to a false moral standard—hence blind follower, or the incapacity to function within their own public regard. What does this kind of disappointment mean? As an icon, they show us what to look forward to. No one looks forward to insignificance or dysfunction—they dash more than just their own dreams. Whether theirs is the immoral pursuit of anti-stature or just plain incompetence, we're better off to take their word for it and find another role model.

We witness others rejecting their own heroism all the time on television. Someone does something great, and one thing their code has disallowed them is pride, so their honor becomes rejecting it. We all feel a brief stab of discomfort when we see someone do that; we can sense its foolishness. We know it is an unnatural act. Starving a spirit is as detrimental as starving a body, yet it is practically an institution. Pride is an axiomatic necessity: its need for a human being is inescapable, yet very little genuine pride is culturally tolerated. Disavowal has been encouraged all along, using repression as if it were an act of pride and strength, and now full paths of self-degradation have been cut. Hell, it's a superhighway. Can you see the joke? They are *still* seeking pride, only by "lead the poodle" means. It's time to catch up with our own highways to self-appreciation, in one extinction-level event.

The Corporate Wringer. In anticipation of a new career, I imagined publishing to be a field of heroes—the realm of ideas—and was I ever wrong. Instead, I see the same error as in all other fields—the clockwork accumulation of capital as central focus, furthering only those who fit the "formula" —unimaginative and without passion, and they wonder why they feel so little in coming to work every morning. Publishing houses and record companies are often founded by someone of vision and talent, but with their retirement, circum to mediocrity.

As the hallmark of non-thought, corporate junkies put faith in a sure thing only. They ride waves created by individual talents, stealing their patterns to develop their string of cookie-cutter corporate stars. They follow a 'go with the stream' and 'don't rock the boat' philosophy that drowns the public in 'me-too' look-alikes, whose style eventually languishes in a mediocrity similar to their own cognitive default. They dismiss talent without investigating an ounce of its depth, but when they do say yes, they force our work into tight timelines and budgets, often making it a rushed product of hostility—not of paced, thoughtful creation. To media executives, it's just a business. They're not interested in art, but more often than not in monopolizing, cornering and barring our way, to force us through their medium. Control of art belongs solely in the hands of the artist, who should be as good at conducting business as he is at his passion. Hint: If you are truly devoted, learning the business side will be easy compared to your medium.

We can't stand before the media executives to *let them* decide whether or not we're photogenic enough to live. Our success isn't up to them. Only the artist *mortally* believes in the value of his effort; only *he* is willing to go without meals to see it through no matter the cost; no matter the time necessary. Thank goodness for the internet and computer technology as we can now circumvent their whole bureaucracy. Helping new talent is wonderful, but if you're a sure thing, you don't need them. By all means use them if a deal makes sense, but remember, the vision is yours and so should be full artistic control, and the bulk of the reward.

The Pinnacle Pose. Fame can come for any reason, just or not, rational or not. It can even be purchased. Among fame's false creation, they copy, shock, steal, even kill; anything to make the news—anything to get attention. The easiest way to become famous is to attack those who are, by violence or scandal. You can work for years to become a rock star, or you can kill one. For the most psychotic of Spirit Murderers, incarceration or death is preferable to anonymity. Assassination for fame is evidence of the most completely controlled social mindset—a spiritual void drawing such a vacuum that no one is safe around them. Their highest value and their very identity is to be known by others, period. It is a higher value than their own freedom, than their own civility and even their own lives.

Down from psychosis to simple neurosis, stealing, copying or riding is next. They write about popular topics without having anything new to say. Any writer looking to pander to your beliefs without challenging you to think is wasting your time. As writers are the foundation of all scripts, this is true for movies as well. Action is just a detail, but it often substitutes for the plot. When so, it's paper-thin and painfully predictable. Implications are rarely passed between actors anymore—just straight dialog. Anything clever nowadays comes in the form of offensive one-liners—a clearly negative bias. Often, drama is introduced through a moral observation that shouldn't shock anyone over eighteen. They sell graphics, beauty and non-stop action: their success banks on advertising rather than quality; on the hype of the product, not the product itself. As in music, they have their own formula: brilliant lights and gorgeous dancers, wild sets and flashy outfits. Barely anyone notices the band after that; anyone could be on stage and it would be considered a great concert. They approach their work not with the question "What do I want to convey to the world?", but "Where is the bandwagon?" Selling empty promises to empty heads, they all earn the name "hack."

As fame is not a fundamental attribute of Man, but a level 4 result of level 3 actions, it is not to be leaned on as a source of self-worth. For the Fear-driven, recognition is not only leaned on, but the meaning of life itself, which with fame, only gets worse. All the weight of their self-worth is shifted to their popularity. They have no identity alone; their pretense means nothing in a mirror. Fear of lost hype drives them to be unusually outlandish, but only deep actions cause lasting interest, while shallow actions draw shallow and temporary gains. Masked as daring, it's actually desperation, and it serves, not to spur deep interest, but to dry and crack their faltering self-image.

Another sign is how they treat money, and how they enjoy leisure. Notice the gaudy malice of wealth blatantly exposed—such as a diamond flashed, but not to be forgotten—or huge gold chains, dangling in their contempt for effort, the fact that no honest effort was expended. Seeking spiritual domination and esteem, they practice the ""I have it and you don't" level 2 motivation of the trailer elite. Posers don't have any deep spiritual values—therefore they don't have any deep spiritual aims. Their interests lie in surface pleasures and cognitive avoidance—sensations such as sex without values, partying which equals the obliteration of consciousness, and money gained without effort—disregarding consideration for cause or consequence. Vacant of any deeper means to conjure feelings of exaltation, his work and pleasure revolves around the greatest number of nerve endings: his groin.

Their entourage is often imposing and unnecessarily violent—permitted the same impertinence as those they guard. Emulating royalty, they clog up the works instead of showing respect for others. Whether it's a commotion they cause intentionally, then to remark "What are *you* looking at?" or a cop who leaves his car blocking a lane when he pulls someone over, it's the same miserable poser fantasy—to impose themselves, leaving others no choice but to acknowledge them. They try to prop up their self-image by making an illogical impact, painfully to be borne, by being involuntarily dominant—the forced center of attention. Such actions and all the fights you hear rap stars getting into are the manifestations of a *social ego.*

Once they've made it, they vent filthy, disgusting habits as if demanding they be equated with success, flaunting their affront to elegance, class and tact. They flip off the cameras and their fans, make threats and play to being "hip" which to them means either not to care about anything, or to be deviant as a standard—but not to identify against what. Remarkably, they have the straightforward, honorable media trying to catch up. The gutter-famous are now as low as they can go, masquerading as self-declared pimps, thugs and whores. The trend has always been down, and it amounts to exactly what it has in the past: nothing. Is there any depravity left to exploit? How should society respond to their arm-flailing, threatening, stature-quest; with fear? Right, give me a break. It's ok to be cool, but not that cool.

It takes a specific kind of person to go searching through sewers for an idol. The crass ignorance of mongrel expression will exist as long as it exists in society to cater to. As long as a guy with a mop has a few extra bucks in his pocket, his spokesman is going to reign, but they don't belong on the Grammy's. What happened to the days when people wouldn't be let near a microphone without grace and some kind of an education? Those of unkempt appearance are now spreading the cancer of their unkempt consciousness. We permit a mix of sweat pants and evening gowns, tank tops and tuxedos—what a disaster. Now everyone closes their eyes and endures the permeation, as the events, their hosts and their executives continue to lose stature and credibility. Wipe your feet on the way out.

There is much more money in the world than there is talent. There is more beauty in the world than there is integrity. The rest are posers, trying to mimic a mindset they don't understand.

The Fear-driven Pattern of Fame. When we reach the zenith of our fame, we're not taught to recognize it as a peak—it *must* be a plateau. We hear we're on top and then that we're slipping, as if anyone in history has ever stayed on the forefront of the consciousness of others. We cannot be ousted; we cannot permit another to be recognized, to match us or to be preferred. They have us measuring our primary worth relative to *others*, subordinating our internal frame, and all it produces is misery and angst—a common response to something self-important, yet outside our control. Fame may wane, but our personal value doesn't have to. It continues to grow at our own pace. We all reach heights of attractiveness and success, coupled with emotional heights we don't wish to part with, but there is no need to buy into the Fear-driven static dream. Look back at the mountains and enjoy the view of what you have achieved.

At any misstep, it's always the end of us as far as the press is concerned. The Self-made never think in such terms. We think, "I've achieved so much, that at one point, the whole world stopped to notice it. Public or private, my life is a continuous ascent." Those who can't enjoy their value independently, *resent* rival talent. They resent up and comers, preferring to murder the chances of youth rather than share the spotlight. They aren't trying to be more, but instead fight for a closed shop and just harm their own standing. They inherently know such a barrier can't be voluntary; it must be forced. No one plateaus; the effort is constant. Artists such as Madonna would have been all but forgotten if they didn't *earn* their staying power, every step of the way.

The Hard Part. We often hear that stars stepped on people to get where they are. I bet that such accusations intend to simply damn celebrities who refused to alter their course in life for any lesser concern. They should clearly be separated from those who stole ideas, material or opportunities, claiming them to be their own. Of course predators will run for moral cover not intended for them, but innocent talent deserves a guiltless refuge. We can only be certain and responsible for our own contribution, and for our own experience of life. Abandoning those who couldn't make the grade is difficult but not wrong, though we may feel guilty, knowing the dream while perhaps born together, was not equal in dedication or talent. If our rise was due to the preference of our following, then we are vindicated.

Newfound fame draws all kinds who knew you before. What keeps them from seeing your value sooner? Very few are willing to recognize the work involved. Like the media brass, they want a sure thing and can only identify it perceptually. Their center of gravity swings outside them from one person to another—the most unstable of Man—and you know inherently not to befriend them, since if you lost popularity you would lose them, just as any fair weather friend. Their focus is not even on you or your virtues, but on what *others* think of you. Having no opinion of their own (of you or of personal values), they substitute mass sentiment as the determiner of their desire for association. You become the vehicle on which they attempt to advance their standing. Having no value to offer you in return, if you permit more than simple recognition and an autograph, the relationship quickly turns to poison. They act as a drain, using you and attempting to sever your virtue by calling it luck, God-given or some other source outside of individual power, responsibility or merit. Granting any expectation beyond a respectful "Congratulations" is asking for trouble. They should know better; don't expect any money. Don't believe our favor could determine your success. It can't. Your success will not come from us; it must come from you.

Such action is not limited to old acquaintances however; there are people out there who just expect too much. They exhibit no comprehension of how *one* must deal with *many*—of how involved a celebrity's schedule and commitments are—and they fail to do their part. Stars can't actually control crowds, and some fans trample others to get close. It gets so hot and cramped that people actually pass out and *die* from it—the best reason to cut an appearance short if you see it happening. The other problem-fan begins by imposing spiritually in the form of a nag, and can become a stalker or a killer. If a fan spent twenty dollars to buy your product and you're averaging five thousand dollars an hour, they've paid for 0.004 percent of your workday's time, or about fifteen seconds worth—enough for an autograph. If true values defined your fame, you are *not* public property. Don't feel bad about giving little else.

It is important not to turn the corner to your arrival and view those you've separated from as flawed or substandard. They have dreams too, even if they haven't defined or reached them yet. Give direction to those who have come to the honest level of requesting help. Perhaps some quick advice will get them there much sooner.

Bad Press. Some imagine the glory of fame as doors opening ahead of you, flash bulbs going off as you enter a room and all eyes on you in appreciation. At its best that's how it is, but there is the unsafe, frightening, nightmare-side as well. Often the problems come not from fans, but from the professionally disrespectful—the paparazzi. Reporters and photographers, in angling for the best shot, pose a physical danger, where stars and their families get pushed and shoved as the press fights to hold their ground. You're forced to stumble down a dark path cluttered with bodies swarming around you, hot, cramped and anything but glamorous. It's like living in a mosh pit. Staking out star's homes, going through their garbage, putting their families in jeopardy, barring their way and hounding them on the street is called *stalking*, and press card or not, should be prosecuted as such. A star's waking up in the morning isn't news. Their leaving the house isn't news. Our destinies can cross paths in a *civil* manner at staged events called press conferences. Outside mutual interests, a private life is to remain just that—private.

Such an abomination is the first wave of contempt a celebrity feels, as subjective reporting then intends to inflict spiritual damage. Fame then is no longer a reward and is more like dealing with ridicule. The flow of their lives is interrupted by those intending to make a living by broadcasting their every action, causing them to feel harassed rather than respected. Without a story, out of hatred and malice they create one—always negative. They focus on the lowest and most dysfunctional happenings, passing its interest off as the culture of our nation. Culture is a vague term that generalizes the overall patterns of life one experiences in daily interactions with others. Media taints true culture as it exemplifies what it wants to—what shocks—and the media by numbers of men, is a minority. With the correct philosophy, this minority can be checked. When commentators, interviewers and public writers know they are going to be judged by a standard available to all and acknowledged by all as a logical and moral expectation, they will either be restrained by it, or seek to live up to it. Mass sentiment can change very quickly with newfound clarity, and the press is *not* the representative of the people. Don't be afraid to slight them if they cross you. As Thomas Jefferson said, "One man with courage is a majority."

Celebrities shouldn't live or die by the press—they should simply shun those who approach with a sneer. Don't give interviews to reporters or organizations you find insincere, vulgar or questionable. Be there for the fans through your own medium. If someone resents me, I know that no matter what I say, they will twist an interview to make their point, honest or not. I try to associate with objective, tactful adults only—those who *enjoy* their lives and their chosen professions and can preform them competently. To the others I could only end up a victim of some kind, so I prefer to remain anonymous. Don't extend their career span by honoring their terms. You don't need the press on your side; what you need is to be happy, and to deal with only those who are mature, tactful and professional.

Misery should never be the price of fame. Fame is not a prison—no one should feel trapped by it. The bitter anger towards the current limitations it

331

imposes taints our view of Man, and must be replaced by new methods of action until interaction is not only tolerable, but positive again. When someone gains the world's reverence, we should show our respect and observe the flow of their action undetected or with the least intrusion, being a part of its grace—not to encumber it. We need to return the glamour of being a celebrity to what it was in the sixties, to the wholesome root of the word itself—a celebration. It would be much cleaner, more innocent and more enjoyable for all.

Chapter Eleven

Institutions of Evil

"I can picture in my mind a world without war, a world without hate. And I can picture us attacking that world, because they'd never expect it."
—Jack Handey

Cowardly groups who practice and preach dysfunctional ideals which necessitate the restraint, parasitism and destruction of other men, are *the* social cancer. They get together to hide. They get together to riot, to steal and to force others to comply with their demands. When men get together to define a formal structure, its design is determined by the fundamental premises held by those involved. If they are of sound mind, it becomes an efficient business style organization. If they are not of sound mind, it becomes a meat-grinder. All Spirit Murdering organizations share the same structure and hierarchy, as they were all designed by the same kind of mind. Some lobby those with political power, while others collectively corner their betters to gain what nature cannot give them: guarantees. Irrational lobbies are the con man's equivalent of the Self-made's patent, copyright and trademark. In such form as subsidies, charters and union membership, they attempt to leave their victims no alternative but to deal with them regardless of their performance, transferring the burden of their instabilities to others. They wish to hold markets captive, permitting them to flourish without running the kind of responsible, profitable ventures that competent men do. They claim their actions are to counter inequities or the evils of Man, but they actually attempt to counter justice; for example, Franklin

Roosevelt's *Economic* Bill of Rights' true target was not monopolistic practice. His metaphysical enemy was existence. His political enemy was freedom.

How well you do in day to day relationships is a strong indication of how your attributes would translate into politics. If you can keep your hands in your own pockets and respect the rights of others, you're right wing. If you make victims of those you encounter or wish to, you're left wing. The premises of a Spirit Murderer are carried through his relationships, his art, his politics and his economics—through all the realms of his action.

Every Spirit Murderer has a different range according to his intellectual efficiency, and this determines the depth of his social affront to integrity. The height of the 1-2 level is religion; the height of the 3-4 level is Communism and socialist principles that infect our government as well, and the height of the 6-8 level is fascist international finance. Of course the Christians believe religion is the highest—a group of people who can't even decide if they are conscious—and can't help but screw up everything above them. Their answer to the supposed injustice of reality is Communism: a plan for prosperity for those who want to ride the backs of the prosperous. What a surprise: with religion opposed to reason and Communism opposed to all boundaries of ownership, we've encountered the source and confirmation that "madness unleashed respects neither reason nor boundaries."

Beyond the intellectual scope of most of society comes the thieving rich of finance: the fathers of our world currency system. There are four general financial categories of Man—the productive rich, the productive middle, the thieving rich and the loafing poor (outside of political oppression, productive people do not stay poor). Every rational man agrees that no one should be paid for doing nothing, and yet, the two latter classes have legal sanction to get away with it. This is the most crucial violation of the social aspects of morality, and while everyone is aware of the Welfare State aspect written into our "national conscience" by one of the greatest fools in American history (When I think of FDR, I can't help but think of James Taggart), few have any knowledge that we are sustaining another more dreadful parasite at the other end of the spectrum.

The Spirit Murderers have a crucial advantage over the Self-made in regard to the whole 1-2, 3-4 and 6-8 cognitive range; they have completed the structure. Through key agencies, they've mastered subversion and unaccountable murder, and have used it to silence the few Self-made in positions of political power over the years who were deep enough to become wise to their game. Once such men are out of the way, they are free to split powers, profits and privileges between themselves and leave the populace to starve.

Isn't it interesting how Czars, dictators and other feudal leaders all get put to death after being ousted by another group, who then takes power and continues the butcher's philosophy? What does this imply? If you have power, you are not held to a rational standard. You are beyond moral judgment until you are overthrown. As with Stalin, all of their actions once they are in power are geared to stave off any advance of those who could threatened their position, and the good of the people falls by the wayside—the Submission/Domination Axis. The same pattern was brought to America, noted by government secrets on certain topics. Their secrets are their defects.

Any default of justice is intended to incite decomposition in causal contacts—and the identification and practice of what *is* the good, is lost in fog. Theft manifests itself in so many unclear ways—making us helpless—and evil helps itself to all the values we've taken our eyes off: our money, our goods, our futures and as in Vietnam—a *for profit* war—even the lives of our children. Yet the abstract world is where the decisions affecting the physical world get made. It is from here that our sons get sent off to war, to die for a cause we may not agree with or even understand. We *have* to care. The same passivity that won't get involved to protect individual political interests, gets them killed.

There are many Spirit Murdering institutions sprinkled throughout the range of cognition. We must be aware of them; our very lives depend on it. Those discussed are the most well known to me, arranged according to their cognitive complexity, least to most. I'll leave you to find, steer clear of and reform, the rest.

Charities and Non-profit Organizations. We see immense smallness in charities as we approach eagerly to do good. We volunteer to help and are given a burden under barked orders—a pushy attitude we resent as a worse imposition than our unpaid effort, and the resentment underlines our every step in the organization. We see that our bright view of the cause is drowned in the quagmire, and that the most miserable are dominant. We see its personnel take anything valuable before the needy see it anyway, and have to ask, "What good is it doing?" The poor are stuck in their patterns, and this doesn't change it. We aren't teaching them new patterns, but perpetuating the old—*catering to it* and losing our compassion in the process.

We give a few hours to charity, abandoning our sensibilities and practicing a death pattern instead, to show and feel that we are good at heart; but by supporting our own existence, we've done that already. If you don't volunteer, perhaps you see them on your way to work standing in intersections, begging at car windows for change. Consider the affront that they enjoy a higher moral status than you, in that their action is viewed as a greater moral virtue than the job you are headed to. It took five minutes to learn to stand, smile, pass out candy and ask for money. Why is it moral? Actually, disconnection from the profit motive is not just the cause of bad managers and bad teachers, but of the misguided everywhere. The profit motive is the *life* motive. Anyone preaching the opposite is preaching dysfunction, dependency and death—that is, the *give* or the *take*—which is why they beg. The *create* is the profit motive. Our work makes their donations possible, but still, their chainless, dead-end action is considered virtuous—while the years spent acquiring our skills used at work every day, which grows in value on its own inertia through time, goes morally silent. Charitable actions, be they government sponsored or otherwise, do nothing to foster living patterns.

335

Everyone should be able to find a way to give value for value; an organization is no different from an individual in this regard. If it has to be pushed with dead capital, then there is something wrong with the plan—in its intention or execution. If there is no natural inclination to support it, it is either flawed or evil. The flawed is to mean it is not conveyed correctly, or at their supporter's cognitive level. All non-profit ventures including all subsidies and nonessential government branches fall into this category. Forced or begged-for monies are an indication of moral default—of a default of judgment and of no clear path between means and ends. Profit-making ventures follow the pattern of life. Any non-profit venture follows its opposite, and subjugated purpose and random dysfunction is always its result. Institutions that need not be concerned about carrying themselves will be misguided. If management cannot find a way around forcing or begging, fire them. If no way can be found, shelve the idea until one can be.

Though unjust criticism is heard against the producers, as contributors, they are often not innocent in this. His own cowardice or dismissal of the subject is equally to blame. To be honest is to take no false action. To invest time, energy or money in what one inherently knows won't work, *is not honest.* Non-profiteers claim to be the healers, the givers, who can see one-tenth the distance of the Self-made, who separate causes from effects to proclaim those who create the benefits that they give away, are *evil.* And likewise, we stand down and never teach what makes it possible for men not to be beggars at the Mission. They claim that incompetence is allowed and is forgivable because it's a nonprofit venture. No kidding. But non-profitable action is no more morally exempt than profitable action. It's not easy to make a profit; profit takes effort. Soundly earned profit is the result of virtuous action; any kind of loss or non-profit is the result of vice—a lack of respect for life. It is treason to support charities who criticize the system and practice of life-furtherance, from which the donations come.

Unions

"The meaning of his bandage, and the meaning of his office, were not to be excepted or to exist, together. It was not a combination for men to live with."
—Atlas Shrugged

The only high profile representatives of the middle class unfortunately are labor unions, who practice and preach policies of purely socialist design. They remove your chains only to put them on your betters, then require you to chain yourself to your brothers. Instead of joining a plan for the greater good, suddenly you're lost among the undifferentiated—among the mean and small— and are then penalized for displaying anything more. You find out that the company is your enemy—that everything you thought made a good employee is now bad—that the lowest around you is now your equal, and your burden. The wolf-pack acknowledges seniority, not performance, disallowing effort to outpace lethargy. It bares its teeth when exposed to any hint of personal accountability. Despite the thinly veiled, murderous smiles welcoming you, you can barely hide from yourself the fact that you've joined a hate group.

I'm not a union member for the same reason I'm not a bigot. I use my own guts and have enough self-confidence to trade in a market with free competition. Even though you may support a union and may believe in brotherhood, I'm sure you can sense its betrayal. It is the deeper brotherhood of all human beings that has been betrayed. When you huddle and protect your clan in violation of rationality—such as supporting internal incompetence by overlooking it while shunning outside success—it is not your opponent's stature that you reveal, it is yours. Unions may have begun as muscle for unfairly treated workers, but are now only a mutation of charity to benefit the worthless and the aspiring worthless. If management thinks they're saving themselves work by collective bargaining, they're wrong. They still maintain a supervisory staff, and all they've done is tied the supervisor's hands and dismissed accountability for those under him. Unions are a collection of *us against them,* 1-2 level Spirit Murderers: malicious guardians of the Submission/ Domination Axis, and that's all.

Great ideas are always forwarded by the men of ability, while looters always try to twist their meaning to secure the undeserved for the non-efforting. Unions damn automation, yet propose no means to remain competitive. You never hear any ideas for improving efficiency; you never hear them addressing the company's competitiveness or considering any sane reason why human beings are in business. Instead we suffer their nineteenth-century reproaches against working conditions. For example, during our country's intellectual pro-communist period, American railways were bullied into focusing on the livelihood of their workers, not on moving freight. The purpose had been lost— that of utilizing every bit of a business's potential in the profitable pursuit of life as an abstract ideal—not the sheer naked survival of some individual workers, and it virtually destroyed the industry.

A business is the dream of one man or a small group of men—*not* the dream of all—except when workers have no dreams. Then they become parasites on others. By pushing all the Mercedes out of the parking lot, they lose their Hondas and never realize why. No business is about its workers. Workers exist in their context, for the product alone. Losing a job is not the equivalent of losing one's life, and there is no such thing as *the right to a job.* The solutions to a country's economic issues are not to be found by generating inefficiency within its industries. With businesses being private, they are already running as efficiently as their owners believe possible. As a nation, the restoration of economic calm is to be found after a shakeout which rids the waste of oversupply, and redistributes workers among the fields were they are actually needed.

No matter their studied Marxist arguments, you can sense the film of malice vented for any greatness, any ability and any honor they encounter. I've never met a union representative who wasn't a twit, among whom the Spanish Inquisition zealot-style is the most disturbing. Their sourcebook is *The Communist Manifesto*—and any other means to mask that they aren't the slugs they are. Preaching unconditional love, he grants it only to others equally undeserving. This love for Man is shown by voting against justice and freedom, and in favor of mercy and enslavement. Often we get shaken by his moral attacks and miss that if he's into reward for non-achievement, then he has disqualified himself from any leadership position.

The truth is they bring *violence* to industry, as unionization is a power organized *specifically* for the disruption of the enterprise. A new individual with good intentions, trying to use sound administrative and moral judgment will find his efforts trounced by the very evil the system is designed to protect. He will be forced into cover-ups, strikes, walk-outs and a host of other immature or hostile activities, shamefully conspiring against good will, where adults embarrass themselves in a psychological predicament children should never have to see.

I can't speak to union members or anyone who preaches protection for fear-ridden incompetents. Within their argument, there is always the premise that some part of my effort belongs to them, that my life is an imposition and their anger is its proof; that I've done something to earn their distrust, to be paid for by relinquishing all the values I generate. Their every debate leans the same way: towards a moral summation that justifies their damnation of the Self-made and the seizure of values, to come upon their land of milk and honey, where the honorable must submit control and succumb to their jubilee—the irrational distribution of wealth. Each member gets to feel he is King for a day, withholding the second half of that adage: *fool for a lifetime*. The maniacally untrusting *are* the untrustworthy, and they reflect it in the limited range of their work, in their malice, in their private lives and in their law. They can never rise, as they appeal to the lowest in Man, and it's only the lowest that come running to such premises. Fear drives them, as no matter how powerful they appear, they lack the key trait of a man—independence. Who has ever stood *alone* to protect their position as a parasite?

There is no transforming a union staff into objective, efficient employees. Due to their subjective, hampered, Fear-driven cognitive pattern, their morale is at an all-time low, intentionally reinforced by Marxist dogma. They're convinced that at work they deserve to sleep, to be drunk, to skip three days a week, to be totally unaccountable for their task, then to proclaim their inestimable worth and strike over compensation. I've seen their petty incivilities first hand; that such people can live with so shameful a disregard for human virtue is an abomination—almost as bad as its tolerance. Is it any wonder that the mob runs the Teamsters, and the Teamsters draw only those who act like crooks openly, or are crooks at heart? If a group wants to unionize—if that is their best answer to workplace issues—you need to build an entirely new staff. I hate incompetence because it is always based on some kind of fraud—even when it is based on cowardice, as cowardice is based on fraud. The only reimbursement for incompetence or intolerable behavior the Self-made have, is exercise of the one line such union membership is designed to prevent: *"You're fired!"*

Extremists

"When a man's life has no value, sometimes death has its price."
—Fistful of Dollars

Religion is partially responsible for terrorism, and not just one faith in particular, but religion as such. Start such a war inside a person, and it soon comes to the outside. Those teaching that independence is evil shouldn't be surprised when kids join gangs. Violating cognition is an act of Spirit Murder, and in an unstable environment it won't be long before it is extrapolated into physical murder. When a consciousness rapidly degenerates, it builds towards an explosion. What happens when children are taught to defy consciousness right from the beginning? Internal anarchy quickly results in external anarchy. They grow confident in being rude and threatening to their parents, but are lost and uncertain when they step outside. By an extension of the same dogma, that negativity is led by a more seasoned force to its ultimate end, and they draw him to his death like a poodle on a string.

Religion is also responsible for perpetuating the tragic melding of cognition with interaction, which leads terrorist minions to their deaths. Religion as well justifies confiscation, sacrifice and destruction for "a good cause," which for a morality where anything goes and no one is to blame, means *any cause they choose*. The advantage they take stems from and feeds on cognitive limitation, and with every religious claim violating the true pattern, terrorist theory is implicitly supported by every mother and grandmother preaching the gospel. Furnish their people with a modern city, and their primitive religious premises would turn it right back into shambles.

A country's citizens would never need to leave their homeland and flee to safe havens if it were not so, if it were not for their non-objective, unrealistically substantiated, unaccountable religious doctrines. Instead of striving for an envisioned future glory, they shoot their citizens in the back while they try to escape the horror, where the trigger is first pulled on rationality—their own cognitive accountability. We hear them say "You have to be willing to sacrifice yourself for the greater good," or, "We cannot see His whole plan," and end up fighting over what it is and what it isn't and who has the authority to say so; but no one can step outside the context of existence itself to make *existential* connections. The only alternative to rationality is violence.

We must grow to the stature of accepting *our own* determinations of moral substance, and that requires a logical standard. Unless we accept that our senses *are* valid, unless we renounce the false-concept of Original Sin—the claim that Man is evil by birth, a scenario not of his choice and therefore outside any logical judgment against him—we invite and *justify* this kind of aggression. An appeased aggressor just becomes more aggressive.

ZEALOTS. Accomplishments determine a man's stature, and destruction only subtracts from it. Where are the great buildings and societies as a result of their philosophy? Ideology is fought not with bombs, but with ideology. Why can't they fight us ideologically? Because theirs is worthless. Was Jesus running around slaughtering his opposition, or was his ministry and following peaceful and voluntary? Jesus wasn't a murdering, threatening Neanderthal. Did the prophets interpret religion so they could rape and kill freely? Did Moses? Who are the extremist's *real* idols then? Who have the terrorists and zealots *really* patterned their lives after? That's right, the prophet's brutal, scavenging enemies. Violence is a confession of cowardice—of intellectual impotence. Listen to their foolish incoherent explanations they hope no one will question. Their veil of dogmatic justification is so thin that they typically have to die or kill their audience before the truth is named—by others or in their own minds. One more dead is one less to convince or to admit the truth of what it is they're doing.

There is no room for zealots in morality. There are no wife-beating, child-molesting, peer and student-threatening, red-faced, fist-shaking convincing tactics that are ever done by rational beings. Such people aren't even in control of themselves—much less their concepts. Society doesn't listen to them anyway. Look into their education and you will find no chain of peace, no capacity for production, no enjoyed independence, only hatred and a mind schooled in murder. Dogma is their justification, and no one buys theirs except the self-hating bomb bait. There is a special place in Hell for those who do not use their head—who practice what they've known was wrong since they were children.

We saw what Spirit Murderer's have to offer the world on September 11th, 2001. We saw their sympathy for the loss of innocent lives as they danced in the streets. This is their perfect world—bombed out cars and buildings—it looks like home to them. This was done by men who have nothing attached to their names but disaster. The only lasting symbolism they've accomplished and my answer to them, is as follows: If you've degenerated to the point where your own death is your most glorious day, odds are high that the world agrees with you.

Note to terrorists: You will answer for this. You will answer on *our* terms for what you've done. You are not heroes; at best, your void of identity nears the criminally insane. Anyone practicing force is at risk of deposition—by force. When you destroy pinnacles instead of aspiring to them, when you make claims of Divine intentions yet by example produce only a sea of blood, then you have chosen an obvious side, and our moral road is clear. We've lived with it long enough; now you have the kind of attention you deserve. We will chase you to the ends of the Earth and rid humanity of your shadow. (It doesn't matter if we haven't managed to kill some fugitive or another. He can spend his life under a rock were he belongs).

What have you ever done that the world can be proud of? As a soldier, ever notice how your dogma directs and trains you to commit atrocities in the name of peace, but never spends any time defining sound living structures of peace, or any civil actions that lead to it? That's because the civilization in America *is* the structure of true, rational, productive peace. The truth is you're a patsy for killers, and you lack the intellectual depth and honorable discipline ever to win. Your great martyrs and the leaders you serve lack it too. They are simply more experienced and subversive failures, and all that keeps them from self-destruction, is *your* destruction. If you want to live, the pattern of *life* is what you must practice. Turn them over and get a job; drop your weapons and join civilization, because the end is coming for your organization—soon.

The Islamic Fundamentalists aren't the only psychotic extremists; we have our own piss-ant American terrorists in the Ku Klux Klan, along with petty militias sprinkled across the nation. Oh, and nice hat. They can't allow themselves to be identified, as the embarrassment of being seen is to admit to everyone, "Yes, I'm *this* stupid." If a man is fool enough to be a bigot, you are better off to be aware of it. If a man is willing to respond with incivility for an inessential characteristic such as color or race, lacking the discipline to define the character of others based on rational convictions, would you want to be exposed to him at all? Laws may stop him from barring transactions with you, but such deceitfulness and irrationality will surface in other areas. Psychological cowardice and dishonesty are never isolated; they are manifested in countless ways. Black or white, Mexican or Italian, bigotry generated from any side is one of the most blatant indications of a fundamental unwillingness to reason, revealing the very lowest of Man.

Slavery was a moral disaster for America, no less atrocious than the savagery of the Dark Ages or the Nazi regime. Every continent has shameful elements in its past, where men became little more than animals. It is never to be tolerated again. So the Klan wants to march peacefully now? Hang it up; you haven't lost our respect, you never had it. There is no such thing as peaceful hatred.

Environmentalism

"That's the thing...about W.A.S.P.'s. They love animals, they can't stand people." —Wallstreet

Why is their focus not on the brilliant sky and our productive harmony under it, but on the small column of smoke coming from a ship's engine? Why do they look, not at the limitless countryside, but at the small rectangle advertising products of free trade along the highways which they also hate? Products of Man *are* products of nature, as Man is not unnatural. Civilization cannot exist harvesting what grows in the wild without our control. A handful of men might be able to survive running through forests, eating berries, building huts from dead branches—but not an industrial society. Sub humans wish men to live without being human, or by the use of human means. More to the point, they wish us *not* to live, or to return us to caves and make us the slaves of their primitive grasp of existence.

Do we see great technological advances out of the Roman Catholic Church? Out of Greenpeace? Out of Ralph Nader? No, only criticism, threats and demands. Their organizations are revenge-based as much as they are wishful. Those who don't create, simply complain about those who do. The advances are provided by the same people who gave us automobiles, computers and running water. They are free to go into business with their energy and ideas, to take away our customers and fix the world. "But I don't have any ideas" they say. Exactly.

They call themselves the "socially conscious"—the *socialists*—sensitive to men's needs, claiming cognizance of every action of mankind, which must not disturb a blade of grass. To tread is wrong in itself; for Man to live is an affront to all that which exists in harmony, *only* without us. Yet as productive men, we tie our lives to the very fabric of nature, as there are only two ways to live—off the land, or off the blood of others. By intellectual default, they promote this last. They slander our system, representing us as the slick salesman who prefers swindling suckers and calls himself a capitalist, but he isn't. He is actually a fascist wannabe—*their* brainchild. The term "businessman" doesn't cover scheming, calculating, wastes of space.

Speaking to the extreme environmentalists, "Let's grant your wish hypothetically, and let you knock down all the smoke stacks. Running errands, you go to the grocery store and stare in horror at the empty shelves. You planned to hit many more stores, but passing a number of closed gas stations, you get an ominous feeling and decide to conserve what's in your tank. Getting the mail at home, you have an emergency tax bill to help cover all the unemployed you've just thrown out of work. Your boss calls to say that a major supplier's factory has been mysteriously shut down, and your products can no longer be made—*you're* out of work too. No more paychecks and no more food, but what do you need them for? It's a beautiful day. You have a blissful, pollution-free world to gaze at while you die."

All elements of an idea must be known in order to maintain its result properly, be it a business, an agricultural supply-line or a philosophy. There is no way to scale back intelligence and still enjoy the use of its products. No expropriation is successful long-term, when the tops are cut down to force solutions to questions the environmentalists have no civil answer for, and no tolerance or mental discipline to reach. They operate from a fixed mind, so they imagine all values to be fixed as well. They see a fixed amount of oil on the planet and a fixed amount of food. They determine that there is only so much to go around and grant no consideration for Man's continuous efficiencies, which extrapolate the preservation, bounty and longevity of raw materials. No faith is placed in Man's mind, because those who focus on this never-ending stream of panicked contrivances have negated theirs.

I remember a story I read somewhere that exemplified the effectiveness of most environmentalists: After spending some $80,000 nursing two seal pups back to health after an oil spill, great fanfare was planned to reintroduce them into the wild. They were released into the ocean, and as TV cameras rolled, both were eaten by a killer whale. We can't control nature, and they certainly have nothing to propose that provides better solutions than ours. Finish college and get a job. Experience and maturity should remove the true cause of your sneer.

To their credit, some have uncovered instances of abuse that are truly deplorable. I've watched footage of Japanese fishing boats cutting fins off sharks and dumping the bodies, leaving them to endure a horrible death. As a pure supporter of free enterprise, a sinking feeling had to ask, "Is this what I represent?" The answer is no. Such waste and inefficiency would be clobbered in a laissez-faire capitalist economy where businesses pay for their raw materials. But they get the fish for nothing—incurring no cost or penalty above honest fishing vessels, for wasting their stock. They wouldn't be so wasteful with ponds they own, but they don't own the ocean. If I was in a ship close by, I wouldn't think twice about putting a torpedo through their hull. Oops! Survival of the fittest. We're best served as capitalists to remain aware of the motives behind what is done in our name. Man's rights do not include rape. It's obvious what they're doing; they're exploiting the cream of the market because it is there to be exploited. My respect for *all* life disallows supporting such heartbreaking, inhumane wastefulness.

An integrated path that respects human life must be formed, and awareness of that is spreading. Civilization must be maintained, and *of course* we must be responsible for our actions—maximizing utilization of the products we draw from the ground or the water—which is simply good business sense. Mankind is *not* in a struggle opposed to nature. One doesn't have to go—it isn't *either/or* anymore. Listen to the Discovery Channel and their pitches for nature are beginning to show respect for industry, which is respect for human life, bringing the environmentalist zealots around to reason, finally.

Religion

"Superstition is a name men give to their ignorance."
—Dragon: The Bruce Lee Story

Religion is considered synonymous with morality, so it must be classified and discussed within *Moral Armor* (kicked around and left to rot in a heap), though a full treatise on morality could be written never mentioning it. The source of morality is not religion.

Most people are far too decent for the morality they have been subjected to. The *naturally*-driven moral desire of mankind has exposed us to religion's poison however, making it a very important issue psychologically. When we contemplate our lives and our actions, how we live and how we affect others in the process, we want to do what is right. We want to be viewed positively. The symbol of a rational philosophy is life and self-esteem. It is not religion or a hero we crave, but esteem in ourselves. Mankind's moral desire is high, and that in part is why many cling to the current cultural standard. But there are two versions of morality: the get away with it side and the earned, rational discipline side.

Have you ever explored a topic and though having many elements defined, still could not put a finger on a thing's essence? It's like trying to figure out a person whose actions keep you confused. You never consider doubting them, but are unable to identify what concept would explain their character. It turns out that they are a liar, and then everything falls into place. Or maybe as a scientist, you make an assumption upon which all of your calculations are based. You know the relationships between all that is affected to be constant, but somehow your calculations are off. Eventually you identify the source of your inquest, and when you take your calculations from the correct starting point, everything works out. It is the same with moral judgment. Centuries have taught us that morality comes from religion and that religion is not to be questioned. Yet when one replaces the claimed source with the nature of existence, moral actions make perfect sense. The only difference is there is nothing in that for any looters. When one accepts the true origin of Man (this Earth) and the actual purpose of morality (the furtherance of human life—primarily your own), everything falls into place. Using a god as the vantage point leaves one chasing one's tail, allowing looters to play middleman and speak in his place. True morality is not at the mercy of interpretations.

As a people, we suffer the bipartisan animosity reared by this moral confusion: the unthinking side which attempts to rigidly follow the popular moral guidance in haughty righteousness, while the independent side wants little to do with its many ludicrous hassles. It's heartbreaking to see people looking for a significance greater than what is glorified by our shallow media glitter—a depth they can enjoy personally and privately—and this is what they find. Society has been stuck in first gear—the gear of common sense, fearing the monotony of mysticism that always seemed to lie beyond it, and with good reason. What rationality prevents, religion permits. Religion has shown what a free reign of its supremacy would mean in the medieval savagery of the Dark Ages, and the paranoid horror of the Salem witch trials. Its naked essence has been seen, and no one wants to get bogged down in another period of mystic ooze. Without an alternative path leading to moral stability, we've stayed in low. They tell us the senses are invalid, but they keep trying to convince us through them. We read that Jesus damns the rich, then damns the unprofitable. He curses the powerful, yet encourages you to show God and men your best. His ministry was voluntary and peaceful, but he threatens you with eternal damnation unless you accept him. How could anyone back an ideology with so many direct contradictions? What has been missing is context, and what makes the riddle of morality clear is the earned versus the unearned, the deserved versus the confiscated, the life-furthering versus the life-destroying.

HEAVEN AND EARTH

In childhood, I was told that heaven was whatever I wanted it to be. As one of Earth's new residents, I knew so little that I wanted, not to determine my surroundings, but to learn about them. If this future world was to revolve around my current grasp, then there was nothing more to learn from that world: no one to look up to and nothing more either could give me. Seeking direction, we huddle under our parents and their supposedly knowledgeable and confident melon guides us to our own epistemological dysfunction. I just knew something was wrong. I wanted to *deserve* the world around me, to *know* I deserved it and that by my developed ability, could reacquire it at will. Why did they think I wanted it for free? Their morality destroyed my happiness in so many ways, it took years to understand why: religion breaks the conceptual chain.

What is it they preach as ideal? What is the image of that utopia they lure you with? Getting everything for nothing; never having to lift a finger. We see the practical result of that in the slums, in welfare offices and in those who *do* pursue it, by pulling insurance jobs, staging accidents and filing nuisance suits. We see it in Islamic Fundamentalism and Third-world slave states, yet an effortless existence is consistently glorified by religion—something no truly moral man would ever want. Afraid to figure this one out, they wish to be masters of an easier world. They claim that if it wasn't for our terrible "human condition," everything would be free. They wish to realize their land flowing with milk and honey, but as these are products of human effort, all they bring about is a land flowing with blood. Their effortless morality might work for ghosts, but what does a ghost need? Nothing. No food, no water, no transportation. We are not ghosts. We should never expect to be granted by a god or by other men what is ours to earn. But such people spend their lives chasing illusions, fatally loyal in treason to Earth and all those they encounter. Their religion has taught them to ignore and defy their own physical natures—to believe some unknowable power will provide—and faithfully, they block out their senses. This is not any Divine Circumstance, but simple neurosis.

We all know that when someone openly embraces religion, there is something tainted about them; something has been lost, as if in prelude to insanity. Their communal gaiety has always made me cringe. Their dreamy ideals are never to be brought down to Earth. Safe in the stagnancy of impossibility and unrevealed incompetence, they feel free to laugh at effort and scoff at experimentation. I've been sickened, listening to the fools put down our world in favor of what they imagine their heaven to be by comparison. Looking around them they say "If this footstool is your heaven, you're not aiming very high." They put down their flesh—their own material existence, their wants, their work, their relationships and their lives. They wipe their feet on all human values. Their rule is "It's not high if I can reach it. It's not deep if I understand," but in life they are a mind looping in panic, achieving nothing. Morality need not carry the distaste in the negation of mind commonly associated to their approach. They declare life to be senseless, and given the way they live, they're right. If life here doesn't matter, then why bother to oppose those who live here and love it? They consider reality to be beside the point, and the point is, their wish. We think and act while they wish and pray, and the more they panic the harder they pray. They encourage us to stop our evil and do what they do, so that we may go to heaven. But they're not going.

HELL

It has always been preached that we risk losing our souls if we pursue knowledge forbidden by the Fear-driven clergy in control of most moral premises—claiming that to defy *them* is to defy God. Funny—the road has been so rewarding since my philosophical departure from their premises, I had forgotten my own conscious acceptance of this burden as well.

Most "thinkers" and religious backers cannot convey anything without deserving to get maced. As no one sane accepts the irrational, they have to inflict their morality. They accomplish this by threats such as purgatory—the worst kind of hell they can project. On the news every evening, we hear of the breakdown of moral fiber in society, the violence, the lawsuits and on Sundays, we get to hear about what pieces of shit we are. We are condemned for our daily greed in that hour long commute, eight hours of disciplined focus and that second hour long commute. They've left us no chance, making us evil by birth (Original Sin). Look at a new born; isn't it evil? It is Man. Notice its fangs, its claws and its violent intentions. Notice its black heart. Imagine the parents of a newborn froggy bearing down on him to say "See those legs? If you were a decent frog, you wouldn't have to hop." Or plant parents saying "If you were a decent plant, you wouldn't have to strive for water, light and air. You wouldn't stretch out to greet its warmth, but be humbled under the sun." Pointing to an uprooted, dried and shriveled weed, they'd say "*That* is virtue before the Lord." Ridiculous and unnatural for other species, that is exactly what the Spirit Murderers have done to Man. The only black hearts are to be found in those who perpetrate such nonsense, grown men whom out of moral carelessness, tell children they are evil—children who cannot even comprehend their evasions, much less their psychotic malice. Children don't know that these anti-concepts are backed by nothing; not the earned grace expected from reaching adulthood, but a pattern mimicked on cue to elicit docility. We listen to their bland, colorless accounts of heroism: sacrifice, self-denial, humbleness and repression, then we get up the next morning and proceed to make all the right moves with no moral credit. We don't redeem ourselves for our weeklong evil by going to church; it's in reverse. It takes five days of virtuous productive action to atone for the moral atrocity of spending our reward of rest and reflection, in a commune of human contempt.

Mysticism relegates the source of all values to the heavens and the source of all evil to Man. They teach us that we are low, filthy creatures whose first impulse is to commit evil. Independent judgment is held as spiritual treason, to be countered with the most horrific retributions in their afterlife. Man's senses are not considered tools to focus, but impediments which blur. We are taught not to trust our senses or other men, but to trust in religion's guiding power alone—the cornerstone of abject dependence. What they try to claim is that if we are provided information by our senses, there is something wrong with us. If pain hurts, if joy feels good, then we are substandard or worse yet, inherently evil. They alter the nature of our fulfillment, adding a lascivious malice we never intended. They exaggerate to where sheer survival is considered hedonistically selfish—and the glutton is always their symbol for use in despising wealth. We humble at what they claim was conveyed, accepting their guilt and looking no further, never to discover that the religious promise of an unearned bounty doesn't lead to any values at all—only to penalties.

<u>Their first rule:</u> Accept that you are evil. Because you sought the tree of knowledge, because you earn your bread by your labor, because you breathe, because you desire intimacy, you are evil. Never mind that all organisms on the planet adhere to this natural pattern; mankind alone must refuse it. You are evil as long as you live by natural human means (Of course, the alternative is to become a mindless savage, devouring those who do).

<u>Their second rule:</u> You can never change. You can never be good and your guilt must be atoned for through a life of service—we'll tell you to whom.

There is no punishing a trait of all men and there is no preexisting human evil. Such an idea violates the very definition of morality—the *choice* to do good or evil. We were all born with a clean slate. No condition or action outside personal choice has moral consideration or weight. Paraphrasing Shakespeare, there is no evil on Earth that only irrationality makes it so. There is no negative tendency or bias either—quite the opposite. If anything our bias is towards the good, as nature points the way. Those who have interpreted Man as evil have given us their own *self*-estimate. It shouldn't need to be said that "the moral is the chosen, not the forced"—Atlas Shrugged, and that those who must *inflict* their morality have always been the most mindless danger. There *is* no Hell beyond what the Spirit Murderers make of life.

Warrior Note: *The good determined by any standard other than life, will achieve its opposite.*

ATHEISM AND SPIRITUALITY

I am an atheist for one main reason: comprehension, and for five secondary reasons: sight, smell, hearing, taste and touch. The beginning of my doubt was spurred while watching *The Blue Lagoon*. It is plausible that children could be shipwrecked and survive to grow up on a desert island, never knowing or remembering the god designed and conveyed by Man. This would drastically affect their life as nothing would question their capacity to deal with the challenge of living. It would bolster the potency of their senses, no longer fixing them on an alternate world and its unknowable, unaccountable requirements. I was immediately envious of the prospect. There would be no questioning human capacities—only using them. It would remove from life the pain of guilt, as guilt would be attached to its only proper and natural moral cause: the unwillingness to carry the burdens of one's own existence by the organic requirements of life.

Religion considers spirituality to be the province of *their* followers, saying its opposite is a shallow, dirty lifestyle, devoid of emotional purity. But no one fights more for their soul than those so willing to relinquish it. The imbecile's devoted stare of non-identity is their tribute to life as they see it— zombies to be steered so long as they are shrouded in their master's concept of the good, which amounts only to the unaccountable approval of others. The Fear-driven have minds dedicated to taking every offshoot of denial; they are focused to escape rational boundaries and consider *that* growth, but disciplined cognitive adherence *is* the moral measure of a man. There is no value in being dressed up by outsiders. If you're not Self-made, you're nothing. Atheism versus spirituality is not an honest alternative. The proper definition of *spirituality* is one's sense of life, who's proper state is exhilaration for personal value and for experiences had by virtuous means, leading to exhilaration for all of life to come. Those holding fast to the sound pattern of cognition are the only ones who have kept their soul, their spirituality and the substance of sovereign identity such a concept implies.

RELIGIOUS EPISTEMOLOGY

"What's burning a city next to tearing the lid off Hell and letting men see it?"
—Atlas Shrugged

Who remembers the song "Because the Bible tells me so?" *That* is the foundation of religious epistemology, and the end of its usefulness. How do we know the things we know? Because the Bible tells us so—a basic "don't ask questions" cognitive violation. Their answer for every happening in the entire length of their epistemological chain can be found in one word: God. That is why no religious group has been responsible for a single advancement in the history of the world. And still they urge us to abandon how far we've come and return to their view of the mind and body as an aborigine sees a skyscraper—just a tall, box-shaped mystical phenomenon. Here is the *actual* epistemological pattern of Christianity: 1) Schooled negation of existence, 2) Voluntary negation of consciousness, 3) Dictation of action, 4) Castration of reward. Look at them; they would never accept that something so complex and important as morality could be so straightforward. They have their students so twisted that most find value in *not* being able to understand a lesson. Centuries of repetition has trained them to expect confusion, boredom and orders; otherwise, they inherently deny a lesson's validity. Their mind responds to rationality like, "This isn't morality. There is no *sense* to morality. The mind as a tool isn't used."

In religion, creative action is replaced with dictated expectations, so the memorization of complex concepts is necessary. Higher concepts in reason are a derivation of walking the chain, but religious concepts respect no existential information. They lead from nowhere to universal harmony, without stopping to ask how. The altruist fog of impossibilities permits non-provable abstract projections that bear no adherence to the 1-4 cognitive process below. Their true fantasy is where anything is possible *morally*. Objectivity *cannot* be subverted, but religion can easily. There is no becoming a victim of reason. There is no need for memorization in rational epistemology beyond storing fundamental elements such as multiplication tables in order to free up registers, permitting quicker abstraction. "Ignorance of the law is no excuse" to the contrary, no rational concepts or laws need be committed to memory; they are intuitive of life. Instead, dictated action removes moral choice, and thus the pride it could generate. Religion creates drones—blind, deaf and dangerous.

Belief means a rational conviction. A rational conviction requires validation, which requires existential referents (things) for the sake of measurement and a means of identification (which requires rationality, which requires sensory perception, assimilation, identification and integration (judgment)). Beliefs require proof. No one *believes* in God. As Ayn Rand said, they do something that takes the place of believing. Call it faith, but they steal the word of the living to give credence to their stance, which is a premise promoting non-identity. Religion has been an improper use of imagination, prompted by the folklore of past generations, none of which reality has shown any evidence of. Beliefs such as the belief in God or of an afterlife have no proof, and therefore no conviction, yet they claim to be sure. How? I would figure that such a concept as *afterlife* makes one value life *less*. I can only be thankful if my loved ones lived well. I cannot benefit myself in life by contemplating the unknowable, and politically, I cannot allow the unknowable to be used as a justification for the slaughter of men or the seizure of my assets on Earth. I can't believe that people would be willing to subordinate their minds to where they couldn't even dance, for a dogma learned from other people—a system whose guidance has been left to the subjectivity of every man who has touched it. How can they grant respect for a system that cannot withstand *any objective validation?*

"Faith in the supernatural, begins as faith in the superiority of others."
—Atlas Shrugged

Faith is acting against your better judgment. Faith isn't the opposite of reason; it is the *negation* of reason. It isn't an alternative to thought, but the absence of thought. Their "higher state of being" doesn't bring what you first expect: a clearer understanding. No, it is a state where cognitive effort for understanding and physical effort for reward is unnecessary. It is a place where they get for nothing, all the values they damn on this Earth. Looking too deeply into anything has long been associated with destroying the feelings of wonder, but what we were given to exalt was not worthy of exaltation. Such men of faith have no chance of reaching integrity. Depth should *bring* wonder, not dissolve it. The pathway to a "higher mode of living," a "higher consciousness," or to "exist on a higher plane," *must* result not in a negation of your senses, but in a greater clarity. It is properly the joy of effort; the pride of competence and ability. It must and can only build on what you already know. A clearer, more concentrated understanding will address your senses in an even more direct and concise way. Those who seek a higher intuitive wisdom must have the ability to address questioning minds with *more* determinate solutions, in a more exacting manner than ever before. If they can't, then back to the ranks they go, until they can.

Instead of working to acquire their prophet's heroic *human* traits, die-hard followers ignore such and mimic instead their impossible marvels, reflecting the superhero worship of their children whom they show such contempt for. They want to raise their hands and part the sea, but refuse to define constructive means to overcome their barriers. They want to magically raise the dead or heal the sick, but won't listen to evidence that stems sickness and the patterns that lead to it. They'll call upon the heavens to guide their lives, but won't hold their emotions in check to think clearly. They're willing to snap their fingers and turn one free meal into ten, but shrug at the prospect of the moral constancy necessary to earn them, or anything else. They have a ruthlessly disciplined imagination, a one way valve that closes at the first touch of reality. They want to believe another conscious power will guide them to their destiny, so they can coast. The only reason to seek an outside source for this is if you are afraid or incompetent. At any time, two key destinies lie before every man: the result of effort and that of sloth. Look down and see whose feet are moving. If they're yours, then so is the decision of where to place them.

A *morality* is a system of life-furthering principles, based on the nature of the entity it intends to preserve—an individual man. It is an endeavor of Man like any other (such as medicine and computer technology), always in some stage of development, subject to constant scrutiny, continually being advanced, focusing in closer and closer for the purpose of furthering the power of individuals and in effect, furthering mankind in the most profitable, bountiful way. *Philosophy* is its proper origin. Philosophy is morality's calculus. Religion is morality's cancer. When the pattern of cognition is overlaid on the text of the bible, it reveals a nightmare of moral contradictions—a psychology and logic as poor as any common novel. In my experience in life and philosophy, all religious edicts result in cognitive dead ends. The only elements of the Bible that can be defined as religious are those which subordinate knowledge to faith and free will to duty. Its valid 'claims to virtue' were hijacked from nature itself. Philosophy is the tree encompassing all of human knowledge. The Bible is just one branch of that tree like *Mein Kampf*, to be reviewed and mostly dismissed. The Bible is a theologist's *entire* tree, and trapped among the goats and sheep herders, he tries to apply their Neanderthal premises to modern life, while somehow assigning the origin of all current and future lessons to itself.

Dealing with those who involve religion in thought has always been a complete waste of time. You can talk to them about normal issues up until the point where they abandon consciousness for their dogma. Over twenty years of study has shown me that no advances come from it as do no moral values, and none ever have—only a mindless hatred of anyone who challenges their illusions. Now, their semi-conscious state feels like death to me—worse than that—like hopeless impotence trapped in a thick fog; the state of never having lived as a man.

People who claim to believe in God have cognitively betrayed themselves, and will betray you and your relationship eventually. It is a lack of moral bravery that must be unlearned. When you come to the current limits of clarity in moral thought, it becomes incomprehensible that anyone could ever waste time considering an unprovable, unobservable alternate universe when this one is as complex as it is. Its scope and implications are difficult to grasp with every weapon you have set to stun! Bible stories are not an adequate foundation for a sound mind. Many aspects of existence held by the mystics for centuries have fallen to science, and morality is the final frontier to be claimed before mankind can progress to the astral level. Make no mistake about it: as long as men remain free, the indeterminate is an endangered species.

EPI-STEMS AND THE ORIGIN OF EXISTENCE

A line you will never hear is "The Vatican discovered in their laboratory today..." Still they say science is way behind religion in this regard, because religion already has an answer to our origin, an answer that took no thought or effort to reach: God. We've all heard of scientists who turned to God after working all their lives to answer fundamental questions of existence, which is used by the church as a full redemption of their faith. Watching a television interview with such a physicist, I was surprised at how unscientific his conclusions were. He didn't use science to validate God, he merely gave up his quest much later than most. I'll say it once: *Rational men do not claim to have answers they don't have; they just keep working on the questions.* Notice that despite this claim, religion must attempt to stay in step with the times, but science and technology *are* the times. The proper philosophy for mankind, for all living entities, their inter-relation and their relation to all existential entities, never has to try and keep up. The proper moral code is the same every morning you wake up. It never changes. Axioms *are*, and that's it. Science and technology are the product of Man's mind, allowed to advance first by our trust in Man's capacity to deal with existence. Religion is just the opposite. It is the product of Man's misuse of the mind. A man's level of faith in a power beyond his grasp is his level of self-mistrust for the task of living.

God as deity is itself a false abstract conception whose only presence is in imagination and folklore. Mysticism is not the subject of that other world; its entirety is an illusory product of Man. Like witnessing fire before it could be identified as a natural, repeatable phenomenon, the flake Neanderthals identified it as having a source outside human grasp: a source possessing volition, an evil intention and the ability to reward or punish by virtue of its unharnessable power. They turned legend into nightmare, stealing the potency and moral value of rational sanity—our living power. The sane ones simply tried to figure out what it was. We've heard their snide remark "For the man of faith, no proof is necessary. For the skeptic, no proof is ever enough." But a rational man seeks enough data to produce a desired result within his realm of action, and no less. Fear-driven Man wants vindication for inaction: "See? Your first experiment failed. Trying is futile; the answer is God. Now I can sit on my ass and wait to die for my reward." Finding the origin of the universe or even proof of a god will not change our sleep cycles, the due dates on our Visa bills or absolve our responsibility for our day to day lives. This is our life's context, whose effort is never to be escaped, jilted or transferred to others.

Responsible thought disallows the trespass of data supposedly borne of a source outside the power of our senses. In order to achieve a solid position in an epistemological chain, an entity, attribute or action must be objectively identified, measured and validated by Man's mind. All differentiation follows this format, as to be intelligible, it must. As all the physical world is scientifically classified into an integrated whole for sensible organized use by Man, so goes the process of identifying all abstract conceptions. The formula of genus and differentia is its essence. In contrast, the Christian point of departure is a perfect person to be emulated. What standard measures his performance? None. Jesus *is* their standard, and his experiences are their context—never to be expanded, verified or questioned. The *true* standard of morality *can* measure his contribution and the net result *is* positive, but there is no convincing a mind that requires no proof. Conviction is not sought by such a mind. In actuality, the religious *reject* the fundamentals of morality, and its full depth requires too much stamina to be digested by them anyway.

I respect Jesus as I respect any great historic figure. Benjamin Franklin, Ayn Rand, Abraham Lincoln and Jesus Christ all considered life sacred, and all had profound knowledge to offer. All were willing to explain themselves and to help others along. As a leader, it's not rational to expect never to be questioned, as a dictator can't handle. To be questioned for a productive purpose such as growth should be no problem, but often Christian followers respond much differently. They treat their leaders like dictators, devoting themselves without question—not to greatness, but to a symbol of greatness—not to an ideal, but to a person. The concept of *dictator* is the Fear-driven political end of melding cognition with interaction; they were set up to accept one. When I see such dedication, it creeps me out. The deepest element of their soul is evasion—look at them in this moment and you will see the spiritual equivalent of a savage. No responsibility for consciousness and none for their body, just a zombie to be steered in the religious trance of self-sacrifice. In their deepest tribute, they still cast their vote to eternally support a leader no matter what they might do in the future, still refusing the commitment to think. Do they say "Have you accepted Jesus as your dictator?" Accepting Jesus doesn't give one the knowledge to practice anything. It is a pledge to be virtuous—nothing more. A moral pledge should be a pledge to actively pursue the *knowledge* necessary to be virtuous—the commitment to fully adhere to a rational process of cognition.

Warrior note: *The purpose of language is to bring existence into precise focus for Man to satisfy the task of life, and to propagate the dissemination of that knowledge. If Man's brain is a living mass, a physical part of Man's body—its driver—without which he cannot exist independently, and if language is a product of Man's mind, with its primary function being a means of structuring into a logical whole—by symbolism—all that which comes within the range of Man's sensate capacity to identify, then it's proper focus is Man's existence on this Earth. In other words, as language is a means of comprehension, it precedes and therefore negates religion as a substitute for comprehension.*

Am I against religion? I'm against anything that substitutes itself for thought. I am against allegiance to any unquestionable precedent. I am against any concept that subordinates or negates the process of rational validation. Just imagine if *Moral Armor* (or any other text) was moved into the end of the Bible—call it *The Final Testament*—what a difference it would have in acceptance. *That* is the power of mixing consciousness with interaction. Thumpers have a long way to go; attaining *rational* conviction is a road that nature has defined, such that each of us must travel it alone.

The religious will just continue practicing what is necessary to live via existential consonance though hampered, while ascribing all errors to themselves and all esteem to their master. Good for them. They'll continue to put their faith in a creed whose every element is known to be dysfunctional, and persist in unquestioning obedience to maintain an image of moral adherence, never questioning the standard to which they adhere. Yet here is the physical world to feel and hear and see, which encompasses the whole of their lives, is the subject of their every conscious moment *and makes possible* their contemplation of the nonexistent. The *true* field of their awareness has a consistent, non-contradictory structure identified by Man and *demonstrable*, step-by-step. It purely respects their means of cognition and gauges their advance with a clear link to the steps that come before and those to follow, as well as those which lie in parallel. Yet it is rejected. I can hear them now: "I disagree with you on the subject of religion." *No you don't.* "Yes I do. My opinion is…" *Only a viewpoint based on sound validation can be classified as an opinion. What you have is an emotionally blind substitute for reason and that isn't rational, so it doesn't count.*

There is no fighting them on their terms. Conversations must flow to make sense—they are an example of walking the epistemological chain. That is why in trying to apply it to life, religious conversations always end in violence or silence, even between believers. This is due to delusional fantasies borne of differing cognitive breaks. What one wants to believe differs from what the other wants to believe, but neither is held to the rules of thought, because neither has accepted that existence exists. Permit a debate and they move into the comfort of mindless inapplicable contemplation, or to mankind's voluntary enslavement.

INTERPRETATION AND HYPOCRISY

Religion has made hypocrites out of people with sincere motives—those who sought no contradictions—a tragic result for an honest effort. *Hypocrisy* is the identification of one's own accepted morality as a fraud, yet acting likewise—in fraud. It *is* the disastrous moral failure that it appears. Instead of continuing to search for truth, we fight the fact that we are human and struggle with the contradiction we've been given. We suffer the embarrassing fact that the structure of faith doesn't work; it has no chain. We're trapped. We want to be moral, but our dogma won't let us live. They foisted hypocrisy on us unnecessarily. We've spent a lifetime of painful contradictions attempting to live up to their standards, while all along we missed the connection between their code and our resulting failures. We don't see that it denies life; that its fundamental intention is to destroy a man, not to foster him. There are two ways to see everything, and the anti-organic, anti-rational, anti-human choice is the evil choice. There is less and less need for martyrdom as a society grows more civil. As martyrdom is their symbol, to keep religion alive, they have to make sure society *doesn't* grow more civil. As Jesus indicated, we can choose the nature of Biblical interpretation ourselves. Those who negate the path to life are the true hypocrites.

Between Spirit Murderer and Self-made Man, both seek to claim virtue, but use religion in very different ways. The loafers quote scripture that justifies stagnation and damns their betters, such as *"The meek shall inherit the Earth"*, *"Pride for wealth is the ultimate evil,"* and, *"It is easier for a camel to pass through the eye of a needle than for a rich man to enter the kingdom of heaven."* In Biblical times, men got rich *only* by over-taxation and plunder, so pride for wealth would have been one step above pride for murder. But shame doesn't apply to wealth earned in a free country where exchange is voluntary—*pride* does. In response, the productive quote scripture that justifies their effort and absolves their guilt. For example: *"Lord, thou deliveredst to me two talents: behold, I have gained two other talents besides them. His lord said unto him, Well done, thou good and faithful servant; thou hast been faithful over a few things, I will make thee ruler over many things: enter thou into the joy of thy lord."* —Matthew 25:23. Another servant was afraid to work with the money he was given, and buried it. He is told to give his money to the most profitable servant and is condemned, *"cast ye the unprofitable servant into outer darkness: there shall be weeping and gnashing of teeth."* —Matthew 25:30. The lethargic strike back with more scripture, *"...he that is the greatest among you shall be your servant. And whosoever shall exalt himself shall be abased; and he that shall humble himself shall be exalted."* —Matthew 23:12. Still, this could mean damnation of a Spirit Murderer's 'stature pose' for others, and approval of Self-made Man's non-esteem seeking, wholesome encounters with others. A sanction of rational self-interest and capitalist freedom can be found in *"Is it not lawful for me to do what I will with my own?"* —Matthew 20:15. Did Jesus tell us to violate our minds? *"Blessed are those who believe without seeing"* could be interpreted as blind faith, or as a sanction of abstraction. Moral *validation* of our senses can be found in *"...blessed are your eyes, for they see: and your ears, for they hear."* —Matthew 13:16. The talent story sanctions the proper value hierarchy of Man, as does the following: *"Let all things be done decently and in order."* —1st Corinthians 14:40.

There is a whole different way to interpret The Bible if you love being alive. Both sides seek moral cover that reflects their ends, but one needs cover and one doesn't. One is a fear-ridden, parasitical slacker whose guilt is valid, while the other's guilt is contrived. The full context of most Bible stories promotes mutual respect, civility and hard work, dissolving the intention of a Spirit Murderer's malicious snippets. With the process of cognition known, it's clear what their doing. Your own conscience must decide which pattern to follow.

Regardless of a person's argument, you can feel who intends to leave you with less. When interpretation must be pitted against objectivity, one side intends to preserve predatory slaughter as an alternative to civility. If any natural part of your body or mind is negated, *run*. It is all there for a reason, and that reason *exposes* their moral corruption. If their god is beyond Man's power to conceive, then there is no reason to listen to them. You can also feel who is interested in your well being—those who desire no power over you or anyone else. He brings you new knowledge to contemplate; he doesn't try to commandeer your will or shut you down. Honorable men do not ride or harass anyone. Self-made Men don't teach "Believe me or else," they teach "See for yourself." Philosophically, I can see the grid system of my work charted out into the future. I can see it superimposed over the past, and how and where the Bible lessons fit. There is a sanction of life and rationality to be found at different cognitive levels of its contexts; all that is necessary is the clarity to find them. I can see its long-term intention to *integrate* moral knowledge, where most present interpretation lends itself to *disintegration*. Learn the grid and the narrow path is no longer so.

PERMEATION

Inauguration into our highest offices take their oath on the Bible as the highest moral tribute they have been shown. This isn't surprising historically; most leaders align themselves with whatever premise is deepest in men. That devotion is reassuring to the extent that one respects the stature of the text. But if it is no longer the highest, remaining faithful to it is frightening. Christianity in our culture, as the religions of societies before us, has permeated everything, shifting all virtue to itself; even the founding of America.

America is not a product of Christianity, but in direct contradiction to it and to any wishy-washy moral uncertainty. This country was founded by those *escaping* religious persecution. Our Constitution clearly separates church and State as a direct result of past experience with tyrannical religious powers witnessed throughout Europe. Our founders were sick of vicious men taking control; religion was intentionally pushed out of the loop of production, law and politics so that men could live. America holds fast to *clear cut* moral standards—first and foremost that Man has a right to live and that his highest value is himself. America was set up so that a man can believe whatever he chooses, without the threat of violence as repercussion for his belief. So long as he respects the basic rights of other men in turn, there are no conflicts. Still, with the Christian morality prevalent in the free world, Christ became our mascot. There was little chance of our justice system not accounting for its charity premises in some way, and the stench of injustice became the foundation for most *abstract* law. Welfare, alimony, antitrust and lobbies are all the mongrel cancer of altruist fantasy, the desire of the ugly to be beautiful, of the sick to be healthy and to gain it all by devouring those who are.

The Bible's initial intention was to lay down the law, which has been superceded in time, depth and quality by Roman, English and American law. The Old Testament measured property values in slaves, oxen and myrrh, things most people cannot relate to, but were significant for that time. Its moral depth was also a reflection of that time. The Ten Commandments as a guide for social action are as poor in implication as the United Nations Bill of Rights. A modern industrial society requires a much more vast and detailed account to dispense justice, which we have in America. Look at Thomas Paine's *The Rights of Man*, Ayn Rand's *Atlas Shrugged* or our own Constitution; these sources give Man a moral clarity no theologist could touch. Due to the nature and depth of its content, the Bible should have been relegated to fable status by now. Look at our civilization compared to those who still practice the primitive Old Testament doctrines. We're not murdering each other en masse—the religious devotees still are. They still preach that selfishness is evil, yet all rational law serves to protect the rights of the individual (the rights of the self). Selling you benefits you won't see for twenty years or until you die is a socialist premise—a pyramid scheme. Religion's actual goal and effectiveness is played out on the battlefields of Islamic nations. When the mind is abandoned, the only means of communication left open is violence. The bloodiest wars are over religious interpretation, which is its logical result.

Religion in political application parallels the propaganda of Socialism. It is a concentration of power—the type of power is not the primary. Whether economic, spiritual or intellectual, cold war soviets are its real children. Socialism is *forced* moral action—a contradiction in terms. The proper moral gauge is based on independent, voluntary action alone. As adherence to the rational process of cognition permeates the field of morality, if you intend to be considered good, you're going to have to think.

JESUS' TRUE CONTRIBUTION

Jesus was a man devoid of pretense. He had the mark of genius so rare in any time—someone who had reached full volitional consciousness—yet he had to depend on 3-4's at best to record and carry his message. Had he lived longer, I'm sure he would have taken his work to the next level. As he grew, he would have resolved its existential contradictions, clarified the true essence of evil and made what he preached more palatable for all. Instead, given the unexplained implications in his word, interpretation was left to those also lacking a proper standard of value from which to extract sound meaning. They relied on that period's cultural standard, with the Submission/Domination Axis as their only reference and key moral conflict. Their solution was to turn the tables and become the dominant, and therefore sacrifice was perpetuated.

He was at odds with the law and at odds with the church. He didn't think the law was helping the people. He didn't think the church was guarding their faith. They were envious. They wanted the love of those he drew voluntarily, and they still want it. Like Judas attempting to exploit his following, they were eager to silence him in order to put words in his mouth. Diminishing the power of the church by fostering independent spirituality was a massive threat to them. The message in his death was "Don't give up your morality. Die for it if necessary, knowing it *is* a question of life or death." By standing mute and adding nothing of his own, he showed what the rulers were all about. What they cannot kill is when this power is an attribute of all men. Challenging the concept of trusting one divine leader for interpretation (the church), versus God being in *every* man—*this* was Jesus' revelation, and one step closer to the truth of *moral* empowerment. For a power seeker, there is no greater threat. If morality was to be an attribute of the individual, next to follow would be self-government and they would be dethroned. They were.

THE TRUTH ABOUT THEM

> *"My karma ran over your dogma."* —bumper sticker

Underneath it all, we've known all along that religion was a license to torture, that they've privately enjoyed our agony, relishing the position of doling out punishment. When death is their symbol and suffering is their standard, who is surprised that they live to torment the rest of us? They are the sadomasochist Spirit Murderers, and religion is their best loved, most complete tool. There isn't a moral action they don't have a penalty for; there isn't a moral violation they are not guilty of. There is no soundly defined, organic and epistemologically based moral premise which religion does not defy. Whether purported now or 2000 years ago, a Spirit Murderer is behind every choice against the flow of natural life. Their job is to stop, condemn, sentence and drag people to their deaths—their historic constant. Give them control even now, and their intentions will have the same medieval end.

Look at their priests: Here is someone under the extreme stress of a vow of celibacy—denied the relief of a natural build up, reminiscent of Chinese water torture—and you wonder why he can't keep his hands out of your five year old's pants. Forced to cover such a debilitating limitation provokes the most radical development for repression and masterful deception. I'd never let my child close to anyone driven nearly insane by a life and reason-negating moral code. The guy is a time bomb. Abolishing this vow and permitting the wholesome, natural expression of sex—for Nuns as well—would virtually wipe out its perverse alternatives, and have a profound impact on their psychological health.

I suffered through their doctrines as a child—the unbelievable violence, the shame of adults whom in answer to their own panic of moral uncertainty, agreed to anything, hysterically forcing us to conform to absurd impossibilities while they sucked up to their own little back-stabbing, political microcosm. We had to memorize what we were expected to believe. We had to practice the lie. The penalty for seeing was being attacked. Like learning to smoke, we had to ignore the convulsions and pretend we loved it. Where reason was not respected, it was the civil and rational who lost. Only those who used lies to pursue plunder and death were good at it; they could move and act unhindered. To them, evasions came natural; from generation to generation it was the continual rebirth of the Socratic Method; of Apartheid; of the Spanish Inquisition. "*Kill your body to free your soul. Accept your own worthlessness. Obey us because only we are privileged to interpret the unknowable. Trust no outsider. Damn enjoyment, damn progress, damn ability. Our perfect world of peace is a cemetery. We will never run out of victims, because someone will always want to live.*"

A long, painful road has brought us to the truth about morality, Man's mind and Man's negation of mind. I submit to you, that it was not a god who told you to violate your own nature—who said you could not think, that you could not protect yourself, that you must allow your life and happiness to be sacrificed and that you are guilty when you've done nothing wrong. It was not a god that told you to spit in your own face, but fear-based men. Men to whom we pay tithes, tithes we imagine disappearing into the heavens to our moral account, but gather instead into their cars, homes and retirement plans. Taking advantage of the directionless, it is used for destruction, fleecing and control. Mass devotion to the unprovable and unaccountable just creates a charlatan breeding ground: men who remind you that you owe someone for your evil, and then maneuver to be the one.

Warrior note: *A guilt accused of all men, leaves no benefactor to atone to.*

In the mean time, watch out for hard-core Christians. Those who openly cling fast to their faith will lie, cheat, force and pretend more than any other type of human. Like Islamic Fundamentalism, their morality lets them get away with anything. If someone chooses religion as their moral operating system, with the structure of cognition known and their violation of it traceable, you'll know why. Whether Buddhism, Judaism or Catholicism, it's all nonsense to the extent that it violates cognition. Socially inept, sacrifice is their mantra and they're always on the lookout for someone to feed to their god. And who is their god? Incoherence. When faced with a dilemma their brain can't handle, the primitive horror of their morality comes right to the surface. They attack, intending to bash you over the head, perhaps thinking on the way, *"Love is my reason! I'll be justified and forgiven afterwards!"* Their anti-reasoning is as follows: *"If we are willing to sacrifice our lives, then everyone else has to be willing to destroy themselves too. If they aren't, we have the right to take matters into our own hands. If they can't see the beauty in our philosophy of destruction, then we'll just have to show them."* Listen carefully to the descriptions of their perfect world: they are enemies of effort, enemies of rational discipline, enemies of Earth and enemies of Man. The cross of death is their symbol, as if to say, *"Blood sacrifice; that's all you need to know."*

The infamy is that if your guardians could start a new world from scratch, *this* is what they would teach that world. Not to develop abilities in order to achieve human values and be the best you can, but cringing at the sight of any greatness, they would teach you to cherish their murderous, occultist stagnation. Trust no dogma whose symbol is death. Only when we see them no longer crucifying their subjects—when their actions reflect their savior, *not* his killers—only when their crosses come down, should we take them seriously. It's not so important how Jesus died. What's important is how he lived. When they return such a great man to the proper setting of life and worship *that*, we'll know they're on the right path.

MAN'S SAVIOR

Should the proper definition of utopia be something we can never reach while we live? *Individualism*, or moral sovereignty is the way to salvation, is responsible for all human progress and will be what leads to peace on Earth, the peace Christianity would not permit. Happiness which proves so elusive has at its core, this essential ingredient withheld by most systems of faith. There is no pretense of humility in true happiness. There is no sense of hypocrisy, living one way while one's moral code demands another. Imagine going to confession and knowing you have no sins to confess. That state of guiltless purity is quite a sensation and quite a worthy goal, but the price is full volitional awareness—the lifelong commitment to stand naked before the truth of cognitive evidence. I won't tell you that you can practice the opposite just by claiming it's right for you, and prosper with an approach that is contrary to life. Be brave and give up the desire to preserve the indeterminate in every important context. You can't win with it anyway; no one ever has, and you will not be the first who will. Follow the rational process of cognition and you will not be confused. You will not be taken advantage of and you will not be immoral. Instead, you will generate the most profound and lasting pride, never to be surrendered again. Face the world alone. Look to *existence* for the answers you seek, as He said: *"Turn over a stone, and you will find me."*

"You know, we're just not reaching that guy."

Education

"How do you explain school to higher intelligence?" —E.T.

Being self-educated in every way, I am often criticized in regard to the validity of my stands and my basic worth as a human being. I've never taken an IQ test. I don't even know if I have a brain according to scholastic precedent. I'm afraid what I'd do with a No. 2 pencil to whoever intended to gauge my cognitive power by asking me "What is the capital of Arkansas?" I refute this misconception in *Moral Armor,* but my response to skepticism is always the same account: A baseball manager was fed up with answering questions about a certain player's value to the team. His response was, "Yep, he can't run, can't hit, can't catch. All he can do is *beat* you."

Anti-philosophy. A host of men throughout history have been declared philosophers, while their thinking consisted of claiming that Man cannot think. From Plato's "We know that we know nothing," to Sartre's "My existence is absurd" (that was true by the way), a long line—Hegel, Marx, Kant, Hume— have been some of the world's most influential minds. The reason is not in the virtue of the authors, but in the vices of their audience. The 'get away with it' mentality is a horde that will crowd around anyone willing to tell them that the 'something for nothing' ideal is a spiritual revelation. With the support of many enthusiastic backers, these men intended to design the perfect society which required nothing from anyone, and succeeded only in destroying our capacity to prove otherwise. They enjoyed the confusion they caused as if it was profound; but is proof of intellectual depth, the contemplation of inconsequential trivia? Even modern professors jump on the band wagon as their only means to feel creative, enjoying the spectacle of leaving their students speechless in response to unanswerable questions, which intend to declare the unreliability and futility of the mind and its sensate capacities. The title of intellectual can only be granted to those who exercise discipline in the use of their intellect; not to those who *evade* its use. Such men have given the field of philosophy the air of unprofessionalism it now has, which is why bus drivers can be so philosophical. Philosophy was meant for 100% practical use, not what we've been subjected to in its name.

Let's question their most common refutation of logic...What has been disapproved? "Everything," they say. Okay, so water is toxic and acid is safe to drink? So human beings no longer need food in order to eat? Fools. What do they intend to accomplish? Why attack reason? The answer is that they have reached their own intellectual tolerance, and to maintain their pretenses, they feel they need you off sound footing. In the context of academia, they have become Spirit Murderers and they intend to deliver you into a void of undifferentiated chaos, hoping you'll never discover their stagnation. When an authority answers a question by introducing any mystical elements, he is side stepping. Mysticism is not the unknown, but the unknowable, safely outside the range of intellectual scrutiny. A better mind and a more complete understanding should have the capacity and tolerance to convey it. Why do they get away with selling obfuscation as revelation? Because Plato and Socrates gave them the idea that rationality is optional, and they ran with it. Fifty years after the most impressive contributions to philosophy were made by Ayn Rand, academics still fail to include her in their courses. That is precisely why this book did not come from a Ph.D.

If I was approached by a group of students exposed to an instructor posing supposedly answerless questions such as "What is an eye?" I would answer as follows: *An eye is an instrument that receives light waves of a certain frequency, allowing detection of universal existents, their motion and their spatial relationships, in regard to its own position.* "What does it do?" *It presents its owner with information regarding entities (animals, plants, men, streets, cliffs) which benefit or threaten it, encompassing all the conditions it may encounter in its pursuit of life.* "What is it for?" *It allows navigation of the Earth's surface for entities designed to employ physical motion to maintain their survival.* "Is what it sees, really there?" *Yes.* "Our teacher said *that* can't be proved. How can we be sure?" *Prove it to him by case study, beginning with the sense of touch. Have every student line up, and one by one, kick him in the ass. Record every "Ow." Divide the number of kicks by the number of Ow's. Repeatability in response to the causal agent should establish a trend for the validation of Man's senses. Repeat the test in a likewise fashion for the remaining senses; you will need a stick, a turd, a trumpet and a doctor. Otherwise, think for yourself.*

How could colleges hope to lure kids with their professors saying things like this? A mathematician doesn't question whether or not humans can add. Ask yourself whether a science that should be focused on the proper development of our tools of cognition—philosophy—should spend its time questioning their validity. Ask yourself what happens to his life if he accepts that they are not. He can no longer drive to class, read a book, hear a lecture or ask a question, get hungry, satisfy that hunger or comprehend anything. He could no longer live. "If we had better vision, would we see something other than what we see right now?" *No, only the precision of what is seen would improve. With better information regarding the object before you, your capacity to differentiate its attributes, to draw conclusions and to deal with it expands, and this is true for our other senses as well.* Look at Benjamin Franklin, his intention to educate society, his motive and the result. Look at Stalin, Mao and Hitler, their removal of education from society, their motive and the result. What intent then, lies behind undercutting Man's *means* of acquiring knowledge? No actions or endeavors of Man are ever to consist of the question whether or not we have any capacity to investigate them, if they are to be considered scientific, philosophical or rational. To close the issue once and for all, *if you ask me a question that attempts to challenge the validity of Man's senses, you'll have to—in good faith—figure out a way to convey it to me without using them.*

Bad Formal Theory. A child is born; in his comprehension of this intriguing new world, it all seems so limitless and so radiantly joyful. He grows into a young adult and discovers that men who lived before him, already have opinions about his subjects of interest and have put caps on achievement. There is a system in place designed not to help him live an unlimited progression, but to trap him and his ambition. "We look upon him with love and only restrict him to keep him from hurting himself or others. *We* know what is best for him." His authorities negate his competence, take his inspiration and tell him what it has to be, and who it has to serve. If he accepts it, his sense of discovery wanes and is bent to discovering the laws of men and their constraints. This is not to extend his freedom, but to limit it, not to foster his best, but to gain his obedience. The rapid pace of his real world experience, open to the sky and the wind, is interrupted and replaced with the snails pace of a stagnant classroom where general information is stuffed into general brains. A well-rounded education becomes the goal for all, which in life is not the *cause* of prosperity, but the *result* of pursuing an individual purpose. Individual purpose is a foreign topic with no guidance whatsoever, having been replaced with the lifeless void of social conformity.

If you remember the freedom of your childhood, everything was new; a wonderful discovery awaited you around every corner. You learned because you wanted to; because it was a stimulating, fascinating, pleasure-filled process. We would sit on a hill, looking out at the limitless Earth, thinking of all we can do. The future promises so much, a promise unbroken until other men impede it. *Life* makes this promise; foolish men take it away. Gathering knowledge only became a chore once we started tripping over adults who felt the need to second-guess our every action. Years later, we find out that we had to do everything twice: first the mindless way and then the *experiential* way, in the real world.

College is not the only way to learn. It does more to pattern people into intellectual lethargy than any other form of teaching. We have patterns of behavior all around us every day, some good, some bad, all of which we have the potentiality to assume and practice. In college for at least four years, you are ingrained to respect an alternate frame of reference (higher authority vs. independent experience) reviewing a static body of knowledge, with success or failure determined not by the free range of what works and what doesn't, but by tests as the only standard of right and wrong, which you then come to accept as the measure of the value of your brain's content (and later, as your self-worth). This, mixed with teacher pleasing (social conformity vs. individual judgment), teaches you to repress, to hold back and to stay in sync with the group. Someone choosing no explicit purpose or goals can manage to cross the street without getting hit, and that's about it. I hated college. The standard college pattern is undue torture for those who know what they want.

If you've had a formal education, looking back, was college the most educational period of your life? Of course not. Why? It lacked application. Most students in college learn the same chain, ten percent of which any of them found useful. Its staunch supporters all remain tied to it in some way. The majority of the furtherance of Man happens outside schools. The best think alone, and discover what the schools are later to teach, but of course not for a long time, while the supposed intellectuals rot in a state of denial over the value of outside accomplishments relative to their own 'elite' clique. They cling to their view of themselves as the cream, while they fall way behind industry. What do the students get out of this?

Teaching people what they don't want to know and have no incentive to learn does not leave them better off. It robs them of time that could be used to further their own aims or discover them, and gives it to that which they don't wish to further. It perverts their expectations and identity as well, conditioning them to believe that they have learned all they need to—all that society expects of them—instilling the delusion that they have joined the cream of that undefined crop—a passionless victory. They become those who are *done learning*, which epistemologically, means *done for*. Outside of the physical sciences and perhaps law, the psychological taint of the standard college pattern is worse than useless. It cripples the cognitive function of Man by implying that mankind's current understanding of existence is on par with the metaphysically given (deserving equal respect with scientific law), but actually, all that which deals with the classification, organization and the present use of mankind's knowledge is subject to change. *Final answers* are not contained in the books; progress dwells in research—the very research students should be trained to conduct into the future.

Flaws in Public Education. Most of the psychological guff spouted by our Departments of Education these days serves to promote failure and complacent stagnation in our public schools. They have reduced expectations to approximations, resulting in intellectual disintegration. They grade on curves instead of assuring competence, making it so easy to pass, that kids learn nothing. They pander to self-esteem instead of instilling *the cause* of self-esteem, a folly the outside world will never cater to. Their psychologists tell us that kids aren't just unruly these days, they are *sick*. They have this disease or that disorder; it couldn't be that they are *kids*. They have to be labeled, drugged and pushed onto a dependency of some kind, informed of their supposed illness—an awareness of which, valid or invalid, is to be carried for life—and altered physically to conform. Whatever the cure, it is not to be sought through education or training, but through penalties. Ironically enough, this coincides with a Cold War Communist infiltration plan called *Psychopolitics*. They have patterned public school more and more, not for independence after graduation, but as if the students will be going on welfare. We have the technology to reverse all these things and yet nothing changes. Why? Spirit Murderers in philosophy—and those who share their malice. The problem is the sociological influence on methodology, and when kids don't perform well under it, regulators do what all socialists propose: variants of force on their victims—threats such as no driver's license, summer school or community service. They blame it on the kids, showing them how inhumane, foolish and downright stupid such adults really are—certainly those in control of this farce.

Mandatory community service for high school students is itself a moral disaster. No vice, be it age, stupidity or addiction justifies involuntary servitude; the psychological ramifications and economic dislocation only foster more evil. Worse yet, nothing justifies altering the natural cognitive state of a child. Educators must hone what they see before them into peaceful, productive independence. The social ramifications are a resultant factor only, and will be obvious.

I'm convinced that the ineffectiveness of public schools stems from their disassociation with the profit motive. Private schools *have* to be good. Public schools are funded regardless, leaving the faculty free to degenerate in countless ways, bickering about salaries rather than showing any concern for the students. Kids shouldn't see adults acting this way. Those of integrity who disagree with the Board belong in the private system, perhaps at a level that does not exist as of yet. All of those selling kids down the river for union demands or senseless board rulings, subjecting them to physical and psychological alteration because it's easier than fulfilling your sacred obligation, you should be ashamed to breathe. Just pass on the dysfunction; welcome to the limitations of the future.

Holier than Thou. Certain professions breed those who believe that their four to six year program such as medical school spans the whole of human knowledge, making them masters over a chain so vast that one hundred lifetimes could not absorb it all. They are wrong, and are known to the rest of us, as twits. Their knowledge, while important, is only a sliver of the total and does not grant them superiority over the rest. Expertise is contextual and is transferable *to an extent*—yet competency in any new realm must be proven. Greatness in one activity won't translate into greatness in others, if one did not translate their means of acquisition. A doctorate doesn't grant total authority over all contexts, any more than musical talent vindicates poor grooming.

The twits equate the undegreed with the unprofessional, as an exclusionist blanket damnation for the rest of mankind. Their gestures imply as if to say, "I don't have to explain myself clearly, because you're not licensed to think." To some extent, their bias rubs off on the general populace, in lowered eyes and humbled dreams, while the world shows countless instances of self-taught, self-made millionaires. After all, it wasn't Dr. Aristotle, Dr. Ayn Rand or Dr. Jesus. So what's true?

Non-degreed people are not second rate citizens. None of the pedigree hoopla they hold over your head is honorable. What are anyone's credentials once they are working? *Results*; and actually, true credentials have never been anything else. The one who does his work the best *is* the best, and there is no consideration other than one's productive accomplishment. The education snob, like the playboy, seeks esteem outside himself by looking down on you. His credentials are a crutch to lean on, in the same manner as a red-faced tantrum intends to lend weight to an opinion. They are the pretense seekers, probably the most boring and miserable of all emotional parasites. Now, it's not wrong to be proud of your education to the extent that it is soundly integrated and honestly achieved. But it is wrong to use it as a shim, in an attempt to lend the pretense of stability to a wobbly perspective.

I have college friends of astounding intellectual capacity, but their educations serve them and continue to expand, as they are all Self-made at heart. The Fear-driven live according to whatever society dictates, which just shows their propensity to be led. They stopped learning when they were told they were "finished." It is their elitist funnel, and huddling for safety, they tend to feel they deserve a closed shop. Classes in sociology have taught them to expect it.

I could have spent this time getting a degree; I wrote *Moral Armor* instead. An undergraduate diploma amounts to 6000 hours of class and study, and in my case, I have over 20,000 hours in philosophy: a Ph.D. can't even touch me. My chain of knowledge is longer and more useful than any university curriculum could provide. It was earned, point by point due to cognitive necessity, in the field. We all work hard, and over time, collect valuable pieces to a vast and complex puzzle—the puzzle of our lives. If we are not stuck in a rut of repetition, every one of us is building a very potent body of life-furthering knowledge—a wealth to be proud of.

Dismal Life Consequences. After a lifetime of self-education, this is a painful question to hear: "Do you have a degree?" It is an automatic ideological conflict, and not the time or place for a debate. I would answer, "*A degree of intelligence? Yes. A college degree? No. Colleges do not teach what I had to learn to write this, and I knew that in advance. What I have is what college is meant to give you—a functional competence in a certain realm. I have a degree of knowledge I can share, which benefits the lives of others with enough value that they are willing to pay me so that I can sustain my own life by it.*" Self-sustenance at the highest level you care to achieve is what education is intended to prepare you for.

It may be statistically valid that those completing a four-year course of study after high school earn more versus those who don't, but statistics are not standards—they are cultural symptoms, effects and results. They get paid more because they are subjectively considered to be more intelligent, which seems a reasonable assumption, though the degree appraises *content* alone—not intellectual efficacy, integrity or the energy necessary to do the work. Having no means to gauge this, requiring a degree substitutes for thought on the part of the hirer. What they want is a release from the responsibility of identifying cognitive value in answering the essential question: "Is this guy good for the company?"

In response to the question "Do you have a degree?" I resort to what I call The "coupon" close. "*No, but I do have a coupon for half-off at Little Caesars. (Looking around to assure privacy) I don't want to imply anything, but if we went out to lunch, you could possibly benefit from the use of this coupon.*" Not in the mood for bribery? Then I'd reply, "*I have the degree of intelligence necessary to perform the work I'm interviewing for, and I'd be glad to prove it.*" If that isn't sufficient, walk. Their desire is not to hire competence, but to avoid thought. Not to choose wisely, but to let an outside force choose for them. If formalities are a deal-breaker, imagine your likely fate in that company anyway, and move on to a better one.

Corporate Dysfunction

"Competition is sin." —John D. Rockefeller

Market inertias sometimes permit mediocre companies to flourish, simply due to under-supplied market segments. Perhaps a mid-level manager sees an opportunity to exploit a niche serving his own employer, and starts his own firm with a competence barely above the coherence to see the opportunity itself. They can go on for years displeasing everyone they encounter and still keep their doors open, as there is no one else to fill the gap. Or maybe the owner is a "lucky sperm" as Donald Trump calls them; born into wealth but not into competence. Sometimes we see a sign of life in their business, only to see it burn out as fast. The brief spurt in such a company's quality is the result of a Living Generator somewhere in the chain. Likely duped into taking the job, the temporary flourish leaves when *he* leaves. While no company can survive completely absent of talent, a company cannot be run by an arm or a leg, and cannot be fundamentally changed without the sanction of its head. When we are employees, we are just limbs. Such an arm can be alive and well, just wiggling away, while the rest is on its death bed. This arm belongs on a healthier body. We cannot mask the entities sickness by attempting to override the confusions of its head. If its head is faulty it will die, and it should die. Outside of corporate bromides, the truth in business for all men in positions of authority is that they work to actualize their own psychological bias towards life or death. As I like to say in consultations, *"The direction of your business is determined by your own psycho-epistemology. We can work to advance your business, or I can help you run it into the ground—whatever the hell you want to do."*

It never ceases to amaze me that the biggest contributor to a profit and loss statement—human resources—has nothing to do with profit and loss. Often, company presidents feel it safe to leave this facet of their business in the hands of some amiable ink-blot specialist. He then restricts the hiring budget and closes his door to the issue of manpower. Employees are then hired by what I call the *"low pay and high hopes"* method, where quality is driven out while schooled incompetence and fresh inexperience is then allowed to destroy the company.

Don't be too upset when organizations don't hire by ability, but only by degree. It's a free country and they can do as they wish. Consider it an opportunity to profit, because they are going in the wrong direction. If they think it's safe to make employment decisions based on nonessentials, then the free market will take a chunk of their profitability away and give it to the quicker, more adapting thinkers—to the displaced producers in that field. Degrees don't make money. If the business is failing, how will it die if MBA is after the president's name? Will it spiral to the left instead of the right? Smart managers assemble teams of the best available, whose selection is based off *ability*. To attract it, you must be able to identify it. To keep it, you must have the deepest regard for it. We must choose our employers by the same means as they choose us, and if the means don't match, watch out!

Irrational Employers. Bad managers tailor their management style to their own cowardice. Often he is thrust into a leadership role by those who escaped the responsibility of judgment by substituting his diploma for their own estimate of his character and capacities. Lacking the courage to define the intellectual framework for the sustenance of independent life, he seeks the protective exoskeleton of a company's hierarchical structure to unwittingly obey. With his fear impairing his ability to distinguish essential profitable actions from inessentials, company policy and supplication replace his judgment.

Unable to do the job and eager to mask it, such managers will sacrifice anything or anyone not to lose it. They eek their way through the organization, jumping when told and responding with "Yes, yes, yes!", pandering to authority without applying a moral-rational filter. They bow above and backstab below, undermining those abler and training their subordinates to do likewise. Corporate dysfunction reveals the same elements found in Communism—the manic pursuit of the sure thing—which is what *all* Fear-driven men do when they are in control. They are tolerated by those above because they are priced right and never make waves above them. They think they're getting a great deal, as they filled the position with a moldable body and came in under budget. Of course, the most important causal agent of a business—its people—become dysfunctional due to low morale and misguided objectives, and no one can figure out why. Permitting such managers in the work hierarchy disrupts proper epistemological flow and results in virtually untraceable, mass inefficiencies. In other words, you get what you pay for. The problem persists because often upper managers were products of the *"low pay and high hopes"* formula as well.

Bad managers expect the supplication of subordinates—the King and Queen syndrome rooted in monarchical times. They expect to be bowed to and to command the whip-driven slave worker who is not to be relied on to think—the mindset that built Nazi industries and China's slave-labor workforce. Instead of promoting independence and exemplifying ability, they design processes to eliminate thought. People are more prone to err if they are not encouraged to exercise their rational faculty. Whenever a supervisor stands in the way of his employee's judgment, whether he is cognizant of it or not, it is an action intended to harm the corporation. Stimulate the mind, and you have their attention and their quality. If you seek supplication instead, your days are numbered. Its worst is when they become abusive, imposing their burden of neurotic unhappiness on a ledge they believe will support it. I'd respond sternly with, *"Listen, I've had enough abuse from my father. I'm not about to take yours."*

With a mindset based on mistrust, they extol working conditions where they can watch our every move. The fish bowl office environment is a sociologically-driven cognitive atrocity. In the study of human efficiency, cognition is the primary to consider; all social aspects are secondary. A mind can handle five elements at most, and having another person in visual range often takes two—first, the perception of the entity and second, the continual identification of its motive—which is a major concentration breaker. A wrong topic of focus—even the effort to block them out—steals a register and taints the other registers. For concentration, all registers must complement by principle. Besides, by making all personal actions *public* actions, it is an attribute of poverty, as privacy is an attribute of wealth. The professional answer is dividers; out of sight, out of mind.

Next, he seizes control whenever workgroups are discussing their approach. Reason to him is vacillation, something he must avoid. His employees comment, *"We get the work done in spite of him, but he doesn't trust us. He wedges in like a sliver and just causes pain until he leaves the loop."* It's not primarily that he doesn't believe in his people, but that he doesn't believe in himself. With no internal frame of moral reference, the fear-based mind panics and operates by the latest business fad. When spooked, he breaks that direction and goes off in another, leaving everyone lost without clear expectations. Employees must operate according to his constantly shifting center of gravity.

Outside the business, he crawls before his corporate customers, submitting to their will regardless of their sanity or the long range impact of their policies on his firm. He rapes his suppliers, abrogating prior agreements that result in lower quality and making it easier for his competition to trounce him. Squeezing every last dime out of each transaction only antagonizes his relations with others: the action is parasitical. He might win on one round of deals, but word spreads fast and his company loses in the long run. To him, no violation of ethics is out of the question once he's in control—lying, pressuring, even annoying his customers to gain a sale or a contact, with deception, telemarketing and personal invasion. He lobbies for unfair advantages and seeks international slave labor to secure the right—not to his own ideas, but to bar the ideas of others from reaching markets he wishes to hold captive. This is predation instead of creation—using others up instead of respecting the pattern of other human lives in turn.

Irrational Employees. Bad managers aren't the only problem; employees are equally prone to functioning primarily from their own fear. On the submissive side of the axis, the employee acts like a captive, relishing any excuse to despise those above him. He focuses on inessentials as well, such as strict adherence to company policy, rank or seniority as substitute for his productive value to the company. He lies, steals, cheats time and takes credit for the work of others, and when hostilities arise, he is defeated in advance, acting like a child being dragged away for a spanking. He forms or joins unions in an "us against them" pose, seeking to wrestle values out of unwilling victims by threat of mob-driven

369

violence, or by holding the company's output for ransom. He hides behind the crowd, muttering animosities under his breath and only emerges to deal a blow once the opposition is down. The collective bargaining of unions *fixes* the Submission/Domination Axis as a business's employee/employer relationship.

An employee does not decide product or corporate direction. At the most he simply provides recommendations, then expedites management's will—that is his proper moral position. His opinion of their motives and policies is irrelevant beyond his own spiritual tolerance for rationality or irrationality. If he has agreed to take their money in exchange for his effort, then they deserve no static from him, and no attitudes.

When we are brought to the state of obeying anyone who expects it without cause, reason or justification, who is at fault? Companies have to be flexible for employees if they expect employees to be flexible for them. Essentially, rational employers pay for *ability*, so there is no need for employees to feel that they hold a weaker position. We need each other, disallowing *either* to take advantage. It doesn't matter if employees are replaceable; *employers are too.*

Spiritual Bankruptcy. We've all had to endure imbeciles who steer our work-lives in exactly the wrong direction. The path we should be on is so clear to us that we can't help but be spiritually inflicted by the deviation. They are so wrapped up in the safety of inessential details, that it seems impossibly as if our human thought process is incompatible, and ours has become null and void in their presence—which is exactly true. Hearing "*I told you to do this; why didn't you?*" we might reply, "*Sorry, I have a habit of doing what makes sense.*" If we don't quit, we have to store the resentment—a bad choice. Most first-time heart attack death victims are job-stress related, so Self-made Man does all he can to reduce work stress. He has the purest respect for rational cognition and no tolerance for its violation. To accept it, the fringe at-risk *dies*. No job is worth harming one's health and one's view of Man. He pays attention to his body; he learns what he can take and what he can't. As an employee, he has his own unwritten policy that says, "*1, 2, 3 and I'm out.*" He identifies who is responsible for the negativity and its level of impact to his inner peace. If the problem is his, he works on it until it no longer unsettles him. If it is outside of him, he counts off the significant violations and then quits. I've been there, threatened by such asinine managers for using common sense, who reply from their management handbook with "*1, 2, 3 and you're out.*" No problem; violate me 1, 2, 3 and I'm gone anyway.

The stupidity and dysfunction of a manager is often so all encompassing that one gets bottlenecked in recounting any specific flaw. They constantly criticize for the neglect of inessential, irrelevant issues such as lunch times, start and stop times, break times, social and work discussions and unnecessary meetings. They can't relax or permit others to. We spend approximately thirty years of our lives in the office—this time should be spiritually positive. If a manager doesn't have the maturity to let his people enjoy their time in the office while they produce for him, he should step down until he gains control of his fear and perhaps sees a psychiatrist. Is anxiety an attribute of the solutions we seek? Of course not. If he brings it, the problem is his.

Even great companies are only great to work for when you can deal comfortably with the management. When management changes, it can very suddenly become a nightmare. In my opinion, managerial retardation is *anti-life* and doesn't deserve our respect, so it's justified and very entertaining to be insolent, when done with grace and style. The key is to have three months salary set aside for when you get fired, because you probably will be. Take one manager for instance...I would sit there thinking, *"Come on, do something stupid...,"* so that I could determine the essential flaws in his pattern, breaking down the most common to identify solutions. In response to hearing some poorly reasoned, short-range direction I'd say, *"Are we doing this to show how much forethought we can avoid?"* Facing the refusal to use current industry standards, defended as *"The old methods still work,"* I'd respond with *"...and we can still shit outside if we want to."* Hearing that we must offer our spare time to those unable to complete their assignments I responded with, *"So our efficiency is to be rewarded with unpaid overtime?"* Eventually I was pushed out: "We're terminating your contract. We have no complaint about your talent; we don't actually have any reasons. We just feel you are a disruptive element, harmful to the company's morale. Now, do you have anything you would like to say?" *"Yes. Morale is a product of management policy. The staff's reaction in support of my comments is the symptom of a problem that does not stem from me; killing the messenger will not resolve it. That's all I have to say. Oh, and your fly is open."* They had a going-away party for me, but needless to say, I wasn't invited.

Life is about fear for them. Business is about money—just *getting* it, so they can stave off their own panic. The idea of fulfillment means nothing but pain and torture to them; any attempt at abstraction results in the folly of altruism—the whole cognitive pattern of the Spirit Murderer—so that is what they bring to others. It's therapeutic to irk the living shit out of them (I've developed so thorough a respect for my own time that I don't bother at this level anymore, but it was fun). It's very powerful to have a mind on the side of the good, secure enough in its own premises to have no fear, and thus be free to remain active and motive-driven. If motives ever get questioned, you don't have to bluff. You lay your cards on the table, and you win.

Fear-driven Government

> *"Men and nations behave wisely once they have exhausted all the other alternatives."* —Abba Eban

Socialism. The governments of Kings, Queens, Imperial Monarchy, Socialist, Communist and Collectivist rule are all just forms of dictatorship—the despotism of unlimited control, which translates into unlimited coercion. There are many styles of government to consider, but in the modern world, only two are prevalent—Socialism, a subversive exaltation of the working class which is the senseless product of Karl Marx and his destructive predecessors, and Capitalism, the product of the Founding Fathers. The ideals of Socialism are just a screen; they are never actually achieved. They permit the looting of rationally gathered, earned wealth, and establish a new structure much lower: the wolf-pack hierarchy and its peril—gang warfare. There is *always* a hierarchy; to be *without* a chain of command is the definition of anarchy. The result of all struggles for power determines the hierarchy's form. Whoever gains control becomes wealthy, if only by comparison to the population—therefore, all irrational governments are forms of fascism.

Most imagine a dictatorship as a super state of arms with rigid rules, but it isn't. The rules flow with expediency, persecuting anyone who has a value to loot, seized under a claimed threat to the party. *They do whatever they want, whenever they want*—the simple pattern of roving criminality, sanctioned by law. Hedonism never sells, but disguise the slaughter of others through *self*-slaughter and aah, now you've got something. Communist governments bank on strangers being able to do what fifty percent of all marriages fail at and which the successful ones don't practice—sacrifice. Even today's Christians who promote and provoke a kinder, gentler slaughter, can't help but conjure the horrifying consequences of abandoning reason.

The mindless, panicked clawing of a dysfunctional animal is called Collectivism or Socialism, on a national scale. These are the butchers of Man, institutionalizing horror to permit themselves the freedom to devour restrained victims. They preach that as Man is an animal, he should be treated like one, that coercion—not mutual respect—is the proper means of obedience. To them disagreement is a sickness, ability is a sickness, and punishment is the cure. Their foggy ideals are based on nothing but clever ways to expropriate, as robbers sympathetic to all incapacities, split up the production generated by those abler. Its inevitable result is degeneration: a cognitive step four loss to the producer resulting in a change of his pattern, which will no longer produce the bounty expected.

Their affront to rational cognition matches that of religion's, substituting obedience to God to that of the State. Socialism sees a man, whether he is doctor or a janitor, as a human body. The same body gets the same payment, regardless of its action. There's no level acknowledged beyond 1-2, which is also inverted. They claim that all work and production is to be shared equally, but the historical truth is that the lives of all citizens are held for ransom as all wealth is funneled through a meat-grinder of centralized control—the most disastrous social theory for Man. They don't intend to participate in a free market by choosing product offerings and therefore supporting the economic survival of the best. No, they intend to decide whether you survive *physically*, as a person. Philosophically, socialists abuse cognitive abstraction in the childish desire not to adhere to reality as long as they are not stopped. Their pattern is simple: disconnect values achieved from effort expended, to take the benefit of the effort. Damn the benefit by claiming it is actually destructive, and then demand atonement through confiscation of the benefit.

A socialist would conclude that if it's good to give and those who don't give voluntarily can be considered evil, then why not make it *involuntary*? They take the concept of a gift—which is light-heartedly given, but only after ones sustenance is addressed and secured—and extrapolate it to demand that everything one has is to be given away in the same fashion, claiming that an even greater thanks will be had—not the panic that actually ensues. If society buys into it, now we're all stealing. They guide us off on a sociological tangent of pity for the criminal's family who will starve if he doesn't rob you, and now the victim is the bad guy. This is the formula for a society's demise, and in essence is the impractical theory of Socialism. It reduces society to where the need or desire of one man becomes a threat to another, consuming half the population through starvation before its inevitable collapse.

Marxism and The Communist Manifesto. Let's go to the horses...mouth. Next to the Bible, no book has had a greater impact on the Spirit Murderers than the Communist Manifesto, written by Karl Marx. Like religion, it permits a medium for any zealot to justify every evil he practices, but on a *world* scale, so it deserves a short refutation here.

Marx acknowledges human coexistence under the Submission/ Domination Axis alone, as does religion—pitting man against man. He split mankind into enemy camps—the *bourgeois* (pronounced boorzh-wah) and the *proletariat*—the fascist ruler and the trampled slave; but the division is wrong. Americans as employees or employers are not fascist; they have no right to use force against each other. The first rights protected by the Constitution are the rights of the individual. No worker is chained to his position *or* to his class; he is free to seek employment elsewhere and free to climb as high as his ambition allows. Marx's favorite word however, is *exploitation*, which in a free nation means productive utilization, not the negative relation he implies. His term *bourgeois* simply means productive Man; his term *proletariat* means the opposite: a fear-ridden, embittered hulk. The foundation of his whole argument against the West is based on a coercion that doesn't exist.

He condemns free trade—the individually decided, mutually beneficial process of exchange, which he considers an affront to *"the numberless indefeasible chartered freedoms"* given by a tyrannical power that claims to handle everything for everyone. When you must sacrifice everything you own, renounce all personal thought, action and speech and be subjected to torture and murder by your supposed guardians, then you have no rights and your life is not free. The foundation of his whole argument for Communism is based as well, on human rights that don't exist.

Struggling with civilization, Marx claims that the productive cannot exist without continuous technological advancement, which is simply the result of minds freed to perform their proper moral function. He laments that *"All fixed, fast frozen relations"* in thought and industry are swept away in Capitalism, and in a fit of honesty, that *"man is at last compelled to face with sober senses his real conditions of life and his relations with his kind."* If you want to stand still and not think, life won't reward you. If you want to pretend, adults won't respect you. Amazingly, he admits that *"narrow-mindedness becomes more and more impossible"*—the true nature of his regret. He condemns productive men for transforming barbaric nations into civilized form, causing *"the barbarian's intensely obstinate hatred of foreigners to capitulate."* He blames the inflation/ deflation cycle on the productive, not on the German-borne fascist element controlling it, claiming it results from *"too much civilization, too much means of subsistence, too much industry, too much commerce."* Nonsense, this stems from a massive expansion of credit, followed by its predatory contraction—strictly a central banking scheme, an institution which Marxism also backs.

He moves on to make a delusional prophecy: that evolution indicates the wealth created will now be seized. *"not only has the bourgeoisie forged the weapons that bring death to itself; it has also called into existence the men who are to wield those weapons—the modern working class—the proletarians."* Marx renews the false division to reinforce his minion's resolve, *"not only are they slaves of the bourgeois class, and of the bourgeois state; they are daily and hourly enslaved by the machine, by the overlooker, and, above all, by the individual bourgeois manufacturer himself."* In Marxism, hatred is the emotional medium. He takes any enjoyment they might feel by proclaiming they must hate; not just everyone else, but the whole intellectual/civil hierarchy and even existence itself through the tools they use. He goes on to say *"The more openly this despotism proclaims gain to be its end and aim, the more petty, the more hateful and the more embittering it is."* A Spirit Murderer couldn't have said it more clearly than that. Despotism is rule by force, which of course free trade isn't. The motive of profit is the motive of life, which *his* isn't. He is right, there is nothing more embittering than serving life, if death is what you want. Marx incites workers to destroy imported goods, to smash their own machinery, to set factories ablaze— all with clear intent: to restore by force, the conditions of the Middle Ages. As a means to this end, he outlines the creation of trade unions to organize *rioting*— not for calm deliberations, whose membership must be ceaselessly expanded to become a political party—the democratic party. He then fuels anarchy by claiming that *"Law, morality, religion, are to him so many bourgeois prejudices, behind which lurk in ambush just as many bourgeois interests."* He goes on to presume that as workers have nothing of their own (untrue), their mission is to destroy all individual property and any means to acquire or maintain it. To destroy everything—now that's a lot of violence.

Marx then claims that the productive cannot lead as they are no longer compatible with a society which *permits* his class to be so rotten. In truth, men are going to be what they want to be. If they must pretend they are slaves in order to shift the moral burden of their slothful disintegration and lust for blood and devastation, we aren't fooled. It's true that honest men are not compatible with the rotten group he claims is society; so who must change? He goes on to say that in order to acquire political control, they must seize the very capital they damn. That if it wasn't for the stress of fair competition which phased out the medieval safeguard of personal monopolies, then for barbarians who wish to remain barbarians, revolt was made inevitable.

A key target of Communism is private property—just as it is for a robber. He asks, *"Does wage labor create any property for the laborer? Not a bit."* Of course if you have a car, a television or a pair of socks, you know this isn't true. Abolishing private property simply means they want it. Deeper, to wipe out private property is to wipe out independence. Next he says, *"In bourgeois society, therefore, the past dominates the present; in communist society, the present dominates the past."* This means that as a rational society follows cause and effect, Communism intends to seize effects, circumventing all causation. In wiping out ability, independence and freedom—the act of production and exchange essential to any civilization—the Self-made is their target. Don't think it's just the rich they're after; their definition of *bourgeois* is *"...the middle-class owner of property. This person must, indeed, be swept out of the way, and made impossible."* He goes on to say that *"...all that it [Communism] does is to deprive him of the power to subjugate the labor of others by means of such appropriation."* Right, no more civil exploitation; it replaces a paycheck with a different kind of incentive: a lash.

Communism intends to break up families, as he claims that all the callous bourgeois parents do is teach children how to survive, which defines a family based *"On capital, on private gain."* He seeks to abolish countries and nationality, killing loyalty and patriotism by claiming *"The working men have no country."* He seeks *"emancipation of the proletariat"*, yet denies the concept of freedom. He intends to end the exploitation of one individual over another, yet when men are not free, they serve someone. He replaces Man's imaginary master with a real one: the State. He claims antagonism will end when they've wiped out the enemy—Hitler's answer as well. Marx thought of everything; he encourages that, *"The charges against communism...are not deserving of serious examination"*, claiming that *"man's ideas, views, and conceptions, in one word, man's consciousness, changes with every change in the conditions of his material existence..."*—*the fixed and the fluid* cognitive delusion of a Spirit Murderer.

Marx sums up by saying they must take all capital and all instruments of production for themselves as the new rulers, then increase rapidly the productive forces he claimed there was too much of. His resulting utopia is described as *"... an association in which the free development of each is the condition for the free development of all."* Who is free? He counsels that the wedge-in for acceptance of Socialism is through Christianity, as they share a common enemy–Man. Cleverly, he counsels against small experiments in Socialism as they indicate failure on any greater scale and counsels as well against any peaceful means of change. As Marx pushes for mass slaughter, nothing less than a total, savage commitment is worthy of the red cause. He exclaims that *"The proletarians have nothing to lose but their chains"*, poetic chains that don't actually exist.

If ever there was an economic treatise built purely on a savage tantrum, this is it. Marx ignores the rudiments of life, of cognition and of social relationships and moves right to unconditional loyalty to an institution he barely defines, other than its intended use of brutality. Marx equates Capitalism with exploitation and greed, yet the term only stands for the voluntary participation of all. Ruthless exploiters? We have chiropractors *for our pets*. Socialism is true greed—the consolidation of power in a single class. His State provides no existential foundation other than pouncing on what other men have made. There is no economic ideology and no constitution, just a delusional dream of taking control of the world. Imagine turning over the nation to the inmates of an asylum, convicted felons and welfare leaches. What would they declare as legal? Confiscation, rape, racial genocide, random murder, pure loyalty or else and censorship, so that no one could speak or reason against them. The result would be a reflection of why they were incarcerated—economic paralysis or collapse under organized looting and wholesale slaughter, benefiting only the most ruthless. They say *"Socialism is the sacrifice of the individual for the benefit of the whole."* If a cannibal could speak, this would be his argument.

Anti-Biological Pretense. Socialism intends to hold all values static for all men, which is in total contradiction with the flow of life itself, with the biological workings of living organisms, with the weather, you name it. Nothing conforms to a fixed sustenance or a fixed pride for Man except the standards—the axioms they evade. Socialism directly violates cause and effect, growth and contraction, and even the process of breathing. It implies that Man's answer to life and every move must be perfect off the bat, with no variation. But we see a dog adjust so it doesn't get stepped on. We correct our path down a hallway so we don't walk into a wall. Their system disallows all independent adjustments as if such were an admission of worthlessness, interrupting the natural pattern of cognition and the flow of life. They say, *"We're happy as we are. We don't need anything. To have needs is to be weak, like the Capitalists. We are complete—the first perfect beings on the planet."* Like a miserable old biddy, they renounce the undefined pattern of life in haughty virtue and then go drink themselves to death. But achievement and happiness are had by conscious effort alone, attained individually to the extent of one's ability and application. They are never achieved by random means and can never be granted to all men by law. All the law can do, is grant the protection necessary to pursue them.

In ancient times, men were limited to the cognitive ability and vision of just one man, such as a king or a priest. If a man out-stepped his authorities and proved more adequate, he was harnessed or put to death, and society was held back as a result. A dictatorship could never keep up in time or depth with the intricate advancements found in every microcosm of human endeavor such as in America, making an attempt at centralized control even more ludicrous. Yet they sell the illusion that they will provide everything for the populace and are supported by the mass that fears to face life alone, condemning the rest to be led by their blind faith. Then they become a nation of haggard bums, urged by their government to "wait just a little longer," for a prosperity that never comes.

Spirit Murderers promote a constant intentional confusion of *free* meaning uncoerced, with *free* meaning something for nothing. They say "This isn't a free country, I haven't gotten anything for free! I've had to work for it, therefore it's a scam." In America *the people* are free, the products aren't, and hence, a massive abundance of products to make life easier. The source of the energy is free to direct it, while the result has a price; this is cause and effect which is simple and fair, honest and natural. In communist countries, the products are free, the people aren't, and hence, no products and no life. They seize the results and wipe out the causes, and any future bounty as a consequence. The 3-4 level pattern of survival is made impossible by Communism. America does not *provide* that level of survival, but simply protects the right of men to pursue it for themselves.

Those who fall for Socialism look to the lifestyles above and imagine being boosted up, but forget that society is a pyramid. Those below far outnumber even *his* level and only the lowest morally, would or could benefit. Under moral inversion, while everyone takes from you, you can take from others; but those of integrity withdraw, participating only as victims, and the honest go without while the scum have a field day. Morality is turned over to professional bums who generate more aches and pains than any doctor can disprove. They manufacture ways of getting in need as their primary ability, milking the welfare state for as many allowances, grants and handouts as they can get away with. The honest pay and the dishonest collect.

Here, we have such groups of people politically dissatisfied with their living conditions, and unwilling to accept self-responsibility, they propose the same communal nightmare, believing they can hide in the pack and reach anonymously into the produce of mankind to survive, while contributing little or nothing at all. Every so many years, college groups schooled in socialist ideals organize "noble" experiments of isolated communal living, all of which are utter failures. Realizing that men turn into cannibals, in panic they permit natural freedoms and improve their conditions immediately. A rational person could see the code itself was wrong, but the irrationalists sit there in a semiconscious stupor, clinging to anti-concepts they hope will save them from their own fears, which is simply the fear of cognition. No, the opposite of their style of regulation is not chaos. Proper regulations are designed to restrain *governments*, not men; to provide direct physical protection to men in regard to other men, not to determine their independent course. Handing to an outside power the task of production and distribution is a declaration of personal incompetence. Following a natural or social disaster, it is only the free, unchecked action of individual entities that allows Man to return to a serene state of calm progression. It is the exercise of unimpeded human action that must be protected by legislation, but socialists answer by giving men so many rights, that no one realizes one half of the rights counteracts the other half. For example, the United Nation's Bill of Rights has thirty articles, where Articles 22, 23, 25 and 29 nullify the rest. The passing of countless inessential laws acts as a net thrown over mankind, smothering all beneath—provoking a moral storm such as the American Revolution, to wipe the slate clean.

Institutions of Evil

In an American free enterprise contrast, once I was ushered into a mass gathering along with hundreds of other employees. Walking into the auditorium, I noticed no huge locks on the doors, as in the Dachau concentration camp showers. Listening to the presentation, I felt no fear; the corporation did not ask for unquestioning trust, but appealed to our rational minds. We were not segregated by our faith, but joined, brought together for our competence. We were not deceived into our deaths, but voluntarily assembled to earn our livings. We were not there to take part in a medieval book burning to remove the threat of intelligence, but were given advanced information—*inside* information on the future of secret programs and of our industry. *This* is the essence of Capitalism in action. I love hearing these rival auto executives publicly claim they'll outdo each other with a faster, more desirable car. It's obvious they're having fun, and that they intend to win by productive genius alone. In Communism they wouldn't exist, but if they did, they would have to plot each other's denouncement, plunder or murder.

The Socialist Utopia. On the way to work and back, you pass hundreds if not thousands of buildings—buildings you'll never enter, but somehow they exist and thrive without you. How does a chandelier or a violin store sustain itself? I've never bought either and most people never will. These buildings and enterprises are made possible on statistical averages; averages made possible only by a free market. You'd never see such a business in a controlled economy. For one, such specializations are the province of passion, conjured by an economic structure that allows men to focus on projects well past bare sustenance.

In a socialist economy, those in control cannot think or operate past day to day survival, which is why only mundane jobs are available, which are then forced on the citizens. Disallowed to think—an action the power seekers have no respect for—the citizens are condemned to face even the natural elements with little preparation and certainly can't afford luxuries. You don't get to peruse a coffee isle with many brands to choose from; you get a paper sack of dirt and beans with COFFEE written on the side, if at all; and all other products are of the same stale, no-brand quality. Everything is rationed, proportionate to party status. Instead of vast supermarkets and countless choices, there is coffee day, bread day, fish day, lard day and each time you get to stand in line for hours—rain, sleet or snow. Every few weeks, you'll notice that their quality drops—the meat is more rancid, the lard is more spoiled, the bread is more stale—and your family's health is deteriorating along with it. Mandatory party activity gets you extra ration cards—subservience lets you live longer. Express an opinion, let anything slip and you're dead. Pride or rationality gets you killed through execution or starvation. Forget about luxuries such as preference, style or fashion; you're lucky to be alive.

Everything you own is now the property of the State. If it's needed more by another or if they have friends that you haven't, you lose it. Soon there will be a family living in your basement, then another taking half of your home. Then you'll be permitted one room, then one corner of the room. Do you imagine your head still held high in sacrifice for the great communal ideal? Are you showing the West a lesson about true brotherhood and prosperity? There is no new construction and no money for maintenance; soon, your home is a slum. If you assume responsibility for repairs or show any leadership skills, you'll be labeled as "bourgeois." You'll end up with a gun to your head, as the State quadruples your taxes. It is safer to wait until they put a gun to your head and direct you.

We hear of the drunken parties of those in good standing; we see their red cheeks and healthy skin, while we are all bones and dark circles. We watch our energy being recklessly consumed without any concern for replenishing, other than a whip on our backs. This is when we learn to hate our brothers for the first time; to hate the actual pattern they practice—life pursued on our blood and through our exhaustion. We begin to meddle in their lives, pushing opinions and imposing embittered wishes over what we cannot control, but are held futilely responsible for. This is when we lose our independence of mind, see each other as a threat and begin to wish others would die.

Censorship. Look at America and her civilized bounty. Look at Iran where they have total control over policy. Listen to their evasive plans for their great world of the future, and look at the murderous result—the spread of terrorism. If socialist dictatorships are so interested in peace, why do they require a purge of every idea which is not theirs? It is the theory that any distrust is disunity—a sickness that must be eradicated in order for the system to survive. Their propaganda conditions a state of paranoia, fearing that any dissention will topple their entire structure; it is weak, true enough. Any pinnacle of public interest outside of their control is a pressure point, to be eliminated. Any other form of power is a threat. Reason is rebellion. Religion told us that reason has nothing to do with morality, as morality is what we are *told* is moral—the province of faith; but no theory disallowing a free exchange of ideas is sincere. That is the structure of the Spirit Murderer, spooked by anything unexpected and uncontrolled; the structure of disrespectful, wishy-washy cognition as law, taken seriously—literally, to the last bloodstained letter. It is through censorship that they disastrously bring politics into the home, infusing youth with a drunken sense of power over their own parents, as a word whispered against the State will get them hauled away. Parents and contrarian thoughts live in fear, as all loyalties and all rational hierarchies are erased in obedience to the State.

The pen *is* mightier than the sword, in some contexts. To the extent that language is perverted, it aids the sword; to the extent that proper concept-formation is obeyed, it prevents the sword's rule. Such poetic subversion spawned the desire for a return to moral accountability in the statement, "Actions speak louder than words," as a way to see through their obfuscations, and it works. Play deaf, watch their actions and you'll come face to face with their true intention—destruction—to not let *anything* remain untrampled. You can read it in their faces. Take away their leader's words and they become plain criminals. You'll witness, not patriotism or God's will, but brutal killings; men driven to lie, steal, torture and murder out of their own hatred for life. Their game will continue as long as no clear, simple bill of human rights damns and restrains their actions; as long as they are able to preserve the indeterminate through language.

Take away the words of Americans and you see peace—people earning their livings as all honest men must. You see not guns and helmets, but sunglasses and brief cases. You see not foxholes and guerrilla warriors, but conference rooms and smooth running industries. You see the style of each successive generation in their flashy cars and fancy clothes; in shapely women and agile men—sculptures with beautiful smiles—the pride of radiant youth enjoying its very existence; a sense of desirability that stretches well into later years for some, and should for all. You see the possibility for this playful vibrancy to grow into wisdom, elegance and great personal power—power over *their own* destinies, to make their lives truly magnificent. You see a culture of respect for each other, and a discipline to work through our problems step by step—rarely resorting to force. You see the mature nature of civility in beings who have accepted that violence is not practical in the pursuit of creation, progress, prized possessions or romance, all of which can bring us so much pleasure in life—*the pursuit of happiness*—sanctioned by law. The positive impact it's had on our physical and spiritual lives was made possible by the longest-range understanding and adherence to *honest* concept-formation by our Founding Fathers, which in turn, realized this great country.

Defection. Altruism does not acknowledge healthy individuals except as livestock, to be churned into a slurry and spread over the needs of the weak. Good and evil becomes not the standard to preserve living entities, but to preserve some living entities in preference to others, and ends in the cannibalism of the best. Humans cannot live as host/parasite. The social alternative between men is not murder or suicide. To be of any use to others, we must first sustain ourselves, in top form if possible. The way to achieve that is to seek and realize our own dreams and needs, thereby setting an example others may follow to fulfill theirs. The most successful men and women all agree: if life is the goal, the highest mind is the final decision-maker in any realm of partners, and without question in the course of their own lives. The correct name to call the non-sacrificing regarding *all* social implications, is...civil.

Soviet citizens know that an American living in a slum is wealthier than any inhabitant of a country disallowing free expression. They know—likely by first hand experience—that poverty is infinitely preferable to the physical and spiritual straight-jacket of Communism, where human beings are reduced to the living-code of ants, unable to use their cognitive tools, tormented by life itself, with no chance to rise.

Moral, productive men *abandon* systems that martyr them. The best leave to find the free-est land as we have seen countless times in history, such as the British "brain-drain." We've witnessed the horrific defections attempted at any cost from *all* socialist countries, substantiated most clearly in the microcosm from East to West Berlin, as children were shot in the back while trying to flee. Such politicians still hide behind the claim that their ideals improve on existence, but the truth is they *defy* existence. No major tenet of theirs follows the natural order of life or permits it; and no sincere intention *ever* affronts nature. Can any socialist premise be supported when you see its citizens running for their lives?

You can only sacrifice your life once, and how many people actually die that way? In our country, where catastrophe is rare and is not sanctioned by law, a few per year. In a communist country, where the able are destroyed for being able, hundreds per day. Another way to comprehend the truth and intention of socialist governments is to compare the results by war percentages: the number killed, the number wounded and the number missing. Socialism would show percentages such as: 20 percent, 50 percent, 10 percent. Capitalism shows percentages such as: .001, .01 and .001, which are a direct result of the American Bill of Rights. So which style of government establishes *true* peace on Earth? Communism is efficient only in horror, perhaps destroying five thousand lives to feed five hundred. The enterprises and institutions of the Self-made do not require fatalities. Communism is actually another name for declaring war on one's own people.

With the most savage resentment of human beings, socialists would line everyone up and physically chop them down to the lowest common denominator, as all must equal all. It sounds ridiculous, but their leaders have acted on such premises, murdering millions before they were stopped. It was Hitler's answer, and do you think there was only one Hitler? Just as many life-hating sadists had to exist to carry out his plans. They would emerge here just as surely, if mindless violence were ever allowed to topple civility in law. For anyone who doubts the true essence of altruist-socialist ideals, Hitler and Stalin gave us the clearest, most accurate examples.

Invasion and Immigration. During the time of the Great Depression, if you were to look to nature, you would see birds and other animals engaged in their pursuits, unhampered. They didn't know there was a depression; somehow it didn't affect the natural world. In Communist countries where the populace starves, wild animals appear as healthy as American animals. Their birds look just like ours. Only the citizens are harmed. Only men suffer, due to artificial barriers erected by other men. It's obvious that such supposed phenomena are man-made and can be stopped. Man may be at risk facing an aggressor or a natural disaster, but he need not choose destructive peril as a constant—subjecting himself or others to avoidable tragedies. Such situations are often *caused* by altruist policy, which in a free capitalist society, are never to be incurred. In countries with looter governments, real tragedies are caused by economic dislocation and oppressive laws which stifle production or steal it, causing famines and widespread bankruptcy, such as Stalin's starvation of the farming communities of Russia, where *ten million people* were killed. Ask anyone living under a socialist system how many times their family's savings has been wiped out by currency inflation, how often their apartment had been ransacked and how many friends and family had been carted away, never to be seen again. In America, we have no emergencies to recover from day after day, and the more sane and less restrictive our social system, the rarer they are to occur. In fact in civil times, the number of proper sacrificial scenarios is exactly...none. The only screaming heard on U.S. soil, is at our amusement parks.

Free countries hold the moral right to invade and emancipate countries held hostage by tyrannical powers, if and when they decide it's reasonably safe to do so. There are many ways to influence governments to correct their violations—embargos, high tariffs, coups—and nothing justifies patience in this regard. They can start being civil, *right now*. The effort of America and England to free Iraq is morally justified on this basis alone, as we are justified in toppling regimes in control of the rest of the world's captive nations, one by one, into the future. Though we have no obligation to free them, all people deserve to be free. We as a nation can consider it an investment in mankind. With a properly executed plan, criminals can be removed from power with the least loss to us, new nations can be added to those who produce abundance, and the people can have the opportunity to live their lives in peace and harmony. There would no longer be any need for them to escape and seek asylum, and there would no longer be any immigration problems in the United States. No one wants to leave their homes anyway; some rulers just make it impossible to stay.

How often have you encountered people who are eager to do things for you—pretending it's selfless—then get pissed when you don't reciprocate? This is the con of altruism. They are still expecting compensation—to trade value for value; all that has changed is a regression in the form of currency. Freedom is the alterative for those who don't wish to trade favors. Man's greatest weapon against men has always been altruism, while Man's greatest tool of civility, has always been reason. With inherent respect for the lives of all men, I'd say to anyone, "I'll carry you to safety on my back, but don't expect to stay there." The maintenance of personal sovereignty is the hallmark of civilization, *not* voluntary enslavement. Conveying a picture of their freedom under a nonsectarian moral standard such as we have in the United States, is crucial to securing a smooth transition. Oppressed foreign citizens have to know exactly what their getting and show respect for it, if we expect them to support our troops.

American Challenges

Life, liberty and the pursuit of happiness has an antithesis: sacrifice, involuntary servitude and its voluntary form: undertaking the duty of service to others. Life is our organic state of being; sacrifice is the destruction of that state. Liberty means legally sanctioned independence; "community first" can only be forced, which is community bondage. The pursuit of happiness shows implicit respect for the purpose of life and a human being's right to live it. The Spirit Murdering moral alternative of "duty to others" doesn't even address it. "Community first" puts relationships as a priority above one's productive capacity—interrelation before comprehension—a metaphysical impossibility.

The living form of sacrifice *is* slavery; the ultimate form of sacrifice is murder. What business do these concepts have, being in our moral code?

If a computer program was asked to define the proper course for a human being and had as input, the course of the Self-made and the Fear-driven, it would see prosperous growth in ever widening circles around the Self-made. It would see the spreading decay around the Fear-driven, and its choice would be obvious. In defining the correct path for mankind, we would put in our current social welfare-capitalist system, morally pure Capitalism, Socialism and every other 'ism.' All styles would preach platitudes and convey ideals which sound surprisingly similar, but the computer could only interpret the specific actions each system would take to achieve those ideals. The winning system would be the one that identifies the indivisible entity it serves—Individual Man—just as science looks to where existence cannot be subdivided further—and then respects the requirements of each individual life. Self-made Man would put in the elements of a sound republic—equality under the law for all men, no unreasonable search and seizure, the right to a fair trial by jury, freedom of speech and peaceable assembly, the right of property and the right of trade. Fear-driven Man would put in the elements of fog and panic—equality not under law, but in all values regardless of personal effort; they would reserve any neurotic action blindly considered necessary to achieve their ideal, such as torture, murder and property confiscation; no one could speak or congregate against their plans; everyone has the *right* to everything, which means nothing; and in their world set free of self-esteem, no one is allowed to outpace anyone else—no one can trade on their own. The computer would quickly define the cannibal nature of the Fear-driven system and reject its consumption and destruction of Man. They would have no chance to con anyone with "Yes, we intend to torture and murder, but ahh, we assure you it's moral and for the best. Here's why."

Essentially, men require all of the same nutrients to survive; they all bleed if you poke them, they all laugh if you tickle them! They all require food, clothes and shelter—the right of property. Most importantly, all are volitional beings, meaning without instinct. In order to survive they must make choices, in order to make choices, their minds must remain free to function and their bodies must remain free to act on that judgment. To interpose another's judgment, is to violate the nature of the entity, to suspend and restrict his tools of survival and to leave him defenseless (which is the argument against welfare).

The differing outcome between the American and French Revolution's was due to the ambiguous policies of the French. They fought for ideals, but never translated them into clear actions and limitations that were to define government procedures. That is the direct intention of the Spirit Murderers: to remain ambiguous. Sound principles prohibit arbitrary structure and felonious expediency. Life is dynamic, growth and contraction are dynamic, but laws are not and cannot be. What kills today, kills tomorrow. Universal truths do not change, and rational law is based *solely* on universal truths. Corrupt men revert back to the same practices whenever they gain control of a government, which is why we've been able to operate off a document that is over two hundred years old. The mechanics are sound and always will be.

When things are set up rationally, it is surprising how easy it is to live, but Spirit Murderers prefer to live and prosper at the expense of others. Mass complacence toward the destruction of the most moral men of a country foretells the potential demise of that society, showing as well its distance to the coherent practice of sound principles. There is no room for those using compulsion for the public good in parallel with the actions of voluntary producers. Compulsion is the fool's substitute for ability.

Predation of Essential Action. Anytime a sound functioning system is in operation, you will find parasites trying to set up shop in order to skim whatever will be tolerated, leaving us flea-bitten with tickets and taxes that are too small to fight. The proper function of a government is to clear the way, maximizing the use of human energy, which is done by protecting that decisions about life and trade will be left in the hands of those who perform them. But generation to generation, we lose track of all that is done to our country, in our name. Our disassociation serves aimlessness, which is always steered by evil. There are two ways to approach societal issues: diligent study or mindless coercion. The response of a Spirit Murderer is always when uncertain, to hurt, maim and kill for whatever they *feel* is right. Then, they close the door on the pursuit of certainty, as if picking up a gun is all one needs to do to solve a problem, as if *their means* were the intent, *not* their claimed end—which is true. Political zealots pose issues they claim will result in poverty, harm and death and propose to solve them with fines, brutality and murder. The intent changes from stupidity to criminality as they enforce these nonessential laws to collect unearned royalties, sprinkling a little Socialism on our freedom of action.

Divorce and Community Property. The concept of *community property* is rooted in Communism itself. To consider a two-million dollar estate to be half-owned by an unemployed spouse with no apparent means is ludicrous. It is not a protection of property rights, but a direct violation of the one who earned it. There is no rational separation between property and the honest effort put forth to acquire it. Both should be able to say "I'm marrying you for *you*, not for your property," signing a document to that effect. If they won't, walk away.

Personally, I wouldn't get married until the legal ramifications are fair and are no longer designed to compel unhappy couples to stay together or to permit one spouse to victimize the other. It should be as painless and easy to separate as it is to get together, *never* requiring each other's consent, or the consent of outsiders. The first right an individual has, is to their own person. The courts should display no bias for or against marriage, or for or against a gender. It is not the government's job to steer or influence them beyond dispensing justice for a specific issue.

All legislative action must serve the inertias of life and its rational progression, as defined by no less than the logic of our forefathers. The concept of justice serves the contextual micro-elements of people's lives, all of which serve their total. The total is not up to the law, but up to each individual, and with just moral conclusions, a judge can see how he contributes to the integrity of the nation.

Traffic Court. We think of justice, law and order as the detective shows portray it—important issues—actual crime. You'll never see them doing a show about traffic or parking tickets. Why? They're unimportant. They thrive not on those who observe the law, but on those who don't.

The actions of the fringe evil have plagued the police force's reputation. Of course such distrust began with the good old boys doing as they pleased, but the negative bias was perpetuated by the burden of irrationality in law itself. The inconsistent moral basis for law provokes disrespect in the public eye for officers who have no choice but to enforce laws they may disagree with. The greatest public experience of irrational law and unjustifiable prosecution resides in our traffic court systems and our antitrust legislation. One feeds on the masses under the guise of their protection, while the other feeds on the best, under the guise of protecting liberty. Both serve channels that further impotent causes and like a cancer, weigh society down with an unnecessary illness, the economic and immoral repercussions that it was their supposed intention to prevent.

The logic they use is a derivative of the Socratic Method, which was abandoned around 370 BC with the influence of Aristotle. It is constantly reborn by those who will do *anything* to win, anything to get away with whatever it is they are after. Its historical infamy came with the Spanish Inquisition. It was abandoned because its intention was not the furtherance of Man, but deception— a means of *beating* other men whose guilt had been decided in advance. In traffic court it goes as follows: The defendant makes a statement, followed by the magistrate reconveying it with a slant to make him appear guilty. This is done at each point to build a case while facts in his favor are ignored or minimized, which is then summarized with a judgment against the defendant. The next time you go, watch. The magistrate will devise false equivocations, twisting everything against the defendant to see him in the worst possible light, while attempting to avoid detection. That is something rats do. I hate to discriminate against youth, but the absence of grey hair on the bench entertains my worst fears. The younger seem to have a lot of conniving to do before they find out it doesn't work—that taking advantage of others only results in self-hatred.

For most citizens, the only brush they *ever* have with the law is traffic citations—a ticket they likely don't deserve. They walk into court expecting to deal with an honorable man and face a con-artist instead. Ask yourself if you like the prospect of being pulled over for doing 52 in a 50 as some counties do. Look at how many roads are posted at 25 to 35 when the eighty-fifth percentile speed shows they should be 40 or 45, making it impossible to live without breaking laws. Notice the cop that sits there and collects $75 to $125 per ticket for no increase in safety—no benefit to the people. Go to court and add up the profits from the small percentage that has the courage to fight. In just one small courtroom, I found it to be over *two million dollars a year*. There is no money in justice; that's why we see fly-by-niter's chosen as magistrates. Harmless traffic violations are a profit center.

Ask yourself if you want photo radar machines planted everywhere, which will suspend your license for minor infractions by the time you get to work—another attempt at an automatic money machine. How many officers would have to be added to watch our every action until we realize our system has turned into the KGB? Ask yourself if rigid conformance to inessential laws is going to make society better, or just clog up the works. *Never* are our rights to be processed away. *Never* are we to be disallowed a fair trial by our peers. If law becomes a penalty handed out by an automated teller, victimizing those it was designed to protect, then *storm the Bastille*. I say always fight—permit no wedge in. Demand a jury trial. Appeal and appeal and waste the court's time while fighting it from the legislative side until the system cracks. None of us should be wasting our time in court over issues that are too asinine for adults to take seriously.

All traffic citations must be based on an infraction of safety—swerving, erratic lane changes, unpredictable turns, failure to yield—actions of an unstable mind that clearly disrupts the flow of others. Fines for false crimes or *victimless crimes* as they are called, just amount to penalties for virtue. Where no loss has been sustained, no penalty can be justly assessed. Adherence to numbers on a sign cannot take the place of the two elements of safe driving: awareness and competence.

Plea Bargaining. In the trend of plea bargaining we see a judge's desire for guilt; we see their complete lack of tolerance to consider cases objectively as facts are considered beside the point, as is justice. They are solely interested in processing penalties so they can move onto the next victim. They corner you morally, and tell you to plead with them—guilty or not—and they will go easy on you. Show them an ounce of pride for truth or any higher standards and they'll throw the book at you.

If a man is willing to break down and submit, they grant him leniency. If he defends himself by coherent, rational moral standards, they make him pay. If his standards are fluid, they allow the law to be fluid. If he allows his moral view to stretch to cover their evil, they will allow the law to stretch, and limit his penalty. They make it clear that he will be *rewarded* for accepting the guilt of the accusation, true or not, and that he will suffer a severe penalty for defending himself. Getting him to plea is their goal—the pattern of submission—not justice. His resistance to injustice justifies their further violation. If he intends to protect himself, to stand and fight for what is his, they use every weapon available against him and hurt him as deeply as they can.

Our courts penalize defendants who won't settle cases in the name of expediency, in defiance of human integrity and without consideration for the validity of the claim. Such a trend is an offense against mankind and justice, serving as a display of moral weakness for fledgling and schooled parasites to take advantage of.

Well, the Self-made are the men who don't plead. We must not allow expediency to tempt us to roll over. Injustice is a seed that once taken root, can destroy any structure built upon it. A moral washout must take place in our courts, and it is this trend and its purveyors who must be flushed. We will teach them that if supplication is what they expect, not to expect men to take them seriously. They can do their job and be impartial, or they can step down.

Runaway Judgments. The Spirit Murderers have used abstract theory against the Self-made, clobbering us with neurotic fantasies of our liability to them. They do this by claiming no cognitive involvement—a pure innocence and absence of mind in the use of products in their own daily life, and that manufacturers are responsible for everything that happens in that abstract range. When the law permits a producer to be held responsible for the actions of consumers regarding the negligent use of their product, it becomes a race to see who can convince a jury to swallow the most monstrous absurdity. If a reader has the driving impulse to poke himself in the head with this book, am I liable? (That's why it's soft cover, for your safety). Obvious product failure resulting in injury is one thing, but when a man drives his car into a pole and then sues GM claiming that because the car didn't *stop him* from steering it into a pole, it is defective, he should be charged with fraud for a frivolous lawsuit, just as he would for insurance fraud.

I recall hearing about a lung cancer case where a jury awarded something like $75 *billion dollars* to a woman who claimed she didn't know smoking was bad for her. This was hailed in the media as "sending a message to the tobacco companies that we aren't going to take it anymore." The company executives were viewed as evil as always, but say fifty thousand people are employed in that industry, all whose financial fate rests on the outcome. Now that the fraud has her prize, these fifty thousand are all thrown out of work, with financial repercussions such as bankruptcies, unemployment and a disruption in the honest services they themselves buy. In that judgment, we take the working capital that represents the living energy of *fifty thousand people* and possibly one hundred years of successful business inertia spread across the entire continent, and dump it on one loser who's done nothing more than get sick by her own stupidity, who was begged to sue by a parasite lawyer stalking the emphysema ward, eager to exploit a new angle. Such lawyers target courts where democratic voters will dominate juries, as such people inherently assume the role of perpetual victim and expect to be granted what doesn't belong to them.

If a premise doesn't serve justice, it doesn't help the country. If ten percent of one's living power is lost, then ten percent is recompense, not *four hundred million times* the level she has achieved in her life, causing a ludicrous economic dislocation, mass bankruptcies and feeding the trailer park desire for the big sourceless payoff. How much can America take? When there is a transfer of wealth from those who produced it to those who didn't, sanctioned by law, it is only a matter of time. As the inertia of irrationality exceeds that of rationality, long term economic plans are abandoned. Cannibalistic legal trends beget others by unsound precedent, as such a slaughter-democracy works to wipe out its own foundation. They claim that life is priceless—an abstract sentiment most would agree with—but try to actualize it in currency by inflicting judgments so large that they wipe out fifty thousand lives to restore one. For the sake of economic stability, judgments must be held to a scale of rational values.

In determining a rational settlement *if any*, we must define what range of action and therefore what percentage of life was permanently lost. Say it was ten percent. With an average life expectancy of 78 years and an example plaintiff's age being 45, the plaintiff would be entitled to 33 years compensation. If their earning power proved to be $50k based on a ten year average, the plaintiff is entitled to 33 x $5k (ten percent per year), or a judgment of $165,000. If the standard of a person's economic worth is considered an improper gauge, then a standard would be chosen such as the poverty or median income level of the nation. Regardless, no jury can be allowed to grant an award outside of all sanity, disrupting the lives of so many. A cap must be placed on all judgments which respect the *true* loss—a range determined by the court for the jury to decide *within*.

Antitrust. Antitrust legislation permits the government to bring charges against any business pricing higher, lower or equal to their competition. Are your eyebrows appropriately raised? Pricing higher is considered *gouging*. Pricing lower is considered *dumping*. Pricing the same is considered *collusion*. As all business activity falls into one of these categories, there is no innocence to be declared other than sanity, and the surest protection for a business is simply never to be successful. Once you stand out, you become a target. The most recent case that comes to mind is the antitrust suit against Microsoft. It is embarrassing that a man as capable as Bill Gates, who has no greater mind to look to for envisioning the future course of his industry, has to sit there and listen to fools theorize about how his business *could* be run. "Experts" with dismal track records by comparison are given the floor to make uncertain projections of what they *feel* would be—it *seems* to them—no problem for Microsoft to adapt to. Such fools think they can better decide the structure of a business they could never have created—and expect him to risk his own money on *their* viewpoint? It must be incredibly demeaning, especially in what is otherwise a free country. A Microsoft representative commented, "We are punished due to our success?" Yes, of course. That is the intention of antitrust legislation. It is anti-*trust*, anti-honest, anti-value and anti-life. It was originally the product of envy—written against the match industry by a jealous senator to destroy a business owner he hated, and the legislation was later institutionalized. It is still a product of envy; there is no other way to use it. Honest legislation is not subjective, but only clear, rational and existentially justifiable. Objective law doesn't attack others by theoretical projections of wrongdoing. It recognizes a clear victim who comes forward with a measurable loss, or it closes the case.

How many class action lawsuits resulting in fifty-seven cents per customer across the nation (if they care to fill out the paperwork and waste a stamp) are going to be filed before officials realize these suits only benefit the lawyers? I have never reviewed a case that was logical for our nation to pursue, or effective in its solution. They have served to restrain trade instead, at times committing the moral horror of jailing business executives for nothing more than providing the public with products they wanted, in a voluntary market. Those who attempt to substitute their judgment for the benefit of others, *harm* their supposed benefactors in that context. If one wants to destroy something, one only need do what *force* intends as *help*. Beware, because such mindless zombies are abound in politics eager to have us finance their crusades, and they intend to help you—even if it kills you.

Lobbies. All in all, special-interest groups aren't wrong—we all have special interests, but the nature of some is certainly immoral. The State is just a group of men, with one critical difference—the capacity to legislate—which means, the right to initiate the use of force against others. When violence is allowed in industry, pull becomes the currency—the hottest commodity—and the easiest to lose control of. This power has been called *government enterprise*, the creation of quasi-governmental agencies that compete with free enterprise, but with a distinct advantage—a guaranteed market. FNMA (known as Fannie-Mae), FRMC (known as Freddie-Mac), none of them should exist.

There are 100 congressmen and 435 house members—all the legislators that companies and cartels will ever need to bribe. When some companies have fifty billion dollars in slush money to ride out recessions, how difficult do you think it is for them to buy legislative favors? The proper separation of the State from economic activity would wipe this lobby pool out of existence. The power to grant monopolies, bar competition and dictate regulations—rational or not—force businessmen into a struggle for legal preferences. As this is a realm without constructive intent, victory goes to the most deceptive, who just sell the country down the river in the process. Laws go to protect the highest bidder and leave moral efficiency for dead until enough of a public uproar is made. It is not the fault of businessmen; while some percentage of men use political subversion to gain business advantages, the rest must finance representatives to protect themselves *from* it. If they want to survive, they must pander to the corrupt system. We are forced to invest in corruption instead of where we want to invest—in scientific and commercial advancements.

Right now, cartels can bribe the few to rob the many, on issues that should never come before the legislature in the first place. If you wonder why nothing changes, it is because such leaders make a business of it. Just as you exercise your honest effort by creating products to sell, benefiting the world in order to sustain yourself, they exercise their intellectual effort by creating opportunities to sell *you* and your current and future production, in order to expand their wealth. Just as you choose raw materials for the composition of your products, you the public are the fodder for their success. You are the value behind any deal they make. They have nothing else to offer, and they work just as hard trying to figure out how to screw you, as we do, sacrificing no one. If a separation of State and trade was a part of our Constitution, the number of people that corrupt men would have to bribe would be unlimited, and therefore impossible.

INSTITUTIONALIZED INDIGENCE

We cringe at the thought of helping the deadbeats in our own families—they are black holes in whom all investment is squandered—but we do it as a nation for those we don't even know. Welfare, subsidies and social security are all the slavery of a faceless victim. With government sponsorship, the do-gooders have combined a tin cup with a gun. These programs have no surplus and never will, which necessitates our continued plunder. The only way not to pay is to ditch the virtue of your effort and join them. When are we going to learn that the leaders who support this kind of dead-end charity are not looking out for *anyone's* best interest? They've built a society that worships pity and need, and all they have to offer the world is their gracious handouts, first taken from the producers. Their pattern of assistance is opposite in design to the life-pattern of capitalist action: recognition of need, self-generated action and fulfillment. The actions taken are actually socialist in design, or *death*-patterns—without intellectual engagement, without self-generation, without continuing value, without lesson and limited to the shortest intellectual range: dealing with the physical matter of consumption. The bleeding hearts only appear that way; the blood is ours.

Welfare. We all start this life as pure consumers. It is our parent's obligation to guide our productive growth before we leave the nest. In many families—through lethargy, evil or just shear stupidity—this is never done. Such parents *dream* of remaining pure consumers, and our welfare laws help them strive to actualize it.

Our government *created* our slums through welfare. If a given number of people never intend to work and are permitted by their financial status to receive a poverty level allotment, they must then seek housing suitable to their aim. They look for the lowest rent or none at all, do no maintenance and let it go to hell. It isn't pretty, but it's free. At the lowest they learn from other parasites to conserve that allotment by paying for every third month's rent, moving by forced eviction every quarter. If welfare pays for seven kids, they have seven before considering birth control, as more kids would be *their* expense. Hence, smart money management combined with absolutely no integrity, provides a complete lifestyle. They create a plethora of democratic cannibal voters versus the statistical average of two children for a moral, self-supporting family. Eventually the overpopulation of losers consumes the capitalist system of slimmer, leaner winners. They exist as little more than a pestilence, and die without ever having deserved the title "Human."

When are we going to learn the principal involved? In consonance with existence, every man must be self-sustaining, which means he must produce his values in order to survive. If he wishes to live in a society of men, he must bring value to them in order to exchange the benefits of *mutual* effort. To grant money to the unproductive without any effort on their part is to deface the currency. Without competence or living will, the money goes into unproductive channels—drugs, alcohol and prostitution—to manifest the kind of rot that plaques our inner cities.

Poverty cannot be physically or emotionally rectified by a bureaucrat in a government office, or by standing in line for a handout. Laws may be written to shift the burden to the innocent, but the fact remains that someone must pay. We as the producers, *provide* the handouts. It's a joke to expect them to have the moral incentive to get off the system on their own. They will pluck from the tree that bears fruit until it doesn't any longer. Continually supporting the poor doesn't help them, it hurts them. It suspends their raticnal faculty and separates them from the proper processes which compose their moral default. Poverty and graft are mental patterns, which welfare breeds and sanctions. It is not further consumption they need to practice—they have that down—but the pattern of living cognition itself. We must reconnect the intellectual bridge of life for those below us which was cut when the welfare-state was created. The clearest moral direction is provided by having men carry their burden of life independently. The only solution is to cut the umbilical. If they have to find other sources to survive, they will.

Social Security. Social Security was a system designed and adopted by the USSR in the 1920's—a plan to steal the wealth of the nation under the guise of caring for them—which was modified and adopted by the United States in 1935 as a moronic answer to the Great Depression. FDR was an idiot. Since then, money is allotted, money gets stolen. Money is borrowed, money is mismanaged. The New Deal with all of its new rights was pure Socialism—and unconstitutional by the way—the asinine generosity of a man giving away other people's money. Such politicians see a world of *consumers* and their programs never account for the *creation* of anything—only of how creation is to be seized. All of their organizations are half-dead by design. A tenet to understand is that no matter what mindless ideal a politician pursues, as soon as you are parted from your money, it is stolen, period, leaving no value to benefit anyone other than those who took it. It's time to take that money back along with our sanction, and return it to the hands that had the capacity to *create* it, and who have the honest objectivity to invest it responsibly. Enough is enough. If you think it is logical, safe or honorable to have faith in the government and then look the other way, just ask any German.

Would you prefer to be fully responsible providing for old age, potential job loss, medical bills and any instance when you may be caught short, in exchange for abolishing laws that require your *involuntary* contribution to funds which you may never even draw on? We have protection in the free market already set up; it is called insurance, and many corporations offer duplicate coverage at a fraction of the cost. How much do you think you're going to see by their management? At a minimum, this should be your account at your bank, managed by you, to be drawn on due to specific essential life requirements—be it medical or financial crisis and ultimately, retirement.

Subsidies. Whatever field is taken over or subsidized by the government, it means the field's products cannot survive in the competitive realm. No private effort then is or can be expended to improve them, or to rid ourselves of them. The forced sanction of a product is just artificial demand, an indication that the product shouldn't exist. An idea as good or not, timely or not, can only be defined by the free market, were supply begins as the dream of a man of action, and demand is the response of each individual's estimate of the product's value to himself.

We stockpile milk to help dairy farmers because it is a product that isn't selling. We market it ourselves to get rid of it, pushing it as a health benefit when next to fluoride, cheese and all other animal products, milk is the worst thing we could put into our bodies. "Got cancer?" The dairy farmers should be transitioning away from products that have been proven harmful, and towards those proven healthy. Set those cows free and grow some vegetables.

What is the insanity surrounding fluoride? Who bought into the slick argument of "Cavities? What you need is industrial waste!" A person can't even touch pure fluoride—*they would die.* The issue revolves around the fact that it is difficult to dispose of industrial waste, so it's easier for corporations if you just eat it. Is common sense that much of a burden? Why don't you follow up that fluoride treatment with a swig of motor oil?

Endless Internal Revenue. In today's world, you would be hard pressed to find anyone who would expect to see the day when income taxes are abolished. Federal income tax is so ingrained a burden, it's practically cultural now. Barely anyone would entertain the serious possibility of ridding ourselves of it, even though our government already collects enough income from other sources to fund its justifiable expenses without them. There may be loopholes to avoid taxes for the informed, but this does not justify the robbery of men who don't know which hoops to jump through. Most of us prosperous souls are too busy furthering our own agendas as we rightfully should be, to constantly be guarding our wallets. There will always be loopholes—for the purpose of survival. A loophole is nature's answer to an anti-concept.

Obviously, your tax burden is a percentage of your income lost. Any public project increases that percentage, removing the self-chosen options which fund your life. If a squirrel's nut is stolen, it doesn't eat—it loses the time and energy that was used to find it. Money is stored energy. All money is human energy, period. If you lose a given amount in taxes, your effort brings you that much less in sustenance. You have to head out into the world that much earlier than otherwise. If you hand over five hundred dollars per week through taxes, do you think you are getting five hundred dollar's worth of assistance in living your life? Do you think you could do better with the money than they have? Combined with the rest of the taxes we pay, we've given up almost half our lives in order to have the government do things for us. Out of a year, we pay almost six months of taxes; *six months* of working with no right to keep the results of our effort; six months of involuntary servitude; and if we don't pay, the rest of our freedom is taken, and for what end?

A society is greatly weakened by over-taxation. The key historical reason for a nation's overrun and collapse is corruptly incurred debt via the corruptly pawned-off responsibility for its recompense—pushed on those who have no say. Fully half the individual income tax receipts go to pay the Federal Reserve for their generous debt-money system, which could be wiped out simply by repealing their charter. The other half can come from cutting welfare. Those two cuts would *eliminate* federal income taxes for all individuals of the nation. There is most certainly a way to bring about reform, given to us by Rome's descent into the Dark Ages, and as recent as Dr. Martin Luther King's abandonment of businesses that discriminate. An organized inertia for fiscal correction begins with a withdrawal of support for those who don't understand, or refuse to. The bloodless answer is tax revolt, as we've seen in local jurisdictions. Let them know that you don't support it either. Let them know that a law supposedly of the people, is not in your name. Think of it as *your* government; *your* instrument; a product of your mind, a tool designed *by you* for a specific purpose, and the more rational that purpose, the closer to harmony with others it becomes. The tax base is just the checkbook of the country, and what it pays for is to be decided by us.

Term Limits. I've been shocked at how many politicians have no fiscal understanding whatever. We all hear of catastrophic government waste, but often it isn't even premeditated; they really have no inkling of sound living patterns—a mindset that goes unlearned in political science, but comes second nature to a professional businessman. Disconnected from the true pattern of cognition, they seem to believe that government magic can turn a dollar's worth of value into limitless wealth; that the government is all powerful and can provide anything they ask if they just seize the funds and discover the magic combination. Federal politicians seem more realistic, but the local politicians are another story. As a result, government projects always look like a few hundred ants trying to push a turd through the mud—never a pretty attempt. They show no practicality and no common sense; their gestures and posturings look strong at times, but are usually directionless and wallow in incompetence. Such people can't handle positions of authority when entering politics straight out of college; often *they don't even know how to live*. College pumps them with socialist theories, which they then attempt to actualize. When a business takes on a similar "no consideration for profitability" design, it falls twice as hard.

A proper government does not make or determine products; its function is as a service entity, maintaining the constancy of life for the living—clearing the way to preserve and improve flow. Look at our roads in many parts of the country such as Detroit; they are a disaster. If politicians can't handle concrete issues (pun intended) then there is no reason to trust them with the abstract ones.

For the reason of core competence, we need to add career politicians to the endangered species list. With term limits for all elected posts—*none* being longer than the chief executive—we can better guarantee that politicians will have spent at least a part of their lives earning a living; and then efficient, responsible action will be second nature to them as they bring it's inertia to office.

"If you have to resort to force, you've already lost." —Sean Connery

Democrats versus Republicans. Spirit Murderers often disguise themselves as vanguards, preaching anti-life or dependency premises which only necessitate the parasitism and destruction of other men. They have twisted the images of power over matter with those of power over men, to where bloody murder is the imagined result of a fully just and civil order. They envision the Self-made, the most moral men, using our freedom to run over those less endowed to our own gain, sacrificing them and living off their blood, which is in direct contradiction with our principles *and* our law, yet their code of domination and submission gives them no imaginable alternative. They believe freedom requires that men turn their backs on the human race instead of what actually happens: invigorated productivity, serene peace and true good will. They imagine us holding a whip when we actually provide the less endowed with safety, privacy and a comfortable living at their level of competence and ambition, with the opportunity for steady advancement. By preaching some kind of half-breed between infirmity worship and productivity, the mass understanding of moral intent dims with infection and their course brings about the exact devastation accused to be the feared theoretical end of the Self-made.

While struggling to make ends meet, the American middle class has always been considered the richest vat to prey upon by corrupt legislators. Every day new laws are passed to place a larger burden on our shoulders, while they placate us with budget controls. Only once in history were there men at the top who set up a system that did not provide them with a cut of our lives in return, but served the longer range profit of a free, productive industrial society. Because of this, the most capable men stood out and rose above the ranks to lead the others with voluntary agreement and mutual respect. But there are those who do not value this respect and do not value voluntary agreements. The men of the shorter range are all around us today, while those of integrity get drowned out in the clamor about altruistic duty. The Spirit Murderers have no tolerance to think, to judge or to weigh rational principles, wishing only to point, shoot and seize. Thankfully, the longest range men gave us an empire that cannot be dissolved by knocking off one man. That governments are instituted among men is the incredible strength of the American Constitution—the distribution of power—and its tenets are what we must further.

By contrast, Fear-driven organizations are designed around the confiscated centralization of energy dispersal—a *mix* of cognition and interaction to complete the *individual* living structure. They portray the masses as feeble and helpless and use our compassion to seek control over everyone. They preach that no man can survive alone and prove it by destroying all those who try. They are hardest on us during the productive phase of our lives when we are the most unique, most significant and most confident. Their laws are designed to penalize these traits to the extent that we exemplify them. While they've withheld our moral value in order to harness us, they have been busy setting up channels for our prosperity.

Republicans view men as mature, capable, strong and responsible; they recognize man's potency. Democrats view men as handicapped, naïve and unhardened, and just look at their supporters—the freebie seekers. They want to *give back* their sovereign power and be taken care of, and likewise view any administration as if it's a dictatorship. The man at the top cannot be responsible for the actions of every person in the chain, or for the issues he inherited; only his handling of those individuals and issues determines his adequacy as a leader. But he is the easiest to see, to blame and to plead before. Older age groups typically turn on the productive middle class that supports them, dropping their integrity to pursue the handouts offered by the Democrats. Who do we see still voting Republican? The ones who thought ahead: the prideful, productive, honest people whom you'd trust with the keys to your home.

Look at the base of a Republican stand versus Democratic on economic issues. Republicans want to reduce taxes, allowing people to keep more of what they make. It is not a grant of money, but simply leaves more of what is theirs *by right* in the productive hands of the nation. Republicans don't give products to the people, they clear the way so men will be free to create products. The Democrats focus on *taking* from the people to provide products for the people because they stubbornly refuse to accept our free market in fear of their own inadequacy, drawing support from those like-mindless, and the result is always the indifferent eyes of a social service worker who—surprise, surprise—treats us as if we are naïve, irresponsible and slow, and grants a pittance that would have been easier to secure on our own.

Fear-driven men dream of a free world where *free* means costing nothing, and will vote for anyone who quests for the sacred combination to make it happen. As long as the public chooses to remain politically and morally naive, Fear-driven intelligence will take advantage of it. There is actually no such thing as a leftist government (unless you define it as fascism)—it's all illusory. Even in Socialism, the little people are *never* in control and in such a system only the leaders stay healthy, warm and fed. When the best are cut down, the moral hierarchy falls and an immoral one is immediately put in its place. It becomes a form of fascism as the wealth of the country is seized and consumed, passing first through the hands of those in power. The clearest semi-plausible leftist government is a democracy—rule not by rationality and the civil needs of Man, but by the wishes of the greatest number. There was a time when the citizenry of England voted itself into Socialism in the name of prosperity. They didn't achieve it. Most democrats live their whole lives and the club they long to brandish never gets passed to them. They see it being used against them instead, in a hundred different ways. Intentional ignorance has no choice but to bash its own head against the wall.

If you notice, those who wish to hold 100% of the population at gunpoint—chained and bridled for the benefit of the unhealthy .001%—have a major dysfunction of their own, and the candidates they support will share this dysfunction. The most consistent political violator of the rational process of cognition at present is certainly found in the Democratic platform. When sacrifice, selfless love and duty to one's brother citizens are preached, those speaking must be removed from office immediately. Be it evil or just naiveté on their part, the resulting destruction will be unavoidable. A call for sacrifice from any leader is a sure sign that he or she must step down. What they preach is all things contrary to heroism, in worship of the dependent. *True leaders exemplify, communicate and support the tenets of independence.* If they cannot properly lead, they must return to the ranks. If they remain, their offspring will flourish—those who hold and strive to justify the mindset of force, dependence and irrationality—con-artists, bums, drug users and pushers, pimps, whores, thieves and killers. Look at the offspring of Benjamin Franklin who are scientists, industrialists, writers, philosophers and teachers. Who is safer to follow? Who are the benefactors of Man? Extrapolate their character—does it hold a link to criminals or to genius? Who do you see standing in support of either?

You don't even have to listen to the reasoning of either side. Just look from far above, watch the men who are producing and see those who produce nothing. See the scuffle between them and watch the assets transfer. Which way do they go? Of course the only way they could, to where the goods are not—towards the parasites. Withhold the penalties they wish to collect from the enforcement of their code and what you will see happening is not the chaos which their propaganda warns of, but that they simply scurry to exploit a new angle, or a new sore.

War and Foreign Policy. We have to wonder why so many nations hate America—it's a massive threat to evil. With our free system so obviously superior to the rest of the world's governments, it is shocking that we've apologized for it instead of flaunting its success. In most instances it has been a backlash by corruption itself, but unfortunately there have been victims of our great strength as well. Since America's inception, attempts have been made to subvert its every facet of wealth—its armies, its economic strength and its international influence have all been bent to serve evil in very powerful ways.

There are many thieving rich in the country who have no intention of honoring the Republic. They want to run things themselves, undermining and dispelling any opposition; they don't care who the President is or what format the citizenship has voluntarily agreed to; they want whatever their interests lean towards to be controlled and determined by them and them alone, and will commit any atrocity to influence those outcomes. Such men exist inside and outside the government and military. One such network has been responsible for practically every major political murder and attempted assassination in America for the last one to two hundred years. The murders of John Kennedy, Robert Kennedy, Dr. Martin Luther King and Malcolm X were among their accomplishments, some of whose killers were paid to stalk other politicians before their historical target was decided. Such organized control is always fascist; to control a network, you have to have the bribe money, and we have the wealthiest fascist network in the world. To a surprising extent, our foreign policy has been controlled by financial powers having no loyalty to our country whatsoever. Even the Cold War was a carefully executed series of engagements planned by this network within both super powers who promote war for profit's sake, and conquest for acquiring land and illegal trades. They are consumed by the psychotic pursuit of dominance—the cognitive replacement for an esteem and stature that their wealth has not given them—a vacuum filled by a vehement wrath towards all those who do not bend to their will.

Even our historical discord with Russia was contrived. Prior to the Bolshevik Revolution, Russians experienced much greater freedom than what was to come. The scourge of Communism was as much their enemy as it is the rest of mankind's; most their citizenry were just decent people caught behind the lines. The Spirit Murderers, through bank-owned and controlled media, stirred up an international controversy between the superpowers to instigate paranoia, which was then to be fought with subversive political structures and fresh new debt. General hatred for the Russians or the Chinese? As an American, I feel nothing of the kind.

They had to secure a draft in the United States to fight the wars they were planning, just as they pushed for our federal income taxes—an involuntary source to bear the brunt of their evil. If the owner of a military contractor (Johnson—Bell Helicopter) is permitted into the oval office, *there is going to be a war*. Imagine the numbers murdered to see their bank accounts grow to unimaginable levels. Imagine all the letters to parents whose sons were lost—they had rows and rows of typists for this task alone—in a room beside accounts receivable, collecting the money piling in via their blood. This is their kind of artificial business—the sure thing, with devastation as gravy. It is no secret that in World War II, both sides were financed by New York banks. Their evil is diabolical; the unspeakable horror of Nazism is exactly what they enact all over the world in order to secure their dominance.

With the murder of John Kennedy, they were able to push us into the planned conflicts that he impeded. Vietnam was our first conquest as a nation—the *real* loss of American life for the *contrived* theory of the Communist domino effect—which was totally false. The war began covertly, defense became *offense* secretly and the public had no choice—about the war, about the draft or about paying for it. Lyndon Johnson could do anything without telling anyone—next to Hoover and Roosevelt, no President has brought the fascist underworld closer to the chief executive position than he did—the closest the United States has come to a dictatorship. As evidence of who was in control, Johnson's "peace with honor" to save face as a country was a typical '*La Cosa Nostra*' poser move. The "War Powers Act" stopped it and the domino theory was invalidated as such governments collapsed on their own, but not before 58,000 Americans were killed, millions of Asians, and one hundred and fifty billion dollars was spent— *three times* that of World War II—without any moral value to the nation or the world as a result. This subversive control is still with us, and must be put to an end.

Trade Agreements. As an immoral extension into 6-8 territory, NAFTA is a screen for slavery. Free-trade can mean unregulated commerce, or it can mean "take what you want without paying for it." Those attempting deceit use one meaning for political cover, while they accomplish the other. Its result is that our markets are unprotected, allowing slave nations to trade without penalties for their human rights violations.

Keep in mind that free exchange does not mean that you get products for free. Free-trade doesn't mean that someone gets a free ride. It means you can trade products without interference from others—mainly governments. No one outside the transaction has the right to stop you, to impose penalties for producing, to subject you to fines for unsubstantiated losses or to direct your actions; the actions, benefits and consequences are yours. Free trade *does not* mean there are no tariffs between nations. Such coalitions as NAFTA and the World Trade Organization *intentionally* suppress that the point of free trade is first and foremost to see *the people* free—protected from other men by a constitutional document guaranteeing their freedom, such as our bill of rights. In every country, their bill of rights must reflect the *American* bill of rights, or it is wrong. It cannot be a plethora of rights that end up simply taking the rights of others, as the United Nations bill of rights does, but a one-sided, government-limiting, individual life-protecting document that all nations must abide by.

To give a looter's government the right to trade with America on equal terms, translates into windfall profits for any nation employing slaves. If immoral men in American corporations can go there and set up shop, it's easy money; such as the situation in China. It is the perfect slave/master relationship. The Chinese army keeps the prisoners in line and their government gets a cut, producing goods to be sold abroad—far away from the murders, the cries, and the filth. That translates into healthy profits on the glossy pages of quarterly reports for international companies and a supposedly better standard of living for Americans, as it masks our true inflationary environment. The arrangement also makes it impossible for honest corporations at home to compete, and permits coercive monopolies to exist in the slave nations—*outside* the range of our laws, while reinforcing uncivil control in those nations. This is the 6-8 Spirit Murderer's idea of social progress.

Free trade was not meant to be a megalomaniac's benefit, but a *citizen's* benefit. What they have put in place today assures that no corrupt regime under the world trade agreements will be penalized for their crimes against humanity. These countries have human rights records that read like that of war, and they will keep churning out casualties as they turn out products by slave labor for the free markets to absorb. Iran exports terrorism, while we export slavery. Who is guiltier? No, most of us have no connection to it, but it is time to see—and to see it end. Until these agreements are redesigned to accomplish what the civilized world would expect of them, they should be abolished.

The Money Vultures

"Madness in great ones must not unwatched go." —Hamlet

All of my adulthood I had been schooled to believe that Socialism was Man's worst offense against Man. With the evidence presented, it appeared to be true; but I eventually identified a force beyond it. It never would have occurred to me, the importance of our system of money. What about it? Money is money. You work to earn it, then spend it to meet your needs. If you're wise, you save a percentage, invest and become financially secure over time. That's all there is to it, right? That's all there *should be* to it, but within the very framework of a monetary system, there is a grave possibility for the subversion of a country's government, the confiscation of its wealth and the enslavement of its people. Most believe that the President is the one responsible for the economy; as evidence, there hasn't been an economic expansion that didn't give rise to a two-term President; but the truth is he has little to do with it. The economy is in the hands of a private monopoly, whom despite our illusions of liberty, control it for their own interests.

As an investor by profession, at a certain point I considered opening a bank. I requested the necessary information from the Federal Reserve and stumbled upon what years later became one of the most important contributions to this book and to my development as a philosopher. I saw that as I scrimped and saved for years to afford the one-hundred thousand dollar Lamborghini in my driveway, as a banker I would only need ten thousand to buy it. I saw that they created money out of *nothing*. I saw no opportunity in joining them—instead it made me angry. I saw a radically unfair advantage in this, and sensed a massive danger. They can buy *anything*, and I had to ask, "Where does such a power lead?" Then I started to read: presidential speeches, congressional memoirs, economic dissertations, anything I could find. In reviewing the historical chain, eventually the picture became clear.

Since then, I've noticed many things about the nature of fractional reserve banks. I learned of Australian mortgages, where a homeowner's entire paycheck is deposited with his mortgage company. He pays his bills throughout the month out of this account, shielding himself from the mortgage interest, which allows the whole loan to be repaid in about *five years*, not the thirty we suffer. Why don't we have this option? I noticed that I paid my boat loan for five years and still owed the same amount. I noticed I had given my mortgage company ten years of payments which were almost pure profit to them, and when I began to have problems along with the rest of the country, received no flexibility from them whatsoever. Instead, I received their intent to foreclose. After giving them roughly $72,000, they were going to throw me out on the street over a matter of *fifteen hundred*. I realized that with the credit budget I'd fallen for, I was renting my lifestyle—that I owned *nothing* of importance, and that they could pull the plug any time they wanted to. More frightening was that I saw a society less aware than I stumbling on to follow, with no hint of the imminent dangers. The bankers have wiped out the savings, retirement plans and dreams of Americans time and time again throughout history, just as they are doing right now. Then I knew that the height of evil wasn't Socialism, it was this.

We've all heard that money is the root of all evil. Morally damning money began for a very practical reason—to take the light off what its corruptors were doing—and was picked up by religion as it suited their own incapacities. But we all know how important money is. Go without money even for a day, and life begins to fall apart. *The freedom to trade is the freedom to live.* Something so individually crucial should never have a private monopoly permitted over it, and we were warned of this from the beginning:

"If the American people ever allow private banks to control the issue of their currency, first by inflation, then by deflation, the banks and corporations that will grow up around [the banks]...will deprive the people of all property until their children wake-up homeless on the continent their fathers conquered."
—Thomas Jefferson, 1809

Our free markets make everything we do, faster, easier and more efficient, but life isn't any more affordable. Couples both have jobs as pride demands, but not just because they wish to, often *they have to*. What one-hundred thousand dollars bought in 1930 costs over one million dollars today, and salaries have not kept pace; our cost of living just keeps going up. At the same time, industry has made our lives easier with advancements in so many fields, it is absolutely mind blowing. Scientists say that ten years from now, we will have a cure for spinal damage. With such radical breakthroughs in science where no problem seems outside our grasp, why is it that we as a people still accept that our financial markets are driven by untold phenomena outside of Man's control?

The answer is simple: Corruption. Corruption rides the back of the most civil tool of exchange Man has ever known—the U.S. dollar. Men have known for *centuries* what a fair monetary system would be comprised of—one that would benefit all of mankind and leave no means to destroy its value—but it has been suppressed to accomplish the most massive abstract crime, whose veil of silence is secured through lies, deceit, propaganda and murder. The chairman of the U. S. House Banking and Currency Committee from 1920 to 1931 had this to say:

"...we have in this country one of the most corrupt institutions the world has ever known. I refer to the Federal Reserve Board and the Federal reserve banks. The Federal Reserve Board...has cheated the Government of the United States and the people...out of enough money to pay the national debt...this evil institution has impoverished and ruined the people of the United States; has bankrupted itself, and has practically bankrupted our government. It has done this through...the corrupt practices of the moneyed vultures who control it."
—Louis T. McFadden, 1932

Imagine a business with no debt, one that simply *creates* debt for others to pay back, whose only function is to collect its income by managing the accounts of its borrowers. Imagine having no product to finance, no competition and no risk. Customers are captives; if they want to live, they must buy, and products are created with the flick of a pen. This is the business of the Federal Reserve.

There are two kinds of banks—privately capitalized banks formed after earning a surplus from successful business ventures along with a *percentage* of depositor reserves, and its inverse—those of the central bank system formed on a multiplier of depositor reserves, which are then *multiplied* by a factor of ten for example, and lent out at interest. The first are *moral* and fully funded. The second are hot air, and account for *ninety percent* of our inflation. Since control was given by government charter to the latter in 1913, they have mostly driven out the wholesome banks and in that time have reduced the original value of an American dollar to about ten cents.

"Most Americans have no real understanding of the operation of the international money lenders...the accounts of the Federal Reserve have never been audited. It operates outside the control of Congress...and manipulates the credit of the United States." —Senator Barry Goldwater

Most people believe the Federal Reserve is just a branch of the government and have no inkling of its *true* nature or motives. Few people know that the Federal Reserve isn't federal at all, but a private corporation with an ill-conceived government charter. The name is a legitimizer, and from its inception had no reserves to speak of. Its structure and ownership stems mainly from European bankers who were eager to take advantage of the New World, causing a struggle for monetary control that has changed hands *eight times* since our country's inception.

From earliest recorded history, mankind has made a stair-step progression in everything but finance. Only half the equation of liberty is accounted for and controlled by the Self-made—through our Constitution. Our technology and standard of living runs a race with currency control, a facet that unless we take over, we will eventually lose to. At the height of mankind's evolution, the central bankers hold the reigns to decimate it or allow it to continue. We have given them the right to create money out of nothing, including the right to *refuse* to lend it to us by nonobjective, private means. If we were in control of money, our cost of living would go down in relation to our advances, but instead, central banking policy has been to increase our burdens while stealing the benefits of our industrialization for themselves. Inflation is just a way of transferring the living benefit of our work to them. If we don't take control of our money, our country will eventually go bankrupt—a mathematical certainty—along with those most able to save her.

Half the wealth of the world sits in the hands of a group of international banking families, but whenever we see lists of the richest bachelors or heirs, they are conspicuously absent. Little publicity is permitted regarding these men and their descendents. Their lives remain private due to the nature of their actions—a shameful accomplishment that must remain hidden. Such combined family wealth represents the world's only *trillionaires*—the last feudal link— the inverted pinnacle of fascist Spirit Murder to which the evasive pattern of cognition, dysfunctional interaction, perversion of exaltation and socialist tyranny all descend to. Such crimes extend directly from common fraud, but being abstract, they are difficult to understand. Discovering the truth, I couldn't believe that adults much older and wiser than I were running around, acting, lying and conniving to put themselves on top. It reminded me of movie scenes where conspirators shoo the women out when the subject is *not* heroic. They can't bear to reveal how small, cowardly and deceitful they actually are. This is what supposedly great men did with their lives? I don't think so; it's something else rats do. They've grown rich through no effort of their own—only by taxing yours.

It is claimed that banking debacles have been the result of incompetence and mismanagement; that most historic events are chance manifestations lacking any single source, but throughout history, a very clear chain of events shows otherwise. Looking back, I'm shocked about what I *didn't* learn in History class, due to a misinformation process called *historical deletion*. Let's take a tour through some of the world's most significant events to decide for ourselves what motives prompted them.

The Revolutionary War and Hyperinflation. Walking the streets of London, Benjamin Franklin was shocked at the number of poverty-stricken unemployed, where the haggard townspeople were reduced to begging. Representing the New England colonies, the London Parliament inquired of Benjamin Franklin how it was that despite economic turmoil in England, the American colonies were doing so well. He responded, *"That is simple. In the Colonies, we issue our own paper money. It is called 'Colonial Scrip.' We issue it in proper proportion to make the goods pass easily from the producers to the consumers. In this manner, creating ourselves our own paper money, we control its purchasing power and we have no interest to pay to no one."*

With the Bank of England horrified by the implications of what the colonies discovered, the British Parliament imposed the Currency Act of 1764, disallowing the colonies to issue paper money and forcing them onto a gold standard. By requiring taxes to be paid in gold, England drained the colonies of currency and severely restrained their trade. Franklin wrote that within a year, the streets looked just like England—filled with beggars and the unemployed, as the money supply had been cut in half. He indicated that despite other abuses, this was in fact the *main* cause of the revolt:

> *"The Colonies would gladly have borne the little tax on tea and other matters had it not been the poverty caused by the bad influence of the English bankers on the Parliament, which has caused in the Colonies hatred of England and the Revolutionary War."*

In the *Declaration of the Causes and Necessity of Taking Up Arms* of July 6, 1775, John Hancock wrote: *"They [the British] have undertaken to give and grant our money without our consent, though we have ever exercised an exclusive right to dispose of our own property."*

The Colonies declared their independence and began printing money again to finance the war. War being a pure expense, its pattern of attrition caused hyperinflation to ensue, and the currency became almost worthless.

A fiat currency often takes the blame for instability or inflation, but what currency *is* safe in war? None. It is the nature of war—of destructive action—that is to blame. Any massive reduction in assets relative to the amount of currency in circulation will result in inflation. Production and consumption must be in balance; a war is *pure consumption*, which is considered the ideal setting by a Spirit Murderer. (If governments loaded every tank with the million dollars it cost to build before they sent it off to be destroyed, perhaps the currency would remain stable).

American Banking History. After the war in 1785, Secretary of the Treasury Alexander Hamilton and his banker friends secured a charter for The Bank of North America, granted in an effort to stabilize the currency. Schooled in European finance, its structure was that of the Bank of England, the original central bank scheme. Conditions did not improve—inflation advanced another seventy percent and four years later, the charter was not renewed.

In 1790, Hamilton proposed another bill which amounted to the same system run by the same people, but was called the First Bank of the United States. Learning from its prior flaws, this time it was drafted with a twenty year term. As before, the years passed with rampant inflation, and once again the bank lost its charter.

Amazingly in 1816, Congress passed yet *another* banking bill—this time called The Second Bank of the United States, and their blatant boom and bust cycle continued; but a mortal enemy was looming on the horizon. President Andrew Jackson was American history's most staunch opponent of immoral banking practices. He considered the bank a massive threat to the safety of the

403

republic, as *"it represented a fantastic centralization of economic and political power under private control. It was a "monopoly" with special privileges, and yet it was not subject to presidential, congressional, or popular regulation."* —Robert V. Remini, Jackson Biographer

As one of the few politicians who understood and was willing to challenge what was going on, he vetoed the bank's renewal bill in one of the most famous speeches of all time. Jackson exhaustively explained the bank's unconstitutional and unpatriotic nature, their desire to skirt taxation and their blatant angling for personal advantages contrary to their declared public objectives:

"More than eight millions of the stock of this bank are held by foreigners... Is their no danger to our liberty and independence in a bank that in its nature has so little to bind it to our country?...Controlling our currency, receiving our public moneys, and holding thousands of our citizens in dependence, it would be more formidable and dangerous than the naval and military power of the enemy."

He went on to distinguish in essence, the moral boundaries of any human institution:

"Distinctions in society will always exist under every just government. Equality of talents, of education, or of wealth cannot be produced by human institutions...every man is equally entitled to protection by law; but when the laws undertake to add to these natural and just advantages artificial distinctions, to grant titles, gratuities, and exclusive privileges,...the humble members of society— the farmers, mechanics, and laborers—who have neither the time nor the means of securing like favors for themselves, have a right to complain of the injustice of their government. There are no necessary evils in government. Its evils exist only in its abuses. If it would confine itself to equal protection, and, as heaven does its rains, shower its favor alike on the high and the low, the rich and the poor, it would be an unqualified blessing. In the act before me there seems to be a wide and unnecessary departure from these just principles." —Andrew Jackson

Nicholas Biddle, head of the Second Bank of the United States, patronized Jackson by pulling what he considered rank: *"This worthy President thinks that because he has scalped Indians and imprisoned Judges, he is to have his way with the Bank. He is mistaken."* Biddle was dubbed "Czar Nikki," and in dictatorial form, eager to assert his will over established and accepted forms of rule, Biddle constricted the money supply and caused a financial panic, claiming it was caused by Jackson's removal of government funds from the bank. It worked initially and brought a censure resolution by the Senate against Jackson, but Biddle was caught publicly boasting about his planned monetary crisis, and the tide reversed. The Governor of Pennsylvania, George Wolf, publicly damned Biddle for bringing "indiscriminate ruin" upon the community. Presidential faith was restored, and on April 4th, 1834, several resolutions were passed by the House of Representatives, among which an investigation was made of the bank's records to discover to what extent the panic had been deliberately instigated by Biddle, including the expectation for his disclosure of all personal loans made to congressmen. Biddle refused to open the bank's records to government scrutiny and refused to testify before congress, and in late 1834 they did not renew the bank's charter. A few weeks later on January 30ᵗʰ, 1835, an attempt was made to assassinate Jackson. Biddle was later arrested and charged with fraud for all the wrongs associated with his previously *sanctioned* monopoly, and was pursued by civil lawsuits for the remainder of his days. When Jackson was asked what his greatest accomplishment as President was, he replied, "I killed the Bank!"

The Civil War. Moving on to a key factor provoking the Civil War, the South had a dishonest and vulnerable economy due to their dependence on the slave trade. Adding to pressure from the North to reform, foreign money powers saw this as a chance to dissolve and possibly *reacquire* the nation.

"The division of the United States into two federations of equal force was decided long before the Civil War by the High Financial Power of Europe. These bankers were afraid that the United States, if they remained in one block and as one nation, would attain economical and financial independence, which would upset their financial domination over the world." —Otto Von Bismarck, Chancellor of Germany, 1876

Financed by the Bank of England, the French and British armies were posted along the Canadian and Mexican borders during the American Civil War. The Russian Czar, Alexander the Second, came to the rescue by stating that any intervention by either force would be considered a declaration of war against Russia. He had refused their control over Russian currency and knew that a reinforced Western Europe would come to threaten Eastern Europe once more.

Lincoln traveled to New York to seek lenders for the Union effort, but was offered only ruinous rates of interest. The Wall Street bankers were tightly linked to the Bank of England and the central bank network; all were eager to see the North lose the war.

"I have two great enemies, the southern army in front of me and the financial institutions in the rear. Of the two, the one in the rear is the greatest enemy. The money power preys upon the nation in times of peace, and conspires against it in times of adversity." —Abraham Lincoln

Back in Washington, Lincoln's counsel suggested he print his own interest-free currency to pay Union troops with—the origin of Greenbacks. The plan was put into effect, and in revelation, prompted Lincoln to exclaim, *"The government should create, issue, and circulate all the currency and credits needed to satisfy the spending power of the government and the buying power of consumers. The privilege of creating and issuing the money is not only the supreme prerogative of Government, but it is the Government's greatest creative opportunity. By the adoption of these principles...the taxpayers will be saved immense sums of interest...Money will cease to be master and become the servant of humanity."*

In the London Times in 1865, a threatened Europe responded with unbelievable and clairvoyant honesty: *"If this mischievous financial policy, which has its origin in the American Republic, shall become permanent, then that government will furnish its own money without cost! It will pay off its debts and be without debt. It will have all the money necessary to carry on its commerce. It will become prosperous without precedent in the history of the world. The brains and the wealth of all countries will go to America. That government must be destroyed or it will destroy every monarchy on the globe!"*

Near the end of the war, suffering a hyperinflation much like that of the Revolutionary War, Lincoln regrettably agreed to pass the National Banking Act of 1864 in an effort to stabilize the currency. The act permitted the creation of money through debt. Still, within a year, Lincoln was murdered. The bankers intended to regain control and put America on a gold standard—gold they controlled—and Lincoln was taking the country in exactly the opposite direction. It was believed that the Vice President, a personal friend of John Wilkes Booth, was an accomplice, noting that protection for the President was removed and phone service in the Capital was cut off at the time of the assassination attempt. The generals who were to accompany the President to the Ford Theater that evening, all withdrew. The President's wife, Mary Lincoln, believed such a conspiracy to be the case, commenting *"As sure as I live, Johnson had some hand in all this."*

In 1866, the national bankers pushed through the Contraction Act under the guise of restoring the prewar currency values, but they went way, way, way past that mark to pay America back for what Jackson did. The post Civil War depression it caused reflected the transition of Rome into the Dark Ages almost verbatim. By 1877 there was open rioting in the streets. As Britain had done to the colonies, the country was put on a gold standard and silver was demonetized. Why? With silver plentiful, the economy was resilient and difficult to manipulate, limiting a central bank's control of money as a weapon for their purposes. The demonetization of silver recovered for them this power.

The paralyzing loss of currency incited a public clamor for relief—greenbacks, silver—whatever would promote recovery, which the bankers had every intention of stamping out. While placating the populace with technical reasons for the depression outside of human control, they were frank in their correspondence amongst themselves. Here we see that those in the American Bankers Association clearly understood the pain of the depression they had caused, and *chose* to let it continue: *"to repeal the act creating bank notes, or to restore to circulation the government issue of money, will be to provide the people with money, and will therefore seriously affect our individual profits as bankers and lenders."*

Not everyone was in the dark about their plans however, and those who spoke out, did so at great personal risk: "*Whosoever controls the volume of money in any country is absolute master of all industry and commerce... And when you realize that the entire system is very easily controlled, one way or another, by a few powerful men at the top, you will not have to be told how periods of inflation and depression originate.*" —President James Garfield in a speech, June of 1881. He was assassinated two weeks later.

Some may recall from history class the great patriotic heroism of J.P. Morgan bailing out the government in the crash of 1907, but the government wasn't in control of the stock market—the bankers were. Preparing the ground for another try, the crash was designed to portray the financial system as unstable under government control, and to show how easily a private banker could come to the rescue—an ability they failed to exercise in all prior history.

The Federal Reserve Act. Deadlocked in controversy, on December 23, 1913 after most members of congress had left for the holidays, a handful of congressmen stayed behind and passed the Federal Reserve Act. President Woodrow Wilson, schooled and backed by the bankers, then signed it into law. Seventy-seven years after The Second Bank of the United States was wiped out, they were back in power.

The Federal Reserve controls the money supply in three ways: 1) Selling or buying U.S. government bonds from the government or in the bond market. To *sell* bonds is to contract the currency, decreasing the supply of money. To *buy* bonds is to inflate the currency, increasing the quantity of money. 2) Raising or lowering bank reserve requirements. To raise reserve requirements is a *tightening* that decreases the money supply, making money harder to obtain. To lower reserve requirements is a *loosening* that increases the money supply and makes loans easier to obtain. 3) Changing the discount rate—the rate that banks borrow money created by the Fed to lend to the public—which cost or savings, is passed on to you. This rate of interest is supposed to reflect the risk of doing business, gauged by the pace and direction of the economy.

These elements are popularly considered essential to control market dynamics, but are little more than layers of coercive control. Their justification was that with this power, depressions could be scientifically prevented. The problem, as congressman Charles A. Lindberg retorted, was that, "*From now on, depressions will be scientifically created.*"

"*To cause high prices, all the Federal Reserve Board will do, will be to lower the rediscount rate...producing an expansion of credit and a rising stock market, then when...businessmen are used to those conditions, it can check prosperity in mid-career by arbitrarily raising the rate of interest.*

It can cause the pendulum of a rising and falling market to swing gently back and forth by slight changes in the discount rate, or cause violent fluctuations by a greater rate variation, and in either case it will possess inside information as to financial conditions and advance knowledge of the coming change, either up or down.

> *This is the strangest, most dangerous advantage ever placed in the hands of the special privilege class by any government that ever existed. The system is private, conducted for the sole purpose of obtaining the greatest possible profits from the use of other people's money. They know in advance when to create panics to their advantage. They also know when to stop panic. Inflation and deflation work equally well for them when they control finance."* —Charles A. Lindberg

Bonds. All of our money is considered *borrowed* money yielding interest, even though it isn't. The banker's wealth is not what we use to run the country and live our lives. The currency is a *fresh* creation, backed by the good faith of the American population. This is how money is created by the Fed: 1) The Federal Open Market Committee (FOMC) approves the purchase of U.S. bonds, which are simply a promise to pay. 2) The bonds are purchased by the Fed. 3) The Fed pays for the bonds with electronic credits added to the bond seller's bank, but these credits are based on nothing—they are created with the flick of a pen. 4) The bank uses the deposits as reserves, and can loan out up to *ten times* the amount of the reserves to new borrowers—all at interest. We see our mortgage interest at perhaps ten percent, but at this reserve ratio it's *one-hundred percent*, and as this leverage to expand or contract the money supply is a tool of *every* central banking system in the world, a worldwide depression can now be engineered.

Anyone can buy bonds, but only the Fed gets them for free, as they *create* the money to buy them. They also create the money—at interest—that all others must use to buy bonds. We hear that it takes money to make money, and under their system, it's true. Central bankers force mankind through an unnecessary toll medium—bonds—where a profit is made from our every action. In the early days of America, men went door-to-door, group to group and sold people on their ventures. They provided rational arguments to active minds, for the possibility of a mutually beneficial, voluntary trade. What bankers have done by monopolizing money, is centralize the asking. No one can use the medium without paying them a cut. Right now, we can only move with their permission. In a natural, moral environment, it takes *energy* to make money. You don't need to wait for anyone's permission—or for a loan approval, to spend your own energy.

> *"We are completely dependent on the commercial banks. Someone has to borrow every dollar we have in circulation, cash or credit. If the banks create ample synthetic money we are prosperous; if not, we starve."* —Robert H. Hamphill, Credit Manager, Atlanta Federal Reserve Bank

The existence of *any* bond must be predicated on an existing financial instrument. The currency must *precede* the bond and not be created *by* the bond, as to retire the bond is to destroy the currency. But the Fed issues currency for bonds as if they are lending, because lending produces interest.

"If our nation can issue a dollar bond it can issue a dollar bill. The element that makes the bond good makes the bill good, also. The difference between the bond and the bill is that the bond lets the money brokers collect twice the amount of the bond and an additional 20 percent, whereas the currency pays nobody but those who directly contribute in some useful way. It is absurd to say that our country can issue $30 million in bonds and not $30 million in currency. Both are promises to pay, but one promise fattens the usurer and the other, helps the people." —Thomas Edison, 1921

Fractional Reserve Banking. Though we've all known paper as our legal form of money and have heard it said that it's the easiest form to inflate, there was another which served as the source of modern institutional counterfeiting: gold.

The concept of *fractional reserve banking* comes from the early days of banking history. Goldsmiths and lenders discovered that they could issue more gold or silver-backed bank notes than their actual holdings in precious metals. As long as public confidence in their business remained, the bank could create as much paper money as it could manage, relative to the customer trends of who would return for redemption of the paper in coin money, and how often. They would establish a safe percentage, and lend this counterfeit money out to collect additional interest.

In our modern equivalent, bonds are created by the Fed at interest and then are multiplied perhaps by a factor of ten at its member banks. This is a purely criminal action. The power to buy and sell is resultant of the power to live—it is the power to trade. The honest sell something which is actually theirs to sell, and buy with money generated by providing value to others. Federal Reserve bankers do not. It's quite simple—with the fractional reserve system, they can buy anything at ten cents on the dollar, and even the ten cents is created from nothing. They have an automatic advantage of *ten times* that of their nearest competitor. Gaining this advantage, they didn't look at business ventures for long. With unlimited funds, they can control whatever they can dream up; a nightmare possibility that must be eradicated.

"Ironically, an agency which can literally swing the market with a sentence was established by the Federal Reserve Act of 1913 to stabilize the workings of the money and credit markets." —Victor Sperandeo, Author and Professional Stock Speculator

To see the ramifications of this policy, look at Japan. In the 1980's it had a reserve ratio of *one-hundred to one* when a BIS (Bank of International Settlements) mandate set the worldwide reserve ratio at eight percent. During the eighties it seemed they could buy anything and did so—flagship office buildings, communications networks and other huge companies. They crashed in 1987 along with us, but they didn't recover—even with *half-percent* interest rates—being a country so bloated with debt, it couldn't move. The bankers then went on to Boom and Bust the rest of the Asian world.

If fractional reserve banking is to stay, then legislation should be passed requiring that all banks holding fractional reserves distribute interest to their customers at the reserve ratio. If they are at a ratio of ten to one and you currently get three percent interest on your money, you will then be entitled to thirty percent. Then the bank will fail. Then via the FDIC, you get to bail yourself out through higher taxes.

Inflation and the Business Cycle. Increasing the money supply drives stock markets up. The public, typically unaware of past lessons, are conditioned to think the prosperity will continue forever, and leverages to the hilt to invest, expand and enjoy it. Interest rates are then used as a ploy to inflate or deflate, *spurring* an economy that is slow or *taming* an economy that is "overheating." As in the financial panics of 1873, 1894 and 1907, the Fed takes the markets down to steal a percentage of the leveraged assets—usually businesses, real estate and by shorting the markets, cash. This is the boom and bust cycle; whoever controls money, defines and controls this cycle. The cycle itself is contrived—a product of fascism.

Currency inflation and deflation is corruption, plain and simple. Products fluctuate independently according to supply and demand. When an essential item becomes scarce, those having product to sell can morally charge whatever the free market is willing to pay. But overall currency devaluation—inflation—can only be brought about by centralized intentional plunder.

Initially, the goods of the country equal the value of the paper currency in circulation, or as a mathematical calculation, Goods = Currency. A corrupt system perhaps doubles the amount of currency by simply printing more. As goods always equal the currency in circulation that buys them, spending the new funds leaves your money's value effectively halved—seen through higher prices.

Honest men produce goods, of which paper money is their socially accepted equivalent. Money creators who produce nothing except the currency itself, yet collect interest on it as if it were *borrowed* from them are counterfeiters, period. The creation of currency out of thin air never benefits anyone. It just makes the existing money worth less. It is supposedly done to "spur men into action," but men don't need fake money to do this. We enjoyed an Industrial Revolution without their fractional reserve inflationary and deflationary fraud. It doesn't help new goods come into existence, it only destroys the value of *existing* goods. Due to our debt-based currency, we are now *forced* to inflate at a rate of *seven billion dollars a day* just to pay the interest we owe.

Immoral finance is just like the fashion industry: they get us to buy in, then change direction again and again, stringing us along year after year to reap the windfall. We've experienced this most recently in the nineties boom, where most were making blind plans to retire through no effort of their own—extrapolating their stock market wealth into oblivion without regard for the cycle. They were not responsible for the bubble's creation, and therefore had no means to recognize the cause of its loss.

Before the cycle was created, economic growth and market activity was more or less linear, and steadily advancing. The system that now exists is designed to destroy itself and to take our citizens with it, as are all quests for the irrational. As money is created as a debt, the interest owed is not created and cannot be paid back without future debt creation. Sure, people do pay off their loans and keep moving forward in life as our economy is so vast, but the net results of these policies aren't immediately evident, and the greater the time frame, the greater the devastation. The money we need to pay our national debt doesn't exist, and cannot be created without bringing *its own* interest to bear—ad infinitum. This process has created debt in a spiraling, compounding nightmare, accumulating now at over *a billion dollars a day* and has wiped out over ninety percent of our currency's value.

Many economists consider the market to be the main driver, as if the ship steers itself; but what is this thing underneath, called a rudder? *The Fed* is the rudder of the economy, and is now the largest creditor of the United States. This is a private system, but only by government charter. It is not a blow to the concept of privatization and deserves no philosophical protection under it. It rather upholds clear parallels to Socialism. The owners of the Federal Reserve are not publicly disclosed. Their meetings are held in secret. They are not bound by insider trading laws. Though private corporations, the Federal Reserve central banks are not even subject to taxation. Financially controlling most the major media, they can cover any subversive activity and string us along economically, coming the closest any private organization can get to censorship. They have a purely no-risk parasitical operation—the shyster's dream made real—and are now the most powerful Spirit Murderers on the planet.

One nation after another has fallen into the clutches of the central bankers—a system purported as beneficial to all. Their altruistic cut in America alone is *360 billion dollars a year* at present, which funds the lives of a handful of banking families, strengthening their fascist grip—our country's largest debt next to Social Security. This is the greatest crime ever perpetrated upon mankind.

After seeing what his passage of the Federal Reserve Act had brought upon the nation, Woodrow Wilson lamented, *"I have unwittingly ruined my country."*

The Internal Revenue Service. If you've ever been in real need, you know that banks aren't into granting faith to anyone. They don't help without having something of equal or greater value to take in case of default. The income tax law, also passed in 1913, acts as collateral for our national debt. The Federal Reserve plan had to be backed by taxing the income of the citizens to support the immense sums of interest it would generate, so we have the Fed to thank for the

Internal Revenue Service as well. Making the citizens pay for it circumvented any concentration of power against them. Prior to this, we had no income taxes to pay. All of the unnecessary welfare burdens placed on us since, grew out of this.

Instead of direct detectable slavery, this is much more furtive—slavery through debt. Currently, the interest paid to the Federal Reserve consumes half the individual income tax receipts and is growing exponentially. Our "tax freedom day" is now June 11th. Close to half our life's work is now spent for ransom.

The Crash of 1929 and the Great Depression. The crash was not accidental. It was not the result of chance. Up until the Federal Reserve Act was passed, the New York banks could only control the reserves of New York. After that, they dominated the reserves of the entire country, and certainly held dominion over the broker margin loans as well. On the morning of October 29th, these loans were suddenly called, and brokers and customers were forced to dump their margined stock in unison, taking everyone else down with them. A number of men involved became rich from the crash and the following monetary contraction. Moving into short positions, cash and gold, Joe Kennedy's wealth for instance went from four million before the crash to one-hundred million by 1935. Similar gains were made by John D. Rockefeller, J.P. Morgan, Bernard Baruch and others who had duped President Wilson into supporting the Federal Reserve Act. After the crash, from 1929 to 1933, the Federal Reserve tightened the money supply by thirty-three percent, reflecting the unemployment rate of the time. As every Fed action made matters worse, there is no masking their intent with the folly of incompetence.

"*The Federal Reserve definitely caused the great depression by contracting the amount of currency in circulation by one-third from 1929 to 1933.*" —Milton Friedman

FDIC. The stock market crash and massive bank failures provoked distrust in the system, prompting the request for deposit insurance in 1933. Federal Deposit Insurance (FDIC) is a government promise to guarantee *all* the banking industry's accounts up to a certain limit, which is a mathematical impossibility. It's like putting a band-aid on a tumor. I was fooled by that one too. I believed that if I spread out my money over a number of banks it would be safe, but the FDIC is a totally illiquid fund, and a direct result of fractional reserve banking. A full reserve law would eliminate the need for this assurance, which actually substitutes as good faith for those with poor reputations, or for new bankers without a track record. We see the sign and we trust that their business is sound. We have no reason to expect misrepresentation, but are we really this simple? They set withdrawal limits on our own money—not to protect us, but to protect the banks *from* us—from the dangers of a run on the bank, which their own fractional reserve policy causes. The reason behind the strict credit policies that

412

can push us into foreclosure so quickly is the anemic nature of their business model. Do yourself a favor and leave the fractional reserve banks behind.

The Gold Standard vs. Fiat Currency. As a one-hundred percent reserve system is the only objective means to stability, a gold standard or other luxury or scarcity good standard is not actually ideal. It allows currency manipulation as the good can easily be cornered and its value heightened or depressed as a result.

Value is determined by context. Gold is only one product with value; it *need not* be the medium of exchange. Anything can be the medium. Scarcity and non-perishability are not essential requirements of the medium; *ease of use and public faith in it* are. How many people *need* gold? How many could live their lives never coming in contact with it? Water on the other hand is something none can do without, and it isn't rare at all. If a group were stranded on a desert island, would some seek food and shelter, while the others dig for gold so the trading could be legitimate? Of course not. When money fails, people trade whatever is needed to live.

Such tremendous advances in technology have created so much wealth that if there were a gold standard, either its value would seriously be inflated due to its scarcity, or trade would seriously be restrained, simply leading to another counterfeit *reserve ratio*. If a reserve ratio is refused, a shortage of gold results in producers being unable to sell what they make. Products then have to be traded for other products they need, wiping out the convenience of money. Supply and demand should be limited to the products available, not extended to the money as well. Just one side of the equation should be variable.

A gold standard is no different than *disallowing* the public to buy gold. It simply means that they *must* buy it, through their government or the cartels that control it, once again taking away their liberties. If they can't get it, they can't trade. A sound bill of rights securing the *voluntary* choice to buy gold or any other non-perishable property, coupled with a rationally quantified fiat or *paper* currency, is all the asset protection we need.

With a gold standard, whoever owns the most gold controls the currency, and its value. Guess who owns the most gold? Central banks own over sixty percent of the world's gold—a monopoly, and not for America's benefit. International bankers have no fatherland and no loyalties. We should leave them with their glittering pile and recover the living energy of mankind. The only time not to trust the fiat money of a land is when one cannot trust its government, the most eloquent example being Britain forcing the American colonies on a gold standard—proof that they didn't trust *themselves* in a good-will relationship with the colonies.

The naïve justification for a gold standard is the desire for a safeguard: to peg the value of paper money to a non-perishable good so that even crooks could handle the regulating of money without being able to counterfeit and therefore inflate it. But the value of gold is moving as well, and nothing is ever crook-proof. *To fix its value from a price rise is to short the benefit of its appreciation. To fix it from a fall is to short its affordability.* Throughout history, this advantage has been used to serve the bankers, not the people. Money should no more be tied to a rare commodity, than air should be withheld from men. In all of my research, I've never seen a satisfactory argument linking gold to monetary stability; it's simply another coercive layer of control with monarchical intent. What is necessary are *public* meetings and moral accountability for a *debt-free* currency, issued by a non-fascist controlled treasury department.

"*Any system which gives so much power and so much discretion to a few men, that mistakes—excusable or not—can have such far-reaching effects, is a bad system. It is a bad system to believers in freedom just because it gives a few men such power without any effective check by the body politic—this is the key political argument against an independent central bank....To paraphrase Clemenceau, money is much too serious a matter to be left to the central bankers.*"
—Milton Friedman

World War II. Just as the American Civil War was provoked by *European* money powers, World War II was planned by *world* money powers while the American people starved. During the currency contraction of 1929-33, the Federal Reserve was funding Hitler's rise. It was the contraction of currency in The West that provoked terror in The East. While allied loans to other countries including Germany were called in the thirties, taking their economies down with ours, the Nazi party was *financed*.

"*The German international bankers have subsidized the present government of Germany and they have also supplied every dollar of the money Adolph Hitler has used in his lavish campaign to build up a threat to the government of Bruening. When Bruening fails to obey the orders of the German international bankers, Hitler is brought forth to scare the Germans into submission...Through the Federal Reserve Board and the Federal reserve banks over thirty billions of American money...has been pumped into Germany...*
The Federal Reserve Board and the Federal reserve banks have pumped so many billions of dollars into Germany that they dare not name the total."
—Louis T. McFadden, 1931

The crippling terms of the Versailles Treaty brought unrest and revolt. No such cannibalistic treaty should have been inflicted on the German people, yet it was characteristic of the pillaging every conqueror was prone to in those days. It wasn't the German countrymen who were to blame for the war, it was the Kaiser; but as countrymen are driven to fight every dictator's wars, they were enslaved to bear its full cost—a dishonorable imposition. Though Germany had already paid for the damage it caused by a transfer to the allies of nine billion dollars worth of gold, Germany was squeezed through a six-month postwar food embargo by the *European* Allies and forced to accept the *thirty-three* billion dollar war debt, which was then repackaged and peddled as a preposterous investment by the Morgan banks in an attempt to pawn off the British and French war debt on the American people. This plan was concealed from the American President, but fortunately, our citizens didn't fall for it. Hitler's response to the Versailles Treaty was one of his few rational moves...he tore it up.

> *"The plan of France was to crush Germany by dismemberment as well as by an impossible indemnity.*
> *If America gets into the question of rectifying the iniquities and injustices of the Versailles treaty, we are likely to...be involved in the war, which is almost sure to come as a result of that treaty."* —Louis T. McFadden, 1931

The bankers were priming the pump for a second world war. Published in 1925, *Mien Kampf* was in print long before Hitler came to power. They knew what kind of a man they were backing—the same kind of destructive loner who serves as pawn for every political assassination. The Blitzkrieg was planned through *our* economic means. Americans paid for their own murder in World War II, as the bullets fired into our children were bought with our own money.

It should be evident that control of a currency implies a great moral responsibility. Hitler's reign never could have come to be if the Federal Reserve had the moral character not to finance him. Why would they support such murderers when the German forces in World War II could've been halted just by calling their loans? Answer: because they are murderers themselves. *Disrespect for life* is what set up such a monetary system, and nothing stimulates indebtedness like war. As a postscript, guess what wasn't destroyed in Hitler's regime? Right—the country's debt.

Central Banks and Central Intelligence. There can be no serious flow of capital without serious intelligence to know what to invest in. Capital is the life-blood of human economies of scale. Every facet of humanity—knowledge, civilization, prosperity and guardianship—follows in the path of Man's investments. It is the flow of money—*serious* capital—that defines civilization and its advances.

We've all seen *Mission Impossible* and other movies tying intelligence operations to the International Monetary Fund, which is majority owned and controlled by the Federal Reserve and the Bank of England, and we know that the major intelligence agency in the United States is the CIA. There *is* substance to the connections. How many more "former heads" of major Wall Street banks need be appointed as Director or Deputy Director of the CIA to make this obvious? As the Federal Reserve unofficially runs the CIA, they have access to the world's best weapons and most advanced technology, and most importantly, they have the money to further their aims.

ASSASSINS

On the street, money is the chief motivator, and the Fed controls it. How much preaching of loyalty or patriotism is necessary to get a lackey to act accordingly, versus offering a surprising amount of money? Certainly the lower levels of intellect are pure cause and effect and don't react readily to abstraction. They can be controlled by this limitation, whereas patriotism or any long range ideal, while perhaps not outside their grasp, is outside their range of activity. The burden of debt is not. Left in the world with no guidance towards rational fulfillment, a future assassin or fall guy clings to the only people who give him a sense of significance well beyond what his person deserves, and who share an impact much greater than his own scope would allow. With tolerance for his confusion and such employment of his malice, he trusts their guidance, and they lead him straight to his own destruction.

On their own, we see simpletons exploiting abstract thought only through lies and religion to cover their wrongs, as with the terrorists. As so, false political motivations only justify their violence. At the lower levels, cash is king and always will be. When the good says "I'll give you pride," and the evil says "I'll give you ten-thousand dollars," they take the money. The loner's dirty work is often *financed* by our own agencies, as American history has shown repeatedly in political assassinations.

From the top down, from central bankers to their assassins, they are all held together by a single tenet—psychological desperation. In the end, the Spirit Murderer's incentive is to see the good perish, before his own demise. Financed members of these agencies have been involved in criminal activity and much whispered conspiracies around the world. We know to trace terrorist funding to stop them. Without money flowing, dead plans stagnate. There is only one group outside this monitoring—the monitors themselves—who use their unlimited wealth to practice unlimited evil, such as revolutions, insurgencies and the assassinations of public figures, including the murder of President Kennedy, all done hidden behind the veil they call *"national security."*

"In the United States today we have in effect, two governments...We have the duly constituted government...then we have an independent, uncontrolled and uncoordinated government in the Federal Reserve System operating the money powers which are reserved to Congress by the Constitution." —Congressman Wright Patman, 1967

With one known head, a horrendously complex conspiracy between multiple agencies becomes no surprise at all; simple even. The *organized crime* bosses of the world know it; the Agency is their biggest customer. It was thought shocking that the CIA and organized crime were united against Castro in the 1960's, until one realizes that the Federal Reserve is in itself the pinnacle of organized crime, whose primary tool is the rank and order of the CIA, where all other bureau and military relationships are bent to follow, including the Pentagon.

Scenarios of political corruption aren't difficult to imagine. A General is given a budget to secure a place on a map. He makes a phone call. He sees out-of-the-way settlements that can be taken over and ruled as a private domain and with a small portion of the money, sends in his troops to secure the area and simply leaves inspection of these provinces off the official military agenda. The intelligence group comes in to establish a system of control from the top down. Legal trades are confiscated for their corporate counterparts, while illegal trades are handed to the Mob. Cover stories are put into the media to mask events. Micro-wars are free to sprout up all over the world as they have in remote locations, all bearing the foulness of a subverted American institution. This is the intelligence community's neurotic substitute for stature; a psychotic euphoria they mislabel as preeminence. Two-thirds of the Central Intelligence operation consists of little more than the paranoid scramble to further politicians funded by the Fed, while they cajole, impede, harass and kill statesmen who act contrary to their plans—acting as an unpatriotic and immoral, political secret police. They've learned a lot from their mistakes, and as Jim Garrison, the prosecutor who clearly implicated the CIA in the Kennedy assassination stated, they can now function with near invisibility, but their motives never change. Spirit Murderers seek any way to take what isn't theirs, ravaging and decimating a world they are incapable of enjoying.

"I spent 33 years in the Marines. Most of my time being a high-class muscle man for big business, for Wall Street and the bankers...I helped purify Nicaragua for the international banking house of Brown Brothers in 1909-1912. I helped make Haiti and Cuba a decent place for the National City Bank boys to collect revenue in. I helped in the rape of half-a-dozen Central American republics for the benefit of Wall Street..." —Major General S. D. Butler, U.S. Marine Corps

The same is done *within* our country, laundering what the government is unknowingly funding through fake business fronts across the nation. They are compelled to kill whenever the democratic process impedes their plans. Political murders are driven by the intention to disrupt or cut off communication that can sway mass sentiment in a manner detrimental to ill motives, parasitical plans and corrupt legislation. Such criminal action cannot pay off everyone however; their activities must remain as shielded and secretive as possible and are vulnerable to any innocent who stumbles upon them. With a small portion of the currency allotted for legitimate purposes, anyone threatening their interests can become the target of a hired mercenary, or of soldiers simply carrying out their orders.

"The high office of President has been used to foment a plot to destroy the American's freedom, and before I leave office I must inform the citizen of his

417

plight." —John F. Kennedy, speaking at Columbia University, ten days before his assassination

Notice how rare news stories have been on the Mafia in the last few decades; that is because they fall under the media and legal protection of the Central Intelligence Agency now. For example, the longer you watch any financial channel or commentary, you will encounter something called a *blackout*. Some sensitive issue of market dynamics is being discussed, and suddenly your television goes black for a few seconds. That's the bankers. The media is regulated to control any skepticism towards the Fed and to extinguish rumors about economic causal factors—anything even hinting towards to the truth must be silenced. They've come as close to fascist tyranny as freedom can be bent. They have legal control over most the media through ownership—their form of censorship. (As free speech is critical to secure our way of life, no media monopoly of any kind—radio, television or newspapers—should exist in a free country).

It is an efficient, centralized, tiered system of evil. Street level crimes are delegated to the local Mob in every city, which is why they can frame or kill someone from across the continent with a phone call. The bankers will kill any leader they don't control; anyone who acts contrary to the plan; even the sons of their own off-spring, as in the case of the Kennedy's. It's interesting that President Kennedy reissued Lincoln's debt-free greenbacks, was against war and issued an executive order to bring all covert operations back under the executive wing to *shatter* the reign of the CIA, as he had promised. As with Lincoln, Kennedy's protection was eliminated and the phones at the White House were out during the assassination. Watch the Zapruder film; that is the beauty they envision for the world. They are cannibals who will eliminate anyone who threatens the ring, and civility is the biggest threat. Notice that Malcolm X was safe until he began preaching a peaceful coexistence. Men such as Martin Luther King—any friend of the people—are automatically an enemy to their illegitimate power. Anyone acting inconsistent with their blind hatred becomes a target. To them I say, "Grow up. You're not acting for the good of *anyone*; you're acting out of fear, envy and weakness. If you have to kill someone who others believe in, ultimately it's because you know the people would never believe in *you*. If you have to murder someone over your issues, make sure it's yourself."

Political murder, overthrows, rigged elections, depressions and their debt-ridden false peace are the rotting epistemological branches that will be cut off by correcting our currency control.

"History records that the money changers have used every form of abuse, intrigue, deceit and violent means possible, to maintain their control over governments by controlling money and its issuance." —James Madison

Still, while such criminality exists as networks within these organizations, the organizations themselves are often sound and necessary. It is the same with banking in general; the Fed must adequately run its key public functions or face losing its charter fast. The FBI, ONI, CIA, KGB—it isn't that they wouldn't exist by some name or another, it is that *bankers* wouldn't be in control of them. Such organizations would fall under and be *fully accountable* to the executive branch of the federal government, whose anti-thesis would be subject to prosecution for espionage and treason.

The furtherance of any institutional edict is propagated by finance, so we must be diligent to assure that the financial source is honorable. Capital is the means of human life in civil society, and *intelligence* will continue to precede its flow.

Rational men can learn a lot from criminals. Weapons can be taken from the enemy and used to fight them. When they develop a pattern of action that is efficient and effective, it can be taken over by sound minds and restored to civil use. These organizations must be government controlled, not private, and fully accountable to the system of checks and balances which our forefathers put in place to ensure no underhanded activity goes undetected. It is paramount that these forces are used with sound judgment. The bankers should be returned to their proper spheres. Either they do something constructive with their lives instead of challenging and undermining our voluntary municipal order, or they should be relegated under the nearest rock.

Sound Money and Sound Banking. Money doesn't grow on trees—and if it did, it couldn't be used as money. Proper money is a tool of trade, naturally governed by a concept known as *the sanctity of contract*. The terms of honor which define a contract are a reflection of a country's civility and legal system. Money is treated as a commodity, but it isn't one. Money is human energy. The nature of your very existence—the morality of how you live—adds or subtracts from the stability of your nation's currency, and indicates its future value. If you see a neighbor's effort amounting to nothing, then the value of his contracts is nothing. If you see vigor, skill and accountability, *that* is someone who supports the currency.

In society, you can be far displaced from a water source, an energy source or a money source, but to benefit from them, the principles behind the transmission of each must remain intact. If you're left without water, life immediately begins to fall apart, as it does without money. Only the proper design and protection of such principles can stabilize a society and allow it to grow beyond bare subsistence. Only the individual freedom to decide what tailored directions each will take, allows so large a society to keep up its momentum. Continued expansion is *predicated* on the elements of cognition.

Stability affords the highest reaches to Man. Whatever is most delicate is last to be created, and first to be lost. Financial contractions hit the longest-range enterprises first, often wiping them out as the 6-8 abstract levels of consciousness are abandoned in a return to the metaphysical range of 1-4.

Money is a social tool implying civility between men. It defines and establishes a relationship between the citizens, a government sanctioned guide for how they will interact. Because money is a contract, control over the definition and issuance of money, like arbitration, must be third party, i.e. government. The value of every product is its remaining useful life set to a standard unit of value, whose goal is to be as steady as science—as in one kilogram, one horsepower, one dollar.

Money can be viewed as a contract between two parties—a promise to deliver goods or services for consideration—that consideration being of equal value, allowing it to be traded with others for products also needed. If you were on a desert island with one other person, *honor* is all you could count on— that you would both put forth your best effort to create values that sustain and improve your lives. If there is no honor, no trade is advisable or possible. Given that most men are honorable, they can write contracts for certain tasks, trading their intentions in advance. If so agreed, this contract can be assigned to other men for products more immediately needed. Thus, the contract is money, and no other medium is necessary. Standardization of monetary units into denominations—ones, fives, tens, twenties and so on, is the only requirement left to facilitate trade.

Just enough currency to make commerce flow freely (estimated by the treasury) and to finance essential government branches should be created—a figure easily computable by a ratio to the populace. No one should have the right to collect interest on money that was not created by their own honest effort. The safe store of value sought by Man is not to be found in a commodity such as gold or silver. It is found in human productivity, that part of a man's life that is spent sustaining his existence. This is an inexhaustible and incorruptible source of wealth—replenished and consumed again, every single day. They say that individuals cannot legally create money, yet anyone who creates a good or service has in effect, created money. Human productivity is what gives all forms of money its value, be it gold, paper or Talley Sticks. The question to ask the Federal Reserve is, "What moral action have you taken to bring this money into existence?"

The job of banking is that of choosing sound investments, originated through the experience of making them. Sound banks are money managers, acting as a safe store of wealth designed to facilitate the exchange of currency— as a check clearing house and a business, not as a jailor; as a friend and fellow businessman who *earns* trust, not as a dictator.

Abstract Arbitrage. There should be only one variable in the value of money. It should not disturb *product* value; it should not be subject to the scarcity of currency or of a precious metal. It should simply gage the products it buys according to quality, supply and demand, so that this fluctuation remains a reflection of the product's value, not the value of the currency itself.

The question of a currency's intrinsic value should arise only when compared to other currencies. As multiple currencies exist, those backed by *honor* and therefore political stability will out-value the others, the freest countries retaining the most consistent and steady value. Such a comparison reveals the value of their *moral code* relative to ours; it is that country's ability to produce—the measure of justice by which its government imparts to private citizens. With all of the stagnant, brutal governments in existence, charts can always be made showing the value of our currency skyrocketing relative to, for instance, Mexican Pesos, or whatever the corrupt South American government comes up with as money this week. They go through currency devaluation after devaluation, constantly running it into the ground through government counterfeit.

Whoever controls money controls the game, and right now, Hell has America on a leash. The Fed is the most powerful central bank in the world due to the freedom of Americans to produce relative to all other nations. We are the most reliable workhorse. Private currency control fundamentally skews the moral gage, so currency must be restored to reflect each government's principles alone. A world currency would be a disaster at this point in time—a white wash of evil, as most governments won't accept that their citizens have a right to live. The EU hasn't stabilized due to the differing laws and corruption of the group of countries attempting it. It had to be pegged to the American dollar, riding *our* virtue for the facade of its stability. They simply masked the fraud, saying "See the American dollar? Us too! Ours is just like it!" By disallowing it to fluctuate relative to honest market forces, they pushed the uncertainty onto what it can buy. Being on par with American currency means it is *our* country that will be looted, and import/export is where the payoff moves for evil. Poor product value will still drop relative to the value of quality products, and their firms will go out of business anyway. It has hidden their inflationary action, making it appear to have the characteristics of ours, which relative values of currency is gauged to define. It is a media move, as hyperinflation and unemployment in their streets cannot be masked. Then they'll take all of Europe the way they took Germany and Japan.

Capitalism, while being the obvious economic choice of the civilized as a practical application of Man's respect for Man, is not impervious to the devastation of an ill-conceived monetary system. The current monetary system of the United States is the most crucial crack in her armor. There should be a separation of politics and business for good reason, as legislation cannot be allowed to be influenced by the desire for unsound gain. *World* currency at this point in history is a method of hijacking the stability afforded by *American* morality. There is worldwide trust in our currency, which is trust in the sound government which paved the way for our prosperity relative to the rest of the world. Free men are the most solid basis for currency, and all countries should follow suit. They must emulate our virtues, not expropriate its result. If we let them steal America's identity, when the mask comes off revealing their horror, we will be left disfigured as well.

421

Our Current Reality. Our monetary system was the first terrorist attack on the United States, and on all countries under their power. We exist now mathematically, in an economic period of parabolic debt expansion. As a country, we are going to be slammed against the wall and handed over to the IMF and the World Bank, just like every other country. Because our government officials have proved they cannot control spending, are too weak to refuse bribes or are too lazy and stupid to comprehend the system, the power will be taken from them and control of our government will officially fall into the hands of our creditors. Evil is impotent you say? *It gained control of our money.* Civilization is not possible without it, and they could pitch us into another Dark Ages if they wanted to. It's time to stop this, and we can't do it without moral clarity. The future of the civilized world depends on it.

Our forefathers cared enough about us to set up this free system of government. It is time for us to think as deeply and as clearly as they did, and care as much about our children's future by expanding our intellectual range. If we fail and fold, everyone must know who is wrong and who is right. If we are forced to live through another period of starvation and stagnation like the Great Depression, it is *critical* that our oppressors do not get our sanction. Ultimately, we can lose only through moral failure.

The current system simply establishes parasites on active Man—it is a harness. To do nothing about a parasite once aware, is to sanction it. We must take from them the power to make money scarce or plenty. We must take from them the power to create money with no balancing creation of value. We must stop paying interest on money we never borrowed in the first place.

"I know of no severe depression, in any country or any time, that was not accompanied by a sharp decline in the stock of money, and equally of no sharp decline in the stock of money that was not accompanied by a severe depression." —Milton Friedman

Their Ultimate Intentions for the World. Their first intention is worldwide central bank domination. Their second is to remove government tariffs in order to avoid controversy between nations, making one neck ready for one leash. NAFTA, WTO and other trade agreements circumvent and ignore true political differences in the treatment of the people. They exploit a play on words, substituting free trade with *free*dom, which permits slave nations to trade on par with civilized nations. Notice that they pay lip service to human rights, but are tolerant of slow or no progress, claiming to be understanding and respectful of their "culture." The truth is they have no concern for human rights and no desire to punish the offenders, as they are often the offenders themselves. Often they own corporations benefiting from the labor of slaves, where factories are financed by central banks, lives are stolen whom the local SS keeps in line and the products hit American shores at unbeatable prices—a system of International Nazism. They are Spirit Murderers: their interest lies in debt, harm, poverty and want; to drain their subjects and witness the misery; to take their joy, to know they caused it and to revel in their impotent power. This system *exists*—such as the Chinese human rights violations and organ trafficking linked to American Corporations that has been recorded and exposed by individuals such as Harry Wu—it is up and operating today.

Their third intention is to have one world currency created from nothing, with no country and no productive value to back it. Already the IMF has its own money called Special Drawing Rights, or SDR's. Riding our productivity like the Eurodollar, they are exchangeable with American money and are fractionally backed by gold. In altruistic goodness, they are being lent to nations overrun with poverty and political corruption, such as Mexico, Africa and the entire Third World. They permit murderers to stay in power in exchange for their patronage—rolling one massive debt over into another while the citizens starve. I'm sure they have charts that project when America will fall back into such medieval savagery as well. My estimate is less than forty years—when the interest we pay them exceeds our individual income tax receipts, and it becomes impossible to live.

American energy is the most profitable to pillage; now they can do it offshore, without interference. As Louis T. McFadden said in 1932, "*They have been peddling the credit of this Government...to the swindlers and speculators of all nations...Give them the flag and they will sell it.*"

The IMF, the BIS and the World Bank make up the three arms of the World Central Bank—the fundamental financial aspects of their scheme are institutionalized and complete.

"*The powers of financial capitalism had another far reaching aim, nothing less than to create a world system of financial control in private hands able to dominate the political system of each country and the economy of the world as a whole. This system was to be controlled in a feudalist fashion by the central banks of the world acting in concert, by secret agreements, arrived at in frequent private meetings and conferences. The apex of the system was the Bank for International Settlements in Basel, Switzerland, a private bank owned and controlled by the world's central banks which were themselves private corporations...Each central bank...sought to dominate its government by its ability to control treasury loans, to manipulate foreign exchanges, to influence the level of economic activity in the country, and to influence cooperative politicians by subsequent economic rewards in the business world.*" —Carroll Quigley, Professor of History at Georgetown University (The professor's only inaccuracy is in defining the *nature* of this power; it is financial *despotism* or simply *fascism*—not capitalism).

The international bankers have proven their worth and intentions, time and time again. Why do we still permit their control? Their system is not only a means of holding human energy for ransom, but is the confiscation and misdirection of human energy, and whoever controls currency, controls human energy. With them in control, no one outside the system is safe. All of mankind's most simple, basic needs are set on a roller coaster while the central bank's subversive juggernaut crushes everything in its path, without the trouble of conscience. Already they are pushing for bankruptcy legislation that will disallow American individuals and corporations to walk away from debt. You will be tied to it for life, no matter the many potential factors involved in a venture's failure, first and foremost being the currency contractions of their dishonest boom/bust cycle. We must assure the *correct* transformation happens, or we will all become slaves as they intend.

Financial Evolution. The central bankers responsible throughout history are just Spirit Murderers like any others, and all that needs to be done is to put in place the legislation to restrain them. Of course, as our country has evolved in reason, the bankers have evolved in treason. They will still win on issues where they have a more clear understanding of what they're after, but elements which determine the fate of the country will no longer be in their hands.

The conspirators weren't and aren't men. Their thirst for power is as morally devoid as the purchase of a lottery ticket. Unearned wealth and the domination of others will never substitute for integrity, as it is the Spirit Murderer's answer to the void caused by its lack; it is their assault on integrity. What it will purchase is what it's always purchased in the past: a parasitical spouse and undeserved luxuries—a giant pretense that draws a chain of less dreadful, less intelligent parasites than themselves to share their medium of mutual contempt. Though they can impress their minions with ostentation, they still reach the end of their lives with a headstone fit for a king and little else—no great inventions to be proud of; no thanks from a world indifferent to their passing. Their unearned and horded fortune becomes a legacy of spiritual destruction, as a life with no tie to its sustenance is a life without purpose—manic and unhappy. All they've accomplished with their ability is to have wasted their lives on borrowed time, and destroyed others along the way.

"I believe that banking institutions are more dangerous to our liberties than standing armies...The issuing power should be taken from the banks and restored to the people, to whom it properly belongs." —Thomas Jefferson, 1809

When foundations are laid poorly, all that is built on them is at risk of collapse. Our monetary system, an abstract conception, must also have a metaphysically sound base. *Honor* is its abstract tangibility. By rebuilding our system on full reserve banking, every girder is real. It must be made impenetrable to evil or it will be subverted, and then is again at risk of collapse. As Andrew Jackson said, the moral code we live by must contain monetary standards that respect all citizens equally, meaning that as Man's nature is best served by sovereignty, the medium through which his energy is spent must share a like design—permitting no concentrated power outside of him to disrupt it. No secret meetings. No subversive political influence. No *means* to engineer depressions. No bending to their neurosis. All must profit by the fairness of the design.

424

How do we solve the problem? All debt-based currencies must be abolished; first in the United States, then in the rest of the world. Replacing Federal Reserve Notes with debt-free notes issued by the Treasury would result in an immediate savings of $360 billion per year. Our income tax burden could be cut in half, with no loss of government services. The concept of fractional reserve banking must be abolished as well. No one gets to generate interest on money they never earned to begin with. Revoke the Federal Reserve's charter, nationalize its assets, and stabilize the currency system with the above amendments. Economic resiliency is found in *freedom*, so remove any opportunity for the Spirit Murderers to affect the individual directly. No central interest rate controls. No inflation booms and contraction busts. Redefine the moral role of the IMF, the BIS and the World Bank. No world currency should exist until all the governments of the world grant *true* liberty and justice for all.

Private central bankers will invent horror stories intending to have us surrender control to them through confusion. As they've done throughout history, they will stage panics in order to blame them on any attempt at honest reform. Don't buy it. Bank crisis's and massive moves in either direction are *planned*. No endeavor of Man—particularly of political design—is outside of Man's capacity. They will show endless statistics that mean nothing and make threats of doom to explain how they cannot keep the economy going without ripping us off. Don't expect them to go quietly. They will crash our markets, call our loans, raise our interest rates, try to murder our leaders and undermine every step we take in the direction of freedom. *This* is the 6-8 battlefield—not the cushy towers of Aristotle vs. Marx—and we *can* win this war, regain our political sovereignty, reinforce our moral standing and bring an end to the goal of psychotic worldwide domination.

It isn't possible that they don't see the nature of their cannibalistic actions, in the presence of all the human greatness they've betrayed. With the power to crash economies, they could *save* them—but they don't. With massive influence at the highest reaches of every government, their concerted effort could have *stopped* the world wars—but it didn't. Their power could pressure tyrannical governments into becoming free societies—but it doesn't. They have no incentives to offer mankind beyond their interest-generated bribes. They have no learned penalties to warn us against, except their private threats of death. We have to wipe out their means in loyalty to the greatness of our own souls, which if it wasn't for the debilitating fear of malicious cowardice, could have been theirs.

I'm here to pay you back for what you did to the people in the post-Civil War depression, the Great Depression and for what you're doing to them right now. This is for Lincoln, for James Garfield and for John Kennedy, who was much more of a man than was his father. For the thousands you've murdered and starved out to keep your precious control. For World War II. For Vietnam. The game is up, *brother*.

We all choose the level of civilization that we will be involved. Such bankers plan to control governments and world inertias. It has been called a

Jewish conspiracy by some in history, but this is irrelevant. There isn't an eager lottery hopeful in the country that wouldn't do the same thing if it served them instead. Rather than plant seeds to see honorable prosperity expand for the benefit of all, they reverse the funnel, seeking to saddle and glean the masses to feed their own psychological trauma. We should be cognizant of our civilization's future, if only because they are. Knowing the intricacies, those of integrity in finance can pinpoint the deeper issues and identify where the dishonest are trying to scam. They can separate the sound practices to be continued, from those to be abolished.

"What we need is an Andrew Jackson to stand, as Jackson stood, against the encroachments of organized wealth." —William Jennings Bryan, Cross of Gold Speech, July 8, 1896

In Andrew Jackson's time, the bankers were entrenched sixteen years deep, and it was difficult to rout them out then. Now, they are *ninety years* deep. They *command* the Justice Department and any media or agency that could be a threat to them. As Congressman McFadden said, *"After 1921 the bankers attained control of the State Department and the Treasury Department and have never relaxed their grip."* Nothing but mass understanding and permission from the American people can uproot them now.

No Presidential platform today is worth a damn unless it includes the removal of American currency control out of private hands, and returns it permanently to the United States Treasury, where it belongs. We are never again to let private banks control and issue currency in our name, thereby permitting a secret government to rise, challenge and undermine the morally sanctioned government agreed upon by all.

As people get smarter, the bankers and bureaucrats will lose control over them. We must see our grace reclaim the levels above, extending as far into abstraction as evil now does. This system must be demolished and replaced for human society to move ahead. Its redefinition is one of the greatest creative opportunities facing us today—it is *historic*. We can cut off the inertia of the past and take prosperity in an entirely new direction; all that is necessary is the vision to do so, and the courage to see it through.

Sources: The Federal Reserve, *The New Economic Disorder* by Larry Bates, *The House of Rothschild* by Naill Ferguson, *The Autobiography of Benjamin Franklin, Money Mischief: Episodes in Monetary History* by Milton Friedman, *On the Trail of the Assassins* by Jim Garrison, *Mein Kampf* by Adolf Hitler, *Banking and Currency and the Money Trust* by Charles A. Lindbergh, *Collective Speeches of Congressman Louis T. McFadden, Tragedy and Hope: A History of The World in Our Time* by Carroll Quigley, *Andrew Jackson* by Robert V. Remini, *The Collapse of Deposit Insurance—and the Case for Abolition* by Richard M. Salsman, *Trader Vic—Methods of a Wall Street Master* by Victor Sperandeo, *The Truth in Money Book* by Theodore R. Thoren and

Richard F. Warner, *The Plot to Kill Lincoln* by Margaret Wendt, *Troublemaker* by Harry Wu. Websites: BankIndex.com, Crtf.org, EsotericWorldNews. net, Gold-Eagle.com, Investigate911.com, TheMoneyMasters.com and Wealth4Freedom.com.

Reclaiming the Earth in Our Name

The complex workings of a man, a relationship or a society that are beyond any centralized power to control, disallow the Spirit Murderer's ideals to succeed—the same complex workings he is neurotically *trying* to control, whose dreamed success was then to be ascribed to himself.

Such people would claim good intentions, perhaps to be followers of Jesus; yet not one of them would hesitate to murder him again if such a friend of the people walked the Earth today. If it meant abandoning their position and the neurotic course of fulfilling their illusions, they would drag him to his death. Jesus, Lincoln, Kennedy, Martin Luther King—it's the same murder over and over again—lovers of freedom, peace and true brotherhood—they've killed them all, and all for the same secret heart-breaking reason—that the world did not revere the killer—envy—evading that they never did anything to justify such mass devotion. They could not follow; they had to be thought great, or destroy all those who are. Their money and their post did not translate into the moral stature that must be earned, and can only be earned through *integrity*. True loyalty is spawned by accountability. To subvert and undermine our civil processes and the civil course of history is to admit they've failed in life.

As long as axiomatic principles are maintained and furthered, it doesn't matter who they kill. They can drop our best leaders and it won't make any difference. Their system of threats, conspiracy and rule by cowardice, fraud and greed for unearned power, is through. Once people know what they are living for, they can assume leadership at will. Such a movement doesn't ultimately have one leader, but a leader in *every* life. The Living Generators will withdraw, and *Moral Armor* will complete them. Sound moral conviction will sweep through the world and take the power back.

We cannot win playing by their rules; the rules must be ours. What do we want to further? The blind acceptance of faith—a pretense we've conceded our joy to, but never embraced—or the discipline of a rational progression of thought, which has made human life, sound relationships and productive civilizations possible? Not moral judgment lost in the sub-categories of Islamic or Christian faith, but a cleaner, clearer, *accountable* standard: life-sustaining premises versus life-taking premises—the principles which brought the United States into being.

All earthbound contextual action must give sole consideration to the earthbound entities involved. All morality is contextual—within the knowable world—as all moral judgment is the *sole* province of reason. What we accept as proof must fall within the range of Man—meaning his typical vocal, auditory and cognitive range, not within his *willingness* to see. Rational men act when the necessary evidence confirms that his causes will reap the expected effects. Morality is concerned with the proper method of producing and accumulating values—*not* with their relinquishment. The next time you hear a call for sacrifice, make sure they jump first. It is senseless for Man to enter a predicament where he has no choice but to come out with less; that wars are necessary for technological advances; that people must die for life to go on—these are cop outs for those who lack the discipline to devise some civil means to reach their goals—and often their goals are equally destructive. To them I say, "*I, as well as existence, am as forgiving as the ocean when you refuse to swim, as healthful as oncoming traffic when you refuse to steer, as charitable as the blow that follows when you turn the other cheek. I am as just as the emotional death you suffer when you answer your own cries with a coward's evasion, instead of a hero's reflection.*"

If they are going to torture us, fine. We must be prepared against those looking to attack any exposed value. Nature takes this into account as well; it is why turtles have shells and why rams have horns. What do we have? Philosophy and the physical ability to actualize our ideals. *Moral Armor* will spawn a generation of steady eyes, with the power and the will to reverse the insanity. We might as well go all the way and be fully what we are. The torture need not come from us. We must stand and be included in a new moral revolution, a brave evaluation of our own motives and actions, gauged to the correct standard of value, as well as awareness of the motives and tactics of our spiritual and mortal enemies. With such a commitment, the whole Submission/Domination Axis that you may have come to accept as having metaphysical validity, will dissolve in the power of your own independence.

Let us step into the light to see our own highest selves. Let us be all we can. It is time to end this inner struggle, the civil war we inherited, which pitted our minds against our bodies and Man against Man. It is time to reintegrate all facets of Man by integrating the full range of human thought and action, to recapture the glory of living. It is time to bring to Man the firm, clean decisiveness and prideful spiritual release that he has always deserved. It is time to master and sanction the spectacular moral power of our own consciousness— our intrinsic frontier.

One wins the battle by gaining sovereign ownership of one's mind. Acknowledging yourself as a *moral* being without pain, or fear, or guilt, in the privacy of your own conscience, rising into the wind to gaze upon the beauty of the world and all we can do, *is* personal deliverance. You have won the battle when you can stand against anyone and say effortlessly, confidently, joyfully, "*This life is mine, and I am going to live it without compromise to the unclean, to the dishonest or to the foolish, to those who want to take my direction from me, and steer my life by the irrational patterns that drive them. I am fortunate to live in a time when this course is open to me, and I am taking full advantage of it. You may speak of other worlds where I will pay a price for my decisions here, worlds you have no proof of, worlds that will subject me to all of the horrors your violent eyes and snarling words can invent. You can have those worlds. I want the only world our senses can validate—this one. No, I don't want or expect the automatic knowledge and unearned rewards that you have baited your hooks with. I only want the power to live my life as I see fit, subjecting no one to violence, fraud or loss, nor submitting to it. Rewards in another world cannot*

429

necessitate pain in this one. The pain is far behind me now, and true happiness lies ahead. Goodbye."

The war will be won when pure motives become the world's precedence. We must clear away the wreckage of institutionalized inequities and redesign what is not consonant with the proper flow of life. If we wish men to live happily on this Earth, we must sanction our own nature and never tolerate its violation. Our Forefathers began their revolution with a Tea Party, and if necessary, so shall we. We win this war, when evil is driven underground by the collective acknowledgment of its shame. We win, when the highest and best are free to lead, when the rest are free to develop, and the preservation of body and spirit is fostered and respected by all.

Damage

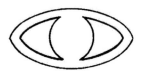

Vision

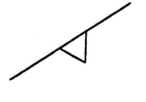

Defense
_____

Moral Armor.

About the Author

Ronald E. Springer has spent over ten years compiling the philosophical data necessary to develop a fully integrated moral code for Man. Twenty thousand hours and almost one million dollars in time went to create *Moral Armor*. The resulting knowledge is the equivalent of about two PhD's—tailored for the direct, practical use of sound moral premises in everyday life.

Outside philosophy, Ron has a background in Real Estate, the Stock Market and Automotive Design. He races exotic cars such as his Lotus Esprit, Lamborghini Countach and Acura NSX, enjoys bicycle freestyle and dabbles in "everything extreme." He spends most of his time researching economics, history, philosophy and psychology, looking to bring new clarity and new armor to Mankind.

Printed in the United States
19300LVS00006B/86